THE LAWS
OF SCOTLAND

———•———

STAIR MEMORIAL
ENCYCLOPAEDIA

Volume 22

THE LAWS
OF SCOTLAND

STAIR MEMORIAL
ENCYCLOPAEDIA

Volume 22

The Law Society of Scotland
Butterworths

Edinburgh   1987

The Law Society of Scotland
The Law Society's Hall, 26 Drumsheugh Gardens, EDINBURGH EH3 7YR

Butterworths
United Kingdom   Butterworth & Co (Publishers) Ltd,
88 Kingsway, LONDON WC2B 6AB and
61A North Castle Street, EDINBURGH EH2 3LJ

Australia   Butterworths Pty Ltd, SYDNEY, MELBOURNE, BRISBANE,
ADELAIDE, PERTH, CANBERRA and HOBART

Canada   Butterworth & Co (Canada) Ltd, TORONTO and VANCOUVER

New Zealand   Butterworths of New Zealand Ltd, WELLINGTON and AUCKLAND

Singapore   Butterworth & Co (Asia) Pte Ltd, SINGAPORE

South Africa   Butterworth Publishers (Pty) Ltd, DURBAN and PRETORIA

USA   Butterworth Legal Publishers, ST PAUL, Minnesota,
SEATTLE, Washington, BOSTON, Massachusetts, AUSTIN, Texas and
D & S Publishers, CLEARWATER, Florida

© The Law Society of Scotland 1987

British Library Cataloguing in Publication Data

The Laws of Scotland: Stair memorial encyclopaedia.
Vol 22
1. Law — Scotland — Dictionaries
I. Law Society of Scotland
344.1108'6   KDC150

ISBN (complete set) 0 406 237 00 X
(this volume) 0 406 237 22 0

Typeset and printed in Scotland by Thomson Litho Ltd, East Kilbride, on Bannockburn Fine Wove made by Guardbridge Papers Co Ltd of Fife and supplied by James McNaughton Paper Group. Bound by Hunter & Foulis Ltd of Edinburgh using cloth supplied by Watson Grange of Linwood, Paisley.

Contributors to this volume

SOCIAL WORK

Anne Black MA (Edin)
Diploma in Applied Social Studies (Nottingham)
Divisional Director of Social Work

SOURCES OF LAW (FORMAL)

LEGISLATION

R B Ferguson LLB, PHD
Lecturer in Law in the University of Dundee

JUDICIAL PRECEDENT

G Maher LLB, B LITT
Lecturer in Jurisprudence in the University of Glasgow

Sir Thomas Smith QC, DCL, LLD, FRSE, FBA
Honorary Bencher of Gray's Inn
Professor Emeritus of Scots Law in the University of Edinburgh

CUSTOM

W David H Sellar BA, LLB, Solicitor
Senior Lecturer in Scots Law in the University of Edinburgh

EQUITY

R B Ferguson

LEGAL LITERATURE

Sir Thomas Smith

SOURCES OF LAW (GENERAL AND HISTORICAL), LEGAL METHOD AND LAW REFORM

T David Fergus MA, LLB
Lecturer in Law in the University of Glasgow

G Maher LLB, B LITT
Lecturer in Jurisprudence in the University of Glasgow

CANON LAW

James J Robertson MA, LLB
Senior Lecturer in Law in the University of Dundee

LAW REFORM

Hugh R M Macdonald Advocate
Formerly a member of the Legal Staff of the Scottish Law Commission

J Charles Mullin LLB, Advocate
Member of the Legal Staff of the Scottish Law Commission
Sir Thomas Smith QC, DCL, LLD, FRSE, FBA
Honorary Bencher of Gray's Inn
Professor Emeritus of Scots Law in the University of Edinburgh
Commissioner, Scottish Law Commission 1965–81

J Fleming Wallace QC, MA, LLB

TIME

David C Coull LLB, PHD, Solicitor

The law stated in this volume is in general that in force on 30 November 1986 but later developments have been noted wherever possible.

Contents

TIME

Abbreviations

AC	Law Reports, Appeal Cases (House of Lords and Privy Council) 1890–
AD	Appellate Division (S Africa) 1910–46
A–G	Attorney-General
ALR	Argus Law Reports (Australia) 1895–1973, and Australian Law Reports 1973–
APS	Acts of the Parliament of Scotland
AS	Act of Sederunt
Act of Adj	Act of Adjournal
Ad & El	Adolphus and Ellis's Reports (King's Bench and Queen's Bench) (England) 1834–42
Adam	Adam's Justiciary Reports 1894–1919
All ER	All England Law Reports 1936–
App Cas	Law Reports, Appeal Cases (House of Lords) 1875–90
App D	Appellate Division (S Africa) 1910–46
App Div	Appellate Division (New York Supreme Court) 1896–1955; 2d, 1955–
Arkley	Arkley's Justiciary Reports 1846–48
Arnot	Arnot's Criminal Trials 1536–1784
Asp MLC	Aspinall's Maritime Law Cases 1870–1943
ATC	Annotated Tax Cases 1922–
Aust	Australia
B & Ad	Barnewall and Adolphus's Reports (King's Bench) (England) 1830–34
B & Ald	Barnewall and Alderson's Reports (King's Bench) (England) 1817–22
B & C	Barnewall and Cresswell's Reports (King's Bench) (England) 1822–30
B & CR	Bankruptcy and Companies Winding up Reports 1918–41
B & S	Best and Smith's Reports (Queen's Bench) (England) 1861–70
BCLC	Butterworths Company Law Cases 1983–
BCR	British Columbia Reports 1867–1947
BILC	British International Law Cases
BTLC	Butterworths Trading Law Cases 1986–
BTR	British Tax Review 1956–
BYIL	British Yearbook of International Law 1920–
Beav	Beavan's Reports (Rolls Court) (England) 1838–66
Bell App	S S Bell's Scotch Appeals (House of Lords) 1842–50
Bell Fol Cas	P Bell's Folio Cases (Court of Session) 1794–95
Bell Oct Cas	P Bell's Octavo Cases (Court of Session) 1790–92
Bing	Bingham's Reports (Common Pleas) (England) 1822–34
Bing NC	Bingham's New Cases (Common Pleas) (England) 1834–40
Biss & Sm	Bisset and Smith's Digest (S Africa)
Bligh	Bligh's Reports (House of Lords) 1819–21
Bligh NS	Bligh's Reports, New Series (House of Lords) 1827–37
Broun	Broun's Justiciary Reports 1842–45
Brown's Supp	Brown's Supplement to Morison's Dictionary of Decisions (Court of Session) 1622–1794

Brown's Syn	Brown's Synopsis of Decisions (Court of Session) 1532–1827
Bruce	Bruce's Decisions (Court of Session) 1714–15
Buchan	Buchanan's Reports (Court of Session) 1800–13
C	Command Papers 1833–99
CA	Court of Appeal
CAR	Commonwealth Arbitration Reports 1905–65
C & P	Carrington and Payne's Reports (Nisi Prius) (England) 1823–41
CB	Common Bench (England) 1845–56
CBNS	Common Bench, New Series (England) 1856–65
CCR	County Court Rules (England)
CL	Current Law 1947–
CLR	Commonwealth Law Reports (Australia) 1903–
CLY	Current Law Year Book 1947–
CMLR	Common Market Law Reports 1962–
CPD	Law Reports, Common Pleas Division (England) 1875–80
Camb LJ	Cambridge Law Journal 1921–
Camp	Campbell's Reports (Nisi Prius) (England) 1807–16
Cd	Command Papers 1900–18
Ch	Law Reports, Chancery Division (England) 1890–
Ch App	Law Reports, Chancery Appeals (England) 1865–75
Ch D	Law Reports, Chancery Division (England) 1875–90
Ch Rob	Christopher Robinson's Reports (Admiralty) (England) 1798–1808
Cl & Fin	Clark and Finnelly's Reports (House of Lords) 1831–46
Cm	Command Papers 1986–
Cmd	Command Papers 1919–56
Cmnd	Command Papers 1956–86
Com Cas	Commercial Cases 1895–1941
Com Dig	Comyn's Digest 1792 (England)
Com LR	Commercial Law Reports 1981–
Coup	Couper's Justiciary Reports 1868–85
Cox CC	Cox's Criminal Cases (England) 1843–1941
Cr App Rep	Criminal Appeal Reports (England) 1908–
Crim LR	Criminal Law Review (England) 1954–
D	Dunlop's Session Cases 1838–62
DC	Divisional Court
D (HL)	House of Lords cases in Dunlop's Session Cases 1838–62
DLR	Dominion Law Reports (Canada) 1912–55; 2d, 1956–67; 3d, 1968–83; 4th 1984–
Dalr	Dalrymple's Decisions (Court of Session) 1698–1718
Deas & And	Deas and Anderson's Decisions (Court of Session) 1829–32
De G & J	De Gex and Jones's Reports (Chancery) (England) 1857–59
De G & Sm	De Gex and Smale's Reports (Chancery) (England) 1846–52
De G F & J	De Gex, Fisher and Jones's Reports (Chancery) (England) 1859–62
De G J & Sm	De Gex, Jones and Smith's Reports (Chancery) (England) 1862–65
De G M & G	De Gex, Macnaghten and Gordon's Reports (Chancery) (England) 1851–57
Dirl	Dirleton's Decisions (Court of Session) 1665–77

Dods	Dodson's Reports (Admiralty) (England) 1811–22
Dow	Dow's Reports (House of Lords) 1812–18
Dow & Cl	Dow and Clark's Reports (House of Lords) 1827–32
Durie	Durie's Decisions (Court of Session) 1621–42
EAT	Employment Appeal Tribunal
E & B	Ellis and Blackburn's Reports (Queen's Bench) (England) 1852–58
E & E	Ellis and Ellis's Reports (Queen's Bench) (England) 1858–61
E B & E	Ellis, Blackburn and Ellis's Reports (Queen's Bench) (England) 1858–60
EC	European Communities
ECHR	European Court of Human Rights
ECJ	European Court of Justice (Court of Justice of the European Communities)
ECR	European Court of Justice Reports 1954–
ECSC	European Coal and Steel Community
EEC	European Economic Community
EG	Estates Gazette 1858–
EGD	Estates Gazette Digest 1902–
EHRR	European Human Rights Reports 1979–
ER	English Reports 1220–1865
Edgar	Edgar's Decisions (Court of Session) 1724–26
Elchies	Elchies' Decisions (Court of Session) 1733–54
Eng Judg	Decisions of English Judges during the Usurpation 1655–61
Eq Rep	Equity Reports (England) 1853–55
Euratom	European Atomic Energy Community
Ex D	Law Reports, Exchequer Division (England) 1875–80
Exch	Exchequer Reports (England) 1847–56
F	Fraser's Session Cases 1898–1906 (preceded by year and volume number); Federal Reporter (USA) 1880–1924; 2d, 1924– (preceded by volume number and followed by year)
FC	Faculty Collection (Court of Session) 1752–1825
F (HL)	House of Lords cases in Fraser's Session Cases 1898–1906
F (J)	Justiciary cases in Fraser's Session Cases 1898–1906
FLR	Federal Law Reports (Australia) 1957–
FSR	Fleet Street Reports 1963–
F Supp	Federal Supplement (USA) 1932–
Falc	Falconer's Decisions (Court of Session) 1744–51
Fam	Law Reports, Family Division (England) 1972–
Ferg	Ferguson's Consistorial Decisions 1811–17
Forbes	Forbes' Journal of the Sessions 1705–13
Fount	Fountainhall's Decisions (Court of Session) 1678–1712
Gaz LR	Gazette Law Reports (New Zealand) 1898–1953
Gil & Fal	Gilmour's and Falconer's Decisions (Court of Session) 1661–66, 1681–86
H & C	Hurlstone and Coltman's Reports (Exchequer) (England) 1862–66

H & N	Hurlstone and Norman's Reports (Exchequer) (England) 1856–62
HC	High Court
HL	House of Lords
HL Cas	House of Lords Cases 1847–66
Hailes	Hailes' Decisions (Court of Session) 1766–91
Hale PC	Hale's Pleas of the Crown 1678
Harc	Harcarse's Decisions (Court of Session) 1681–91
Hawk PC	Hawkin's Pleas of the Crown
Home	Clerk Home's Decisions (Court of Session) 1735–44
Hume	Hume's Decisions (Court of Session) 1781–1822
ICJ	International Court of Justice
ICJR	International Court of Justice Reports
ICLQR	International and Comparative Law Quarterly Review 1952–
ICR	Industrial Cases Reports (England) 1972–
IH	Inner House
ILJ	Industrial Law Journal
ILR	Irish Law Reports 1838–50
ILT	Irish Law Times 1867–
ILT Jo	Irish Law Times Journal 1867–
IR	Irish Reports 1893–
IRLR	Industrial Relations Law Reports 1972–
ITR	Industrial Tribunal Reports 1966–78
Imm AR	Immigration Appeal Reports 1972–
Irv	Irvine's Justiciary Reports 1851–68
J	Justice
JC	Justiciary Cases 1917–
J Juris	Journal of Jurisprudence 1857–91
JLSS	Journal of the Law Society of Scotland 1956–
JP	Justice of the Peace Reports (England) 1837–
JP Jo	Justice of the Peace and Local Government Review (England) 1837–
JPL	Journal of Planning Law 1948–53; Journal of Planning and Property Law 1954–72; and Journal of Planning and Environment Law 1973–
J Shaw	J Shaw's Justiciary Reports 1848–51
JR	Juridical Review 1889–
Jur Soc P	Juridical Society Papers 1858–74
KB	Law Reports, King's Bench Division (England) 1900–52
KIR	Knight's Industrial Reports (England) 1966–75
K & W Dic	Kames' and Woodhouselee's Dictionary of Decisions (Court of Session) 1540–1796
Kames Rem Dec	Kames' Remarkable Decisions (Court of Session) 1716–28
Kames Sel Dec	Kames' Select Decisions (Court of Session) 1752–68
Kilk	Kilkerran's Decisions (Court of Session) 1738–52
LA	Lord Advocate
LC	Lord Chancellor
LCJ	Lord Chief Justice
LGR	Knight's Local Government Reports 1902–

LJ	Law Journal newspaper (England) 1866–1965; Lord Justice
L J-C	Lord Justice-Clerk
LJ Ch	Law Journal, Chancery (England) 1831–1946
LJ Ex	Law Journal, Exchequer (England) 1831–75
L J-G	Lord Justice-General
LJKB	Law Journal, King's Bench (England) 1900–52
LJP	Law Journal, Probate, Divorce and Admiralty (England) 1875–1946
LJPC	Law Journal, Privy Council 1865–1946
LJQB	Law Journal, Queen's Bench Division (England) 1831–1900
LJR	Law Journal Reports (England) 1947–49
LQR	Law Quarterly Review 1885–
LR A & E	Law Reports, Admiralty and Ecclesiastical (England) 1865–75
LRCCR	Law Reports, Crown Cases Reserved (England) 1865–75
LRCP	Law Reports, Common Pleas (England) 1865–75
LR Eq	Law Reports, Equity (England) 1865–75
LR Exch	Law Reports, Exchequer (England) 1865–75
LRHL	Law Reports, House of Lords (England and Ireland) 1866–75
LR Ir	Law Reports, Ireland 1877–93
LR P & D	Law Reports, Probate and Divorce (England) 1865–75
LRPC	Law Reports, Privy Council 1865–75
LRQB	Law Reports, Queen's Bench (England) 1865–75
LRRP	Law Reports, Restrictive Practices 1957–
LR Sc & Div	Law Reports, House of Lords (Scotch and Divorce) 1866–75
LS Gaz	Law Society's Gazette (England) 1903–
LT	Law Times Reports (England) 1859–1947
LT Jo	Law Times newspaper (England) 1843–1947
LTOS	Law Times Reports, Old Series (England) 1843–59
LVAC	Lands Valuation Appeal Court
Land Ct	Scottish Land Court
Law Com	Law Commission (England)
Ll L Rep	Lloyd's List Law Reports 1919–50
Lloyd's Rep	Lloyd's List Law Reports 1951–67; Lloyd's Law Reports 1968–
Lyon Ct	Court of the Lord Lyon
M	Macpherson's Session Cases 1862–73
M (HL)	House of Lords cases in Macpherson's Session Cases 1862–73
MLR	Modern Law Review 1937–
MR	Master of the Rolls
Mac & G	Macnaghten and Gordon's Reports (Chancery) (England) 1849–52
MacF	MacFarlane's Jury Trials (Court of Session) 1838–39
Macl & R	Maclean and Robinson's Scotch Appeals (House of Lords) 1839
Maclaurin	Maclaurin's Arguments and Decisions 1670–1770
Macq	Macqueen's House of Lords Reports 1851–65
Misc	New York Miscellaneous Reports 1892–1955; 2d, 1955–
Mor	Morison's Dictionary of Decisions (Court of Session) 1540–1808

Mun LR	Municipal Law Reports 1903–13
Murr	Murray's Jury Court Cases 1815–30
NI	Northern Ireland Law Reports 1925–
NLJ	New Law Journal (England) 1965–
NY	New York Court of Appeals Reports 1847–1955; 2d, 1956–
NYS	New York Supplement 1888–1937; 2d, 1938–
NZ	New Zealand
NZLR	New Zealand Law Reports 1883–
NZULR	New Zealand University Law Review 1963–
OCR	Ordinary Cause Rules
OH	Outer House
OJ	Official Journal of the European Communities; C, Information; L, Legislation
OLR	Ontario Law Reports 1901–30
OR	Ontario Reports 1931–73; 2d, 1974–
P	Law Reports, Probate, Divorce and Admiralty Division (England) 1890–1971
P & CR	Planning and Compensation Reports 1949–67; Property and Compensation Reports 1968– (England)
PC	Judicial Committee of the Privy Council
PD	Law Reports, Probate, Divorce and Admiralty Division (England) 1875–90
PL	Public Law
Pat	Paton's House of Lords Appeal Cases 1726–1821
Paters	Paterson's House of Lords Appeals 1851–73
Pitc	Pitcairn's Criminal Trials 1488–1624
QB	Queen's Bench Reports (England) 1841–52 (volume number precedes)
QB	Law Reports, Queen's Bench Division (England) 1891–1901, 1952– (year precedes)
QBD	Law Reports, Queen's Bench Division (England) 1875–90
QC	Queen's Counsel
R	Rettie's Session Cases 1873–98
RA	Rating Appeals 1965–
RC	Rules of the Court of Session
R (HL)	House of Lords cases in Rettie's Session Cases 1873–98
R (J)	Justiciary cases in Rettie's Session Cases 1873–98
RPC	Reports of Patents, Designs and Trade Marks Cases 1884–; Restrictive Practices Court
RRC	Ryde's Rating Cases (England) 1956–
RSC	Rules of the Supreme Court (England)
RTR	Road Traffic Reports 1970–
RVR	Rating and Valuation Reports (England) 1960–
Robert	Robertson's Scotch Appeals (House of Lords) 1707–27
Robin	Robinson's Scotch Appeals (House of Lords) 1840–41
S	P Shaw's Session Cases 1821–38
SA	South African Law Reports 1947–
SALJ	South African Law Journal

SAL Rev	South African Law Review
SAR	South African Supreme Court Reports 1881–92
S & D Just	Shaw and Dunlop's Justiciary Cases 1819–31
SC	Session Cases 1907–; Supreme Court
SCCR	Scottish Criminal Case Reports 1981–
SC (HL)	House of Lords cases in Session Cases 1907–
SC (J)	Justiciary Cases in Session Cases 1907–16
SCLR	Scottish Civil Law Reports 1987–
SCOLAG	The journal of the Scottish Legal Action Group
SCR	Summary Cause Rules
SI	Statutory Instruments
SJ	Scottish Jurist 1829–73
SLCR	Scottish Land Court Reports in Scottish Law Review (1913–63) (preceded by year and volume number), and Scottish Land Court Reports 1982– (preceded by year)
SLCR App	Appendix to the annual reports of the Scottish Land Court 1963–
SLG	Scottish Law Gazette 1933–
SLJ	Scottish Law Journal and Sheriff Court Record 1858–61
SLM	Scottish Law Magazine and Sheriff Court Reporter 1862–67
SLR	Scottish Law Reporter 1865–1925
SL Rev	Scottish Law Review and Sheriff Court Reporter 1885–1963
SLT	Scots Law Times 1893–1908 (preceded by year and volume number), and 1909– (preceded by year)
SLT (Land Ct)	Scottish Land Court Reports in Scots Law Times 1964–
SLT (Lands Trib)	Lands Tribunal for Scotland Reports in Scots Law Times 1971–
SLT (Lyon Ct)	Lyon Court Reports in Scots Law Times 1950–
SLT (Notes)	Notes of Recent Decisions in Scots Law Times 1946–1981
SLT (Sh Ct)	Sheriff Court Reports in Scots Law Times 1893–
SN	Session Notes 1925–48
SO	Standing Orders
SPLP	Scottish Planning Law and Practice 1980–
SR & O	Statutory Rules and Orders
SRR	Scots Revised Reports 1707–1873, 1898–1908
STC	Simon's Tax Cases 1973–
Scot Law Com	Scottish Law Commission
Sh & Macl	P Shaw and Maclean's House of Lords Appeal Cases 1835–38
Sh App	P Shaw's Scotch Appeals (House of Lords) 1821–26
Sh Ct Rep	Sheriff Court Reports in Scottish Law Review 1885–1963
Shaw Just	P Shaw's Justiciary Reports 1819–31
Shaw Teind	P Shaw's Teind Court Decisions 1821–31
Sim	Simon's Reports (Chancery) (England) 1826–52
Sim & St	Simon & Stuart's Reports (Chancery) (England) 1822–26
Sim NS	Simon's Reports, New Series (Chancery) (England) 1850–52
Smith LC	Smith's Leading Cases (England)
Sol Jo	Solicitors' Journal (England) 1856–
Stair Rep	Stair's Reports (Court of Session) 1661–81
Stair Soc	Stair Society
State Tr	State Trials 1163–1820

State Tr NS	State Trials, New Series 1820–58
Stuart	Stuart, Milne and Peddie's Reports (Court of Session) 1851–53
Swin	Swinton's Justiciary Reports 1835–41
Syme	Syme's Justiciary Reports 1826–29
TC	Tax Cases 1875–
TLR	Times Law Reports (England) 1884–1952
TR	Taxation Reports 1939–
Taunt	Taunton's Reports (Common Pleas) (England) 1807–19
Term Rep	Term Reports (England) 1785–1800
US	United States Supreme Court Reports 1754–
VATTR	Value Added Tax Tribunal Reports 1973–
V-C	Vice-Chancellor
VLR	Victorian Law Reports 1875–1956
VR	Victorian Reports 1870–72, and 1957–
Ves	Vesey Junior's Reports (Chancery) (England) 1789–1817
Ves Sen	Vesey Senior's Reports (Chancery) (England) 1747–56
WALR	West Australian Law Reports 1898–1959
WAR	Western Australian Reports 1960–
W & S	Wilson and Shaw's House of Lords Cases 1825–34
WLR	Weekly Law Reports (England) 1953–
WN	Law Reports, Weekly Notes (England) 1866–1952
WR	Weekly Reporter (England) 1852–1906
WS	Writer to the Signet
WWR	Western Weekly Reports (Canada) 1911–1950, and 1955–
West	West's House of Lords Reports 1839–41
White	White's Justiciary Reports 1885–93
YB	Year Books

Table of Statutes

Table of Orders, Rules and Regulations

Table of Other Enactments

Table of Cases

A

References are to paragraphs

References are to paragraphs

References are to paragraphs

E

F

References are to paragraphs

G

References are to paragraphs

References are to paragraphs

References are to paragraphs

M

References are to paragraphs

References are to paragraphs

Q

R

References are to paragraphs

References are to paragraphs

References are to paragraphs

References are to paragraphs

Supplementary Table of Cases

SOCIAL WORK

1. THE DEVELOPMENT AND CO-ORDINATION OF SOCIAL WORK SERVICES

1. Historical perspective. Social work services provided by public authorities have a short history in comparison with those provided by the medical and legal professions or by churches. The hallmark of a social work service is its direct concern with the personal needs and well-being of the individual. Such care and concern is by no means modern: charitable organisations and religious orders have provided social care over the centuries.

Early social services adopted an environmental focus with social reformers like Lord Shaftesbury and Octavia Hill pressing for improvements in the conditions in which people lived and worked. The aim of these services was to improve the sanitary or, generally speaking, the physical surroundings of the individual, and thus indirectly led to better public health and amenities of life. From these broad aims there developed in the twentieth century the more specific aim of personal social services provision. The well-being of individual citizens was a growing concern[1], and the care of children who were deprived or delinquent and of those people with a physical or mental handicap was identified as a vital component of a social service. Until the mid-twentieth century, much of this individual provision was made by charitable or voluntary organisations with the public provision being directed to poor law relief with its consequent social stigma for the recipients.

Since then, the scope of social services has extended rapidly from the mere provision of material benefits by the state to a wide range of individually focused services which attempt to meet varied personal needs. However, the expansion of the individual social work services and the involvement of public authorities bring dangers of depersonalisation and of a bureaucratic response to the very critical problems faced by individuals. The problems are not ones which can be solved merely by providing material benefits but are problems where personal maladjustments and emotional distress need understanding personal approaches. Social work services have to be able to work with basic human relationships between an individual and his family or his workplace or his wider community. To undertake this kind of work, adequate training and support for social work personnel must be made available. The needs of the individual seeking social work help must also be set in the wider social context, and sensitivity to social trends and a changing environment is constantly required.

The stresses involved in coping with the distress of some individuals can be high and social workers frequently face unknown and sometimes violent situations when dealing with the wide range of people who seek their help or are directed to them for help. Much social work involves risks. In particular, the assessment of the level of risk faced by a client, particularly if that client is a child, has to be thorough and careful. Time is often short to make these assessments with no possibility of deferring a judgment to study precedents or ponder possible solutions.

Action to reduce or remove dangers from children at risk of abuse has to be immediate, and public criticism abounds not only when a social worker fails to act to protect a child but also when social workers intervene in situations where danger initially appeared likely but which, after more extensive examination, proved not to be potentially dangerous. The statutes within which social workers must operate are capable of wide interpretation, and judicial decisions often highlight the variety of child care practices within families which are deemed by some to be totally acceptable but are considered by others to be wholly unacceptable. Perhaps this is most evident in the variety of opinions as to what is reasonable physical chastisement.

As services have developed the classes of recipients of social work services have widened: no longer are public services only for the poor or disadvantaged, but they span the whole community.

1 T S Simey *Principles of Social Administration* (1937) Ch 1.

2. Early legislative regulation. The watershed for much social work provision occurred in 1947 and 1948. The National Health Service (Scotland) Act 1947 was designed to promote a comprehensive health service in Scotland[1]. Improvements in the physical and mental health of the community, and in the prevention, diagnosis and treatment of illness were key objectives. Local health authorities were given specific responsibilities for providing services later transferred to social work authorities. These were services designed to assist with the care or after-care of persons suffering from illness or mental deficiency, including domestic help at home[2].

The National Assistance Act 1948 spanned the material and emotional aspects of welfare by providing for a system to give assistance to any person in need through an income maintenance service and also by providing for the welfare of claimants seeking income maintenance. Alongside the income maintenance services, welfare departments were set up. These departments were also charged with providing residential accommodation for the aged or infirm or other persons in need[3]. The local authority could also provide welfare services through officers visiting at home those who were incapacitated in some way, and making available to them assistance and advice.

The third major statute which shaped modern social work services was the Children Act 1948. This Act gave local authorities clear duties to provide care for children deprived of a home life. The duties, although wide-ranging, focused on arrangements for placing and supervising the placing of children into care away from their parents. The stress on maintaining children with their own parents, if that could be achieved, was not given much impetus by this Act[4].

Each local authority was required to set up a children's committee and appoint a children's officer, on whom were laid the duty to supervise children separated from their parents[5]. In 1963 the functions of local authorities were expanded to encompass more general advice and guidance to families experiencing problems within the community, and impetus was given to the promotion of the welfare of the whole family rather than just individual members[6].

Another early Act shaping the services to young children and aiming to prevent their well-being from suffering through inadequate care was the Nurseries and Child-Minders Regulation Act 1948. This Act laid duties on local health authorities to monitor the care of children under five who were cared for on a daily basis either in groups or individually. Registration of people caring for young children was introduced, as well as registration of premises where children were to be cared for[7]. The Act was designed to reduce the numbers of unsuitable placements of young children for long hours with strangers, often at high cost to their parents.

Thus separate departments within local health authorities and local authorities were working independently from 1948 until the enactment of the Social Work (Scotland) Act 1968 (c 49). The departments often carried overlapping functions and while from the early 1960s a variety of efforts to set up better co-ordinating machinery was emerging, none achieved the integration which the social work services really required to be effective in terms of time, skill and resources.

1 National Health Service (Scotland) Act 1947 (c 27), s 1(1) (repealed; see now the National Health Service (Scotland) Act 1978 (c 29), s 1(1)).
2 National Health Service (Scotland) Act 1947, ss 27, 28 (repealed).
3 National Assistance Act 1948 (c 29), s 2(1)(a) (repealed).
4 As to the general duty of local authorities to care for children, see the Children Act 1948 (c 43), Pt I (ss 1–10) (repealed).
5 Ibid, ss 39, 41 (repealed).
6 Children and Young Persons Act 1963 (c 37), s 1 (repealed).
7 Nurseries and Child-Minders Regulation Act 1948 (c 53), s 1.

3. First moves towards a co-ordinated social work service. Within a year of the enactment of the Children Act 1948 (c 43) a working party of officials of the Home, Health and Education Departments of England and Wales and Scotland was appointed to consider whether local authorities could do more to prevent the neglect and ill-treatment of children in their own homes. The conclusions of the working party were contained in circulars to local authorities[1]. No new statutory powers were recommended: instead, the working party advised better co-ordination of the use of existing statutory and voluntary services. Each authority was urged to consider designating an officer to be responsible for co-ordinating services for children's welfare at home. In 1954 local authorities were again urged to use local health facilities and personnel to prevent the break-up of families[2].

Three influential reports presaged the major changes in the shape of social work in Scotland in the 1960s[3]. These were to determine the future services to be provided by local authorities to ensure a comprehensive social services provision without unnecessary duplication and which had ease of access for those seeking help.

1 Scottish Home Department circular 7497.
2 Department of Health circular 77/1954.
3 As to these reports, see paras 4, 5, below.

4. The McBoyle Committee. The McBoyle Committee presented its report *Prevention of Neglect of Children* in January 1963[1]. This report drew largely on the earlier recommendations of the Ingleby Committee in England and Wales[2]. There was general agreement by the McBoyle Committee with the major recommendations of the Ingleby Committee, namely:

'(1) There should be a general duty laid upon local authorities to prevent or forestall the suffering of children through neglect in their own homes, and local authorities should have power to do preventive casework and provide material needs that cannot be met from other sources; these powers should be vested generally in the local authority.

(2) Arrangements for the detection of families at risk should be over the widest possible front and we urge recognition of the need for early reference of cases and the need for impartiality in and a measure of independence for those responsible for diagnosis.

(3) There should be a statutory obligation on all local authorities to submit for ministerial approval schemes for the prevention of suffering of children through neglect in their own homes; it should be made clear to which government department a local authority should look for advice or approval on matters of co-ordination.

(4) We urge the importance of further study by the Government and the local interests concerned of the reorganisation of the various services concerned with the family'[3].

The McBoyle Committee identified some ways which it saw as improving services to children at risk[4]. It suggested that greater stress should be put on services aimed at keeping children at home rather than requiring them to come into care. Local authorities should provide guidance and assistance to families in their own homes on both personal and domestic matters.

The committee suggested the setting up of family advice centres to which members of the public could come for help. Other centres could provide training for parents to help them to manage their parenting and domestic tasks more effectively. Local authorities should have the power to provide material assistance to families where such assistance was not available from any other statutory agencies. To enable local authorities to exercise such powers effectively, the committee felt that local authorities should have powers to conduct research into all matters relevant to the discharge of these powers. The committee saw that these additional powers would ensure that a comprehensive preventive service was available to the community.

The recommendations did not include an amalgamation of the different departments which could contribute to these services but recommended machinery for the co-ordination of policies, services and information. The committee identified the local authority children's committees as appropriately being given the responsibility for the co-ordination of preventive work. It also recommended a variety of additional duties and powers which local authorities should be given to tackle the prevention of neglect of children and family breakdown. The formation of a comprehensive family welfare service was seen as a desirable long-term aim.

1 *Report of the Committee of the Scottish Advisory Council on Child Care* (1963) (Cmnd 1966).
2 *Report of the Committee on Children and Young Persons* (1960) (Cmnd 1191).
3 Cmnd 1966, para 6, quoting from the Report of the Ingleby Committee.
4 Cmnd 1966, paras 29–33.

5. The Kilbrandon Committee. The publication of the report of the McBoyle Committee was followed closely by the report of the Kilbrandon Committee whose remit had been 'to consider the provisions of the law of Scotland relating to the treatment of juvenile delinquents and juveniles in need of care or protection or beyond parental control and, in particular, the constitution, powers and procedure of the courts dealing with such juveniles'[1].

The committee recommended that all juvenile courts should be abolished and that a panel or panels for juvenile offenders and young people in need of care or protection should be set up for each education authority area[2]. The referral of children to such panels should be at the instance of an independent official to be known as the 'reporter'. This would limit the rights of police and local authorities to bring cases to legal proceedings directly but would require all cases to be directed via this new official[3].

The Kilbrandon Committee argued for a new statutory department — the 'social education department' — which would act as the executive arm of the children's panel[4]. The provision of treatment and care either in the community or in residential schools would also fall to this new department. The committee recommended that the powers of the existing children's departments should be transferred to new social education authorities, but it did not specifically locate adoption services. One may ponder what the shape of social work would have become if these recommendations had been implemented, as these new social education departments would have been of massive size with wide responsibilities, but would have excluded some key individual social services.

1 *Report of the Committee on Children and Young Persons, Scotland* (1964) (Cmnd 2306), para 1.
2 Ibid, paras 68–76.
3 Ibid, paras 98–102.
4 Ibid, paras 241–242.

6. Proposals for a co-ordinated social work service. Very shortly after the completion of the deliberations of the Kilbrandon Committee, the Secretary of State for Scotland sought the views of relevant professions on the proposals. The major criticism which emerged was that the proposed social education department focused too narrowly on children and that, in consequence, the broader range of services for families might well suffer.

By selecting recommendations from the McBoyle and Kilbrandon Reports and subsequent responses to them, Scotland proceeded to prepare for major reorganisation of local authority services. The government's proposals for change were contained in *Social Work and the Community* and were published as a basis for discussion with a view to comprehensive legislation later[1]. Within these proposals social work departments with wide responsibilities were introduced, avoiding the possibility of a narrow child care focus which Kilbrandon had presented.

The powers and responsibilities proposed for these new departments were clearly stated:

> 'The existing powers of local authorities to provide advice and assistance, and to promote welfare, are set out mainly in the National Health Service (Scotland) Act 1947, the National Assistance Act 1948, the Children Act 1948, the Mental Health (Scotland) Act 1960, the Education (Scotland) Act 1962 and the Children and Young Persons Act 1963. These powers will be continued, with the adjustments necessary to fit the new organisation. They are already very wide, and only two substantial groups of people appear not to be fully covered. Services for old people under the National Assistance Act are limited to the provision of accommodation, meals and recreation. For adults who are not aged, handicapped, ill or parents of young children, there is at present no express power by which a local authority may at its own hand provide personal advice and guidance. It is proposed that the local authority should in future have power to provide all citizens, of whatever age or circumstances, with advice and guidance in the solution of personal and social difficulties and problems'[2].

The proposals were aimed to provide a better co-ordinated social work service, rather than the piecemeal existing situation which led to confusion and overlap. The social work department should not, the proposals suggested, be subordinated to any existing local authority department. It should provide community and residential services, and persons seeking social work help should be able to approach 'one door' and not be directed from one agency to another seeking help. Thus the existing separate departments offering help to children, families, the elderly, the mentally ill, the handicapped and offenders would be amalgamated into this one social work department. These proposals were presented to Parliament in October 1966.

1 *Social Work and the Community* (1966) (Cmnd 3065).
2 Ibid, para 7.

7. Central advisory services. Because of the complexity of the social work services and their provision within a local authority setting, where little experience of professional service delivery existed, the proposals also contained a commitment to setting up a central professional advisory service. This service was to be provided by the government and was to be set up before the new legislation was enacted. Central government brought together its existing inspectorates for child care, approved schools, probation and welfare, and in March 1967 the Social Work Services Group was formed. The group was attached to the Scottish Education Department for financial appropriations and accountability, but directly responsible to ministers for the implementation of the Social Work (Scotland) Act 1968[1].

The Social Work Services Group has remained within the Scottish Education Department and provides an advisory service to social work departments on a range of professional practice and policy issues. The group has a major input to the promulgation of new legislation and regulations, and is involved with local authorities in training and advice on various topics. The oversight role which the group carries links with the responsibilities of central government to contribute to the services provided by local authorities through the rate support grant. The needs of vulnerable groups like children and the elderly affect the level of rate support grant and advisers in the Social Work Services Group carry responsibilities to question local authorities about whether the level of service provided is commensurate with the money allocated. Such individually focused calculations are complex within an agency which has been specifically set up to provide services across the range of needs. People with very different problems often live within one family and will receive services from one social worker — where service to one family member stops and another begins is not easily calculated! Local authorities must provide the Social Work Services Group with a range of statistical information which is analysed and published and provides the basis for future planning of services and expenditure. The wide powers invested in the Secretary of State by the Social Work (Scotland) Act 1968 are frequently carried out by members of the group. Regulations prepared by the Secretary of State with the advice of the group provide the basis for much social work practice and procedure.

For example, recent regulations include provision for the boarding out and fostering of children[2], while some predate the formation of the group but are still in force[3]. Regulation, inspection, training and research are enshrined in the powers of the Secretary of State within the Social Work (Scotland) Act 1968[4], and duly authenticated officers acting on his behalf are required to exercise his powers[5]. While the Social Work Services Group fulfils these duties, the direct inspectorial role carried out by the inspectorate of the Department of Health and Social Security in England and Wales is much less evident in Scotland. Certain incidents must be reported to the Secretary of State, and in practice investigation of those incidents falls to members of the Social Work Services Group. The large administrative component within the group further underlines the regulatory and legislative focus of the group, while the professional social work staff carry a more limited training and advisory role.

1 *Social Work and the Community* (1966) (Cmnd 3065), para 55.
2 Boarding Out and Fostering of Children (Scotland) Regulations 1985, SI 1985/1799.
3 Eg the Administration of Children's Homes (Scotland) Regulations 1959, SI 1959/834.
4 Social Work (Scotland) Act 1968 (c 49), s 5.
5 Ibid, s 6 (amended by the Children Act 1975 (c 72), s 108(1)(a), Sch 3, para 50; Criminal Law Act 1977 (c 45), s 63(1), Sch 11, para 13; Adoption (Scotland) Act 1978 (c 28), s 66(2), Sch 3, para 10; Local Government and Planning (Scotland) Act 1982 (c 43), s 66(2), Sch 4, Pt II).

8. The Social Work (Scotland) Act 1968. The Social Work (Scotland) Act 1968 received the royal assent on 26 July 1968 and much of the Act came into force on 17 November 1969[1]. The Act is as wide ranging in its provisions as were the recommendations contained in *Social Work and the Community*[2].

The new departments carrying out social work functions were based initially on counties, counties of cities and large burghs[3] — fifty-two in all. Since the local government reorganisation of 1975 the organisation of social work services has been based instead on regional or islands councils[4]. Additional functions were given to social work departments at that time; in particular, responsibility for social work provision in hospitals and prisons.

The Social Work (Scotland) Act 1968 brought together services previously provided by probation, child care, welfare and mental health officers. The sum of responsibilities became wider as several functions of the local health authorities were also transferred to the social work departments[5]. These included duties to register premises and persons caring for young children, and they provide after-care services for people who have been suffering from illness[5].

The 1968 Act requires each local authority to appoint a social work committee to which stand referred all the functions required to be carried out by social work departments[6]. As social work departments have such extensive areas of duties and responsibilities and such wide interests, the major social work committee will generally form some sub-committees to which a range of functions may be delegated[7]. These sub-committees may deal with different types of social work provision, for example residential services, area team services, policy and planning and voluntary organisation funding. Alternatively, they may carry responsibility for the full range of services but be split into different client groupings, for example services to the elderly, to children, to handicapped persons and to offenders. As the legislation is framed, all functions of the local authority relating to social work stand referred to the social work committee[8] and, as numerous duties and responsibilities are involved, delegation of many of the duties is made to appropriate officers of the authority. Such schemes of delegation require to be presented to the full committee to ensure that officers of the authority are legally empowered to carry out those duties and to exercise the powers which are contained within the Act. For example the local authority has power to recommend to a children's hearing that a review should be held in respect of the care of a particular child[9]. This power must be specifically delegated to a senior officer within the social work department if the social workers involved with the child and his family are to be legally entitled to request the reporter to a children's hearing to arrange a review, without approaching the social work committee to sanction every request.

The regional or islands council must also appoint a director of social work to run the social work department[10]. The Secretary of State has power to prescribe conditions for his qualifications and suitability[11]. In Scotland one condition is that the director of social work must hold a recognised professional social work qualification[12], a condition which does not pertain in England and Wales.

1 Social Work (Scotland) Act 1968 (c 65), s 98(1); Social Work (Scotland) Act 1968 (Commencement No 2) Order 1969, SI 1969/1274.
2 Cmnd 3065 (1966): see para 6 above.
3 Social Work (Scotland) Act 1968, s 1 (as originally enacted).
4 Ibid, s 1 (amended by the Local Government (Scotland) Act 1973 (c 65), ss 161, 214(2), Sch 20, Sch 27, Pt II, para 183). For the regional and islands councils, see s 1, Sch 1, Pt I.
5 See the Social Work (Scotland) Act 1968, s 1(4).
6 Ibid, s 2(1).
7 Local Government (Scotland) Act 1973, Sch 20, para 2.
8 Social Work (Scotland) Act 1968, s 2(2) (prospectively amended by the Disabled Persons (Services, Consultation and Representation) Act 1986 (c 33), s 12(2)).
9 Social Work (Scotland) Act 1968, s 48(2).
10 Ibid, s 3(1).
11 Ibid, s 3(2); Qualifications of Directors of Social Work (Scotland) Regulations 1978, SI 1978/1284.
12 See ibid, Schedule.

9. The structure and organisation of social work departments. The organisation and structure of social work departments is not prescribed, apart from the requirement to have a director of social work[1]. The Social Work (Scotland) Act 1968 requires the local authority to provide adequate staff to assist the director of social work[2], but the numbers of staff and structure of departments is left to individual authorities.

Authorities have organised their services in a variety of ways but the primary objective must be to ensure that services are adequate for and available to those people who require them. Regional authorities which include large centres of population have provided local social work offices, area or district offices, in sufficient numbers to prevent people seeking help from having to travel long distances for advice or assistance. In rural areas there will be fewer local offices but social workers will require to travel great distances to visit those people seeking their help and advice. In small communities social workers may have an office within community centres or medical centres.

Regional social work departments organise their management in a diversity of ways. Several regions have appointed depute directors who fill the role of the director in his absence and also carry key functions to ensure the efficient operation of the department's work. Regions also have assistant directors who are in charge of either a geographical section of the department which is responsible for the full range of social work services in that area, or a functional section of the department, for example residential provision, administration, training or community social work provision.

If the department is one with a large staff then again senior managers directly accountable to assistant directors may hold posts with either geographical or functional responsibilities. Social workers are generally grouped in teams serving a specific geographical area and deal with all the requests for advice and assistance presented to them from the community they serve. Social workers are supervised by a more experienced social worker who may help them with the complex decisions which have to be made about vulnerable clients needing help or care. Local offices will also have organisers of the home help service located in them. The home help service is a most important provision for assisting elderly, sick or disabled people to cope independently within their own homes[3].

Local offices will also have occupational therapists working from them, providing a range of services to disabled people. The provision of services is required to enhance the independence of disabled and sick people and to aid them with daily living[4]. Occupational therapists have a different training from that of social workers to equip them to understand the nature and effect on clients of disability and chronic illness, and to be able to suggest practical aids and adaptations to property which can allow the disabled person a fuller life. Close co-operation with housing authorities is vital in planning and providing accommodation which is suitable for people with a substantial handicap. The manager of these different workers may be called a team leader or an area officer. His role is to ensure that the provision of social work services to his geographical area is adequate and of a satisfactory standard. He is accountable to senior managers for the services provided, and must inform senior managers of the need for resources of staff and finance to enable him to fulfil the duties laid on the department to provide social work services in that area.

Administrative services are most important to complement the social work services and to administer the complex financial transactions which are consequential on many social work services. For example, families in the community who care for children as foster parents must receive proper recompense, equipment and clothing for the child; home help services require payment from clients; and staff must have access to personnel advice and receive their salaries regularly.

Since local government reorganisation in 1975, social work services must also be provided in hospitals and prisons. The presence of a social worker within a medical team in hospitals is important to ensure that patients facing serious illness or receiving treatment can be supported by appropriate social work services. This could involve arranging alternative care for young children where a parent is in hospital, or home-help support for an elderly person whose regular caregiver is in hospital. Several specialist treatment units, for example severe head injuries wards and kidney transplant units, will have a social worker solely to work as a member of the team of staff caring for the patients.

Within a prison, the social work unit provides advice and assistance to prisoners and their families. The families of persons in prison frequently need assistance with housing or financial matters following committal to prison of, perhaps, the breadwinner. Many prisoners will be seen at their own request, while others will be identified by prison staff as having particular anxieties and problems which a social worker may be able to alleviate.

Although much of the legislation relating to social work provision lays duties, and not merely powers, on departments their ability to fulfil those duties may be limited by the resources available to them. The finances available are seldom adequate to provide services in sufficient depth or variety for the plethora of needs presented by modern society. Regional councils and local offices are therefore faced with making decisions about priorities both in terms of services and location, and many duties may remain unfulfilled.

1 Social Work (Scotland) Act 1968 (c 49), s 3(1): see para 8 above.
2 Ibid, s 3(7).
3 As to the home help service, see ibid, s 14 (amended by the National Health Service (Scotland) Act 1972 (c 58), s 64(2), Sch 7, Pt II, and the Health and Social Services and Social Security Adjudications Act 1983 (c 41), s 30, Sch 10, Pt I). See also para 14 below.
4 Chronically Sick and Disabled Persons Act 1970 (c 44), s 2 (amended by the Local Authority Social Services Act 1970 (c 42), s 14(1), Sch 2, para 12, and the Local Government Act 1972 (c 70), s 272(1), Sch 30); Chronically Sick and Disabled Persons (Scotland) Act 1972 (c 51), s 1. See also para 23 below.

10. Social work and voluntary organisations. Much social service provision is made by voluntary organisations. They often have a specialist focus and have built up skills and knowledge with special needs groups in the community, for example, blind persons, deaf persons, stroke victims or with people who share a common problem or interest, for example, single parents, widows and parents of children with severe handicaps. Voluntary organisations in terms of social work legislation are bodies (other than public or local authorities) the activities of which are carried on otherwise than for profit[1].

The Secretary of State may make grants or loans to voluntary organisations who are carrying out functions which are required by the Social Work (Scotland) Act 1968[2]. The local authority similarly may make grants or loans or contributions to voluntary organisations whose sole or primary purpose is to promote social welfare[3]. The local authority may also make premises or equipment, transport or staff available to such organisations, whether by way of gift, loan or otherwise[4]. As a local authority embraces many departments, the sole power to make grants or loans does not rest with social work departments. Education departments may make loans or grants to groups who provide activities in the community for young people or families. Many education departments offer rent-free premises to groups for mothers and toddlers or to day clubs for senior citizens. Throughout the Social Work (Scotland) Act 1968 but most particularly in the provisions relating to general social welfare services and the provision of residential establishments[5] voluntary organisations may form an integral part of the social services provision for a local authority area. In services to the chronically sick or disabled, voluntary resources are frequently harnessed to provide recreational activities, provisions of meals and holidays.

Funding by a social work department to a voluntary organisation may range from meeting all the staffing and running costs of a small specialist agency to making a grant of a few hundred pounds to assist a small local specialist group to rent premises for its meetings. It is by a network of statutory and voluntary provision that the needs of the many individuals and groups who require help with the day-to-day pressures of living can best be met. Close partnership between voluntary organisations and local authorities is required to prevent duplication and competition for scarce resources. The collaboration is encouraged by the legislative provisions of the Act of 1968[6].

Health boards also have a role in contributing to the services provided by local authorities. This was strengthened in 1983. Health boards may provide money to assist with certain services provided by the social work department, for example special educational and day care facilities for handicapped persons and residential facilities[7].

Local authorities must from year to year decide what level of services they are able to provide within the resources available to them. To enhance the level of provision they must co-operate closely with voluntary organisations, health boards and district authorities to enhance provision for those most in need, and by joint planning ensure that the services are as effective as possible.

1 Social Work (Scotland) Act 1968 (c 49), s 94(1).
2 Ibid, s 10(1) (amended by the Children Act 1975 (c 72), s 108(1)(a), Sch 3, para 51(a), and the Adoption (Scotland) Act 1978 (c 28), s 66(2), Sch 3, para 11).
3 Social Work (Scotland) Act 1968, s 10(3). Such an organisation includes an approved adoption agency: s 10(3A) (added by the Children Act 1975, Sch 3, para 51(b)).
4 Social Work (Scotland) Act 1968, s 10(4).
5 Ie ibid ss 12, 59.
6 See eg ibid, ss 10(4), 59(2)(c).
7 See the National Health Service (Scotland) Act 1978 (c 29), s 16A (substituted by the Health and Social Services and Social Security Adjudications Act 1983 (c 41), s 2).

11. The training of social workers. In the 1950s there was a small number of courses offering specialist training to social workers, principally in mental health and medical social work. The direction of present social work training was set by the influential committee chaired by Dame Eileen Younghusband which reported in 1959. The Younghusband Report stressed the need for foundation courses linked with vocational courses later which would develop skills in social work rather than impart purely theoretical knowledge[1]. Local authorities were also urged to develop in-service training opportunities for their staff.

The recommendations were widely accepted and universities developed social science courses which prepared students for professional specialist courses later. Training for social workers also developed outwith universities in colleges of education. The Younghusband Report stressed the importance of national standards in training, and recommended that to achieve this a central training council in social work should be established, funded by public money[2]. The council was to be responsible for the recognition of all training courses and for setting appropriate standards for the assessment of a student's performance[3]. Throughout the 1960s courses at a basic level and at a postgraduate level developed in many universities and colleges. Most postgraduate courses remained of a narrow and specialist nature, reflecting the various different departments that existed before the Social Work (Scotland) Act 1968. Courses thereafter offered a generic experience and qualification (Certificate of Qualification in Social Work (CQSW)). Integral to all social work courses is the practical application of theory to practice. This is achieved by each student being required to undertake three or four periods of supervised work experience in different social work settings.

In 1971 the central body recommended by Younghusband was established, namely the Central Council for the Education and Training of Social Workers (CCETSW). CCETSW promotes relevant training, approves courses and encourages applicants to present themselves for training. Members of CCETSW are appointed by the Secretary of State, and the council consists of a chairman and no more than twenty-five other members[4].

Since 1976 many local authorities have been joining together to provide in-service training leading to a Certificate in Social Service. This certificate course has been particularly relevant for staff in residential and day-care units and managers of home-care services. The pattern of this course is for the person to remain within his own workplace but attend college regularly and have directed periods of study and supervision.

Training for the future is subject to scrutiny. A single qualifying award in social work is to be introduced in the early 1990s. It is currently recommended that the period of training should extend to an extra year, making a three-year period of training. The extension of the period of training is seen by CCETSW to be necessary to equip social workers better 'to meet the demands of rapidly changing social conditions and new forms of service delivery'[5]. The content of these three-year courses should ensure 'an appropriate balance . . . of study in an educational institution; supervised practice, in placement, in employment, or in both'[5].

If further specialised training is required for social workers it is recommended that this should be considered only after a relevant period in employment and that specialist courses should be provided both within social work departments and in colleges or universities. Specialist training is mandatory for social workers undertaking duties in terms of the Mental Health (Scotland) Act of 1984. The persons appointed as mental health officers must be able to show competence, qualification and experience in mental health[6]. The Secretary of State is empowered under the Social Work (Scotland) Act 1968 to provide courses for training social workers, and to fund such courses[7].

1 *Working Party Report on Social Workers in Local Authority Health and Welfare Services 1959* (The Younghusband Report), paras 870, 891.

2 Ibid, para 875.
3 Ibid, para 876.
4 Health and Social Services and Social Security Adjudications Act 1983 (c 41), s 10, Sch 3.
5 CCETSW Resolution dated 20 September 1985.
6 Mental Health (Scotland) Act 1984 (c 36), s 9(3), (4).
7 Social Work (Scotland) Act 1968 (c 49), s 9.

12. Conclusions. Social work departments as part of regional and island councils have extensive duties and powers to fulfil in order to try to meet the needs of many and varied groups and individuals in their area. Duties laid on local authorities demand that services are provided, and services require resourcing if they are to be adequate and effective. The balance between need and resource is seldom in equilibrium and social workers have not only to assess the individual needs of people seeking their help but also set them in some order of priority for receiving help as long as demand exceeds resources.

Services must continue to go to the most vulnerable individuals and groups so that their welfare may be enhanced and deterioration of their difficulties may be halted and so that the aims of the Social Work (Scotland) Act 1968 to promote social welfare in every community may come closer to realisation.

2. GENERAL DUTIES OF SOCIAL WORK DEPARTMENTS

13. Advice, guidance and assistance. The keystone of the Social Work (Scotland) Act 1968 is the provision that local authorities are required 'to promote social welfare by making available advice, guidance and assistance on such a scale as may be appropriate for their area, and . . . to provide or secure the provision of such facilities (including the provision or arranging the provision of residential and other establishment) as they may consider suitable and adequate'[1]. Such assistance is to be given to persons specified more fully in subsequent provisions of the Act[2].

The advice, guidance and assistance can thus be made available directly by the local authority or it may arrange that some services and facilities are provided by other bodies. For example, Dr Barnardo's may provide residential units for children in need of care; the Church of Scotland may provide residential homes for elderly persons; a voluntary organisation may provide counselling services for specific groups of people, for example, CRUSE for widows and Age Concern for elderly persons. The statute defines clearly the scope of this provision as limited to certain persons who can be identified as a child under eighteen or 'persons in need'[3].

Where a child under eighteen is involved, if assistance in kind or, in exceptional circumstances, cash is being considered, the local authority must satisfy itself that the assistance is likely to reduce the need (1) to take a child into care; (2) to keep him in care, or (3) to be referred to a children's hearing[4].

When the Social Work (Scotland) Act 1968 was first implemented 'persons in need' were to include those (a) in need of care because of infirmity, youth or age; (b) suffering from illness or mental disorder or substantially handicapped; (c) rendered homeless or in need of temporary accommodation; (d) persons prescribed by the Secretary of State as needing assistance from the local authority[5]. The duty to provide help to homeless persons was later removed by the Housing (Homeless Persons) Act 1977[6], the direct provision of help to homeless persons being replaced by a duty on local authorities to co-operate with housing authorities to give advice to homeless people and other assistance as appropriate[7]. The provision of assistance is further restricted when a person in need is involved in that assistance may be given in cash only where exceptional circumstances exist which must, unless a person under eighteen is involved, also constitute an emergency for the person in need[8]. The local authority must also consider the person's eligibility for assistance from any other statutory body and the availability of that assistance at the time of need[9]. The legislation places a duty on local authorities to have regard to these aspects[10], and thus a person in receipt of statutory benefits may still be eligible for assistance if there are exceptional circumstances in the particular emergency which mean that the person has residual problems which require assistance. Any assistance given may be given unconditionally or be subject to repayment[10]. Further considerations about the appropriateness of assistance require the local authority to assess whether assistance in the form considered would (i) avoid the local authority being caused greater expense than in giving other types of assistance, or (ii) avoid aggravation of the person's needs which, if left without help, would be likely to cause the authority greater expense at a later date[11].

This particular provision of the Social Work (Scotland) Act 1968 is frequently equated with cash payments to divert emergencies, but it does form the basis for much of the services of a social work department to families in the community where work is undertaken to prevent children from coming into care, or to elderly persons to make it possible for them to continue to live at home. The provision of appropriate facilities to promote social welfare will include many residential as well as day facilities, for example children's centres where a child with health or developmental problems may receive daily care and where parents are encouraged to participate in a range of activities to enhance their capabilities as parents.

1 Social Work (Scotland) Act 1968 (c 49), s 12(1).
2 Ibid, s 12(2).
3 Ibid, s 12(2). As to the meaning of 'person in need', see below.
4 Ibid, s 12(2)(a).
5 Ibid, s 94(1) (as originally enacted).
6 Housing (Homeless Persons) Act 1977 (c 48), s 20(4), Schedule.
7 Ibid, s 9(1).
8 Social Work (Scotland) Act 1968, s 12(2)(b).
9 Ibid, s 12(3).
10 Ibid, s 12(4).
11 Ibid, s 12(2)(b).

14. Home help and laundry services. Every local authority must provide a home help service on a scale that is adequate to the needs of its area[1]. Home helps provide care to persons in need or to expectant mothers so that they may remain at home[2]. Domestic help forms the basis of the home help service but, particularly with housebound persons, the regular presence of the home help is of great value to monitor their well-being and to provide assistance with laundry, housework, shopping and cooking. The home help service may be provided without charge, or appropriate charges may be made by the local authority[3].

In addition, the local authority may provide laundry facilities to households receiving home help services or who could be eligible for them[4]. This service assists people caring for elderly or disabled persons where incontinence is a problem and where managing laundry is increasingly difficult. Both these services play a key part in maintaining persons in need within the community rather than requiring them to be placed in residential care.

1 Social Work (Scotland) Act 1968 (c 49), s 14(1).

2 Ibid, s 14(1). For the meaning of 'person in need', see para 13 above.
3 Ibid, s 87(1), (1A) (substituted by the Health and Social Services and Social Security Adjudications Act 1983 (c 41), s 18).
4 Social Work (Scotland) Act 1968, s 14(1).

15. Miscellaneous powers. The local authority may make arrangements for the burial or cremation of people who were in local authority care at the time of their death or who were receiving assistance from the local authority immediately before their death[1]. Expenses for burials and cremations may be recovered from the estate of the deceased person or from a person liable to maintain the deceased person at the time of his death[2]. The local authority may make payments to assist parents, relatives or other persons connected with the person whose funeral is being arranged by the local authority, to attend the funeral[3].

The local authority may also make payments to parents and relatives to enable them to visit a child who has been placed in care[4]. Guidance from the Secretary of State laid stress on the need to ensure that parents had regular contact with their children in care[5], and this power enables the local authority to assist with the costs of such visits which otherwise might cause undue hardship to the parent to maintain.

1 Social Work (Scotland) Act 1968 (c 49), s 28(1).
2 Ibid, s 28(2) (amended by the Social Security (Consequential Provisions) Act 1975 (c 18), s 1(3), Sch 2, para 35).
3 Social Work (Scotland) Act 1968, s 29(2).
4 Ibid, s 29(1).
5 *Code of Practice – Access to Children in Care or Under Supervision in Scotland* (1983).

16. Provision of residential and day care facilities. Local authorities must provide and maintain suitable residential and other establishments which will assist them in carrying out their various duties to persons in need[1]. These establishments may be provided directly by the local authority or jointly with another local authority or through voluntary organisations which will set up and run a range of establishments[2]. Finance for capital expenditure on establishments is frequently provided by central government on a loan basis, repayment being required within sixty years[3]. Local authorities must ensure that there is provision for young people who need secure accommodation[4]. These secure units are required for those young people where physical and structural controls are necessary to prevent further deterioration of the young person's behaviour. Specific powers are given to the Secretary of State to make grants to local authorities to ensure that this kind of accommodation is available[5].

The operation of all residential and day care establishments is closely governed by regulations made by the Secretary of State[6]. Such regulations set out the standards of accommodation and equipment desired, the management required and the inspection duties of local authorities for residential establishments provided by voluntary organisations[7].

Before admitting residents, any unit not run by the local authority must apply to the local authority for registration[8]. The local authority must then visit the premises and be satisfied about the fitness of the person to manage, the adequacy of the staff to run the establishment, the accommodation's suitability for the purpose it is to fulfil and the general conduct of the establishment[9]. If satisfied about the staffing, accommodation and conduct the local authority may proceed to register the establishment[10]. If, however, the applicant seeking registration is found to be unfit by reason of age or character, or if the premises are unsuitable or the proposed staffing levels insufficient, then registration may be refused[10]. If it is decided that registration should be refused the local authority must send a notice by the recorded delivery service not less than fourteen days before refusing the application for registration to the applicant[11]. The applicant then has a right to be heard[12], usually by the social work committee, which will receive reports from its officers about registration of or refusal to register establishments. After hearing the applicant, the local authority may decide that registration should be refused, and a notice about the refusal must again be sent to the applicant[13]. Appeal by the applicant thereafter is to an appeal tribunal whose constitution is set out by law[14]. This appeal must be brought within twenty-one days of the date of the notice of refusal to register the establishment[15].

The local authority may remove persons from an establishment which it has refused to register during the twenty-one-day period of appeal[16]. The primary aim of the local authority through its social work department must be to ensure the safety and well-being of any persons resident in an establishment assessed to be unsuitable for the care of those persons.

Where the local authority registers an establishment, the inspection of the establishment will be carried out subsequently by officers of the local authority[17]. The local authority must also ensure that persons in registered establishments are visited from time to time in the interests of the well-being of those persons[18]. The social work department will provide advice and support to people running establishments in its area on a regular basis. Its role is much wider than the narrow inspection of conditions of care and premises which is required by the legislation.

1 Social Work (Scotland) Act 1968 (c 49), s 59(1).
2 Ibid, s 59(2).
3 Ibid, s 59(3).
4 Ibid, s 59(1), read with s 58A (added by the Health and Social Services and Social Security Adjudications Act 1983 (c 41), s 8(4)).
5 Social Work (Scotland) Act 1968, s 59A (added by the Children Act 1975 (c 72), s 72).
6 See eg the Administration of Children's Homes (Scotland) Regulations 1959, SI 1959/834.
7 See the Social Work (Scotland) Act 1968, s 60 (amended by the National Health Service (Scotland) Act 1978 (c 29), s 109, Sch 16, para 29, and the Health and Social Services and Social Security Adjudications Act 1983, s 8(3)).
8 Social Work (Scotland) Act 1968, ss 61(1), (2), 62(1), (2).
9 Ibid, s 62(3).
10 Ibid, s 62(3) proviso.
11 Ibid, s 64(1).
12 Ibid, s 64(2).
13 Ibid, s 64(3).
14 Ibid, s 64(4), Sch 5.
15 Ibid, s 64(5).
16 Ibid, s 65(1).
17 Ibid, s 67.
18 Ibid, s 68.

3. MAJOR DUTIES TO SPECIFIC GROUPS OF CLIENTS

(1) CHILDREN AND YOUNG PERSONS

17. General duties. The social work department has major duties relating to children and young people. The local authority must provide care for children in its area who appear to be under seventeen and have neither parent nor guardian, or where the parent or guardian is prevented by illness or other circumstances from providing adequate care[1]. The test in decisions about whether a local authority should be involved in caring for the child rests on whether the actual intervention of the authority is necessary to protect the interests of the child. It is important to remember that many children deprived of care by their parents will be very adequately looked after by relatives with no need of assistance from the local authority.

Once a child is received into its care, the local authority must try to rehabilitate the child with his parents, friends or other family members wherever this is consistent with the child's welfare[2]. To care for children the social work department must provide a range of services including residential homes and families in the community who are suitable and skilled in looking after other people's children[3]. The social work department is required by regulations to assess very carefully the suitability of carers who look after other people's children[4]. Certain categories of persons are excluded as foster parents and a variety of checks must be made on the suitability of families before the social work department may place a child in their home[5]. Similar regulations cover the placement of children by their parents with strangers[6] and the placement of children under five with carers[7]. The primary aim of the regulations is to try to ensure that no one is permitted to care for someone else's child unless he can offer adequate care and has no previous record of convictions for violence, particularly to children, which would render him unsuitable for the task[8]. The visiting of children placed in homes other than their own is also regulated, and different timescales apply according to the type of care which is being provided[9].

1 Social Work (Scotland) Act 1968 (c 49), s 15(1).
2 Ibid, s 15(3).
3 Ibid, ss 20, 21 (amended by the Children Act 1975 (c 72), s 79; Child Care Act 1980 (c 5), s 89(2), Sch 5, para 21; Health and Social Services and Social Security Adjudications Act 1983 (c 41), s 9, Sch 2, paras 4, 5).
4 See eg the Nurseries and Child-Minders Regulation Act 1948 (c 53), the Foster Children (Private Fostering) (Scotland) Regulations 1985, SI 1985/1798, and the Boarding Out and Fostering of Children (Scotland) Regulations 1985, SI 1985/1799.
5 Ibid, reg 7(1), Schedule.
6 Foster Children (Private Fostering) (Scotland) Regulations 1985.
7 Nurseries and Child-Minders Regulation Act 1948, ss 1, 2.
8 Boarding Out and Fostering of Children (Scotland) Regulations 1985, reg 7(1), Schedule.
9 As to the care of children generally, see CHILDREN AND YOUNG PERSONS.

18. Planning for a child's care. All decisions relating to a child in its care must be made by the social work department, giving first consideration to the need to safeguard and promote the child's welfare throughout his childhood[1].

Social workers must be fully conversant with the emotional and physical needs of children so that they can make decisions which will safeguard the child. This kind of decision requires the exercise of balancing the child's safety at home and his well-being there with the possible risks of moving him to a different family. This type of decision will be shared with others and, particularly where compulsory removal is sought, a justice of the peace, children's hearing or sheriff will make the decision but the social worker must provide the evidence and assessment to assist with that decision. Beside the social work assessment of the child's needs, consideration must be given to the most appropriate legal basis for the child's care. Freeing for adoption procedures[2] provides opportunities in legal terms to resolve dilemmas and disagreements about whether adoption is in the child's best interests prior to the child or a new family committing themselves to this course of action. Legal delays in hearing these cases have extended the processes with consequent distress for the natural parents and damaging uncertainty for the child, who is often existing in limbo, with natural parents unable to care for him but unwilling to release him to other parents. The absence of timescales for such important decisions prevents social work departments from making the most effective plans for a child. Similar disagreements between natural parents and social work authorities in the children's hearing process have strict timescales which allow clear planning to take place.

1 Social Work (Scotland) Act 1968 (c 49), s 20(1) (substituted by the Children Act 1975 (c 72), s 79, and amended by the Health and Social Services and Social Security Adjudications Act 1983 (c 41), s 9, Sch 2, para 4).
2 As to freeing a child for adoption, see the Adoption (Scotland) Act 1978 (c 28), s 18 (amended by the Health and Social Services and Social Security Adjudications Act 1983, Sch 2, para 40).

19. Adoption services. Adoption services form a large part of the responsibilities of a social work department towards children, either by the direct provision of services or by co-operation with approved adoption agencies[1]. Local authorities and voluntary organisations must work together to provide a comprehensive range of services to mothers seeking advice about placing their children for adoption, families seeking to adopt a child, and adopted persons seeking information about their background[2].

The selection process of persons wishing to adopt which must be followed by social work departments and voluntary organisations is contained in regulations[3]. The organisation of decision making is regulated within these procedures to ensure that most careful consideration is given by authorities to all steps of the process; for example decisions to place a child for adoption or to accept persons as adopters must be made by a panel of persons selected for their experience and skills[4].

To assist the court with its decisions about whether to grant a particular adoption order the local authority must provide reports on all placements not made by an adoption agency[5]. Where the placement is by an adoption agency (including a local authority), the agency itself must prepare a report to the court on the suitability of the application and how it safeguards the welfare of the child[6].

1 As to adoption generally, see 'Adoption' in FAMILY LAW.
2 Adoption (Scotland) Act 1978 (c 28), s 1.
3 Adoption Agencies (Scotland) Regulations 1984, SI 1984/988.
4 Ibid, regs 11–13, 18.
5 Adoption (Scotland) Act 1978, s 22(1).
6 Ibid, s 23.

20. Custody applications. The social work department must provide the court with reports where a custody application[1] is made by any person who is not the parent of a child for whom application is made[2]. The person seeking custody must notify the social work department of his application, and a social worker must then visit to assess the situation and report to the court on whether an award of custody would be in the best interests of the child[2].

1 As to custody applications in respect of children generally, see FAMILY LAW.
2 Children Act 1975 (c 72), s 49(1), (2).

21. Children's hearings. The local authority must establish a panel for its area to consider children who may be in need of care and protection[1]. The local authority must appoint an officer, known as a reporter, to arrange children's hearings and undertake other duties which may be assigned[2]. It is also the responsibility of the local authority to ensure that the reporter has adequate staff[3], and suitable accommodation which must be separate from criminal courts and police stations[4].

Social work departments work very closely with the reporter and children's hearing by provision of social background reports on children referred to a hearing as in need of compulsory measures of care. Where children are assessed as requiring care which encompasses protection, control, guidance and treatment[5] the supervision will fall to a social worker. The work with the child and his family will involve supporting them by advice and guidance and arranging for reviews of the supervision requirement by a children's hearing as appropriate[6].

The provision of care will include the establishment and running of a range of residential and day centres for young people[7]. Day centres offer day-by-day care to pre-school children and their families and try to reduce the risk of children requiring to be cared for apart from their parents on a more permanent basis. These children may include children at risk of abuse by their parents where the assistance of staff and relief of pressure on parents will reduce the risks.

For older children services such as those envisaged by the Kilbrandon Committee will be provided in some areas[8]. The focus will be on social education for these young people to divert them from delinquency and to help them with the preparation for adulthood.

1 Social Work (Scotland) Act 1968 (c 49), s 33. As to the panels, see Sch 3 (amended by the Local Government (Scotland) Act 1973 (c 65), ss 214(2), 237(1), Sch 27, Pt II, para 187, Sch 29; Local Government (Scotland) Act 1975 (c 30), s 33; Law Reform (Miscellaneous Provisions) (Scotland) Act 1985 (c 73), s 24).
2 Social Work (Scotland) Act 1968, s 36(1) (amended by the Local Government (Scotland) Act 1973, Sch 27, Pt II, para 185(a), Sch 29).
3 Social Work (Scotland) Act 1968, s 36(6).
4 Ibid, s 34(3).
5 As to the tests, see ibid, s 32 (amended by the Children Act 1975 (c 72), s 108(1), Sch 3, para 54; Solvent Abuse (Scotland) Act 1983 (c 33), s 1; Health and Social Services and Social Security Adjudications Act 1983 (c 41), s 8(1)).
6 Social Work (Scotland) Act 1968, s 20A (added by the Children Act 1975, s 80).
7 Social Work (Scotland) Act 1968, s 21 (amended by the Child Care Act 1980 (c 5), s 89(2), Sch 5, para 21, and the Law Reform (Miscellaneous Provisions) (Scotland) Act 1985, s 59(1), Sch 2, para 9). See also the Social Work (Scotland) Act 1968, s 59.
8 As to the Kilbrandon Committee, see para 5 above. As to other services for older children, see CHILDREN AND YOUNG PERSONS.

22. Children at risk of abuse. Social work departments carry heavy responsibilities towards children at risk of abuse, whether that abuse is physical, emotional or sexual. If a social worker receives information from any source, whether anonymous or identified, he must investigate the information received unless he is satisfied that such investigation is unnecessary[1]. These investigations must be carried out in a very short time so that damage is not done to a child through lack of speedy investigation. Some investigations will lead the social worker to ask a justice of the peace or a sheriff for a warrant to remove the child to a place of safety where investigations indicate that an offence has been committed against the child or that there is likely to be unnecessary suffering or serious impairment of a child's health because of a lack of parental care[2]. Wherever a child appears to be in need of compulsory measures of care the social worker must give the reporter what information he can about the child[3]. Invariably when a place of safety warrant has been obtained the reporter must be involved and a hearing convened on the first lawful day after the child's detention in a place of safety[4].

Children at risk require the services of many agencies and professionals and the government issues regular circulars of guidance about this work. The central government circulars all recommend that local authorities set up area review committees with representatives from the police, education departments, health services, reporter to the children's hearing, voluntary child care organisations and social work departments. These committees are charged with the duty to consider the most effective way of co-ordinating services to protect children at risk of abuse. Social work departments will also draw up notes of guidance to staff about their responsibilities in this highly sensitive and stressful area of work.

1 Social Work (Scotland) Act 1968 (c 49), s 37(1A)(a) (added by the Children Act 1975 (c 72), s 83(a)).
2 Social Work (Scotland) Act 1968, s 37(2) (substituted by the Children Act 1975, s 83(b)).
3 Social Work (Scotland) Act 1968, s 37(1A)(b) (as added: see note 1 above).
4 Ibid, s 37(4) (amended by the Criminal Procedure (Scotland) Act 1975 (c 21), s 461(1), Sch 9, para 42).

(2) HANDICAPPED PERSONS

23. General duties. Social work services to persons suffering from a mental or physical handicap were included in the general services to people with infirmity, disability or mental disorders until the enactment of specific legislation relating to services to persons with a chronic illness or disability. Legislation for England and Wales was enacted in 1970[1], and the provisions were extended to Scotland two years later[2].

Every local authority with social work responsibilities must inform itself of the number of persons in its area who are persons in need in terms of the Social Work (Scotland) Act 1968 so far as it relates to chronic illness or disability, and of the need for services for those persons who are identified as chronically sick or disabled[3]. The authority must also publish general information about services for disabled people and ensure that any person using any of these services is also informed of any other services relevant to his need[4]. Identified within the legislation is a wide range of services which local authorities must provide if they decide that those services are necessary to meet the needs of such persons[5]. The level and range of provision is very varied across Scotland, and financial resources are seldom sufficient to ensure that the full range of services is available to all the disabled people who could benefit from them.

1 Chronically Sick and Disabled Persons Act 1970 (c 44).
2 Chronically Sick and Disabled Persons (Scotland) Act 1972 (c 51), s 1.
3 Chronically Sick and Disabled Persons Act 1970, s 1(1), applied by s 29(2) (substituted by the Chronically Sick and Disabled Persons (Scotland) Act 1972, s 1(1), which is prospectively amended by the Disabled Persons (Services, Consultation and Representation) Act 1986 (c 33), s 12(1)). For the meaning of 'person in need', see para 13 above.
4 Chronically Sick and Disabled Persons Act 1970, s 1(2), as so applied (prospectively amended by the Disabled Persons (Services, Consultation and Representation) Act 1986, s 9).
5 Chronically Sick and Disabled Persons Act 1970, s 2(1), as so applied.

24. Specific services. The Disabled Persons (Services, Consultation and Representation) Act 1986 seeks to place duties on local authorities to specify why necessary services are not being provided[1] and to encourage disabled persons or their representatives to make representations about the lack of service[2]. The Act also requires local authorities to consider the ability of the current carer for a disabled person when determining what services may be necessary[3].

Some of the services which social work departments should provide are practical assistance at home (for example home helps and laundry), aids to daily living (for example minor articles to allow a disabled person to be independent such as adapted taps on sinks), recreational or educational facilities, assistance for travel to and from facilities, adaptations to housing to secure independence, safety or convenience (for example ramps, extra toilet and shower facilities accessible to a disabled person), assistance with holiday provision for disabled persons, meals at home and telephone installations[4].

Social work departments discharge many of these duties by employing occupational therapists to visit disabled people in their homes. They make an assessment of the person's needs and recommend what kind of aids and help will be necessary to meet the person's needs. Some services, particularly the provision of meals at home, will be carried out in close co-operation with voluntary organisations like the Women's Royal Voluntary Service.

The social work department must provide, or arrange for the provision of, residential and day care establishments for those disabled or chronically sick persons who can no longer remain at home but for whom hospital care is not required[5]. Day centres will incorporate therapy for disabled persons to try to ensure that full use is made of all the skills that they have. In providing services for the chronically sick or disabled, social work departments work closely with the education and health authorities and with housing authorities in adapting houses to be suitable for use by disabled persons.

1 See the Disabled Persons (Services, Consultation and Representation) Act 1986 (c 33), s 3. The Act comes into force on such date or dates as the Secretary of State may by order appoint: s 18(2). At the date at which this volume states the law no such date had been appointed.
2 See ibid, ss 1–3.
3 Ibid, s 8.
4 See the Chronically Sick and Disabled Persons Act 1970 (c 44), s 2(1), applied by s 29(2) (substituted by the Chronically Sick and Disabled Persons (Scotland) Act 1972 (c 51), s 1(1), which is prospectively amended by the Disabled Persons (Services, Consultation and Representation Act 1986, s 12(1)). As to the duties of local authorities to consider the needs of disabled persons, see ss 3, 4 of the 1986 Act.
5 See the Social Work (Scotland) Act 1968 (c 49), ss 12(1), 59(1).

(3) ELDERLY PERSONS

25. General duties. Services to elderly persons must be provided by social work departments in terms of their duty to promote welfare by offering advice, guidance and assistance to persons in need — specifically in this section of the title to those in need through age or infirmity[1]. Linked with this general duty are the specific responsibilities for the provision of residential facilities[2]: a large proportion of residential resources in any local authority is used to provide residential care for elderly people who can no longer be cared for at home.

1 Social Work (Scotland) Act 1968 (c 49), s 12(2)(b). For the meaning of 'person in need', see para 13 above.
2 Ibid, s 59(1).

26. Home help service. The social work department must provide a home help service to persons in need because of their age and infirmity[1]. Again a high percentage of persons receiving a home help service are sixty-five and over. The home help service offers a significant level of care to elderly persons within their own homes and is instrumental in maintaining elderly people safely at home, reducing the stress of care on family members and reducing the need for the elderly person to be admitted to residential care.

Linked with a home help service the social work department may provide a laundry service to cope with the problem of severe incontinence which may accompany age and increasing frailty[1]. This service is not an obligatory one and is difficult to administer and organise in sparsely populated areas.

1 Social Work (Scotland) Act 1968 (c 49), s 14: see para 14 above. For the meaning of 'person in need', see para 13 above.

27. Home meals service. The duty to make provision of meals to house-bound and disabled people also rests with the social work department. The provision of meals constitutes assistance in kind to persons in need[1] where the provision of meals would be instrumental in avoiding the local authority being caused greater expense by either providing other services (for example residential care) or aggravating that person's need and causing greater expense at a later date to the local authority to meet these needs.

1 Social Work (Scotland) Act 1968 (c 49), s 12(2)(b). For the meaning of 'person in need', see para 13 above.

28. Residential and day services. Services provided by the social work department to elderly persons constitute a major part of the total expenditure of most departments. The need for residential accommodation has increased rapidly, and residential units of varying size form a large part of the total residential care provision of a social work department.

The local authority must provide and maintain such residential establishments as are required to meet the needs of elderly persons within its area[1]. Much provision for the elderly is made by private individuals, registered companies and voluntary organisations. The social work department must register any such establishments where the sole or main object is to accommodate persons in need[3]. Financing elderly persons in private or voluntary accommodation rests with the persons themselves if their income is sufficient, or with the Department of Health and Social Security if they have insufficient income to meet the costs. A social work department is not permitted to supplement the costs of the care of the elderly in such establishments[3].

Day care provision is increasing with the social work department providing some places where elderly persons can attend on a daily basis, receive meals, assistance perhaps with bathing and have contact with other persons of similar age.

1 Social Work (Scotland) Act 1968 (c 49), s 59(1).
2 Ibid, s 61. For the meaning of 'person in need', see para 13 above.
3 See the Supplementary Benefit (Requirements) Regulations 1983, SI 1983/1399, reg 9(6).

29. Compulsory care. Despite the provision of services by health personnel, voluntary organisations and social work departments, some elderly persons reject all these services although they are incapable of caring adequately for themselves. Some may require compulsory removal from their homes because their circumstances have become dangerous to themselves and others. These circumstances arise where persons are suffering from grave chronic disease or, being aged, infirm or physically incapacitated, are living in unsanitary conditions and are unable to devote to themselves, and are not receiving from other persons, proper care and attention[1].

Where a medical officer investigates the circumstances of an elderly person and finds that person in the circumstances outlined above and assesses that it is necessary in that person's interests or for the prevention of injury to the health of, or serious nuisance to, other persons, to remove the elderly person, he will ask the social work department to arrange for the person's removal[2]. The social worker must apply to the appropriate summary court for an order authorising a named officer from the social work department to remove the person to a suitable hospital or other place[3]. The person in charge of the hospital or suitable place must be heard in court or have been given seven clear days' notice to state whether he can or cannot receive the person to be removed[4]. The person for whom the order is sought must also be given seven days' notice of the court hearing[5]. Once an order is granted the person may be removed and detained for up to three months, although the court has power to extend that period[6].

The person who has been removed may, when a period of at least six weeks has elapsed from the making of the order, apply to the court for the order to be revoked[7].

Where the circumstances of the person for whom removal is deemed necessary are such that a delay of seven days would be too damaging, notice by the local authority to the person involved may be waived if the medical officer of the local authority and another medical practitioner certify that it is necessary in the interests of the elderly person that he or she be removed without delay[8]. Where the situation is an emergency, the person in charge of the appropriate establishment may give verbal agreement and not require to give written agreement[9]. The emergency order may be granted by the sheriff for the area in which the person to be removed currently resides[10]. The emergency order can last for only three weeks[11]. The court may, however, reconsider the application before the expiry of that period and extend the order if necessary. The social worker must try to reduce the distress for the person being subjected to compulsory removal and involve any family or friends who might assist with the person's removal and subsequent care.

The local authority must provide temporary protection for the property of elderly persons if they are removed under a compulsory order[12]. This duty requires the local authority to take reasonable steps to prevent or mitigate the loss or damage to moveable property of the person who has been removed by an order of the court[12]. Reasonable expenses in carrying out this function may be recovered by the social work department from the person himself or from anyone liable to maintain him[13]. This may require the social worker to search a house for any valuable items or money stored in the property and ensure they are stored safely by being deposited in a bank or other secure place as soon as possible after the person's removal from the house[14].

1 National Assistance Act 1948 (c 29), s 47(1).
2 Ibid, s 47(2) (amended by the National Health Service (Scotland) Act 1972 (c 58), s 64(1), Sch 6, para 83(a)).
3 National Assistance Act 1948, s 47(2), (3).
4 Ibid, s 47(3) proviso.
5 Ibid, s 47(7)(a).
6 Ibid, s 47(4).
7 Ibid, s 47(6).
8 National Assistance (Amendment) Act 1951 (c 57), s 1(1).
9 Ibid, s 1(2).
10 Ibid, s 1(3), (5).
11 Ibid, s 1(4)(a).
12 National Assistance Act 1948, s 48(1).
13 Ibid, s 48(3).
14 For powers of entry, see ibid, s 48(2).

(4) PERSONS WITH MENTAL DISORDERS

30. Mental illness. The local authority must provide services for persons suffering from or recovering from mental disorder[1]. These services include the provision of residential accommodation[2] and after-care services[3]. After-care services may be provided in co-operation with appropriate health boards or voluntary agencies[4].

Within a psychiatric hospital a social worker will provide a counselling and advice service as part of the psychiatric team involved in caring for a mentally ill patient. The social work department must provide in each area a sufficient number of people appointed to discharge the functions of mental health officers in relation to the compulsory admission and detention of people in a psychiatric hospital[5]. From a day to be appointed by order special competence in dealing with persons suffering from a mental disorder must be demonstrated by persons wishing to be appointed as a mental health officer[6]. From such a day no mental health officer previously appointed may continue to act as such unless he is approved by the local authority and that authority is satisfied that he has competence in dealing with persons suffering from mental disorder and that he has such qualifications, experience and competence as the Secretary of State may direct[7]. The role, function and legal status of a mental health officer is distinct from the other range of functions a social worker may perform. The duties of an appointed mental health officer are carried out by that officer as a specific and named person and the functions are not originally vested in the local authority and delegated to its officers.

The main function of the mental health officer is to set in motion the procedures for compulsory admission of a person to a psychiatric hospital where the person's mental health demands that action[8]. The mental health officer must be satisfied on the basis of his social work assessment that the detention of the person in hospital is the most appropriate way of providing for his care and treatment[9]. Social work reports about the person's situation are prepared and an application then processed to the court to seek the removal and detention of the person suffering from a mental illness[10]. Where a mental health officer has not taken part in a compulsory admission to hospital the social work department must be informed by the hospital and a mental health officer must then interview the patient and provide a report on the patient's social circumstances to the responsible medical officer and to the Mental Welfare Commission for Scotland, not later than twenty-one days after the person's admission to hospital[11]. Where the admission is required as an emergency, the responsible medical officer should seek the consent of a relative of the patient to this course of action, but, if no relative is available, the consent of a mental health officer should be sought[12]. Consultation with a mental health officer may be sufficient, depending on the degree of urgency with which the patient requires to be admitted to hospital. In an emergency admission the local authority should be notified if no responsible relative is available to safeguard the patient's property[13]. The duty of the local authority in the absence of a relative is to safeguard both the moveable and heritable property of the person admitted[13]. The tasks performed by social workers acting as mental health officers contribute to the total care and treatment of the patient and assist the medical staff in carrying out their functions by relieving the patient of some anxieties about his property.

Persons suffering from mental illness are also included in the primary social work legislation as 'persons in need'[14], and many of the social work services are provided to the families of patients by social workers to help people suffering from a mental illness to function more independently in the community and to gain support from other people who are experiencing or have experienced a similar illness.

1 Mental Health (Scotland) Act 1984 (c 36), ss 7, 8. 'Mental disorder' means mental illness or mental handicap however caused or manifested: s 1(2). See further MENTAL HEALTH.
2 Ibid, s 7(1)(a).
3 Ibid, s 8(1).
4 Ibid, s 8(2).
5 Ibid, s 9(1).
6 Ibid, s 9(3). At the date at which this volume states the law no such day had been appointed.
7 Ibid, s 9(4).
8 Ibid, s 19(3).
9 Ibid, s 19(4).
10 See ibid, ss 19(6), 21.
11 Ibid, s 22(3).
12 Ibid, s 24(1), (2).
13 See the National Assistance Act 1948 (c 29), s 48, and the Mental Health (Scotland) Act 1984, s 92(2).
14 For the meaning of 'person in need', see para 13 above.

31. Mental handicap. Mental handicap is included in the definition of 'mental disorder' contained in the primary mental health legislation[1]. As with persons suffering from mental illness, people with a mental handicap may be provided with a range of services by the social work department. Provision of residential and day units for people suffering from a mental handicap is seldom adequate for the number of people needing these services. Social work initiatives to support people with a mental handicap in the community rather than in a hospital are many, but not yet enough to enable all the people currently living in hospitals, but who could live satisfactorily in the community, to make this transition. Shared flats, accommodation with a supportive and skilled landlady and small community houses all offer opportunities for people with a mental handicap to live a more ordinary life with greater freedom and independence.

The social work department must make a variety of provisions to provide or secure the provision of suitable training and occupation for persons suffering from mental handicap who are over school age[2]. This duty is fulfilled by providing a range of day facilities which offer training and sheltered employment opportunities to people over school age suffering from a mental handicap. The social work department must be informed by the education authority not less than one month and not more than six months before the child reaches school-leaving age that a particular pupil will require the services of the social work department on leaving school[3]. At the same time the child's parent must be notified of the education department's decision that their child suffers from a mental handicap such that he may benefit from the services which a local authority provides[3]. The social work department will then assess the child's individual needs in conjunction with education and health personnel to decide which day facility is most likely to meet the young person's needs and whether such a place is available. Necessary transport to social work facilities must also be provided[4]. Local authorities may join with voluntary organisations to fund special facilities for people with particular handicaps[5]. The level of provision of day training facilities is seldom adequate for those persons who require them, and some people will remain in hospitals and institutions longer than their level of care would indicate.

Social work departments also provide respite care to families with a person suffering from mental handicap. These services usually consist of an arrangement whereby the parents of a child with a mental handicap can request periods of relief from the day-to-day care of a handicapped child. The child will be placed with another family, chosen by the social work department, which has been assessed as suitable to undertake the task[6]. Some children, because of the severity of their handicap or behaviour, may be accommodated in a residential unit or hospital for relief care.

Social work departments play a key role in applications to the sheriff for the guardianship of a person aged over sixteen who is suffering from mental disorder of a nature or degree which warrants his reception into guardianship and where it is necessary in the interests of his welfare that he be received into guardianship[7]. A mental health officer must be involved in the making of the guardianship application to the sheriff and must be satisfied that the application is appropriate and that the opinions of the patient's relatives have been taken into account[8]. Medical recommendations must be presented to the sheriff before the application may be approved[9]. The person named in the application as guardian may be the social work department or someone it has chosen to act as guardian or any other person approved by it so to act[10]. The powers vested in the person named as guardian are substantial. The guardian or local authority may require the patient to live in a particular place, and to attend for training, education or medical treatment, and may require that access be given to the person under guardianship by any medical practitioner or mental health officer[11]. Once an application for guardianship has been approved the social work department, if named as guardian, must visit the person regularly to ensure his well-being and to consider the continued appropriateness of a guardianship order[12]. The order must be reviewed at six-monthly intervals until the end of the first year of guardianship, and thereafter annually[13].

1 Mental Health (Scotland) Act 1984 (c 36), s 1(2): see para 30, note 1, above.
2 Ibid, s 11(1).
3 Education (Scotland) Act 1980 (c 44), s 65(1).
4 Mental Health (Scotland) Act 1984, s 11(2).
5 Ibid, s 11(3).
6 Boarding Out and Fostering of Children (Scotland) Regulations 1985, SI 1985/1799, reg 7.
7 Mental Health (Scotland) Act 1984, ss 36, 37(1), 40.
8 See ibid, s 38.
9 Ibid, s 37(3).
10 Ibid, s 37(2).
11 Ibid, s 41(2).
12 See ibid, s 43(2), and the Mental Health (Specified Treatments, Guardianship Duties etc) (Scotland) Regulations 1984, SI 1984/1494, reg 5.
13 Mental Health (Scotland) Act 1984, s 47(1), (2).

(5) PERSONS APPEARING BEFORE A COURT, RELEASED FROM PRISON, ON PROBATION OR UNDER COMMUNITY SERVICE ORDERS

32. Persons appearing before a court. Social background reports, usually called 'social inquiry reports' to differentiate them from reports prepared for a children's hearing, must be made available by the social work department to any court which requires such a report to assist with the disposal of a case[1]. The Streatfield Report and the Morison Report outlined key aspects of these social inquiry reports[2]. The Morison Report recommended that reports should cover the following matters:

'Essential details of the offender's home surroundings and family background; his attitude to his family; and their response to him; his school and work record; and their spare-time activities; his attitude to employment; his attitude to his present offence; his attitude and response to previous forms of treatment following any previous convictions; detailed histories about relevant physical and mental conditions; an assessment of personality and character'.

The discretion which courts enjoy to call for reports is extensive, but there are certain situations when social inquiry reports must be called for before sentence may be given.

In both solemn and summary procedure the court has the power to adjourn the case for the purpose of enabling inquiries to be made or of determining the most suitable method of dealing with the case[3]. Adjournments are time-limited and may not be made for a single period exceeding three weeks[4]. Parallel inquiries to those of the social worker may also be requested into medical aspects of a person's background. The obligatory nature of reports formerly related only to young offenders, but the Criminal Justice (Scotland) Act 1980 extended obligatory reports to all first offenders who had not previously been imprisoned prior to any sentence of imprisonment being imposed[5]. The requirement is that the court obtains such information as it can about the offender and takes that information into account in deciding the disposal of the case[5]. These reports are prepared by social workers and must be available to the court at the date of the person's appearance.

A sentence of imprisonment may not be imposed on a person under twenty-one although a sentence of detention may be passed upon a person who is not less than sixteen[6]. Before imposing any sentence of detention the court must similarly consider information placed before it by an officer of the local authority[7]. Where detention on a male is for at least twenty-eight days but not exceeding four months the detention will be in a detention centre[8]. For other periods of detention for young persons under twenty-one, detention will be in a young offender's institution[8]. A copy of any report prepared by a social worker for a court must be given to the offender or to his solicitor[9]. Where a child is appearing in an adult court, then a copy of any report must be given to his parent or guardian[9].

Reports do not follow a standard format across Scotland, but the content is largely similar. The report should express an opinion to the court if the writer is able and competent to do this. 'The most appropriate opinion, if any is to be offered, is one relating to the offender's suitability for probation. In particular, the court's concern is with the degree of probability that probation will divert the offender from further crime. At all times, the offering of an opinion is related to the social and rehabilitative possibilities of any suggested disposal'[10]. The report will be prepared by a social worker for the area where the offender usually resides. Interviews will be held with the offender and, where possible, his family, to try to present to the court a full picture of the offender's background and current circumstances. Access to an offender by a social worker may be problematic, although where a person is also on bail a condition relating to the person's availability for the purpose of being interviewed to prepare a social inquiry report may be inserted by the court[11]. The social worker must explain to the person on whom the report is being prepared the requirement of the court for information and the possible consequences of non-co-operation or delay. If there is serious non-co-operation or refusal or delay the social worker must report this to the appropriate judge.

1 Criminal Procedure (Scotland) Act 1975 (c 21), ss 179, 380 (amended by the Bail (Scotland) Act 1980 (c 4), s 5, and the Criminal Justice (Scotland) Act 1980 (c 62), s 83(2), Sch 7, paras 36, 59).
2 *Report of the Interdepartmental Committee on the Business of the Higher Criminal Courts* (the Streatfield Report) (Cmnd 1289) (1961); *Report of the Interdepartmental Committee on the Probation Service* (the Morison Report) (Cmnd 1650) (1962).
3 Criminal Procedure (Scotland) Act 1975, ss 179(1), 380(1) (as amended: see note 1 above).

4 Ibid, ss 179(1) proviso, 380(1) proviso.
5 Criminal Justice (Scotland) Act 1980, s 42(1).
6 Criminal Procedure (Scotland) Act 1975, s 207(1), (2) (substituted by the Criminal Justice (Scotland) Act 1980, s 45(1)).
7 Criminal Procedure (Scotland) Act 1975, s 207(4) (as so substituted).
8 Ibid, s 207(5) (as so substituted).
9 Ibid, ss 192, 393.
10 G Moore and C Wood *Social Work and Criminal Law in Scotland* (1981) pp 42, 43.
11 Bail (Scotland) Act 1980, s 1(2)(d).

33. Children appearing in court. Social workers have specific duties in relation to children appearing in an adult court. Where the young person is aged under sixteen or between sixteen and eighteen and currently on supervision as a result of a children's hearing, the court will request advice from a children's hearing as to a suitable disposal, or the court may remit the case in its entirety to the children's hearing for a decision about whether and what compulsory measures of care are required[1]. This will entail a background report being prepared by a social worker for the appropriate children's hearing, to assist the hearing in assessing the best advice to present to the court or to deal with the case in its totality.

The restrictions on the placement of young people under twenty-one in prison[2] require courts to seek the advice and resources of the local authority in the provision of appropriate accommodation for a young person remanded by a court for further inquiries. Where the young person remanded is under sixteen the court must commit him to the local authority for care in a place of safety and not to prison[3]. However, where the young person is over sixteen, or is a child aged between fourteen and sixteen, and the court certifies him to be so unruly or depraved that committal to a place of safety would not be a safe disposal, the court may commit him to a remand centre or, if a remand centre is not available, to prison[4].

'Place of safety' means any residential or other establishment provided by a local authority, a police station, or any hospital or surgery or other suitable place where the occupier is willing to care for the child on a temporary basis[5]. Detention of any child is regulated by statute, which places restrictions on using secure accommodation to detain a child unless certain requirements are fulfilled[6]. Unless the child has a history of absconding or is likely to damage himself or others if not detained, secure accommodation may not be used[7]. The decision about the need for secure accommodation is laid on the director of social work or a senior member of his staff in conjunction with the person in charge of the unit where secure accommodation is provided[8]. Any secure accommodation for children must be registered by the Secretary of State as necessary and suitable[9].

Where any child is to be brought before a court, the chief constable for the area must send notification of the child's appearance to the local authority[10]. Through the social worker the authority must make necessary investigations and supply the court with a report about the child's home surroundings, including an education report, to assist the court in disposing of the case[11].

Where a court has convicted a child of an offence and the sentence is a specific period of detention under the direction of the Secretary of State[12], the actual placement of the child and his supervision will generally be passed to the appropriate local authority. If the detention was following solemn procedures the child's eventual release is dependent on the Secretary of State advised by the Parole Board for Scotland[13], although the social work department will provide a social background report on the child's home and family circumstances to the Parole Board. In summary procedures the social worker will be closely involved with the child's care and with the plans of the Secretary of State and the residential unit for his release so that guidance and support may be offered to the child and his family before and after his release[14].

1 Criminal Procedure (Scotland) Act 1975 (c 21), ss 173(3), 373 (s 173(3) being amended by the Criminal Justice (Scotland) Act 1980 (c 62), s 83(2), Sch 7, para 35).
2 As to the restrictions on the imprisonment of young people, see the Criminal Procedure (Scotland) Act 1975, s 23, and s 207 (substituted by the Criminal Justice (Scotland) Act 1980, s 45(1)).
3 Criminal Procedure (Scotland) Act 1975, ss 23(1)(a), 24(1), 297(1).
4 Ibid, ss 23(1)(b), 24(2), 297(2).
5 Social Work (Scotland) Act 1968 (c 49), s 94(1), applied by the Criminal Procedure (Scotland) Act 1975, s 462(1).
6 See the Social Work (Scotland) Act 1968, ss 58A–58G (added by the Health and Social Services and Social Security Adjudications Act 1983 (c 41), s 8(4), and amended by the Law Reform (Miscellaneous Provisions) (Scotland) Act 1985 (c 73), s 26).
7 Social Work (Scotland) Act 1968, s 58A(3) (as so added).
8 Secure Accommodation (Scotland) Regulations 1983, SI 1983/1912, reg 7.
9 Ibid, reg 3.
10 Criminal Procedure (Scotland) Act 1975, ss 40(1), 308(1).
11 Ibid, ss 40(2), 308(2).
12 See ibid, s 413 (summary trial), and s 206 (substituted by the Criminal Justice (Scotland) Act 1980, s 44) (trial on indictment).
13 See the Criminal Justice Act 1967 (c 80), s 61 (amended by the Criminal Justice (Scotland) Act 1980, Sch 7, para 18, and the Criminal Justice Act 1982 (c 48), s 77, Sch 14, para 19).
14 Social Work (Scotland) Act 1968, s 27(1)(b)(ii).

34. Probation. Every local authority must provide certain services to courts and to offenders. The two aspects of the service which social work departments must provide are (1) the provision of reports to the court; (2) supervision and provision of advice, guidance and assistance for (a) people under supervision by a court, (b) people released from prison or any other form of detention, and (c) people subject to community service orders or probation orders requiring them to perform unpaid work[1].

A probation order is an order which requires an offender to be under supervision for a period to be specified by the court[2]. This period may be not less than one year but not more than three[2]. The making of a probation order is not seen as a sentence by the court but places the offender on an order which is an order of a court. The social work department must carry out the order of the court by undertaking supervision of the offender[3]. Each probation order lays requirements on the person subject to it:

(1) to be of good behaviour;
(2) to conform to the directions of the supervising officer; and
(3) to inform the supervising officer at once of any change of residence or place of employment.

These requirements consequentially shape the role of the social worker in relation to a person placed on probation. The social worker must ensure that the person placed on a probation order understands it and the conditions within it. The social worker must ensure that the probationer receives and signs a copy of the order and the social worker retains a copy of the order as evidence of the contract into which the person has entered. A major part of the work of the social worker is giving general advice and assistance in all areas of the life of the probationer. If the court has added specific requirements (for example to find employment, to abstain from alcohol or to reside in a particular place), the social worker must assist the probationer to fulfil the requirements.

The social work department may provide special accommodation for offenders through its general powers to provide a range of residential accommodation[4]. Work within social work hostels will be aimed to reduce the likelihood of the offender committing another offence, and to counsel on any particular problems, for example addiction to drugs or alcohol. A requirement to carry out unpaid work may be attached to a probation order, but only if the offender is over sixteen and has committed an offence which is punishable with imprisonment and the offender consents to such an order[5]. Before making this condition the social worker must have reported to the court that the offender is suitable to perform work under such an order[5].

Where the probationer fails to adhere to the requirements of the probation order the social worker must decide what action is required. It may be sufficient to warn the probationer of the possible consequences of breaching the order. If the social worker assesses that a warning is unlikely to alter the probationer's conduct, the social worker may initiate proceedings in the court which originally made the probation order to have the probation order breached. The social worker must place before a court the information which forms the basis for the action. The social worker must then swear on oath before the appropriate judge that the information is true[6]. On hearing this statement the court must decide, if action to breach the order is authorised, the method of bringing the person to court[6]. The court officials then make the necessary administrative arrangements to cite the probationer to appear in court or to issue a warrant for his arrest[6]. If the case is contested the social worker must give evidence at the hearing to support the breach of the order. The social worker also retains a clear role in assisting the court with an opinion about the kind of disposal that may be appropriate and submits a report on the current circumstances of the offender. If the person on probation commits another offence, the social worker must inform the court which made the order and the court administration will then deal with the matter[7]. To assist the court the social worker may provide a report which addresses the likelihood of the probation order being able to be sustained despite the further offence.

Probation may also be ended by the supervising social worker applying to the court for an early discharge of the order because of the good behaviour of the probationer and progress made[8]. The probationer may also apply to the court for an early discharge of the order[8]. The social worker will usually be cited to appear in such proceedings, but the court may discharge the order whatever the advice of the supervising officer may be.

1 See the Social Work (Scotland) Act 1968 (c 49), s 27(1) (amended by the Community Service by Offenders (Scotland) Act 1978 (c 49), s 14, Sch 2, para 1).
2 Criminal Procedure (Scotland) Act 1975 (c 21), ss 183(1), 384(1), 462(1).
3 Ibid, ss 183(3), 384(3).
4 As to the general powers to provide residential accommodation, see the Social Work (Scotland) Act 1968, s 59.
5 Criminal Procedure (Scotland) Act 1975, ss 183(5A), 384(5A) (added by the Community Service by Offenders (Scotland) Act 1978, s 7).
6 Criminal Procedure (Scotland) Act 1975, ss 186(1), 387(1).
7 See ibid, ss 187, 388.
8 Ibid, ss 185(1), 386(1), Sch 5, para 1.

35. Parole. The local authority must provide a service to offer supervision and to provide advice, guidance and assistance to persons released from prison or detention where those persons are required to be under supervision or on licence[1].

Parole was introduced to Scotland by the Criminal Justice Act 1967[2]. Parole involves the release of a person before the normal date of discharge, and is thus a period during which the offender is regarded as still serving his sentence, although in the open community.

The social worker's role in parole starts several months before the possible release of an offender, when the social worker provides a home circumstances report to the local review committee of the appropriate prison. The social worker must identify what the likely home circumstances of the offender will be on his release, with particular emphasis on what support will be available both from the offender's family and from the social work department. If parole is granted the social worker must supervise the offender, who continues to serve his sentence although at liberty in the community. A parole licence is issued to the offender and to the social worker. The licence contains conditions very similar to those in a probation order, namely to keep his supervising officer in touch with any changes of address or employment and to be of good behaviour. Additional requirements may be added to a parole licence where specific accommodation or treatment is identified as essential. The duties of the supervising officer are extensive, and the Parole Board for Scotland underlines the need to help the individual released from prison to resettle in the community. This may well involve the social worker in helping the offender to find accommodation, and, if possible, employment, and to assist with suggestions about the use of his leisure time.

People who are released while serving a life sentence have a very long contract with their supervising officer — indeed many life parolees have outlived their supervising officer as the parole licence for a person on a life sentence lasts for life!

The social worker holding the parole licence carries no discretion in what action to take if the parolee commits a further offence. An offence must be reported immediately to the Prisons Division of the Scottish Home and Health Department for consideration by the Secretary of State. The social worker may submit a view about the likely successful continuation of parole, but the decision to recall the parolee to prison to continue his sentence there rests exclusively with the Secretary of State.

1 Social Work (Scotland) Act 1968 (c 49), s 27(1)(b)(ii).
2 As to the general provisions relating to parole, see the Criminal Justice Act 1967 (c 80), ss 59–64.

36. After-care. After-care by a social worker is statutory only for a small group of offenders, namely young offenders serving sentences of more than six months[1]. Social workers may, however, offer voluntary after-care to anyone released from a penal institution should social work resources permit this. After-care is obligatory for:
(1) persons imprisoned in young offenders' institutions with sentences of up to eighteen months, who will be subject to statutory after-care for six months following release; and
(2) young offenders serving eighteen months or more in a young offenders' institution and not released on parole, who will be subject to statutory after-care for twelve months[2].
Any after-care licence ceases to have effect on the licensee reaching twenty-three years of age[3].

In the case of the release of a child who has been detained under section 206 of the Criminal Procedure (Scotland) Act 1975[4] but who has not been released on licence, the Secretary of State may give notice to the child that he is to be under the supervision of an officer (usually a social worker) specified by the Secretary of State[5]. This supervision may not continue after a period of twelve months has elapsed since the child's release[6].

The social worker must prepare reports for the institution prior to the offender's release, with details of the offender's home circumstances. Immediately on release the social worker must interview the offender and deal with any immediate problems as well as planning future work. The social worker must inform the Secretary of State that the offender has reported following his release and thereafter notify the Secretary of State of any changes in the licence, be it change of supervising officer or commission of a further offence.

Social workers must perform their two-pronged role of assisting and supporting the person on licence or parole to re-establish himself in his family or community but also to be clear about the social control role in the concept of licence which seeks to ensure that the person's release does not place other individuals at risk. No after-care should start at the point of release but should have been planned over the period of the person's detention.

Within penal institutions social work staff are also deployed by the local authority. They have an important role in linking the offender and the supervising officer prior to release and in identifying aspects of work which will require to be done to assist with a successful transition from prison to community.

After-care supervision may also be required in respect of children detained in terms of section 206 of the Criminal Procedure (Scotland) Act 1975, who have been released on licence[7]. The social worker will require to supervise the young person either for the rest of the period until the original sentence would have expired or for twelve months from the release date, whichever is later[8]. Supervision of children released on after-care will require the social worker to make early contact with the child and his family and the staff of the institution where he is residing. The social worker may provide accommodation on release in a variety of places, either with a family specially trained to help troubled young people or within a small residential unit.

1 Criminal Justice (Scotland) Act 1963 (c 39), s 12(2) (substituted by the Criminal Justice (Scotland) Act 1980 (c 62), s 45(2), Sch 5, para 2). This provision applies to young offenders sentenced under the Criminal Procedure (Scotland) Act 1975 (c 21), s 207 or s 415 (each substituted by the Criminal Justice (Scotland) Act 1980, s 45(1)): Criminal Justice (Scotland) Act 1963, s 12(1) (substituted as in the case of s 12(2)).
2 Ibid, s 12(2)(b) (as so substituted).
3 Ibid, s 12(4) (as so substituted).
4 The Criminal Procedure (Scotland) Act 1975, s 206, was substituted by the Criminal Justice (Scotland) Act 1980, s 44.
5 Criminal Procedure (Scotland) Act 1975, s 206A(1) (added by the Law Reform (Miscellaneous Provisions) (Scotland) Act 1985 (c 73), s 45(1)).
6 Criminal Procedure (Scotland) Act 1975, s 206A(2) (as so added).
7 As to release on licence, see ibid, s 206(2)–(4) (as substituted: see note 4 above).
8 Ibid, s 206(4) (as so substituted).

37. Fine supervision. Fine supervision is sometimes imposed on an offender by a court where time is allowed for the payment of the fine. The court may order that the offender is under the supervision of a social worker or such other person as the court may appoint, who will provide assistance and advice to the person in the payment of his fine within the timescale set by the court[1].

1 Criminal Procedure (Scotland) Act 1975 (c 21), s 400(1), which is applied to compensation orders by the Criminal Justice (Scotland) Act 1980 (c 62), s 66(1), (2).

38. Community service. A community service order is an order of a court which requires an offender to perform unpaid work in the community for a specified number of hours[1]. In 1975 the government asked four areas of the country to experiment with community service for offenders as one require-ment within a probation order. Following successful reports on these experi-mental schemes provision was made '. . . for the performance of unpaid work by persons convicted or placed on probation'[2]. Its strength is to provide another option for disposing of cases where imprisonment would otherwise have ensued. Orders may be made on anyone of or over sixteen who is convicted of an offence punishable by imprisonment, other than where the offence has a fixed penalty[3]. The person involved must consent to such an order before it may be made[4]. The hours of unpaid work to be performed must be specified and cannot be less than forty hours or more than 240 hours[5]. Before the court may impose an order to perform community service a social worker must provide a back-ground report on the offender and his circumstances and provide an assessment of his suitability to perform unpaid work for the community[6]. If the court decides to make a community service order the local authority must assign or appoint an officer to supervise the order[7]. The offender must report regularly to the officer appointed and, as with probation orders, report any changes in address or employment[8]. The main requirement on the offender is that he carries out the specified number of hours of unpaid work[8].

The social work department must seek out suitable forms of unpaid work which must be for the benefit of the community, and preferably the community which is local to the offender. The social worker responsible must assess the skills and aptitudes of the offender and attempt to match those skills with the work available. Some offenders may be well suited to work with community groups, conservation programmes or with individuals who, because of age or disability, need assistance with decorating or gardening.

If the offender fails to comply with the requirements of the community service order, the social worker must decide whether to initiate proceedings for a breach of the order[9]. The situations in which a breach of the order may be committed are:

(1) failure to perform the unpaid work as instructed;
(2) failure to complete the ordered number of hours within twelve months;
(3) failure to perform work satisfactorily;
(4) failure to report changes in address or employment.

The administrative process is the same as that for breach of a probation order[10].

Provision is also made for unpaid work within the context of a probation order with the social worker responsible for finding suitable unpaid work for the offender to perform and for supervising the performance of the work as well as the wider aspects of a probation order[11].

Community service schemes continue to be developed across Scotland and are substantially financed by central government. The social work department must report annually to the Secretary of State on the progress of the schemes as well as submitting full statements of expenditure and predicted expenses of the scheme to be eligible for further grants towards maintaining a community service scheme[12].

The role of the social worker supervising a community service order is different in some respects from that of a social worker supervising a probation order. Once the assessment of the offender's suitability for being placed on a community service order has been made, the major function of the social worker becomes the supervision of the offender's work performance. The issues for the offender become reparation to the community through unpaid work and deprivation of personal time by undertaking this work. Social work-ers supervising offenders within a community service scheme are often assisted by skilled craftsmen who work with offenders on projects, and the social worker may delegate aspects of the supervision of the offender to these people or to a voluntary organisation for whom the offender is carrying out work.

1 Community Service by Offenders (Scotland) Act 1978 (c 49), s 1(1).
2 Ibid, long title.
3 Ibid, s 1(1).
4 Ibid, s 1(2)(a).
5 Ibid, s 1(1).
6 Ibid, s 1(2)(c).
7 See ibid, s 2(1)(b).
8 Ibid, s 3(1).
9 See ibid, s 4(1).
10 As to breach of a probation order, see para 34 above, and the Criminal Procedure (Scotland) Act 1975 (c 21), ss 186, 187, 387, 388 (ss 186(2), 387(2) being amended by the Community Service by Offenders (Scotland) Act 1978 (c 49), s 8).
11 Criminal Procedure (Scotland) Act 1975 (c 21), ss 183(5A), 384(5A) (added by the Community Service by Offenders (Scotland) Act 1978, s 7(b)).
12 See the Social Work (Scotland) Act 1968 (c 49), ss 27(1)(b)(iii), 27A (added by the Community Service by Offenders (Scotland) Act 1978, ss 9, 14, Sch 2, para 1).

SOURCES OF LAW (FORMAL)

1. LEGISLATION

(1) THE CONCEPT OF LEGISLATION

(a) Introduction

101. Problems of definition. The word 'legislation' may be used to refer to the process of enacting laws or to the laws which are the product of such a process. Legislation as a 'source of law' is legislation in the latter sense. Any attempt at a definitive statement of the attributes of legislation in this sense is unlikely to be wholly successful: legislation is not necessarily abstract or general or prospective or innovative, although it is commonly all of these things[1]. Nevertheless legislation in the modern Scottish legal system typically displays features which may be contrasted with those typically evinced by other sources of law[2].

1 See S A Walkland *The Legislative Process in Great Britain* (1968) pp 9, 10; D R Miers and A C Page *Legislation* (1982) pp 1, 2.
2 See paras 103 ff below. Legislation has no single feature that differentiates it from all other sources of law; rather different features of legislation differentiate it from different sources of law.

102. Identity of the enacting agency as a criterion. An alternative approach is to identify legislation by 'the formal criterion of the identity of the enacting agency'[1]. This can only succeed if one somehow already knows what agencies are to be regarded as legislative in character. In the context of the modern Scottish legal system there are various agencies whose legislative character is a matter of common consent[2], and hence it is possible to proceed by examining the formal attributes of the norms produced by these agencies[3].

1 B Akzin 'Legislation: Nature and Functions' in *International Encyclopaedia of Social Sciences* (1968) vol 9, p 222.
2 Further, the legislative competence of these agencies is a product of constitutional history.
3 See paras 116 ff below.

(b) Legislation and Contract

(A) COMPARISON BETWEEN LEGISLATION AND CONTRACT

103. Parallel between legislation and contract. The parallel between legislation and contract as sources of legally valid norms has often been remarked upon. 'There is an obvious analogy between agreement and legislation — the former being the private and the latter the public declaration and establishment of rights and duties'[1]. Making a contract can be regarded as 'the exercise of limited legislative powers by individuals'[2]. On this view freedom of contract implies a delegation to individual citizens of 'a piece of sovereignty which enables them to participate constantly in the law making process' which is thereby 'decentralised'[3].

1 J W Salmond *Jurisprudence* (12th edn, 1966 by P J Fitzgerald) p 338.
2 H L A Hart *The Concept of Law* (1961) p 94.
3 F Kessler 'Contracts of Adhesion — Some Thoughts about Freedom of Contract' (1943) 43 Columbia Law Rev 629 at 641.

104. Formal difference between legislation and contract. While contractual activity may thus be visualised as a sort of private law-making, there remains a paramount formal distinction between legislation and contract. The legal validity of a purely contractual norm depends upon the 'voluntary' consent or acquiescence of the party against whom it is asserted: 'Conventional [that is, contractual] law is the product of agreement, and therefore is law for none except those who have consented to its creation'[1]. The validity of a legislative norm, on the other hand, need not depend upon consent; such a norm may be validly imposed *in invitos*, willy-nilly (*ius cogens*). In reality, of course, by no means all legislation imposes involuntary obligations; the legislature, forbearing to exercise its full power, may authorise contracting out (*ius dispositivum*)[2].

1 J W Salmond *Jurisprudence* (12th edn, 1966 by P J Fitzgerald) p 124. This statement, of course, does not consider *ius quaesitum tertio*.
2 See paras 121 ff below.

105. Generality. Legislative norms are not inherently general in their coverage of persons, and contractual norms are not inherently individual. A legislative norm may address a single case[1], while thousands of persons may be parties to a single contract or to a series of identical contracts. The most that can be said is that legislative norms are typically more general in their coverage than contractual norms. This reflects the characteristically different concerns of legislators and contracting parties, and also the practical difficulty of propagating norms whose legal effect depends on the assent of each person who is to be bound thereby.

1 D R Miers and A C Page *Legislation* (1982) pp 2, 3.

(B) CONTRACTUAL SIMULATION OF LEGISLATION

106. Introduction. While the resemblance between a public Act of general application and a contract negotiated between two private individuals may appear slight, under favourable conditions contract may be used to effect legal patterns very similar to those characteristically produced by legislation. For example, the constitution of Lloyd's is comparable to that of The Stock Exchange, yet the former rests on a private Act of Parliament[1], the latter on a contract among the members of The Stock Exchange[2].

1 Lloyd's Act 1982 (c xiv).
2 Until 1986 the constitution of The Stock Exchange was based on the Deed of Settlement of 31 December 1875, as altered by special resolutions, coupled with The Stock Exchange Rules (New Markets Final Version: 27 October 1986). Thereafter The Stock Exchange became the International Stock Exchange, a company registered with limited liability.

107. Contracts of adhesion[1]. To identify 'voluntary' consent as the cardinal factor differentiating between contract and legislation[2] is to place a heavy burden on the concept of voluntariness. Classical contract law presupposes a clear distinction between sovereignty or *imperium*[3] (capable of creating *ius cogens*) and mere bargaining power, and denies that the exercise of the latter — even if one-sided — vitiates consent. If, on the other hand, we are disposed to regard consent procured by economic pressure as nugatory, it is but a short step to argue that 'unequal' bargaining power is quasi-legislative and that the contracts in which it finds expression are tantamount to legislation by the stronger party. Particularly in relation to standard contract forms, this argument became a juristic commonplace long ago[4]. A representative formulation is advanced by Jaffe:

> '... the great complexes of property and contract which constitute our modern industrial machine, the monopolistic associations of capital, labor, and the professions which operate it, exert under the forms and sanctions of law enormous powers of determining the substance of economic and social arrangements, in large part irrespective of the will of particular individuals'[5].

Such arguments are overstated because they take for granted the supposedly monopolistic character of modern economic life, and fail to explicate the crucial notion of unequal bargaining power which is highly problematic in the context of a competitive market[6]. Nevertheless, where for one reason or another a single contractor or a trade association occupies a dominant position an opportunity is afforded to use contract as an instrument for the planned ordering of economic relations on a wide scale. When used in this way, contract performs a function commonly ascribed to legislation[7]; but the plausibility of asserting that contracts of adhesion and legislation in the form of *ius cogens* are functionally equivalent depends on the extent of the economic hardship entailed by a refusal to contract[8].

1 See generally Rakoff 'Contracts of Adhesion — An Essay in Reconstruction' (1983) 96 Harvard Law Rev 1173.
2 See para 104 above.
3 R David 'Sources of Law', para 137, in *International Encyclopaedia of Comparative Law*, vol II, ch 3.
4 See eg M Cain and A Hunt *Marx and Engels on Law* (1979) pp 101, 102 (Engels); M Weber *Law in Economy and Society* (New York, 1954 ed M Rheinstein) pp 188, 189; C K Allen *Law in the Making* (7th edn, 1964) p 545.
5 L Jaffe 'Law Making by Private Groups' (1930) 51 Harvard Law Rev 201 at 220. For a more extreme version, see Kessler 'Contracts of Adhesion' (1943) 43 Columbia Law Rev 629 at 640.
6 R Posner *Economic Analysis of Law* (2nd edn, 1977) pp 84–88; Trebilcock 'The Doctrine of Inequality in Bargaining Power: Post-Benthamite Economics in the House of Lords' (1976) 26 Univ Toronto LJ 359.
7 Eg by F A Hayek *Law, Legislation and Liberty* (1973), vol I, ch 6.
8 As to government contracts, see paras 234, 235 below.

108. Model terms and conditions. By no means all standard form contracts are contracts of adhesion. Some standard contract forms are no more than models devised by professional or trade associations for adoption or imitation by contracting parties to the extent that they find this course of action convenient[1]. As such they plainly perform a similar function to legislative codes (for example, the Sale of Goods Act 1979 (c 54)) which set out implied terms while preserving freedom of contract (*ius dispositivum*). The main difference is that such legislative codes apply unless one contracts out, whereas to gain the benefit of model terms and conditions one must contract in. Even this distinction does not always hold: the Uniform Laws on International Sales Act 1967 (c 45) applies to a transaction only if the parties contract in[2].

1 For examples, see J Tillotson *Contract Law in Perspective* (2nd edn, 1985) pp 113–123.
2 See para 123, note 1 below.

(c) Legislation and Custom

109. Contrast between legislation and custom. Two main characteristics serve to differentiate legislation from custom. First, legislation is laid down or posited, whereas custom grows gradually[1]. Legislation is thus the deliberate artefact of identifiable human agencies, whereas custom is a by-product of human interaction. Secondly, with legislation it is the *ipsissima verba* (actual words used) that count: 'If we want to know what those words mean, we look first at the words themselves and not at some expression of a more or less equivalent thought to be found somewhere else in the literature of the law'. With custom, on the other hand, except in the case of 'judicial custom', there is 'no authoritative verbal declaration of the terms of the custom; it expresses itself not in a succession of words, but in a course of conduct'[2].

1 A W B Simpson 'The Common Law and Legal Theory' in *Oxford Essays in Jurisprudence* (2nd ser, 1973, ed A W B Simpson) at pp 80, 81.
2 L L Fuller *Anatomy of the Law* (1971) p 64.

(d) Legislation and Precedent

110. Judicial legislation. The claim that setting a precedent can be regarded as an act of 'judicial legislation' has been a familiar one since the Benthamite polemic against the old idea that the common law is customary in character and that judicial decisions are declarations of custom. The concept of judicial legislation highlights the well-worn observation that through their decisions appellate judges sometimes occasion the development of new law. But to push the analogy further is unhelpful or even misleading. Even when new law emerges from it, the *process* of adjudication is as a rule markedly different from the process of legislation[1]. Moreover, the *products* of these processes — precedent and statute — evince different qualities as 'sources of law', our concern here.

1 However, the procedure for passing private Acts of Parliament is an interesting hybrid.

111. Authority and validity. We speak of and handle statutes and precedents in different ways. In the first place, statutes and precedents are authoritative in different ways. The authority of a statute is absolute: a statute is 'valid' or it is nothing. With precedents, however, talk of validity sounds out of place. The authority of a precedent is a matter of degree. Precedents are more or less 'persuasive'; they have to be weighed. Some (not necessarily decisions of the supreme court) are 'leading cases'; others are not. It might be urged that a 'binding' precedent is equivalent to a valid statute, but this suggestion founders on the observation that a valid statute binds all judges while a binding precedent binds only those who occupy an inferior position in the judicial hierarchy. In the final analysis — that is, in the supreme court — there are no binding precedents.

112. Fiat and justification. A further point is that the validity of a statute rests exclusively on legislative fiat. As long as a legislator does not exceed his powers, the validity of his legislation is wholly independent of the cogency or weakness of any justification that might be advanced in support of it. The putative reasons for a statute may bear upon its interpretation, but cannot affect its authority, which is derived from the legislator's imprimatur alone[1]. The authority of a precedent, on the other hand, is not merely a function of judicial decree. Rather the degree of authority attributed to a precedent depends in part on the quality of the reasoned argument through which the judge seeks to justify his ruling. Thus it is that whereas a statute has no authority beyond the jurisdiction for which it was enacted, a precedent, by virtue of the strength of its reasoning, may be viewed as persuasive in jurisdictions other than the one in which it was set.

1 Of course this statement does not hold good when legislative power conferred for one specific purpose is purportedly exercised for another.

113. *Ipsissima verba*. The exact words (*ipsissima verba*) of a statute have the force of law. But the propositions of law for which a precedent is 'authority' are altogether more elusive; there is and can be no definitive statement of the common law or any part thereof. As Simpson puts it: 'There exists no context in which a judicial statement to the effect that this or that is the law confers the status of law on the words uttered[1]; or, in Fuller's words,

> 'In the common law it is not too much to say that the judges are always ready to look behind the words of a precedent to what the previous court was trying to say, or to what it would have said if it could have foreseen the nature of the cases that were later to arise, or if its perception of the relevant factors in the case before it had been more acute. There is, then, a real sense in which the written words of the reported decisions are merely the gateway to something lying behind them that may be called, without any excess of poetic licence, "unwritten law"'[2].

Thus precedents are legitimately susceptible to techniques of elaboration such as analogical extension for which there is comparatively little scope in relation to statutes[3].

1 A W B Simpson 'The Common Law and Legal Theory' in *Oxford Essays in Jurisprudence* (2nd ser 1973, ed A W B Simpson) p 86. As to judicial precedent, see paras 247 ff below.
2 L L Fuller *Anatomy of the Law* (1971) p 130.
3 'What the appellant is saying . . . is that, if A, B and C are included expressly in a statutory definition, the legislature intended, and the Courts must uphold, that X and Y and Z and anything else that is analogous to A or B or C should also be included by implication in that definition. No authority was cited for this proposition and I can find no reason for applying it here': *Boyd v A Bell & Sons Ltd* 1970 JC 1 at 7, 1969 SLT 156 at 159, per Lord Justice-Clerk Grant. See also P S Atiyah 'Common Law and Statute Law' (1985) 48 MLR 1, especially at 8; and contrast N MacCormick *Legal Reasoning and Legal Theory* (1978) p 194.

114. Acts encrusted with precedent. This contrast is not, however, absolute. An old Act may become so heavily encrusted with precedent that it is in effect assimilated or absorbed by the common law. A notorious example was the Bankruptcy Act 1621[1], directed against fraudulent alienation to the prejudice of creditors of bankrupts, which was extended by analogy to various cases not literally within its ambit: its provisions were regarded 'rather as examples than as restrictions'[2]. 'Whatever the literal meaning of the statutory words' old Scots Acts are to be read in the light of *contemporanea expositio*, which was sometimes so free that it 'cannot be reconciled with the words of the Act'[3]. Perhaps more surprisingly, there is high judicial authority in England for the view that the provisions of the Sale of Goods Act 1893[4], which its authors hoped would more or less supersede the common law[5], are to be treated as 'illustrations' of the application to simple types of contract of general principles for ascertaining the common intention of the parties — illustrations which are to be applied 'by analogy' in cases beyond the immediate contemplation of the draftsman in 1893[6]. The rationale for this approach is presumably that (from an English point of view) the Sale of Goods Act was supposed to be no more than a restatement of the common law.

1 The Bankruptcy Act 1621 (c 18) was repealed by the Bankruptcy (Scotland) Act 1985 (c 66), s 75(2), Sch 8.
2 Sir George Mackenzie, quoted in *Thomas v Thomson* (1865) 3 M 1160 at 1165.
3 W M Gloag and R C Henderson *Introduction to the Law of Scotland* (8th edn, 1980 by A B Wilkinson and W A Wilson) p 6.
4 The Sale of Goods Act 1893 (c 71) was repealed and replaced by the Sale of Goods Act 1979 (c 54).
5 R B Ferguson 'Legal Ideology and Commercial Interests: The Social Origins of the Commercial Law Codes' (1977) 4 BJLS 18.
6 *Christopher Hill Ltd v Ashington Piggeries Ltd* [1972] AC 441 at 501, [1972] 1 All ER 847 at 882, HL, per Lord Diplock.

115. Repetition of dicta. Conversely, a judicial dictum may achieve virtually canonical status by virtue of its incessant repetition in later cases. The outstanding example is Baron Alderson's famous formulation of 'the rule in *Hadley v Baxendale*'[1], which tends to be quoted almost as if it were a legislative text.

1 *Hadley v Baxendale* (1854) 9 Exch 341 at 354.

(2) THE FORM OF ACTS OF PARLIAMENT

116. British legislative ethos. Although Acts of Parliament are the paramount source of law in Scotland as in the rest of the United Kingdom[1], they have never been regarded as a ubiquitous or comprehensive source, still less as an exclusive one. Statutes are of course decisive in relation to matters which they address expressly or by clear implication[2], but Scots lawyers do not see legislation as a reservoir of principles and analogies upon which to draw when a novel case is to be decided[3]. The common law of Scotland, on the other hand, is viewed as pervasive in the sense that it is held to be capable of generating legal solutions to unprecedented cases through the application of established principles to novel circumstances. In this respect at least, modern Scotland falls within the common law tradition rather than that of the codified civil law wherein it remains true that judges and jurists are 'not at ease unless they can invoke one or more texts of enacted law to justify or support the legal solution which they recommend'[4]. In the United Kingdom as a whole legislation has been regarded as a means of effecting changes in the law rather than as the form in which all major principles and rules ought to be cast.

1 See para 120 below.
2 Where a comprehensive statutory code covers a situation, it is an impermissible exercise of the judicial function to go beyond the statutory provisions by applying common law principles: *Pioneer Aggregates (UK) Ltd v Secretary of State for the Environment* [1985] AC 132 at 141, [1984] 2 All ER 358 at 363, HL, per Lord Scarman.
3 See paras 113, 114 above.
4 R David and J E C Brierley *Major Legal Systems in the World Today* (2nd edn, 1978) p 97.

117. Consequences of British legislative ethos. This conception of legislation has conditioned the British approach to the drafting and rationalisation of legislation. Statutes tend to contain detailed stipulations rather than broad statements of principle. Further, rationalisation in the form of codification, understood as a systematic and fairly comprehensive legislative restatement of a branch of the law, synthesising previously enacted rules with those of common law extraction, has been largely neglected[1].

1 The enactment of the commercial law codes (the Bills of Exchange Act 1882 (c 61), the Partnership Act 1890 (c 39), the Sale of Goods Act 1893 (c 71) (now the Sale of Goods Act 1979 (c 54)) and the Marine Insurance Act 1906 (c 41)) was an attempt to pass legislation which would in most cases preclude resort to other sources of law on the matters with which the legislation dealt: see *Bank of England v Vagliano Bros* [1891] AC 107 at 144, 145, HL, per Lord Herschell. In practice this aim has been defeated: in order to discover the law, the courts still roam over a vast number of authorities, including ones that predate the codifying legislation. See A L Diamond 'Codification of the Law of Contract' (1968) 31 MLR 361. See further para 114 above.

118. Rationalisation of the corpus of statutes. Whereas the impulse to codify has been weak, various steps have been taken to facilitate access to up-to-date legislative texts. In particular, statute law revision Acts have been passed to excise 'obsolete, spent, unnecessary or superseded' enactments[1]; statute law repeal Acts are passed to get rid of enactments that are suppposedly 'no longer of practical utility'[2]; consolidation Acts are passed to integrate into one Act the various enactments relating to a particular subject; and the *Statutes in Force* are published to make available a version of statutory texts, arranged according to subject matter, in which all repeals and amendments are incorporated.

1 See eg the Statute Law Revision Act 1966 (c 5), long title.
2 See eg the Statute Law (Repeals) Act 1986 (c 12), long title.

119. Rationalisation of the structure of individual statutes. The internal structure of individual Acts of Parliament has also undergone rationalisation.

The modern practice of dividing statutes into parts, and sections into subsections and paragraphs, thereby facilitating citation and interpretation, was inaugurated in the middle of the nineteenth century[1]. The virtual disappearance of preambles reflects the modern view that the authority of a statute can be neither enhanced nor diminished by the strength of the reasons for its enactment[2]. The value of preambles as an aid to interpretation is in any event doubtful if they enshrine statements of policy that are not fully reflected in the substantive provisions enacted[3], or if the substantive provisions accommodate considerations of policy other than those avowed in the preamble[4].

1 C P Ilbert *Legislative Methods and Forms* (1901) pp 68, 69.
2 See further para 112 above.
3 See eg the Parliament Act 1911 (c 13).
4 See further *The Preparation of Legislation* (Cmnd 6053) paras 11.6–11.8.

(3) THE AUTHORITY OF ACTS OF PARLIAMENT

(a) The Supremacy of Statute

120. The legislative supremacy of Parliament. The legislative supremacy and omnicompetence of Parliament was not acknowledged without qualification in the seventeenth and eighteenth centuries[1]. In modern times, however, axiomatic status has, at any rate until recently, generally been attributed uncritically to the dogma of Parliamentary sovereignty as expounded by Dicey[2]. In the last few decades that dogma has been subjected to much critical scrutiny[3], above all with respect to the Union of England and Scotland[4] and the Accession of the United Kingdom to the European Communities[5]. Nevertheless it remains the fundamental postulate on the basis of which the relationship of statute to other sources of law[6] has, by and large, been elaborated.

1 Eg Bankton's view that legislation cannot be retrospective: Bankton *Institute* I, 1, 61. As Mitchell observes, 'For the most part what were formerly asserted to be limitations upon the legislative capacity of Parliament have become presumptions of interpretation': J D B Mitchell *Constitutional Law* (2nd edn, 1968) p 66.
2 A V Dicey, *Introduction to the Study of the Law of the Constitution* (10th edn, 1959 by E C S Wade) c 1: see the remarks of Lord Guthrie in *MacCormick v Lord Advocate* 1953 SC 396 at 403, 1953 SLT 255 at 259. Cf K W B Middleton 'New Thoughts on the Union' (1954) 66 JR 37 at 39.
3 See generally CONSTITUTIONAL LAW, vol 5, paras 308 ff.
4 See paras 144 ff below.
5 See paras 202 ff below.
6 See paras 121 ff below.

(b) Statute and Contract

(A) INTRODUCTION

121. *Ius cogens* and *ius dispositivum*. Statute being the paramount source of law in the United Kingdom, an Act of Parliament may itself provide (explicitly or implicitly) that its own provisions may be overridden by norms emanating from elsewhere. In the context of contract this possibility is recognised in the distinction between *ius cogens* and *ius dispositivum*. A statutory provision is *ius cogens* if it stipulates a legal consequence which is mandatory, so that the legal consequence is necessarily entailed irrespective of the expressed intention of the contracting parties, as long as their transaction or relationship falls within the scope of the relevant provision. A statutory provision is *ius dispositivum*, on the other hand, if the legal consequence it stipulates may be averted by an agreement of the contracting parties to that effect, even though their transaction or relationship falls within the scope of the provision concerned. In short, the question is whether or not the statutory provision admits of 'contracting out'.

122. Contracting out and avoidance. Contracting out in this sense can be distinguished from the 'avoidance' or circumvention of a statutory provision. Whereas contracting out and avoidance may sometimes be actuated by similar motives, there is an important formal distinction between them. In the case of avoidance, the arrangement entered into by the contracting parties purports to fall beyond the ambit of the statutory provision in question; it will be contended that the provision does not address the particular kind of transaction or relationship into which the parties have entered. Thus, formally at least, avoidance is perfectly consistent with the overriding character of a statutory provision. In the case of contracting out, however, a statutory provision, even though it covers the transaction or relationship in question, is purportedly superseded by a contract term; subordinate status is attributed to a legislative text, on the footing that this accords with the intention of the legislature. This latter phenomenon is our concern here.

123. Express provisions as to contracting out. The question whether contracting out is permissible or not may be put beyond doubt by an unequivocal declaration in the statute itself. So, for example, where the intention of the legislature is to permit contracting out, a statute may provide that the consequences it stipulates may be negatived or varied by express agreement, or by the course of dealing between the parties, or by usage[1]. Conversely, where the intention of the legislature is to prohibit contracting out, a statute may declare void any contract term purporting to exclude or restrict liability for breach of the obligations arising from the statute[2], or it may incorporate the formula 'Notwithstanding any agreement to the contrary...'[3].

1 Eg the Sale of Goods Act 1893 (c 71), s 55 (repealed). The Uniform Laws on International Sales Act 1967 (c 45) goes further in that it governs the contract only if the parties contract in: the Uniform Law on Sales has 'the force of law' in the United Kingdom (s 1(2)), but it applies to a contract of sale 'only if it has been chosen by the parties to the contract as the law of the contract' (s 1(3)).
2 Eg the Unfair Contract Terms Act 1977 (c 50), s 20(1).
3 For a list of provisions that prohibit contracting out, see 44 Halsbury's Laws of England (4th edn) para 951.

(B) THE IMPLICATION OF LEGISLATIVE INTENTION AS TO CONTRACTING OUT

124. *Quilibet potest renunciare juri pro se introducto.* In the absence of an unequivocal expression of legislative intention on the question of contracting out, the maxim *quilibet potest renunciare juri pro se introducto*[1] (a person may renounce a right which exists solely for his own use or benefit) comes into play[2]. This asserts a qualified presumption in favour of the permissibility of contracting out. 'The onus is always on those who assert that the Court is not to enforce a contract which is *ex facie* good, save on grounds of law substantial enough to outweigh the paramount policy of the law that people should keep faith and fulfil their promises'[3]. In short, the presumption is in favour of freedom of contract[4]. But this presumption is reversed when the matter is one in which the public has an interest. For 'no man can renounce a right of which his duty to the public and the claims of society forbid the renunciation'[5].

1 F A R Bennion *Statutory Interpretation* (1984) ss 11, 12.
2 *Johnson v Moreton* [1980] AC 37 at 58, [1978] 3 All ER 37 at 47, HL, per Lord Hailsham of St Marylebone.
3 *Fender v St John-Mildmay* [1938] AC 1 at 37, 38, [1937] 3 All ER 402 at 424, HL, per Lord Wright.
4 *Kennedy v Johnstone* 1956 SC 39 at 49, 1956 SLT 73 at 81, per Lord Sorn.
5 *Hunt v Hunt* (1862) 4 De GF & J 221 at 233, per Lord Westbury, applied in *Ayr Harbour Trustees v Oswald* (1883) 10 R (HL) 85, 8 App Cas 623.

125. Competing conceptions of public interest. The notion of a public interest, upon which the permissibility of contracting out may turn, is, however, highly equivocal[1]. The elusiveness of the public interest criterion is most readily apparent in cases of putative unequal bargaining power where the question arises whether there is a public interest in statutory rights conferred upon supposedly weaker parties such as tenants, employees and consumers. The answer is likely to turn on the prevailing economic philosophy of the judiciary. Most recently, a comparatively paternalistic outlook has found expression whereby the notion of unequal bargaining power is taken at face value, and a public interest may well be discerned in rights conferred by protective legislation. This outlook is well exemplified by a dictum of Lord Hailsham of St Marylebone:

'The truth is that it can no longer be treated as axiomatic that, in the absence of explicit language, the courts will permit contracting out of the provisions of an Act of Parliament where that Act, though silent as to the possibility of contracting out, nevertheless is manifestly passed for the protection of a class of persons who do not negotiate from a position of equal strength, but in whose well being there is a public as well as a private interest. Such Acts are not necessarily to be treated as simply *"jus pro se introductum"*, a "private remedy and a private right" which an individual member of the class may simply bargain away by reason of his freedom of contract. It is precisely his weakness as a negotiating party from which Parliament wishes to protect him'[2].

In the past, however, a more robust liberal outlook sometimes actuated judicial decisions on contracting out. On this view, people of full age and sound mind were assumed to be able to look after their own interests, and were not lightly to be released from contracts freely entered into merely because they agreed to give up rights conferred by statute. So, for example, in a case where the question was whether a workman might by contract surrender his right to claim compensation from his employer for personal injuries under the workmen's compensation legislation[3], Field J said:

'There is no suggestion that the contract was induced by fraud, or by force, or made under duress, and it was not a naked bargain made without consideration . . . . It is at least doubtful whether, where a contract is said to be void as against public policy, some public policy which affects all society is not meant. Here the interest of the employed only would be affected. It is said that the intention of the legislature to protect workmen against imprudent bargains will be frustrated if contracts like this one are allowed to stand. I should say that workmen as a rule were perfectly competent to make reasonable bargains for themselves'[4].

It remains to be seen whether modern currents in economic thought[5] will reinvigorate the nowadays somewhat attenuated presumption in favour of freedom of contract. That it is not rejected out of hand in Scotland is apparent in the context of family provision on divorce[6].

1 The extreme malleability of the notion is evident eg in *National Westminster Bank Ltd v Halesowen Presswork and Assemblies Ltd* [1972] AC 785 at 808, 809, [1972] 1 All ER 641 at 652, HL (public interest discerned in right to set off under the Bankruptcy Act 1914 (c 59), s 31). Contrast the Report of the Review Committee on Insolvency Law and Practice (Cmnd 8558) para 1342 ('no sound reason of policy' for prohibition of contracting out).

2 *Johnson v Moreton* [1980] AC 37 at 60, [1978] 3 All ER 37 at 49, HL.

3 Employers' Liability Act 1880 (c 42) (repealed).

4 *Griffiths v Earl of Dudley* (1882) 9 QBD 357 at 362, 363, DC. This was doubted in *Admiralty Comrs v Valverda Owners* [1938] AC 173 at 185, [1938] 1 All ER 162 at 168, HL, per Lord Wright, and in *Johnson v Moreton* [1980] AC 37 at 57, 58, [1978] 3 All ER 37 at 47, HL, per Lord Hailsham of St Marylebone.

5 See eg R Posner *Economic Analysis of Law* (2nd edn, 1977).

6 See eg *Dunbar v Dunbar* 1977 SLT 169; *Thompson v Thompson* 1981 SC 344, 1982 SLT 521; and *Elder v Elder* 1985 SLT 471. Cf the Family Law (Scotland) Act 1985 (c 37), s 16(1).

126. Status of the maxim *quilibet*. It must not be forgotten that in relation to statutory provisions the maxim *quilibet potest renunciare juri pro se introducto*[1] is no more than a presumption of statutory interpretation. Even in the absence of an unequivocal expression of legislative intention that presumption may be strengthened or rebutted by inferences drawn from the legislative text itself.

1 See para 124 above.

127. Implication from wording of statute. In principle, an intention to permit or forbid contracting out might be inferred from a contrast in the wording of different sections of a statute[1]. But where some sections of an Act expressly countenance contracting out while others expressly prohibit it, plainly no inference can legitimately be drawn as to Parliament's intention in relation to sections which are silent on the question of contracting out[2]. Moreover, in the context of a codifying statute, random recognition in certain sections of the principle that contracting parties are at liberty to express their contractual intentions as they please does not suffice to support the contrary proposition that the absence of such recognition in another section implies the absence of freedom of contract[3].

1 Ie where one section of an Act expressly authorises contracting out while another is silent, or where one section expressly prohibits contracting out while another is silent.

2 *Johnson v Moreton* [1980] AC 37, [1978] 3 All ER 37, HL. But contrast the questionable reasoning in *Kennedy v Johnstone* 1956 SC 39, 1956 SLT 73, where the question was whether a tenant might contract out of the Agricultural Holdings (Scotland) Act 1949 (c 75), s 20 (for which see AGRICULTURE, vol 1, para 788). Section 20 itself being silent on this question, Lord President Clyde (at 44 and at 78) and Lord Sorn (at 49 and at 81) argued that the permissibility of contracting out might be inferred from the fact that other sections of the Act expressly ruled out the possibility of contracting out of them. But it appears to have been overlooked that further sections (eg ss 13, 31(2)) expressly countenanced the possibility of contracting out. Thus their Lordships might equally have drawn the opposite inference.

3 *Ooi Book Leong v Citibank NA* [1984] 1 WLR 723 at 730, PC, per Lord Brightman.

128. Implication from object of statute. An intention to permit or forbid contracting out may also be inferred from the object imputed to a statutory provision[1]. A party cannot contract out of a statutory provision — even one exclusively in his own favour — when so to permit would reinstate the mischief which the statute was designed to remedy and render the statutory provision a dead letter. Accordingly in such circumstances the maxim *quilibet potest renunciare juri pro se introducto* can have no bearing[2].

1 'Wherever there is a question whether there can be contracting out or waiver of statutory provisions, the problem must be solved on a consideration of the scope and policy of the particular statute': *Admiralty Comrs v Valverda Owners* [1938] AC 173 at 185, [1938] 1 All ER 162 at 167, HL, per Lord Wright.
2 *Johnson v Moreton* [1980] AC 37 at 68, 69, [1978] 3 All ER 37 at 55, 56, HL, per Lord Simon of Glaisdale. Contrast *Kennedy v Johnstone* 1956 SC 39, 1956 SLT 73.

(c) Statute and Custom

129. Stair. The modern subordination of custom to statute was not clearly acknowledged by Stair, if indeed he recognised it at all. According to Stair, 'we are ruled in the first place by our ancient and immemorial customs, which may be called our common law'. He adduces various examples, such as primogeniture, and describes them as 'anterior to any statute, and not comprehended in any, as being more solemn and sure than those are'. Then 'in the next place' come our statutes or Acts of Parliament 'which, in this, are inferior to our ancient law, that they are liable to desuetude, which never encroaches on the other'[1].

These remarks certainly furnish strong support for the view that Stair, in contrast to most other Scottish jurists, accorded primacy as a source of law to ancient custom[2]. Nevertheless, there is reason to believe that Stair's position was somewhat ambivalent. If custom is regarded as superior to statute, the doctrine of desuetude requires no special justification; it is just a logical consequence of custom's superiority. And yet Stair does appear to seek an alternative theoretical basis for the doctrine:

'... we differ from the English, whose statutes of parliament, of whatsoever antiquity, remain ever in force till they be repealed.... But with us, the Lords of Session being by their institution authorized with power to make rules and statutes to be observed in the manner and order of proceeding in, and administration of justice[3]...; therefore, as to the matter of justice, their authority by their institution is utterly to decide and determine, but [ie without] appellation to the king or parliament[4]... Before the first institution appeals were in force, in place whereof reduction succeeded, so that the Lords' decreets upon debates, being [final][5] are irreducible upon allegeance of iniquity, and extend, not only to the interpretation of acts of parliament, but to the derogation thereof, especially so far as concerns the administration of justice, which is specially committed to them'[6].

This is not an easy passage, but its location in Stair's text makes it clear that it is intended to furnish a statutory rationale for the power of the Court of Session to disregard statutes fallen into desuetude. Two arguments seem to be interwoven by Stair: first, that the Lords' power derives from their statutory capacity to make rules and statutes respecting the administration of justice; and secondly, that by virtue of statute they have inherited from King and Parliament the power enjoyed by the Parliament to override their own acts. Stair's argument is obscure and strained; but that he felt impelled to make it is significant because it suggests that Stair, like later writers, apprehended the tension between the doctrine of desuetude and the authority of the 'positive laws of sovereigns'[6], and sought to reconcile them without detracting from the authority of the latter.

1 Stair *Institutions* I, 1, 16.
2 D M Walker, Introduction to Stair *Institutions* (2nd edn of 1693, 1981 ed D M Walker) p 27; H L MacQueen 'Mackenzie's *Institutions* in Scottish Legal History' (1984) 29 JLSS 498 at 500. As to custom generally, see paras 355 ff below.
3 College of Justice Act 1532 (APS II, 335, c 2); College of Justice Act 1540 (APS II, 371, c 10).

4 Procedure before Lords of the Session Act 1457 (c 3).
5 The text of the second edition has 'formal', but the context makes it obvious that this is a misprint. The first edition described the Lords' decisions as 'final and irrevocable'.
6 Stair *Institutions* I, 1, 16.

130. Mackenzie. Jurists after Stair sought to solve this problem mainly by founding on the tacit consent of the sovereign. As 'a king's man and believer in the royal prerogative'[1], Mackenzie naturally favoured this solution, but even so accepted the doctrine of desuetude only grudgingly, as his treatment of it in the context of criminal law makes clear. Criminal statutes, he conceded, might run into desuetude 'so far that they cannot be the foundation of a criminal pursuit for former transgressions':

> 'since the people who know not law so much by reading the books of statutes as by seeing the daily practice of the country should not be ensnared by pursuits upon old buried laws, which scarce lawyers study or know. Nor can the people be thought to have contemned what they cannot be presumed to have known. And our judicators, by ordaining such ancient laws to be renewed by proclamations, do confess that before these proclamations these laws were not binding: for else the renewing them had been unnecessary. And if it were otherwise, we have so many penal statutes now in desuetude that the lieges would be certainly ruined by them'[2].

But Mackenzie refuses to acknowledge that the desuetude of a statute is tantamount to its repeal: 'I think that desuetude cannot *in futurum* abrogate a crime and enervate the law altogether, *since the Parliament only can rescind their own laws*: nor should the people, nay nor our judges, be made legislators'[3]. In support of this position Mackenzie cites the *Codex Iustinianus*: '*Consuetudinis ususque long-aevi non vilis auctoritas est, verum non usque adeo sui valitura momento ut aut rationem vincat aut legem*'[4]. To paraphrase: the authority of longstanding custom is not inconsiderable, but not so great as to prevail over reason or statute. Mackenzie concludes:

> 'it seems absurd that it should be lawful to the people to loose themselves from the laws made against themselves, and to gain impunity by frequent repetition of their faults, or to be able to free themselves from punishment by contemning these laws by which they are inflicted'[5].

We see, therefore, that Mackenzie's deference to the authority of the legislator, coupled with his sensibility that a full-blown doctrine of desuetude is hard to square with that authority, leads him to propound a heavily qualified doctrine of desuetude in criminal law.

1 H L MacQueen 'Mackenzie's Institutions in Scottish Legal History' (1984) 29 JLSS 498 at 500, note 2.
2 Mackenzie *Laws and Customs* I, 1, 3 (spelling and punctuation modernised).
3 Emphasis added.
4 *Codex Iustinianus* VIII, 52.
5 Mackenzie *Laws and Customs* I, 1, 3.

131. Bankton. Bankton also relies in part on the notion of the sovereign's tacit consent: 'many of our old statutes have run into desuetude, a contrary usage for a long course of time acquiesced to by the lawgivers being a tacit abrogation of them, and this is expressly declared to be law with us by an old statute'[1]. It is not clear what statute Bankton has in mind[2]. In any event, Bankton's attitude to desuetude is scarcely more generous than Mackenzie's. For:

> 'if these laws concern the publick policy of the kingdom, a disuse of them past memory, or a contrary practice, regularly will not derogate from them: a custom against such laws will always remain erroneous, and cannot be established by any length of time . . .'[3].

And Bankton, like Mackenzie, cites the *Codex Iustinianus*.

1 Bankton *Institute* I, 1, 60.
2 Bankton cites 'P 1593 c 136'. The 12mo edition, James VI, includes an Act 1592 c 136 (Record edition, James VI, Act 1592 c 52) on the reduction of redemptions, but this has no obvious bearing on desuetude. Bankton may have been thinking of the Act 1592 c 45 (Record edition; not in the 12mo edition) on the printing of Acts of Parliament, but this Act does not truly bear out his statement.
3 Bankton *Institute* I, 1, 60.

132. Erskine. The tacit consent of the supreme power is also the basis of the doctrine of desuetude in Erskine's jurisprudence:

> 'Custom, as it is equally founded in the will of the lawgiver with written law, hath the same effect. Hence . . . as a posterior statute may repeal or derogate from a prior, so a posterior custom may repeal or derogate from a prior statute, even though that prior statute should contain a clause forbidding all usages that might tend to weaken it; for the contrary immemorial custom sufficiently presumes the will of the community to alter the law in all its clauses, and particularly in that which was intended to secure it against alteration; and this presumed will of the people operates as strongly as their express declaration'[1].

1 Erskine *Institute* I, 1, 45.

133. Conclusion. It may be observed that this theory of desuetude contains nothing that inherently limits its application to the Acts of the old Scots Parliament. Yet it has never been doubted that the legislation of the United Kingdom Parliament is like that of the English Parliament in that desuetude has no bearing upon its validity. This is not to be regretted. Whatever its legal rationale, the real basis of the doctrine of desuetude, as Mackenzie apprehended, was its practical usefulness. As long as the statute book of Scotland remained a shambles cluttered with the debris of the centuries, the doctrine of desuetude made sound sense. Not only was it invoked in an appreciable number of reported cases[1], but there must have been occasions when the desuetude of a statute was so manifest as to render litigation on it inconceivable. However, systematic statute law revision is a more sure method of dealing with the debris of the past, and its institution[2] rendered the doctrine of desuetude obsolescent[3]. Today it may be regarded as virtually redundant.

1 For a list of cases in which desuetude was canvassed, see W C Smith 'Desuetude' (1895) 7 JR 173 at 176, 177.
2 The Statute Law Revision (Scotland) Act 1906 (c 38) repealed the bulk of the material in question.
3 The most recent case is *Brown v Edinburgh Magistrates* 1931 SN 90, 1931 SLT 456, OH.

(d) Statute and Precedent

(A) INTRODUCTION

134. Subordination of precedent to statute. It is axiomatic that precedent is subordinate to statute as a source of law. Nevertheless the interaction of the authority of precedent and the superior authority of Acts of Parliament raises certain problems which are discussed in the paragraphs which follow.

(B) PRECEDENT AS A GLOSS UPON STATUTE

135. General principle. In ordinary circumstances a precedent which embodies a judicial interpretation of an Act of Parliament has as much or as little authority as any other precedent emanating from the court that set the precedent on the Act. So an inferior court may be bound by such a precedent[1], and its interpretation of the Act in question controlled thereby.

1 Alternatively a superior court may find such a precedent persuasive: see eg *Nicol's Trustees v Sutherland* 1951 SC (HL) 21, 1951 SLT 201.

136. Limits of general principle. A precedent glossing a statute may be regarded as binding or persuasive only if it is not inconsistent with the statute that it purports to gloss: 'No court is entitled to throw over the plain words of a statute by referring to a previous judicial decision. When there is a conflict between a plain statute and a previous decision, the statute must prevail'[1]. In such extraordinary circumstances it is a logical consequence of the supremacy of statute that even an inferior court must prefer statute to ostensibly binding precedent[2]. But in practice it can scarcely ever be possible for an inferior court to be certain that an otherwise binding precedent purporting to elaborate a statutory provision in fact contradicts it. Accordingly it may be concluded that the passage of time has not impaired the value of Bankton's summary of the issue:

> 'The decisions or resolutions of our superior courts of justice declare what is common law with us, but, when they concern the sense or interpretation of a statute in observance, they cannot influence subsequent judgments, except so far as they are supported by the statute; so that, if they are neither founded in the words, reason or intent of the act, (if any such judgments there be) they cannot be regarded in parallel cases. The rule laid down by the emperor, *non exemplis, sed legibus judicandum*, must then be followed by all courts of justice; but otherwise former precedents, as to the interpretation of a statute, where the sense is doubtful, must have weight with the judges in the subsequent decisions thereon, that the law may not be uncertain . . .'[3].

1 *Farrell v Alexander* [1976] QB 345 at 359, [1976] 1 All ER 129 at 137, CA, per Lord Denning MR, approved on this point [1977] AC 59 at 97, [1976] 2 All ER 721 at 746, HL, per Lord Edmund-Davies.
2 Contrast *Farrell v Alexander* [1977] AC 59 at 91, 92, [1976] 2 All ER 721 at 741, 742, HL, per Lord Simon of Glaisdale.
3 Bankton *Institute* I, 1, 20 (Observations on the law of England, p 41).

(C) STATUTORY ENDORSEMENT

137. The concept of statutory endorsement. Parliament being sovereign, an Act of Parliament may ratify or endorse a precedent, thereby elevating it (whatever court set it) above the ordinary hierarchy of precedents and endowing it with the authority of statute. The question of statutory endorsement has in practice usually arisen when some statutory word or phrase, having been glossed in a precedent, is re-enacted in a successor Act or in a statute *in pari materia*. Such re-enactment has sometimes been held to imply that Parliament has endorsed the precedent in question, making it absolutely binding on all courts[1].

1 Eg *Edinburgh Water Co v Hay* (1854) 1 Macq 682, HL; *Barras v Aberdeen Steam Trawling and Fishing Co Ltd* 1933 SC (HL) 21, 1933 SLT 338.

138. The doctrine of statutory endorsement. The doctrine of statutory endorsement has been authoritatively expressed as follows:

'Where the language of a statute has received judicial interpretation and Parliament again employs the same language in a subsequent statute dealing with the same subject-matter, there is a presumption that Parliament intended that the language so used by it in the subsequent statute should be given the meaning which meantime has been judicially attributed to it. Parliament, in short, is to be presumed to have given statutory effect to the judicial interpretation so as to render it binding on the Courts as if it had been expressly enacted in an interpretation section'[1].

This doctrine does not apply to consolidation Acts since consolidation legislation affords Parliament no opportunity to reconsider the Acts being consolidated[2]. Nor is statutory endorsement to be inferred from the mere fact that the legislature, while amending other sections of the Act in question, has neglected to amend the section in which the glossed words appear[3].

1 *Barras v Aberdeen Steam Trawling and Fishing Co Ltd* 1935 SC (HL) 21 at 50, 1933 SLT 338 at 353, per Lord Macmillan.
2 *Haigh v Charles W Ireland Ltd* 1974 SC (HL) 1 at 33, 40, 1974 SLT 34 at 38, 42. See also *R v Chard* [1984] AC 279 at 292, [1983] 3 All ER 637 at 641, HL.
3 *Nicol's Trustees v Sutherland* 1951 SC (HL) 21 at 25, 1951 SLT 201 at 203. See also *R v Chard* [1984] AC 279 at 292, [1983] 3 All ER 637 at 641, HL.

139. Competing formulations of the doctrine. In the *Barras* case[1] two of their Lordships adopted the formulation by James LJ of the doctrine of statutory endorsement:

'Where once certain words in an Act of Parliament have received a judicial construction in one of the Superior Courts, and the Legislature has repeated them without alteration in a subsequent statute, I conceive that the Legislature must be taken to have used them according to the meaning which a Court of competent jurisdiction has given to them'[2].

In the same case, however, Lord Macmillan chose a more cautious formulation:

'If this rule were to be treated as a canon of construction of absolute obligation, I can see that it might have very far-reaching and possibly undesirable consequences. ... I find it rather a strain to have to believe that the reputed omniscience of Parliament extends to every decision of the Courts. What if the interpretative decision has never been reported? And what if Parliament has repeated language which has been construed in contrary senses by Courts of co-ordinate jurisdiction in England and Scotland? In my view the rule of interpretation which I am discussing affords only a valuable presumption as to the meaning of the language employed in a statute. Where a judicial interpretation is well-settled and well-recognised, the rule ought doubtless to receive effect, but it must, I think, be a question of circumstances whether Parliament is to be presumed to have tacitly given statutory authority, say, to a single judgment of a competent Court, so as to render that judgment, however obviously wrong, unexaminable in this House. After all, there is another rule of statutory interpretation of not less, if not indeed of higher authority, of which Parliament must be equally taken to be aware — namely, Lord Wensleydale's "golden rule"[3] that in construing statutes the grammatical and ordinary sense of the words is to be adhered to, unless it leads to some absurdity, repugnance, or inconsistency. For myself, I prefer the later form in which James LJ himself restated his rule in the case of *Greaves v Tofield*[4] as follows: "If an Act of Parliament uses the same language which was used in a former Act of Parliament referring to the same subject, and passed with the same purpose, and for the same object, the safe and well-known rule of construction is to assume that the Legislature when using well-known words upon which there have been well-known decisions uses those words in the sense which the decisions have attached to them". To the rule as so stated I am prepared whole-heartedly to subscribe'[5].

1 *Barras v Aberdeen Steam Trawling and Fishing Co Ltd* 1933 SC (HL) 21 at 27, 1933 SLT 338 at 339, per Viscount Buckmaster, and at 44 and at 350, per Lord Warrington of Clyffe.
2 *Ex parte Campbell, Re Cathcart* (1869) LR 5 Ch App 703 at 706, LJJ.
3 *Grey v Pearson* (1857) 6 HL Cas 61 at 106; *Caledonian Rly Co v North British Rly Co* (1881) 8 R (HL) 23 at 30.
4 *Greaves v Tofield* (1880) 14 Ch D 563 at 571, CA.
5 *Barras v Aberdeen Steam Trawling and Fishing Co Ltd* 1933 SC (HL) 21 at 50, 1933 SLT 338 at 353.

140. Conclusion. Although, in view of the competing views expressed therein, the *Barras* case[1] is 'a thoroughly unsatisfactory authority for any rule of statutory construction of general application'[2], Lord Macmillan's approach to the doctrine of statutory endorsement is preferable because it accords with modern principles of statutory interpretation[3]. The presumption of statutory endorsement is therefore a comparatively weak one, and this weakness is underlined by the fact that it has been 'acted on so rarely, in comparison with the number of occasions on which it could have been applied if it were completely valid'[4].

1 *Barras v Aberdeen Steam Trawling and Fishing Co Ltd* 1933 SC (HL) 21, 1933 SLT 338.
2 *R v Chard* [1984] AC 279 at 291, [1983] 3 All ER 637 at 641, HL, per Lord Diplock.
3 *R v Chard* [1984] AC 279 at 295, [1983] 3 All ER 637 at 644, HL, per Lord Scarman. However, in *Farrell v Alexander* [1977] AC 59 at 91, [1976] 2 All ER 721 at 740, 741, HL, Lord Simon of Glaisdale said that the mere statutory repetition of language which has been the subject of previous judicial interpretation is 'entirely neutral' in its implications.
4 W H D Winder 'The Interpretation of Statutes subject to Case Law' (1956) 58 JR 93 at 102, 103.

(D) STATUTORY ABROGATION

141. Introduction. Provided its words are aptly chosen, the legislature can overturn the rule of law which emerges from a judicial decision. So, for example, the decision in the *Burmah Oil* case[1] was negatived by the War Damage Act 1965[2]; and the immediate legal effect of the ruling in *Brown v Inland Revenue*[3] that solicitors must account to their clients for interest earned on clients' money was neutralised by statutory means[4].

1 *Burmah Oil Co (Burma Trading) Ltd v Lord Advocate* 1964 SC (HL) 117, 1964 SLT 218.
2 War Damage Act 1965 (c 18), s 1.
3 *Brown v Inland Revenue Comrs* 1964 SC (HL) 180, 1964 SLT 302.
4 See now the Solicitors (Scotland) Act 1980 (c 46), s 36, and the Solicitors (Scotland) Accounts Rules 1981, r 11.

142. Statutory derogation from common law principles. The elusive character of the common law raises a question. Since the juridical norm for which a judicial decision is 'authority' can commonly be formulated at various levels of abstraction and generality — ranging from a fairly narrow 'rule' to a comparatively broad 'principle' — may a precedent continue to be regarded as an authoritative source of principles and analogies after a specific rule for which it was authority has suffered legislative reversal? The general rule is that a precedent does not lose its authority merely because one of its legal implications has been overturned by the legislature; by and large 'the courts tend to regard the statutory reversal of judicial decisions as not affecting the underlying principles of those decisions'[1]. Rather it is usually conceived that Parliament has created a specific statutory exception to a general common law principle. So, for example, the *Burmah Oil* case[2] is still authority for the broad principle that the Crown cannot lawfully take or destroy the property of one of Her Majesty's subjects without paying compensation for it, and has been followed[3] as such, notwithstanding the passage of the War Damage Act 1965 (c 18). So also *Brown v Inland Revenue*[4] remains an authority on the duties of fiduciaries, and as such is to be followed or distinguished[5] but not disregarded.

1 P S Atiyah 'Common Law and Statute Law' (1985) 48 MLR 1 at 12.
2 *Burmah Oil Co (Burma Trading) Ltd v Lord Advocate* 1964 SC (HL) 117, 1964 SLT 218.
3 *Nissan v Attorney-General* [1968] 1 QB 286 at 341, [1967] 2 All ER 1238 at 1244, CA, per Lord Denning MR.
4 *Brown v Inland Revenue Comrs* 1964 SC (HL) 180, 1964 SLT 302.
5 *Potters v Loppert* [1973] Ch 399, [1973] 1 All ER 658.

143. Statutory abrogation of common law principles. On the other hand, the view is occasionally taken that a statutory intervention is so far-reaching that it has destroyed root and branch a common law principle founded on a whole series of cases. In *Broom v Morgan*[1] Denning LJ rejected an attempt to argue by analogy from the cases upon which the doctrine of common employment was based: that doctrine, he said, has now been 'abolished by statute'[2], and accordingly it 'should be disregarded in the same way as if it had never been enunciated'[3]. The outstanding Scottish example of this phenomenon is *Beith's Trustees v Beith*[4], where Lord President Cooper felt able not to follow a decision of seven judges in 1875[5] on the irrevocability *stante matrimonio* of a trust created by a marriage contract. The decision of 1875 has been a side effect of common law rules subsequently overridden by emancipatory legislation[6], by virtue of which the 'old' common law of the restricted capacity of the married woman in relation to property rights had 'passed into legal history'. Thus, although we owe respect to previous decisions of superior or equal authority, 'we also owe respect to Acts of Parliament; and if subsequent statutes have deprived a decision of its whole content, we have no duty to echo outmoded and superseded conceptions'[7].

1 *Broom v Morgan* [1953] 1 QB 597, [1953] 1 All ER 849, CA.
2 Law Reform (Personal Injuries) Act 1948 (c 41), s 1. See also the long title of the Act.
3 *Broom v Morgan* [1953] 1 QB 597 at 609, [1953] 1 All ER 849 at 854, CA. As to the effect of the repeal of a statute abrogating a common law principle, see para 163 below.
4 *Beith's Trustees v Beith* 1950 SC 66, 1950 SLT 70.
5 *Menzies v Murray* (1875) 2 R 507.
6 Married Women's Policies of Assurance (Scotland) Act 1880 (c 26); Married Women's Property (Scotland) Act 1881 (c 21); Sex Disqualification (Removal) Act 1919 (c 71); Married Women's Property (Scotland) Act 1920 (c 64).
7 *Beith's Trustees v Beith* 1950 SC 66 at 71, 72, 1950 SLT 70 at 73. As P S Atiyah observes of similar cases, the change here effected by Lord President Cooper is 'in the nature of a consequential amendment': 'Common Law and Statute Law' (1985) 48 MLR 1 at 23. See also para 354 below. The rule enabling a woman to create an alimentary liferent in her own favour, which survived Lord Cooper's judgment, ceased to have effect under the Law Reform (Husband and Wife) (Scotland) Act 1984 (c 15), s 5(1)(a).

(e) Fundamental Law

(A) THE UNION LEGISLATION AS FUNDAMENTAL LAW

144. Introduction. The axiomatic status of the view that Parliament is a sovereign and omnicompetent legislature, so that ordinary Acts of Parliament are the highest source of law in the United Kingdom and as such beyond legal challenge, has in Scotland been questioned in *MacCormick v Lord Advocate*[1] and in subsequent scholarly inquiries.

  1 *MacCormick v Lord Advocate* 1953 SC 396, 1953 SLT 255. See CONSTITUTIONAL LAW, vol 5, paras 349 ff.

145. The Union agreement as a constituent document. The thesis to be examined is that the vires of the United Kingdom Parliament are hedged in by fundamental law which cannot lawfully be overridden. This putative fundamental law is to be found in the Treaty of Union, the Acts of Union passed by the English and Scottish Parliaments[1], and associated legislation, most notably the Act for Securing the Protestant Religion and Presbyterian Church Government in Scotland[2]. These instruments, it is contended, form a constituent document: 'The main relevance of the Union Agreement was and is as a basic constituent document — a new and revolutionary *Grundnorm* for a new state'[3].

  1 Ie the Union with Scotland Act 1706 (c 11), and the Union with England Act 1707 (c 7).
  2 Protestant Religion and Presbyterian Church Act 1707 (c 6).
  3 T B Smith *Short Commentary on the Law of Scotland* (1962) pp 52, 53; T B Smith *Studies Critical and Comparative* (1962); T B Smith *Basic Rights and their Enforcement* (1979). Cf J D B Mitchell *Constitutional Law* (2nd edn, 1968) pp 69, 70; D M MacCormick 'Does the United Kingdom have a Constitution? Reflections on *MacCormick v Lord Advocate*' (1978) 29 NILQ 1–19. See CONSTITUTIONAL LAW, vol 5, paras 338 ff.

146. Intention of Union legislation. Certainly it can be argued that the Union legislation was intended by its authors to impose constraints on the legislative acts of the United Kingdom Parliament. In Lord Cooper's words:

'. . . the Treaty and the associated legislation, by which the Parliament of Great Britain was brought into being as the successor of the separate Parliaments of Scotland and England, contain some clauses which expressly reserve to the Parliament of Great Britain powers of subsequent modification, and other clauses which either contain no such power or emphatically exclude subsequent alteration by declarations that the provision shall be fundamental and unalterable in all time coming, or declarations of a like effect. I have never been able to understand how it is possible to reconcile with elementary canons of construction the adoption by the English constitutional theorists of the same attitude to these markedly different types of provisions'[1].

So, for example, the Treaty of Union expressly authorises the alteration by the Parliament of Great Britain of both public and private Scots law, while stipulating that 'no alteration be made in Laws which concern private Right except for the evident utility of the subjects within Scotland'[2]; and requires that the Court of Session 'remain in all time coming within Scotland as it is now constituted by the Laws of that Kingdom'[3]. The Act for securing the Protestant Religion and Presbyterian Church Government ordains that it shall be 'held and observed in all time comeing as a fundamental and essential condition of any Treaty or Union to be concluded betwixt the two Kingdoms without any alteration thereof or derogation thereto in any sort for ever'[4].

1 *MacCormick v Lord Advocate* 1953 SC 396 at 411, 1953 SLT 255 at 262.
2 Treaty of Union between Scotland and England 1707, art 18.
3 Ibid, art 19.
4 Protestant Religion and Presbyterian Church Act 1707 (c 6).

(B) OBJECTIONS TO THE FUNDAMENTAL LAW THESIS

147. The institutional writers. On one reading, such provisions as those quoted in the preceding paragraph establish fundamental law. This was certainly Bankton's view of their effect:

> 'Acts of parliament against the power of subsequent parliaments bind not; but 'tis declared by the 42 Edward III c 5[1] that any statute made against the *magna charta* or *charta de forrestis*, shall be void; and the same may be said as to the substantial articles of the treaty of union, which is as the great charter of the liberties of both kingdoms united into one'[2].

Erskine, on the other hand, was adamant that any Parliament has an unlimited power to abrogate the legislation of former Parliaments[3], and this despite the fact that, as Mitchell observes, phrases such as 'in all time coming' and 'for ever' were of common occurrence in Scottish Acts of Parliament[4].

1 The reference is to the Confirmation of the Charters Act 1368 (c 1).
2 Bankton *Institute* I, 1, 25 (Observations on the law of England). See also I, 1, 51.
3 Erskine *Institute* I, 1, 19. Stair *Institutions* IV, 1, 61 takes a similar view of the powers of the old Scots Parliament.
4 J D B Mitchell *Constitutional Law* (2nd edn, 1968) p 70.

148. Dicey. In any event, to concede that the legislators of 1707 intended to create fundamental law does not entail the concession that this has indeed been the legal effect. From Dicey's point of view, the 'undoubted legal fact'[1] of Parliamentary sovereignty reduced the attempts at entrenchment not to futility but to political symbolism. The declaration of immutability in the Act for Securing the Protestant Religion, for example, is said to represent 'the conviction of the Parliament which passed the Act of Union that the Act for the security of the Church of Scotland ought to be morally or constitutionally unchangeable even by the British Parliament'. Thus such a declaration could do no more than morally strengthen political opposition to any future change[2].

1 A V Dicey *Introduction to the Study of the Law of the Constitution* (10th edn, 1959 by E C S Wade) p 64. Cf CONSTITUTIONAL LAW, vol 5, para 340.
2 A V Dicey and R S Rait *Thoughts on the Union between England and Scotland* (1920) p 253.

149. The Universities (Scotland) Act 1853. The thesis that the instruments of the Union created fundamental law must cope with the difficulty raised by the enactment of the Universities (Scotland) Act 1853 (c 89), which ostensibly did away with the requirement entrenched as unalterable in the Act for Securing the Protestant Religion that professors of the Scottish universities should avow the Presbyterian Confession of Faith. The Act of 1853 has been explained away in a number of ways. According to Middleton, 'A single instance . . . or even several instances, cannot prove that Parliament was entitled to do what it did, especially when the alteration was such that little opposition to it could be expected'[1]. If it follows that the 1853 Act and its successors are legal nullities the conclusion is, to say the least, controversial. Smith, however, suggests that what happened in 1853 'might be regarded *pro tanto* as a revolution by consent'.

He adds: 'It does not follow that all other purported repeals of terms of the Union would be so generally accepted'[2]. His suggestion, therefore, is not that this 'revolution by consent' established the doctrine of Parliamentary sovereignty, but that it validated only this particular derogation from fundamental law. This is not unarguable, but it may be observed that there is nothing in the 'constituent documents' themselves to found such an approach, and quite conceivably one of the intentions of the authors thereof may have been to protect certain institutional arrangements from the back-sliding of subsequent generations of the Scots themselves, as well as from the interference of the English. Mitchell's approach is different in that he does not concede that the Act of 1853 cannot be reconciled with the Act for Securing the Protestant Religion. Constituent documents, he says, are to be interpreted flexibly — 'Words like "ever" or "never" in such contexts must be read in a relative sense' — and allowance must be made for changes in ideas[3]. 'Thus the thing which is "entrenched" is not... anything which is absolutely constant'[4]. Mitchell is right that posterity will always interpret constitutional provisions according to its own lights, but even so the language of the Act for Securing the Protestant Religion is so uncompromising and unequivocal that not even the most strained and tendentious interpretation could square it with the sequence of legislation starting in 1853 which has, after all, purportedly repealed part of the earlier Act[5].

1 Middleton 'New Thoughts on the Union' (1954) 66 JR 37 at 43. See also at 49.
2 T B Smith 'The Union of 1707 as Fundamental Law' in *Studies Critical and Comparative* (1962) pp 1–27 at p 14. See also T B Smith *Short Commentary on the Law of Scotland* (1962) p 56; and CONSTITUTIONAL LAW, vol 5, paras 346–348.
3 J D B Mitchell *Constitutional Law* (2nd edn, 1968) pp 71, 74.
4 *Mitchell* p 72.
5 The offending words were expressly struck out by the Statute Law Revision (Scotland) Act 1964 (c 80), Sch 1 (repealed by the Statute Law (Repeals) Act 1974 (c 22), Schedule, Pt XI). See also the Statute Law Revision Act 1948 (c 62), Sch 1.

(C) THE COMPETENCE OF JUDICIAL REVIEW

150. Judicial review of validity. A further question is whether it is competent for a court to review the validity of a statute alleged to be in breach of the fundamental law of the Union. In Lord Cooper's words, 'it is of little avail to ask whether the Parliament of Great Britain "can" do this or that, without going on to inquire who can stop them if they do'[1]. In *MacCormick v Lord Advocate* Lord Cooper himself took the view that the courts could not entertain any challenge to Parliament's legislative competence in respect of matters of 'public right'[2]. In respect of matters of 'private right', and also the position of the Court of Session itself, he reserved his opinion[3]. However, in *Gibson v Lord Advocate* Lord Keith observed that

> 'the question whether a particular Act of the United Kingdom Parliament is or is not "for the evident utility" of the subjects within Scotland is not a justiciable issue in this court. The making of decisions upon what must essentially be a political matter is not part of the function of the court, and it is highly undesirable that it should be.... A general inquiry into the utility of certain legislative measures as regards the population generally is quite outside its competence'[4].

Even if they were not obiter, these remarks would not establish that a Scottish court can never ask whether an Act of Parliament is *ultra vires* by virtue of the terms of the Union Agreement. Even if this inquiry is beyond the jurisdiction of the courts, that is not logically fatal to the contention that an Act in contradiction of a fundamental term of the Union is void[5]. But for practical purposes the two issues cannot be separated: who cares whether an Act is 'really' invalid if the courts will brook no denial of its ostensible validity?

1 *MacCormick v Lord Advocate* 1953 SC 396 at 412, 1953 SLT 255 at 263.
2 1953 SC 396 at 413, 1953 SLT 255 at 263. A similar line was taken in *Sillars v Smith* 1982 SCCR 367, 1982 SLT 539, where, however, the effect of the Union Agreement between Scotland and England 1707 was neither argued nor considered.
3 *MacCormick v Lord Advocate* 1953 SC 396 at 412, 1953 SLT 255 at 263.
4 *Gibson v Lord Advocate* 1975 SC 136 at 144, 1975 SLT 134 at 137.
5 J D B Mitchell *Constitutional Law* (2nd edn, 1968) p 88.

(D) CONCLUSION

151. Assertion and proof. To reach a conclusion, one may start with Mitchell's remark that 'the accepted doctrines in relation to Parliament have, essentially, grown up as beliefs founded upon assertion rather more than upon proof'[1]. This is no doubt true of the dogma of Parliamentary sovereignty, but it is not necessarily a weakness. The consensus on the dogma was until quite recently so strong, at least in England, that one might well have said that *communis error facit ius*. Besides, it is too much to ask of any *Grundnorm* that it should be capable of rational 'proof'. From a strictly legal point of view, the *Grundnorm* pulls itself up by its own bootstraps; its legal validity is postulated, not demonstrated. The dogma of Parliamentary sovereignty can be explained and understood only in historical terms, as the product of political and ideological factors.

In the final analysis, the case for regarding the Union Agreement between Scotland and England as fundamental law also rests on assertion rather than proof. From the fact that the United Kingdom Parliament was brought into being by the Union instruments it does not follow that it must forever after be limited by them. If Parliament was ever bound, it may have emancipated itself imperceptibly long ago[2]. The legislation of 1853[3] on that view is only evidence that the emancipation had already occurred.

1 J D B Mitchell *Constitutional Law* (2nd edn, 1968) p 91.
2 Cf G Maher 'The Identity of the Scottish Legal System' 1977 JR 21 at 28, note 19.
3 Ie the Universities (Scotland) Act 1853 (c 89): see para 149 above.

152. Academic logic and political realism. Nor can it be said on that interpretation that a refusal to attribute superior status to the instruments of the Union represents the triumph of academic logic over political realism[1]. Political realism may well require a different assessment of the Statute of Westminster 1931 (c 4) or the European Communities Act 1972 (c 68). *MacCormick v Lord Advocate* has understandably been seized upon by juridical nationalists as a symbol of Scotland's legal nationhood[2]. Others consider that it is romanticism, not realism, to attribute fundamental status to a set of historic documents after 250 years and more: an English expert in the field of public law has observed 'the truth is that the Treaty was made too early, and the argument has been raised too late'[3] for the fundamental law thesis to prevail. This may be so. He does not, however, discuss earlier assertions in Scotland of the fundamental nature of the Union Agreement nor explain why passage of time should in itself invalidate legal argument. Nevertheless, time may change constitutional realities and the distribution of power among the organs of government. The status of the Union Agreement today is an unresolved question which may never be resolved. As A W Bradley observes, 'not all arguments challenging the orthodox view of Parliamentary sovereignty in Scotland are at all far fetched... But arguments founded upon the binding character of the Treaty of Union have not yet been upheld by the Scottish courts'[4].

1 Cf *MacCormick v Lord Advocate* 1953 SC 396 at 412, 1953 SLT 255 at 263, per Lord President Cooper.
2 *MacCormick v Lord Advocate* was, of course, litigated by political nationalists on, it must be said, the thinnest of legal pretexts. The court did not consider that it raised the issue of validity of legislation. See also *Sillars v Smith* 1982 SCCR 367, 1982 SLT 539, in which the Union Agreement was not under consideration.
3 H W R Wade *Constitutional Fundamentals* (1980) p 33.
4 A W Bradley 'The Sovereignty of Parliament — in Perpetuity?' in J Jowell and D Oliver (ed) *The Changing Constitution* (1985). See CONSTITUTIONAL LAW, vol 5, paras 344–351, 358–360.

(4) THE OPERATION OF ACTS OF PARLIAMENT

(a) Enactment and Commencement

153. Enactment. The normal form of the enacting formula is 'Be it enacted by the Queen's most Excellent Majesty, by and with the advice and consent of the Lords Spiritual and Temporal, and Commons, in this present Parliament assembled, and by the authority of the same, as follows'[1]. What follows the enacting formula is thereby endowed with legal validity[2], and the legal validity of a genuine statute[3] cannot be impugned. The courts cannot look behind the enacting formula; questions of procedural irregularity or fraud in the passage of a Bill, whether public or private, are for Parliament alone[4].

1 In the case of Bills governed by the Parliament Acts 1911 and 1949, the formula is 'Be it enacted by the Queen's most Excellent Majesty, by and with the advice and consent of the Commons in this present Parliament assembled, in accordance with the provisions of the Parliament Acts 1911 and 1949, and by authority of the same, as follows': Parliament Act 1911 (c 13), s 4(1) (amended by the Parliament Act 1949 (c 103), s 2(2)).
2 Before Lord Brougham's Act (the Interpretation of Acts Act 1850 (c 21)) (repealed), each separate portion of an Act would be preceded by words of enactment. Now every section of an Act takes effect as a substantive enactment without introductory words: Interpretation Act 1978 (c 30), s 1.
3 Authentic copies of all public Acts since 1849, printed on vellum and signed by the Clerk of the Parliaments, are stored in the House of Lords and the Public Record Office: see 44 Halsbury's Laws of England (4th edn) para 825; Craies *Statute Law* (7th edn, 1971 by S G G Edgar) pp 45, 46. As to private Acts, see para 168, note 1 below.
4 *Edinburgh and Dalkeith Rly Co v Wauchope* (1842) 1 Bell App 252, 8 Cl & Fin 710, HL; *British Railways Board v Pickin* [1974] AC 765, [1974] 1 All ER 609, HL.

154. The preamble. A preamble (where there is one) contains a recital, narrative or rehearsal of avowed legislative motives, and precedes the enacting formula. Accordingly the preamble is not, strictly speaking, part of the Act[1], although under certain circumstances the preamble may be resorted to as an aid to construction[2]. Since the preamble does not enjoy the force of law, assertions of fact or of law contained therein are not conclusive although the onus of refuting such assertions lies on those who wish to controvert them[3]. Of course an assertion of law or fact enacted in the body of an Act cannot be gainsaid, no matter how false or objectionable.

1 *Renfrew County Council v Orphan Homes of Scotland Trustees* (1898) 1 F 186 at 191, 6 SLT 229, per Lord President Robertson.
2 See INTERPRETATION OF STATUTES, DEEDS AND OTHER DOCUMENTS.

3   *R v Haughton Inhabitants* (1853) 1 E & B 501 at 516, per Lord Campbell. As to recitals in private Acts, see *Edinburgh and Glasgow Rly Co v Linlithgow Magistrates* (1859) 3 Macq 691, HL.

155. Commencement. The mere passing of an Act does not necessarily bring its provisions into force. Enactment is therefore to be distinguished from commencement[1].

The time at which an Act or enactment comes into force depends upon the intention of the legislature as manifested in the Act itself[2]. In some cases a particular date is specified by the Act in question. In other cases the Act empowers Her Majesty or a government minister to appoint a date by order. Provision is frequently made for different provisions to be brought into force at different times or by different means[3]. Where an Act (or any provision thereof) which does not come into force immediately on its enactment confers power (for example to make subordinate legislation), that power may be exercised, and any instrument made thereunder may be made so as to come into force, at any time after the passing of the Act so far as may be necessary or expedient for the purpose of (1) bringing the Act (or any provision thereof) into force, or (2) giving full effect to the Act (or any provision thereof) at or after the time when it comes into force[4].

Where an Act makes no provision for its coming into force, it comes into force at the beginning of the day on which it receives the royal assent[5].

1   'Commencement' in relation to an Act or enactment means the time when the Act or enactment comes into force: Interpretation Act 1978 (c 30), Sch 1.
2   Thus an Act may be retrospective in operation if the intention of the legislature is expressed clearly enough: see 44 Halsbury's Laws of England (4th edn) paras 921–926; Craies *Statute Law* (7th edn, 1971 by S G G Edgar) pp 387–406.
3   Where provision is made for an Act or a provision to come into force on a particular day, it comes into force at the beginning of that day: Interpretation Act 1978, s 4(a).
4   Ibid, s 13(a), (b).
5   Ibid, s 4(b).

(b) Expiry and Repeal

156. Duration. Leaving aside the effect of desuetude[1], the duration of an Act depends upon the intention of the legislature as manifested in the Act itself and in subsequent Acts. An enactment may be temporary — that is, it may stipulate that it is to cease to have effect at a specified time — in which case it will expire automatically at that time. In the absence of such a stipulation an enactment continues to enjoy the force of law indefinitely — that is, until repealed expressly or impliedly.

1   As to desuetude, see paras 129 ff above.

157. Express repeal. An enactment (whether temporary or of indefinite duration) may be expressly repealed by any words in a later Act (whether temporary[1] or of indefinite duration) which clearly evince the intention to abrogate the enactment in question[2]. Express repeal of a statute or any of its provisions may also be effected by delegated legislation, provided the necessary power has been conferred by an enabling Act. On the traditional view of Parliamentary sovereignty no Act can be rendered immune from the possibility of subsequent repeal[3].

1 On general principle there seems to be no reason why express words of repeal in a temporary Act should not be taken at face value; but see 44 Halsbury's Laws of England (4th edn) para 963. Likewise there is no legal reason why a private or local and personal Act should not effect the express repeal of a public general Act.
2 An Act may be repealed in the session of Parliament in which it was passed: Interpretation Act 1978 (c 30), s 2.
3 Stair *Institutions* IV, 1, 61; Erskine *Institute* I, 1, 19; A V Dicey *Introduction to the Study of the Law of the Constitution* (10th edn, 1959 by E C S Wade) pp 64–70.

158. Implied repeal. An enactment is impliedly repealed by a later Act[1] of indefinite duration if it is impossible to reconcile the provisions of the latter with the former[2]: *leges posteriores priores contrarias abrogant*. Before repeal can be inferred by implication, actual repugnancy between the provisions of the two enactments must be proved in whole or in part, and repeal by mere implication is not easily to be presumed[3]. Where an enactment cannot be reconciled with a subsequent temporary enactment the obvious solution is to hold that the effect of the latter is suspensory rather than abrogatory. On the traditional view of Parliamentary sovereignty no Act can be rendered immune from the possibility, albeit in some cases remote, of repeal by implication[4].

1 It may also be impliedly repealed by later subordinate legislation, provided the power to repeal has been conferred by the parent Act.
2 See eg *Ross v Ross* (1894) 22 R 174, 2 SLT 349; *Randall v Renton* (1902) 5 F (J) 16, 10 SLT 495.
3 *Bain v Mackay* (1875) 2 R (J) 32 at 36, per Lord Justice-Clerk Moncrieff.
4 *Vauxhall Estates Ltd v Liverpool Corpn* [1932] 1 KB 733; *Ellen Street Estates Ltd v Minister of Health* [1934] 1 KB 590, CA.

159. Effect of repeal. At common law a repealed enactment is to be treated, except with regard to actions concluded while it was still law, as if it had never been passed[1]. But this principle has been progressively circumscribed by the provisions of interpretation legislation since 1850[2]. The relevant provisions are now enacted in the Interpretation Act 1978[3]. Not all of the relevant provisions of this Act, however, apply to Acts passed before 1979[4].

1 See eg *Surtees v Ellison* (1829) 9 B & C 750; *Kay v Goodwin* (1830) 6 Bing 576.
2 Interpretation Act 1889 (c 63), ss 11, 38 (repealed).
3 See the Interpretation Act 1978 (c 30), ss 15–17.
4 For the application of the Interpretation Act 1978 to Acts passed prior to its commencement (on 1 January 1979), see s 22(1), Sch 22, Pt I (paras 1–5). For its application to subordinate legislation, see s 23(1), (2), (4), Sch 2, Pt II (paras 6, 7).

160. Effect of repeal on subordinate legislation. Upon the repeal of an enabling Act subordinate legislation deriving its validity from that Act necessarily loses its force[1] unless its lapse is prevented by a saving provision[2].

1 See eg *Inglis's Trustees v Macpherson* 1910 SC 46, 1909 2 SLT 363.
2 As to the effect of repeal and re-enactment on subordinate legislation, see para 164 below.

161. Effect of repeal on accrued rights etc. Unless the contrary intention appears, the repeal of an enactment does not (1) affect the previous operation of the enactment repealed or anything duly done or suffered under that enactment; (2) affect any right, privilege, obligation or liability acquired, accrued or incurred under that enactment; (3) affect any penalty, forfeiture or punishment incurred in respect of any offence committed against that enactment; (4) affect any investigation, legal proceeding or remedy in respect of any such right, privilege, obligation, liability, penalty, forfeiture or punishment[1]. Any such investigation, legal proceeding or remedy may be instituted, continued or enforced, and any such penalty, forfeiture or punishment may be imposed, as if the repealing Act had not been passed[2].

1 Interpretation Act 1978 (c 30), s 16(1)(b)–(e), which applies, by virtue of s 22(1), Sch 2, para 3, to Acts passed after the year 1889. For judicial interpretation of this provision, see *Moray County Council v Maclean* 1962 SC 601, 1962 SLT 236, OH; *Apostolic Church Trustees v Glasgow District Council (No 2)* 1978 SLT (Lands Trib) 17.
2 Interpretation Act 1978, s 16(1). See also note 1 above.

162. Effect of repeal of repealing enactment. Where an Act repeals a repealing enactment, the repeal does not revive any enactment previously repealed unless words are added reviving it[1].

1 Interpretation Act 1978 (c 30), s 15, which applies, by virtue of s 22(1), Sch 2, para 2, to Acts passed after the year 1850.

163. Effect of repeal on the common law. Where an Act repeals an enactment which superseded the common law in relation to a particular matter a question arises as to whether the common law is revived by the repeal of the enactment in question. The Interpretation Act 1978 provides that 'unless the contrary intention appears' the repeal of an enactment does not 'revive anything not in force or existing at the time at which the repeal takes effect'[1], and these words seem wide enough to cover the common law[2]. But if Parliament repeals a statute which superseded the common law without making fresh statutory provision for the matter in question, a contrary intention (that is, an intention to revive the common law) must surely be inferred; for Parliament cannot be thought to have intended to create a legal vacuum. So, for example, freedom of contract at common law is revived when a legislative scheme derogating from it is abrogated.

1 Interpretation Act 1978 (c 30), s 16(1)(a), which, by virtue of s 22(1), Sch 2, para 3, applies to Acts passed after the year 1889.
2 Craies *Statute Law* (7th edn, 1971 by S G G Edgar) p 355.

164. Repeal and re-enactment. Where an Act repeals a previous enactment and substitutes provisions for the enactment repealed, the repealed enactment remains in force until the substituted provisions come into force[1]. Where an Act repeals and re-enacts, with or without modification, a previous enactment then, unless the contrary intention appears, in so far as any subordinate legislation[2] made or other thing done under the enactment so repealed, or having effect as if so made or done, could have been made or done under the provision re-enacted, it is to have effect as if made or done under that provision[3].

1 Interpretation Act 1978 (c 30), s 17(1), which, by virtue of s 22(1), Sch 2, para 2, applies to Acts passed after the year 1850. Further, where an Act repeals and re-enacts, with or without modification, a previous enactment, then, unless the contrary intention appears, any reference in any other enactment is to be construed as a reference to the provision re-enacted: s 17(2)(a), which, by virtue of Sch 2, para 3, applies to Acts passed after the year 1889. In the application of s 17(2)(a) to Acts passed after 1978 the reference to 'any other enactment' includes any deed or other instrument or document: s 23(3).
2 'Subordinate legislation' means Orders in Council, orders, rules, regulations, schemes, warrants, byelaws and other instruments made under any Act: ibid, s 21(1).
3 Ibid, s 17(2)(b), which, by virtue of s 22(1), applies to Acts passed after 1978.

165. Effect of expiry. The general saving provision of the interpretation legislation[1] applies to the expiry of a temporary enactment as if it were repealed by an Act[2]. In consequence the expiry of a temporary enactment does not affect rights accrued etc under that enactment[3]. In consequence also, the expiry does not, unless the contrary intention appears, revive anything not in force or existing at the time at which it takes effect[4]. If a temporary enactment is held to have suspended rather than abrogated earlier legislation[5], a contrary intention (that is, an intention that the earlier legislation should revive) will presumably be inferred.

1 Interpretation Act 1978 (c 30), s 16(1), which, by virtue of s 22(1), Sch 2, para 3, applies to Acts passed after the year 1889.
2 Ibid, s 16(2) which, by virtue of s 22(1), applies to Acts passed after 1978.
3 See para 161 above.
4 Interpretation Act 1978, s 16(1)(a).
5 See further para 158 above.

166. Continuing Acts. Where a Bill for the continuation in force of an expiring Act is introduced in the Parliamentary session in which the Act would expire, but does not receive the royal assent until after the date of expiry, the continuing Act takes effect from the date of expiry unless it provides otherwise[1]. However, no punishment, penalty or forfeiture may be imposed for breaking, between the date of expiry and the date of the royal assent, the Act continued[1].

1 Acts of Parliament (Expiration) Act 1808 (c 106).

(c) Promulgation, Proof and Citation

167. Promulgation. An Act of Parliament is legally valid by virtue of its enactment alone[1]; promulgation is not necessary to validate an Act or to bring it into force[2].

1 See para 153 above.
2 Craies *Statute Law* (7th edn, 1971 by S G G Edgar) p 33. Until the sixteenth century Acts of the old Scots Parliament were proclaimed in the county towns, burghs and baron courts: Proclamation of Acts of Parliament Act 1425 (c 21); Proclamation of Acts of Parliament Act 1457 (c 39). However, the Proclamation of Acts Act 1581 (c 37) provided that proclamation at the market cross of Edinburgh should suffice and that the legislation should come into force forty days thereafter.

168. Proof. Every Act is a public Act to be judicially noticed as such, unless the contrary is expressly provided by the Act[1].

1 Interpretation Act 1978 (c 30), s 3, which, by virtue of s 22(1), Sch 2, para 2, applies to Acts passed after the year 1850. A private Act passed before 1851 requires to be proved unless it provides that it is to be judicially noticed as a public Act.

169. Citation. An Act may be cited by reference to its short title, either with or without a reference to its chapter number. Alternatively an Act may be cited by reference to the regnal year or years of the Parliamentary session in which it was passed and to its chapter number[1]. The chapter numbers of Acts passed after 1962 are assigned by reference to the calendar year and not the session in which they are passed, and such Acts may be cited accordingly[2].

Acts of the old Scots Parliament are traditionally cited by reference to the calendar year and chapter number. Short titles were conferred upon such old Scots Acts as were thought to be still in force by the Statute Law Revision (Scotland) Act 1964[3].

1 Statutory warrant for these modes of citation could formerly be found in the Interpretation Act 1889 (c 63), s 35(1) (repealed). There is no corresponding provision in the Interpretation Act 1978 (c 30).
2 Acts of Parliament Numbering and Citation Act 1962 (c 34), s 1.
3 Statute Law Revision (Scotland) Act 1964 (c 80), s 2, Sch 2.

(d) Territorial Extent

170. Application to Scotland. An Act of Parliament may expressly stipulate that its provisions do or do not apply to Scotland. In the absence of an express stipulation, the presumption is that the statute in question extends to the whole of the United Kingdom. The presumption that an Act extends to Scotland is strengthened if Northern Ireland, but not Scotland, is expressly excluded from the operation of the Act[1]. The presumption that an Act extends to Scotland is also strengthened if it deals with interests and considerations of policy that obtain equally on either side of the border[1]. On the other hand, the whole tenor of an Act may be such as to suggest that its application to Scotland was not contemplated by the legislature[2]. Thus the presumption in favour of applicability to Scotland may be rebutted if it can be inferred from allusions to English officials and procedure, and from the use of English terminology, that an Act has in view the law and practice of England only[3]. But it is difficult to found the same inference on a mere isolated departure from Scots phraseology[4]. In practice, by virtue of improvements in the technique of drafting Parliamentary Bills, doubt about applicability to Scotland is unlikely to arise in relation to modern legislation.

1 *Perth Water Comrs v M'Donald* (1879) 6 R 1050.
2 *Westminster Fire Office v Glasgow Provident Investment Society* (1888) 15 R (HL) 89 at 94, 13 App Cas 699 at 716, per Lord Watson.
3 *Levy v Jackson* (1903) 5 F 1170 at 1172, 11 SLT 268 at 269, per Lord Justice-Clerk Macdonald.
4 *Dunlop v Goudie* (1895) 22 R (J) 34.

(5) PREROGATIVE LEGISLATION

171. Character and forms. Parliamentary legislation is legislation by the sovereign in Parliament; prerogative legislation on the other hand derives its authority from the sovereign alone, although it is most commonly effected in the form of an Order in Council[1]. Prerogative legislation is primary legislation[2], but it can always be overridden or superseded by an Act of Parliament[3].

1 Prerogative Orders in Council purport to be made by and with the advice of the Privy Council: see eg the Requisitioning of Ships Order 1982, printed in Statutory Instruments 1982, p 1693. Contrast royal proclamations, eg Trading with the Enemy Proclamation 1914. As to the publication of royal proclamations, see the Order in Council of 22 February 1978, r 7, printed in III SR & O (Rev) 1948, p 1009 (substituted by the Crown Office (Commission of the Peace and Royal Proclamations) Rules 1975, SI 1975/622, r 3). In any event a royal proclamation is valid in law if published in the London Gazette, Edinburgh Gazette and Belfast Gazette: Crown Office Act 1877 (c 41), s 3.

2 *Council of Civil Service Unions v Minister for the Civil Service* [1985] AC 374 at 399, [1984] 3 All ER 935 at 942, HL, per Lord Fraser of Tullybelton.

3 As to the supersession of prerogative by statute, see para 174 below.

172. Scope. The scope of the legislative aspect of the prerogative has been largely determined by the political and constitutional struggles of the seventeenth century. The prerogative does not confer upon the Crown any general power to legislate other than through Parliament. In normal times it cannot be used to change or suspend common law or statute[1]. It may, however, be invoked when there will be no derogation from the rights of the subjects[2], and legislation to regulate the colonies, the armed forces and the Civil Service[3] may be founded on the prerogative. The scope of the legislative aspect of the prerogative in times of extreme stress and peril, as may arise for example in war[4], is undoubtedly greater and may well extend to any measures necessary to meet the immediate exigencies of the situation[5].

1 *Proclamations Case* (1611) 12 Co Rep 74; Claim of Right 1689 (c 28); *Grieve v Edinburgh and District Water Trustees* 1918 SC 700, 1918 2 SLT 72.

2 Eg the creation of the Criminal Injuries Compensation Scheme: see *R v Criminal Injuries Compensation Board, ex parte Lain* [1967] 2 QB 864, [1967] 2 All ER 770, DC.

3 Eg the Civil Service Order 1982.

4 See eg the Trading with the Enemy Proclamation 1914, and the Requisitioning of Ships Order 1982.

5 *Grieve v Edinburgh and District Water Trustees* 1918 SC 700 at 709, 1918 2 SLT 72 at 76, per Lord Dundas; *Burmah Oil Co (Burma Trading) Ltd v Lord Advocate* 1964 SC (HL) 117 at 121, 122, 1964 SLT 218 at 220, 221, per Lord Reid. But even in war, 'Anxiety to get a thing quickly done because the doing of it has been too long delayed does not provide an occasion for the exercise of the royal prerogative': *Grieve v Edinburgh and District Water Trustees* above at 706 and at 74, per Lord Ormidale (Ordinary). On the question of compensation, see the *Burmah Oil* case above, and the War Damage Act 1965 (c 18), s 1.

173. Reviewability. In the *Civil Service Unions* case[1] the House of Lords held that, in the absence of overriding considerations of national security, the exercise of a power conferred upon a minister by a prerogative Order in Council[2] was in principle amenable to judicial review. This case is not authority for the proposition that a direct legislative exercise of prerogative power (that is, the actual making of an Order in Council under the prerogative) is similarly reviewable. Nevertheless there are dicta in the case which suggest that some of their Lordships might be prepared to countenance this development in a later case[3]. Such an extension of judicial review would, however, run counter to authority of great weight[4]. Moreover, whereas judicial review of the exercise of a power conferred by statute or by prerogative legislation can be rationalised as being based on the implied intention of the legislator that the power conferred should be exercised fairly, this rationale cannot cover judicial review of prerogative legislation itself which is primary legislation just as an Act of Parliament is.

1 *Council of Civil Service Unions v Minister for the Civil Service* [1985] AC 374, [1984] 3 All ER 935, HL.

2 Civil Service Order 1982, art 4.

3 *Council of Civil Service Unions v Minister for the Civil Service* [1985] AC 374 at 407, [1984] 3 All ER 935 at 948, HL, per Lord Scarman, at 410 and at 950, 951 per Lord Diplock, and at 417, 418 and at 955, 956 per Lord Roskill. Contrast that case at 398 and at 942 per Lord Fraser of Tullybelton, and at 423, 424 and at 960 per Lord Brightman.

4 These were enumerated by Lord Fraser of Tullybelton in *Council of Civil Service Unions v Minister for the Civil Service* [1985] AC 374 at 398, [1984] 3 All ER 935 at 941, 942, HL.

174. Supersession of prerogative by statute. An Act of Parliament may expressly supersede or expressly save a prerogative power to legislate. Where an Act covers the same ground as a prerogative, but does not make express provision in respect of that prerogative, the inference to be drawn as a rule is that the Act curtails and supersedes the prerogative to the extent that they overlap[1].

1 *Attorney-General v De Keyser's Royal Hotel Ltd* [1920] AC 508 at 526, HL, per Lord Dunedin (prerogative curtailed), at 539, 540 per Lord Atkinson (prerogative abridged and in abeyance), at 561, 562 per Lord Sumner (prerogative abated and superseded), and at 576 per Lord Parmoor (prerogative taken away or abridged). Contrast that case at 554 per Lord Moulton. See also *Sabally and N'Jie v Attorney-General* [1965] 1 QB 273 at 295, [1964] 3 All ER 377 at 381, CA, per Lord Denning MR (prerogative swallowed up), and contrast that case at 299 and at 384 per Russell LJ. As to the effect of an Act superseding or curtailing a prerogative power, see para 163 above. Cf S A de Smith *Constitutional and Administrative Law* (4th edn, 1980) p 140.

(6) SUBORDINATE LEGISLATION

(a) Introduction

175. The concept of subordinate legislation. Subordinate legislation is legislation made, directly or indirectly[1], under powers conferred by an Act of Parliament or by prerogative legislation. The legislative power of the sovereign in Parliament (or, within the sphere of the prerogative, of the sovereign alone) rests on no ulterior legal authority; the authority of primary legislation is original and inherent. The legislative power of the maker of subordinate legislation on the other hand is delegated power[2], ultimately referable to the provisions of an Act of Parliament or prerogative legislation; the authority of subordinate (or secondary) legislation is derivative. From this it follows that, whereas the validity of any Act of Parliament is beyond question[3], subordinate legislation is valid only in so far as its maker does not go beyond the powers conferred upon him; and in legal proceedings there is as a rule[4] nothing to prevent an inquiry into the validity of some item of subordinate legislation[5].

1 In the case of subdelegated legislation it is made indirectly.
2 Hence subordinate legislation is commonly called 'delegated legislation'.
3 See para 153 above.
4 For a modern attempt to preclude judicial review of the validity of subordinate legislation, see eg the Education (Scotland) Act 1980 (c 44), s 114(2) (amended by the Education (Scotland) Act 1981 (c 58), s 15, Sch 6, para 13; Education (Scotland) Act 1981 (Commencement No 1) Order 1981, SI 1981/1557, art 4), which provides that an instrument containing or giving effect to a scheme under the Education (Scotland) Act 1980, Pt IV (ss 87–97), is to be conclusive evidence that the scheme is within the scope of, and was made in conformity with, the Act, and that the validity of the scheme is not to be questioned in any legal proceedings whatever. For the probable effect of such a provision, see *Ex parte Ringer* (1909) 25 TLR 718. As to the effect of a stipulation in an enabling Act that an instrument under the Act is to have effect 'as if enacted in this Act', see *Institute of Patent Agents v Lockwood* (1894) 6 R (HL) 219, 2 SLT 106. Contrast *R v Minister of Health, ex parte Yaffe* [1931] AC 494, HL.
5 See generally ADMINISTRATIVE LAW.

(b) Statutory Instruments

176. Definition. All statutory instruments are documents by which power conferred by Parliament to make subordinate legislation is exercised; but not all such documents are statutory instruments. Three classes of document are defined as statutory instruments:

(1) where the Statutory Instruments Act 1946 or an Act passed after 1947 confers power to make, confirm or approve orders, rules, regulations or other subordinate legislation on Her Majesty in Council, and that power is expressed to be exercisable by Order in Council, any document by which that power is exercised is a statutory instrument[1];

(2) where that Act of 1946 or an Act passed after 1947 confers such power on a minister of the Crown, and that power is expressed to be exercisable by statutory instrument, any document by which that power is exercised is a statutory instrument[2];

(3) where an Act passed before 1948 confers power to make statutory rules[3] on any rule-making authority[4], any document by which that power is exercised after 1947 is (subject to certain exceptions[5]) a statutory instrument[6].

In addition, any Act of Parliament may stipulate that a power conferred by it to make subordinate legislation is to be exercised by statutory instrument, even though in the absence of such a stipulation the exercise of the power in question would not be by statutory instrument by virtue of the threefold definition above[7].

1 Statutory Instruments Act 1946 (c 36), s 1(1)(a).
2 Ibid, s 1(1)(b).
3 Ie statutory rules within the meaning of the Rules Publication Act 1893 (c 66), s 4 (repealed), the broad effect of which was to bring rules of court and rules, regulations and byelaws made by the various organs of the central government within the definition of 'statutory rules'.
4 Ie any rule-making authority within the meaning of ibid, s 4 (repealed), by virtue of which such an authority included every authority authorised to make statutory rules.
5 Statutory Instruments Act 1946, s 8(1)(d). See also the Statutory Instruments Regulations 1947, SI 1948/1. The main proviso is that the document must be legislative rather than executive in character: reg 2(1)(a).
6 Statutory Instruments Act 1946, s 1(2).
7 So eg the powers of the Chief Registrar of Friendly Societies under the friendly societies legislation are exercisable by statutory instrument: Friendly Societies Act 1974 (c 46), s 119(2). As to acts of adjournal and acts of sederunt, see para 187 below.

177. Making and commencement of statutory instruments. Where (as is always the case) provision is made for a statutory instrument to come into force or operation on a particular day, it comes into force at the beginning of that day[1]. Statutory instruments whose parent legislation requires them to be laid[2] before Parliament[3] may be made so as to come into operation before being laid if this is 'essential'[4]; but otherwise they must be laid prior to coming into operation[5].

1 Interpretation Act 1978 (c 30), ss 4(a), 23 (1). Every copy of any statutory instrument which was required to be laid before Parliament after being made which is sold by the Queen's Printer must bear on its face a statement showing the date of its coming into operation: Statutory Instruments Act 1946 (c 36), s 4(2)(a).
2 As to the meaning of references to 'laying', see the Laying of Documents before Parliament (Interpretation) Act 1948 (c 59), s 1(1).
3 Where an instrument is required to be laid before the House of Commons only, references to Parliament are to be read as references to the House of Commons: Statutory Instruments Act 1946, s 7(2).
4 In this case the Lord Chancellor and the Speaker of the House of Commons must be notified and furnished with an explanation: ibid, s 4(1). As to the procedure where there is a vacancy in either office, see the Laying of Documents before Parliament (Interpretation) Act 1948, s 2.
5 Statutory Instruments Act 1946, s 4(1).

178. Statutory instruments subject to annulment. Where the parent Act provides that any statutory instrument made under it is to be subject to annulment in pursuance of a resolution of either House of Parliament, such an instrument must be laid, and comes into force on the day stipulated, but if either House within the period of forty days[1] beginning with the day on which it is laid resolves that an Address be presented to Her Majesty praying that the instrument be annulled, then no further proceedings may be taken under the instrument which, moreover, may be revoked by Order in Council[2]. Revocation (and indeed the resolution itself) cannot, however, prejudice the validity of anything previously done under the instrument or the making of a new instrument[2].

1 In reckoning this period, no account is to be taken of any time during which Parliament is dissolved or prorogued or during which both Houses are adjourned for more than four days: Statutory Instruments Act 1946 (c 36), s 7(1).
2 Ibid, s 5(1).

179. Draft to be laid before Parliament. Where, on the other hand, the parent Act provides that a draft of any statutory instrument to be made under it is to be laid before Parliament[1], but does not prohibit the making of the instrument without the approval of Parliament, forty days[2] must be allowed to expire before the instrument is made[3]. If within the forty-day period either House resolves that the instrument is not to be made[4], then no further proceedings may be taken on the draft, although this is without prejudice to the laying before Parliament of a new draft[5].

1 See para 177, notes 2, 3 above.
2 The forty days begin with the day on which a copy of the draft is laid before each House of Parliament, or, if such copies are laid on different days, with the later of the two days: Statutory Instruments Act 1946 (c 36), s 6(1). As to certain periods excluded, see para 178, note 1 above.
3 Ibid, s 6(1). In the case of an Order in Council, the forty days must expire before the draft is submitted to Her Majesty in Council: s 6(1).
4 In the case of an Order in Council, either House resolves instead that the Order be not submitted to Her Majesty: ibid, s 6(1).
5 Ibid, s 6(1).

180. Affirmative procedures. The Statutory Instruments Act 1946 does not make positive provision for statutory instruments subject to affirmative procedures, but of course parent legislation may stipulate that an instrument is not to come into operation until approved by resolution, or that an instrument is to become inoperative after a certain period if not approved by resolution, or that a draft instrument is not to be made unless approved by resolution.

181. Revocation. Statutory instruments may be revoked by Act of Parliament, or by subordinate legislation if the parent Act has conferred the necessary power[1]. Unless the contrary intention appears, a power to make subordinate legislation by way of statutory instrument implies a co-extensive power to revoke, amend or re-enact any instrument made under the power[2].

1 Where a statutory instrument is revoked by Act of Parliament the general savings provisions in the Interpretation Act 1978 (c 30) apply: s 16. They also apply where a statutory instrument is revoked by subordinate legislation made after 1978: s 23(1).
2 Ibid, s 14(b), which, by virtue of s 22(1), applies to powers conferred by Acts passed after 1978. As to Acts passed after 1889 authorising the making of rules or regulations, see ss 14(a), 22(1), Sch 2, para 3.

182. Expiry. The expiry of temporary statutory instruments entails the same legal consequences as the expiry of temporary statutes[1].

1 See para 165 above. Where an expiring statutory instrument was made after 1978 the general savings provisions of the Interpretation Act 1978 (c 30), s 16, apply: see s 23(1).

183. Lapse. The repeal of a parent Act necessarily extinguishes all statutory instruments made under it, unless they are specially saved[1].

1 As to repeal and re-enactment, however, see para 164 above.

184. Promulgation. Immediately after being made, statutory instruments must be sent to the Queen's Printer, who must (except in certain cases[1]) print and sell copies of them as soon as possible[2]. In a criminal prosecution for a contravention of a statutory instrument printed and sold by the Queen's Printer, it is a defence to prove that the instrument had not been issued by Her Majesty's Stationery Office at the date of the alleged contravention unless it is proved that at that date reasonable steps had been taken for the purpose of bringing the purport of the instrument to the notice of the public, or of persons likely to be affected by it, or of the person charged[3]. But a failure to issue an instrument which ought to have been issued does not invalidate it or render it inoperative[4].

1 As to the exceptions, see the Statutory Instruments Regulations 1947, SI 1948/1, regs 5–8, and 44 Halsbury's Laws of England (4th edn) para 986.
2 Statutory Instruments Act 1946 (c 36), s 2(1).
3 Ibid, s 3(2). Her Majesty's Stationery Office publishes lists showing the date upon which every statutory instrument printed and sold by the Queen's Printer was first issued by that office, and in any legal proceedings a copy of any such list purporting to bear the imprint of the Queen's Printer (with which the Stationery Office imprint is equated by virtue of the Documentary Evidence Act 1882 (c 9), s 2) is to be received in evidence as a true copy, and an entry therein is conclusive evidence of the date on which any statutory instrument was first issued by the Stationery Office: Statutory Instruments Act 1946, s 3(1).
4 *R v Sheer Metalcraft Ltd* [1954] 1 QB 586, [1954] 1 All ER 542. The reasoning is that if a failure to issue invalidated an instrument or rendered it inoperative, the Statutory Instruments Act 1946, s 3(2), which provides a qualified defence, would be redundant: *R v Sheer Metalcraft Ltd* above at 590, 591 and at 545, per Streatfeild J. However, the Statutory Instruments Act 1946, s 3(3), provides that nothing in s 3 is to affect any enactment or rule of law relating to the time at which any statutory instrument comes into operation, and in *Johnson v Sargant & Sons* [1918] 1 KB 101 at 103, Bailhache J held that a statutory order did not come into operation 'before it was known'. See further Lanham 'Delegated Legislation and Publication' (1974) 37 MLR 510; Campbell 'The Publication of Delegated Legislation' [1982] PL 569; and Lanham 'Publication of Delegated Legislation' [1983] PL 395.

185. Proof of statutory instruments. Statutory instruments, being part of the general law of the realm, are presumed to be known to everybody and are therefore within judicial notice[1].

1 *Macmillan v M'Connell* 1917 JC 43, 1917 2 SLT 26, especially at 54 and at 32.

186. Citation of statutory instruments. Any statutory instrument may, without prejudice to any other mode of citation, be cited by the number given to it by the Queen's Printer[1] and the calendar year[2].

1 Statutory Instruments Act 1946 (c 36), s 2(1). The Queen's Printer proceeds to the numbering in accordance with regulations made under the Act: s 2(1). See the Statutory Instruments Regulations 1947, SI 1948/1, reg 3.
2 Statutory Instruments Act 1946, s 2(2).

187. Acts of adjournal and acts of sederunt. Various statutes confer powers upon the judges of the High Court of Justiciary and the Court of Session to lay down rules of adjectival law. Acts of adjournal are the subordinate legislation of the High Court[1]; and acts of sederunt are the subordinate legislation of the Court of Session[2]. Both are statutory instruments where made in exercise of powers conferred by statutes passed after 1947[3].

Until the middle of the eighteenth century it seems to have been regarded as legitimate for the judges of the Court of Session to legislate on matters of substantive law through the medium of acts of sederunt. So, for example, the Bankruptcy Act 1621 (c 18) was a ratification of an act of sederunt made in 1618[4]. An act of sederunt of 1662[5], the Act anent executors-creditors, was never ratified by Parliament, but was nevertheless considered to be part of the established law of Scotland[6]. It is not easy to discern the legal basis of such acts. The College of Justice Act 1540, ratifying the institution of the College of Justice, gave the judges power 'to make sik actes, statutes and ordinancis, as they sall thinke expedient, for ordouring of proces, and haistie expedition of justice', but this language does not seem well framed to cover the declaration and alteration of substantive law[7]. The specious rationalisation proffered by Bankton was that unratified acts of sederunt were not 'laws', but merely 'rules, which the lords propose to themselves to follow'. However, 'where acts of sederunt, in matters of right, have, for a long course of time, inviolably obtained as laws, they become customary laws, and therefore require no statute to establish them'[8].

At the same time it was also apparently acknowledged that the judges had in them, by law, 'the superintendency and regulation of all matters relating to provisions and vivres' in respect of the city of Edinburgh[9], in exercise of which power the Court of Session took it upon itself to regulate such things as the sale of beer in the city[10]. Again the legal basis of this assertion of legislative power is obscure: the judges appear to have been content to declare that they were proceeding in conformity to the practice of their predecessors, that is, on the basis of custom[11].

1 The principal enabling Act in this connection is the Criminal Procedure (Scotland) Act 1975 (c 21), ss 282, 457.
2 The principal enabling Act in this connection is the Administration of Justice (Scotland) Act 1933 (c 41), s 16. The main subordinate measure is the Act of Sederunt (Rules of Court, Consolidation and Amendment) 1965, SI 1965/321.
3 Law Reform (Miscellaneous Provisions) (Scotland) Act 1966 (c 19), s 10.
4 W Alexander *Abridgment of the Acts of Sederunt* (1838) p xi.
5 AS 28 February 1662.
6 *Alexander*, p xii. See also pp xi–xiv.
7 However, cf Stair's invocation of the College of Justice Act 1540 (c 10) in connection with the doctrine of desuetude: Stair *Institutions* I, 1, 16; see para 129 above.
8 Bankton *Institute* I, 1, 73. See, to the same effect, Erskine *Institute* I, 1, 40.
9 *Acts of Sederunt of the Lords of Council and Session from 15 January 1553 to 1794* (1806), Pt II, pp 88, 89, Information and Memorial of Mr Duncan Forbes, His Majesty's Advocate, 29 July 1725.
10 See eg ibid, Pt II, p 87 (AS 8 July 1725).
11 Eg ibid, Pt II, p 85 (AS 13 November 1717), and p 87 (AS 8 July 1725). On the other hand, the action taken by the court in connection with the brewers' strike of 1725 (Pt II, pp 88–90) was characterised by Kames as an exercise of the *nobile officium*: see further paras 430, note 6, below.

(c) Other Subordinate Legislation

(A) OTHER GOVERNMENTAL SUBORDINATE LEGISLATION

188. Status of other subordinate instruments. Statutes conferring legislative powers upon the Privy Council or ministers of the Crown need not and do not invariably stipulate that the documents by which these powers are exercised are to be statutory instruments[1]. The legal effect of subordinate instruments other than statutory instruments made by the government depends on the provisions of the parent legislation (which may be such as to deprive the subordinate instrument of normal legislative force[2]), but the mere fact that a subordinate instrument is not in the form of a statutory instrument cannot *per se* detract from its legislative character[3].

1 Eg the contingent power of the Secretary of State to make byelaws under the Water (Scotland) Act 1980 (c 45), s 73, is not exercisable by statutory instrument.
2 As to statutory codes of practice, see paras 195 ff below.
3 As to whether the immigration rules made under the Immigration Act 1971 (c 77), s 3(2) (see HC Paper (1979–80) no 394), are properly regarded as subordinate legislation, see *R v Secretary of State for Home Affairs, ex parte Hosenball* [1977] 3 All ER 452, [1977] 1 WLR 766, CA; *Pearson v Immigration Appeal Tribunal* [1978] Imm AR 212, CA; *R v Immigration Appeal Tribunal, ex parte Nathwani* [1979–80] Imm AR 9, DC. But see contra *R v Chief Immigration Officer, Heathrow Airport, ex parte Bibi* [1976] 3 All ER 843 at 848, [1976] 1 WLR 979 at 985, CA, per Roskill LJ. On the view expressed in the text it is irrelevant that the immigration rules do not take the form of a statutory instrument; it is not, however, irrelevant that they are expressed to be rules 'as to the practice to be followed in the administration' of the Immigration Act 1971: s 3(2). See further IMMIGRATION AND EXTRADITION.

(B) LOCAL AND PUBLIC AUTHORITY BYELAWS

189. Making and confirmation of byelaws. Many statutes confer powers upon local authorities or public authorities to make byelaws governing matters falling within their sphere of competence. The manner of enacting byelaws in any particular case of course depends on the precise stipulations of the parent statute. Nevertheless among such statutes a characteristic pattern can be discerned. Typically the legislation designates a 'confirming authority' — commonly a government minister — and provides that the byelaws of the propounding authority are not to have effect until confirmed by that person[1]. The confirming authority may consider the policy and expediency of byelaws submitted for confirmation[2], and may confirm them with or without modification or refuse to confirm them[3].

1 See eg the Transport Act 1962 (c 46), s 67(5); Local Government (Scotland) Act 1973 (c 65), s 202(3); Airports Authority Act 1975 (c 78), s 9(4); Water (Scotland) Act 1980 (c 45), Sch 1, para 24.
2 *Glasgow Corpn v Glasgow Churches' Council* 1944 SC 97, 1944 SLT 317. Matters of policy and expediency are germane to the decision of the confirming authority even if he is a judge rather than a politician: *Glasgow Corpn v Glasgow Churches' Council* above.
3 See eg the Local Government (Scotland) Act 1973, s 202(10); Airports Authority Act 1975, Sch 2, para 5; Water (Scotland) Act 1980, Sch 1, para 29.

190. Publicity, commencement and authenticity. Parent legislation characteristically makes provision for publicity, commencement and authenticity of byelaws. Typically the authority making the byelaws must give public notice of its intention to apply for confirmation at least one month before applying, and for at least one month before the application is made copies of the byelaws should be made available for inspection and purchase by anyone[1]. Any person aggrieved who wishes to object to the byelaws has one month after the giving of public notice in which to notify his objection and its basis in writing to the confirming authority, who must take such objections into consideration before the confirmation[2]. The confirming authority is empowered to fix the date on which the byelaws are to come into operation; but if no date is fixed, they come into operation at the expiration of one month from the date of their confirmation[3]. Copies of the confirmed byelaws must be printed and made available for inspection and purchase[4]. Byelaws are authenticated by means of the common seal of the authority making them[5]; and the production of a copy of a byelaw purporting to be made by the relevant authority upon which is indorsed a certificate purporting to be signed by the appropriate officer of the authority stating that the byelaw was made by the authority, that the copy is a true copy of the byelaw, that on a specified date the byelaw was confirmed by the confirming authority, and the date, if any, fixed by the confirming authority for the coming into operation of the byelaw is sufficient evidence of the facts stated in the certificate[6].

1 See eg the Transport Act 1962 (c 46), s 67(6)–(8) (twenty-eight days); Local Government (Scotland) Act 1973 (c 65), s 202(4)–(6); Airports Authority Act 1975 (c 78), s 9, Sch 2, paras 2–4; Water (Scotland) Act 1980 (c 45), Sch 1, paras 25–27.

2 See eg the Transport Act 1962, s 67(6) (representations within twenty-eight days); Local Government (Scotland) Act 1973, s 202(7), (8); Airports Authority Act 1975, Sch 2, para 2 (representations); Water (Scotland) Act 1980, Sch 1, para 28.

3 See eg the Transport Act 1962, s 67(9); Local Government (Scotland) Act 1973, s 202(10); Airports Authority Act 1975, Sch 2, para 5; Water (Scotland) Act 1980, Sch 1, para 29.

4 See eg the Transport Act 1962, s 67(10); Local Government (Scotland) Act 1973, s 202(11); Airports Authority Act 1975, Sch 2, para 6; Water (Scotland) Act 1980, Sch 1, para 30.

5 See eg the Local Government (Scotland) Act 1973, s 202(3); Airports Authority Act 1975, Sch 2, para 1; Water (Scotland) Act 1980, Sch 1, para 24.

6 See eg the Transport Act 1962, s 67(11); Local Government (Scotland) Act 1973, s 204; Airports Authority Act 1975, Sch 2, para 7; Water (Scotland) Act 1980, Sch 1, para 31.

191. Confirmation and validity. Confirmation of a byelaw is no bar to its challenge in a court of law on an allegation that its making was *ultra vires* of the propounding authority[1]. But a challenge founded on an imputation of un-reasonableness to a byelaw can only succeed nowadays upon a case of great strength, and where the byelaw is one which requires and has received confirmation the court will be loath to substitute its own judgment for that of the confirming authority[2].

1 *Glasgow Corpn v Glasgow Churches' Council* 1944 SC 97 at 125, 1944 SLT 317 at 330, per Lord Justice-Clerk Cooper. See generally LOCAL GOVERNMENT.

2 *Robert Baird Ltd v Glasgow Corpn* 1935 SC (HL) 21, 1935 SLT 369. See also *Da Prato v Partick Magistrates* 1907 SC (HL) 5, 14 SLT 874; *Aldred v Miller* 1925 JC 21, 1925 SLT 33. Contrast *Dunsmore v Lindsay* (1903) 6 F (J) 14, 11 SLT 545.

192. Revocation of byelaws. In general, where an Act passed after 1889 confers power to make byelaws it implies, unless the contrary intention appears, a power, exercisable in the same manner and subject to the same conditions or limitations, to revoke, amend or re-enact any byelaw made under the power[1].

The local government legislation, however, allows the revocation of byelaws without resort to the confirming authority. All that is necessary for the revocation of a local authority byelaw is that notice of the proposed revocation should be given in a local newspaper, and that objections to the proposal should be taken into account by the local authority before the resolution of revocation is passed[2]. But it is not competent to revoke, separately from the set of byelaws containing it, any byelaw which was inserted into the set of byelaws by, or which otherwise wholly or substantially derives from, a modification made by the confirming authority³. Nor is it competent to revoke any byelaw if the effect of the revocation would be to widen the scope of any other byelaw⁴.

1 Interpretation Act 1978 (c 30), ss 14(a), 22(1), Sch 2, para 3.
2 Local Government (Scotland) Act 1973 (c 65), s 202C(2), (3) (added by the Civic Government (Scotland) Act 1982 (c 45), s 110(3)). Byelaws which are revoked cease to have effect on the date of their revocation unless a later date is specified in the resolution: Local Government (Scotland) Act 1973, s 202C(4) (as so added). As to the register of byelaws, see para 193, note 2 below.
3 Ibid, s 202C(5) (as so added). Nor is it competent to revoke, separately from the byelaw containing it, any part of a byelaw which was inserted into the byelaw by, or which otherwise wholly or substantially derives from, a modification made by the confirming authority: s 202C(5) (as so added).
4 Ibid, s 202C(6) (as so added). Nor is it competent to revoke any part of any byelaw if the effect of the revocation would be to widen the scope of the remaining part of the byelaw: s 202C(6) (as so added).

193. Review of local authority byelaws. Not later than 1 July 1994¹ or ten years from the coming into force of a byelaw which a local authority has the power to revoke or amend, whichever is the later, that authority must review that byelaw and do so thereafter at intervals of not more than ten years².

1 Ie ten years from the coming into force of this provision: see the Civic Government (Scotland) Act 1982 (Commencement) Order 1983, SI 1983/201, art 3.
2 Local Government (Scotland) Act 1973 (c 65), s 202A (added by the Civic Government (Scotland) Act 1982 (c 45), s 110(3)). A local authority must keep a register of all byelaws which it has power to revoke or amend, containing a description of them, the dates when they were confirmed, the dates when they came into operation, and the date when they were last reviewed: Local Government (Scotland) Act 1973, s 202B(1), (2) (as so added).

(C) AUTONOMIC LEGISLATION

194. Character and scope. Many self-governing bodies corporate, standing outside the structure of government, have the power, conferred upon them by Act of Parliament or by royal charter, to lay down byelaws, regulations or the like. Norms created by the exercise of such powers have been characterised as 'autonomic' or 'autonomous' legislation¹. Such norms often stand on the borderline between legislation and contract². Where the power conferred is power to bind only members of the corporation, so that the eventuating legislation is binding only 'intra the corpus of the corporation'³, the contractual aspect of the phenomenon is prominent⁴. The byelaws of a corporation cannot bind non-members thereof unless the governing Act or charter confers the power to bind them⁵, or unless they contract to be bound⁶. The legislative character of autonomic legislation is more evident where power is given to bind outsiders⁷, in which case any byelaw that takes full advantage of this power is plainly 'not an agreement, but a law binding on all persons to whom it applies, whether they agree to be bound by it or not'⁸. But where legislation expressly confers upon a corporation powers which it, as the owner of property, could have exercised without any express statutory authority (for example a power to regulate access to the facilities of the corporation), the powers expressly given must be treated as implying a prohibition against the exercise of the more extensive rights which the corporation would otherwise have enjoyed by virtue of its ownership of property⁹.

1 J W Salmond *Jurisprudence* (12th edn, 1966 by P J Fitzgerald) p 123; C K Allen *Law in the Making* (7th edn, 1964) p 542.

2 As to the concepts of legislation and contract, see paras 103 ff above.

3 _Glasgow University v Faculty of Physicians and Surgeons_ (1840) 1 Robin 397 at 432, per Lord Brougham.

4 Thus articles of association of registered companies are not generally regarded as legislative in character. But contrast _Salmond_ p 124.

5 _Dodwell v Oxford University_ (1680) 2 Vent 33; _Butchers' Co v Morey_ (1790) 1 Hy Bl 370.

6 _London Association of Shipowners and Brokers v London and India Docks Joint Committee_ [1892] 3 Ch 242 at 255, CA, per Lindley LJ, at 266 per Bowen LJ, and at 268 per Kay LJ.

7 Eg the powers enjoyed by Associated British Ports by virtue of the application to most of its harbours, by local legislation, of the Harbours, Docks and Piers Clauses Act 1847 (c 27), ss 83–90.

8 _London Association of Shipowners and Brokers v London and India Docks Joint Committee_ [1892] 3 Ch 242 at 252, CA, per Lindley LJ.

9 [1892] 3 Ch 242 at 251, CA, per Lindley LJ, applied in _J H Pigott & Son v Docks and Inland Waterways Executive_ [1953] 1 QB 338, [1953] 1 All ER 22.

(d) Statutory Codes of Practice

195. Introduction. Whether statutory codes of practice are properly to be regarded as subordinate legislation is a question incapable of definitive resolution. Against attributing legislative character to them it can be observed that the norms promulgated in statutory codes of practice are non-mandatory (that is, not legally binding in their own right), and that such codes are commonly couched in everyday language which might well be seen as out of place in a statute or statutory instrument. On the other hand, statutory codes of practice are general in scope and issued on the authority of primary legislation[1]. Typically, moreover, they are subject to a Parliamentary procedure comparable to that applied to statutory instruments and are brought into 'effect' or 'operation' on a day appointed by statutory instrument[2].

1 Contrast those non-statutory codes of practice that are sponsored by a public official who is under a statutory duty to encourage their issue, eg under the Fair Trading Act 1973 (c 41), s 124(3) (Director-General of Fair Trading), or the Data Protection Act 1984 (c 35), s 36(4) (Data Protection Registrar).

2 See eg the Employment Protection Act 1975 (c 71); s 6(4)–(8); Race Relations Act 1976 (c 74), s 47(4)–(7); Employment Act 1980 (c 42), s 3(4), (5).

196. Functions. Since they are not legally binding _per se_, a major potential advantage of statutory codes of practice from a governmental point of view is the opportunity they afford to economise on a scarce resource — the coercive might of the state. The use of statutory codes is an attempt to achieve governmental ends through 'education', persuasion and 'voluntary' compliance[1]. At the same time it is accepted that statutory codes may legitimately be framed in language that might be regarded as inappropriate in a formal legislative text. Thus statutory codes are often exhortatory in tone, use comparatively simple language, and may lack the precision commonly associated with legislation proper. The main potential drawback of such codes is of course their inability to exact conformity as a matter of direct legal obligation.

1 A C Page 'Self-Regulation and Codes of Practice' [1980] JBL 24 at 25.

197. Status of statutory codes in general. As a rule[1] the legal status of a statutory code of practice is specified in the statute on the authority of which it is to be promulgated. No single formula is in universal use, but a certain amount of common ground can be discerned in the statutory provisions and the case law[2]. This is because the prototype of modern statutory codes is the Highway Code, first promulgated on the authority of the Road Traffic Act 1930 for the 'guidance' of road users[3]. The Highway Code 'is not binding as a statutory regulation; it is only something which may be regarded as information and advice to drivers'[4]. Modern statutory codes are partially modelled on its example. Although they are promulgated on the authority of a statute, they are not thereby themselves endowed with statutory authority. They are not statutory instruments, although they may be brought into force by statutory instruments.

1 It is not an invariable rule: see the Social Work (Scotland) Act 1968 (c 60), s 17E (added by the Health and Social Services and Social Security Adjudication Act 1983 (c 41), s 7.
2 See Lord Campbell of Alloway 'Codes of Practice as an Alternative to Legislation' [1985] Statute Law Rev 127; A Samuels 'Codes of Practice and Legislation' [1986] Statute Law Rev 29.
3 Road Traffic Act 1930 (c 43), s 45(1) (repealed).
4 *Croston v Vaughan* [1938] 1 KB 540 at 551, 552, [1937] 4 All ER 249 at 252, CA, per Greer LJ.

198. The Highway Code. The non-mandatory character of the Highway Code is established by a stipulation that a person's failure to observe a provision thereof 'shall not of itself render that person liable to criminal proceedings'[1]. The legal significance of the code is merely that in any proceedings such a failure may be relied upon 'as tending to establish or to negative any liability which is in question'[1]. Thus breach of the code is not necessarily negligent[2]. 'Nor is it sufficient excuse for any person to say, in answer to a claim for negligence, that he carrried out every provision of the code'[3]. This much is uncontroversial, but in *Powell v Phillips* judicial depreciation of the Highway Code may have been carried too far. The code, it was said, is no more than a codification of common sense: 'It is . . . clear that a breach creates no presumption of negligence calling for an explanation . . .'[4]. In the context of that case this dictum was unnecessary inasmuch as a wholly adequate explanation for the breach of the code was available. In any event, it is submitted that a breach of the code must call for an explanation, in the sense that it must place an evidential burden upon the infractor; if not, how could it be relied upon as (in the words of the parent Act) 'tending to establish or to negative' liability?

1 Road Traffic Act 1972 (c 20), s 37(7) (substituted by the Transport Act 1982 (c 49), s 60).
2 *Joseph Eva Ltd v Reeves* [1938] 2 KB 393 at 403, [1938] 2 All ER 115 at 119, CA, per Sir Wilfrid Greene MR.
3 *Croston v Vaughan* [1938] 1 KB 540 at 552, [1937] 4 All ER 249 at 252, CA, per Greer LJ.
4 *Powell v Phillips* [1972] 3 All ER 864 at 868, CA, per Stephenson LJ.

199. Industrial relations codes. The various industrial relations codes of practice follow in part the example of the Highway Code. The standard formula in industrial relations legislation has three elements[1]. First it is provided that a failure on the part of any person to observe any provision of the code of practice 'shall not of itself render him liable to any proceedings'. Secondly it is stipulated that the code itself 'shall be admissible in evidence' in proceedings before a tribunal. And thirdly it is stipulated that any provision of the code which appears to the tribunal to be relevant to 'any question' arising in the proceedings 'shall be taken into account in determining that question'. In relation to the question of unfair dismissal the judicial approach has paralleled that displayed vis-à-vis the Highway Code. Thus non-compliance with the code does not necessarily render a dismissal unfair. A failure to follow a procedure prescribed in the code may lead to the conclusion that a dismissal was unfair, but of course it depends on the circumstances of each individual case[2].

The industrial relations codes of practice, as we have seen, must be taken into account (where relevant) by tribunals. A question arises as to the legal effect of this requirement in relation to provisions of a code of practice which purport to 'explain' the existing law. If a code of practice glosses a common law principle or a statutory provision, does that gloss have any authority? In other words the question is whether it is an argument in favour of a particular reading of the law that it has been adopted by a code of practice. In a memorandum laid before the House of Commons Employment Committee in 1980, the Rt Hon Enoch Powell contended that issues of principle are raised by

> 'extensions and interpretations of statute, which the courts are directed to "take into account". The result is a species of unconstitutional legislation, whereby the executive and the respective Houses create what may or may not (depending on the force of "take into account") be law by making statements which neither have the benefit of the ordinary parliamentary process of debate and scrutiny nor have become the law of the land in proper form'[3].

In reply the Secretary of State for Employment insisted that the standard statutory formula 'makes it quite clear that the Codes do not extend the law or create new offences'[4]. If 'evidence' means evidence of fact and 'any question' means question of fact and not question of law, then this reply is formally correct. But it is also somewhat disingenuous: statutory codes of practice are intended to exert and do sometimes exert an influence on the judicial application of legal rules and principles[5].

1 See the Industrial Relations Act 1971 (c 72), s 3 (repealed); Sex Discrimination Act 1975 (c 65), s 56A(10) (added by the Race Relations Act 1976 (c 74), s 79(4), Sch 4, para 1); Employment Protection Act 1975 (c 71), s 6(11); Race Relations Act 1976, s 47(10); Employment Act 1980 (c 42), s 3(8).

2 *Lewis Shops Group v Wiggins* [1973] ICR 335, NIRC; *W Devis & Sons Ltd v Atkins* [1977] AC 931 at 955, [1977] 3 All ER 40 at 48, HL, per Viscount Dilhorne (approving *Earl v Slater and Wheeler (Airlyne) Ltd* [1973] 1 All ER 145, [1973] 1 WLR 51, NIRC). See F P Davidson *The Judiciary and the Development of Employment Law* (1984) pp 72–74.

3 House of Commons Employment Committee *The Legal Immunities of Trade Unions and other related matters: Minutes of Evidence* (HC Paper (1979–80) no. 462–vii) Memorandum submitted by the Rt Hon J Enoch Powell, para 2.

4 House of Commons Employment Committee *The Legal Immunities of Trade Unions and other related matters: Draft Codes of Practice on Picketing and the Closed Shop: Observations by the Secretary of State for Employment on the Second Report* (HC Paper (1979–80) no. 848).

5 See eg *Thomas v National Union of Mineworkers (South Wales Area)* [1985] ICR 886 at 920, 921, [1985] 2 All ER 1 at 26, 27, per Scott J.

200. Health and safety at work codes. Codes of practice approved under the Health and Safety at Work Act etc 1974 carry more weight than other statutory codes of practice in that commission of the *actus reus* of certain offences under the Act is to be taken as proved by proof of a breach of the relevant provision of an approved code, unless the court is satisfied that the requirements of the law were observed 'otherwise than by way of observance of that provision of the code'[1]. This appears to impose a probative burden upon the accused once a breach of the relevant code provision has been established.

1 Health and Safety at Work etc Act 1974 (c 37), s 17(2).

201. Statutory guidance. Sometimes legislation authorises the Secretary of State to give 'guidance' to a body as to how it should discharge its statutory functions. If the statutory requirement is merely to 'have regard' to the guidance issued, then there is no obligation to comply with the guidance. Once regard has been had to the guidance, departure from it is quite lawful[1]. This, of course, does not hold good if the statutory provision in question stipulates that the guidance is to be binding[2]. Guidance given on the authority of a statutory provision must be consistent with all the requirements of the statute in question[3], as well as with the law of the land.

1 *De Falco v Crawley Borough Council* [1980] QB 460 at 477, 478, [1980] 1 All ER 913 at 921, CA, per Lord Denning MR; *R v Police Complaints Board, ex parte Madden* [1983] 2 All ER 353 at 374, [1983] 1 WLR 447 at 471, per McNeill J.
2 See eg the Policyholders Protection Act 1975 (c 75), s 2(1).
3 *Laker Airways Ltd v Department of Trade* [1977] QB 643, [1977] 2 All ER 182, CA.

(7) EUROPEAN COMMUNITY LEGISLATION

(a) Form and Classification

(A) FORM

202. Obligation to give reasons. Community legislative acts must state the reasons on which they are (ostensibly) based[1]. The rationale of this requirement, which is in marked contrast to modern practice with respect to United Kingdom legislation[2], is inter alia to facilitate judicial review[3]. The obligation to give reasons is satisfied in the case of legislative acts (as opposed to acts of individual application) by a broad account of the general situation leading to the adoption of the act and the general objectives that it is intended to achieve. There is no need to set out in detail the circumstances which prompted the adoption of the act[4].

1 EEC Treaty, art 190; Euratom Treaty, art 162; ECSC Treaty, art 15, 1st para.
2 See para 119 above.
3 Case 24/62 *Germany v EEC Commission* [1963] ECR 63, [1963] CMLR 347, ECJ.
4 Case 5/67 *W Beus GmbH & Co v Hauptzollamt München* [1968] ECR 83 at 95, [1968] CMLR 131 at 145, ECJ.

203. Structure of legislative acts. Community legislation typically has the following structure. First there is the title which conveys the class to which the act belongs (for example regulation or directive[1]), the identity of the adopting authority (for example the EC Council or EC Commission[2]), the date of the act, a summary description of its subject-matter, and a serial number (for example 64/221). Next there is the preamble which reiterates the identity of the adopting authority, recites the enabling provisions under which the act is made, refers to the Commission's proposal (if any) and to the opinions (if any) of the European Parliament (the Assembly) or the Economic and Social Committee[3], and avows reasons for the act. There follow the substantive provisions (the text) of the act, at the end of which there is (in the case of a regulation[4]) an affirmation that the act is binding in its entirety and directly applicable in all member states, or (in the case of a directive[5]) a statement of to whom the act is addressed. Finally there comes the place and date of the act's adoption and the signature of the relevant president. In the main[6] adherence to this pattern is a matter of practice rather than legal obligation.

1 As to the classification of Community legislation, see paras 204 ff below.
2 As to the legislative authorities of the European Communities, see EUROPEAN INSTITUTIONS.
3 As to the Parliament and the Social Committee, see EUROPEAN INSTITUTIONS.
4 The same applies to a general decision of the ECSC.

5 The same applies to a recommendation of the ECSC.
6 This is subject to the requirement to state reasons (see para 202 above) and to refer to any proposals or opinions which were required to be obtained pursuant to the Community treaties: EEC Treaty, art 190; Euratom Treaty, art 162; ECSC Treaty, art 15, 1st para.

(B) REGULATIONS AND ECSC GENERAL DECISIONS

204. Regulations. A regulation has general application; it is binding in its entirety and is directly applicable in all member states[1]. Direct applicability entails that regulations automatically enjoy the force of law in member states, and override incompatible rules of national law[2]. No special national legislation (primary or secondary) is needed to bring regulations into force within national legal systems; indeed national legislation to implement a regulation is not only redundant but also contrary to the Community treaties if it would create an obstacle to the direct applicability of the regulation or conceal its Community nature or jeopardise its simultaneous and uniform application throughout the common market[3]. It is of course otherwise when the regulation itself requires implementing measures to be taken[4].

1 EEC Treaty, art 189, 2nd para; Euratom Treaty, art 161, 2nd para.
2 Case 106/77 *Amministrazione delle Finanze dello Stato v Simmenthal SpA* [1978] ECR 629, [1978] 3 CMLR 263, ECJ. See further para 213 below.
3 Case 39/72 *EC Commission v Italy* [1973] ECR 101 at 114, [1973] CMLR 439 at 456, ECJ; Case 50/76 *Amsterdam Bulb BV v Produktschap voor Siergewassen* [1977] ECR 137, [1977] 2 CMLR 218, ECJ.
4 Case 128/78 *EC Commission v United Kingdom* [1979] 419, [1979] 2 CMLR 45, ECJ.

205. ECSC general decisions. The ECSC Treaty speaks not of regulations but of 'decisions', which are expressed to be binding in their entirety[1]. The jurisprudence of the European Court of Justice distinguishes between individual decisions and general decisions[2], attributes legislative character to general decisions and equates them with regulations[3].

1 ECSC Treaty, art 14, 2nd para.
2 Ie on the strength of ibid, art 15. See also art 33. As to individual decisions, see para 211 below.
3 Case 8/55 *Fédération Charbonnière de Belgique v High Authority* [1954–56] ECR 245, ECJ; Case 13/57 *Wirtschaftsvereinigung Eisen- en Stahlindustrie v High Authority* [1957–58] ECR 265, ECJ.

(C) DIRECTIVES AND ECSC RECOMMENDATIONS

206. Directives. A directive is binding, as to the result to be achieved, upon each member state to which it is addressed, but leaves to the national authorities the choice of form and methods[1]. Thus, subject to what will be said below[2], directives are not directly applicable and acquire the force of law within national legal systems only by virtue of national implementing measures.

1 EEC Treaty, art 189, 3rd para; Euratom Treaty, art 161, 3rd para.
2 See para 208 below.

207. Implementation of directives. Each member state addressed by a directive is under an obligation to achieve the result stipulated therein by the date stipulated therein. The freedom of choice enjoyed by member states with respect to the form and methods of implementation is constrained by their obligation to choose the form and methods best calculated to ensure the effectiveness of the directive in question[1]. It is possible for a directive to be so detailed that member states are left virtually without latitude as to the wording of the implementing measure[2]. Moreover the implementation of directives requires their translation into binding provisions; the obligation to implement cannot be discharged by mere administrative practices or guidelines[3].

1 Case 48/75 *Royer* [1976] ECR 497 at 519, [1976] 2 CMLR 619 at 643, ECJ.
2 Case 38/77 *Enka BV v Inspecteur der Invoerrechten en Accijnzen, Arnhem* [1977] ECR 2203, [1978] 2 CMLR 212, ECJ.
3 Case 96/81 *EC Commission v Netherlands* [1982] ECR 1791, ECJ; Case 97/81 *EC Commission v Netherlands* [1982] ECR 1819, ECJ; Case 300/81 *EC Commission v Italy* [1983] ECR 449, [1984] 2 CMLR 430, ECJ.

208. Non-implementation of directives. A failure to implement a directive timeously may of course be raised before the European Court of Justice[1]. In addition, however, the court's jurisprudence establishes that the concept of direct effect is not confined to regulations and treaty articles but that directives are capable of becoming directly effective, that is, of conferring enforceable rights upon individuals vis-à-vis the member states. In particular, a directive which remains unimplemented by a member state upon the expiry of the time allowed for its implementation may be held to have become, by virtue of the default of the member state, directly effective in the sense that it may be enforced in the national courts against the state by persons upon whom its proper implementation would have conferred enforceable rights[2]. Direct effectiveness cannot, however, be attributed to provisions conferring upon member states discretionary power of a character that precludes enforcement by national courts[3]. It is not easy to discern in any particular provision of the Community treaties any substantial foundation for the doctrine of the contingent direct effectiveness of directives (as opposed to regulations and treaty provisions); the doctrine seems to rest primarily on the court's policy of enhancing the efficacy (*l'effet utile*) of Community measures[4].

1 See EUROPEAN INSTITUTIONS.
2 Case 9/70 *Grad v Finanzamt Traunstein* [1970] ECR 825, [1971] CMLR 1, ECJ; Case 33/70 *SACE SpA v Italian Ministry for Finance* [1970] ECR 1213, [1971] CMLR 123, ECJ; Case 41/74 *Van Duyn v Home Office* [1974] ECR 1337, [1975] Ch 358, ECJ; Case 148/78 *Pubblico Ministero v Ratti* [1979] ECR 1629, [1980] 1 CMLR 96, ECJ.
3 Case 6/64 *Costa v ENEL* [1964] ECR 585, [1964] CMLR 425, ECJ. But see also Case 41/74 *Van Duyn v Home Office* [1974] ECR 1337, [1975] Ch 358, ECJ, and Case 43/75 *Defrenne v SA Belge de Navigation Aérienne* [1976] ECR 455, [1976] 2 CMLR 98, ECJ.
4 See eg Case 41/74 *Van Duyn v Home Office* [1974] ECR 1337, [1975] Ch 358, ECJ.

209. ECSC recommendations. ECSC recommendations are binding as to the aims to be pursued but leave the choice of the appropriate methods for achieving these aims to those to whom the recommendations are addressed[1]. Such recommendations are therefore parallel to directives except that they may be addressed to individual persons as well as to member states.

1 ECSC Treaty, art 14, 3rd para.

(D) DECISIONS AND ECSC INDIVIDUAL DECISIONS

210. Decisions. A decision is binding in its entirety upon those to whom it is addressed[1]. Decisions therefore lack the general applicability of regulations, and if generality is the hallmark of legislation, decisions appear to be 'executive' or 'administrative' rather than legislative in character. However, it is not always easy to draw the line[2]. Decisions may be addressed to member states or individual persons.

  1 EEC Treaty, art 189, 4th para; Euratom Treaty, art 161, 4th para.
  2 The question of the character of a Community act can arise in relation to the EEC Treaty, art 173, 2nd para, which gives any natural or legal person the right to institute procedings against a decision addressed to that person or against a decision which, although in the form of a regulation or a decision addressed to someone else, is of direct and individual concern to the former: see eg Case 64/69 *Compagnie Française Commerciale et Financière SA v EC Commission* [1970] ECR 221, [1970] CMLR 369, ECJ. Contrast Case 100/74 *Société CAM SA v EC Commission* [1975] ECR 1393, ECJ. See further ADMINISTRATIVE LAW, vol 1, paras 210 ff.

211. ECSC individual decisions. ECSC individual decisions are binding in their entirety[1].

  1 ECSC Treaty, art 14, 2nd para. For the distinction between individual and general decisions, see para 205 above.

(b) Authority

(A) LEGISLATIVE COMPETENCE OF THE COMMUNITIES

212. Extent of legislative power. Various articles of the Community treaties confer specific legislative powers on various Community institutions. In addition, however, the EEC Treaty provides that if action by the Community should prove necessary to attain, in the course of the operation of the common market, one of the objectives of the Community and the treaty has not provided the necessary powers, then the EC Council, acting unanimously on a proposal from the Commission and after consulting the European Parliament, is to take the appropriate measures[1]. This broad residual power may not be invoked where power to adopt the requisite legislative act is clearly conferred elsewhere in the treaty; but it may be exercised in relation to a matter explicitly addressed elsewhere in the treaty if the power there conferred is considered inadequate, or (for the sake of legal certainty) if the precise extent of the power conferred elsewhere is unclear[2].

  1 EEC Treaty, art 235. There are parallel provisions in the Euratom Treaty, art 203, and the ECSC Treaty, art 95. As to the objectives of the Community, see the EEC Treaty, art 2, the Euratom Treaty, arts 1–3, and the ECSC Treaty, arts 2–4.
  2 Case 8/73 *Hauptzollamt Bremerhaven v Massey-Ferguson GmbH* [1973] ECR 897, ECJ.

(B) PRECEDENCE OF COMMUNITY LEGISLATION

213. The Community standpoint. The European Court of Justice holds that Community law is independent of, and superior to, national law and that the member states have made over a portion of their sovereignty to the institutions of the Communities[1]. It is a fundamental principle of Community jurisprudence that directly applicable or directly effective Community legislation prevails over incompatible rules of national law, and this holds good whether the offending national rule was introduced before or after the relevant Community provision: 'The transfer by the States from their domestic legal system to the Community legal system of the rights and obligations arising under the Treaty carries with it a permanent limitation of their sovereign rights against which a subsequent unilateral act incompatible with the concept of the Community cannot prevail'[2]. Incompatible national rules are inapplicable: thus not only are national legislators under an obligation to repeal them or not to pass them[3], but also national courts must not apply them[4].

1 Case 26/62 *NV Algemene Transport- en Expeditie Onderneming van Gend en Loos v Nederlandse Tarief Commissie* [1963] ECR 1, [1963] CMLR 105, ECJ.
2 Case 6/64 *Costa v ENEL* [1964] ECR 585 at 594, [1964] CMLR 425 at 456, ECJ; Case 106/77 *Amministrazione delle Finanze dello Stato v Simmenthal SpA* [1978] ECR 629, [1978] 3 CMLR 263, ECJ.
3 Case 167/73 *EC Commission v France* [1974] ECR 359, [1974] 2 CMLR 216, ECJ.
4 Case 106/77 *Amministrazione delle Finanze dello Stato v Simmenthal SpA* [1978] ECR 629, [1978] 3 CMLR 263, ECJ.

214. The United Kingdom standpoint. From a United Kingdom point of view the authority of Community legislation in the United Kingdom currently depends upon the European Communities Act 1972 (c 68). Section 2(1) provides that all such rights, powers, liabilities, obligations and restrictions from time to time created or arising by or under the Community Treaties, and all such remedies and procedures from time to time provided for by or under the treaties, as in accordance with the treaties are without further enactment to be given legal effect or used in the United Kingdom are to be recognised and available in law, and allowed and followed accordingly. Community legislation is made 'under the Treaties'; hence the capacity of such legislation to be directly applicable and to have direct effects is to be recognised, but only in so far as this accords with the treaties. However, section 3(1) provides that, for the purposes of all legal proceedings, any question as to the meaning or effect of any of the treaties, or as to the validity, meaning or effect of any Community instrument is, if not referred to the European Court of Justice, to be for determination as a question of law in accordance with the principles laid down by and any relevant decision of that court. Accordingly United Kingdom courts must recognise the precedence of Community law as expounded by the Court of Justice, and also the contingent direct effect of directives whether or not their direct effect is securely founded in the text of the treaties.

Section 2(4), which provides that any enactment passed or to be passed is to be construed and have effect subject to the foregoing provisions of section 2, appears to be an attempt to entrench section 2(1). Plainly, in view of the traditional conception of Parliamentary sovereignty, and in particular the doctrine that any Act of Parliament is liable to be abrogated (or derogated from) by subsequent Acts (whether expressly or by implication[1]), the status of this provision is problematic. United Kingdom enactments posterior to the 1972 Act have already been held inapplicable by virtue of their incompatibility with Community provisions predating the enactments in question[2]. A possible rationale of these decisions is that there was nothing in the enactments in question to indicate that Parliament intended to amend the European Communities Act 1972. For the foreseeable future it is likely to remain the case that Parliament's recognition of Community law by one enactment (the 1972 Act) can be withdrawn by another, either expressly or by necessary implication[3].

1 See paras 157, 158 above.
2 *Macarthys Ltd v Smith* [1979] 3 All ER 325, CA (later proceedings [1981] QB 180, [1981] 1 All ER 111, CA); *Re an Absence in Ireland* [1977] 1 CMLR 5, NIC; *MacMahon v Department of Education and Science* [1983] Ch 227 (direct applicability of relevant Community provisions not contested).
3 *Macarthys Ltd v Smith* [1979] 3 All ER 325 at 334, CA, per Lawton LJ, and at 329, per Lord Denning MR. See however *Garland v British Rail Engineering Ltd* [1983] 2 AC 751 at 771, [1982] 2 All ER 402 at 415, HL, per Lord Diplock. Cf CONSTITUTIONAL LAW, vol 5, para 354.

(c) Operation

(A) ENTRY INTO FORCE

215. Regulations and ECSC general decisions. Regulations enter into force on the date specified in them or, if no date is specified, on the twentieth day following their publication[1]. Parallel arrangements apply to ECSC general decisions[2].

1 EEC Treaty, art 191, 1st para; Euratom Treaty, art 163, 1st para.
2 The ECSC Treaty, art 15, 3rd para, provides that general decisions take effect by the mere fact of publication: thus there is no need to notify individually the parties concerned. Article 15, 4th para, requires the High Authority (now the EC Council) to determine how it is to be implemented. This was done by ECSC High Authority Decision 22/60 (OJ 1960, p 1248 (S edn (2nd Ser) VIII, p 13)), art 6, which provides that unless otherwise stipulated general decisions take effect on the twentieth day following their publication.

216. Other legislative acts. Directives and decisions take effect upon being notified to those to whom they are addressed[1]. ECSC recommendations when general in character are governed by the same arrangements as ECSC general decisions[2].

1 EEC Treaty, art 191, 2nd para; Euratom Treaty, art 163, 2nd para.
2 See para 215, note 2 above.

217. Retrospectiveness. It is possible for Community legislation to be retrospective where there is a legitimate reason for retrospectiveness, but the European Court of Justice will disallow retrospective effects that offend against the principle that legitimate expectations must be protected[1].

1 Case 37/70 *Rewe-Zentrale des Lebensmittel-Großhandels GmbH v Hauptzollamt Emmerich* [1971] ECR 23, [1971] CMLR 238, ECJ; Case 1/73 *Westzucker GmbH v Einfuhr- und Vorratsstelle für Zucker* [1973] ECR 723, ECJ; Case 98/78 *Racke v Hauptzollamt Mainz* [1979] ECR 69, ECJ.

(B) PARTICIPATION, PROMULGATION, AMENDMENT AND REPEAL

218. Participation. Under various provisions of the EEC Treaty the EC Council may not adopt the legislation it is empowered to enact unless the EC Commission has submitted to it a proposal in respect thereof[1]. In the absence of a proposal such legislation could not enjoy the force of law. Likewise various provisions require consultation with the European Parliament[1]. In such cases the proper consultation of the Parliament is an essential procedural requirement, and failure to observe it renders the legislative act in question null and void[2].

1 See eg the EEC Treaty, art 235.
2 Case 138/79 *Roquette Frères SA v EC Council* [1980] ECR 333, ECJ.

219. Publication and notification. Regulations and ECSC decisions and recommendations (where general) must be published in the Official Journal of the European Communities[1], and cannot take effect until so published[2]. Directives and decisions cannot take effect until notified to the persons to whom they are addressed[3]; in practice these too are published.

1 EEC Treaty, art 191, 1st para; Euratom Treaty, art 163, 1st para; cf the ECSC Treaty, art 15, 3rd and 4th paras, and see ECSC High Authority Decision 22/60 (OJ 1960, p 1248 (S edn (2nd Ser) VIII, p 13)), art 5.
2 Case 185/73 *Hauptzollamt Bielefeld v König* [1974] ECR 607, ECJ.
3 EEC Treaty, art 191, 2nd para; Euratom Treaty, art 163, 2nd para; ECSC Treaty, art 15, 2nd para.

220. Amendment and repeal. The power to amend or repeal Community legislation is implicit in the power to enact it.

(C) IMPLEMENTATION IN THE UNITED KINGDOM

221. Implementation by subordinate legislation. Where (as in the case of directives) Community legislation requires implementation at national level, this may of course be done within the United Kingdom by means of an Act of Parliament. In addition, however, United Kingdom legislation makes provision for the implementation of Community legislation by means of subordinate legislation. Such legislation may be made for the purpose of implementing any Community obligation of the United Kingdom, or enabling any such obligation to be implemented, or of enabling any rights enjoyed or to be enjoyed by the United Kingdom to be exercised[1]. It may also be made for the purpose of dealing with matters arising out of or related to any such obligation or rights, or the operation of section 2(1) of the European Communities Act 1972[2]. Such legislation may not, however, impose or increase taxation, have retrospective effect, subdelegate legislative power[3] (other than the power to make procedural rules for a court or tribunal) or create any major new criminal offence[4]. Subject to this qualification, subordinate legislation made for these Community purposes may include any such provision of any such extent as might be made by Act of Parliament[5].

1 European Communities Act 1972 (c 68), s 2(2)(a).
2 Ibid, s 2(2)(b). The power may be exercised by Order in Council or by ministerial or departmental regulations in the form of a statutory instrument: s 2(2), Sch 2, para 1; see para 176 above. As to s 2(1), see para 214 above.
3 However, a power to give directions as to matters of administration is not to be regarded as a legislative power: ibid, Sch 2, para 1(2).
4 Ibid, Sch 2, para 1(1)(a)–(d). There is no power to create any new criminal offence punishable with imprisonment for more than two years or punishable on summary conviction with a fine of more than level 5 on the standard scale (if not calculated on a daily basis) or with a fine of more than £100 a day: Sch 2, para 1(1)(d) (amended by the Criminal Law Act 1977 (c 45), s 32(3), and the Criminal Justice Act 1982 (c 48), ss 40, 46).
5 European Communities Act 1972, s 2(4).

222. Community objects and obligations. In the exercise of any statutory power or duty[1], including any power to give directions or to legislate by means of orders, rules, regulations or other subordinate instrument, the person entrusted with the power or duty may have regard to the objects of the Communities and to any Community obligation of the United Kingdom or any rights enjoyed by the United Kingdom under the Community Treaties[2].

1 This provision therefore applies not just to powers and duties arising under the European Communities Act 1972 (c 68), but also to powers and duties arising under any Act of Parliament or subordinate instrument.
2 Ibid, s 2(2).

(8) ERSATZ LEGISLATION

(a) Ersatz Legislation in general

(A) THE ROLE OF ERSATZ LEGISLATION

223. Policy and enactment. Formally speaking (and leaving aside legislation by virtue of the royal prerogative), legislation in the United Kingdom is a function of the Queen in Parliament and of those upon whom the legislature has conferred a portion of its legislative authority. But of course the reality is different. By and large, since the government normally commands a majority in the House of Commons, 'legislation is in practice a function of government'[1]. Nevertheless, in order to legislate validly the government must adhere to the recognised form: government policy still requires parliamentary enactment if it is to be clothed with the force of law.

1 D R Miers and A C Page *Legislation* (1982) p 12.

224. Ersatz legislation and its advantages. Sometimes, however, governments seek to simulate legislation by promulgating norms which they hope will be respected, without submitting to the discipline of the enacting process. It may be found expedient to substitute such 'ersatz' legislation[1] for the real thing for several reasons. First, legislative time being finite, room can be found in the parliamentary programme for only a limited number of legislative projects. Hence governments naturally exploit non-legislative methods of giving effect to their policies. Secondly, the amendment of legislated norms is as a rule more cumbersome than the adjustment of ersatz legislation, since there need be no formalities associated with the latter[2]. So ersatz legislation may be used in order to retain 'flexibility'. Thirdly, a government may view the mobilisation of Parliament for the enactment of legislation as politically risky or impracticable, especially when it cannot be sure of its own supporters or when it is a minority government[3].

1 Cf the notion of 'soft law'in international relations: see T Gruchella-Wesienski 'A Framework for understanding "Soft Law"' (1984) 30 McGill LJ 37.
2 Sometimes, however, ersatz legislation has been the subject of resolutions passed by the House of Commons, eg the former Fair Wages Resolutions. See further para 234 below.
3 See the discussion by E Page *Central Government Instruments of Influence upon Services delivered by Local Government* (PhD thesis, Strathclyde University 1982) ch 6.

(B) BASES OF ERSATZ LEGISLATION

225. Introduction. If ersatz legislation is to be more than an expression of wishful thinking on the part of the government it must be linked with means of exerting influence over those whom it addresses. The main bases of ersatz legislation may be identified as governmental economic power, official discretion in the administration of laws, and consensus. It is to be observed that in practice these bases are not mutually exclusive; rather they interact with one another in varying proportions. It is to be observed also that ersatz legislation as a phenomenon does not exist wholly independently of the formal legal order; on the contrary, the exploitation of governmental economic power and of official discretion in the administration of laws both take place within a framework of common law and statute which affords a degree of latitude to the government, and the promulgation of ersatz legislation commonly takes advantage of the room for manoeuvre inherent in the existing framework of laws.

226. Governmental economic power. The wealth that the government puts at its own disposal is an important resource in this connection[1], since its disbursement can be made dependent on the would-be recipient's satisfaction of conditions stipulated by the government but not set out in formal legislation. Government money gives the government leverage which can be exerted through government contracts, grants and guarantees[2].

1 See R S Summers 'The Technique Element in Law' (1971) 59 Calif LR 733 at 739–741 (the public benefit conferral technique); T C Daintith 'The Function of Law in the Field of Short-term Economic Policy' (1976) 92 LQR 62 at 76–78; T C Daintith 'Legal Analysis of Economic Policy' (1982) 9 J Law and Society 191 especially at 210–216.
2 See paras 234–237 below.

227. Official discretion in the administration of laws. A further possible basis of ersatz legislation is the latitude enjoyed by the government — *de facto* if not *de jure* — in deciding how or indeed whether statutory provisions are to be implemented. Where an activity requires official permission, and the decision to license or authorise is at the discretion of a government department, a favourable exercise of discretion can be made dependent on conformity to requirements additional to those stipulated in the statutory scheme[1]. A somewhat different case is where citizens are in effect relieved of a statutory obligation or liability, without its formal repeal, by governmental forbearance in enforcement. A notorious instance is the extra-statutory concessions of the Inland Revenue[2].

1 See paras 236, 237 below.
2 See paras 241–243 below.

228. Consensus. Ersatz legislation might also proceed, albeit rather insecurely, on the basis of a broad consensus among those involved that norms promulgated should be honoured. Such a consensus might be the fruit of negotiations between the government and affected interest groups, eventuating in a mutually satisfactory accord[1]. Alternatively, a government might try to rely on its 'moral authority' (perceived legitimacy) or on public support for the actual substance of the norms declared by it.

1 See paras 244–246 below.

(C) WEAKNESSES OF ERSATZ LEGISLATION

229. Introduction. While it is inherent in the idea of ersatz legislation that it can be regarded as a substitute for formal legislation, it must not be thought that it is always or even usually an entirely satisfactory substitute. The advantages of ersatz legislation are purchased at a price.

230. Coverage of ersatz legislation. Most ersatz legislation gains its efficacy by playing on someone's dependence on governmental largesse or favour. But the extent to which economic actors depend upon the government's grace varies markedly, as does the extent to which they enjoy countervailing bargaining power. As Turpin remarks in relation to the power derived from the magnitude of expenditure on government contracts:

> 'It is possible to exaggerate the extent of this governmental power and its distribution over the several sectors of industry is unequal. In some the government's share of purchases is minimal, in others it is dominant or amounts to virtual monopoly. This inequality in the incidence of the power is a significantly limiting factor in the use of procurement as an instrument of policy'[1].

Mutatis mutandis, this point is applicable to all manifestations of governmental grace. Ersatz legislation is likely to bear unevenly upon those whom it addresses.

1 C Turpin *Government Contracts* (1972) p 246.

231. Coverage of formal legislation. Legislation, on the other hand, is in principle potentially uniform and universal in its formal application. It may govern all equally, irrespective of individual degrees of susceptibility to governmental blackmail, browbeating, bribery, blandishments etc. However, this contrast is of course greatly diminished if one looks at legislation 'in action' rather than legislation 'in the books', since there are bound to be derogations from uniformity and universality in the actual enforcement of legislation.

232. The use of coercion. While the loss of a government contract, or of a grant or a licence, by virtue of non-compliance with ersatz legislation may entail fairly serious economic consequences for the infractor, there are certain sanctions which may not be imposed in support of a governmental policy unless that policy has been given legal effect through legislative enactment[1]. Above all, ersatz legislation cannot be enforced through expropriation or imprisonment.

1 T C Daintith 'Legal Analysis of Economic Policy' (1982) 9 J Law and Society 191 at 210–216.

233. Legitimacy. From a legal point of view, the significance of parliamentary enactment is that it confers legal validity upon what is enacted. From a sociological point of view, the process of enactment may also confer legitimacy. That is, it may be felt that parliamentary enactment is a more or less democratic process and that, accordingly, statutes are entitled to be respected and honoured. Such feelings might account for a measure of conformity to legislation duly enacted.

Ersatz legislation, on the other hand, bypasses the enacting process, and this fact may diminish the extent to which the citizens are prepared to attribute legitimacy to it. Ersatz legislation is always liable to be stigmatised as 'unconstitutional' or 'contrary to the rule of law'.

(b) Particular Types of Ersatz Legislation

(A) GOVERNMENT CONTRACTS

234. Policy clauses in government contracts. Government contracts have been exploited as an instrument of government policy in three main areas. First, between 1891 and 1983 a series of Fair Wages Resolutions passed by the House of Commons prompted government departments to insert into their contracts a clause requiring contractors to pay their employees wages at the generally prevailing level[1]. Secondly, government contracts have since 1969 committed contractors not to engage in unlawful racial discrimination[2]. Thirdly, for a comparatively brief period in the latter half of the 1970s, government contractors had to undertake to comply with the incomes policy[3]. Plainly the potential of government procurement as an instrument of policy is not confined to these areas[4].

1 B Bercusson *Fair Wages Resolutions* (1978); 47 Halsbury's Laws of England (4th edn) para 262.
2 See L Lustgarten *Legal Control of Racial Discrimination* (1980) pp 155–159.
3 See R B Ferguson and A C Page 'Pay Restraint: The Legal Constraints' (1978) 128 NLJ 515; T C Daintith 'Regulation by Contract: The New Prerogative' [1979] CLP 41.
4 See generally C Turpin *Government Contracts* (1972) ch 9.

235. Consequences of breach. Where a contract has been entered into, breach of a policy clause is of course breach of contract, and as such is attended by those legal consequences stipulated if not by the contract itself then by the general law of contract. Of equal or greater significance in this connection, however, is the government's common law freedom to contract or not, which enables it to 'blacklist' (that is, refuse to do business with) anyone who has failed to comply with the policy in question[1].

1 However, note Daintith's view that European Community directives on public contracts could, if exploited by contractors, 'seriously inhibit the use by government of the procurement process as an instrument of regulation in aid of general economic and social policies': T C Daintith 'Regulation by Contract: The New Prerogative' [1979] CLP 41 at 50. As to these directives, see 51 Halsbury's Laws of England (4th edn) paras 11.74 ff.

(B) DISCRETIONARY REQUIREMENTS

236. 'Quasi-legislative' character. Any statutory conferment of discretion upon a government minister affords the government an opportunity to stipulate the conditions upon whose fulfilment it is prepared to exercise its discretion in a particular way. This *de facto* power to lay down discretionary requirements 'resides implicitly in any delegation of administrative discretion'[1]. Such discretionary requirements are not, of course, law *stricto sensu*, but merely a statement of government policy. However, for someone who depends upon a favourable exercise of discretion, this formal distinction may be a fine one. Accordingly the 'quasi-legislative' character of discretionary requirements has long been recognised[2]. For example, the regulation of authorised unit trusts was formerly effected[3] through the imposition of extra-statutory conditions which had to be satisfied if authorisation was to be gained[4]. Under the Financial Services Act 1986 it is contemplated that the making of a designation order in connection with overseas collective investment schemes will be conditional upon the satisfaction of certain extra-statutory requirements[5].

A further illustration is furnished by the 'pay limits' laid down by the government from 1975 to 1978. Observance of these limits was stipulated as a prerequisite of receiving discretionary government assistance under various statutory schemes[6].

1 H Parris *Constitutional Bureaucracy* (1969) p 193.
2 *Parris* p 193.
3 Ie the now-repealed Prevention of Fraud (Investments) Act 1958 (c 45), s 17(1) (amended by the Authorised Unit Trust Schemes Regulations 1976, SI 1976/195).
4 This practice was upheld in *Allied Investors' Trusts Ltd v Board of Trade* [1956] Ch 232, [1956] 1 All ER 162.
5 Financial Services Act 1986 (c 60), s 87(2).
6 *The Attack on Inflation* (1975) (Cmnd 6151) para 22; R B Ferguson and A C Page 'Pay Restraint: The Legal Constraints' (1978) 128 NLJ 515.

237. Legality. Discretionary requirements, and administrative decisions founded upon them, are by no means inherently unlawful. There is nothing in the law to prevent reliance upon a 'carefully formulated policy' in the exercise of an administrative discretion conferred by statute[1]. However, first, the discretionary requirements upon which an administrative decision is based must not be inconsistent with the legislative purpose of the relevant statutory provisions; nor must they actuate the exercise of a discretionary power upon irrelevant grounds[2]. In this connection, of course, everything depends upon an imputation of legislative purpose, and therefore turns on the construction of the individual statute in question. Secondly, even if the requirements formulated pass the above test, the decision-maker must not 'shut his ears to an application', although

> 'a Ministry or large authority may have had to deal already with a multitude of similar applications and then they will almost certainly have evolved a policy so precise that it could well be called a rule. There can be no objection to that, provided the authority is always willing to listen to anyone with something new to say . . .'[3].

1 *Re Findlay* [1985] AC 318 at 335, [1984] 3 All ER 801 at 828, HL, per Lord Scarman.
2 See generally S A de Smith *Judicial Review of Administrative Action* (4th edn, 1980 by J M Evans) pp 325–343.
3 *British Oxygen Co Ltd v Minister of Technology* [1971] AC 610 at 625, [1970] 3 All ER 165 at 170, 171, HL, per Lord Reid.

(C) CIRCULARS

238. Variety of circulars. Circulars are no more than a medium through which the government communicates with those whom it wishes to address. As one might expect, therefore, circulars are extremely varied in function and diverse in legal character. The role of circulars within the Civil Service, where the Crown gives binding instructions to its own servants, must be distinguished from their role vis-à-vis those extraneous to central government, that is, public authorities, local authorities and members of the public. In relation to these latter groups some circulars do no more than convey more or less factual information, while others offer interpretations and elaborations of the law, or urge the adoption of a specific policy, or indicate the manner in which the government proposes to exercise its own discretion[1].

1 For an analysis of the contents of a sample of circulars addressed to local authorities, see E Page *Central Government Instruments of Influence upon Services delivered by Local Government* (PhD thesis,

Strathclyde University 1982). See generally R Baldwin and J Houghton 'Circular Arguments: The Status and Legitimacy of Administrative Rules' [1986] PL 239.

239. General principle. Leaving aside internal Civil Service documents, the general legal principle is that circulars have no legal effect[1]. Indeed the legality of the advice or guidance embodied in a circular may be tested against statute and common law[2].

1 See eg *Inglis v British Airports Authority* 1978 SLT (Lands Trib) 30; *Newbury District Council v Secretary of State for the Environment* [1981] AC 578 at 621, [1980] 1 All ER 731 at 756, HL, per Lord Scarman.
2 See eg *Royal College of Nursing of the United Kingdom v Department of Health and Social Security* [1981] AC 800, [1981] 1 All ER 545, HL; *Gillick v West Norfolk and Wisbech Area Health Authority* [1986] AC 112, [1985] 3 All ER 402, HL.

240. Qualifications. This general principle is, however, subject to two qualifications. First, where a statute authorises the issue of directions or the like these are sometimes embodied in the form of a circular[1]. Again, it is not unheard of for a power to sub-delegate powers to be exercised by means of a circular[2]. Secondly, a circular may gain legal recognition by indirection. For example, if a circular sets out the criteria according to which a government minister proposes to exercise his discretion, that circular may give rise to legitimate expectations on the part of those to whom it is addressed; and reaching a decision otherwise than on the stated criteria may be held to be unfair and contrary to natural justice[3]. Again, if a statutory provision requires a government minister to apply a broad standard in exercising his powers, a circular may assume quasi-legislative status by indicating how the minister intends to give effect to the standard enshrined in the statute. A case in point is the guidance on expenditure by local authorities issued by the Secretary of State for Scotland. Since expenditure in excess of the guidelines is liable to be considered 'excessive and unreasonable', and excessive and unreasonable estimated expenses can be countered by a reduction of the rate support grant[4], the guidance is buttressed by legal support in a roundabout way. The same example illustrates the exploitation of governmental economic power within a permissive statutory framework.

1 See eg *Palmer v Inverness Hospitals Board of Management* 1963 SC 311, 1963 SLT 124.
2 C K Allen *Law and Order* (3rd edn, 1965) pp 189–192.
3 *R v Secretary of State for the Home Department, ex parte Asif Mahmood Khan* [1985] 1 All ER 40, [1984] 1 WLR 1337, CA. On the related issue of personal bar/estoppel, see 1 Halsbury's Laws of England (4th edn) para 24.
4 Local Government (Miscellaneous Provisions) (Scotland) Act 1981 (c 23), s 14.

(D) INLAND REVENUE EXTRA-STATUTORY CONCESSIONS

241. Quasi-legislative character. Extra-statutory class concessions made by the Board of Inland Revenue may be regarded as quasi-legislative in character in that they purport to authorise 'departure from the strict requirements of tax law' by remitting tax 'in circumstances applying generally to specified classes or groups of taxpayers'[1]. The ostensible rationale behind extra-statutory concessions is that they 'mitigate the unforeseen or unintended effects of tax legislation'; they are made when the Board of Inland Revenue considers that 'a rigid application of the relevant tax law would produce unintended or inequitable results or otherwise present difficulties'[2]. Most extra-statutory concessions are published in a booklet[3], but some remain unpublished for various reasons, 'including limited applicability, transience and the risk of abuse'[4].

1 Report of the Comptroller and Auditor General on the Appropriation Accounts 1980–81 (HC Paper (1981–82) no. 76–IX) para 60.
2 Ibid, paras 56, 60.
3 Inland Revenue booklet IR 1, to which there are annual supplements.
4 Report cited in note 1 above, para 63.

242. Legality. The legality of extra-statutory concessions is highly problematic in view of the provisions in the Claim of Right 1689 (c 28) and the Bill of Rights 1688 (c 2) negating the suspending power[1]. The suggestion that such concessions have a legal basis in section 1 of the Taxes Management Act 1970 (c 9), which places the relevant taxes 'under the care and management' of the Inland Revenue, and in various other statutory provisions[2], imposes excessive strain on the statutory language in question. Extra-statutory concessions have no real statutory foundation[3]. In these circumstances it has been repeatedly urged that constitutional propriety would be best served by putting extra-statutory class concessions on a statutory footing. In some cases this has been done. But in other cases the Inland Revenue takes the view that the concessions are inappropriate for statutory cover because of their 'transient character', 'provisional nature' or 'negligible cost', or because of the 'complexity of the legislation required'[4]. It may be surmised that in one or two cases there is a desire to avoid the critical scrutiny of the parliamentary legislative process[5].

1 See para 172 above.
2 Inland Revenue Regulation Act 1890 (c 21), s 1(2); Income and Corporation Taxes Act 1970 (c 10), s 115(2).
3 *Vestey v Inland Revenue Comrs* [1980] AC 1148, [1979] 3 All ER 976, HL. See also D W Williams 'Extra-Statutory Concessions' [1979] BTR 137. In the light of *R v Inland Revenue Comrs, ex parte National Federation of Self-Employed and Small Businesses Ltd* [1982] AC 617, [1981] 2 All ER 93, HL, and *R v HM Treasury, ex parte Smedley* [1985] QB 657, [1985] 1 All ER 589, CA, the difficulty of establishing title and interest to sue might not be insuperable. See, however, A Sumption 'Vestey v Inland Revenue Commissioners' [1980] BTR 4 at 11.
4 Report of the Comptroller and Auditor General on the Appropriation Accounts 1980–81 (HC Paper (1981–82) no. 76–IX) paras 62, 63.
5 See eg Concession A2 (meal vouchers) and Concession A6 (miners: free coal and allowances in lieu) in Inland Revenue booklet IR 1 (1980).

243. Contrast with statements of practice. Statements of practice represent the Inland Revenue's 'understanding of the law and the practical way in which they propose to give effect to it'[1]. In principle, therefore, there are two important distinctions between extra-statutory concessions and statements of practice. First, extra-statutory concessions derogate from the text of the statute, supposedly to give effect to its spirit; statements of practice, on the other hand, merely gloss the statutory text. Secondly, it has yet to be shown that extra-statutory concessions are in practice justiciable; the interpretation embodied in a statement of practice, on the other hand, may be contested in litigation by a taxpayer disadvantaged thereby and subordinated to the authoritative interpretation of the court.

1 Report of the Comptroller and Auditor General on the Appropriation Accounts 1980–81 (HC Paper (1981–82) no. 76–IX) para 68.

(E) SOCIAL CONTRACTS

244. Usage. The idea of the social contract is a familiar philosophical device[1]. In the 1970s, however, the phrase was borrowed to describe a series of understandings between the Labour government, the Trades Union Congress and the

Confederation of British Industry. More generally, any bargain struck between the government (other than in its capacity as an employer) and the representatives of interest groups such as trade unions, trade associations, or federations of trade unions or associations might be regarded as a 'social contract'. Social contracts in this sense are very likely to be viewed by those who participate in their formulation as an alternative to regulation through formal legislation, and this indeed may be one of the incentives to participation. Incomes policy of course supplies the leading illustration of the use of social contracts, but their use in connection with private insurance is also important enough to merit notice[2].

1 See eg J Rawls *A Theory of Justice* (1972) p 11.
2 See also R Baggott 'By Voluntary Agreement: The Politics of Instrument Selection' (1986) 64 Public Admin 51.

245. Incomes policy. Intermittent resort to social contracts as a vehicle of incomes policy was a characteristic feature of the years between 1945 and 1980[1]. Political problems and economic distortions attend the implementation of any incomes policy. This is not the place to review the difficulties which are common to statutory and voluntary policies alike. A distinctive strength of the social contract approach, however, is that it can be represented as being compatible with the 'tradition' of voluntarism in British industrial relations, in terms of which negotiated agreements binding in honour only enjoy greater legitimacy than legislative regulation. The countervailing weakness is, of course, the voluntary character of the social contract, which raises problems of coverage. Those who are more or less willing to adhere voluntarily may be demoralised and materially prejudiced by the behaviour of those who do not; thus one rogue elephant can precipitate a stampede. For this reason incomes policy between 1975 and 1978, although ostensibly founded on a bilateral or tripartite social contract, was 'voluntary' rather than voluntary, inasmuch as voluntary compliance with the pay norm was reinforced by the manipulation of statutory price controls and the government's economic power[2].

1 Eg the bargain of 1948, described as 'a kind of extra-governmental legislation': S H Beer *Modern British Politics* (1965) p 205.
2 See R B Ferguson and A C Page 'Pay Restraint: The Legal Constraints' (1978) 128 NLJ 515. Voluntary compliance with a pay norm may also be facilitated by legislation conferring immunity for breach of contract upon employers who break their contracts of employment in order to honour the pay norm; hence the enactment of the Remuneration, Charges and Grants Act 1975 (c 57), s 1.

246. Private insurance. There is a long history of agreements between the government and insurance trade associations by virtue of which new benefits have been conferred on various classes of people without any formal enhancement of their strict legal entitlements[1]. The most important of these agreements in modern times — the Motor Insurers' Bureau agreements[2] — are drafted in the style of formal contracts, and are legally enforceable between the government and the Motor Insurers' Bureau Ltd. But in truth the legal character of the agreement is quite incidental, for as Atiyah says, 'it is almost unthinkable' that the bureau would violate the scheme, 'and if it did so there is not much doubt that the whole scheme — or some alternative — would be put onto a statutory footing'[3].

1 R K Lewis 'Insurers' Agreements not to enforce Strict Legal Rights: Bargaining with Government and in the Shadow of the Law' (1985) 48 MLR 275.
2 The agreements are reproduced in *Butterworths Insurance Law Handbook* (2nd edn, 1985) paras 824 ff.
3 P S Atiyah *Accidents, Compensation and the Law* (3rd edn, 1980) p 289.

2. JUDICIAL PRECEDENT

Note by General Editor

After it had been agreed that the General Editor and Mr G Maher should write this section as co-authors, Mr Maher prepared the original draft which the General Editor largely accepted — even when it conflicted with views which he had expressed in his Doctrines of Judicial Precedent in Scots Law *(1952). On some matters the co-authors hold or held divergent opinions, and where these could not be reconciled alternative solutions have been offered or the view favoured by consulted judges has been preferred. The credit for this section is substantially due to Mr Maher. Advice from Lord Cameron and Lord Hunter was particularly valued.*

(1) INTRODUCTION

(a) The Nature of Judicial Precedent

247. Meaning of 'judicial precedent'. The core idea of judicial precedent is that when a court or tribunal is considering a point calling for decision it is proper for it to have regard to decisions on similar points which have been reached previously by that court or tribunal or by other courts. Precedent in this broadest sense is not a feature of reasoning confined to law but applies to all decision-making institutions. What is of special significance in the field of judicial precedent is that sets of rules, at times of a complex nature, have developed which specify when a court or tribunal may or must look to previous decisions and what aspects of previous decisions the court or tribunal is bound to regard. A further striking feature of precedent in the legal field is the notion that in certain circumstances a court may be bound to apply a previously-reached decision. A distinction may accordingly be drawn between judicial precedent in a wide sense, which relates to the broad notion of precedent as a form of decision-making, and precedent in a narrow sense, which is concerned with the conditions in which a court must apply a previous decision irrespective of its views of the merits of that previous decision. This narrower sense of judicial precedent is expressed in the maxim *stare decisis et non quieta movere* or *stare decisis*. A specialised, although inaccurate[1], sense of *stare decisis*, which under the influence of English law is commonly used, is that of the absolute binding quality of even a single prior decision.

1 D J Hurst 'The Problem of the Elderly Statute' (1983) 3 Legal Studies 21 at 24, 25.

248. Justification for judicial precedent. The reasons and justifications for judicial precedent are but specialised illustrations in the judicial sphere of arguments for any system of precedent[1]. Generally speaking, judicial precedent is justified by the manner in which it provides for certainty in decisions over a period of time, and by the notion of fairness implicit in treating those in legally similar positions in similar ways. Precedent, especially in its narrower sense, can also be understood as a requirement of the rule of law or the principle of legality, namely that judges as unelected officials, who are accountable to no other organ of government, should, in a democracy, have no legislative power and should implement the law as promulgated. On the other hand, judicial precedent can be criticised for not succeeding in achieving certainty and so failing to provide for reliance on law as promulgated. A more fundamental source of criticism is that judicial precedent may achieve formal justice only at the cost of working substantive injustice and of perpetuating a bad rule merely because of a doubtful decision in the past. As Lord Pitfour declared, 'some judges are like the old bishop who having begun to eat the asparagus at the wrong end did not choose to alter'[2].

1 T B Smith Dictionary of the History of Ideas III, 27.
2 *Sinclair v Sinclair* (1768) 1 Hailes 247 at 248, cited by A A Paterson *The Law Lords* (1982) p 159.

(b) Historical Introduction

249. Outline. The present position of Scots law in relation to judicial precedent[1] represents a noticeable difference from the approaches adopted in previous epochs, and is also one which, it has been argued, is inconsistent with the fundamental tenets of the Scottish legal tradition. In merest outline, the evolution of precedent in Scotland can be presented in the following way: Prior to the institution of the College of Justice in 1532, there is no certain view as to the nature of judicial precedent. During the seventeenth and eighteenth centuries case law did come to be recognised as playing a part in the legal system, but the core idea of such case law was that a tract of decisions provided evidence of binding judicial custom. However, in the nineteenth century Scots law moved closer towards the position of English law (arguably under the influence of English law), and precedent in a broad sense was replaced by something akin to *stare decisis*. In the present century this stricter and narrower approach has prevailed and, if anything, has intensified, despite weighty and authoritative criticisms against it[2].

1 By way of historical introduction, see generally SOURCES OF LAW (GENERAL AND HISTORICAL). For a general historical survey, see J C Gardner 'Judicial Decisions as a Source of Scots Law' (1941) 53 JR 33.
2 See particularly Lord Cooper *Selected Papers 1922–1954* (1957).

250. Precedent prior to the sixteenth century. Little can be said with certainty about precedent in Scotland prior to the sixteenth century. The chief reason for this lack of understanding is that our knowledge about the legal system at this time depends upon scanty historical records which give a far from complete picture. What is available is a variety of court registers which record the actual decreets or decisions made by the courts, but these records in themselves give no indication of the use, if any, to which previous decisions were put in deciding these later cases. However, it is reasonable to surmise that in this period there was nothing like precedent in any formal sense. In the first place, the registers of decreets lacked accessibility and, further, did not contain all the information about decisions which would be necessary for their use in later cases. A second reason to suppose that precedent could only have existed in a very loose form is that the current conceptions of what counted as law and what would be likely to influence judicial decisions required little by way of reference to previously decided cases. In a society in which law was linked centrally to the concept of custom and in which direct appeal to religious authority was accepted, cases were referred to in order to establish title rather than as precedents[1]. Moreover the administration of justice for much of Scottish legal history was tied up with considerations of political influence and financial persuasion. In these circumstances, consideration of prior decisions would have been beside the point.

1 Cooper *Select Scottish Cases of the XII Century* p xxv; G W S Barrow 'The Scottish Justiciar in the Twelfth and Thirteenth Centuries' 1971 JR 97.

251. Precedent in the sixteenth and seventeenth centuries. The establishment of a College of Justice by James V in 1532, an event of special significance for the general development of the Scottish legal system, paved the way also for developments in judicial precedent. The practice developed on the institution of the Court of Session of one of the Senators of the College of Justice being responsible for maintaining a record of the decisions made by the court. This practice gave rise to a new form of legal literature, the 'Practicks', which were records of decisions designed for the private use of judges in order to promote consistency in their decisions[1]. As the noting of cases in Practicks grew, early cases were incorporated into the various collections. Thus Balfour's *Practicks*, which were compiled in 1539, noted decisions of the middle of the previous century. Furthermore Practicks themselves became of two different types. The first sort contained merely notes of decisions, usually set out in chronological order, while the second type in addition noted relevant statutes, excerpts from *Regiam Majestatem*, and practical comments. The former, the so-called 'decision Practicks', continued to be made until the seventeenth century, when they were replaced by law reports in something more like their modern form. The 'digest Practicks' can be seen as early forms of general textbooks and provided the model for the later work of the Institutional writers.

Despite these developments, judicial precedent in this era was still very loose in form. Craig's *Jus Feudale* of 1603, published in 1645, contains references to only seventy-three cases in over one hundred pages of text. This contrasts markedly with English works of a much earlier period, such as Bracton's *De Legibus* (1250–1266) which cites more than 500 cases. However, by the end of the seventeenth century some firmer indication is given of the role and nature of cases in stating the law, and of their place in deciding later cases. Mackenzie wrote 'Our unwritten law comprehends the constant tract of decisions past by the Lords of Session which is considered as law, the Lords respecting very much their own decisions, and tho' they may, yet they use not to recede from them except upon grave considerations'[2]. Stair saw precedent in the same manner: 'But there is much difference to be made betwixt a custom by frequent decisions and a simple decision, which hath not the like force'[3].

For writers such as Mackenzie and Stair case law was not unimportant as a form of legal authority. On the contrary, cases were a crucial indicator of binding custom, and the requirement that there must be a number or tract of decisions before such custom could be noted led in turn to discussion of a range of cases on any point of law which was being examined. Recent writings have discredited the erroneous view that Stair did not cite cases as authority, and it has been calculated that upward of 2,300 decisions of the Court of Session are cited in the *Institutions*[4]. But the real issue in understanding the conception of case law used by Stair is not revealed simply by looking at the number of cases which he cites. Rather the core idea of precedent subscribed to by both Mackenzie and Stair was that cases in themselves do not state the law and thus are not necessarily binding in later cases. Rather cases are important items of evidence of custom which is binding on judges, and it is the idea of judicial custom which explains the overriding binding force of law. Until well into the eighteenth century custom or binding practice was seen as the predominant form of law[5], and for judges previous cases were important only in indicating what was the custom or practice which judges had to respect in deciding later cases. During the eighteenth century, however, the notion that custom was the dominant form of law declined in influence. Commentators have noted that in the writings of eighteenth century jurists such as Forbes, Bankton, Erskine and Kames statements of precedent as practice or custom continued to be made, but this view begins to be interspersed with the competing view that law is the declaration of the will of the sovereign and that case law is by its nature declaratory of law and as such is binding, irrespective of whether a case represents part of judicial practice. Erskine stated in his *Institute*, published in 1773,

> 'Decisions, therefore, though they bind the parties litigating, create no obligations on the judges to follow in the same track, if it shall appear to them contrary to law. It is, however, certain, that they are frequently the occasion of establishing usages which, after they have gathered force by a sufficient length of time, must, from the tacit consent of the state, make part of our unwritten law. What has been said of decisions of the Court of Session is also applicable to the judgments pronounced upon appeal by the House of Lords: for in these that august court acts in the character of judges, not of lawgivers; and consequently their judgments, though they are final as to the parties in the appeal, cannot introduce any general rule which shall be binding either on themselves or inferior courts. Nevertheless, where a similar judgment is repeated in this court of the last resort, it ought to have the strongest influence on the determinations of inferior courts'[6].

Two other factors in the development of precedent in the eighteenth century were that cases became better and more systematically reported and that writers began to make references to cases in a more copious way than is found in the works of Craig or even of Stair.

1 For a fuller discussion, see H McKechnie 'Practicks' in *Sources and Literature of Scots Law* (Stair Soc vol 1, 1936) pp 25–41.
2 Mackenzie *Institutions* I, i, 10.
3 Stair *Institutions* I, 1, 16. For Stair's connecting his view of case law to a conception of law as custom, see I, 1, 15.
4 H David *Introduction à l'Étude du Droit Écossais* (Paris 1972) pp 333, 334; K Luig 'The Institutes of National Law' 1972 JR 193 at 221, 222; W D H Sellar 'English Law as a Source' in *Stair Tercentenary Studies* (Stair Soc vol 33, 1981) pp 140, 146–149.
5 For the doctrine, strange to modern eyes, that the best form of statute is that which merely declares the tested custom of the land, see Stair *Institutions* I, 1, 15.
6 Erskine *Institute* I, 1, 47.

252. Precedent in the nineteenth century. During the nineteenth century precedent in a formal and relatively rigid sense took form in Scots law. Various contributing factors to this development have been identified, but it should be remembered that in England, where precedent, in a formal although not necessarily strict sense, had existed for centuries before the appearance of judicial precedent in Scotland, a similar trend towards *stare decisis* was apparent. This point is worth noting because commentators have tended to take the view that the adoption of *stare decisis* in Scotland arose under the influence, both direct and indirect, of an already developed English system. However, it is more likely the case that moves from looser forms of precedent towards *stare decisis* occurred contemporaneously in both Scotland and England and that each was caused by the same broad factor, namely changing conceptions of the nature of law and of law-making authority, rather than one system borrowing directly from the other. Nevertheless the approach to judicial precedent in the two systems did not converge, and in some important respects, such as the reference to legal principles and the binding element in previous decisions (the so-called *ratio decidendi*), the two systems still differ markedly.

Four broad factors can be found in the development of precedent in nineteenth century Scots law, namely improvements in law reporting[1], reforms of the Court of Session[2], the influence of the House of Lords[3] and changing conception of law[4].

1 See para 253 below.
2 See para 254 below.
3 See para 255 below.
4 See para 256 below.

253. Nineteenth-century improvements in law reporting. During the eighteenth century the former decision Practicks gave way to law reports in something like their modern form[1]. However, in the eighteenth century a variety of different sorts of case report still existed. Some (such as the collected decisions of Kames and Hume) were simply reports made by judges and practitioners of cases in which they had been involved. A second type consisted of encyclopaedic collections of many or all cases ranging back over all available records of decisions, the most famous example of this sort of law report being Morison's *Dictionary of Decisions*. A third type of law report were collections made by the Faculty of Advocates for use by the Bar. This last type, although irregular in appearance and often incomplete in content, was to provide the model for a new series of reports in the early nineteenth century, the *Session Cases*[2], which contain comprehensive and full reports of all major decisions in the Scottish courts.

Better reporting of decisions did not necessarily cause stricter attitudes towards case law in Scotland. If there is a causal connection, it is more likely to be in the opposite direction, for there would be little point in either bar or jurists wishing to be better informed of decided cases unless cases had come to be seen as more than mere adminicles of evidence of judicial custom.

1 For a full discussion, see J S Leadbetter 'The Printed Law Reports 1540–1935' in *Sources and Literature of Scots Law* (Stair Soc vol 1, 1936) pp 42–58. As to decision Practicks, see para 251 above.
2 The first five series are known by the names of the editors, namely Shaw (1821–1838), Dunlop (1838–1862), Macpherson (1862–1873), Rettie (1873–1898) and Fraser (1898–1906), and are cited by their initials (S, D, M, R and F). Thereafter the reports are known simply as *Session Cases* (SC).

254. Nineteenth-century reforms of the Court of Session. Various reforms in the constitution and procedure in the Court of Session also indicate the changes in judicial precedent in the nineteenth century. Until then the court comprised fifteen judges of whom at least nine sat on any matter of importance and the Lord President had a casting vote in the event of an equal vote[1]. In 1808 the court was divided into two Divisions[2] and in 1810 permanent judges of the Outer House were introduced[3]. In 1825 this change was put on a permanent footing and the court was constituted into two Divisions of the Inner House, with four judges in each Division, while the Outer House was manned by the remaining seven judges as permanent Lords Ordinary[4], reduced in 1830 to five[5]. It has been suggested[6] that one result of these changes was that judges acting in smaller Divisions or singly, and not as a full collegiate body, had greater opportunity to deliver fuller and more carefully prepared written opinions. The casting vote of the Lord President who had to control the discussions of the 'Haill Fifteen' does not seem to have been exercised since the reorganisation. Certainly by the early nineteenth century the Court of Session began to formulate criteria for which decisions by the court were to be treated as binding on its new constituent parts. In 1828 it was accepted by a Division that a decision of the Whole Court was binding on it[7].

Another change in Court of Session procedure which has been pointed to in argument for the growth of stricter doctrines of precedent is the abandonment of detailed written pleadings and their replacement with oral argument. However it is not clear that this reform in itself was the occasion for any change towards either precedent or even towards the nature of the reporting of decisions[8].

1 James Boswell *The Earlier Years* p 333; *Report of Opinions of Court of Session: Archibald Douglas v Duke of Hamilton* 15 July 1767.
2 Court of Session Act 1808 (c 151), s 1.
3 Court of Session Act 1810 (c 112), s 29.
4 Court of Session Act 1825 (c 120), s 1.
5 Court of Session Act 1830 (c 69), s 20.
6 J S Leadbetter 'The Printed Law Reports 1540–1935' in *Sources and Literature of Scots Law* (Stair Soc vol 1, 1936) p 45. For descriptions of uncontrolled procedures in decision-making before reform, see James Boswell *The Earlier Years* p 333; James Boswell *The Ominous Years* (ed Ryskamp-Pottle) pp 217, 218; H Cockburn *Memorials of His Time* p 127.
7 *Rose v Drummond* (1828) 6 S 945. Smith notes that this case is not decisive of the issue whether a decision of the Whole Court is binding on a later Whole Court: T B Smith *The Doctrines of Judicial Precedent in Scots Law* (1952) p 28. See further para 292 below.
8 J S Leadbetter 'The Printed Law Reports 1540–1935' in *Sources and Literature of Scots Law* (Stair Soc vol 1, 1936) p 45; Gardner (1941) 53 JR 62–64.

255. The influence of the House of Lords in the nineteenth century. Various commentators have attributed much of the blame for the imposition of an alien doctrine of *stare decisis* into Scots law to the influence of the House of Lords as an appellate court[1]. But it is necessary to make clear the ways in which the House of Lords could have, and did, influence Scottish courts on judicial precedent. Certainly after a period of hostility on the part of the Court of Session, decisions of the House came to be treated as binding precedents on the Court of Session, but this development can largely be explained by the idea of the role of appellate jurisdiction. Although it is arguable that decisions of the House of Lords in Scottish appeals imported into Scots law many doctrines of substantive law which were purely English in origin and inconsistent with Scottish legal principle[2], it is not so readily apparent how the House could have imposed the English approach to *stare decisis* on doctrines of precedent in the Court of Session. In any case, precedent in the nineteenth-century English legal system, although narrower than the Scottish conception of judicial practice, was itself in the process of developing towards *stare decisis*. This process was not finalised in the House of Lords until almost the beginning of the present century in the *London Tramways* case[3].

1 T B Smith *The Doctrines of Judicial Precedent in Scots Law* (1952) p 10 (a view which he would now modify); Lord Cooper *Selected Papers 1922–1954* (1957) pp 206, 251.
2 For a spirited but exaggerated statement of this claim, see A Dewar Gibb *Law from Over the Border* (1950). It is significant that Gibb, despite the evident hostility he displays towards the House of Lords as a court of appeal, does not hold the House responsible for the Scottish adoption of *stare decisis*. His only discussion of *stare decisis* (at p 55) is in the context of whether the House is bound by pre-1707 decisions of the Court of Session.

3 *London Tramways Co Ltd v London County Council* [1898] AC 375, HL, further discussed in paras 270 ff below.

256. Changing conceptions of law in the nineteenth century. A further reason why precedent became stricter in operation during the nineteenth century lies in changed attitudes towards the nature of law and legal authority. By the end of the eighteenth century the notion that law was essentially a matter of custom or practice had been substantially replaced with the view that law was the expression of the will of the law-maker or sovereign. Thus legislation, whatever its content, was to be accepted as making law. Judges also were accorded a legislative role by their power to decide cases, and consequently it became important to determine in detail how cases had been decided previously as giving form to the rules and principles of law. Accordingly, cases were given an importance as forms of statements of the law, and nineteenth-century textbooks from Hume at the end of the eighteenth century to Bell at the beginning of the nineteenth and to the more modern classical writers at the end of that century, such as McLaren and Fraser, treat cases as stating the law and not merely as indicating binding custom.

It might be thought that the changing attitudes to precedent apparent in the nineteenth century should be reflected in a court's attitude to older decisions. If the High Court of Justiciary or the Court of Session in the eighteenth century could by developing judicial custom have discarded a precedent as no longer serviceable, it would seem somewhat paradoxical and anachronistic that centuries later it should be sacrosanct and should be accorded the same reverence in the courts of the twentieth century as if it had been pronounced after modern doctrines of precedent had developed. Much as pre-Union statutes may be impliedly repealed by desuetude and contrary use, early precedents, for example regarding obsolete categories of delict, might also be regarded as spent. Yet both in the High Court and in the Court of Session the factor of anachronism in the rules of precedent has never been fully considered[1].

A further feature of judicial precedent in the nineteenth century appears in the judges' concern when deciding cases to state the law in the manner of laying down principles. This feature is largely to be explained by the dearth of law-making from other sources. During the period when the Institutional writings had immediate relevance as contemporary statements of the law, there was less need for attention to particular decided cases[2]. Whether or not Scots law would have developed a code based on the Institutional works but for the Union of 1707 and the extent to which cases would have had significance in a code-based system are matters for conjecture, but it is clear that, for much of the nineteenth century, case law was required as a means of providing flexibility to law in terms of changing social and economic circumstances. Accordingly a feature common to both Scots and English law in the nineteenth century was the formulation of broad principles of law by judicial decision. This feature does not, however, lead to flexibility in doctrines of precedent. On the contrary, it requires cases to be accorded a central importance in order to obtain the full effect of decided cases as ways of providing flexibility.

1 See eg the consideration of *HM Advocate v Macgregor* (1773) Mor 11146 in *Sugden v HM Advocate* 1934 JC 103, 1934 SLT 465. See also *M'Kendrick v Sinclair* 1972 SC (HL) 25, 1972 SLT 110.
2 See eg the Preface to Kames *Dictionary of Decisions* (1741): 'What greater service to his country can a lawyer in high estimation perform than bring their (*scil* decisions) substance into a new institute leaving nothing to the student but to consult the originals when not satisfied with his author. This may indeed require a new institute every century or two'.

(2) GENERAL ASPECTS OF JUDICIAL PRECEDENT

(a) Precedent and Other Sources of Law

257. Introduction. In order to assess the role of precedent in modern Scots law, it is necessary to place precedent in the general context of the Scottish legal system. A constant point of controversy is the extent to which courts both do and should follow previous cases as binding authority, but it is thought that in historical and contemporary contexts alike this issue cannot be examined in isolation from the workings of the general legal system. Indeed it can be argued that the extent to which case law needs to be flexible or strict in nature depends in large part on how other sources of law operate to formulate and state law and on the legitimacy accorded to all sources of law. Thus in a society in which custom is taken as the dominant form of law (and this was true of Scotland until well into the eighteenth century), precedent need be no more than a particular example of custom as law (that is, judicial practices over a tract of cases as indicating law).

However, where law is taken as a form of expression of the will of the law-giver, precedent can also be seen as a form of this sort of law-making by the judiciary. But if primacy is given to statute as a means of reformulating legal doctrine, there is less apparent need or justification for law-making powers to lie in the hands of judges, although it may be thought that as interpreters of statute they determine its meaning and scope. The flexibility or rigidity of the workings of precedent can accordingly be taken to be in inverse ratio to the flexibility or rigidity of other sources of law. An extension of this point can also be suggested, namely that within a hierarchy of courts, the tendency of a court at any level in the hierarchy towards flexibility or rigidity will depend on the relative flexibility or rigidity adopted by courts at other levels. For example, since 1966 the House of Lords has assumed the power to overrule its own prior decisions in certain circumstances[1], and the existence of this power might partly explain the growing tendency of the Court of Session to adopt a stricter approach to precedent.

1 See *Practice Statement* [1966] 3 All ER 77, [1966] 1 WLR 1234, HL, and paras 283 ff below.

258. Precedent and legislation. A fundamental feature of British constitutional law, as accepted by the Scottish as well as the English courts, is that legislation is the primary source of law in the sense that, subject to a few possible restrictions imposed by the Union Agreement which created Parliament, statute law can override law created by any other source[1]. Connected to this feature is the separate but related argument that in a democracy law-making is a function for the politically accountable legislature, whereas the task of the non-elected judiciary is to declare pre-existing law. These points combine in the view, found in many cases, that judges do not feel free to disregard earlier cases, while accepting the substantive merits of so doing, on the ground that to do so would be in effect to make, and not merely declare, law — a function which is better left to Parliament. In *Dick v Falkirk Burgh*[2] the Inner House refused to depart from the admittedly unsatisfactory precedent of the House of Lords decision of *Darling v Gray & Sons*[3]. Lord Justice-Clerk Wheatley observed: 'I would only add that I, too, appreciate the doubts and misgivings which nowadays attach to the effect of that decision and the injustices which follow from it. If these are well-founded the remedy lies not in the efforts of this Court to find a notional distinction where no real distinction lies, but with a higher authority, be that Parliament or the House of Lords with their current power to overrule the previous decisions of the House'. Similar views about the propriety of judges making essentially policy decisions about overruling established rules of law can be found in cases from earlier times. For example in *Preston v Preston*[4] Lord President Cooper pointed to several fundamental defects in the law of matrimonial property and suggested that a desirable solution would be the reintroduction of the old conception of *communio bonorum*. However, Lord Cooper considered that this was an issue more suited to reform by legislation.

A corollary of the argument that judges in dealing with precedent should not 'legislate' is that where an issue calls for fundamental consideration then that issue should be left for an appropriate law-reforming body to consider. In *M'Kendrick v Sinclair*[5] Lord Reid accepted that the existing law on the range of persons entitled to raise an action of damages for the death of a relative[6] had stood too long to be reversed by the House of Lords but that the matter was one which should be considered by the Scottish Law Commission.

However, in the field of criminal law (which is still substantially the creation of common law and little regulated by statute), Scottish judges have been less ready to recognise that Parliament must have the dominant role in law-making. In *Watt v Annan*, which developed substantially the crime of shameless indecency, Lord Cameron offered the opinion that if precise boundaries or limits were to be placed on the process of expanding the reach of the crime of shameless indecency, then that would be a matter for the legislature[7]. In the *Khaliq* case the High Court of Justiciary was unimpressed by arguments that the imposition of criminal liability for selling solvents for others to use for toxic effects was a matter which should be left to Parliament[8]. However, in both cases the court claimed to base its decisions on flexible principles of existing law and not on purely legislative considerations.

1 See *Gibson v Lord Advocate* 1975 SC 136, 1075 SLT 134, and *Sillars v Smith* 1982 SCCR 367, 1982 SLT 539. Some Scottish judges have conjectured that statutes may not be lawful where they are inconsistent with certain provisions of the Union Agreement: see especially *MacCormick v Lord Advocate* 1953 SC 396 at 411, 1953 SLT 255 at 262, per Lord President Cooper, and the discussion by T B Smith 'The Union of 1707 as Fundamental Law' in *Studies Critical and Comparative* (1962) p 1; *Basic Rights and Their Enforcement* (New Delhi, 1979), pp 11, 57–64; and N MacCormick 'Does the United Kingdom have a Constitution?' (1978) 29 NILQ 1.

2 *Dick v Falkirk Burgh* 1976 SC (HL) 1 at 4, 1975 SLT 110 at 112, 113, per Lord Justice-Clerk Wheatley. See also at 11 and at 116, per Lord Fraser.

3 *Darling v Gray & Sons* (1892) 19 R (HL) 31, *sub nom Wood v Gray & Sons* [1892] AC 576, HL.

4 *Preston v Preston* 1950 SC 253, 1950 SLT 196. For a recent illustration, see *Robertson v Turnbull* 1980 SC 108 at 116, 1979 SLT 182 at 186, OH, per Lord Maxwell, and 1980 SC 108 at 135, 1982 SLT 96 at 104, 105, per Lord Stott.

5 *M'Kendrick v Sinclair* 1972 SC (HL) 25, 1972 SLT 110.

6 Ie as stated in *Eisten v North British Rly Co* (1870) 8 M 980, 42 SJ 575.

7 *Watt v Annan* 1978 JC 84, 1978 SLT 198.

8 *Khaliq v HM Advocate* 1983 SCCR 483, 1984 SLT 137.

259. Precedent and juristic writing. The relative flexibility or strictness of the operation of judicial precedent depends in part on how flexible or rigid are other sources of law in stating and restating law. This is apparent in the context of the relationship between precedent and juristic writing in Scots law. The period when precedent in Scots law was still of a fairly flexible nature coincided with the emergence of the Institutional works, especially those of Stair, Erskine, Bell and Hume, which were regarded as statements of basic principles of law[1]. Accordingly there was relatively less need for precedent to be regarded as an important source of law or to be relatively rigid in operation. However, it was during the period when the Institutional writings began to lose their broad contemporary relevance, in the later part of the nineteenth century, that precedent was needed to adapt law to changed circumstances. Such a role for judge-made law also required a greater degree of stability in the mode of its creation and in its effect, and also recognition that precedent should override inconsistent statements in juristic writings.

This position in broad terms remains the case at the present day. Institutional writings remain authoritative sources, but their relevance is diminishing. Professor Black has observed of the current approach to legal argument:

> 'Certainly during the present century practitioners have been in use to treat judicial decisions rather than institutional works as the first (and too often today, the only) sources of authority to which resort will be made. Citation of the institutional writers, even in such areas as obligations, property and family law in which their authority would seem to be still the most clearly of contemporary relevance, has become the exception and not the rule. The hunt is for decided cases with facts as similar as possible to those giving rise to the instant dispute rather than for an institutional statement of principle from which a solution to that dispute can be obtained by deduction'[2].

Despite this assessment, it is still true that in appropriate cases, judges and practitioners continue to look to Institutional writings for guidance. For instance, in the *Sloans Dairies* case[3] the court examined a large number of writings in considering the issue of passage of risk of destruction of property in sale of heritage. Lord Dunpark's judgment contains a detailed study of the views of Stair, Bell and Erskine to discover whether Scots law had adopted the rule of Roman law embodied in the maxim *periculum rei venditae nondum traditae est emptoris*. In the *Brennan* case[4] a Full Bench of the High Court of Justiciary accepted Hume's views on the meaning of insanity in law, despite the extensive developments of philosophical and medical thought on mental illness in the nineteenth and twentieth centuries. On the other hand, in the *Duffy* case[5] the trial judge, Lord Robertson, refused to apply Hume's position that a charge of rape was incompetent in respect of a woman complainer alleging rape by her husband, and justified this course partly by appeal to changes in the position of marriage and the status of women since Hume's time.

Since the era of the so-called Institutional writers there has been no continuation of a more or less equal partnership between the judiciary and legal authors in developing the law. Circumstances have changed the relationship[6].

1 For a useful discussion of the development of the idea of writings having Institutional status, see J W G Blackie 'Stair's Later Reputation as a Jurist' in *Stair Tercentenary Studies* (Stair Soc vol 33, 1981) p 207. As to Institutional writers and the authority to be accorded to legal literature, see paras 439 ff below.
2 R Black, review of Stair's *Institutions* (1981 edn) 1981 SLT (News) 283, 284. Professor Black has expanded on this observation in 'Principle and Precept in Scots Law' 1982 JR 31.
3 *Sloans Dairies Ltd v Glasgow Corpn* 1977 SC 223 at 237, 238, 1979 SLT 17 at 22, 23.
4 *Brennan v HM Advocate* 1977 JC 38, 1977 SLT 151.
5 *HM Advocate v Duffy* 1982 SCCR 182, 1983 SLT 7.
6 See T B Smith 'Authors and Authority' 1972 JSPTL 3; W A Wilson 'Knowing the Law and Other Things' 1982 JR 259 at 267; and T B Smith 'Authors as Authority' *Huldigungsbundel Paul van Warmelo* (Pretoria 1984) p 180.

260. Precedent and custom. Custom in its most general sense has little application in modern Scots law. In a narrower sense, however, custom has two quite different implications for judicial precedent. The first is that precedent is but a form of judicial custom and it is the idea of custom which explains both the range and the binding force of precedent. However, it is not clear that this conception of custom has any application to issues of judicial precedent except in a historical context.

A second way in which custom plays some part in present case law concerns custom in the sense of trade or professional practices. This sense of custom does have some application in matters of interpretation of commercial contracts but it is certainly not seen as a ground in itself for departing from previous cases. In *Winston v Patrick*[1] the Second Division rejected averments founded on normal conveyancing practice that a clause which appeared in the missives of sale of heritage, but which did not appear in the subsequent disposition, did create at least personal obligations on the parties. The court held that any such normal practice did not affect the general rule that the disposition superseded prior dealings between the parties in matters of heritable property, nor did it cause the case to fall within one of the recognised exceptions to that general rule.

1 *Winston v Patrick* 1980 SC 246, 1981 SLT 41.

(b) Precedent and Law Reporting

261. Reported cases. It is relevant to consider how cases are stored and made available for citation and consideration in later cases. In Scotland most reported cases are to be found in the *Session Cases* and *Scots Law Times* series, although Scottish cases are also to be found in specialised reports on United Kingdom aspects of law (for example the *Industrial Tribunal Reports*). Because the judges revise the opinions to be published in *Session Cases* and counsel's arguments are stated, that series enjoys a favoured status[1]. Nevertheless reference may certainly be made to cases not reported in the standard series of reports. For example in the *Wills' Trustees* case[2] the House of Lords considered an 1867 case reported in the *Elgin and Morayshire Courier*[3]. The *Wills' Trustees* case also shows that where a report of a case is in any way inadequate, as occurs especially but not exclusively with many older cases, the court will examine the various background papers to the case in order to discover what were the issues and what was the basis of the decision reached. Before the House of Lords heard argument in the *Wills' Trustees* case, considerable research had been done to amplify the report of *Grant v Duke of Gordon*, as reported by Morison and by Paton[4]. This amplification included the production of interlocutors pronounced at various stages in that case, the Session papers, and manuscript notes of the judges who heard the case.

1 D M Walker *The Scottish Legal System* (5th edn, 1981) p 365.
2 *Wills' Trustees v Cairngorm Canoeing and Sailing School Ltd* 1976 SC (HL) 30 at 162, 1976 SLT 162 at 212.
3 *Seafield v Jamieson* (1867) Elgin and Morayshire Courier, 26 July.
4 *Grant v Duke of Gordon* (1781) Mor 12820, 2 Pat 582.

262. Unreported cases. Scottish law reporting has been subjected to critical scrutiny in recent years[1]. Some points raised, such as instances of delay in publication and the unsatisfactory style of layout of the reports (and each of these features can be thought to contrast unfavourably with the corresponding English position) seem peripheral. A more serious problem relates to the criteria adopted in deciding whether a case should be reported or not, and instances can be cited of important cases which are reported only in unusual or inaccessible places or which remain totally unreported. For example, a Full Bench decision of the High Court of Justiciary in *HM Advocate v Hayes*[2], which concerns the issue of automatism in criminal law, an area on which there is very little Scottish authority, is still unreported and can be found only in a casebook for students which was published in 1980[3]. Much of the case law in criminal law was for long contained in Crown Office circulars, and only in 1980 did these circulars become readily available to members of the legal profession[4]. With the appearance of the specialised series *Scottish Criminal Case Reports*, it is to be hoped that all criminal cases of importance will appear in reported form, but there are still instances of cases which lay down basic principles of criminal law, such as most of the law of conspiracy[5], which have remained unreported in full. In the *Finlayson* case[6] the High Court of Justiciary decided that a medically supervised decision to switch off a life support machine did not break the causal link between the action of the accused and the death of the victim. This very issue had arisen in an earlier unreported case[7], but no reference was made to this previous decision in either argument or the opinions of the court in the *Finlayson* case.

Occasionally an unreported case which has been cited to a court may be reported as an appendix if the later case is itself reported. For example, in 1977 in the *Albyn Properties* case[8] the First Division followed a hitherto unreported case of 1971, which now appears as an appendix to the *Session Cases* report of the *Albyn Properties* case[9]. Even cases which are reported may not be reported in full on all significant aspects. In the *Crédit Chimique* case[10] the Lord Ordinary consulted the Session papers of an earlier reported case[11] to determine the weight to be attached in that case to the element of warrant of arrest, a matter not apparent in the reported versions of the case. The *Session Cases* report of *Morrisson v Robertson*[12] omits reference to the fact that conviction of theft was pleaded in the case, thus misleading the First Division in *MacLeod v Kerr*[13].

1　S E Woolman 'Reporting of Cases' (1980) Scolag Bulletin 45, p 83.
2　*HM Advocate v Hayes* High Court of Justiciary, Edinburgh, October and November 1949.
3　C H W Gane and C N Stoddart *A Casebook on Scottish Criminal Law* (1980) pp 214, 215.
4　See (1980) 25 JLSS 132.
5　See the cases of *Wilson, Latta* and *Rooney* (Glasgow High Court 1968) and *Milnes* (Glasgow High Court 1971); and the discussion in G H Gordon *Criminal Law of Scotland* (2nd edn, 1978) pp 200–204.
6　*Finlayson v HM Advocate* 1979 JC 33, 1978 SLT (Notes) 60.
7　*Lafferty v HM Advocate* (June 1973), discussed in C H W Gane and C N Stoddart *A Casebook on Scottish Criminal Law* (1980) pp 59, 60.
8　*Albyn Properties Ltd v Knox* 1977 SC 108, 1977 SLT 41.
9　*Glasgow Heritable Trust Ltd v Donald* 1977 SC 113. For similar examples, see *M'Kay v Scottish Airways Ltd* 1948 SC 254, 1948 SLT 402; and *Ayr Town Council v Secretary of State for Scotland* 1965 SC 394, 1966 SLT 16.
10　*Crédit Chimique v James Scott Engineering Group Ltd* 1979 SC 406 at 414, 1982 SLT 131 at 135, 136.
11　*Société du Gaz de Paris v Les Armateurs français SA* 1926 SC (HL) 13, 1926 SLT 33.
12　*Morrisson v Robertson* 1908 SC 253, 15 SLT 697. The report in *Scots Law Times* includes a reference to theft. Inspection of the productions in this case includes an extract conviction of theft. See (1967) 12 JLSS 306, 346; W A Wilson 'Knowing the Law and Other Things' 1982 JR 259 at 268, 269; G H Gordon *Criminal Law of Scotland* (2nd edn, 1978) p 492.
13　*MacLeod v Kerr* 1965 SC 253, 1965 SLT 358.

263. Modern law reporting and data bases. It has already been observed that there is a connection between precedent and law reporting in that a reliable and accurate series of law reports is a prerequisite for any system of precedent. However, the view has been put by the Scottish courts that counsel have a duty to make reference to all relevant cases, whether or not these are reported. As Lord Guthrie said, 'The authority of a case depends not upon whether it is to be found in a series of reports but upon the fact that it is a judicial decision'[1]. A factor which may prove to have a profound effect on the further development of precedent in Scotland is the new, computerised methods of storage and retrieval of cases. In earlier times, application of precedent was virtually impossible because no or inadequate records existed. In the near future precedent may break down because too many cases are recorded.

In 1986 a law database, known as *Lexis*, is available in Britain. Modern Scottish material is included in it[2], and all future decisions by courts in Scotland, or at least those of the higher courts, will be stored on this base. Each of the two major features of these new forms of recording cases, namely storage and retrieval, has important implications for judicial precedent. In the first place, it allows for the keeping of *all* cases from the earliest recorded previously decided cases to all or most decisions as they are handed down. Secondly, retrieval of this material will enable reference to *every* recorded case on any point, and such reference can be made available within a matter of seconds. The possibility then exists for courts to be flooded with an excess of previous decisions, and mechanisms will be needed for dealing with this overabundance of authority. Writing in 1936 Lord Macmillan observed: 'The portentous growth of reported cases in modern times is threatening a breakdown of the rule of *stare decisis*. When decisions become innumerable how can any judge be certain that he is not infringing a binding precedent by his judgment?'[3] Similar views were later expressed by Lord Cooper[4]. It has also been suggested by an eminent American legal scholar that the movement known as American Legal Realism, which resulted in the breakdown of the then existing rigid system of precedent in the United States of America, was caused in part by the introduction of a near universal system of reports of court decisions[5].

As yet, partly no doubt because Scottish material is only marginally covered by the new storage and retrieval systems, the Scottish courts have not expressed any attitude to case law in the context of the new computerised databases. Significantly, however, as coverage of English law in databases increased, the House of Lords in English appeals has made a number of statements suggesting changed attitudes towards precedent. In *Lambert v Lewis*[6], the House warned of the dangers of counsel citing a plethora of cases which did no more than illustrate accepted principles of law; and in the *Roberts Petroleum* case[7] the House repeated this point and further ruled that in future it would decline to allow transcripts of unreported judgments of the Court of Appeal to be cited except in certain circumstances. In this case Lord Diplock expressly noted the role of computerised databases in leading to this increase in the citation of (otherwise) unreported cases. It is not clear how the Scottish courts will react to these problems but it seems clear that some response may be necessary. Lord Keith associated himself with the statement of Lord Diplock in the context of English appeals to the House of Lords.

1 *Leighton v Harland and Wolff Ltd* 1953 SLT (Notes) 36, OH.
2 Ie the full text of *Session Cases* and *Scots Law Times* reports from 1950, and *Scottish Criminal Case Reports* from 1981, together with recent unreported Court of Session transcripts.
3 Introduction to J C Gardner *Judicial Precedent in Scots Law* (1936) p ix.
4 See eg Lord Cooper *Selected Papers 1922–1954* (1957) pp 248, 250 'Defects in the British Judicial Machine'.
5 G Gilmore 'Legal Realism: Its Cause and Cure' (1961) 70 Yale LJ 1037 at 1041.
6 *Lambert v Lewis* [1982] AC 225 at 274, 275, [1981] 1 All ER 1185 at 1189, 1190, HL.
7 *Roberts Petroleum Ltd v Bernard Kenny Ltd* [1983] 2 AC 192, [1983] 1 All ER 564, HL, especially at 200–202 and at 566–568, per Lord Diplock. For discussion, see N H Andrews 'Reporting Case Law: Unreported Cases, the Definition of a *Ratio* and the Criteria for reporting Decisions' (1985) 5 Legal Studies 205.

(c) Legal Argument and Legal Writing

264. Use of cases in legal argument and legal writing. Recognition of the extent to which precedent is regarded as stating the law in the present day Scottish legal system is apparent in the use made of cases in legal argument and legal writing. Although legal argument in decided cases is only briefly reported, if at all, it is clear that considerable importance is given to previously decided cases when presenting argument as to what is the current law of Scotland. The *Nordic Travel* case[1] concerned the issue of fraudulent preferences in the law of bankruptcy and more particularly the question whether cash payments of trade debts made by a limited company prior to its liquidation to another, and associated, company was a fraudulent preference at common law. Before the First Division, the reclaimers referred to Bell and four other writers, and also referred the court to, and discussed in detail, eighteen previously decided cases. The respondents cited three of the same text writers as did the reclaimers, and also referred to fifteen cases, not all of which were the same as those cited by the reclaimers.

Cases also feature in a major way in current writing in Scots law. The most general textbook, D M Walker's *Principles of Scottish Private Law* (3rd edn, 1982) cites more than 40,000 cases, many of them non-Scottish in origin. Other works, written with the explicit aim of introducing the general principles of Scots law, also use considerable numbers of cases. For example, T B Smith's *Short Commentary on the Law of Scotland* (1962) refers to more than 2,500 cases. In these and other books, cases tend to be cited as direct authorities for the various propositions of law stated in the text. For practising lawyers and legal scholars alike, therefore, cases, although they may be criticised, are treated as statements of the law. Indiscriminate citation of English case law unbalanced by other comparative material may consequently distort presentation and decision in a Scottish context.

1 *Nordic Travel Ltd v Scotprint Ltd* 1980 SC 1, 1980 SLT 189.

(3) THE HIERARCHY OF COURTS

(a) Precedent and Appellate Jurisdiction

265. Use of precedent in appeals. The operation of precedent depends in large part on the relationship between the various courts whose decisions are to be considered as authorities (binding or otherwise) in later cases. Where courts are related in the structure of a hierarchy, especially where the lower courts are linked to the higher ones in terms of appellate jurisdiction, the decisions of the higher courts are usually regarded as binding precedents in the lower courts. It has been suggested that the role of appellate jurisdiction, especially of the House of Lords, played a major part in the development of a stricter approach to case law in the Scottish legal system[1], and the notion of appellate jurisdiction also helps to explain those occasions where decisions of a hierarchically superior court do not bind lower courts (for example Outer House decisions not binding the sheriff court). However, appellate jurisdiction is not the sole explanation or justification for precedent. The reason why appellate jurisdiction has led to the development of case law as binding in nature is that otherwise there would be the risk of confusion and uncertainty if lower courts did not follow the law as stated in the previous decisions of the higher courts, especially where it is likely that the higher court itself would apply its own prior decisions. This point was made by the Lord Chancellor in 1972 in an English appeal in the House of Lords: 'The fact is, and I hope that it will never be necessary to say so again, that in the hierarchical system of courts that exists in this country, it is necessary for each lower tier, including the Court of Appeal, to accept loyally the decisions of the higher tier'[2]. However, this reason by itself relates only to the practicality of a court system with a hierarchical structure and is not the sole basis for precedent, as the only possible rationale it offers by itself is that litigants will be put to unnecessary expense if they are forced to resort to the higher courts to obtain a judgment denied to them by a lower court unwilling to apply a precedent of the higher court. Thus where matters of appellate jurisdiction do not arise (for example with the extent to which one Division of the Inner House of the Court of Session is bound by the decisions of the other Division), other considerations (such as fairness, formal justice and the principle of legality) may come directly into play.

1 J C Gardner *Judicial Precedent in Scots Law* (1936) pp 37–57.
2 *Broome v Cassell & Co Ltd* [1972] AC 1027 at 1054, [1972] 1 All ER 801 at 809, HL, per Lord Hailsham of St Marylebone LC. Sir Rupert Cross discusses the possible meanings of 'necessary' in this dictum of Lord Hailsham in 'House of Lords and Rules of Precedent' in P M S Hacker and J Raz (eds) *Law, Morality and Society* (1977) pp 145, 147.

(b) Precedent and the European Community

266. Introduction. The rules and practices of precedent in the Scottish courts are subject to possible qualifications in any case concerning a matter within the scope of the law of the European Communities[1]. There are three broad features of the connection between precedent and Community law which should be noted: preliminary rulings[2]; precedent in the European Court of Justice[3]; and European dimensions of precedent in the Scottish courts[4].

1 This is defined for the purposes of Scots law by the European Communities Act 1972 (c 68), ss 1, 2.
2 See para 267 below.
3 See para 268 below.
4 See para 269 below.

267. Preliminary rulings. Where a Scottish court has referred a point of Community law to the European Court of Justice for a preliminary ruling[1], the ruling given by the Court of Justice is authoritative of the matter referred and must be applied by the Scottish court in the case in which the reference arose. Any question as to the meaning or effect of any of the Community treaties or the validity, meaning or effect of any Community instrument is to be treated as a question of Community law[2].

1 Ie under the EEC Treaty, art 177, or the Euratom Treaty, art 150, or, although it is less extensive in scope, the ECSC Treaty, art 41.
2 European Communities Act 1972 (c 68), s 3(1).

268. Precedent in the Court of Justice. The European Court of Justice, despite its practice of tending to follow its own previous decisions, does not hold itself bound by them[1]. Interestingly in light of the thesis advanced above that the relative flexibility of precedent is in inverse ratio to the flexibility of other sources of law, some commentators[2] have suggested that the reason why the Court of Justice has adopted a flexible approach to precedent lies in the virtual impossibility of amendment of the Community treaties. The fact that the court is not bound by its own decisions (and is not reluctant to depart from them if it thinks necessary) is an important factor to be borne in mind when a national court is considering whether to make a reference for a preliminary ruling, even on a matter on which the Court of Justice has previously made rulings.

In addition, several features of case law in the Court of Justice present a contrast with the Scottish position[3]. The features of precedent often thought central to British practices often remain implicit rather than explicit in the approach of the Court of Justice. Thus previous cases are sometimes followed and incorporated into later judgments, without being referred to by name. Even where a prior case is not followed in a later case, this may be done without the court explicitly stating that it is overruling its previous decision. Furthermore, there is little discussion of such matters as 'distinguishing' or 'finding the *ratio*' of cases. Another noticeable feature is that the opinions of the advocates general are accorded a form of authority in later cases, although these opinions do not strictly speaking form part of the judgment of the court[4].

1 See eg Case 4/69 *Alfons Lütticke GmbH v EC Commission* [1971] ECR 325, ECJ, overruling Case 25/62 *Plaumann & Co v EC Commission* [1963] ECR 98, [1964] CMLR 29, ECJ, discussed in T C Hartley *The Foundations of European Community Law* (1981) pp 508–511.
2 See eg L N Brown and F G Jacobs *The Court of Justice of the European Communities* (2nd edn, 1983) p 278.
3 See the discussion by T Koopmans in D O'Keefe and H G Schermers (eds) *Essays in European Law and Integration* (1982) p 11; *Brown and Jacobs* pp 276–281.
4 *Brown and Jacobs* pp 279, 280; *Hartley* pp 57, 58.

269. The European dimension of precedent in the Scottish courts. In a case with a Community law element in which a preliminary ruling has not been made, a Scottish court must decide the matter involved in accordance with the principles laid down in previous decisions of the European Court of Justice[1]. Where such principles or any ruling from a decision of the European Court of Justice conflict with a decision of a Scottish court (including the House of Lords), a Scottish court must disregard the earlier decision of the Scottish court and apply the principles or rules laid down by the Court of Justice[2].

Cases stating views on issues of Community law decided by the courts of other member states and by other courts in the United Kingdom have at most only mildly persuasive authority in Scotland. Thus any views expressed by English courts, including the House of Lords in an English appeal, could be disregarded by the Scottish courts if the Scottish courts consider that these views do not cohere with the general principles laid down by the Court of Justice. Thus it is unlikely that the decision of the English Court of Appeal in the *Bulmer* case[3], in which guidelines on when a court must or should make a reference for a preliminary ruling were laid down, would be followed in Scotland, the decision having attracted widespread criticism that it displays misunderstanding of the nature of preliminary rulings[4].

1 European Communities Act 1972 (c 68), s 3(1).
2 Case 146/73 *Rheinmühlen-Düsseldorf v Einfuhr- und Vorratsstelle für Getreide und Futtermittel* [1974] ECR 33, [1974] 1 CMLR 523, ECJ; Case 166/73 *Rheinmühlen-Düsseldorf v Einfuhr- und Vorratsstelle für Getreide und Futtermittel* [1974] ECR 139, [1974] 1 CMLR 523, ECJ.
3 *H P Bulmer Ltd v J Bollinger SA* [1974] Ch 401, [1974] 2 All ER 1226, CA.
4 L N Brown and F G Jacobs *The Court of Justice of the European Communities* (2nd edn, 1983) pp 170, 171; A A Paterson and T St J N Bates *The Legal System of Scotland: Cases and Materials* (2nd edn, 1986) p 144.

(c) Precedent and the House of Lords

(A) THE HOUSE OF LORDS AS A COURT

270. Introduction. Before considering the ways in which decisions of the House of Lords affect current practice of precedent in Scotland, something must first be said about the identity of the House as a court. Given the House's role in constitutional and general legal matters, it is surprising perhaps to discover that it is not altogether clear in what capacity the House sits as a court, and in particular whether the House is to be characterised as a Scottish court or alternatively as a United Kingdom court.

The issue has tended to arise in certain specific contexts. Thus, for example, writers previously looked to the question of the nature of the House as a court to discover whether or not the doctrine, enunciated in the English appeal in the *London Tramways* case[1] that the House was bound by its own prior decisions, applied to Scotland (although since 1966 this problem is purely speculative). Another context for considering the nature of the House as a court is the issue whether and to what extent decisions of the House in English appeals are binding on Scottish courts. For example, in the *Virtue* case[2] Lord President Inglis characterised as an error taking the House as sitting at one time as a Scottish Court and at another as an English Court. Instead, the Lord President saw the House as an imperial court of appeal for the United Kingdom, administering at various times the law of Scotland, the law of England and the law of Ireland. His Lordship used this point to support his view that where the House of Lords deals with a general principle of law in an English appeal, that case can in certain circumstances be binding on Scottish courts. However the issues involved here are quite separable, even if they are not always separated. Although views on the nature or identity of the House of Lords as a court may have implications for the argument that a Scottish court can, or ought to, disregard decisions of the House in English appeals, these views do not determine the scope of application of decisions of the House of Lords.

1 *London Tramways Co Ltd v London County Council* [1898] AC 375, HL; Lord Kilbrandon 'The House of Lords and the Scottish Law Commission' (1967) 83 LQR 176; T B Smith 'Law Reform in Scotland' (1975) 35 LaLR 927 at 943.
2 *Virtue v Alloa Comrs of Police* (1873) 1 R 285 at 296, 297.

271. The House as a national or a United Kingdom court. On the first issue, the identity of the House of Lords as a court, the choice lies between taking the House as sitting at different times as a Scottish, and as an English and as an Irish, court; or, alternatively, as a United Kingdom court. This second alternative is itself open to differing interpretations in that the House could be viewed as a United Kingdom court which applies different systems of law in appeals from different jurisdictions or at least in some respects as a court applying one system of law (namely United Kingdom law) divided into different sub-systems. Authority exists for all these competing propositions. For example, in the *Virtue* case Lord President Inglis took the House to be an imperial (that is, a United Kingdom) court[1], whereas Lord Deas in a dissenting judgment saw the House as a Scottish court when dealing with Scottish appeals[2]. Academic opinion too is divided on this issue[3]. However, although there is no clear solution to this issue, there are certain agreed characteristics concerning the House of Lords as a court of appeal which may be relevant in seeking the answer.

1 *Virtue v Alloa Comrs of Police* (1873) 1 R 285 at 296, 297.
2 (1873) 1 R 285 at 301.
3 Contrast D M Walker (*The Scottish Legal System* (5th edn, 1981), p 372), who seemingly takes the House to be a Scottish court when dealing with Scottish appeals, with T B Smith (*The Doctrines of Judicial Precedent in Scots Law* (1952) p 49), who favours the United Kingdom court view.

272. Judicial knowledge of national laws. In appeals before the House of Lords, all matters of Scots law, English law and the law of Northern Ireland are treated as matters of law within their Lordships' judicial knowledge[1]. This is so no matter what may be the originating forum of the appeal, and whether or not any evidence as to the law of other United Kingdom systems was led in the courts below. In *Elliot v Joicey*[2], an appeal to the House from the English Court of Appeal, it was pointed out by Lord Macmillan during argument before the House that the issue in question raised a matter of Scots law rather than, as had been assumed by all sides in the courts below, a matter of English law. The appeal was decided on the basis of Scots law, which thus had not been argued before the courts below. In a more recent English appeal, *MacShannon v Rockware Glass Ltd*[3], the House repeated the point that it was entitled and indeed bound to take judicial notice of Scots law in English appeals, no matter what finding of fact as to Scots law had been arrived at in the inferior courts. The issue in *MacShannon* was whether the English courts should order a stay of proceedings of actions for personal injuries brought against English employers by resident Scotsmen who had been injured at work in Scotland. Both Scottish Lords of Appeal in Ordinary delivered speeches. In the course of their speeches, all of their Lordships had to pronounce upon the nature of aspects of Scots and English civil proceedings and it could be argued that these observations on Scots and English civil proceedings are binding on Scottish and English courts respectively in subsequent cases.

However, the view that these observations have only high persuasive authority for the Court of Session but are not absolutely binding seems preferable and more rational. No Scottish Lord of Appeal nor Scottish counsel might have been involved. When *Elliot v Joicey* was first considered by the First Division in *Allan's Trustees v Allan*[4] — a case which is quite inadequately reported — they welcomed Lord Macmillan's exposition of the law in the House of Lords but declined to accept the House of Lords decision as a binding precedent. While paying tribute to the great abilities of Sir Wilfred Greene as counsel in the *Elliot* case, the Lord President asked pertinently what qualifications he had to argue the law of Scotland. The question has general relevance. More recently when an English Lord of Appeal pressed Scottish counsel to indicate whether Scots and English law were identical on the matter in issue, Lord Fraser of Tullybelton intervened to indicate that Scottish counsel (unless also of the English Bar) were not qualified to make any such concession[5]. Thus, although the House of Lords may take judicial notice of Scots law in an English appeal for the purposes of that appeal, it would jeopardise the coherence of Scots law if it were to be determined conclusively by a decision of the House of Lords, especially if it has sat without the assistance of Scottish law lords or counsel. A Scottish court should be regarded as entitled rather than obliged to accept a decision of the House of Lords in an English appeal as a precedent.

1 See eg *Cooper v Cooper* (1885) 15 R (HL) 21 at 26, 31, 13 App Cas 88 at 101, 109.
2 *Elliot v Joicey* 1935 SC (HL) 57, [1935] AC 209.
3 *MacShannon v Rockware Glass Ltd* [1978] AC 795 at 815, 821, [1978] 1 All ER 625 at 633, 638, HL. The Dean of the Faculty of Advocates represented one of the parties in this English appeal.
4 *Allan's Trustees v Allan* 1949 SLT (Notes) 3, discussed by T B Smith (who was present at the argument) *The Doctrines of Judicial Precedent in Scots Law* (1952) p 61.

5 *GUS Property Management Ltd v Littlewoods Mail Order Stores Ltd* 1982 SLT 533, HL (information communicated by counsel in the appeal). See also T B Smith 'Authors as Authority' in *Huldigungsbundel Paul can Warmelo* (Pretoria 1984) pp 180, 181.

273. The House and its own precedents. A second area of relevance in considering the nature of the House of Lords as a court is the practice of the House as far as concerns its own precedents which cut across the boundaries of Scottish, English and Irish law. In the *London Tramways* appeal[1] the issue presented to the House in argument was whether it was bound by two earlier cases heard together. Of these two earlier cases, one was Scottish[2] and the second, which merely declared that the issue was governed by the Scottish appeal, was English[3]. This approach might possibly suggest that the House makes no distinction in dealing with issues of precedent as to the originating forum of its own previous decisions. On the other hand, the preferable view may be that even in interpreting statutory provisions applicable to Great Britain or the United Kingdom, although it is highly probable that the House will accept an interpretation adopted in an English appeal as appropriate to be followed in a subsequent Scottish appeal (and conversely), it is not strictly bound to do so. There may be some relevant ground for not doing so, since statute law is set in a general context of common law. Thus expressions such as 'property', unless closely defined for the purposes of an Act concerned, for example, with sale of goods, may have substantially different meanings in Scots and English law. Similarly with so-called 'general principles' of law, unless these have been closely scrutinised in the general context of a particular jurisdiction, it would be inappropriate to extrapolate a precedent pronounced in an appeal concerned with a different jurisdiction. There is probably more sensitivity to such matters than hitherto. Thus, although in *McIntyre v Armitage Shanks Ltd*[4] the House adopted a statutory interpretation pronounced in a prior case, Lord Fraser was careful to indicate that it was not formally binding in a Scottish appeal.

1 *London Tramways Co Ltd v London County Council* [1898] AC 375, HL.
2 *Edinburgh Street Tramways Co v Lord Provost of Edinburgh* (1894) 21 R (HL) 78, [1894] AC 456.
3 *London Street Tramways Co v London County Council* [1894] AC 489, HL.
4 *McIntyre v Armitage Shanks Ltd* 1980 SC (HL) 46 at 62, 1980 SLT 112 at 119, per Lord Fraser of Tullybelton.

274. Similarities and divergencies in national laws. The practice of the House of Lords on precedent since 1966 also has some relevance in determining the nature of the House as a court. Although the Netherlands Supreme Court invokes the concept of the 'common core' of neighbouring legal systems as an aid to construing the Civil Code[1], the House of Lords — disregarding in general comparative jurisprudence except from systems based on the English common law — uses its appellate jurisdiction to assimilate (and usually but not invariably to anglicise) the solutions to legal questions raised in the distinct jurisdictions from which appeal lies to the House of Lords. In this sense at least it acts as a United Kingdom court oriented towards English law. In so far as the law to be applied is case law, including decisions on Great Britain or United Kingdom statutes, the overwhelming majority of English as compared with Scottish cases reported is reflected in the decisions of the House of Lords.

1 I Kisch 'Statutory Construction in a New Key' in *XXth Century Comparative and Conflicts Law* (Leyden 1962) p 262.

275. Constitutional law. In certain areas of law the House of Lords has accepted that it is desirable that Scots and English law should provide similar solutions. This approach is favoured, for example, in the field of constitutional law. In *Conway v Rimmer*[1] the House in effect overruled the earlier English case of *Duncan v Cammell, Laird & Co Ltd*[2] on the matter of Crown privilege on disclosure of documents, and preferred the approach of Scots law as accepted by the House in *Glasgow Corporation v Central Land Board*[3]. In *Conway v Rimmer* both Lord Reid and Lord Upjohn stated that this was an area in which Scots and English law should not diverge unnecessarily[4]. On the other hand, on the important issue as to the effect of the Union Agreement of 1707 on pre-Union legislation conferring rights of nationality in the states superseded by the Union, divergent solutions have been recognised. The *Prince Ernest* case[5] illustrates the potential dangers of applying legal solutions to Scotland by decisions of the House of Lords in an English appeal, after a hearing at which Scottish interests are not represented. The Prince claimed British nationality under a pre-Union English Act of 1705[6] which had granted English nationality to descendants of the Electress Sophia ostensibly to encourage them to study the laws and customs of England. In 1822 the House of Lords in a Scottish appeal had rejected the appellants' claim to British nationality based on a pre-Union Scottish Act conferring Scottish nationality on those who fulfilled certain conditions[7]. An article discussing the relevance of that decision[8] was brought to the notice of the Attorney-General by Lord Simonds, who presided at the *Prince Ernest* appeal, but the Attorney-General declined to argue the point — which clearly caused embarrassment to the Law Lords who had to decide the appeal. Lord Kilbrandon later conjectured that the Attorney-General feared 'a faint flavour of federalism. For this or for some other reason, the Attorney-General refused to take the point, which Lord Simonds at least seemed to have thought a winner'[9]. Lord Normand, who sat at the appeal, expressed his indignation subsequently and observed 'the only way in which this matter could have been determined properly was by actions raised against the Attorney-General in England and against the Lord Advocate in Scotland and for the processes to have been conjoined in appeals to the House of Lords'[10]. Certainly it seems contrary to principle that the constitutional law of any jurisdiction should be determined in proceedings in which the public interest is not represented. This is particularly relevant in the context of the Union Agreement of 1707, but it is submitted that in principle no aspect of Scots law — especially in the field of constitutional law — should be conclusively determined in proceedings which did not originate in the Scottish courts.

1 *Conway v Rimmer* [1968] AC 910, [1968] 1 All ER 874, HL.
2 *Duncan v Cammell, Laird & Co Ltd* [1942] AC 624, [1942] 1 All ER 587, HL.
3 *Glasgow Corpn v Central Land Board* 1956 SC (HL) 1, 1956 SLT 41.
4 *Conway v Rimmer* [1968] AC 910 at 938 and at 990, [1968] 1 All ER 874 at 879 and at 912, 913, HL.
5 *Attorney-General v Prince Ernest Augustus of Hanover* [1957] AC 436, [1957] 1 All ER 49, HL.
6 Princess Sophia Naturalization Act 1705 (c 4).
7 *Macao v Officers of State* (1822) 1 Sh App 138.
8 T B Smith 'British Nationality and the Union of 1707' 1956 SLT (News) 89.
9 Lord Kilbrandon *Scots Law seen from England* (Child & Co Lecture) (1980) pp 1, 2.
10 Letter to T B Smith.

276. Application of 'general principles'. The desire to reduce differences between Scots law and English law is at the root of decisions by the House of Lords on occupiers' liability[1] and *forum non conveniens*[2]. However, it is equally clear that where Scots and English law openly differ, as with the law on exemplary damages[3], this approach has less application. In some areas of law the House has asserted its right to apply the principles of English law as general or universal principles, sometimes with disastrous consequences. Thus in 1858 in imposing the doctrine of common employment on Scots law Lord Cranworth declared: 'But if such be the law of England, on what ground can it be argued not to be the law of Scotland? The law as established in England is founded on principles of universal application, not on any peculiarities of English jurisprudence'[4]. Ninety years after English lawyers had discovered that the doctrine was peculiar to their system, this 'universal principle' was abolished by statute[5], and Scots law was restored to the *status quo*. The view that pronouncements of the House of Lords in English appeals on 'general principles' should be accepted by the Scottish courts should be viewed with considerable scepticism because of the vagueness of the concept. Most legal systems in developed countries are faced with similar problems and may or may not reach similar conclusions. However, the conceptual approach may be very different. For example, the law of Scotland for damage caused by *culpa* or fault is based on the developed *lex Aquilia* comprehending deliberate and negligent harm, whereas English law developed separate remedies for deliberate and negligent harm. Mistaken extension of English concepts to Scots law frustrated the logical development of the Scots law of reparation in such fields as liability for economic loss and delictual remedies complementing those available in contract[6]. Although the *lex Aquilia* and the English tort of negligence flow from divergent sources, their solutions now merge in principles of liability for harm caused by negligence, but not if extrapolated to the context of wilful harm.

The decision of the House of Lords in *Donoghue v Stevenson*[7], which is generally regarded both in Scotland and England as constituting a new point of departure for the law, was probably not strictly binding as a precedent in either jurisdiction, since it was decided in a Scottish appeal on counsels' concession that Scots and English law were identical on the matter in issue. No English counsel would have conceded or indeed comprehended that the matter in issue involved the scope of *culpa* in the evolved *lex Aquilia*. The only reference made to *culpa* was by Lord Atkin. Nevertheless the decision substantially reinstates principles latent in the concept of *culpa* which had been recognised in Scots law but frustrated by involvement with English doctrines. After *Donoghue v Stevenson* these principles were developed primarily by the House of Lords in English appeals such as the *Hedley Byrne* case[8] until the Scottish appeal in *Junior Books Ltd v Veitchi Co Ltd*[9]. In such a situation it is suggested that a Scottish court should probably feel free to accept as a 'general principle' to be preferred to Scottish precedents an interpretation by the House of Lords in an English appeal — in so far as this interpretation rejected those English doctrines which had been superimposed on the law of Scotland and had adapted and developed constructions consistent with the principles of Scots law as it stood before they had been rejected by the House of Lords in a Scottish appeal or by the Court of Session relying on the views of the House of Lords expressed in English appeals. Whether such a course should be open to a Lord Ordinary or sheriff or only to a Division of the Court of Session is debatable. However, if the sole *ratio* of a Scottish precedent is clearly reliance on a doctrine of English law which the English courts themselves have rejected, there seems no sound reason for a single judge to continue to apply it[10].

1 See *Herrington v British Railways Board* [1972] AC 877 at 897, [1972] 1 All ER 749 at 756, 757, HL, per Lord Reid. This development was detrimental to Scots law: see T B Smith 'Full Circle: The Law of Occupiers' Liability in Scotland' in *Studies Critical and Comparative* (1962) p 154.
2 *The Atlantic Star* [1974] AC 436, [1973] 2 All ER 175, HL; *The Abidin Daver* [1984] AC 398, [1984] 1 All ER 470, HL.
3 *Broome v Cassell & Co Ltd* [1972] AC 1027 at 1114, 1134, [1972] 1 All ER 801 at 860, 861, 877, HL.
4 *Bartonshill Coal Co v Reid* (1858) 3 Macq 266 at 285.
5 Law Reform (Personal Injuries) Act 1948 (c 41).

6 T B Smith *Studies Critical and Comparative* (1962) pp 80, 89, 189; A Wilkinson and A D M Forte 'Liability for Pure Economic Loss' 1983 JLSS 148, and 'Pure Economic Loss — A Scottish Perspective' 1985 JR 1.
7 *Donoghue v Stevenson* 1932 SC (HL) 31, 1932 SLT 317.
8 *Hedley Byrne & Co Ltd v Heller & Partners Ltd* [1964] AC 465, [1963] 2 All ER 575, HL.
9 *Junior Books Ltd v Veitchi Co Ltd* 1982 SLT 492, [1983] 1 AC 520, HL.
10 See the references in note 6 above; and *Report on Negligent Misrepresentation* (Scot Law Com Consultative Memorandum no. 92). Since negligent harm by misrepresentation is merely a sub-category of harm caused by *culpa* in the sense of negligence, it might be thought that *Manners v Whitehead* (1898) 1 F 171 was treated with undue deference. This problem required correction by statute. See the Law Reform (Miscellaneous Provisions) (Scotland) Act 1985 (c 73), s 10.

277. 'Cross-border' precedents. It is not easy to lay down in advance those areas where as a matter of public policy the House of Lords will consider that Scots and English law should be treated as substantially identical and the House's own practice in following 'cross-border' precedents does not provide any clear indication. However, the fact that such precedents are accorded authority indicates that the House considers its own role as going beyond acting as an appellate court from the courts of a particular jurisdiction.

Taking the House as separate Scottish and English courts or regarding it as exercising separate jurisdictions might possibly explain a puzzling feature of the use made by the House of its 1966 power[1] to refuse to follow its own precedents. In the English appeals of *Herrington v British Railways Board*[2] and *The Albazero*[3], the House, although not formally overruling previous decisions, so distinguished the prior cases that commentators have argued that in effect the 1966 power was used. In each case the prior precedent in question was a decision of the House in a Scottish appeal[4] (paradoxically both the Scottish precedents were decisions of the House of Lords which reversed the Court of Session and in effect imposed solutions of English law). It may be that the House regards itself as not able formally to overrule its own Scottish precedents in later English cases. Certainly to date there is no case involving use of the 1966 power in which a Scottish precedent has been overruled in a subsequent English appeal, or an English precedent overruled in a Scottish appeal.

1 *Practice Statement* [1966] 3 All ER 77, [1966] 1 WLR 1234, HL: see paras 283 ff below.
2 *Herrington v British Railways Board* [1972] AC 877, [1972] 1 All ER 749, HL.
3 *The Albazero* [1977] AC 774, [1976] 3 All ER 129, HL.
4 These were respectively *Dumbreck v Robert Addie & Sons (Collieries) Ltd* 1929 SC (HL) 51, 1929 SLT 242, and *Dunlop v Lambert* (1839) 6 Cl & Fin 600, HL. For further discussion, see G Maher 'Scots Law and the 1966 Practice Statement' 1981 SLT (News) 181 at 182, 183. In the *Addie* case Lord Reid commented on the unfavourable reception of the House of Lords decision by Scots lawyers, but in *The Albazero* the *Dunlop* case was not specifically identified as a Scottish decision.

278. Conclusion. It is submitted that on proper analysis when it exercises appellate jurisdiction the House of Lords sits as a United Kingdom court applying the law of Scotland, England and Ireland, as appropriate, according to the jurisdiction from which the appeal in question originated. The Appellate Committee reports to the whole House which is unquestionably a United Kingdom institution. Similarly the Judicial Committee of the Privy Council has advised on appeals from the jurisdictions where the common law is Roman-Dutch or based on a code derived from French law as well as from jurisdictions whose legal system is based on English law. It would be inappropriate for an ultimate appellate court to pronounce binding rulings in law for any jurisdiction except in an appeal originating from that jurisdiction. However, pronouncements in appeals from other jurisdictions may have persuasive force. These factors do not fragment the ultimate court into a plurality of courts nor constitute it an arbiter of 'imperial' or United Kingdom law applicable without question by the courts of the jurisdictions from which appeal lies.

(B) BINDING EFFECT OF HOUSE OF LORDS DECISIONS ON SCOTTISH COURTS

279. Introduction. A separate, but not always separated, question from the identity of the House of Lords as a court is the effect of decisions of the House as binding precedents on other courts. As far as concerns decisions of the House in Scottish appeals, it is accepted that those decisions are binding on all Scottish civil courts[1], although at least since 1966[2], and possibly even before then, they do not bind the House of Lords itself in subsequent Scottish appeals. The question as to the extent, if any, to which the House's decisions bind Scottish criminal courts is considered subsequently[3].

1 This point is so much reflected in the practice of the Scottish courts as to require little explicit statement, but for examples of formal recognition, see *Stewart v Agnew* (1823) 1 S 413 at 433; *Virtue v Alloa Comrs of Police* (1873) 1 R 285 at 293, 299, 300.
2 See *Practice Statement* [1966] 3 All ER 77, [1966] 1 WLR 1234, HL.
3 See paras 302 ff below.

280. Effect in Scotland of non-Scottish decisions. What is not altogether clear is the effect on Scottish civil courts of decisions of the House given in earlier English or Irish appeals. In the seven judge *Virtue* case[1], the Inner House split four-three on the issue whether it should follow a more recent decision of the House of Lords in an English appeal rather than follow an earlier Scottish decision by the House. The majority held that the Court of Session should follow the English decision. Lord President Inglis was of the view that where the House is dealing with principles of law common to both Scots and English law, the decisions of the House are binding on Scottish courts even where delivered in English appeals. However, Lord Justice-Clerk Moncrieff, who was also in the majority, took the view that the Court of Session in such circumstances was entitled, although not necessarily bound, to follow English decisions of the House on matters of 'general jurisprudence'[2]. The minority judges in the *Virtue* case argued that English decisions of the House were conclusive as to English law, but that only Scottish decisions by the House could be binding on the Scottish courts[3].

In assessing these pronouncements it is important to bear in mind the legal background in which the *Virtue* case arose[4]. In a Scottish appeal, *Duncan v Findlater*[5], the House of Lords reversed the earlier Scottish rule concerning the liability of public trustees for the negligence of their employees, and gave as their reason for so doing the need to make Scottish practice the same as English practice. However, in the later English *Mersey Docks* appeal[6], the House declared the English rule to be that which was understood to be the Scottish rule prior to 1839. Accordingly, in these circumstances, as in other cases where the House of Lords had reversed an earlier decision of the Court of Session but subsequently altered its view on English appeals, there were good grounds for the majority in the *Virtue* case to look for reasons for following the *Mersey Docks* case rather than the *Duncan* case in that the English precedent of the House of Lords embodied a rule more consistent with Scottish legal principle than did the House's Scottish precedent.

1 *Virtue v Alloa Comrs of Police* (1873) 1 R 285.
2 (1873) 1 R 285 at 297, 304. See also Lord Benholme at 302, who talks of the court being entitled to apply English decisions concerning principles of universal application under imperial statutes.
3 (1873) 1 R 285 at 299, per Lord Cowan, at 300 per Lord Neaves, and at 302 per Lord Deas.
4 For a fuller discussion, see T B Smith *The Doctrines of Judicial Precedent in Scots Law* (1952) pp 56–58.
5 *Duncan v Findlater* (1839) Macl & R 911, 6 Cl & Fin 894, HL.
6 *Mersey Docks and Harbour Board Trustees v Gibb* (1866) LR 1 HL 93.

281. Non-Scottish decisions entitled to consideration. However, despite these explanations of the reasoning in the *Virtue* case[1], the opinion has been expressed in a number of subsequent cases that English decisions of the House of Lords may be entitled to consideration by the Scottish courts. In the *Orr Ewing* case[2] Lord President Inglis expressed the view that although it was the case that the Court of Session was bound by the House's decisions even in English or Irish appeals dealing with common or general principles of law, it was otherwise when the House was in previous cases administering a law different from, or antagonistic to, the principles of Scots law. In that case the Court of Session held that a prior English decision of the House, being based on the practice of the English Court of Chancery, was not binding on the Scottish courts. When the case came before the House of Lords on appeal, Lord Selborne LC made the following general pronouncement:

> 'A decision of this House, in an English case, ought to be held conclusive in Scotland, as well as England, as to questions of English law and jurisdiction which it determined. It cannot, of course, conclude any question of Scottish law, or as to the jurisdiction of any Scottish Court in Scotland. So far as it may proceed upon principles of general jurisprudence, it ought to have weight in Scotland; as a similar judgment of this House on a Scottish appeal ought to have weight in England. If, however, it can be shown that by any positive law of Scotland, or according to authorities having the force of law in that country, a different view of the proper interpretation, extent, or application of those principles prevails there, the opinions on those subjects, expressed by noble and learned Lords when giving judgment on an English appeal ought not to be held conclusive in Scotland'[3].

1 *Virtue v Alloa Comrs of Police* (1873) 1 R 285: see para 280 above.
2 *Orr Ewing v Orr Ewing's Trustees* (1884) 11 R 600 at 636.
3 *Orr Ewing v Orr Ewing's Trustees* (1885) 13 R (HL) 1 at 3, 4, 10 App Cas 453 at 499.

282. Non-Scottish decisions generally not binding in Scotland. In *Glasgow Corporation v Central Land Board*[1], Lord Normand stated that a decision of the House in an English appeal in which no question of Scots law fell to be decided was not to be treated as binding on Scottish courts. The most recent explicit examination of this issue is the Inner House *Dalgleish* case[2]. Here Lord Justice-Clerk Wheatley stated that one instance where a House of Lords decision in an English case should be regarded as a binding precedent in the Scottish civil courts was where the decision involved a United Kingdom statute which has equal or similar applicability in both countries. His Lordship added:

> 'Since we have in Scotland our own system of law, then in my opinion no legal issue in Scots law should be held to be governed by a House of Lords decision in an English appeal, unless the point is based on legislation which has equal applicability and force in both countries, or has been decided by an authoritative and binding court to be exactly the same and have the same legal significance in both countries'[3].

To illustrate the effect of this approach by the Scottish courts to non-Scottish House of Lords decisions, the *Dalgleish* case itself can be considered. In that case the Lord Ordinary held that he was entitled to look at, but was not bound by, the English *West* case[4] on the issue of the effect of unconsciousness of loss of faculties on assessment of damages for personal injuries. In the Inner House, this approach to the *West* case was approved. Lord Wheatley stated that there were differences in the attitudes of Scots and English law so that the legal systems did not necessarily apply the same general principles[5]. The *Dalgleish* case is also an interesting example of a case where the Inner House gave a substantive judgment of an issue which had become moot, or, as the Lord Justice-Clerk termed it, 'academic'.

In the *Commerzbank* case[6] the First Division refused to follow an old Scottish decision of the House of Lords in *Hyslops v Gordon*[7], which had reversed the Court of Session, because conditions which then existed no longer applied, and followed the later English *Miliangos* appeal[8], in which the position of Scots law had not been argued before the House, nor was the *Hyslops* case cited to it. However, in the House Lord Fraser of Tullybelton stated that the principles applied in the *Miliangos* case to justify overruling a prior English case, namely loss of rationale owing to changed circumstances, might well apply also to the *Hyslops* case. Though the grounds for refusing to follow the House's ruling in a Scottish appeal were indicated in an English appeal, the English case was not regarded as binding. Here again the Court of Session substantially restored Scots law to what it had been accepted as being before the intervention of the House of Lords.

In *Miller & Partners v Edinburgh Corporation*[9] the Second Division accepted, without holding itself bound by, a decision of the House of Lords in the English *West Midlands* case[10]. This case concerned the issue of compensation in connection with compulsory purchase, a matter on which appeal to general or common principles appears to be clearly desirable.

The Exchequer jurisdiction of the Scottish courts is founded on English law. In the *Glasgow Police Athletic Association* case[11] the House of Lords held that, for purposes of the law of income tax, the English law of charity was to be regarded as part of Scots law and not as foreign law. However, Lord Normand also pointed out that what was incorporated into Scots law was the substantive English law of charities and not the English practice of precedent, and accordingly that Scottish courts 'are technically not bound by the decisions of the English courts in the matter of charities, and it is not improper for them to discuss or criticise English decisions'[12]. What this position leaves open is the status as precedents in Scots law of decisions on the law of charities made by the House of Lords in English appeals.

Although the constitutional status of the House of Lords as a court and the binding effect of its decisions in appeals from different jurisdictions have not been conclusively determined, it is submitted that Lord Justice-Clerk Wheatley's formulation is in essence correct. There may be specialties where, as in the Exchequer jurisdiction regarding charities, English law is superimposed upon Scots law. However, decisions of the House of Lords are not otherwise strictly binding on the Scottish courts unless pronounced in Scottish appeals. Their Lordships' interpretation of statutes applicable to Great Britain or the United Kingdom pronounced in English or Irish appeals will be followed in Scotland unless, after argument in the Scottish courts, grounds for a different construction because of the context of Scots law are established. This is a matter for the Scottish courts and cannot be predetermined. The same approach may be justified in relation to some 'general principles' of law, although any lawyer who had experience of comparative jurisprudence would regard this concept with caution. General extrapolation from a principle acceptable in particular circumstances may not be justified. Unless a legal proposition has been argued by counsel professionally qualified to state the relevant arguments, its generality cannot be accepted without subsequent scrutiny by a Scottish court. A concession by counsel that the laws of Scotland and England are identical on an issue cannot constitute a decision as a binding precedent for future litigants. If processes originating in Scotland and England are conjoined in the House of Lords, the decision would, however, seem to constitute a binding precedent in both jurisdictions.

1 *Glasgow Corpn v Central Land Board* 1956 SC (HL) 1 at 16, 17, 1956 SLT 41 at 45, 46.
2 *Dalgleish v Glasgow Corpn* 1976 SC 32, 1976 SLT 157.

3 1976 SC 32 at 52, 1976 SLT 157 at 159. See also that case at 59 and at 161 per Lord Kissen.
4 *H West & Son Ltd v Shephard* [1964] AC 326, [1963] 2 All ER 625, HL.
5 *Dalgleish v Glasgow Corpn* 1976 SC 32 at 53, 1976 SLT 157 at 159, 160.
6 *Commerzbank AG v Large* 1977 SC 375, 1977 SLT 219.
7 *Hyslops v Gordon* (1824) 2 Sh App 451, HL.
8 *Miliangos v George Frank (Textiles) Ltd* [1976] AC 443, [1975] 3 All ER 801, HL.
9 *Miller & Partners v Edinburgh Corpn* 1978 SC 1.
10 *West Midland Baptist (Trust) Association (Inc) v Birmingham Corpn* [1970] AC 874, [1969] 3 All ER
     172, HL.
11 *Inland Revenue Comrs v Glasgow Police Athletic Association* 1953 SC (HL) 13 at 21, 1953 SLT 105 at
     106, 107, per Lord Normand. Lord Reid, at 29 and at 110, talks of this as an example of
     'legislation by reference'.
12 1953 SC (HL) 13 at 22, 1953 SLT 105 at 106, 107.

(C) BINDING EFFECT OF HOUSE OF LORDS DECISIONS ON THE HOUSE

283. The 1966 Practice Statement on judicial precedent. In 1966 the
House of Lords issued a Practice Statement on judicial precedent[1] in which it
was declared that the House would modify its then practice, as declared in the
English *London Tramways* appeal[2], of treating itself bound by its own previous
decisions. Although the House recognised that precedent did provide a degree
of certainty in the law and allowed for the orderly development of legal
doctrine, their Lordships proposed that in the future they would 'depart' from a
previous decision when it appeared right to do so.
    The making of the Practice Statement has been described as a 'natural and
probable consequence' of a plan of action to free the House of Lords from the
London Tramways rule[3]. By the mid-1960s the House's approach to precedent
had been criticised both by jurists and by judges and in its First Programme of
Work the Scottish Law Commission proposed that it should be made clear, if
necessary by legislation, that the *London Tramways* rule did not apply to Scottish
appeals to the House of Lords. It is now commonly accepted that it was this
initiative taken by the Scottish Law Commission which resulted in the announcement of the Practice Statement.

1 *Practice Statement* [1966] 3 All ER 77, [1966] 1 WLR 1234, HL.
2 *London Tramways Co Ltd v London County Council* [1898] AC 375, HL: see para 270 above.
3 Lord Kilbrandon 'The House of Lords and the Scottish Law Commission' (1967) 83 LQR 176.
   For an instructive account of the background to the making of the Practice Statement, see
   A A Paterson *The Law Lords* (1982) pp 146–151.

284. Effect of the Practice Statement. The fact that the House of Lords was
liberated from the doctrine of the *London Tramways* case[1] by means of a practice
statement[2] issued by the House determined the issue, much discussed prior to
1966, of how, if at all, the *London Tramways* rule could be abolished. Although
hints of attack on the validity of dealing with this matter by way of a practice
statement were made by counsel in a case shortly after it was issued[3], the
propriety of what was done is no longer a real issue. One of their Lordships,
Lord Simon of Glaisdale, has in speeches in reported cases referred to the
Practice Statement as a constitutional 'convention' which as an announcement
by the Lord Chancellor must be taken as having had the approval of the
executive and to which no objection was raised in Parliament[4]. In 1978 Viscount
Dilhorne proffered the explanation of the basis of the Practice Statement that the
House of Lords as part of a legally illimitable Parliament could not in law bind
itself for the future[5], and he made the further point (his target being the Court of
Appeal in England, led by Lord Denning MR) that this ground for freeing a

court from self-imposed restriction of precedent was not available to any other court. However, this view can be criticised for its very presupposition that there are no legal limits on parliamentary activity[6]. Furthermore, there is merit in the view that the basis for the House of Lords adopting a less rigid approach to its own prior cases is that any court (unless directed otherwise by statute) is free to provide for its own procedures and practices. It is submitted that issues of parliamentary 'sovereignty' are irrelevant to the question of the extent to which any Scottish court is bound by its own prior decisions[7].

1 *London Tramways Co Ltd v London County Council* [1898] AC 375, HL.
2 *Practice Statement* [1966] 3 All ER 77, [1966] 1 WLR 1234, HL.
3 *Broome v Cassell & Co Ltd* [1972] AC 1027 at 1038, HL (in argument).
4 *R v Knuller (Publishing, Printing and Promotions) Ltd* [1973] AC 435 at 485, [1972] 2 All ER 898 at 927, 928, HL. Cf also *Miliangos v George Frank (Textiles) Ltd* [1976] AC 443 at 472, [1975] 3 All ER 801 at 816, 817, HL.
5 *Davis v Johnson* [1979] AC 264 at 336, [1978] 1 All ER 1132 at 1146, HL.
6 See T B Smith 'The Union of 1707 as Fundamental Law' in *Studies Critical and Comparative* (1962) pp 1–27, and CONSTITUTIONAL LAW, vol 5, paras 338 ff.
7 See paras 286 ff, 296 ff, 302 ff, below.

285. Application of the Practice Statement. Although the Practice Statement of 1966[1] states that the House of Lords will depart from prior decisions when it appears right to do so, since 1966 a number of principles have been laid down by the House as to when the use of the power assumed in 1966 is or is not appropriate[2]. Indeed the cases in which these principles are laid down are themselves treated as precedents for the House when the issue of the 1966 power arises in later cases. In the *Vestey* case[3] Lord Wilberforce stated that 'the discretion conferred by the Practice Statement of 1966 is a general one. We should exercise it sparingly and try to keep it governed by stated principles'. A number of such principles have been identified by commentators. The most significant are as follows:

(1) The power is to be used sparingly, and will not be used merely because a prior case is questionable or even wrong[4]. However, where a prior case, although not wrong at the time of its decision, has lost its underlying rationale, that case may be overruled[5].

(2) A prior case may be overruled where its application would lead to injustice to the litigants in the instant case[6]; and, conversely, lack of injustice to the litigants in following a precedent is argument for not overruling it[7].

(3) A prior decision which has been relied on as stating the law will not easily be overruled[8]. Accordingly cases which have stood for some time will tend to be followed in later cases unless good reasons can be given for overriding the consideration of not disturbing a settled rule[9]. On the other hand, a case which has recently been the subject of decision by the House is unlikely to be overruled by the House in a subsequent case raising the same issue[10].

(4) The 1966 power will rarely be used where the issue is the interpretation of a statute as construed in a prior decision of the House[11].

(5) A prior decision will not be overruled where the rule in that case has been approved by Parliament, at least when it is reasonable to assume that Parliament could have changed the law but refrained from doing so[12].

(6) The 1966 power should not be used to overrule a prior case in circumstances which would involve the House in a type of law reform which should be carried out by Parliament, suitably advised by a law reform body[13]. However, the dividing line between topics fit for judicial lawmaking or development and those appropriate only for parliamentary activity is by no means clear. Among the topics which the House has thought not appropriate for judicial creativity are jurisdiction[14], personal injuries damages[15] and

canons of construction[16]. On the other hand, the House has used its power to overrule its prior decisions on the issues of judgments in currencies other than sterling[17], exemplary damages[18] and the range of persons able to sue in respect of injuries to a deceased relative[19]. In *M'Kendrick v Sinclair*[20] Lord Reid, although noting criticisms of the rule deriving from the *Eisten* case[21], thought that the rule was too firmly established to be overruled by the House but suggested that it should be considered by the Scottish Law Commission.

The way in which these principles concerning the use of the 1966 power are balanced and weighed against each other is illustrated by the sole Scottish case decided prior to 1986 in which the power has been used[22]. In *Dick v Falkirk Burgh*[23] the House overruled the *Darling* case[24], which was authority for the rule that an action of damages could not be raised by the relatives of a person who had raised an action in respect of his injuries but who had died before that action was heard. Lord Wilberforce noted that the *Darling* case had stood for eighty years and that the law of damages was properly a matter for legislative rather than judicial change. However, his Lordship felt that these considerations were overridden by appeal to the principle of the need to avoid doing injustice to the present litigants. The need to do justice in the instant case was also mentioned by Lord Kilbrandon who further pointed out that the rule in question was not one on which much reliance had been placed.

1 *Practice Statement* [1966] 3 All ER 77, [1966] 1 WLR 1234, HL.
2 For a full discussion of these principles, see A A Paterson *The Law Lords* (1982) pp 134–169; G Maher 'Statutory Interpretation and Overruling in the House of Lords' [1981] Stat L Rev 88.
3 *Vestey v Inland Revenue Comrs* [1980] AC 1148 at 1178, [1979] 3 All ER 976 at 989, HL.
4 *Jones v Secretary of State for Social Services* [1972] AC 944 at 966, 996, [1972] 1 All ER 145 at 149, 174, HL; *Miliangos v George Frank (Textiles) Ltd* [1976] AC 443 at 480, [1975] 3 All ER 801 at 823, 824, HL; *Fitzleet Estates Ltd v Cherry* [1977] 3 All ER 996 at 999, 1002, 1003, [1977] 1 WLR 1345 at 1349, 1353, HL; *Vestey v Inland Revenue Comrs* [1980] AC 1148 at 1178, 1187, [1979] 3 All ER 976 at 989, 995, 996, HL.
5 *Miliangos v George Frank (Textiles) Ltd* [1976] AC 443, [1975] 3 All ER 801, HL.
6 *The Johanna Oldendorff* [1974] AC 479 at 552, [1973] 3 All ER 148 at 171, 172, HL; *Miliangos v George Frank (Textiles) Ltd* [1976] AC 443 at 467, 501, [1975] 3 All ER 801 at 812, 813, 841, HL; *Dick v Falkirk Burgh* 1976 SC (HL) 1 at 21, 29, 1976 SLT 21 at 24, 28, 29; *R v Camplin* [1978] AC 705 at 724, [1978] 2 All ER 168 at 179, 180, HL; *Vestey v Inland Revenue Comrs* [1980] AC 1148 at 1174, 1196–1198, [1979] 3 All ER 976 at 986, 1003–1005, HL.
7 *Jones v Secretary of State for Social Services* [1972] AC 944 at 966, 1025, [1972] 1 All ER 145 at 149, 197, 198, HL; *Fitzleet Estates Ltd v Cherry* [1977] 3 All ER 996 at 1000, 1002, 1003, [1977] 1 WLR 1345 at 1350, 1353, HL.
8 *Dick v Falkirk Burgh* 1976 SC (HL) 1 at 20, 29, 1976 SLT 21 at 23, 24, 28, 29; *Vestey v Inland Revenue Comrs* [1980] AC 1148 at 1175, 1186, 1196, [1979] 3 All ER 976 at 987, 994, 995, 1003, HL.
9 *Lynall v Inland Revenue Comrs* [1972] AC 680 at 690, 702, 704, [1971] 3 All ER 914 at 924–927 HL; *M'Kendrick v Sinclair* 1972 SC (HL) 25 at 55, 1972 SLT 110 at 114; *R v Knuller (Publishing, Printing and Promotions) Ltd* [1973] AC 435 at 455, 463, 466, [1972] 2 All ER 898 at 903, 909, 910, 912, HL; *Taylor v Provan* [1975] AC 194 at 227, [1974] 1 All ER 1201 at 1223, 1224, HL; *Hesperides Hotels Ltd v Aegean Turkish Holidays Ltd* [1979] AC 508 at 536, 541, [1978] 2 All ER 1168 at 1174, 1175, 1179, HL; *Lim Poh Choo v Camden and Islington Area Health Authority* [1980] AC 174 at 189 [1979] 2 All ER 910 at 919, 920, HL. See also the Privy Council case of *Geelong Harbor Trust Comrs v Gibbs Bright & Co* [1974] AC 810 at 820, PC.
10 *Duport Steels Ltd v Sirs* [1980] 1 All ER 529, [1980] 1 WLR 142, HL, where the House pointed out that *Express Newspapers Ltd v McShane* [1980] AC 672, [1980] 1 All ER 65, HL, was binding on the Court of Appeal, with Lord Edmund-Davies adding (at [1980] 1 All ER 548, [1980] 1 WLR 165): 'In reality, though not in strict law, it is also presently binding on this House'. In *R v Shivpuri* [1986] 2 All ER 334, HL, the House overruled its recent decision in *Anderton v Ryan* [1985] AC 560, [1985] 2 All ER 355, HL, on the interpretation of the Criminal Attempts Act 1981 (c 47), s 1.
11 *Jones v Secretary of State for Social Services* [1972] AC 944 at 966, [1972] 1 All ER 145 at 149, HL; *R v Knuller (Publishing, Printing and Promotions) Ltd* [1973] AC 435 at 490, [1972] 2 All ER 898 at 932,

HL; *Taylor v Provan* [1975] AC 194 at 218, [1974] 1 All ER 1201 at 1215, 1216, HL; *Vestey v Inland Revenue Comrs* [1980] AC 1148 at 1186, 1187, 1196, [1979] 3 All ER 976 at 994–996, 1003, HL.

12 *Jones v Secretary of State for Social Services* [1972] AC 944 at 1025, [1972] 1 All ER 145 at 197, 198, HL; *R v Knuller (Publishing, Printing and Promotions) Ltd* [1973] AC 435 at 464, 466, 489, [1972] 2 All ER 898 at 910–913, HL (but cf Lord Reid at 455 and at 903, and Lord Diplock at 480 and at 923, 924); *R v Hyam* [1975] AC 55 at 71, [1974] 2 All ER 41 at 49, HL; *Taylor v Provan* [1975] AC 194 at 216, 221, [1974] 1 All ER 1201 at 1213, 1214, 1218, 1219, HL.

13 *R v Knuller (Publishing, Printing and Promotions) Ltd* [1973] AC 435 at 454, 489, [1972] 2 All ER 898 at 902, 932, HL; *R v Hyam* [1975] AC 55 at 69, 80, [1974] 2 All ER 41 at 47, 57, HL.

14 *Hesperides Hotels Ltd v Aegean Turkish Holidays Ltd* [1979] AC 508 at 537, 541, 544, [1978] 2 All ER 1168 at 1175, 1176, 1179, 1182, HL.

15 *Lim Poh Choo v Camden and Islington Area Health Authority* [1980] AC 174 at 182, 189, [1979] 2 All ER 910 at 913, 914, 919, 920, HL.

16 *Air-India v Wiggins* [1980] 2 All ER 593 at 597, [1980] 1 WLR 815 at 820, HL.

17 *Miliangos v George Frank (Textiles) Ltd* [1976] AC 443 at 469, 470, [1975] 3 All ER 801 at 814, 815, HL.

18 *Broome v Cassell & Co Ltd* [1972] AC 1027 at 1128, [1972] 1 All ER 801 at 872, HL, but cf Lord Kilbrandon at 1133 and at 876.

19 *Dick v Falkirk Burgh* 1976 SC (HL) 1 at 21, 29, 1976 SLT 21 at 24, 28, 29.

20 *M'Kendrick v Sinclair* 1972 SC (HL) 25 at 55, 1972 SLT 110 at 114. See also Lord Kilbrandon at 69 and at 121.

21 *Eisten v North British Rly Co* (1870) 8 M 980, 42 SJ 575.

22 For a fuller discussion, see G Maher 'Scots Law and the 1966 Practice Statement' 1981 SLT (News) 181.

23 *Dick v Falkirk Burgh* 1976 SC (HL) 1, 1975 SLT 110.

24 *Darling v Gray & Sons* (1892) 19 R (HL) 31, sub nom *Wood v Gray & Sons* [1892] AC 576.

(d) Precedent and the Court of Session

286. The collegiate nature of the Court of Session. The key to understanding precedent in the Court of Session is to recognise the nature of the court as a collegiate court rather than as a hierarchy of related courts. In *Purves v Carswell*[1] it was pointed out that all decrees issued by the court are decrees of the Court of Session, and a single judge in issuing a decree exercises a delegated jurisdiction. In that case Lord President Dunedin also made the following important observations about the essentially collegiate nature of the court:

'Originally the Court all sat as one Court, and the so-called Outer House was not really in any sense a separate Court, but was simply a place where one of the fifteen Judges sat for the presentation of cases, just as another sat in the Bill-Chamber. All that changed in 1808[2]. The Court was made to sit in two Divisions, and the Judges were appropriated to the two Divisions, the First Division consisting of the Lord President and seven Judges, and the Second Division of the Lord Justice-Clerk and six Judges; and these appropriated Judges, Ordinary Judges as they were called, sat in rotation in the Outer-House to prepare cases as had been originally done by one of the old fifteen. The next alteration that came was, that instead of each of the Ordinary Judges doing that work in rotation, the four junior Judges of the first Division and the three junior Judges of the Second were taken for the work, the others being allowed to remain in the Divisions without going to the Outer House[3]. Inasmuch as that reform could not be carried out without the consent of the Judges concerned, there was provision made for a transition stage. And then ... it was provided "as soon as five junior Ordinary Judges shall officiate as permanent Lords Ordinary in the manner herein directed three Judges in either Division shall be a quorum in the Inner House; and the other Judges of the Court of Session shall be relieved from attendance in the Outer House, and from performing the duties of Lords Ordinary therein"[4], and that alteration stands to this day. Your Lordships will see that this leaves the position of the Inner-House Judges just the same as it was in the days of the old fifteen, excepting that they are not compellable to do ordinary Outer-House work'.

1 *Purves v Carswell* (1905) 8 F 351 at 354, 13 SLT 708 at 709.
2 Court of Session Act 1808 (c 151), ss 1–6.
3 Court of Session Act 1810 (c 112), s 29; Court of Session Act 1825 (c 120), s 1.
4 Court of Session Act 1810, s 32.

287. Report from the Outer House to the Inner House. The Court of Session still retains a number of features which reflect its collegiate nature and which have implications for precedent in the court. For example, in a case in the Outer House the Lord Ordinary may report any incidental matter or the whole cause to the Inner House. These reports tend to occur whenever some question of difficulty or importance arises which calls for an authoritative decision, or to clarify a practice about which doubts have arisen[1].

Thus in *Gould v Gould*[2] the Lord Ordinary noted a practice regarding evidence as to the means of the parties in the context of financial provisions on divorce, as stated in the earlier case of *Marshall v Marshall*[3]. The Lord Ordinary noted that this practice, though common, was one about which considerable doubts existed, and accordingly felt the matter as one proper to report to the Second Division. After consultation with the judges of the First Division, the Second Division held that the practice in question was not necessary. In *Kerr v John Brown & Co Ltd*[4] the Inner House expressly approved of the decision of the Lord Ordinary to report to the Inner House the appropriate mode of inquiry in certain actions of damages for personal injuries. The Lord Ordinary had felt himself bound by prior decisions of the Inner House on this issue, and took the view that if the mode of inquiry was to be altered this could only be done by the Inner House and not by the Lord Ordinary, and for this reason the matter was to be reported. In *Caldwell v Caldwell*[5] the Lord Ordinary had issued a warrant for the delivery of a child in traditional terms which seemed to imply that procurators fiscal and police had a duty to execute the warrant. This interpretation was opposed by the Crown in argument before the Lord Ordinary, who reported the matter to the Inner House, which held that the terms of such warrants should be amended to make clear that they imposed no duty of enforcement on the police or fiscal.

1 See D Maxwell *The Practice of the Court of Session* (1980) pp 243, 244.
2 *Gould v Gould* 1966 SC 88, 1966 SLT 130.
3 *Marshall v Marshall* 1965 SLT (Notes) 17.
4 *Kerr v John Brown & Co Ltd* 1965 SC 144, 1965 SLT 237. For other examples, see *Borland v Borland* 1947 SC 432, 1947 SLT 242; *Gallagher v National Coal Board* 1962 SLT 160; *Commerzbank AG v Large* 1977 SC 375, 1977 SLT 219; *Huggins v Huggins* 1981 SLT 179.
5 *Caldwell v Caldwell* 1983 SLT 610.

288. Hearing by a larger court or consultation with other judges. A second feature of the collegiate nature of the Court of Session which has important implications for the practice of judicial precedent in the court is that in any case before the Inner House, including one where a matter has been reported by a Lord Ordinary, the case may be heard by a larger court or alternatively one Division may consult other judges, normally the judges of the other Division[1]. Either of these procedures may be adopted in cases of difficulty or importance. Although parties to a case may present a motion (for example requesting that a previous decision be reconsidered) calling for a rehearing by a larger court or for more judges to be consulted[2], litigants have no right to demand that a case be dealt with in this way[3].

1 D Maxwell *The Practice of the Court of Session* (1980) pp 507–509.

2 In *Galloway v Galloway* 1947 SC 330, 1947 SLT 300, the judges of the First Division indicated that had there been a motion asking for a larger court to be convened to reconsider a case binding on the Division, that motion would have been granted.

3 *William Baird & Co Ltd v Stevenson* 1907 SC 1259, 15 SLT 291.

289. Effect of collegiate nature on authority. The core idea behind these methods of dealing with cases is that a truly authoritative decision of the Court of Session is one which is rendered by the court clearly in its collegiate capacity. This feature, that the authority of decisions is connected to the collegiate nature of the court, was recognised in the various nineteenth-century statutes which reformed the Court of Session. For example, the Court of Session Act 1825 provides that in order to preserve uniformity in the decisions of the court and to settle doubtful questions of law, a Division may direct a case to be heard by a Whole Court[1]. By the Court of Session Act 1868, in cases of difficulty or importance, which according to the practice existing in 1868 might have been referred to the Whole Court, the case may be dealt with by a court of seven judges[2], presumably on the view that a decision of a court of seven judges in 1868 represented a decision of the majority of Court of Session judges.

However, in present practice convening all judges of the Court of Session would present such extreme practical difficulties as to be only theoretically possible. The last reported instance of a Whole Court decision made by all the judges was a case which was heard in 1940 by all existing thirteen judges[3]. Most cases which are heard by a Fuller Court in current practice are decided by a bench of seven judges. In the *Connell* case[4] the Second Division, after consultation with the judges of the First Division, distinguished but did not formally overrule an earlier case[5] which was itself decided by one Division after consultation with the other and which was described in the *Connell* case as a 'decision of authority'. In the *Cochrane* case[6] a court of seven judges was convened to reconsider two prior cases decided by the Second Division which were declared to be overruled by the decision in the *Cochrane* case[7]. In *Myles*[8] the Second Division consulted the First Division before ruling that all petitions in charitable trusts must be presented to the Inner House, a matter on which doubts in the profession had been noted. The *Rieley* case[9] was heard by a bench of seven judges (described in the reports as a Full Bench) to give an authoritative ruling on the competency of amending the record to cover material change of circumstances following a proof in an action for damages for personal injuries.

The present constitution of the Court of Session, which derives from a number of changes in the nineteenth century, leaves intact the collegiate nature of the court and also provides for mechanisms to allow the court, as a collegiate body, to give authoritative decisions. It is submitted that the authority of a decision of the court as a binding precedent in later cases is directly related to that decision being a decision of a collegiate court. Thus it is clear that decisions of the Whole Court are binding on the Divisions of the Inner House and all judges of the Outer House. As early as 1828 it was accepted that a Division was bound by a decision of the Whole Court, even though doubts were felt about the prior decision[10]. In the *Hargrave* case[11] the Second Division held itself bound by the decision of a court of seven judges in the *Miller* case[12]. In the *Hargrave* case there was an interesting disagreement within the Division as to the extent of the binding quality of the earlier case. Lord Young held that the *Miller* case was contrary to established principle and as such did not bind the Division. However Lord Trayner, who agreed that the *Miller* case was wrongly decided, felt that a judge of a Division was nonetheless bound by it: 'I do not share the opinion that a Judge may disregard an authoritative decision, simply because he does not concur in it. If each judge, or each Court proceeded upon that principle, our rules of law would become uncertain and confused. *Stare decisis* is a safer principle so long as the precedent stands unreversed. I accordingly in this case give effect to the law as it stands upon the decided cases, and out of deference to their authority'[13]. Lord Moncreiff did not express any view as to the correctness of the *Miller* case, but held that, as a decision of a court of seven judges, the Division was bound by it. He added, however, that if the case was to be reconsidered that was a matter for the Whole Court.

1 Court of Session Act 1825 (c 120), s 23.
2 Court of Session Act 1868 (c 100), s 60.
3 *Bell v Bell* 1940 SC 229, 1940 SLT 241. See also *Wright v Bell* (1905) 8 F 291, 13 SLT 633, also decided by all thirteen judges of the court.
4 *Connell v Connell* 1950 SC 505, 1950 SLT 308.
5 *Bridges v Bridges* 1911 SC 250, 1911 1 SLT 12.
6 *Cochrane's Executrix v Cochrane* 1947 SC 134, 1947 SLT 69.
7 *Cochrane's Executrix v Cochrane* 1947 SC 134 at 140, 147, 1947 SLT 69 at 72, 75, overruling *Denholm's Trustees v Denholm's Trustees* 1907 SC 61, 14 SLT 394, 1908 SC 255, 15 SLT 589; and *Heavyside v Smith* 1929 SC 68, 1929 SLT 45.
8 *Myles* 1951 SC 31, 1951 SLT 63.
9 *Rieley v Kingslaw Riding School* 1975 SC 28, 1975 SLT 61.
10 *Rose v Drummond* (1828) 6 S 945.
11 *Hargrave's Trustees v Schofield* (1900) 3 F 14, 8 SLT 201.
12 *Miller's Trustees v Miller* (1890) 18 R 301.
13 *Hargrave's Trustees v Schofield* (1900) 3 F 14 at 16, 17.

290. Inner House decisions binding on the Outer House. Another feature of precedent which is clearly indicated in the law reports is that decisions of a Division of the Inner House are binding on all judges in the Outer House. For example, in a case in the Outer House[1] Lord Fraser expressed dissatisfaction with a decision of the First Division in an earlier case[2] but stated that the decision was binding upon him and upon any judge sitting in the Outer House, whatever his own opinion on the matter might be.

1 *Hunter v Glasgow Corpn* 1971 SC 220.
2 *Boyle v Glasgow Royal Infirmary and Associated Hospitals Board of Management* 1969 SC 72, 1969 SLT 137.

291. Decisions of Whole or Fuller Court and of Divisions. Without question decisions of the Whole Court or a bench of seven (or more) judges are binding on the Divisions and on the Outer House, and decisions of the Divisions are binding on judges in the Outer House. The rationale which is suggested for these clearly established aspects of practice is that a decision of the court which is more clearly a decision of the court as a collegiate body than the part of the court which is considering the present case is binding on that part of the court. What is less clear, however, is the binding authority which is to be accorded to previous decisions of a part of the court which is of equal collegiate status with the part of the court in the instant case. Only in cases of decisions of the Outer House, which are not binding on later Outer House judges, is this broad issue free from doubt.

292. Whether Whole Court binds Whole Court. At the highest level of the court the question can be posed whether a decision of the Whole Court is absolutely binding on a later Whole Court, or whether alternatively a later Whole Court has the freedom to overrule any decision of the Court of Session. This issue has never arisen directly for decision. The most relevant authority is

Yuill's Trustees v Thomson[1], where the Second Division ordered that the Whole Court should be convened to consider a case concerning an issue in the law of trusts 'with special reference to the decision pronounced in the case of *Miller's Trustees v Miller*'[2], which case was decided by a court of seven judges by a majority of five to two. The view taken by the consulted judges in the *Yuill* case was that the *Miller* case should not be reconsidered. In a joint opinion by Lord President Balfour, Lord Adam, Lord McLaren, and Lord Kinnear, it was stated that the House of Lords was the only court competent to review the *Miller* case, although somewhat inconsistently their Lordships also accepted that there may be certain circumstances in which it would be proper to reconsider a question of law which had been decided by a court of seven judges. At the same time their Lordships held that section 60 of the Court of Session Act 1868[3] had the effect that a decision of the court of seven judges is equivalent to a decision of the Whole Court and also that the *Miller* case must be taken as the final decision of the issue in the Court of Session. All four judges in their joint opinion also accepted that the *Miller* case had been correctly decided, and this was the sole ground put forward by Lord Kincairney in a separate judgment for following the prior case. Lord Kincairney also suggested that the authority of the *Miller* case may have been weakened by the fact that it was by a majority decision (and thus not a decision of the majority of the Whole Court as it existed in 1890). Lord Kyllachy concurred with the views expressed by the Lord President and his colleagues in their joint opinion as to the competency of questioning the *Miller* case, and also indicated that he accepted the intrinsic merits of that decision. Lord Stormonth Darling concurred in the opinion of Lord Kyllachy and Lord Pearson in that of Lord Kincairney. Lord Low held that the *Miller* case was correctly decided but expressed no opinion as to the competency on reconsidering it.

However, different views were expressed in the opinions of the Second Division. Lord Justice-Clerk Macdonald accepted that the *Miller* case was rightly decided and was to be followed, but disagreed with the view that a decision of a court of seven judges must in all circumstances be regarded as equivalent in authority to decisions of the Whole Court. His Lordship mentioned the point that such a decision may not represent the majority view of the Whole Court. Lord Young, consistently with his position in the *Hargrave* case[4], simply by-passed the issue of the binding quality of the *Miller* case and held that it was wrongly decided. Lord Trayner, who also commented upon the *Miller* case in the *Hargrave* case, repeated that he considered the *Miller* case to have been wrongly decided but that, as the court in the present case had decided that it was in fact correctly decided and must be taken as binding, he would acquiesce in applying it in the present case. Lord Moncreiff accepted that, as the court had now held that the *Miller* case was correctly decided and applied to the present case, he was bound by it. He added that he thought it was competent for a decision of a court of seven judges to be reconsidered by a Whole Court.

The issue whether a decision of the Whole Court is binding on a later Whole Court was not directly in issue in the *Yuill* case, in which the issue was whether a decision of a court of seven judges could be reconsidered by a larger court. Some of the opinions in that case do appear to favour the view that decisions of the Whole Court cannot be reconsidered at all by the Court of Session, but at the same time it must be said that other opinions suggest that a Whole Court decision is possibly open to later reconsideration where the prior case was a majority decision or one reached other than on unanimous grounds. There is also the issue, which was never before the court in the *Yuill* case, whether a later Whole Court can overrule a prior Whole Court decision where the later Whole Court consists of a greater number of judges than in the earlier court[5].

There is no settled practice on these matters, and principle pulls in different directions. On the one hand, mere number of judges seems less relevant than the extent to which a decision of the court is a decision of the court in its full collegiate capacity. Clearly, in present day circumstances a Whole Court of twenty-three judges could overrule a decision of a Full Bench of seven or even of thirteen judges, but neither of these is necessarily of the same authority as a unanimous decision of the Whole Court, and it does not follow that a unanimous court of twenty-three judges could overrule a prior unanimous decision of thirteen judges sitting as a Whole Court.

The desirability of the Court of Session as a collegiate body having the power to overrule its own prior decisions depends to a large extent on the weight to be given to such factors as certainty in statement of the law and reliance placed on promulgated law (factors which weighed heavily in the *Yuill* case) and also the possibility of a review of a Whole Court decision elsewhere. Although the House of Lords will not overrule a Court of Session decision merely because doubt has been cast on it, especially where a decision has been followed in the court for many years[6], the House has clear authority to do so, and it is submitted that the existence of appeal to the House of Lords weakens the argument for the Court of Session having power to overrule its own prior decisions[7]. It is thought that, in any case, this whole problem is mainly speculative in that any matter important enough to involve the convening of a Whole Court would probably also be of sufficient importance as to involve appeal to the House of Lords. On the other hand, it must be said that the decision to appeal to the House of Lords lies solely in the hands of the litigants, who may be unable or unwilling to take the risk of appeal to the House because of the extra expense involved, whereas convening a Whole Court, although administratively very costly, is within the control of the court and not so costly to litigants as appeal to the House of Lords[8]. Accordingly to leave the power to overrule decisions of the Whole Court solely in the hands of the House of Lords might be to leave open the chance that unsatisfactory precedents will not be authoritatively considered with a view to overruling.

1 *Yuill's Trustees v Thomson* (1902) 4 F 815, 10 SLT 169.
2 *Miller's Trustees v Miller* (1890) 18 R 301.
3 As to the Court of Session Act 1868 (c 100), s 60, see para 289, text to note 2 above.
4 *Hargrave's Trustees v Schofield* (1900) 3 F 14, 8 SLT 201: see para 290 above.
5 Cf T B Smith *The Doctrines of Judicial Precedent in Scots Law* (1952) p 30.
6 See D Maxwell *The Practice of the Court of Session* (1980) p 5, citing *Kirkpatrick's Trustees v Kirkpatrick* (1874) 1 R (HL) 37; *Nicol's Trustees v Sutherland* 1951 SC (HL) 21, 1951 SLT 201; and *Cole-Hamilton v Boyd* 1963 SC (HL) 1, 1963 SLT 157.
7 The decision of the Whole Court of thirteen judges in *Bell v Bell* 1940 SC 229, 1940 SLT 241, was reversed on appeal to the House of Lords: see 1941 SC (HL) 5, 1941 SLT 273.
8 The parties will have the expense of paying counsel and solicitors for the rehearing (or continued hearing) before the Whole Court. 'It is necessary, however, to note that this valuable power to remit to a larger Court usually proves expensive for the litigants and is resorted to as a rule only when substantial sums or interests are involved. There is a limit to law reform at the expense of the individual': T B Smith *The Doctrines of Judicial Precedent in Scots Law* (1952) p 21.

293. Whether Division binds Division. A second level of precedent where no obvious indication is given by locating its source as the collegiate authority of the Court of Session is the binding effect of a Division of the Inner House in subsequent cases before either Division. The law reports contain expressions by judges to the effect that such cases both are and are not necessarily binding[1]. However, most of the cases which point to Divisions not being bound by previous decisions of a Division were decided in the nineteenth century and early part of the present century. For example, in *Earl of Wemyss v Earl of Zetland* Lord Young stated: 'I should like to say that I do not approve of any judgment of any Division as conclusive on Scots law. If it should happen to be thought wrong on further consideration either by the same Division or by another Division, I am not of opinion that it is necessary to summon the Whole Court, or that nothing but an Act of Parliament will correct an error which has been fallen into'[2].

On the other hand, most cases in the twentieth century which touch upon this issue indicate that a Division does regard itself as bound by a prior decision of either Division, and that if a decision is to be reconsidered that is a matter for a fuller bench or the Whole Court. In *Galloway v Galloway*[3] Lord President Cooper stated: 'If a motion had been made to us for the reconsideration of *Thomson v Bowater*[4] by a larger Court, I should have been disposed for myself to have acceded to that motion, but no such motion has been made; and, as *Thomson v Bowater* is directly in point in relation to the question which the reclaimers desire to have reviewed, namely the refusal of the two items in the specification, it appears to me that we have no option but to follow *Thomson v Bowater* and so hold the reclaiming motion to be competent'. The Administration of Justice (Scotland) Act 1933 abolished the right of parties to choose a Division[5]. This right seemed to recognise grounds for discrimination between the qualities of a particular quorum of judges which may have been reflected in regard for the precedents of each Division.

Commentators are agreed that recent practice has developed into a clear rule that decisions of one Division are binding on either Division in later cases. T B Smith, writing in 1952, accepted that the practice was now well established that decisions of one Division will normally be treated as binding on both[6]. More recently it has been asserted: 'There have been a number of dissenting voices, particularly in the older cases. This would seem to suggest that one time (possibly even as late as the 1930s) there was no settled practice on the question and no consensus amongst the judges. Nevertheless the practice of the judges for the last 50 years seems to have crystallised. Divisions nowadays do regard themselves as bound by previous Divisional decisions and a larger court is convened if it is felt that the earlier decision ought to be reconsidered'[7].

Most commentators, in addition to stating current practice, also raise the issue whether a Division should, at least in some circumstances, be free to depart from a previous decision of a Division[8]. When parties are before a Division of the Court of Session, they might seem entitled to expect that the court in that constitution will adhere to its declared rules as stated by that level of the court, or, in other words, that each Division will follow precedents of a Division. The various mechanisms described above expressly allow for a more authoritative (as more collegiate) decision of the court to review rules declared by Divisions. It is thought that there are good reasons for the court to maintain its existing practice whereby a Division follows earlier decisions made at the level of the Divisions, and that all issues of review of decisions of the Division are for the court in a fuller collegiate capacity.

1 T B Smith *The Doctrines of Judicial Precedent in Scots Law* (1952) pp 23–28.
2 *Earl of Wemyss v Earl of Zetland* (1890) 18 R 126 at 130. See also *Lord Advocate v Young* (1898) 25 R 778, 5 SLT 375, where it is stated that a Division is not bound by a previous decision of a Division on the interpretation of a statute.
3 *Galloway v Galloway* 1947 SC 330 at 331, 332, 1947 SLT 300 at 301, 302. See also Lord Moncrieff at 332 and at 301.
4 *D C Thomson & Co Ltd v W V Bowater & Sons Ltd* 1918 SC 316, 1918 1 SLT 200, a decision of the First Division.
5 Administration of Justice (Scotland) Act 1933 (c 41), s 5.
6 *Smith*, p 28.
7 A A Paterson and T St J N Bates *The Legal System of Scotland* (2nd edn, 1986) pp 328, 329.
8 *Smith*, p 28. The author would not now maintain the position there stated.

294. Decisions of an Extra Division. Commentators have not expressly considered the authority of decisions of an Extra Division. By statute, the Lord President has power to direct any three judges of the Court of Session to sit as a Division of the Inner House, and it is declared that any reference in an Act or Act of Sederunt to a Division of the Inner House is to be construed as including a reference to such an Extra Division[1]. In recent times, because of pressure of work on the Inner House, there is increasing resort to convening of an Extra Division[2]. The question then arises of the authority which is to be accorded to decisions of an Extra Division as binding precedents in later cases. There is no suggestion that in practice decisions of an Extra Division are treated differently from decisions of the permanent Divisions by judges in either the Outer House or the Inner House. It is submitted that a decision of an Extra Division is equal in collegiate authority to any decision by a permanent Division and thus the arguments outlined above for treating Divisional decisions as binding on later Divisions and on Lords Ordinary apply equally to decisions of Extra Divisions.

1 Administration of Justice (Scotland) Act 1933 (c 41), s 2(1).
2 See eg *Cliffplant Ltd v Kinnaird* 1981 SC 9, 1082 SLT 2, overruled in *Scottish Discount Co Ltd v Blin* 1986 SLT 123, for which purpose a court of seven judges was convened. Until the middle of the present century the First and Second Divisions met with four judges, but now normally sit with three. The Divisions often include a Lord Ordinary from the Outer House.

295. Decisions of the Outer House. The final level of application of precedent in the Court of Session which requires to be considered is the authority to be given to decisions of judges in the Outer House. Here the current practice is quite clear: a judge in the Outer House is in no way bound by previous decisions by Outer House judges, and although such prior decisions will often be followed, a Lord Ordinary in a subsequent case is free to depart from them. For example, in *Galbraith v Galbraith*[1] Lord Wheatley, sitting in the Outer House, refused to follow the prior Outer House case of *Warden v Warden*[2]. However, in the *Galbraith* case Lord Wheatley did not simply state his disagreement with the *Warden* case as sufficient to justify his not following it. Rather, in a full opinion, his Lordship indicated that the approach in the *Warden* case was dispproved of by the House of Lords in a more recent English appeal[3], and although noting that this appeal was not technically binding on Scottish courts, Lord Wheatley held that there were good reasons for preferring the reasoning of that case to that in the *Warden* case. In a subsequent case in the Outer House[4], Lord Robertson held that he was not bound by either the *Warden* or the *Galbraith* case but that for the same reasons as given by Lord Wheatley he followed the approach of the *Galbraith* case.

Another illustration of the Outer House approach is the *Collins* case[5], in which Lord Grieve refused to follow an earlier Outer House decision[6]. He did not think it sufficient simply to express disagreement with the prior decision, but gave a number of reasons for not following the case.

The position of Outer House precedent, then, is that decisions of an Outer House judge do not bind other Outer House judges but that where they are not to be followed normally reasons will be given for this course. It might be thought that the arguments about the importance of formal justice apply also to the practice of precedent in the Outer House, and it is true that considerable uncertainty has arisen as to a number of matters where Outer House judges have refused to follow each other's decisions[7]. A decision of the Outer House is, however, the weakest form of a decision of the Court of Session as a collegiate court. Moreover, one of the accepted criteria for the proper reporting of a case to the Inner House is where there is divergence of practice in the Outer House so that an authoritative decision can be obtained, and it may be that this mechanism, if fully used, will obviate any apparent injustice in Outer House decisions not binding other Outer House judges.

1 *Galbraith v Galbraith* 1971 SC 65, 1971 SLT 139, OH.
2 *Warden v Warden* 1951 SC 508, 1951 SLT 406, OH.
3 *Indyka v Indyka* [1969] 1 AC 33, [1967] 2 All ER 689, HL.
4 *Bain v Bain* 1971 SC 146, 1971 SLT 141, OH.
5 *Collins v South of Scotland Electricity Board* 1977 SC 13, 1977 SLT 93, OH.
6 *M'Bay v Hamlett* 1963 SC 282, 1963 SLT 18, OH.
7 See eg A A Paterson and T St J N Bates *The Legal System of Scotland* (2nd edn, 1986) pp 329.

(e) Precedent and the Civil Jurisdiction of the Sheriff Court

296. Introduction. It is surprising that no detailed study has yet been made of the workings of judicial precedent in the sheriff court. The most extensive discussion is that by Gardner, which is chiefly concerned with the historical development of sheriff court practice on case law and is dealt with in two brief passages in his book[1]. This lack of examination is surprising because of the range of civil jurisdiction which the sheriff court possesses and because of the key role played by the court in the day-to-day running of the Scottish judicial system[2]. Many areas of Scots law, for example consumer diligence and lawburrows, are dealt with mainly or solely at the level of the sheriff court. Most of the cases on diligence in the latter half of the twentieth century, including cases of great significance in both legal and social terms, are sheriff court decisions. Although arrangements for reporting sheriff court decisions may not be altogether satisfactory, some of the judgments which are reported are notable contributions to the law[3].

A partial explanation for this lack of attention to precedent in the sheriff court may be that present practice on precedent in that court is of relatively recent origin. Gardner notes that it was not always the case that sheriff courts held themselves bound by the decisions of the Court of Session, and even by the mid-nineteenth century it was unsettled whether sheriff courts were *absolutely* bound by decisions of the superior courts[4]. Gardner advances the view that the greatest influence in the development of a settled practice on precedent in the sheriff court was the effect of the appellate jurisdiction exercised over sheriff court decisions by the Inner House and indirectly by the House of Lords.

The nature of the sheriff court in the system of Scottish courts provides the key to appreciating the operation of precedent in that court. Because of the possibility of appeal to the Inner House (and from there to the House of Lords) from decisions of sheriffs and sheriffs principal, there are practical constraints on the sheriff court to have regard to decisions of the Inner House and of the House of Lords. A sheriff, however, is not bound to accept the views of a Lord Ordinary[5].

The nature of the sheriff court largely determines the authority to be accorded by a sheriff to other sheriff court decisions. Scotland is divided into six sheriffdoms, each with its own sheriff principal and each further divided into a number of sheriff court districts. Apart from the sheriff principal, sheriffs are (notionally) attached to a sheriff court within a sheriff court district. Although administration of the sheriff court lies in the hands of central government, each sheriff court is not simply one branch of a larger court. Rather the sheriff court is meant to be a local court, organised into respective sheriffdoms, and to a great extent the nature of the sheriff court brings out the relative autonomy which sheriffdoms and sheriff courts have in respect of each other.

1 J C Gardner *Judicial Precedent in Scots Law* (1936) pp 39–42, 57, 58. Walker discusses precedent in the sheriff court in one paragraph (D M Walker *The Scottish Legal System* (5th edn, 1981) p 375), and Smith deals with the matter only incidentally (T B Smith *The Doctrines of Judicial Precedent in Scots Law* (1952) pp 19, 91, 92, 105).
2 The Civil Judicial Statistics Scotland 1982 (Cmnd 9235) reveal that 16,501 actions were raised in the Court of Session General Department, 11,674 Outer House divorce actions were heard and 1,684 petitions were brought. In the sheriff court 22,536 actions with General Department business were raised, 98,799 summary cause actions and 52,373 miscellaneous actions.
3 See eg the decision of Sheriff I D Macphail in *Morrow v Neil* 1975 SLT (Sh Ct) 65, on the remedy of lawburrows.
4 *Gardner* pp 39–42.
5 See eg *Foster v Craigmillar Laundry Ltd* 1980 SLT (Sh Ct) 100, although in this instance it is somewhat surprising that the sheriff rejected the reasoning of the Lord Ordinary.

297. Decisions of the House of Lords. The present practice of precedent in the sheriff court is in many ways settled, but as to a number of issues there still remains a degree of uncertainty. It is clear, however, that decisions of the House of Lords in Scottish appeals are binding on sheriffs principal and on sheriffs. For example in *Boomsma v Clark and Rose Ltd*[1] the sheriff accepted that, on the matter of construction of exemption clauses in contracts, he was bound to apply the approach set out by the House of Lords in *Smith v UMB Chrysler (Scotland) Ltd*[2].

As regards decisions of the House of Lords in non-Scottish appeals, although there has been little explicit discussion of this issue, Gardner states that where in English or Irish appeals the House is construing a United Kingdom statute or where it is stated by the House that the law is the same for the whole United Kingdom, then the House's decision binds the sheriff court[3]. But no authority is given for this view, which seems unconvincing. It is submitted that the problem is identical to that of the authority of such cases in the Court of Session, and that a similar answer applies to the issue as concerns the sheriff court[4]. In *More v Boyle*[5] the sheriff refused to follow a dictum of Lord Watson in the English appeal *Bradford Corporation v Pickles*[6] to the effect that the doctrine of *aemulatio vicini* was no longer part of the law of Scotland because this dictum was inconsistent with institutional authority, with subsequent Inner House decisions and with academic opinion.

1 *Boomsma v Clark and Rose Ltd* 1983 SLT (Sh Ct) 67.
2 *Smith v UMB Chrysler (Scotland) Ltd* 1978 SC (HL) 1, 1978 SLT 21.
3 J C Gardner *Judicial Precedent in Scots Law* (1936) p 57.
4 See paras 279 ff above.
5 *More v Boyle* 1967 SLT (Sh Ct) 38.
6 *Bradford Corpn v Pickles* [1895] AC 587 at 597, HL.

298. Decisions of the Court of Session. Decisions of the Inner House of the Court of Session are binding on sheriffs principal and on sheriffs. The reports contain many illustrations of this feature of precedent[1]. In *Luke v Little*[2] the sheriff followed the Inner House decision of *Kaye v Hunter*[3], although he accepted that that decision was inconsistent with the approach of the English courts in the interpretation of the Firearms Act 1968 (c 31). Where a sheriff is deciding an appeal from a decision of an electoral registration officer, he is bound by decisions of the Registration of Voters Appeal Court[4].

There is no appellate link between the sheriff court and the Outer House. It is clear that Outer House decisions do not bind sheriffs principal or sheriffs, though lack of appellate jurisdiction may not be the sole explanation; judges in the Outer House themselves are not bound by Outer House decisions[5]. However, sheriffs will often follow them as highly persuasive and will disregard Outer House decisions only for good reasons. Thus in *Foster v Craigmillar*

Laundry Ltd[6] the sheriff did not apply a dictum of the Lord Ordinary[7] because he considered that the views of the Lord Ordinary were inconsistent with decisions of the Inner House which were binding on the sheriff. In *Hardie v Hardie*[8] the sheriff did not follow an Outer House decision[9] on the view that the Lord Ordinary had decided the case *per incuriam* in the absence of reference to relevant statutory authority. In the *Lossie Hydraulic* case[10] the sheriff referred to three decisions[11] as 'authorities in the Outer House of the Court of Session which I consider must govern my decision in this case'. However, it is clear from his opinion that the sheriff accepted these cases as authority because of their intrinsic correctness, not as a matter of precedent.

1 See eg *Lawrence Jack Collections v Hamilton* 1976 SLT (Sh Ct) 18 (following *Dalgliesh v Scott* (1822) 1 S 506); *Ulferts Fabriker AB v Form and Colour Ltd* 1977 SLT (Sh Ct) 19 (following *Smith and Archibald Ltd v Ryness* 1937 SLT (News) 81); *City Bakeries Ltd v S and S Snack Bars and Restaurants Ltd* 1979 SLT (Sh Ct) 28 (following *Henderson v Grant* (1896) 23 R 659, 3 SLT 311); *Hodgmac Ltd v Gardiners of Prestwick Ltd* 1980 SLT (Sh Ct) 68 (following *Crear v Morrison* (1882) 9 R 890); *South of Scotland Electricity Board v Carlyle* 1980 SLT (Sh Ct) 98 (following *Jack v Waddell's Trustees* 1918 SC 73, 1917 2 SLT 235); and *Duggie v A Tulloch & Sons Ltd* 1983 SLT (Sh Ct) 66 (following *Cook v Crane* 1922 SC 631, 1922 SLT 397).
2 *Luke v Little* 1980 SLT (Sh Ct) 138.
3 *Kaye v Hunter* 1958 SC 208.
4 *Dumble v Borders Electoral Registration Officer* 1980 SLT (Sh Ct) 60 at 61.
5 See para 295 above.
6 *Foster v Craigmillar Laundry Ltd* 1980 SLT (Sh Ct) 100.
7 *John Kenway Ltd v Orcantic Ltd* 1979 SC 422, 1980 SLT 46, OH.
8 *Hardie v Hardie* 1984 SLT (Sh Ct) 49.
9 *Whiteford v Gibson* (1899) 7 SLT 233, OH.
10 *Lossie Hydraulic Co v Ecosse Transport Ltd* 1980 SLT (Sh Ct) 94 at 96.
11 *Ganley v Scottish Boatowners Mutual Insurance Association* 1967 SLT (Notes) 45, OH; *Ellon Castle Estates Co Ltd v Macdonald* 1975 SLT (Notes) 66, OH; *Foxley v Dunn* 1978 SLT (Notes) 35, OH.

299. Sheriff court decisions binding on sheriff principal. The practice of sheriff court cases being regarded as binding in the sheriff court itself is well settled. A distinction is made between decisions by a sheriff principal and by a sheriff. A sheriff principal is not bound by any decision of a sheriff, whether of the same or a different sheriffdom. Nor is a sheriff principal bound by a decision of a sheriff principal of a different sheriffdom[1]. In *Spencer v Spencer*[2], the sheriff principal of Grampian, Highland and Islands sheriffdom said of *Milne v Milne*[3], decided by the sheriff principal of Glasgow:

'Notwithstanding the great respect which is owed to any pronouncement on such a matter by Sir Allan Walker QC, I find it impossible to agree with his decision in that case. Since the decision is not binding in this sheriffdom I must act on the views which I have formed and entertain the appeal'.

Shortly after the decision in the *Spencer* case, the same issue came before the sheriff principal of North Strathclyde, who also preferred not to follow *Milne v Milne*[4].

It is not clear whether a sheriff principal is bound by his own previous decisions or by the decisions of his predecessors[5]. He will normally follow such decisions, but may not be absolutely bound to do so. In the *City Bakeries* case[6] the sheriff principal of Glasgow followed a case[7] decided by a previous sheriff principal of Glasgow, but this does not appear to have been done as a matter of binding precedent.

1 See eg *Troc Sales Ltd v Kirkcaldy District Licensing Board* 1982 SLT (Sh Ct) 77, not following *Muir v Chief Constable of Edinburgh* 1961 SLT (Sh Ct) 41, 77 Sh Ct Rep 30.
2 *Spencer v Spencer* 1983 SLT (Sh Ct) 87.
3 *Milne v Milne* 1964 SLT (Sh Ct) 28.

4 See *Lamberton v Lamberton* 1984 SLT (Sh Ct) 22.
5 In *Hill v McMillan* 1980 SLT (Sh Ct) 3, a sheriff principal distinguished his own views expressed
   in a case which he decided as a sheriff-substitute.
6 *City Bakeries Ltd v S and S Snack Bars and Restaurants Ltd* 1979 SLT (Sh Ct) 28.
7 *New Day Furnishing Stores Ltd v Curran* 1974 SLT (Sh Ct) 20.

300. Sheriff court decisions binding on sheriff. Decisions of a sheriff principal are binding on all sheriffs within the sheriffdom concerned. Although he
no longer maintains this view, Smith has stated that decisions of a sheriff
principal are normally followed by sheriffs in his sheriffdom while the sheriff
principal holds office[1], but this puts the matter too narrowly. The binding
nature of decisions of a sheriff principal within the sheriffdom is more absolute
than Smith suggested, and there is no reason to believe that decisions have less
force after a sheriff principal has demitted office. In the *City Bakeries* case[2] a
sheriff in Glasgow accepted as binding authority a decision by an earlier
Glasgow sheriff principal[3]. The binding nature of a sheriff principal's decision is
established in a number of cases. In *Edwards v Lothian Regional Council*[4] a sheriff
in Lothian and Borders said:

> 'My view of the matter is supported by the judgment of Sheriff Principal F W F
> O'Brien QC in *Kilbarthan Primary School Parents Association v Strathclyde Regional
> Council* (1976, unreported). Sheriff Principal O'Brien was not when he decided the
> said case sitting as sheriff principal of this sheriffdom so that his decision would
> perhaps not technically be binding on me'.

In *Lothian Regional Council v T*[5] a sheriff accepted as binding authority the
decision of his sheriff principal in *Lothian Regional Council v H*[6], but distinguished that case as being one decided on its own facts in an area of law where
regard to individual circumstances of each case was of importance.

    However, the extent of the binding quality of a decision of a sheriff principal
is limited to his own sheriffdom. Sheriffs will treat decisions of sheriffs principal
from other sheriffdoms as persuasive but not as binding, and where such a
decision is thought to be wrong it will not be followed[7].

    Decisions by a sheriff are not binding authority on any other sheriff, whether
or not in the same sheriffdom. The reports contain many examples of sheriffs
not following decisions of other sheriffs[8]. An illustration of the confusion which
can result from sheriffs departing from decisions of other sheriffs is in the area of
ranking following on from the diligence of inhibition. In the *McGowan* case[9] a
sheriff refused to follow the *Allan* case[10]. The *McGowan* case was followed and
the *Allan* case was not followed in the *Ferguson* case[11]; but in the *Abbey National*
case[12] the sheriff followed the *Allan* case and thought the decision in the
McGowan case wrong.

    A sheriff is not bound by his own previous decisions. In *Smillie v Hamilton
Burgh Licensing Court*[13], there was cited to the sheriff one of his own previous
decisions[14]. The sheriff stated that he would not rely on his own *ratio decidendi* in
the previous case but on the various authorities cited to him in the case before
him.

    A sheriff principal can overrule a decision of a sheriff only of his own
sheriffdom[15].

1 T B Smith *The Doctrines of Judicial Precedent in Scots Law* (1952) p 19. He would not now assert this
   view.
2 *City Bakeries Ltd v S and S Snack Bars and Restaurants Ltd* 1979 SLT (Sh Ct) 28.
3 *New Day Furnishing Stores Ltd v Curran* 1974 SLT (Sh Ct) 20. The same point is illustrated by
   Allison's (Electrical) Ltd v McCormick 1982 SLT (Sh Ct) 93, following *Cantors Ltd v Hardie* 1974
   SLT (Sh Ct) 26.
4 *Edwards v Lothian Regional Council* 1980 SLT (Sh Ct) 107 at 110.

5 *Lothian Regional Council v T* 1984 SLT (Sh Ct) 74.
6 *Lothian Regional Council v H* 1982 SLT (Sh Ct) 65.
7 See eg *North West Securities Ltd v Barrhead Coachbuilders* 1975 SLT (Sh Ct) 34 (not following *FC Finance Ltd v Langtry Investment Co Ltd* 1973 SLT (Sh Ct) 11); *Astor Dance Club v Chief Constable of Strathclyde* 1977 SLT (Sh Ct) 43 (not following *Free Gardeners (East of Scotland) Social Club v Chief Constable of Edinburgh* 1967 SLT (Sh Ct) 80). In the *Astor Dance Club* case the sheriff said (at 40) 'I considered that although the decision in the *Free Gardeners* case was persuasive, it was not an authority binding upon me'. See also *Lothian Regional Council v B* 1984 SLT (Sh Ct) 83 (not following *Central Regional Council v Mailley* 1977 SLT (Sh Ct) 36).
8 See eg *Merchants Facilities (Glasgow) Ltd v Keenan* 1967 SLT (Sh Ct) 65 (not following *United Dominions Trust (Commercial) Ltd v Hayes* 1966 SLT (Sh Ct) 101); *Watt v Grampian Regional Council* 1980 SLT (Sh Ct) 80 (not following *Hartley v Scottish Omnibuses Ltd* 1978 SLT (Sh Ct) 35); *Luke v Little* 1980 SLT (Sh Ct) 138 (not following *Hamilton v Chief Constable of Strathclyde* 1978 SLT (Sh Ct) 69); *Aberdeen District Council v Christie* 1983 SLT (Sh Ct) 57 (not following *Edinburgh District Council v Parnell* 1980 SLT (Sh Ct) 11); *Hardie v Hardie* 1984 SLT (Sh Ct) 49 (not following *Torbet v Morrison* (1902) 18 Sh Ct Rep 183, and *Shanks v Shanks* (1910) 27 Sh Ct Rep 57); *Lothian Regional Council v B* 1984 SLT (Sh Ct) 83 (not following *Strathclyde Regional Council v D* 1981 SLT (Sh Ct) 34).
9 *McGowan v A Middlemas & Sons Ltd* 1977 SLT (Sh Ct) 41.
10 *George M Allan Ltd v Waugh's Trustees* 1966 SLT (Sh Ct) 17.
11 *Ferguson and Forster v Dalbeattie Finance Co* 1981 SLT (Sh Ct) 53, which was decided prior to the *Abbey National* case cited in note 12 below.
12 *Abbey National Building Society v Shaik Aziz* 1981 SLT (Sh Ct) 29.
13 *Smillie v Hamilton Burgh Licensing Court* 1975 SLT (Sh Ct) 45.
14 *Russo v Hamilton Licensing Court* 1971 SLT (Sh Ct) 63. See also *British Relay Ltd v Keay* 1976 SLT (Sh Ct) 23.
15 *Love v Montgomerie and Logan* 1982 SLT (Sh Ct) 60.

301. The Sheriff of Chancery. The Sheriff of Chancery is seemingly not bound by previous decisions of the sheriff. In *Robertson*[1] the Sheriff of Chancery stated his agreement with the decision in *McBryde*[2], in which the earlier decision of *Waterston*[3] was not followed.

1 *Robertson* 1980 SLT (Sh Ct)73.
2 *McBride* 1975 SLT (Sh Ct) 25.
3 *Waterson* 1947 SLT (Sh Ct) 73, 64 Sh Ct Rep 34.

(f) Precedent and the Criminal Courts

(A) DECISIONS OF THE HOUSE OF LORDS AND OF ENGLISH COURTS

302. Introduction. As a preliminary to examining the operation of precedent in the two main criminal courts in Scotland, the High Court of Justiciary and the sheriff court[1], it is desirable to consider the effect of decisions of the House of Lords and of the English criminal courts on the criminal courts in Scotland. A significant difference between the structures of the hierarchy of the Scottish civil and criminal courts is that by decision of the House itself and by statute no appeal lies to the House of Lords from the criminal courts[2]. However, decisions of the House of Lords are not without persuasive authority in the criminal courts and will be treated with appropriate respect in matters of statutory construction and general law. In *Sillars v Smith*[3] a defence was raised to a charge of vandalism under the Criminal Justice (Scotland) Act 1980[4] to the effect that that Act had no constitutional force in Scotland. The High Court of Justiciary rejected this ground of appeal by stating that the issue whether a Scottish court could challenge the *vires* of an Act of Parliament which had gone through the whole parliamentary process, had received the royal assent and had been brought into force had been 'definitely answered by two Scottish cases'[5].

1 The lowest level of criminal courts in Scotland is the district court. Although in terms of bare statistics the district court handles a significant number of cases, virtually nothing is known about the operation of precedent in that court. Cases from the district court are rarely reported. G H Gordon *Criminal Law of Scotland* (2nd edn, 1978) cites only one case from a court below the level of the sheriff court, *Stevenson v Rankin* (June 1962), an unreported decision of Oban Police Court.

2 *MacKintosh v HM Advocate* (1876) 3 R (HL) 34, 2 App Cas 41; Criminal Procedure (Scotland) Act 1975 (c 21), ss 262, 281. See the discussion in *Criminal Appeals in Scotland* (Cmnd 7005 (1977)) p 79. The judicial determination was not based on such certain grounds as is often supposed.

3 *Sillars v Smith* 1982 SCCR 367, 1982 SLT 539. For criticism of the substantive decision in this case, see A C Evans 'Parliamentary Sovereignty and the Scottish Courts' (1983) 28 JLSS 168.

4 Criminal Justice (Scotland) Act 1980 (c 62), s 78.

5 Ie *Edinburgh and Dalkeith Rly Co v Wauchope* (1842) 1 Bell App 252, 8 Cl & Fin 710, HL (on appeal from the Court of Session); and *MacCormick v Lord Advocate* 1953 SC 396, 1953 SLT 255. The dicta quoted from the latter case did not in fact concern the *vires* of an Act of Parliament.

303. Matters of constitutional or civil law. Although the *jurisdiction* of criminal courts in Scotland is now restricted to matters of criminal law, this is not an invariable rule[1]. In the law of theft, as Sheriff Gordon observes, 'whether or not A is the owner of a thing at the relevant time falls to be decided by the civil law of property'[2]. However, the civil law has sought to restrict the scope of the *vitium reale* resulting from theft, while recognising that theft may be given a wider consideration in the criminal law than forcible or clandestine appropriation of the property of another[3]. Thus the meaning of 'property' and 'theft' are somewhat confused in Scots law, and this would not necessarily be resolved by a decision of the Court of Session being approved on appeal by the House of Lords and observations being made on the criminal aspects of the law. The criminal courts do have a duty to apply and take judicial notice of the law of Scotland generally. Accordingly Scottish criminal courts may have to decide a case chiefly on the basis of a principle of constitutional law (as in *Sillars v Smith*[4]) or of civil law. For example, a statute may impose liability without expressly stating whether that liability is civil or criminal or both. If an action in delict were raised under that statute and a decision on liability was reached by the House of Lords, it is probable that the decision of the House on the question of the type of liability imposed would be regarded as binding on the criminal courts if a prosecution under the same statute were later brought[5].

Although at the present time it is unusual for criminal courts to decide matters of constitutional or civil law, it is submitted that where any such matter does arise in a criminal case the High Court of Justiciary and the sheriff court would feel bound to apply relevant decisions of the House of Lords in a Scottish appeal unless there was a distinction between the civil and criminal effects of the issue determined. The lack of appellate jurisdiction from the High Court of Justiciary to the House of Lords does not necessarily of itself preclude House of Lords decisions from being strictly binding on the Scottish criminal courts, for, as noted, appellate jurisdiction is not the sole rationale for the Scottish practice of binding precedent. Nevertheless the authority which the High Court of Justiciary would accord to decisions of the Court of Session on a matter of private law is linked to the weight to be accorded to House of Lords precedents in these matters. Probably the High Court would not regard itself as absolutely bound in a criminal case by decisions of the Inner House on a matter of public or civil law. However, criminal courts will follow appropriate precedents of the civil courts of higher or equal standing unless strong grounds exist for not doing so. On such questions as police powers of arrest, some of the leading cases are decisions of the Inner House[6]. It would be highly undesirable for the development of Scots law if Inner House or Full Bench decisions of the Court of Session were to be disregarded by the criminal courts as being erroneous statements of public (other than criminal) or private law.

This issue may gain added relevance by the terms of the Civil Jurisdiction and Judgments Act 1982 (c 27). It has been argued that under that Act the criminal courts in Scotland have, in certain circumstances, jurisdiction in actions of reparation[7]. Although this view has been challenged[8], if it is correct (and this may require a decision of the House of Lords), then there will be need for a clear statement of the binding effect on the criminal courts of decisions of the civil courts in matters of reparation.

1 There was overlapping jurisdiction of the High Court and the Court of Session in forgery (Hume *Commentaries* I, 162–168), and appellate civil jurisdiction was conferred on circuits of the High Court by several statutes, now repealed, from the Heritable Jurisdictions (Scotland) Act 1746 (c 43) to the Small Debt (Scotland) Act 1837 (c 41) (repealed by the Sheriff Courts (Scotland) Act 1971 (c 58), ss 35(2), 46(2), Sch 2, Pt II). See also the question of compensation orders under the Criminal Justice (Scotland) Act 1980 (c 62).
2 G H Gordon *Criminal Law of Scotland* (2nd edn, 1978) p 484.
3 *Gordon*, pp 494–496; *Brown v Marr* (1880) 8 R 427; *Protection of the Bona Fide Onerous Acquirer of Another's Property* (Sc Law Com Consultative Memorandum no. 27 (1976)) pp 42–49, 51–54; W A Wilson 'Knowing the Law and Other Things' 1982 JR 259 at 268, 269.
4 *Sillars v Smith* 1982 SCCR 367, 1982 SLT 539.
5 Cf *Nimmo v Alexander Cowan & Sons Ltd* 1967 SC (HL) 79, 1967 SLT 277, where Lord Pearson notes that where statute imposes civil and criminal liability, although the standard of proof may differ in criminal and civil proceedings the incidence of the burden of proof is the same.
6 See eg *Peggie v Clark* (1868) 7 M 89, 41 SJ 52.
7 R Black *Civil Jurisdiction: the New Rules* (1983) pp 24, 25; J H C Morris *The Conflict of Laws* (3rd edn, 1984) p 83; T C Hartley *Civil Jurisdiction and Judgments* (1984) pp 52, 53.
8 See G Maher 'Concurrent Criminal and Civil Jurisdiction' (1984) 29 JLSS 492; A E Anton *Civil Jurisdiction in Scotland* (1984) pp 79, 80, 184.

304. English decisions on criminal law. Scottish criminal courts are not bound by decisions of any English court on criminal matters, even by decisions of the House of Lords (and *a fortiori* of the Criminal Division of the Court of Appeal), even if the English decisions related to a statute applicable throughout the United Kingdom. Especially on matters of statutory interpretation they will be considered with respect.

In *Dalgleish v Glasgow Corporation*[1] Lord Justice-Clerk Wheatley noted that the interpretation by the House of Lords of a United Kingdom statute pronounced in an English appeal would in general be accepted by the Scottish court, but added:

'I note in parenthesis that this does not apply to appeals in criminal cases in Scotland, where the ultimate court of appeal is the High Court of Justiciary or the Court of Criminal Appeal, and decisions of the House of Lords in criminal cases in England are not binding on these Scottish courts even in relation to the interpretation of United Kingdom statutes applicable equally in both countries'.

For example, in *Ritchie v Pirie*[2] the High Court of Justiciary preferred to apply two earlier Scottish cases rather than follow the House of Lords decision of *Rowlands v Hamilton*[3] on the construction of a United Kingdom Act[4]. In such cases the Scottish courts may note the unfortunate effect if different interpretations are given to the same United Kingdom statute by Scottish and English courts, but take the view that the authority of English cases depends solely on their intrinsic correctness in the question of construction. The Scottish interpretation of the statute providing exceptions to the rule forbidding attack on the character of the accused[5] has been criticised by the House of Lords in an English appeal[6], but it is clear that the Scottish courts continue to adhere to the approach set out in *O'Hara v HM Advocate*[7].

Where an English appeal to the House of Lords on a matter of criminal law relates to a matter other than the construction of a United Kingdom statute, the authority of the House of Lords decision is at most highly persuasive. In *Brennan v HM Advocate*[8] a Full Bench of the High Court of Justiciary overruled two earlier decisions of the High Court which had followed the English appeal of *Director of Public Prosecutions v Beard*[9] on the topic of the effect of intoxication on criminal responsibility. In the *Brennan* case the court pointed out that the rule in *Beard* was based on different principles from that of the Scottish rule, and that the *Beard* case had very little authority in the Scots law on this topic.

The principle that English cases possess persuasive authority only in the Scottish criminal courts is further illustrated by cases in which decisions of the English Court of Appeal have been disregarded in Scotland. In *Kelly v MacKinnon*[10] the High Court of Justiciary refused to follow the Court of Appeal decision in *R v Freeman*[11] on the construction of a United Kingdom Act[12] although the English court, in reaching its decision, had attempted to follow what it thought to be the approach of the Scottish courts as stated in the sheriff court case of *Muir v Cassidy*[13]. In *Keane v Gallacher*[14] the High Court refused to follow a Court of Appeal decision[15] on the issue of the quantity of drugs required to constitute the offence of unlawful possession[16] of drugs. In a later English case[17] the House of Lords preferred the approach of the Scottish Court to that of the Court of Appeal.

In *Thomson v HM Advocate*[18] the High Court disregarded several English cases on the defence of duress[19] on the ground that they were inconsistent with statements in Hume's *Commentaries* on the limits of the defence of coercion in Scots law[20]. In *Ferguson v HM Advocate*[21] the High Court refused to follow the Court of Criminal Appeal decision in *R v Gibbon*[22] on the question of competency of abandoning an appeal where no prior notice had been given, although the English rule of court considered in *Gibbon* was in the same terms as the provisions of the Scottish statute.

1 *Dalgleish v Glasgow Corpn* 1976 SC 32 at 52, 1976 SLT 157 at 159.
2 *Ritchie v Pirie* 1972 JC 7, 1972 SLT 2, especially at 14 and at 7, 8.
3 *Rowlands v Hamilton* [1971] 1 All ER 1089, [1971] 1 WLR 647, HL.
4 Ie the Road Safety Act 1967 (c 30), s 1(1) (repealed).
5 Criminal Procedure (Scotland) Act 1975 (c 21), ss 141(1)(f)(ii), 346(1)(f)(ii), re-enacting the Criminal Evidence Act 1898 (c 36), s 1(f)(ii).
6 *R v Selvey* [1970] AC 304 at 338, [1968] 2 All ER 497 at 507, HL.
7 *O'Hara v HM Advocate* 1948 JC 90, 1948 SLT 372. For a general discussion, see R L C Hunter 'Imputations on the Character of Prosecution Witnesses' 1968 JR 238. In *Templeton v McLeod* 1985 SCCR 357, 1986 SLT 149, a five-judge court purported to follow *O'Hara v HM Advocate* although the effect of its decision is to assimilate Scots and English law.
8 *Brennan v HM Advocate* 1977 JC 38, 1977 SLT 151.
9 *Director of Public Prosecutions v Beard* [1920] AC 479, HL.
10 *Kelly v MacKinnon* 1982 SC 94, 1983 SLT 413.
11 *R v Freeman* [1970] 2 All ER 413, [1970] 1 WLR 788, CA.
12 Ie the Firearms Act 1968 (c 27), s 57(1).
13 *Muir v Cassidy* 1953 SLT (Sh Ct) 4.
14 *Keane v Gallacher* 1980 JC 77, 1980 SLT 144.
15 *R v Carver* [1978] QB 472, [1978] 3 All ER 60, CA.
16 Ie under the Misuse of Drugs Act 1971 (c 38), s 5.
17 *R v Boyesen* [1982] AC 768, [1982] 2 All ER 161, HL.
18 *Thomson v HM Advocate* 1983 SCCR 368, 1983 SLT 682.
19 These included *R v Hudson* [1971] 2 QB 202, [1971] 2 All ER 244, CA.
20 Hume *Commentaries* I, 53.
21 *Ferguson v HM Advocate* 1980 JC 27, 1980 SLT 21.
22 *R v Gibbon* (1946) 31 Cr App Rep 143, CCA.

(B) PRECEDENT AND THE HIGH COURT OF JUSTICIARY

305. Introduction. Some writers have suggested that one distinguishing feature about precedent in criminal courts is that, contrasted with civil litigation, much more is at stake in criminal matters, given the essentially stigmatic nature of criminal conviction and the possible penalties in loss of liberty and property[1]. This feature has, however, no single clear implication, for it supports the importance of both finality and certainty in the law and of justice in the individual case. The balance of these factors calls for a system of precedent which is on the whole strict but which allows for flexibility on issues of importance. It is thought that doctrines of precedent in the High Court of Justiciary provide a means of ensuring this balance.

  1 See eg T B Smith *The Doctrines of Judicial Precedent in Scots Law* (1952) pp 46, 47, 105; R Cross *Precedent in English Law* (3rd edn, 1977) pp 116–118.

306. The collegiate nature of the High Court of Justiciary. As is the case with the Court of Session, the key to understanding precedent in the High Court of Justiciary lies in the essentially collegiate nature of the court. The High Court of Justiciary was explicitly founded as a collegiate court to consist of the Lord Justice-General, the Lord Justice-Clerk and a specified number of Lords Commissioners of Justiciary[1]. Subsequent legislation was concerned with requisite quora for the court to hear cases, but the essentially collegiate nature of the court remains the same today.

  1 See the Courts Act 1672 (c 40).

307. Effect of collegiate nature on authority. As with the question of precedent in the Court of Session, the authority of a decision of the High Court of Justiciary reflects the extent to which a decision was given by the court in its collegiate capacity. This feature is seen in the practice of convening a larger court than the normal quorum of three when a point of importance or difficulty falls to be decided[1]. In *Kirkwood v HM Advocate*[2] the Whole Court with the exception of two of their Lordships considered and accepted an argument about the limits of the plea of diminished responsibility. In *Thom v HM Advocate*[3] a Full Bench of five judges decided a case concerning the competency of the Crown serving an indictment on an accused after it had given him notice of no further proceedings in respect of the charge.

  1 See also the Criminal Procedure (Scotland) Act 1975 (c 21), s 113(4).
  2 *Kirkwood v HM Advocate* 1939 JC 36, 1939 SLT 209.
  3 *Thom v HM Advocate* 1976 JC 48, 1976 SLT 232.

308. Decisions of court of greater collegiate authority. The practice has emerged that decisions of the High Court of Justiciary of greater collegiate authority than the court in its present constitution are treated as binding on the court. Furthermore, as T B Smith notes[1], there has also grown up the practice that a quorum of the court regards itself as bound by a previous decision of a court of equal number. A decision can be overruled or not followed (if otherwise in point) only by the court sitting with a larger quorum than that of the earlier decision. The only exceptions to the rule that decisions of equal levels of collegiate authority are binding are at the levels of the Whole Court (although this is not clear) and of the single judge.

As concerns the Whole Court, the chief source of discussion is the case of *Sugden v HM Advocate*[2], but it must be admitted that this case does not provide a clear answer to the question of the extent to which a Whole Court is bound by previous decisions of a Whole Court. The issue directly before the court in the *Sugden* case was whether vicennial prescription of crime formed part of the law of Scotland. This in turn involved consideration of the question whether *HM Advocate v Macgregor*[3] was authority for the proposition that vicennial prescription was part of Scottish criminal law and what was the binding effect of the *Macgregor* case on the present court. The *Macgregor* case had been decided in 1773 by all six judges of the High Court (less the Lord Justice-General, an office not then held by a legally qualified person) and was referred to in the *Sugden* case as a decision of the Whole Court[4]. As with the *Macgregor* case, the *Sugden* case was itself heard by the Whole Court except the Lord Justice-General (although no indication is given in the reports of the reason for his absence). Unfortunately, there was no unanimity among their Lordships in the *Sugden* case on any of the issues facing the court.

Seven of their Lordships[5] held that the *Macgregor* case was not authority for vicennial prescription of crime, a doctrine which they also stated had no other basis in Scots law, but three of this group[6] stated that the court could in any case now overrule the *Macgregor* case. Four judges[7] held that vicennial prescription of crime was part of Scots law, that the *Macgregor* case was authority for that view and that that case could not now be departed from. Lord Moncrieff accepted that the *Macgregor* case was authority for vicennial prescription of crime and could not be overruled but held that the doctrine did not apply to the facts of the instant case.

In these circumstances it is difficult to say whether the *Sugden* case is authority for the view that a Whole Court can review a decision of an earlier Whole Court. There was a plurality of five[8] for the view that the *Macgregor* case could not be reviewed, whereas only three judges[9] held that it could be reversed. But four of the majority judges did not give any opinion on this issue.

Of the judges who favoured the view that the *Macgregor* case could be overruled, the most direct statements were made by Lord Murray and Lord Anderson. Lord Murray commented:

> 'Even if *Macgregor's* case, however, be regarded as having decided the question, I am of opinion, contrary to the argument submitted for the appellant, that it is open to this Court, if it thinks fit, to overrule it. No authority was referred to in support of the view that the traditional rule which, theoretically at least, prevails in the House of Lords applies in Scotland, so as to prevent the High Court of Justiciary from reconsidering a former judgment'[10].

Lord Anderson argued as follows:

> 'I am clearly of opinion that we have power to reverse. There might have been difficulty (although I do not think it would have been insurmountable) if the whole 'Fifteen' had been Commissioners of Justiciary and parties to the decision. But a Court of twelve judges is now considering the judgment of a Court of six, and I have always understood that, by our settled practice, a larger Court could review the decision of a Court which was fewer in number. Moreover, any doubt as to our competency to review the decision in *Macgregor* would seem to be removed by the provisions of the Criminal Appeal (Scotland) Act 1926, which empower the High Court of Justiciary, sitting as a Court of Criminal Appeal, to determine any question of law raised by a prisoner's appeal[11]. The determination of the question of law may involve, as it does in the present case, the validity of a standing decision'[12].

As against this the joint opinion of Lord Mackay, Lord Wark and Lord Carmont stated:

'The decision in the case of *Macgregor* was a decision of the Whole Court. In our opinion that decision is binding upon this Court, and, even if it were not, we should be of opinion that the rule of law there recognised ought not to be disturbed... We respectfully differ from the view that this Court, sitting in virtue of the provisions of the Criminal Appeal (Scotland) Act 1926, is vested with wider powers to interpret or alter the law than ordinarily reside in the High Court of Justiciary. The Court of Appeal set up by the 1926 Act is the Justiciary Court. If the decision in the case of *Macgregor* would otherwise have been binding upon the High Court in the exercise of its original jurisdiction, we are of opinion that it is equally binding upon the High Court sitting in the exercise of the appellate jurisdiction conferred by the statute'[13].

It is submitted that on the issue of the power of the High Court as a court of appeal under statutory jurisdiction, this latter view is to be preferred to that of Lord Anderson.

1 T B Smith *The Doctrines of Judicial Precedent in Scots Law* (1952) p 42.
2 *Sugden v HM Advocate* 1934 JC 103, 1934 SLT 465.
3 *HM Advocate v Macgregor* (1773) Mor 11146.
4 *Sugden v HM Advocate* 1934 JC 103 at 116, 1934 SLT 465 at 472, 473, per Lord Hunter, at 133, 135 and at 482, 483 per Lord Mackay, Lord Wark and Lord Carmont; cf at 129 and at 480 per Lord Moncrieff.
5 Ie Lord Justice-Clerk Aitchison, Lord Anderson, Lord Blackburn, Lord Morison, Lord Murray, Lord Fleming and Lord Pitman.
6 Ie Lord Anderson, Lord Morison and Lord Murray.
7 Ie Lord Hunter, Lord Mackay, Lord Wark and Lord Carmont.
8 Ie Lord Moncrieff, Lord Hunter, Lord Mackay, Lord Wark and Lord Carmont.
9 Ie Lord Anderson, Lord Morison and Lord Murray.
10 *Sugden v HM Advocate* 1934 JC 103 at 127, 128, 1934 SLT 465 at 479.
11 See the Criminal Appeal (Scotland) Act 1926 (c 15), s 2 (repealed, and replaced by the Criminal Procedure (Scotland) Act 1975 (c 21), s 254).
12 *Sugden v HM Advocate* 1934 JC 103 at 124, 1934 SLT 465 at 477.
13 1934 JC 103 at 135, 136, 1934 SLT 465 at 484.

309. Whether Whole Court binds Whole Court. The issue still remains whether a Whole Court decision can be overruled by a later and larger Whole Court. To this question, there is as yet no definite answer, and the *Sugden* case[1] only supplies part of the argument, not the solution. However, in considering this issue two points seem of special relevance.

The first point is an issue of principle, namely whether the High Court of Justiciary should have the power to reverse its own decisions. During argument in the *Sugden* case, counsel for the appellant, when asked to provide authority for the view that the *Macgregor* case[2] could not be reversed, is reported to have replied with little confidence[3]: 'I have no authority except that the House of Lords does not review its own decisions, and this is the supreme Court of Scotland'. One advantage in the House of Lords not being bound by its own decisions would seem to be that it now permits that flexibility available at the highest level of the Scottish civil courts which allows for proper regard to be given to prior decisions at lower levels[4]. Moreover, the need to balance certainty and flexibility is a particularly acute one in the field of criminal justice, and the best solution would appear to be that the High Court sitting as a Whole Court should, as the supreme criminal court, be able to review its own decisions, so as to permit adherence to decided cases at the lower levels of the court.

The second point is that this whole issue may have little or no practical importance. There cannot be many decisions in the books laid down by the Whole Court and possibly none of the doctrines and principles which might call for reconsideration in the future is based on a Whole Court decision. It is in any event exceedingly unlikely that a Whole Court would ever be convened in the future (unless solely to decide on the power to review a Whole Court decision), so that it is also unlikely that there will be further Whole Court decisions which might give rise to later doubts. Since it is clear that a larger Full Bench can overrule a decision of a smaller Full Bench, the High Court already possesses the means of ensuring flexibility without upsetting settled law and there may be no need for any doctrine on the powers of the Whole Court to review previous Whole Court decisions.

A further consideration was not fully explored in the *Sugden* case because the judges who considered themselves bound by the *Macgregor* case also approved of the decision itself. It may be thought that the Whole Court should not feel bound to accept a decision as strictly binding if it had been promulgated in an era — as was the *Macgregor* case — when no single decision was regarded as absolutely binding by the court which formulated it[5].

1 *Sugden v HM Advocate* 1934 JC 103, 1934 SLT 465: see para 308 above.
2 *HM Advocate v Macgregor* (1773) Mor 11146: see para 308 above.
3 See J C Gardner *Judicial Precedent in Scots Law* (1936) p 49.
4 See para 257.
5 See para 256.

310. Fuller Bench may overrule smaller Fuller Bench. The proposition that a larger Full Bench of the High Court of Justiciary can overrule a prior decision of a smaller Full Bench is illustrated by a good number of cases. In *Smith of Maddiston Ltd v Macnab*[1] a Full Bench of nine judges was convened to decide a matter of construction of road traffic regulations on the meaning of causing or permitting the use of a vehicle not complying with the regulations. An appeal had been made to the High Court from a decision of the sheriff, who felt bound to apply the decision of the High Court in *Hunter v Clark*[2]. Although the court in *Hunter v Clark* consisted of three judges, the Lord Justice-General in that case stated that the issue before the court was analogous to that decided by the seven-judge case of *Mitchell v Morrison*[3] and it was this observation which led to the convening of a court of nine judges in the *Smith v Maddiston* case. In the event, the court decided that *Hunter v Clark* and *Mitchell v Morrison* were clearly distinguishable and overruled *Hunter v Clark* without having to review *Mitchell v Morrison*. In *Brennan v HM Advocate*[4] a Full Bench of seven judges overruled two previous decisions on the issue of the effect of self-induced intoxication on criminal responsibility, *HM Advocate v Campbell*[5] (a decision of Lord Justice-Clerk Scott Dickson sitting as a trial judge) and *Kennedy v HM Advocate*[6] (a decision of five judges). In the *Brennan* case the court held that the *Campbell* case had erroneously applied principles of the English law of murder to this issue and pointed out that in the *Kennedy* case the court had upheld this approach because of concessions made in argument, a factor which necessarily detracts from the authority of any decision as a precedent.

It is also accepted practice that a Full Bench can overrule a decision made by a bench of three judges. In *Macmillan v M'Connell*[7] a seven-judge bench overruled *M'Avoy v Cameron*[8], a decision of three judges who had with reluctance considered themselves bound by a previous three-judge decision. In *Marshall v Clark*[9], a Full Bench of five judges noted that a number of cases of three-judge authority were in conflict with each other and that two of these decisions[10] had been rarely followed and much criticised. Both cases were overruled. In *Hall v Associated Newspapers Ltd*[11] a Full Bench of five judges was convened to consider the correctness of *Stirling v Associated Newspapers Ltd*[12], a decision of three judges on the limits of contempt of court involving reporting by newspapers. In the *Hall* case the court disapproved of some of the reasoning in the *Stirling* case but stated that the decision was sound and correctly represented the law of Scotland. However, the court expressly disapproved of some of the dicta in the judgment in the *Stirling* case as suggesting too extensive a jurisdiction of the court on the issue of contempt by prejudicial publication.

1 *Smith of Maddiston Ltd v Macnab* 1975 JC 48, 1975 SLT 86.
2 *Hunter v Clark* 1956 JC 59, 1956 SLT 188.
3 *Mitchell v Morrison* 1938 JC 64, 1938 SLT 201.
4 *Brennan v HM Advocate* 1977 JC 38, 1977 SLT 151.
5 *HM Advocate v Campbell* 1921 JC 1, 1920 2 SLT 317.
6 *Kennedy v HM Advocate* 1944 JC 171, 1945 SLT 11.
7 *Macmillan v M'Connell* 1917 JC 43, 1917 2 SLT 26.
8 *M'Avoy v Cameron* 1917 JC 1, 1916 2 SLT 169.
9 *Marshall v Clark* 1957 JC 68, 1958 SLT 19.
10 *Allan v Howman* 1918 JC 50, 1918 1 SLT 181, and *Morrison v Ross-Taylor* 1948 JC 74, 1948 SLT 257.
11 *Hall v Associated Newspapers Ltd* 1979 JC 1, 1978 SLT 241.
12 *Stirling v Associated Newspapers Ltd* 1960 JC 5, 1960 SLT 5.

311. Decisions of bench of equal number. The corollary of the practice of convening a larger court to hear matters of importance or to review decisions by a smaller bench is that decisions of a bench of equal number are binding on the High Court of Justiciary. In *O'Neill v Wilson*[1] a Full Bench of five judges sought to distinguish (on possibly questionable grounds) rather than overrule a previous five-judge decision[2]. In *M'Avoy v Cameron*[3] a three-judge bench accepted with reluctance the decision of *Todd v Anderson*[4], and took the view that that case could be reconsidered only by a larger court (which happened shortly afterwards[5]). In *Ritchie v Pirie*[6] a three-judge bench preferred to follow the approach on an issue of statutory interpretation made in the previous decision of *Wood v Brown*[7] rather than follow the House of Lords in an English appeal[8]. Lord Wheatley added that in any case *Wood v Brown*, a decision of three judges, was binding on the court and could be reviewed only by a larger court[9].

1 *O'Neill v Wilson* 1983 SCCR 265, 1983 SLT 573. For critical comments, see the notes by Sheriff Gordon at 1983 SCCR 272–276; and C N Stoddard 'The Immunity Rule' (1983) 28 JLSS 453.
2 *HM Advocate v Dreghorn* (1806) Burnett *Treatise on the Criminal Law of Scotland* p 82, App lxvii.
3 *M'Avoy v Cameron* 1917 JC 1, 1916 2 SLT 169.
4 *Todd v Anderson* 1912 SC (J) 105, 1912 2 SLT 217.
5 *Macmillan v M'Connell* 1917 JC 43, 1917 2 SLT 26. See para 310 above.
6 *Ritchie v Pirie* 1972 JC 7, 1972 SLT 2.
7 *Wood v Brown* 1969 SLT 297.
8 *Rowlands v Hamilton* [1971] 1 All ER 1089, [1971] 1 WLR 647, HL.
9 *Ritchie v Pirie* 1972 JC 7 at 14, 1972 SLT 2 at 7, 8.

312. Decisions of a single judge. Much as a decision by a Lord Ordinary does not bind another in the Court of Session, so also rulings by a single judge do not bind other Lords Commissioners of Justiciary sitting alone. The reasons for this policy are even more apparent in the High Court than the Court of Session. At a criminal trial a judge may not be able to take a matter to avizandum, a circuit court library may be very limited, and there may be no opportunity to consult a colleague. Moreover, especially on circuit, it may be fortuitous what unreported statements of the law by single judges are available to the court. T B Smith[1] and D M Walker[2] cite *HM Advocate v Higgins*[3] for the proposition that rulings by single judges in the High Court do not bind others. Although pronouncements of single judges have undoubtedly developed the criminal law in modern times, the view that they do not constitute binding precedents in the High Court is accepted in modern practice. For example, Lord Walker's views[4] on the admissibility of evidence of statements by the accused were not accepted by his colleagues, nor did Lord Stewart's views on insanity induced by drugs commend themselves to other judges[5].

1 T B Smith *The Doctrines of Judicial Precedent in Scots Law* (1952) p 41.
2 D M Walker *The Scottish Legal System* (5th edn, 1981) p 375.
3 *HM Advocate v Higgins* 1914 SC (J) 1, 1913 2 SLT 258. Lord Johnson declined not only to follow Lord Deas but also other collegiate decisions on the matter, eg *HM Advocate v M'Lean* (1876) 3 Coup 334.
4 *HM Advocate v Christie* 1961, 3 November (unreported). See D B Smith 'A Note on Judicial Examination' 1961 SLT (News) 179; J W R Gray 'Police Interrogation and the Trial within a Trial' 1970 JR 1.
5 *HM Advocate v Aitken* 1975 SLT (Notes) 86.

(C) PRECEDENT AND THE CRIMINAL JURISDICTION OF THE SHERIFF COURT

313. Introduction. As is the case with the sheriff court as a court of civil jurisdiction, very little detailed attention has been paid to the operation of precedent in the criminal side of the sheriff court. This is surprising given the extensive jurisdiction in criminal matters, both solemn and summary, which is possessed by the sheriff court. Moreover, as Sheriff Gordon points out at the beginning of his work on *Criminal Law*: 'It should also be noted that the vast bulk of serious crime is dealt with in Glasgow sheriff court, and that cases there are hardly ever reported unless appealed'[1].

Commentators are agreed on the general workings of precedent in the sheriff court on its criminal side, and the cases illustrate the types of decision which are, and those which are not, treated as binding.

1 G H Gordon *Criminal Law of Scotland* (2nd edn, 1978) p 4, note 6.

314. Collegiate decisions of the High Court of Justiciary. It is clear that decisions of the High Court of Justiciary in a collegiate capacity (that is, with a quorum of three or more judges) are binding on sheriffs in criminal trials. In *Farrell v Stirling*[1] the sheriff accepted as binding authority the controversial High Court decision in *HM Advocate v Cunningham*[2], but sought to distinguish that case on somewhat dubious grounds. In *Herron v Nelson*[3], which concerned the elements constitutive of corroboration, the sheriff followed the decision of the seven-judge Full Bench in *Morton v HM Advocate*[4], despite the fact that to do so was to disregard practice in that sheriff court and was possibly also to act inconsistently with a decision of a Full Bench of five judges in *Gillespie v Macmillan*[5]. The sheriff noted that the *Gillespie* case had not been cited to him but that in that case no doubt had been cast on the decision in the *Morton* case, which accordingly was fully binding in the present case.

In *Tudhope v Lawson*[6] the sheriff refused to follow dicta in two High Court of Justiciary decisions[7] on the question of computation of time relating to the beginning of summary proceedings. The learned sheriff noted that those High Court decisions contained dicta inconsistent with the view which he favoured, but held that the matters before him had not fallen for decision by the High Court in either of the cases. The sheriff also took note of older authorities[8], which he accepted as authoritative support for his decision[9].

1 *Farrell v Stirling* 1975 SLT (Sh Ct) 71.
2 *HM Advocate v Cunningham* 1963 JC 80, 1963 SLT 345. For a recent reversal of a sheriff's refusal to follow this case, see *Carmichael v Boyle* 1985 SCCR 58, 1985 SLT 399.
3 *Herron v Nelson* 1976 SLT (Sh Ct) 42.
4 *Morton v HM Advocate* 1938 JC 50, 1938 SLT 27.
5 *Gillespie v Macmillan* 1957 JC 31, 1957 SLT 283.

6 *Tudhope v Lawson* 1983 SCCR 435.
7 *Beattie v M'Kinnon* 1977 JC 64, and *Smith v Peter Walker & Son (Edinburgh) Ltd* 1978 JC 44.
8 Eg *Frew v Morris* (1897) 24 R (J) 50, 4 SLT 342.
9 For further illustrations of sheriffs holding themselves bound by collegiate decisions of the High
   Court of Justiciary, see *Pirie v Rivard* 1976 SLT (Sh Ct) 59 (following *Coogans v MacDonald* 1954
   JC 98, 1954 SLT 279); *Lockhart v Stokes* 1981 SLT (Sh Ct) 71 (following *Hay v HM Advocate* 1968
   JC 40, 1968 SLT 334); *Smith v Downie* 1982 SLT (Sh Ct) 23 (following *Robertson v Smith* 1980 JC
   1, 1979 SLT (Notes) 51); *MacPhail v Clark* 1982 SCCR 395, 1983 SLT (Sh Ct) 37 (following *Paton
   v HM Advocate* 1936 JC 19, 1936 SLT 298, and *Quinn v Cunningham* 1956 JC 22, 1956 SLT 55);
   and *Tudhope v Stirrup* 1982, 19 April, Glasgow Sheriff Court, Crown Office Circular A40/82
   (following *Scott v Annan* 1981 SCCR 172, 1982 SLT 90).

315. Decisions of trial judges of the High Court of Justiciary. The position concerning the authority to be accorded to decisions of trial judges of the High Court of Justiciary is less clear. Such decisions are not necessarily reported, unless as background to a decision of the High Court considering the case with a fuller quorum. It would seem to be the case that sheriffs are free to disregard decisions of trial judges of the High Court where they view those decisions as wrong. However, they rely on them as persuasive authority to be treated with respect. In *Tudhope v Grubb*[1] the sheriff was faced with the unusual defence of necessity and accepted a statement on the defence of coercion by Lord Keith[2]. On the other hand, in *HM Advocate v Swift*[3] the sheriff was faced with the situation where the accused had made statements to the police, which had been tape-recorded. At the trial the sheriff held that the tape was inadmissible and the question arose whether it was competent for the Crown to lead oral evidence from the police officers who had taken the statements. The sheriff held the evidence to be admissible but noted:

> 'There was some discussion to the effect that Lord Jauncey may have reached a different conclusion on this point in a High Court case in Dundee[4]; if that is so, I can only apologise but I have been unable in the time available to me to trace any report of such a decision'[5].

1 *Tudhope v Grubb* 1983 SCCR 350.
2 *HM Advocate v Docherty* 1976, June, Glasgow High Court (unreported).
3 *HM Advocate v Swift* 1983 SCCR 204.
4 *HM Advocate v McFadden* (1980) 1983 SCCR 208n.
5 *HM Advocate v Swift* 1983 SCCR 204 at 206. At 209 Sheriff Gordon notes: 'As will be seen, Lord
   Jauncey's view of the law differs from that of Sheriff Younger: a binding authority is still
   awaited'.

316. Decisions of other sheriffs. Sheriffs are not bound by decisions of single judges of the High Court. What is even clearer is that sheriffs sitting in their criminal jurisdiction are not bound by decisions of the sheriff court. It should be noted, however, that the reports contain many illustrations of sheriffs following previous decisions of the sheriff court[1], although this is not done as a matter of binding precedent. In *Tudhope v Stirrup*[2] the sheriff followed *Pirie v Rivard*[3] and also *Scott v Annan*[4], in which the High Court of Justiciary approved the decision in the *Pirie* case. In the later sheriff court case it was noted that only the High Court decision was authoritative.

There are also many illustrations of sheriffs expressly refusing to follow decisions of other sheriffs in criminal cases. In *Farrell v Stirling*[5] the sheriff refused to follow a sheriff's decision[6] on the onus of proof of the defence of automatism and took the view that that decision was inconsistent with the approach of the High Court in the important case of *Lambie v HM Advocate*[7]. In *Tudhope v Laws*[8] on a question of construction relating to the powers of health and safety inspectors[9], the sheriff noted a prior sheriff court case[10] and stated:

'In that case, which bore marked similarities to the present, Sheriff Scott Robinson reached the opposite conclusion to mine. The case is not distinguishable, and I must therefore record my disagreement with the view taken by the learned sheriff in that case'[11].

1 See eg *McLeod v Morton* 1982 SLT (Sh Ct) 102 (applying *MacLean v Riddell* 1960 SLT (Sh Ct) 35, 76 Sh Ct Rep 73); *Smith v Holt* 1983 SCCR 175 (following *MacNeill v Calligan* 1973 SLT (Sh Ct) 54); *Tudhope v Morrison* 1983 SCCR 262 (agreeing with but distinguishing *MacNeill v Robertson* 1982 SCCR 468).
2 *Tudhope v Stirrup* 1982 Crown Office Circular A40/82.
3 *Pirie v Rivard* 1976 SLT (Sh Ct) 59.
4 *Scott v Annan* 1981 SCCR 172, 1982 SLT 90.
5 *Farrell v Stirling* 1975 SLT (Sh Ct) 71.
6 *Stevenson v Beatson* 1965 SLT (Sh Ct) 11.
7 *Lambie v HM Advocate* 1973 JC 53, 1973 SLT 219.
8 *Tudhope v Laws* 1982 SLT (Sh Ct) 85.
9 Health and Safety at Work etc Act 1974 (c 37), s 20.
10 *Skinner v John G McGregor (Contractors) Ltd* 1977 SLT (Sh Ct) 83.
11 *Tudhope v Laws* 1982 SLT (Sh Ct) 85 at 88. For further illustrations of sheriffs not following prior sheriff court decisions, see *Smith v Downie* 1982 SLT (Sh Ct) 23 (not following dicta in *Tudhope v Barlow* 1981 SLT (Sh Ct) 94); and *Tudhope v Lawson* 1983 SCCR 435 (not following *S* 1979 SLT (Sh Ct) 37).

317. Decisions of higher civil courts. *Tudhope v Lawson*[1] illustrates how the sheriff court sitting in its capacity as a criminal court is bound by relevant decisions of the higher civil courts, unless they conflict with decisions of the High Court. That case concerned the computation of time for the bringing of prosecutions under the Trade Descriptions Act 1968 (c 29). The sheriff noted but did not follow two High Court cases[2], taking the view that the High Court in those cases was considering different issues from that in the instant case. The sheriff held himself bound by certain older authorities, namely *Ashley v Rothesay Magistrates*[3], a decision of the First Division of the Court of Session, and *Frew v Morris*[4], in which the High Court of Justiciary followed the *Ashley* decision.

1 *Tudhope v Lawson* 1983 SCCR 435.
2 Ie *Beattie v M'Kinnon* 1977 JC 64, and *Smith v Peter Walker & Son (Edinburgh) Ltd* 1978 JC 44.
3 *Ashley v Rothesay Magistrates* (1873) 11 M 708, 45 SJ 440.
4 *Frew v Morris* (1897) 24 R (J) 50, 4 SLT 342.

318. Decisions of English criminal courts. Decisions of the English criminal courts are not binding on sheriffs, even where the English decisions involve the interpretation of United Kingdom statutes. In *Copeland v Sweeney*[1], which concerned the construction of 'special reasons' against disqualification for drink-drive offences, the sheriff refused to follow two English decisions[2]. On an issue of the meaning of 'driving', the sheriff in *Lockhart v Smith*[3] followed the approach of the High Court in *Ames v MacLeod*[4] in preference to a decision of a five-judge bench of the English Court of Appeal[5]. However, sheriffs are prepared to follow English authority where this has intrinsic value (that is, rather than as a matter of binding precedent). In *Tudhope v Barlow*[6] the sheriff, in attempting to make sense of a charge of 'shameless indecency', looked at several decisions of the Court of Appeal and of the House of Lords on the English law of obscene publications.

1 *Copeland v Sweeney* 1977 SLT (Sh Ct) 28. See also *Skinner v Ayton* 1977 SLT (Sh Ct) 48, which also concerned 'special reasons', and in which the sheriff noted a number of inconsistent English decisions and preferred the approach in *Pugsley v Hunter* [1973] 2 All ER 10, [1973] 1 WLR 578, DC.

2 *R v Baines* (1970) 54 Cr App Rep 481, CA; *Taylor v Rajan* [1974] QB 424, [1974] 1 All ER 1087, DC.
3 *Lockhart v Smith* 1979 SLT (Sh Ct) 52.
4 *Ames v MacLeod* 1969 JC 1.
5 *R v MacDonagh* [1974] QB 448, [1974] 2 All ER 257, CA.
6 *Tudhope v Barlow* 1981 SLT (Sh Ct) 94.

(D) LORD ADVOCATE'S REFERENCES

319. Power to refer point of law. Mention must be made of the power of the Lord Advocate to refer a point of law for the opinion of the High Court[1]. This power arises only where a person has been tried on indictment and acquitted[1], and the High Court's opinion in no way affects the acquittal[2]. The power of reference of a point of law is similar to that of the Attorney-General in England[3] and was based on a recommendation of the Thomson Committee on Criminal Appeals in Scotland[4], which favoured the introduction of the power as a means of gaining certainty on difficult points of law, especially on matters on which there existed conflicting decisions.

1 Criminal Procedure (Scotland) Act 1975 (c 21), s 263A(1) (added by the Criminal Justice (Scotland) Act 1980 (c 62), s 37).
2 Criminal Procedure (Scotland) Act 1975, s 263A(5) (as so added).
3 Criminal Justice Act 1972 (c 71), s 36.
4 *Criminal Appeals in Scotland*, Third Report (Cmnd 7005 (1977)), ch 4.

320. Exercise of power to refer. On a number of occasions the Court of Appeal in England has expressed its view as to the purpose and proper use of the Attorney-General's power to refer a case. In *Attorney-General's Reference (No 1 of 1975)* Lord Widgery LCJ stated:

'It would be a mistake to think, and we hope people will not think, that references by the Attorney-General are confined to cases where very heavy questions of law arise and that they should not be used in other cases. On the contrary, we hope to see this procedure used extensively for short but important points which require a quick ruling of this Court before a potentially false decision of law has too wide a circulation in the courts'[1].

In other cases, the Court of Appeal has pointed out that the power can be used only in respect of issues arising from the actual case which led to the acquittal, not on general theoretical problems of law, no matter how interesting[2].

In its first encounter with the use of the Lord Advocate's power of reference, the High Court of Justiciary did not express any view as to the proper occasions for the use of the power or of the effect of its own decisions in cases involving the reference on the development of the criminal law[3]. That case concerned the issue of the admissibility of statements made by a suspect in the course of an interview by police officers, where the interview was recorded on tape. Although the High Court's opinion clarified a number of points, it has been noted that the court did not deal with all problems connected with the leading of evidence of tapes and/or transcripts[4].

The second reported instance of the Lord Advocate's reference concerned the question whether the crime of perjury could be committed where a witness had falsely denied that he had made a statement to the police where that statement had been obtained unfairly[5]. In deciding this question the court expressly disapproved a passage in the standard work on criminal law, but the judgments contain no discussion on the proper criteria for the use of the Lord Advocate's power of reference.

Although the power to refer a point of law for the opinion of the High Court is not one which is likely to be exercised often, the existence of the Lord Advocate's reference has considerable implications for any examination of judicial precedent in Scotland, for it is assumed, either explicitly or implicitly, by commentators and the High Court itself, that the opinion of the court in deciding an issue before it by means of the Lord Advocate's reference is a binding decision as a statement of the law of Scotland. Indeed the power of reference would be pointless if the court's opinion lacked binding force. However, it must be borne in mind that the decision of the High Court, although based on facts arising in an actual case, has no effect on that case, and thus always concerns an issue which is moot or hypothetical. These features have led English commentators to question the status of Attorney-General's references as precedents[6], a problem which is particularly acute in the light of the distinction in English law between the *ratio decidendi* and *obiter dicta* of a case. Whatever view is taken of the binding effect of precedent in Scotland, it must be capable of explaining how Lord Advocate's references can have binding force as precedents[7].

1 *Attorney-General's Reference (No 1 of 1975)* [1975] QB 773 at 778, [1975] 2 All ER 684 at 685, 686, CA.
2 *Attorney-General's Reference (No 4 of 1979)* [1981] 1 All ER 1193, [1981] 1 WLR 667, CA.
3 *Lord Advocate's Reference (No 1 of 1983)* 1984 SCCR 62, 1984 SLT 337.
4 See the commentary by Sheriff Gordon at 1984 SCCR 70, 71.
5 *Lord Advocate's Reference (No 1 of 1985)* 1986 SCCR 329, disapproving G H Gordon *The Criminal Law of Scotland* (2nd edn, 1978) para 48–14.
6 See J Jaconelli 'Attorney-General's References—A Problematic Device' [1984] Crim L Rev 543, especially at 547–549.
7 See further para 344 below.

(g) Precedent and Other Civil Courts

321. The Scottish Land Court. The Scottish Land Court holds itself bound by the decisions of superior Scottish courts. In the case of the binding effect of decisions of the Court of Session, this practice stems in part from the appellate jurisdiction which the Inner House exercises over decisions of the Land Court. However the Land Court has also followed decisions of the House of Lords in Scottish appeals, even though no appeal from a decision of the court can ultimately be heard by the House. Thus in *Cameron v Duke of Argyll's Trustees*[1] the Land Court approved statements on methods of statutory interpretation made in two Scottish House of Lords appeals[2], and in *Haddo House Estate Trustees v Davidson*[3] the court held itself bound by the decision of another House of Lords decision[4]. In the last resort the judges of any court may determine what authority they will accept, and, if no appellate tribunal can overrule that determination, it becomes the practice of the court until it adopts a different practice.

The binding quality of decisions of the Inner House of the Court of Session is illustrated by a number of cases. In *Callander v Watherston*[5] the Land Court applied *Campbell's Trustees v O'Neill*[6]. In *Cameron v Duke of Argyll's Trustees*[7] the court declined to follow the decision of the Full Court of the Court of Session in *M'Neill v Duke of Hamilton's Trustees*[8] to the extent that that decision had been superseded by statute[9], but on the separate issue of the fair rent of croft land the *M'Neill* case was held to be still an authority. In *Craig*[10] the Land Court in terms stated that it was bound to follow a decision of the Inner House in *Donaldson's Hospital Trustees v Esslemont*[11], although the House of Lords later reversed the Inner House on different grounds.

As regards the binding effect of its own decisions, the Land Court will usually follow its decisions but is not bound to do so, and has the power to overrule unsatisfactory precedents without waiting for the Inner House to do so. There are many cases in the reports where the court has followed its own decisions[12]. However, there are also cases, although few in recent times, where the court has refused to follow its prior decisions. In *Chisholm v Campbell Orde*[13] the court 'respectfully dissented' from its views in *Stuart v Duke of Richmond and Gordon*[14]. In *Georgeson v Anderson's Trustees*[15] the court declined to overrule the decision in the *Chisholm* case as the relevant submission had been withdrawn by the litigants, but the court did state that it should reconsider its decision if that case were founded on in the future. In *Niven v Cameron*[16] the court did not follow *M'Isaac v Orde's Trustees*[17] as that decision was inconsistent with its more recent decisions.

The Scottish Land Court sits both as a divisional court and as a full court of four members. The practice is that the court as a divisional court follows its own decisions given as a full court. In *Fulton v Noble*[18] the court noted that there had been divergences of approach by divisional courts to the full court case of *Campbell v Duke of Argyll's Trustees*[19] and stated:

'The time has therefore come, due to these divergencies of view, for the full court not only to reiterate what was said in *Campbell*, namely that the word 'conveyance' appearing in the 1976 Act[20] may include either a disposition simpliciter or a feu disposition; but also to give guidelines as to the circumstances in which one or the other is appropriate. This is so that divisional courts may in future direct in their orders, after hearing argument where necessary, which form of conveyance is appropriate to the particular circumstances of the case. Simply leaving it open to the parties to decide is likely to give rise to subsequent dispute as indeed has occurred in the present case'[21].

The court is willing to adopt the reasoning in decisions by English courts as persuasive wherever it considers this to be appropriate. In *Cameron v Duke of Argyll's Trustees*[22] the court followed two decisions of the Court of Appeal and an English decision of the House of Lords[23] on a question of general valuation law. In the same case the court, in considering the proper approach to statutes which provide only a general framework to be filled by decisions of the courts, looked at three English cases[24]. A decision of the English Divisional Court[25] was followed in *Leask v Grains*[26]. In *Haddo House Estate Trustees v Davidson*[27] the Land Court felt that it could not disregard an English House of Lords decision[28], but was able to distinguish it on the basis of the separate *persona* of a partnership in Scots law.

1 *Cameron v Duke of Argyll's Trustees* 1981 SLT (Land Ct) 2 at 8.
2 *Heriot's Trust Governors v Caledonian Rly Co* 1915 SC (HL) 52, 1915 1 SLT 347; and *Nimmo v Alexander Cowan & Sons Ltd* 1967 SC (HL) 79, 1967 SLT 277.
3 *Haddo House Estate Trustees v Davidson* 1982 SLT (Land Ct) 14 at 17.
4 *Woolfson v Strathclyde Regional Council* 1978 SC (HL) 90, 1978 SLT 59.
5 *Callender v Watherston* 1970 SLT (Land Ct) 13 at 16.
6 *Campbell's Trustees v O'Neill* 1911 SC 188, 1910 2 SLT 392.
7 *Cameron v Duke of Argyll's Trustees* 1981 SLT (Land Ct) 2.
8 *M'Neill v Duke of Hamilton's Trustees* 1918 SC 221, 1918 1 SLT 265.
9 Ie the Crofters (Scotland) Act 1961 (c 58), s 5.
10 *Craig* 1981 SLT (Land Ct) 12 at 15.
11 *Donaldson's Hospital Trustees v Esslemont* 1925 SC 199, 1925 SLT 92. The same case was held binding in *Eagle Star Insurance Co Ltd v Simpson* 1984 SLT (Land Ct) 37, 1984 SLCR 1.
12 See eg *Gordon v Rankin* 1972 SLT (Land Ct) 7 (following *Stewart v Moir* 1965 SLT (Land Ct) 11); *Somerville v Watson* 1980 SLT (Land Ct) 14 (following *McLaren v Lawrie* 1964 SLT (Land Ct) 10); *Ross v Donaldson* 1983 SLT (Land Ct) 26 (following *Austin v Gibson* 1979 SLT (Land Ct) 12); *Eagle Star Insurance Co Ltd v Simpson* 1984 SLT (Land Ct) 37, 1984 SLCR 1 (following *Allan-Fraser's Trustees v Macpherson* 1981 SLT (Land Ct) 17).

13 *Chisholm v Campbell Orde* (1920) 8 SLCR 36 at 39.
14 *Stuart v Duke of Richmond and Gordon* (1916) Report by Scottish Land Court for the year 1916 (Cd 8626 (1917)) p 51.
15 *Georgeson v Anderson's Trustees* (1944) 33 SLCR 44.
16 *Niven v Cameron* (1938) 27 SLCR 23.
17 *M'Isaac v Orde's Trustees* (1928) 16 SLCR 83.
18 *Fulton v Noble* 1983 SLT (Land Ct) 40.
19 *Campbell v Duke of Argyll's Trustees* 1977 SLT (Land Ct) 22.
20 Ie the Crofting Reform (Scotland) Act 1976 (c 21), s 1(1).
21 *Fulton v Noble* 1983 SLT (Land Ct) 40 at 41.
22 *Cameron v Duke of Argyll's Trustees* 1981 SLT (Land Ct) 2.
23 *West Midland Baptist (Trust) Association (Inc) v Birmingham Corpn* [1970] AC 874, [1969] 3 All ER 172, HL; *W and S (Long Eaton) Ltd v Derbyshire County Council* (1975) 31 P & CR 99, CA; *Hoveringham Gravels Ltd v Chiltern District Council* [1979] RVR 252, CA.
24 *Magor and St Mellons Rural District Council v Newport Corpn* [1952] AC 189, [1951] 1 All ER 839, HL; *Kammins Ballrooms Co Ltd v Zenith Investments (Torquay) Ltd* [1971] AC 850, [1970] 2 All ER 871, HL; *H P Bulmer Ltd v J Bollinger SA* [1974] Ch 401, [1974] 2 All ER 1226, CA.
25 *Evans v Roper* [1960] 2 All ER 507, [1960] 1 WLR 814, DC.
26 *Leask v Grains* 1981 SLT (Land Ct) 11.
27 *Haddo House Estate Trustees v Davidson* 1982 SLT (Land Ct) 14.
28 *Jackson v Hall* [1980] AC 854, [1980] 1 All ER 177, HL.

322. The Court of Exchequer. A Court of Exchequer with the same power and authority as the Court of Exchequer in England was instituted in Scotland in implement of the Union Agreement of 1707[1], and in 1856 was merged with the Court of Session[2]. However, the court was not abolished as such, and specialties attend exchequer causes when the Court of Session is sitting as Court of Exchequer[3]. Some of these specialties affect the practice of precedent in the Exchequer Court.

The general position is that the court is bound by decisions of the House of Lords in Scottish appeals and is also bound by its own decisions. Moreover, the court tends also to follow decisions of the Court of Session on general matters of private law which arise in cases before it. These points are illustrated in several cases. In *Clark's Trustees v Lord Advocate*[4] the court followed the House of Lords decision in the revenue case *Allan's Trustees v Lord Advocate*[5]. This latter case was also followed in *Kerr's Trustees v Lord Advocate*[6]. The House of Lords decision in *Inland Revenue Comrs v Richard's Executors*[7] was followed in *Cleveley's Investment Trust Co v Inland Revenue Comrs*[8]. House of Lords decisions on areas of law other than revenue law are also followed in exchequer causes in appropriate cases. In the *Allan* case[9] the court applied a test on the nature of the *ius quaesitum tertio* laid down by Lord Dunedin in *Carmichael v Carmichael's Executrix*[10]. In *Thomson's Trustees v Inland Revenue Comrs*[11] a particular canon of statutory construction, laid down by the House of Lords in English appeals[12], was applied to cover the effect of the Law Reform (Miscellaneous Provisions) (Scotland) Act 1966 (c 19) on the interpretation of the Trusts (Scotland) Act 1961. In the same case it was pointed out that certain decisions of the Court of Session and of the House of Lords on the construction of the 'Thellusson' Act 1800[13] (which the 1961 Act re-enacted) were authoritative for the court.

The court treats its own decisions as binding in future cases. In *Drummond v Inland Revenue Comrs*[14] the court held that it was bound by its prior decisions of *Donald v Inland Revenue Comrs*[15] and *Inland Revenue Comrs v Grant*[16]. Furthermore, in his judgment Lord President Cooper made this observation about the nature of the Exchequer Court and precedent in that court:

'In the closing speech in this case the Solicitor-General invited us to convene a larger Court to reconsider *Donald*. I reserve my opinion as to whether such a course is open to this Court sitting as the Court of Exchequer. Even on the assumption that such a course is open, I should be opposed to its adoption in the circumstances described above, especially as I consider that, if it is thought desirable to have the whole question reviewed, that should be done by the House of Lords, whose decisions on a United Kingdom taxing statute would be universally binding'[17].

From this observation by Lord Cooper, T B Smith infers that a stricter doctrine of precedent operates in exchequer causes than in other types of litigation before the Court of Session[18]. Where grounds exist for distinguishing a prior decision, the Court of Exchequer may, of course, refuse to follow a decision. Moreover, in the *Kerr* case[19] the court noted that on certain matters before the House of Lords in the *Allan* case[20] and before the Court of Session in the *Clark* case[21] decisions were made on the basis of concessions by the Crown. In the *Kerr* case doubt was cast on whether these concessions had been rightly made, and Lord Fraser expressly stated that because of the concessions the cases were not binding on the court[22]. This view of the effect of concessions would seem applicable to decisions generally. In *Lord Advocate v Young*[23] the court declined to follow *Gosling v Brown*[24] on the ground that that decision had to some extent been superseded by subsequent legislation. However, both Lord President Robertson and Lord McLaren stated as a further reason that the court was not bound by a single decision on the construction of a statute[25]. This attitude on the lack of the binding effect of a single decision on a matter of statutory interpretation has not survived in current practice, either in exchequer causes or in the Court of Session generally.

In exchequer causes, relevant Court of Session decisions will be followed. In the *Allan* case[26] the court followed the decision of *Cameron's Trustees v Cameron*[27] on the nature of the *ius quaesitum tertio*, and in the *Thomson* case[28] the court followed several Court of Session decisions on the law of accumulations[29].

Brief note should be made of the law of charities which is to be applied in exchequer causes. In *Glasgow Trades House v Inland Revenue Comrs* Lord Cameron stated:

> 'In order to ascertain what in the law of Scotland is a charity for the purposes of the Income Tax Acts it is necessary to refer to the preamble of an English statute[30] passed in the reign of Queen Elizabeth I, in the sixteenth century, for a totally different purpose, which survives only in the Mortmain and Charitable Uses Act 1888[31], and thereafter to consider a wide complex of decisions in the House of Lords, the Court of Appeal and the Court of Chancery'[32].

It does not appear, however, that these English decisions must be followed by the court as a matter of binding precedent, and the court would seem to have power to criticise and refuse to follow them[33].

1 Treaty of Union between Scotland and England 1707, art 19.
2 Exchequer Courts (Scotland) Act 1856 (c 56), s 1.
3 See D Maxwell *The Practice of the Court of Session* (1980) pp 636 ff.
4 *Clark's Trustees v Lord Advocate* 1972 SC 177 at 184, 1972 SLT 190 at 195.
5 *Allan's Trustees v Lord Advocate* 1971 SC (HL) 45, 1971 SLT 62.
6 *Kerr's Trustees v Lord Advocate* 1974 SC 115, 1974 SLT 193.
7 *Inland Revenue Comrs v Richard's Executors* 1971 SC (HL) 60, 1971 SLT 107.
8 *Cleveleys Investment Trust Co v Inland Revenue Comrs* 1975 SC 283, 1975 SLT 237.
9 *Allan's Trustees v Lord Advocate* 1970 SC 10, 1970 SLT 73 (revsd 1971 SC (HL) 45, 1971 SLT 62).
10 *Carmichael v Carmichael's Executrix* 1920 SC (HL) 195, 1920 2 SLT 285.
11 *Thomson's Trustees v Inland Revenue Comrs* 1978 SC 206; affd 1979 SC (HL) 74, 1979 SLT 166.
12 *Ormond Investment Co v Betts* [1928] AC 143, HL; *Inland Revenue Comrs v Dowdall, O'Mahoney & Co Ltd* [1952] AC 401, [1952] 1 All ER 531, HL.
13 Ie the Accumulations Act 1800 (c 98) (repealed and re-enacted by the Trusts (Scotland) Act 1961 (c 57), s 5).
14 *Drummond v Inland Revenue Comrs* 1951 SC 482, 1951 SLT 347, especially at 492 and at 351, 352.
15 *Donald v Inland Revenue Comrs* 1922 SC 237, 1922 SLT 204.

16 *Inland Revenue Comrs v Grant* 1943 SC 528, 1944 SLT 89.
17 *Drummond v Inland Revenue Comrs* 1951 SC 482 at 488, 489, 1951 SLT 347 at 349, 350.
18 T B Smith *The Doctrines of Judicial Precedent in Scots Law* (1952) p 35. For a recent example of the
    court holding itself bound by a previous decision, see *Will v Inland Revenue Comrs* 1980 SC 208 at
    288, 299, 303, 305, sub nom *Stevenson's Executors v Lord Advocate* 1981 SLT 336 at 337–340,
    following *Royal Bank of Scotland v Lord Advocate* 1977 SC 116, 1977 SLT 45.
19 *Kerr's Trustees v Lord Advocate* 1974 SC 115, 1974 SLT 193.
20 *Allan's Trustees v Lord Advocate* 1971 SC (HL) 45, 1971 SLT 62.
21 *Clark's Trustees v Lord Advocate* 1972 SC 177, 1972 SLT 190.
22 *Kerr's Trustees v Lord Advocate* 1974 SC 115 at 130, 1974 SLT 193 at 200, 201.
23 *Lord Advocate v Young* (1898) 25 R 778, 5 SLT 375.
24 *Gosling v Brown* (1878) 5 R 755.
25 *Lord Advocate v Young* (1898) 25 R 778 at 786, 5 SLT 375.
26 *Allan's Trustees v Lord Advocate* 1970 SC 10, 1970 SLT 73.
27 *Cameron's Trustees v Cameron* 1907 SC 407, 14 SLT 719.
28 *Thomson's Trustees v Inland Revenue Comrs* 1978 SC 206; affd 1979 SC (HL) 74, 1979 SLT 166.
29 *Lord v Colvin* (1860) 23 D 111, 33 SJ 55; *Hutchinson v Grant's Trustees* 1913 SC 1211, 1913 2 SLT
    31; *Watson's Trustees v Brown* 1923 SC 228, 1923 SLT 70.
30 Charitable Uses Act 1601 (c 4) (repealed).
31 Mortmain and Charitable Uses Act 1888 (c 42), repealed by the Charities Act 1960 (c 58),
    ss 38(1), 48(2), Sch 7, Pt II. Thus it is seemingly the English common law of charities which
    applies.
32 *Glasgow Trades House v Inland Revenue Comrs* 1970 SC 101 at 114, 1970 SLT 294 at 301.
33 See *Inland Revenue Comrs v Glasgow Police Athletic Association* 1953 SC (HL) 13, 1953 SLT 105,
    and cf the discussion in para 282 above.

323. The Lands Valuation Appeal Court. The Lands Valuation Appeal
Court hears appeals from determinations of local valuation appeals committees
on issues of valuation. The normal quorum of the court is a single judge of the
Court of Session, although in certain circumstances the former quorum of three
judges will hear cases[1]. A possible consequence of this change in the quorum of
the court is that single judges of the court will hold themselves bound by
decisions of a three-judge court and that a fuller court will be convened in all
cases where the question of overruling a prior decision of the court is in issue.

In previous times it was thought that the court issued an opinion relating only
to the valuation of the heritable subject in which the matter arose in the
particular case[2]. However, the court has expressly approved the practice of
assessors and valuation appeals committees following the principles laid down
in the court's decisions[3].

The court has accepted that it has the power to overrule its own prior
decisions, but it has stressed that strong grounds must exist before this power
will be exercised[4]. The court's approach towards its practice in relation to prior
decisions is best explained in the judgment of Lord Salvesen in *Glasgow Parish
Council v Glasgow Assessor*:

> 'It was not seriously contended that it is incompetent for us to review a judgment
> pronounced in this Court, whether by the Judges who now constitute the tribunal or
> by their predecessors. It was, however, urged with much force that it is desirable to
> have continuity in the principles which the Court from time to time lays down, and
> I agree that we should not reconsider any judgment pronounced in this Court unless
> we came to be clearly of opinion that it was erroneous, and that its application would
> lead to inequitable results. It cannot be affirmed of any Court that its decisions are
> infallible; nor is it the practice of the Court of Session or the Justiciary Court to
> follow blindly all the decisions which have been pronounced in these Courts. It is
> true that, so far as these Courts are concerned, a decision of importance is not usually
> reconsidered, except by a fuller bench than that which originally pronounced it,
> although cases might be cited where one Division of the Court of Session has refused
> to follow the decision of the other, and that without consultation with the other

Division, or has deliberately reversed a decision which it regarded as erroneous without recourse to a larger tribunal. In this Court there is no machinery by which we can call to aid other judges; but that does not relieve us from the duty of reconsidering a decision which we think contrary to the law which we are bound to administer'[5].

In the same case, Lord Johnston noted that the need for flexibility in the application of precedent arose from the fact that there was no further appeal from the decision of the court[6].

Although the court may overrule its prior decisions, its practice is generally to follow them. The court has accepted that fundamental principles of the law of valuation cannot be by-passed by the court. In *Occidental Inc v Orkney Assessor*[7] members of the court expressly noticed the difficulties associated with the contractor's principle of valuation but thought that it was too firmly established to be overturned.

Where prior decisions have been overruled the court has given indications of the sort of grounds which can justify not following earlier cases. In the *Glasgow Parish Council* case[8] the court refused to follow *Edinburgh Parish Council v Edinburgh Assessor*[9] on the ground that the earlier decision was based on a misunderstanding of the authorities, and a similar reason was given in *Inverness-shire Assessor v Cameron*[10] for overruling *Inverness-shire Assessor v Mackay*[11]. In the *Cameron* case it was also pointed out that in the *Mackay* case some of the points in the judgments had not been developed in the argument of counsel[12]. In *National Commercial Bank of Scotland Ltd v Fife Assessor*[13] the court refused to follow a previous decision which was inconsistent with a trend of authority in other cases. The court is more likely to overrule a prior decision where that decision was recently given and has not led to established practice on the basis of the case[14]. It is not necessary that the overruling court be unanimous, even in respect of a precedent which was decided by a unanimous court[15]. In *Renfrewshire Assessor v Hendry*[16] the court noted that a prior decision[17] contained two competing views on a particular issue, and the court expressed its preference for the view which it would now adopt.

One particular aspect of the court's practice which deserves attention is its attitude towards the binding quality of decisions of the House of Lords. As there is no appeal from decisions of the Lands Valuation Appeal Court, there is no basis for House of Lords decisions having binding force on the grounds of appellate jurisdiction. The position at present appears to be that the court is ready to follow decisions of the House in Scottish appeals but that this is not done strictly as a matter of binding precedent, and where a decision of the House of Lords has no intrinsic value for the question before the court, the court may decline to follow the House's decision. Where a decision of the House in an English appeal relates to a point of law which is common to, or similar in, Scots and English law, the decision is likely to be applied by the court.

In *Angus Assessor v Dundee Society for the Blind*[18] the court followed the House of Lords decision in *Almond v Birmingham Corpn*[19], but this decision was consistent with earlier decisions of the court itself. In the *Occidental* case[20] the court applied a dictum of Lord Dunedin in *Hines v Eastern Counties Farmers' Co-operative Association Ltd*[21] on a matter of the construction of a statute applicable to both Scotland and England. On the other hand, in the *Glasgow Parish Council* case[22] the court held that it was not bound by *Lambeth Overseers v London County Council*[23]. Lord Johnston noted: 'I cannot, however, accept the judgment in the *Lambeth* case as binding on this court. It is not a judgment of the House of Lords sitting in a Scots appeal, nor is it a judgment on the statute which we are administering'.

The position concerning the binding force of House of Lords decisions on the Lands Valuation Appeal Court has been complicated by the court's decision in *Aberdeen Assessor v Collie*[24], where the court overruled its prior decision of *Inland Revenue Comrs v Gunn, Collie and Topping*[25], and preferred to follow the House of Lords decision of *Finn v Kerslake*[26], an English appeal in which the *Gunn* case had been criticised. The *Collie* case concerned the construction of a statute similar in both Scotland and England, and the court put forward the consideration of consistency in interpretation as justifying its overruling its prior decision. But another weighty consideration with the court in the *Collie* case was the view which it apparently took of the House of Lords at that time as the 'infallible' interpreter of the law, albeit its decisions were not technically binding on the court. This view is brought out in the ironic words of Lord Sands, which have been quoted too often and too uncritically:

> 'It is quite true that we are a supreme tribunal in valuation matters, and our judgments are not subject to review by the House of Lords; and, accordingly, in a technical sense, the judgments of the House of Lords may not be binding upon us. But there is one thing that is binding upon us and that is the law, and the House of Lords is an infallible interpreter of the law. A batsman, who, as he said, had been struck on the shoulder by a ball, remonstrated against a ruling of lbw; but the wicket-keeper met his protest by the remark: "It disna' maitter if the ba' hit yer neb; if the umpire says yer oot yer oot". Accordingly, if the House of Lords says "this is the proper interpretation of the statute", then it is the proper interpretation. The House of Lords has a perfect legal mind. Learned Lords may come or go, but the House of Lords never makes a mistake. That the House of Lords should make a mistake is just as unthinkable as that Colonel Bogey should be bunkered twice and take 8 to the hole'[27].

However, this last consideration — which had dubious relevance in the context stated — has no weight since the House of Lords *Practice Statement* on precedent in 1966[28], and the approach taken in the *Collie* case should be taken as exceptional. In any event it is to be considered in the context of the court's acknowledged power to reject its own prior decisions.

1 Valuation of Lands (Scotland) Amendment Act 1867 (c 80), s 8; Valuation of Lands (Scotland) Amendment Act 1879 (c 42), s 7 (both amended by the Rating and Valuation (Amendment) (Scotland) Act 1984 (c 31), s 13).

2 *Inverness-shire Assessor v Cameron* 1938 SC 360 at 369, 1938 SLT 259 at 261, 262, LVAC.

3 *Glasgow Assessor v Watson* 1920 SC 517 at 524, 1920 2 SLT 262 at 265, 266, LVAC; *Aberdeen Assessor v Collie* 1932 SC 304 at 310, 1932 SLT 128 at 129, LVAC; *Inverness-shire Assessor v Cameron* 1938 SC 360 at 369, 1938 SLT 259 at 261, 262, LVAC; *National Commercial Bank of Scotland Ltd v Fife Assessor* 1963 SC 197 at 203, 207, 1963 SLT 329 at 332–334, LVAC.

4 *Glasgow Parish Council v Glasgow Assessor* 1912 SC 818 at 829, 1912 1 SLT 157 at 161, LVAC; *Glasgow Assessor v Watson* 1920 SC 517 at 525, 1920 2 SLT 262 at 266, LVAC; *Inverness-shire Assessor v Cameron* 1938 SC 360 at 369, 378, 384, 1938 SLT 259 at 261, 262, 266, 267, 270, LVAC; *Deeside Poultry Ltd v Aberdeenshire Assessor* 1967 SC 328 at 346, 1967 SLT 110 at 115, LVAC.

5 *Glasgow Parish Council v Glasgow Assessor* 1912 SC 818 at 840, 1912 1 SLT 157 at 167, 168, LVAC. This passage must now be read subject to possible changes following from the quorum of the court being a single judge.

6 *Glasgow Parish Council v Glasgow Assessor* 1912 SC 818 at 829, 1912 1 SLT 157 at 161, LVAC.

7 *Occidental of Britain Inc v Orkney Assessor* 1978 SC 231 at 253, 256, 1979 SLT 60 at 74–76, LVAC.

8 *Glasgow Parish Council v Glasgow Assessor* 1912 SC 818 at 835, 1912 1 SLT 157 at 164, 165, LVAC.

9 *Edinburgh Parish Council v Edinburgh Assessor* 1910 SC 823, 1910 1 SLT 290, LVAC.

10 *Inverness-shire Assessor v Cameron* 1938 SC 360 at 373, 384, 385, 1938 SLT 259 at 264, 270, 271, LVAC.

11 *Inverness-shire Assessor v Mackay* 1936 SC 300, 1936 SLT 113, LVAC.

12 *Inverness-shire Assessor v Cameron* 1938 SC 360 at 385, 1938 SLT 259 at 271, LVAC.

13 *National Commercial Bank of Scotland Ltd v Fife Assessor* 1963 SC 197, 1963 SLT 339, LVAC (not following *Simpson v Selkirkshire Assessor* 1948 SC 270, 1948 SLT 221, LVAC).

14 *Glasgow Parish Council v Glasgow Assessor* 1912 SC 818 at 841, 1912 1 SLT 157 at 165, LVAC; *Inverness-shire Assessor v Cameron* 1938 SC 360 at 371, 1938 SLT 259 at 262, 263, LVAC.

15 *Inverness-shire Assessor v Cameron* 1938 SC 360 at 370, 1938 SLT 259 at 262, LVAC.
16 *Renfrewshire Assessor v Hendry* 1969 SC 211, LVAC.
17 *Stirlingshire Assessor v Forrest-Hamilton* [1963] RA 214, 4 R & VR 187, LVAC.
18 *Angus Assessor v Dundee Society for the Blind* 1969 SC 342 at 346, LVAC.
19 *Almond v Birmingham Corpn* [1968] AC 37, [1967] 2 All ER 317, HL.
20 *Occidental of Britain Inc v Orkney Assessor* 1978 SC 231 at 248, 1979 SLT 60 at 72, LVAC.
21 *Hines v Eastern Counties Farmers' Co-operative Association Ltd* [1931] AC 456, HL.
22 *Glasgow Parish Council v Glasgow Assessor* 1912 SC 818 at 835, 1912 1 SLT 157 at 164, 165, LVAC.
23 *Lambeth Churchwardens and Overseers v London County Council* [1897] AC 625, HL.
24 *Aberdeen Assessor v Collie* 1932 SC 304, 1932 SLT 128, LVAC.
25 *Inland Revenue Comrs v Gunn, Collie and Topping* 1930 SC 389, 1930 SLT 296, LVAC.
26 *Finn v Kerslake* [1931] AC 457, HL.
27 *Aberdeen Assessor v Collie* 1932 SC 304 at 311, 312, 1932 SLT 128 at 130, LVAC.
28 *Practice Statement* [1966] 3 All ER 77, [1966] 1 WLR 1234, HL: see paras 283–285 above.

324. The Lands Tribunal for Scotland. The Lands Tribunal for Scotland holds itself bound by appropriate decisions of superior Scottish courts. For example, in general questions of land law and conveyancing the tribunal has followed decisions of the Inner House[1] and of the House of Lords[2]. In *Evans v Glasgow District Council*[3] and *Park Automobile Co v Strathclyde Regional Council*[4] the tribunal followed decisions of the Inner House on questions of disturbance payments claimed on compulsory purchase. In the second of these cases the tribunal also noted the distinction between remoteness of damage and mitigation of loss as expressed in the *Liesbosch* case[5], which had in turn referred to the *Clippens Oil* case[6]. In *Keith v Texaco Ltd*[7] the tribunal followed the approach to statutory interpretation set out in two House of Lords decisions[8].

Although it is not clear that the Lands Valuation Appeal Court is a 'superior' court to the Lands Tribunal, in *Ness v Shannon*[9] the tribunal followed the decision of that court in *Ferguson v Glasgow Assessor*[10].

As regards its own decisions, the clear practice of the tribunal is to follow its own precedents, and the reports contain many illustrations of this practice[11]. An explicit statement of the tribunal's approach to precedent was made in *Robertson v Church of Scotland General Trustees*[12], a case which had been brought as a test case to challenge the decision in *McVey v Glasgow Corpn*[13]. In the *Robertson* case the tribunal stated:

> 'We have to indicate at this stage that this Tribunal, for the sake of consistency, feels that it should endeavour to follow its own legal decisions — especially where reached (as in *McVey*) by a large tribunal. Only where a legal decision has been given by a small tribunal might we exceptionally be persuaded — following the practice of the Court of Session — to convene a fuller tribunal to review it'.

This practice does not commit the tribunal to following all previous decisions, and on occasion the tribunal might be prepared to reconsider a decision. Moreover, where a previous case can genuinely be distinguished, the tribunal will do so and not follow on that basis. The reports provide several illustrations[14].

The tribunal is also prepared to accept as persuasive authority decisions of the English courts which deal with matters common to, or similar in, Scots and English law[15]. In *Keith v Texaco Ltd*[16] the tribunal followed the approach, set out by the House of Lords in the English *Black-Clawson International* appeal[17], that in construing a statute the courts are permitted to consult various sorts of *travaux préparatoires* to determine the 'mischief' which the statute was designed to remedy. The tribunal looked at the Report of the Halliday Committee on Conveyancing Legislation and Practice[18] to determine the mischief at which section 1 of the Conveyancing and Feudal Reform (Scotland) Act 1970 (c 35) was aimed. However, in *Inglis v British Airports Authority*[19] the tribunal held that the *Black-Clawson* rule did not allow consideration of a departmental memorandum designed to give guidance on the scope of the Act which was to be construed in the case before the tribunal.

Where appropriate, the tribunal will consider decisions from other jurisdictions. In *Smith v Strathclyde Regional Council*[20] the tribunal took note of, and approved, the decision of the Northern Ireland Lands Tribunal in *McGonigal v Department of Environment for Northern Ireland*[21], and in *O'Donnell v Edinburgh District Council*[22] the tribunal applied a dictum of Griffith CJ in *Spencer v Commonwealth of Australia*[23].

   1 *Murrayfield Ice Rink Ltd v Scottish Rugby Union* 1972 SLT (Lands Trib) 20 at 21 (following *Swans v Western Bank* (1866) 4 M 663, 38 SJ 346); *Smith v Taylor* 1972 SLT (Lands Trib) 34 at 36 (following *Alexander v Stobo* (1871) 9 M 599, 43 SJ 311); *James Miller & Partners Ltd v Hunt* 1974 SLT (Lands Trib) 9 (following *Napier v Spiers Trustees* (1831) 9 S 655, SJ 458, and *Duncanson v Giffen* (1878) 15 SLR 356); *Bachoo v George Wimpey & Co Ltd* 1977 SLT (Lands Trib) 2 at 4 (following *Howard de Walden Estates Ltd v Bowmaker Ltd* 1965 SC 163, 1965 SLT 254).
   2 *Co-operative Wholesale Society v Ushers Brewery* 1975 SLT (Lands Trib) 9 at 11 (following *Tailors of Aberdeen v Coutts* (1840) 1 Robin 296, HL, and *Aberdeen Varieties Ltd v James F Donald (Aberdeen) Cinemas Ltd* 1940 SC (HL) 52, 1940 SLT 374); *Bachoo v George Wimpey & Co Ltd* 1977 SLT (Lands Trib) 2 at 4 (following *Earl of Zetland v Hislop* (1882) 9 R (HL) 40).
   3 *Evans v Glasgow District Council* 1978 SLT (Lands Trib) 5 (following *Glasgow Corpn v Anderson* 1976 SLT 225).
   4 *Park Automobile Co v Strathclyde Regional Council* 1984 SLT (Lands Trib) 14 at 19 (following *Venables v Department of Agriculture for Scotland* 1932 SC 573, 1932 SLT 411, and *Aberdeen District Council v Sim* 1983 SLT 250).
   5 *Liesbosch Owners v Edison Owners* [1933] AC 449, HL.
   6 *Clippens Oil Co Ltd v Edinburgh and District Water Trustees* 1907 SC (HL) 9, 15 SLT 92.
   7 *Keith v Texaco Ltd* 1977 SLT (Lands Trib) 16.
   8 *Heriot's Trust Governors v Caledonian Rly Co* 1915 SC (HL) 52, 1915 1 SLT 347; *Nimmo v Alexander Cowan & Sons Ltd* 1967 SC (HL) 79, 1967 SLT 277.
   9 *Ness v Shannon* 1978 SLT (Lands Trib) 13 at 16.
  10 *Ferguson v Glasgow Assessor* 1977 SLT 142, LVAC.
  11 See eg *Murrayfield Ice Rink Ltd v Scottish Rugby Union* 1972 SLT (Lands Trib) 20, which has been followed in *Smith v Taylor* 1972 SLT (Lands Trib) 34, *Bolton v Aberdeen Corpn* 1972 SLT (Lands Trib) 26, and *James Miller & Partners Ltd v Hunt* 1974 SLT (Lands Trib) 9. Further, *Ware v Edinburgh District Council* 1976 SLT (Lands Trib) 21 followed *Renfrew's Trustees v Glasgow Corpn* 1972 SLT (Lands Trib) 2, and was itself followed in *Smith v Strathclyde Regional Council* 1982 SLT (Lands Trib) 2. Further examples of the tribunal following its own decisions are *Co-operative Wholesale Society v Ushers Brewery* 1975 SLT (Lands Trib) 9 (following *Coles' Executors v Inland Revenue* 1973 SLT (Lands Trib) 24); *Blythswood Friendly Society v Glasgow District Council* 1976 SLT (Lands Trib) 29 (following *McVey v Glasgow Corpn* 1973 SLT (Lands Trib) 15); *Bachoo v George Wimpey & Co Ltd* 1977 SLT (Lands Trib) 2 (following *McArthur v Mahoney* 1975 SLT (Lands Trib) 2); *Keith v Texaco Ltd* 1977 SLT (Lands Trib) 16 (following *Blythswood Friendly Society v Glasgow District Council* above); and *Park Automobile Co v Strathclyde Regional Council* 1984 SLT (Lands Trib) 14 (following *Smith v Strathclyde Regional Council* above).
  12 *Robertson v Church of Scotland General Trustees* 1976 SLT (Lands Trib) 11 at 12.
  13 *McVey v Glasgow Corpn* 1973 SLT (Lands Trib) 15.
  14 *Co-operative Wholesale Society v Ushers Brewery* 1975 SLT (Lands Trib) 9 (distinguishing *Manz v Butter's Trustees* 1973 SLT (Lands Trib) 2, and *Owen v MacKenzie* 1974 SLT (Lands Trib) 11); *Keith v Texaco Ltd* 1977 SLT (Lands Trib) 16 (distinguishing *McArthur v Mahoney* 1975 SLT (Lands Trib) 2); *O'Donnell v Edinburgh District Council* 1980 SLT (Lands Trib) 13 (distinguishing *MacDonald's Representatives v Sutherland District Council* 1977 SLT (Lands Trib) 7).
  15 See eg *Bolton v Aberdeen Corpn* 1972 SLT (Lands Trib) 26 at 30 (applying *Re Munday's Application* (1953) 7 P & CR 130, Lands Trib, and *Re Chandler's Application* (1958) 9 P & CR 512, Lands Trib); *Evans v Glasgow District Council* 1978 SLT (Lands Trib) 5 (applying *Harvey v Crawley Development Corpn* [1957] 1 QB 485, [1957] 1 All ER 504, CA).
  16 *Keith v Texaco Ltd* 1977 SLT (Lands Trib) 16.
  17 *Black-Clawson International Ltd v Papierwerke Waldhof-Aschaffenburg AG* [1975] AC 591, [1975] 1 All ER 810, HL.
  18 Cmnd 3118 (1966).
  19 *Inglis v British Airports Authority* 1978 SLT (Lands Trib) 30.
  20 *Smith v Strathclyde Regional Council* 1982 SLT (Lands Trib) 2 at 6.
  21 *McGonigal v Department of the Environment for Northern Ireland* [1976] RVR 56.

22 *O'Donnell v Edinburgh District Council* 1980 SLT (Lands Trib) 13 at 16.
23 *Spencer v Commonwealth of Australia* (1907) 5 CLR 418.

325. The Lyon Court. The Lord Lyon has jurisdiction to reduce his own decrees[1]. The Court of Session has sustained its jurisdiction to review proceedings in the Court of the Lord Lyon[2], and from the Court of Session appeal may be taken to the House of Lords[3]. The view was expressed in *M'Donnell v M'Donald*[4] that before an action of reduction of a Lyon Court decree may be pursued in the Court of Session remedy must first be sought in the Lyon Court. Certainly that court still proceeds on the basis that it can overturn its own decrees[5]. Probably as a corollary of this power of reduction any Lord Lyon in office would regard previous decisions of the Lyon Court as persuasive authority only. However, Lyon would regard himself as bound by precedents of the House of Lords, the Court of Session and the High Court of Justiciary. The mere fact that a decision of the Court of Session was reached in the eighteenth century will not reduce its authority as a binding precedent.

It is clearly the practice of Lyon to follow as binding authority decisions of the House of Lords in Scottish appeals and of the Court of Session. For example, the House of Lords decision of *Stewart Mackenzie v Fraser-Mackenzie*[6], and the Inner House decisions of *M'Donnell v M'Donald*[7] and *Maclean of Ardgour v Maclean*[8] have been followed in many Lyon Court cases. However, Lyon may be able to distinguish decisions as being inconsistent with authority and refuse to follow them for that reason. In the *Smollet of Bonhill* case[9] Lyon stated:

'It is now necessary to comment upon two cases on the matter (*Hunter v Weston*[10]; *Munro's Trustees v Spencer*[11]). I cannot hold that either of these was a proper interpretation of the Law or is binding upon this Court. I do not consider the circumstances in either are such as to make them entitled to be received for the modern and (un-Scottish) doctrine of *stare decisis*. One was allowed to proceed on fundamental misapprehensions; and in neither case was the Court proceeding, as it ought (both on principle of law and on the precedent laid down in *Forlong*[12]) by having first before it a decision of the Lyon Court'.

Lyon also pointed out that both decisions were incompatible with the express principles of later Court of Session decisions. In *The Law Society of Scotland*[13] Lyon distinguished, and so declined to follow, *Royal College of Surgeons v Royal College of Physicians*[14]. The reports contain examples of Lyon following previous decisions of the Lyon Court[15]. Lyon has also recognised the importance of decided cases in stating the law. In the *Macnab of Macnab* case[16] in 1957 he stated:

'In view of the confusion of thought which has supervened on certain of these matters some twenty years ago, this court had been at pains, during the past fifteen years, to lay down with particular care the fact and law upon which such jurisdiction is exercised and the relative principles-of-law, and the practice which has come down through the ages. It appeared that the inclusion of the more important of such findings in each parchment was to be useful to the Chiefs and clans in realising the nature and circumstances of the exercise of such jurisdiction. Now that these have been repeated in so many cases published in *The Scots Law Times* and in treatises on clan law in current books, it appears no longer necessary to reiterate what is now well known, readily accessible, and has been so satisfactorily applied in so many different circumstances to so many different cases. Accordingly, I do not propose in future to burden decrees with such reiteration of general facts and principles of law. It will be sufficient, as in ordinary causes, to confine the findings in law and fact to those applicable to the particular case under the court's consideration'.

Lyon would be unlikely to gain assistance from decisions of other courts of persuasive authority. In England the comparable court to that of Lyon is the High Court of Chivalry, a civil court which, being almost defunct, avoided the reform of the civil law courts of England in the nineteenth century. The High Court of Chivalry has only sat once since 1737, and when it did so in 1954 Lord Chief Justice Goddard sat as Surrogate of the Earl Marshal of England[17]. In his judgment Lord Goddard discouraged proceedings before this court and expressed the view that it should be put upon a statutory basis. Despite the virtual desuetude of the English jurisdiction and the relative activity of the Lyon Court, the Earl Marshal's College of Arms in London pretends to operate an imperial jurisdiction in relation to countries of the Commonwealth and to act as arbiter concerning the law of arms in matters on which the views of the Lord Lyon should have equal authority[18].

1 *Dundas v Dundas* 28 Feb 1757, papers in Lyon Court and Interlocutor 20 Dec 1756, *Lyon Court Books; Alexander Gordon* 3 Dec 1813, Lyon Register II, 104; *Adams of St Bennetts Castle* 24 Dec 1923, Lyon Register xviii, 57.
2 *M'Donnell v M'Donald* (1826) 4 S 371; *Cunninghame v Cunyngham* (1849) 11 D 1139.
3 *Stewart Mackenzie v Fraser-Mackenzie* 1922 SC (HL) 39, 1922 SLT 18; *Dunbar of Kilconzie* 1986 SLT 463, HL.
4 *M'Donnell v M'Donald* (1826) 4 S 371 at 376, per Lord Robertson.
5 See reduction of a Matriculation of Arms of Robert Hinde-Douglas in the *Public Register of All Arms and Bearings in Scotland* vol 29, fol 52. These proceedings followed the petition at the instance of the Procurator Fiscal to the Court of the Lord Lyon. By an interlocutor of 18 July 1966 the Lord Lyon rescinded and annulled the matriculation, which had proceeded on an interlocutor of Lord Lyon Sir Francis Grant dated 1 Dec 1930.
6 *Stewart Mackenzie v Fraser-Mackenzie* 1922 SC (HL) 39, 1922 SLT 18. This was followed in eg *Rear-Admiral Lachlan Donald Mackintosh of Mackintosh* 1950 SLT (Lyon Ct) 2; *Rt Hon Sir Donald Patrick Trevor Grant of Grant, Lord Strathspey* 1950 SLT (Lyon Ct) 17; *Lt-Gen Sir Gordon Holmes Alexander MacMillan of MacMillan* 1953 SLT (Lyon Ct) 5; *Lewis Gretton Grahame of Duntrune and Claverhouse* 1960 SLT (Lyon Ct) 2; *Dame Maureen Daisy Helen Dunbar of Hempriggs, Baroness* 1966 SLT (Lyon Ct) 2; *Lady Ruthven of Freeland* 1977 SLT (Lyon Ct) 2.
7 *M'Donnell v M'Donald* (1826) 4 S 371, followed in eg *Rear-Admiral Lachlan Donald Mackintosh of Mackintosh* 1950 SLT (Lyon Ct) 2; *Duncan Alexander Eliott Mackintosh of Mackintosh-Torcastle* 1950 SLT (Lyon Ct) 5; *Rt Hon Alexander Godfrey, Lord Macdonald* 1950 SLT (Lyon Ct) 5; *Maj-Gen Alexander Patrick Drummond Telfer Smollett of Bonhill* 1959 SLT (Lyon Ct) 3; *Earl of Selkirk* 1985 SLT (Lyon Ct) 2.
8 *Maclean of Ardgour v Maclean* 1941 SC 613, 1942 SLT 46, followed in eg *Duncan Alexander Eliott Mackintosh of Mackintosh-Torcastle* 1940 SLT (Lyon Ct) 5; *Rt Hon Alexander Godfrey, Lord Macdonald* 1950 SLT (Lyon Ct) 8; *Capt Alwyne Arthur Compton Farquharson of Invercauld* 1950 SLT (Lyon Ct) 13; *Lt-Gen Sir Gordon Holmes Alexander MacMillan of MacMillan* 1953 SLT (Lyon Ct) 5; *Patrick Gascoigne Munro of Foulis* 1953 SLT (Lyon Ct) 15; *Hugres Diarmid Ian Campbell-Gray, 22nd Lord Gray* 1959 SLT (Lyon Ct) 2; *Sir Hugh Vere Huntly Duff Munro-Lucas-Tooth, Baronet* 1965 SLT (Lyon Ct) 2.
9 *Maj-Gen Alexander Patrick Drummond Telfer Smollet of Bonhill* 1959 SLT (Lyon Ct) 3 at 6 (see also at 12). A similar point about the lack of binding quality of the two cases in question was made in *Sir Hugh Vere Huntly Duff Munro-Lucas-Tooth, Baronet* 1956 SLT (Lyon Ct) 2 at 5.
10 *Hunter v Weston* (1882) 9 R 492; J H Stevenson, *Heraldry in Scotland* p 74.
11 *Munro's Trustees v Spencer* 1912 SC 933, 1912 1 SLT 395.
12 *Forlong* (1880) 7 R 910.
13 *The Law Society of Scotland* 1955 SLT (Lyon Ct) 2 at 4.
14 *Royal College of Surgeons of Edinburgh v Royal College of Physicians of Edinburgh* 1911 SC 1054, 1911 2 SLT 134.
15 See eg *Rt Hon George Alexander Eugene Douglas, Earl Haig* 1950 SLT (Lyon Ct) 26 (followed in *Lt-Gen Sir Gordon Holmes Alexander MacMillan of MacMillan* 1953 SLT (Lyon Ct) 5); *Rear-Admiral Lachlan Donald Mackintosh of Mackintosh* 1950 SLT (Lyon Ct) 2 (followed in *George Kenneth Stewart Fergusson of Dunfallandy* 1953 SLT (Lyon Ct) 2); *Lt-Gen Sir Gordon Holmes Alexander MacMillan of MacMillan* above (followed in *Sir Arthur Herman Munro of Foulis-Obsdale* 1955 SLT (Lyon Ct) 5); *Sir Arthur Herman Munro of Foulis-Obsdale* above (followed in *Sir Hugh Vere Huntly Duff Munro-Lucas-Tooth, Baronet* 1965 SLT (Lyon Ct) 2).
16 *Archibald Corrie Macnab of Macnab and Kinnel* 1957 SLT (Lyon Ct) 2 at 3. See also *Sir Hugh Vere Huntly Duff Munro-Lucas-Tooth, Baronet* 1965 SLT (Lyon Ct) 2 at 10.
17 *Manchester Corpn v Manchester Palace of Varieties Ltd* [1955] P 133, [1955] 1 All ER 387, High Ct of Chivalry.
18 Cf 'Pretensions of English Law as Imperial Law' in CONSTITUTIONAL LAW, vol 5, paras 711 ff.

326. The Registration of Voters Appeal Court. The practice of the Registration of Voters Appeal Court is in general to follow its own decisions, but the court has not yet had to decide whether it is absolutely bound by them. As there is no further appeal from the court, it may well be that the court would hold itself free to review a prior decision which was thought to be unsatisfactory. The court will follow decisions of the Court of Session and of the House of Lords on any points of general law which arise before it.

Most of the reported decisions of the court are concerned with the issue of the interpretation to be given to the meaning of 'general nature of occupation' which entitles a person to be treated as an absent voter[1]. In *Daly v Watson*[2] the court pointed out that certain statements in its decision in *Craig v Mitchell*[3] had to be read in their proper context but that they did correctly state the law. The court also applied the general principles set out in *Keay v MacLeod*[4] to the instant case. In *Frame v Brydon*[5] the court referred to its decisions in *Craig v Mitchell* and *Daly v Watson*, and in the later case *Marr v Robertson*[6] it applied the general principles as set out in those cases and in *Frame v Bryden* itself. *Keay v MacLeod, Daly v Watson* and *Frame v Bryden* were also cited by the court in *MacCorquodale v Bovack*[7].

In *Strathclyde Electoral Registration Officer v Boylan*[8] the issue before the court was whether an untried prisoner in prison qualified as an absent voter. No Scottish authorities were cited by the court, which did note[9]: 'We were referred to three old cases, including two Irish appeal cases, but these were concerned with very different Acts and circumstances and we found little assistance from them. On the other hand we did find some assistance from the observations of the Judges in *Fox v Stirk*[10]'. In *Scott v Phillips*[11], where the issue was the nature of residence necessary to qualify for registration on the electoral register, the court declined to follow *Fox v Stirk*. Dicta in that case ignored some of the general principles applicable to the issue and, moreover, disregarded the Scottish case of *Ferris v Wallace*[12], which did correctly set out the relevant principles.

Decisions of the court are binding on sheriffs who hear appeals from decisions of electoral registration officers[13].

1 Representation of the People Act 1983 (c 2), s 19(1)(b)(i), substantially re-enacting the Representation of the People Act 1949 (c 68), s 12(1)(b)(i).
2 *Daly v Watson* 1960 SC 216, 1960 SLT 271, RAC.
3 *Craig v Mitchell* 1955 SC 399, 1955 SLT 369, RAC.
4 *Keay v MacLeod* 1953 SC 252, 1953 SLT 144, RAC.
5 *Frame v Brydon* 1964 SC 242, 1964 SLT 266, RAC.
6 *Marr v Robertson* 1964 SC 448, 1965 SLT 14, RAC.
7 *MacCorquodale v Bovack* 1984 SLT 328, RAC.
8 *Strathclyde Electoral Registration Officer v Boylan* 1980 SC 266, RAC.
9 1980 SC 266 at 268.
10 *Fox v Stirk and Bristol Electoral Registration Officer* [1970] 2 QB 463, [1970] 3 All ER 7, CA.
11 *Scott v Phillips* 1974 SLT 32, RAC.
12 *Ferris v Wallace* 1936 SC 561, 1936 SLT 292, RAC.
13 *Dumble v Borders Electoral Registration Officer* 1980 SLT (Sh Ct) 60 at 61.

327. The Restrictive Practices Court. The Restrictive Practices Court was instituted by the Restrictive Trade Practices Act 1956[1]. Although the court has a different constitution depending on whether a case before it originates in Scotland or in one of the other law districts of the United Kingdom[2] and although there is a correspondingly different appeal structure from decisions of the court (in Scotland appeal lies to the Court of Session[3]), the court is essentially a United Kingdom court. This feature of the court is relevant when considering the practice of precedent which it follows.

In principle, as a number of appellate courts can hear appeals from decisions of the court, all relevant decisions of such courts are binding on the court no matter whether it is sitting in Scotland or elsewhere. In the Scottish case *Re Scottish Master Monumental Sculptors' Association's Agreement*[4] the court, in considering whether it had jurisdiction in respect of an agreement which had been varied after the reference to the court, followed a decision of the House of Lords in an English appeal[5] and two decisions of the Court of Appeal[6]. In that case the court also considered two decisions of the court in English cases[7]. In *Re Scottish Daily Newspaper Society's Agreement*[8] the court distinguished a Court of Appeal decision[9], and in *Re Scottish Daily Newspaper Society's Agreement (No 2)*[10] the court followed on one point, and distinguished on another, a House of Lords decision on an English appeal[11].

The court has made a number of explicit observations concerning its practice in relation to its own decisions. In the English case *Re Electrical Installations at the Exeter Hospital Agreement*[12] the court stated that it was desirable to adopt a consistent approach to its construction of the Restrictive Trade Practices Act and that where it was faced with conflicting decisions of its own, it would follow the general trend of those decisions. This 'preponderance of judicial reasoning' approach to prior decisions was expressly approved by the court in the Scottish case, *Re Scottish Daily Newspaper Society's Agreement*[13], which followed decisions of the court in two English cases[14]. In the first reported decision of the court in a Scottish case, *Re Wholesale and Retail Bakers of Scotland Association's Agreement*[15], the decision in an English case[16] was followed. An English decision was also followed in the Scottish case, *Re Scottish Daily Newspaper Society's Agreement (No 2)*[17]. In one reported Scottish case, *Re Mallaig and North West Fishermen's Association's Agreement*[18], no cases were cited to the court in argument nor referred to in the court's judgment.

In an English case, *Re National Sulphuric Acid Association's Agreement*[19], the court faced the situation where a number of points put to it in argument had become, in its own words, 'academic' because of the court's decisions on other matters in that case. The court refused to decide these points and stated that it was undesirable for it to express views on questions of law which were merely speculative, even where these points had been fully argued.

1 Restrictive Trade Practices Act 1956 (c 68), s 2(1) (repealed), continued in the Restrictive Practices Court Act 1976 (c 33), s 1(1).
2 See ibid, s 2.
3 Ibid, s 10(1)(b).
4 *Re Scottish Master Monumental Sculptors' Association's Agreement* (1965) LR 5 RP 437, RPC (Sc).
5 *Re Newspaper Proprietors' Agreement* (1964) LR 4 RP 361, [1964] 1 All ER 55, HL(E).
6 *Schweppes Ltd v Registrar of Restrictive Trading Agreements* (1965) LR 5 RP 103, [1965] 1 All ER 195, CA; *Re Crane Makers' Association's Agreement* (1965) LR 5 RP 264, [1965] 2 All ER 561, CA.
7 *Re British Waste Paper Association's Agreement* (1963) LR 4 RP 29, [1963] 2 All ER 424, RPC (E & W); *Re Birmingham Association of Building Trades Employers' Agreement* (1963) LR 4 RP 54, [1963] 2 All ER 361, RPC (E & W).
8 *Re Scottish Daily Newspaper Society's Agreement* (1971) LR 7 RP 379, RPC (Sc).
9 *Re Blanket Manufacturers' Association's Agreement* (1959) LR 1 RP 271, [1959] 2 All ER 630, CA.
10 *Re Scottish Daily Newspaper Society's Agreement (No 2)* (1972) LR 7 RP 401, RPC (Sc).
11 *Re Newspaper Proprietors' Agreement* (1964) LR 4 RP 361, [1964] 1 All ER 55, HL(E).
12 *Re Electrical Installations at the Exeter Hospital Agreement* (1970) LR 7 RP 102, [1971] 1 All ER 347, RPC (E & W).
13 *Re Scottish Daily Newspaper Society's Agreement* (1971) LR 7 RP 379 at 396, 397, RPC (Sc).
14 *Re British Waste Paper Association's Agreement* (1963) LR 4 RP 29, [1963] 2 All ER 424, RPC (E & W), and *Re Electrical Installation at the Exeter Hospital Agreement* (1970) LR 7 RP 102, [1971] 1 All ER 347, RPC (E & W).
15 *Re Wholesale and Retail Bakers of Scotland Association's Agreement* (1959) LR 1 RP 347, 1960 SLT 130, RPC (Sc).
16 *Re Yarn Spinners' Agreement* (1959) LR 1 RP 118, [1959] 1 All ER 299, RPC (E & W).

17 *Re Scottish Daily Newspaper Society's Agreement (No 2)* (1972) LR 7 RP 401, RPC (Sc), following
     Re Federation of Wholesale and Multiple Bakers' (Great Britain and Northern Ireland) Agreement (1960)
     LR 1 RP 387, [1960] 1 All ER 227, RPC (E & W).
18 *Re Mallaig and North West Fishermen's Association's Agreement* (1970) LR 7 RP 178, RPC (Sc).
19 *Re National Sulphuric Acid Association's Agreement* (1963) LR 4 RP 169 at 238, 239, [1963] 3 All ER
     73 at 96, 97, RPC (E & W). This does not, it is considered, imply that where several grounds may
     justify a conclusion any necessarily become academic after one has been stated.

328. Tribunals in general. Many areas of law, usually created by statute and
normally concerned with the promotion of conceptions of welfare unknown to
the common law, are dealt with at least in the first place by specialised tribunals
rather than through the normal system of courts. The nature of these tribunals
has implications for their approach to precedent. Most tribunals apply statute
law which is uniform throughout Great Britain or the United Kingdom, and
many have a marked relaxation in the formality of proceedings before them (a
feature which reflects the fact that representation before them is often by lay
persons rather than by qualified lawyers). For these reasons tribunals tend to
adopt a flexible approach towards following previous decisions, especially their
own, but also seek to apply decisions of superior courts throughout Britain to
keep the interpretation and application of the law on a uniform basis.

329. The Employment Appeal Tribunal. The Employment Appeal Tribunal, which is a British court, is bound on matters of Scots law by decisions of
the House of Lords and of the Inner House of the Court of Session, and on
matters of English law by decisions of the House of Lords and of the Court of
Appeal[1]. Decisions of the Outer House, of the High Court in England and of the
former National Industrial Relations Court are not binding on the Employment
Appeal Tribunal, but are of high persuasive value[2].

1 *Portec (UK) Ltd v Mogensen* [1976] ICR 396 at 400, [1976] 3 All ER 565 at 568, EAT.
2 For the practice of the National Industrial Relations Court in relation to its own decisions, see
   Chapman v Goonvean and Rostowrack China Clay Co Ltd [1973] ICR 50 at 58, [1973] 1 All ER 218 at
   224, 225, NIRC; *Dewar and Finlay Ltd v Glazier* [1973] ICR 572 at 579, NIRC.

330. Industrial tribunals. Industrial tribunals in Scotland are bound by decisions of the House of Lords in Scottish appeals, and of the Inner House and
Outer House of the Court of Session[1]. A tribunal is also bound by decisions of
the Employment Appeal Tribunal in both Scottish and English appeals, but not
by decisions of other industrial tribunals[1]. However, the Employment Appeal
Tribunal has warned that industrial tribunals must avoid over-rigid approaches
to prior decisions binding on them and that their first duty is to apply the terms
of the statute upon which a case before them is based. In *Anandarajah v Lord
Chancellor's Department*, the Employment Appeal Tribunal stated:

'The objective of Parliament, when it first framed the right not to be unfairly
dismissed and set up a system of Industrial Tribunals (with a majority of lay
members) to administer it, was to banish legalism and in particular to ensure that,
wherever possible, parties conducting their own case would be able to face the
Tribunal with the same ease and confidence as those professionally represented. A
preoccupation with guideline authority puts that objective in jeopardy. It should
seldom be necessary (and may sometimes even be unwise) for an Industrial Tribunal
to frame its decision by reference to any direction other than the express terms of the
statute'[2].

1 See W Leslie *Industrial Tribunal Practice in Scotland* (1981) p 203.
2 *Anandarajah v Lord Chancellor's Department* [1984] IRLR 131 at 132, EAT.

331. Social security tribunals. The practice of precedent in relation to the various bodies or tribunals dealing with matters of social security have been stated in explicit fashion in reported decisions[1]. The adjudicative bodies which deal with matters of social security have been reformed by the Health and Social Services and Social Security Adjudications Act 1983[2]. However, it is likely that the new bodies will continue the practices in relation to precedent followed by their predecessors. In *Decision CI 440/50* it was held that an insurance officer was not bound by his own previous decisions on claims under the Social Security Acts, and this applies now to the binding effect of decisions of adjudication officers on other adjudication officers. In *Decision R(I) 12/75*, an important decision of three commissioners, several features of precedent were approved[3]:

(1) adjudication officers and social security appeal tribunals must follow decisions of a Social Security Commissioner and of tribunals of commissioners;

(2) where decisions at the level of commissioners conflict, adjudication officers and social security appeal tribunals must prefer a decision of a tribunal of commissioners to that of a single commissioner, and will normally rely only on reported decisions[4], but if these principles do not eliminate the conflict, the adjudication officer or social security appeal tribunal has a discretion which decision to follow;

(3) a single commissioner must follow a decision of a tribunal of commissioners and, although not strictly obliged to do so, should also normally follow decisions of other single commissioners;

(4) adjudication officers, social security appeal tribunals and commissioners are all bound to follow decisions on points of principle of the higher courts, both Scottish and English[5].

An appeal at the level of commissioners may be heard by a tribunal of three rather than by a single commissioner to resolve conflict of prior decisions of commissioners[6].

1 See further R Micklethwait *The National Insurance Commissioners* (1976) pp 73–75; A I Ogus and E M Barendt *The Law of Social Security* (2nd edn, 1982), 595, 596; *Social Security Appeal Tribunals, a Guide to Procedure* (1985) App 5.

2 See the Health and Social Services and Social Security Adjudications Act 1983 (c 41), s 25, Sch 8, para 1, and Sch 8, paras 2–31 (amending the Family Income Supplement Act 1970 (c 55), ss 6, 8; Social Security Act 1975 (c 14), ss 97, 104, 108–110, 112, 113, 115, 117, Schs 10, 12, 13, 20; Supplementary Benefits Act 1976 (c 71), ss 2, 10; Social Security Act 1980 (c 30), s 15; and Social Security and Housing Benefits Act 1982 (c 24), Schs 2, 3). The effect is that the functions of the former insurance officers, benefit officers and family income supplement officers are now exercised by adjudication officers, and the functions of the former local tribunals and appeal tribunals are now exercised by social security appeal tribunals.

3 The decision refers to decisions which bind insurance officers and national insurance appeal tribunals. The statement of practice in the text has been modified to refer to the successor institutions of these bodies. The former supplementary benefit appeal tribunals followed the same rules of precedent as were followed by national insurance local appeal tribunals: *Ogus and Barendt* p 611.

4 See *Ogus and Barendt* (2nd Cum Suppt B 53).

5 See *Decision R(U) 8/80*.

6 *Decision R(U) 1/66*, para 8.

332. Pensions appeal tribunals. Decisions of the Court of Session and also of the nominated judge of the High Court in England (which is the equivalent English body for hearing appeals in pensions cases) are binding on pensions appeal tribunals. It has been stated in English cases that the doctrine of *stare decisis* does not apply in its strictest form in war pension cases[1], and it is probably the case that in pensions appeals the Court of Session is not bound by its own prior decisions or by decisions of the nominated judge of the High Court in England.

1 *James v Minister of Pensions* [1947] KB 867, [1947] 2 All ER 432; *Minister of Pensions v Higham* [1948] 2 KB 153, [1948] 1 All ER 863.

333. The Transport Tribunal. It has been held by the Court of Appeal in England that the Transport Tribunal, which has jurisdiction in both Scotland and England, should not regard itself as absolutely bound by its own decisions as to do so would be inconsistent with its duty to consider each appeal before it on its merits[1].

1 *Merchandise Transport Ltd v British Transport Commission* [1962] 2 QB 173 at 186, 192, 193, 207, 208, [1961] 3 All ER 495 at 500, 506, 507, 518, 519, CA.

(4) THE BINDING ELEMENT IN PRIOR DECISIONS

(a) The *Ratio Decidendi*

334. Introduction. Hitherto in this discussion the binding nature of prior decisions has been explained in relation to the rules or practices adopted by courts in respect of decisions of that same court or of other courts in the judicial hierarchy. However, when it is asserted that a decision is binding on later courts, explanation is still required to show what it is about the prior decision which has this binding quality. Writing in 1952 T B Smith pointed to the surprising fact that although in relation to English law this topic was a much canvassed one, 'no Scottish jurist has essayed the task of examining in detail or even in substantial outline that aspect of precedent known as the *ratio decidendi*'[1].

1 T B Smith *The Doctrines of Judicial Precedent in Scots Law* (1952) p 67.

335. The nature of the *ratio decidendi*. Little detailed attention has been paid to the nature of the *ratio decidendi* in relation to the actual practices of the Scottish courts[1], although recent writings on the judicial process have made valuable contributions to understanding the nature of the binding element in prior decisions, the *ratio decidendi*. By '*ratio decidendi*' is implied a reason or rule of law formulated by a court as a necessary basis for its determination of the legal issues raised by the material facts submitted for adjudication. However, the expression '*ratio decidendi*' is used in two senses[2]. In its first sense it is a legal rule or proposition which is formulated, expressly or by necessary implication, solely in the context of the opinions expressed in the instant case and the manner of its disposal. In the second sense ascertainment of the rule or proposition of law may be assisted by construing the opinions of the court in the instant case in the context of the law as expressed in other consistent authority, preceding or subsequent. The task of determining the *ratio* is not confined to the individual case, but — unless it conflicts with it — is also concerned with its consistency with other authority. Thus in the second sense — but not in the first — the scope of a *ratio decidendi* will reflect developments in the law. In the present context, however, it is proposed to use '*ratio decidendi*' chiefly in the second of the two senses noted. This is because this sense has greater accord with the traditional emphasis which Scots law gives to underlying principle rather than to individual rule[3]. Furthermore this sense of '*ratio decidendi*' suggests a more accurate description of the nature of legal reasoning than does the former sense. When a case is cited as authority for a proposition, the proposition is not advanced in isolation from the rest of legal authority but rather as a proposition of law which is in general conformity with that authority. Using '*ratio decidendi*' in this sense, the factors discussed in the following paragraphs[4] seem to explain the nature of the binding quality of cases in the practice of precedent in the Scottish courts.

1 See, however, the discussion of precedent in N MacCormick *Legal Reasoning and Legal Theory* (1978) pp 82–86, 134–138, 213–228. The particular value of Professor MacCormick's analysis is that many of his illustrations are taken from Scottish cases. See also the valuable discussion of W A Wilson 'Dealing with Decisions' in his *Introductory Essays on Scots Law* (2nd edn, 1984) p 78.
2 Recent commentators have accepted that *ratio decidendi* has this dual meaning: see A A Paterson and T St J N Bates *The Legal System of Scotland* (2nd edn, 1986) pp 329, 330.
3 It is significant that the rather inconclusive debate among English academic lawyers on the problem of 'finding the *ratio decidendi*' tended to use '*ratio decidendi*' in its narrower sense. See eg the debate between J L Montrose and A W B Simpson in (1957) 20 MLR 124, 413, (1958) 21 MLR 155. For a general discussion of this question in English law, see R Cross *Precedent in English Law* (3rd edn, 1977) pp 38–50.
4 The seven factors are discussed in paras 336–340, 341–343 and 344 below.

336. The *ratio decidendi* as a proposition of law. First, the *ratio decidendi* of a case is the element of principle which is binding in later cases and as such is a proposition of law which the decision in the case embodies or illustrates. However, not every decided case necessarily has a *ratio* in this sense, while some decisions may have more than one such *ratio*.

337. Who discovers the *ratio decidendi*? Secondly, the problem of discovering or finding the *ratio decidendi* of a case is a problem, not for the court or tribunal which made the decision, but for the court or tribunal in *later cases* which is seeking to determine what, if anything, it is about the earlier case that is now binding on it.

   Although the present discussion is in terms of later courts looking for the *ratio* of earlier cases, the issue of finding the *ratio* is also of concern to others who deploy legal reasoning. This makes *a fortiori* the point that the problem of formulating the *ratio decidendi* is not one for the court which makes the decision in question.

338. The context of the decision. Thirdly, in ascertaining the *ratio decidendi* of a case, the decision should be construed in the context of the general law of which the decision in question is part. If its statement of principle clearly conflicts with that context — as when relevant authorities have not been cited to the court which decided it — the case will be treated as wrongly decided. On the other hand the judicial process would be unduly prolonged and elaborated if a court had to consider a penumbra of existing authority which was merely peripherally relevant to every proposition of law stated by it which might fall to be considered in the future. Thus in *Sillars v Smith*[1] the High Court of Justiciary dismissed an appeal on the grounds that the *vires* of an Act of Parliament which had gone through the whole parliamentary process and had received the royal assent cannot be challenged in a Scottish court. This statement of law was made against the background of the argument submitted to the court that the Order in Council repealing the Scotland Act 1978 (c 51) was invalid. Literally the language of the court could extend to purported legislation conflicting with fundamental provisions of the Union Agreement of 1707. That, however, was a hypothesis to which the judges never had their minds directed, nor did they ever consider it. The *ratio* of the decision accordingly is limited by the context of the general law.

1 *Sillars v Smith* 1982 SCCR 367, 1982 SLT 539.

339. Who searches for the *ratio decidendi*? Fourthly, the search for a proposition of law in a decision (that is, its *ratio decidendi*) in the context of related
authority is a search made by the later court, not by the court deciding the
precedent. Developments in the law since the date of the case's actual decision
may broaden or restrict the *ratio* implicit in the court's earlier formulation of a
proposition. Thus, following the decision of the House of Lords in *Donoghue v
Stevenson*[1], a narrow and wide *ratio* competed for recognition. The case could
have been construed narrowly to imply merely that manufacturers of a product
sold for consumption owe a duty of care to the ultimate consumer or user and
that the duty could be excluded by opportunity for intermediate inspection. On
the other hand it could be construed to imply a much wider potential expansion
of *culpa* encapsulated in Lord Atkin's generalisation of the neighbourhood
principle. Immediately after the case the restrictive interpretation gained some
support, but, in the event, in situations involving physical harm at least, the *ratio*
has been interpreted to recognise a duty of care generally unless some valid
justification for its exclusion can be shown[2]. As Lord Reid observed in the
Dorset Yacht case[3]: 'In later years there has been a steady trend regarding the law
of negligence as depending on principle so that, when a new point emerges, one
should ask not whether it is covered by authority, but whether recognised
principles apply to it. *Donoghue v Stevenson* may be regarded as a milestone, and
the well-known passage in Lord Atkin's speech[4] should I think be regarded as a
statement of principle'.

1 *Donoghue v Stevenson* 1932 SC (HL) 31, 1932 SLT 317.
2 Glanville Williams and B A Hepple *Foundations of the Law of Tort* (1976) p 90; J W Salmond and
  R F V Heuston *Law of Torts* (18th edn, 1981) p 184; J G Fleming *Law of Torts* (6th edn, 1983)
  p 132.
3 *Home Office v Dorset Yacht Co Ltd* [1970] AC 1004 at 1026, 1027, [1970] 2 All ER 294 at 297, HL.
  See also *Anns v Merton London Borough Council* [1978] AC 728 at 757, [1977] 2 All ER 492 at 503,
  HL, per Lord Wilberforce: 'I believe that the conception of a general duty of care, not limited to
  particular accepted situations, but extending generally over all relations of sufficient proximity,
  and even pervading the sphere of statutory functions of public bodies, had not [in 1940] become
  fully recognised. Indeed it may well be that full recognition of the impact of *Donoghue v Stevenson*
  in the latter sphere only came with the decision of this House in *Home Office v Dorset Yacht Co
  Ltd*'. These interpretations were confirmed in the context of Scots law in *Junior Books Ltd v
  Veitchi Co Ltd* 1982 SLT 492, [1983] 1 AC 520, HL.
4 His Lordship did not identify the passage, but presumably he was referring to 'Who, then, in
  law, is my neighbour? The answer seems to be — persons who are so closely and directly affected
  by my act that I ought reasonably to have them in contemplation as being so affected when I am
  directing my mind to the acts or omissions which are called in question': *Donoghue v Stevenson*
  1932 SC (HL) 31 at 44, 1932 SLT 317 at 323, per Lord Atkin.

340. Consistency of *ratio decidendi* with decision. Fifthly, in searching for a
ratio decidendi an important requirement is that the *ratio* must be consistent with
the actual determination or disposal of the case by the court. This appears from
the dissenting speech of Lord Dunedin in *The Mostyn*[1]:

> 'Now, when any tribunal is bound by the judgment of another court, either superior
> or co-ordinate, it is, of course, bound by the judgment itself. And if from the
> opinions delivered it is clear — as is the case in most instances — what the *ratio
> decidendi* was which led to the judgment, then that *ratio decidendi* is also binding. But
> if it is not clear, then I do not think it is part of the tribunal's duty to spell out with
> great difficulty a *ratio decidendi* in order to be bound by it'.

1 *The Mostyn* [1928] AC 57 at 73, HL. A similar point was made by Lord Blanesburgh at 99.

341. The opinions of the judges. Sixthly, in determining the _ratio decidendi_ of a prior decision, a court will also look at the opinions of the judges who decided the case, but these opinions do not necessarily contain the _ratio_ as an explicit statement and the opinions may in some situations be disregarded by later courts as too wide, too narrow or as inaccurate as a statement of the _ratio_ of the case. In _The Mostyn_[1] Lord Dunedin also made the point in discussing _Wear v Adamson_[2]:

> 'It remains for two purposes. First, for the judgment itself and, second, for the opinions of the noble Lords, which are entitled to the greatest respect. Now, the judgment is binding. What, therefore, I think is our duty on this occasion is to consider the statute for ourselves in the light of the opinions, diverging as they are, and to give an interpretation; but that interpretation must necessarily be one which would not, if it was applied to the facts of _Wear v Adamson_, lead to a different result'.

In a Scottish appeal[3] Lord Blackburn made the following observation:

> 'For when it appears that a case clearly falls within the _ratio decidendi_ of the House of Lords, the highest Court of Appeal, I do not think it competent for even this House to say that the _ratio decidendi_ was wrong. It must, however, in my opinion, always be open to a party to contend that the differences between the facts in the case under discussion and those in the case on which the decision in the House of Lords proceeded are so material as to prevent his case from falling within the _ratio decidendi_ of the House, even though the opinions of the noble and learned Lords who decided the case in the House are so worded as to seem to apply equally to the facts in the case then under discussion; for unless those differences in fact did exist in the case in this House, or at least the possibility of their existence was prominently brought forward, I think the House cannot be taken to have decided that such differences in fact might not make a material distinction in law'.

In a later Scottish appeal[4] Lord Selborne LC made a similar point:

> 'The reasons which learned Lords who concurred in a particular decision may have assigned for their opinions have not the same degree of authority with the decisions themselves. A judgment which is right, and consistent with sound principles, upon the facts and circumstances of the case which the House had to decide, need not be construed as laying down a rule for a substantially different state of facts and circumstances, though some propositions, wider than the case itself required, may appear to have received countenance from those who then advised the House. With this preface, I think it right to say that all three decisions of this House, to which I have referred, appear to me capable of being explained and justified upon consistent principles'.

1 _The Mostyn_ [1928] AC 57 at 74, HL, cited by Lord President Cooper in _Beith's Trustees v Beith_ 1950 SC 66 at 70, 1950 SLT 70 at 72.
2 _Wear River Comrs v Adamson_ (1877) 2 App Cas 743, HL.
3 _Houldsworth v City of Glasgow Bank_ (1880) 7 R (HL) 53 at 62.
4 _Caledonian Rly Co v Walker's Trustees_ (1882) 9 R (HL) 19 at 21.

342. The _ratio decidendi_ where the judges differ. In a case determined by a plurality of judges, some of whom may dissent as to the result or reject only certain pleas in law or arguments for the successful party, there may be particular difficulty in determining the true _ratio decidendi_ of the case[1]. Five judges of the House of Lords usually hear appeals. Lord A may sustain a plea in law for reasons stated, Lord B may sustain another relevant plea for reasons explained by him and Lord C may argue that the appellant should succeed on both pleas and explain his reasoning. Lords D and E may dissent, rejecting both pleas in law accepted by the majority. If, on the other hand, Lord C holds for the appellant on the plea of law and grounds favoured by Lord A but rejects those favoured by Lord B, the latter's view is rejected by a majority of the House. A subsequent court might well interpret the *ratio* to be contained in the highest common factor of the opinions expressed in the speeches delivered, although it might on more dubious ground seek to ascertain the *ratio* from the speech which seemed most consistent with the general context of the law as hitherto recognised. There is, of course, available the solution favoured by Lord Dunedin in *The Mostyn*[2] that where no clear *ratio* (in his sense) could be extracted from the opinions it was not for the later court to insist on finding one.

1 For further discussion of this problem, see R Cross 'The Ratio Decidendi and a Plurality of Speeches in the House of Lords' (1977) 93 LQR 378.
2 *The Mostyn* [1928] AC 57 at 73, HL.

343. Obiter dicta. When a statement is made in an opinion in a case which is not directly derivable from the proposition said later to form its *ratio decidendi*, that statement is an *obiter dictum*. In *Neilson v Wilson*[1] Lord President Inglis noted that:

> 'every expression of a judicial opinion must be read *secundum subjectam materiam*; and it would be as unfair to apply an opinion given on a case where there is no previous constitution of a debt to another case where the obligation is constituted by written instrument, as it is to read judgments delivered in the latter kind of cases as intended to apply to and include the former'.

In determining whether a statement made by a judge in his opinion is a formulation of the *ratio* (or is a statement consistent with the *ratio*) or, on the other hand, is merely *obiter*, it must be stressed that a case may have more than one *ratio* and that various statements within one judgment may be consistent with the various *rationes*. This point was made by Lord Wheatley sitting as Lord Ordinary in *Glasgow Corpn v Lord Advocate*[2] when, in discussing *Wilson and M'Lellan v Sinclair*[3], his Lordship noted:

> 'while it is true that the appeal had been decided on the primary ground referred to above, it should be noted that the Lord Chancellor prefaced his opinion on this matter by the words "But there are other circumstances in this case, and I shall only refer to one or two, which make it perfectly clear that there can be no affirmance of any part of the decree". It seems to me that with that preamble what follows is not really *obiter* but is an additional ground for holding that the appeal should be sustained, and it is noteworthy that the headnote to the report seems to view it in that light. If a Judge rejects an argument on three grounds, each one of which would be fatal to the argument, it may be a matter of chance or preference which ground is stated first. In these circumstances I doubt whether the second and third grounds can be said to be truly *obiter*'.

This opinion of Lord Wheatley also illustrates that *obiter* statements are not entirely lacking in force as statements of legal principle. His Lordship was there concerned with the issue of whether an error of law founded an action based on a *condictio indebiti*, and examined a number of cases on the *condictio indebiti* where courts were faced with issues of error of fact but had made observations about error of law. Lord Wheatley found persuasive 'this chain of judicial opinion even if only *obiter*' to the effect that Scots law did not extend the *condictio indebiti* to error of law[4].

1 *Neilson v Wilson* (1890) 17 R 608 at 613. In *Fortington v Lord Kinnaird* 1942 SC 239 at 271, 1943 SLT 24 at 38, Lord Mackay referred to 'the excellent law that things said by judges (even if not entirely *obiter*) fall to be read *secundum subjectam materiam*, and that to read them in any wider sense is dangerous and false law'.

2 *Glasgow Corpn v Lord Advocate* 1959 SC 203 at 216, 1959 SLT 230 at 236, 237.
3 *Wilson and M'Lellan v Sinclair* (1830) 4 W & S 398, HL.
4 *Glasgow Corpn v Lord Advocate* 1959 SC 203 at 219, 1959 SLT 230 at 238.

344. Defining the issue in the earlier case. Seventhly, a crucial element in formulating the *ratio decidendi* of a prior decision is to identify the issue that that case decided. It is sometimes said that what the later court must do is to ascertain the material facts of the precedent case, and an influential theory of the *ratio* in English law, that of Professor A L Goodhart, restricts the *ratio decidendi* of a case to the proposition or propositions of law based on the facts of the case which are treated as material by the judge deciding it[1]. Goodhart's approach does not, however, fit easily with certain aspects of Scottish procedure[2]. In the first place, the doctrine of relevancy in Scottish procedure requires decisions to be made on law applicable to facts pleaded but not yet proved. It is, of course, true that a judge may well treat certain averments as material and others not so. In procedure by special case, parties are not in dispute as to facts but are seeking an authoritative decision solely on a point of law. Parties put forward an agreed statement of facts, and again, the court may well treat some of these facts as material and others not so. However, in neither situation need evaluation of facts correspond to Goodhart's tests. The courts have warned that they will not decide purely hypothetical issues[3], but may decide questions which have become moot by the time of decision, and if the issue has become moot between the decision at first instance and the hearing of the appeal, the question of the correctness of the decision at first instance is relevant to the issue of liability for expenses. An important illustration of a decision on a matter of legal principle without direct consequences for the parties involved is the duty of the High Court of Justiciary to decide a question brought by means of the Lord Advocate's reference, when, no matter the decision of the court, the accused's acquittal will remain unaffected[4].

Facts as such do not determine precedents, for facts will always vary from case to case, even if only as to the identity of parties and the dates of litigation. Rather what is important for a later court in deciding whether it is bound by a prior case is the identity or similarity of the issue before the earlier court to the issue facing it now. Material facts will certainly be an element in formulating the issue but it is only one element and is not to be confused with the issue. This point was made by Lord Finlay in *Craig v Glasgow Corpn*[5]:

> 'I am not going to compare the facts of *Jackson's* case[6] or the facts of *Wakelin's* case[7] with the facts of the present case; it seems to me that no inquiry is more idle than one which is devoted to seeing how nearly the facts of two cases come together. The use of cases is for the propositions of law they contain; and it is no use to compare the special facts of one case with the special facts of another for the purpose of endeavouring to ascertain what conclusion you ought to arrive at in the second. Authorities so used would really very much encumber the administration of justice'.

This process of defining the issue or issues in a prior case, it must be noted, is one for the later court to perform, and it is a means whereby a court can avoid having to follow a prior decision which it does not favour by 'distinguishing' the issue in that case from the issue in the case before it. For example, in *Shand's Trustees v Shand's Trustees*[8] the court distinguished *Brydon's Curator Bonis v Brydon's Trustees*[9] as being one where the facts were very special and where the issue in the present case was not a live issue in the earlier case. In *McIldowie v Muller*[10] the court distinguished *Finlay v Finlay's Trustees*[11] as being one of a number of cases the abstractable principle of which, when read in its own context, indicated that it did not apply to the present case.

1　For a discussion and criticism of Professor Goodhart's views, see R Cross *Precedent in English Law* (3rd edn, 1977) pp 66–76.
2　T B Smith *The Doctrines of Judicial Precedent in Scots Law* (1952) pp 76–81.
3　*Glasgow Navigation Co Ltd v Iron Ore Co Ltd* 1910 SC (HL) 63 at 64, 1910 1 SLT 345 at 347.
4　Ie under the Criminal Procedure (Scotland) Act 1975 (c 21), s 263A (added by the Criminal Justice (Scotland) Act 1980 (c 62), s 37): see paras 319, 320 above. For an illustration of a court dealing with a point which had become moot, see *Dalgleish v Glasgow Corpn* 1976 SC 32, 1976 SLT 157.
5　*Craig v Glasgow Corpn* 1919 SC (HL) 1 at 10, 11, 1919 1 SLT 131 at 134, 135.
6　*Metropolitan Rly Co v Jackson* (1877) 3 App Cas 193, HL.
7　*Wakelin v London and South Western Rly Co* (1886) 12 App Cas 41, HL.
8　*Shand's Trustees v Shand's Trustees* 1966 SC 178 at 183, 1966 SLT 306 at 308, 309.
9　*Brydon's Curator Bonis v Brydon's Trustees* (1898) 25 R 708, 5 SLT 355.
10　*McIldowie v Muller* 1979 SC 271 at 276, 277, 1982 SLT 154 at 156, 157.
11　*Finlay v Finlay's Trustees* 1948 SC 16, 1948 SLT 182.

345. *Ratio decidendi* and the hierarchy of courts. To appreciate how the process of finding the *ratio decidendi* of a previous decision operates in practice, it is important also to note the position in the hierarchy of courts occupied by the respective courts deciding the precedent and the instant case. Where a court is bound to apply a decision of a court superior to it, or co-ordinate with it, in the hierarchy of courts, it will require to give special reasons for holding itself not bound to follow that particular decision. Judicial precedent is not to be accounted for solely in terms of appellate jurisdiction and a hierarchy of courts. Good reasons of principle exist for a court following prior decisions, even of courts equal to it, or lower than it, on the judicial hierarchy. Accordingly the practice has developed of a court giving justifying reasons for not applying a prior decision even when not bound to apply it.

This feature of giving reasons for not applying decisions which are not in any event binding in terms of *stare decisis* is most dramatically illustrated by the practice of the House of Lords in respect of its own decisions which since 1966 are no longer binding on the House in later cases[1]. In the *Vestey* case[2] Lord Wilberforce noted that 'the discretion conferred by the practice direction of 1966 is a general one. We should exercise it sparingly and try to keep it governed by stated principles'. It is clear that principles of fairness, in treating like cases alike, and of legality, that is applying previously declared law, explain the practice of courts giving justifying reasons for not following prior decisions, whether or not the particular rules of *stare decisis* require precedent to be followed.

1　*Practice Statement* [1966] 3 All ER 77, [1966] 1 WLR 1234, HL: see paras 283 ff above.
2　*Vestey v Inland Revenue Comrs* [1980] AC 1148 at 1178, [1979] 3 All ER 976 at 989, HL.

(b) Reasons for not following Prior Decisions

346. Introduction. It is probably not possible to give a complete and exhaustive list of the reasons justifying a court in not following prior decisions, but the factors discussed in the following paragraphs are among those to which appeal is most typically made.

347. Different issues in the respective cases. The most common justifying reason adduced for not following a prior decision is to argue that the issue in that decision is different from that now facing the court. In *Inverurie Magistrates v Sorrie*[1], the court consulted the Session papers to discover the background to *MacLeod v Davidson*[2], which was distinguished. In *Turner's Trustees v Turner*[3] the court distinguished *Jamieson's Trustees v Jamieson*[4] as a case decided on its own particular facts. A more recent example is *Lawrence Building Co Ltd v Lanarkshire County Council*[5], where the court pointed to the differences in the issues before it and those before the court in *Varney (Scotland) Ltd v Lanark Burgh*[6] as allowing it to distinguish the prior case.

1 *Inverurie Magistrates v Sorrie* 1956 SC 175 at 181, 182, 1956 SLT (Notes) 17 at 18.
2 *MacLeod v Davidson* (1886) 14 R 92.
3 *Turner's Trustees v Turner* 1961 SLT 319 at 321, 322.
4 *Jamieson's Trustees v Jamieson* (1899) 2 F 258, 7 SLT 279.
5 *Lawrence Building Co Ltd v Lanarkshire County Council* 1978 SC 30, 1979 SLT 2.
6 *Varney (Scotland) Ltd v Lanark Burgh* 1976 SLT 46.

348. Prior case not consistent with existing authority. The *ratio decidendi* is the proposition of law which the case states. If this *ratio* is inconsistent with the law as already settled it may be overruled by a court which has power to do so, or not followed by a court which lacks this power. A case which has no clear discernible *ratio* may be ignored. Indications that a decision lacks this element of consistency with authority are that it has been rarely followed in later cases and that it has not received recognition or welcome in the textbooks. In *Fortington v Lord Kinnaird*[1] the Inner House overruled the decision in *Drummond v Bell-Irving*[2] as being inconsistent with the cases examined by the court in the later case. In *Sinclair's Trustees v Sinclair*[3] the case of *M'Kenzie v Holte's Legatees*[4] was held not to have the wide *ratio* claimed for it, as there was no trace that it had such a *ratio* in any books of authority. Similarly in *Cochrane's Executrix v Cochrane*[5] the court overruled *Denholm's Trustees v Denholm's Trustees*[6] as it was not consistent with any other case and, except in one case, it had not been followed. It was also pointed out that the decision had not been approved by textbook writers and had been viewed with distaste by later courts. In *Shand's Trustees v Shand's Trustees*[7] it was noted that *Brydon's Curator Bonis v Brydon's Trustees*[8] had not been followed in any later case and was distinguished by the court.

1 *Fortington v Lord Kinnaird* 1942 SC 239, 1943 SLT 24.
2 *Drummond v Bell-Irving* 1930 SC 704, 1930 SLT 466.
3 *Sinclair's Trustees v Sinclair* 1942 SC 362 at 365, 1942 SLT 168 at 169.
4 *M'Kenzie v Holte's Legatees* (1781) Mor 6602, 2 Feb 1781 FC.
5 *Cochrane's Executrix v Cochrane* 1947 SC 134, 1947 SLT 69.
6 *Denholm's Trustees v Denholm's Trustees* 1907 SC 61, 14 SLT 394, 1908 SC 255, 15 SLT 589.
7 *Shand's Trustees v Shand's Trustees* 1966 SC 178 at 184, 1966 SLT 306 at 309.
8 *Brydon's Curator Bonis v Brydon's Trustees* (1898) 25 R 708, 5 SLT 355.

349. Prior decision given *per incuriam*. A particular way of demonstrating that a decision lacks consistency with general legal authority is to show that it was made without proper regard to legal authority which would have affected the decision and which is still binding authority. In *Mitchell v Mackersy*[1] the court overruled *Gray's Trustees v Royal Bank of Scotland*[2] as having been made without reference to the leading House of Lords decision, *Globe Insurance Co v Mackenzie*[3]. Lord Kyllachy noted:

> 'Now, in these circumstances we might have had some difficulty as to our procedure if there had been no judgment of this Court subsequent to the case of *Gray's Trustees* — no judgment reaffirming the law as laid down in the case of *The Globe Insurance Co.* I am not sure that even on that assumption we should have been justified in ignoring, or hesitating to give effect to, a judgment of the House of Lords, a judgment plainly applicable and of indisputable authority. But we are I think relieved of any difficulty on that head by the fact that, in a case which shortly

followed the case of *Gray's Trustees* — I refer to the case of *Stewart's Trustee v Stewart's Executrix*[4] — the decision in *The Globe Insurance Co's* case was considered and its authority recognised'[5].

In *Currie's Trustees v Collier*[6] it was pointed out that *Normand's Trustees v Normand*[7] was difficult to justify, and that the leading case of *Carleton v Thomson*[8] was not among the cases cited by the court in that case. Similarly, in *Copeland v Gillies*[9] the High Court of Justiciary noted that observations by Lord Justice-General Clyde in *MacLeod v Woodmuir Miners' Welfare Society Social Club*[10] had been made without his attention having been brought to the case of *Clark v Stuart*[11], a case which had been followed subsequent to *MacLeod*[12].

1 *Mitchell v Mackersy* (1905) 8 F 198, 13 SLT 570.
2 *Gray's Trustees v Royal Bank of Scotland* (1895) 23 R 199, 3 SLT 168.
3 *Globe Insurance Co v Mackenzie* (1850) 7 Bell App 296, 22 SJ 625, HL.
4 *Stewart's Trustee v Stewart's Executrix* (1896) 23 R 739, 4 SLT 17.
5 *Mitchell v Mackersy* (1905) 8 F 198 at 200, 13 SLT 570 at 570.
6 *Currie's Trustees v Collier* 1939 SC 247 at 252, 1939 SLT 117 at 119, 120.
7 *Normand's Trustees v Normand* (1900) 2 F 726, 7 SLT 430.
8 *Carleton v Thomson* (1867) 5 M (HL) 151, 39 SJ 640.
9 *Copeland v Gillies* 1973 SLT 74.
10 *MacLeod v Woodmuir Miners' Welfare Society Social Club* 1961 JC 5, 1960 SLT 349.
11 *Clark v Stuart* 1950 JC 8, 1949 SLT 461.
12 See *Bell v Hogg* 1967 JC 49, 1967 SLT 290.

350. Age of, and lack of reliance on, prior case. A further indication that a prior decision has little by way of an extensive *ratio decidendi* is that the case has been little relied on as correctly stating the legal position on a matter. Where, however, there has been reliance on a case, this is usually taken to mean that the *ratio* of the case as relied upon will continue to be binding. At times the issue of reliance is confused with that of the age of the case. The age of a case *in itself* has, however, little relevance in determining whether the case should or should not now be followed. Continuing to follow a case which has been followed in the past seems justified on general considerations of fairness. It may indeed have established some important and seminal principle of law.

In *Donnelly v Donnelly*[1] Lord Justice-Clerk Thomson stated: 'I doubt if the most fanatical devotee of judicial precedent would regard *Logan v Wood*[2], however pointed and in point, as binding on us'. However, it has been pointed out[3] that Lord Thomson's judgment in the *Donnelly* case is consistent with *Logan v Wood*, and Lord Patrick explicitly states that the case forms a trend of authority which must now be regarded as settled law. In *Laing and Irvine v Anderson*[4] Lord President Inglis stated, in discussing *Bruce v Jack*[5], that 'I should not allow a single obscure judgment to stand in the way of pronouncing a decision in accordance with the light which we now have'. However, it is clear that *Bruce v Jack* was not followed, not simply because of its age, but because of its lack of consistency with binding authority. Certainly courts do not hesitate to apply old judgments where necessary. For example, in *Yuill's Trustees v Maclachlan's Trustees*[6], the House of Lords reversed a judgment of the Inner House for not having given sufficient weight to *Boyd's Trustees v Earl of Home*[7], albeit Lord Macmillan had to deduce the *ratio* in this case from the report of counsel's argument. In *Jacksons (Edinburgh) Ltd v Constructors John Brown Ltd*[8] the decision was based on the case of *Duncan v Arbroath Town*[9], which had not been cited in argument.

The role of reliance as adding to the strength of a case in terms of its binding effect is illustrated by *Cochrane's Executrix v Cochrane*[10], where Lord President Normand said:

'It is said, however, that it[11] has stood a long time in the books and that its age should save it. If a case, even though it may be thought to have been wrongly decided, has stood long in the books and if it may be supposed to have been used as a guide by conveyancers, that may be a good reason for allowing it to remain undisturbed. But it is scarcely to be believed that any conveyancer has taken the *Denholm's* mutual settlement as a model style. It is a decision which runs counter to the legal conception of a fee'.

On the other hand, in *Baird v Baird's Trustees*[12] it was noted that in *Mackenzie's Trustees v Lord Kilmarnock's Trustees*[13] Lord President Dunedin suggested that *Alves v Alves*[14] should be reviewed by the House of Lords when the occasion arose. Subsequently Lord Normand took the view that the time had passed when such a review was permissible as property had been enjoyed by persons whose right depended on the validity of the rule in the *Alves* case. Nevertheless Lord Keith of Avonholm reserved his opinion on this point. In *Shand's Trustees v Shand's Trustees*[15] the court followed *Perret's Trustees v Perret*[16] which, it was noted, had been followed as a binding authority in many cases and had stood unchallenged for almost sixty years.

The point does not seem to have been fully argued that — especially if a case had seldom been relied on subsequently — it is anachronistic to attach more weight to seventeenth and eighteenth-century decisions today than would have been accorded before doctrines of *stare decisis* had evolved and when case law was merely an aspect of developing learned or judicial custom.

1 *Donnelly v Donnelly* 1959 SC 97 at 102, 1959 SLT 327 at 330.
2 *Logan v Wood* (1561) Mor 5877, Balfour *Practicks* 95.
3 W A Wilson *Introductory Essays on Scots Law* (2nd edn, 1984) p 79.
4 *Laing and Irvine v Anderson* (1871) 10 M 74 at 76, 44 SJ 53.
5 *Bruce v Jack* (1670) 1 Brown's Supp 609.
6 *Yuill's Trustees v Maclachlan's Trustees* 1939 SC (HL) 40, 1939 SLT 233.
7 *Boyd's Trustees v Earl of Home* (1777) Mor 42.
8 *Jacksons (Edinburgh) Ltd v Constructors John Brown Ltd* 1965 SLT 37, OH.
9 *Duncan v Arbroath Town* (1668) Mor 10075, 1 Stair Rep 563.
10 *Cochrane's Executrix v Cochrane* 1947 SC 134 at 147, 1947 SLT 69 at 75.
11 Ie *Denholm's Trustees v Denholm's Trustees* 1907 SC 61, 14 SLT 394, 1908 SC 255, 15 SLT 589.
12 *Baird v Baird's Trustees* 1956 SC (HL) 93 at 108, 1956 SLT 274 at 277.
13 *Mackenzie's Trustees v Lord Kilmarnock's Trustees* 1909 SC 472, 16 SLT 676.
14 *Alves v Alves* (1861) 23 D 712, 33 SJ 354.
15 *Shand's Trustees v Shand's Trustees* 1966 SC 178 at 184, 1966 SLT 306 at 309.
16 *Perrett's Trustees v Perrett* 1909 SC 522, 1909 1 SLT 302.

351. Points conceded in argument. A further indication that a possible *ratio decidendi* of a decision is not consistent with legal authority is that in the argument before the court points of law had been conceded or that a key point had not in fact been argued. In *Aldridge v Simpson-Bell*[1] the Lord Ordinary refused to follow the Inner House decision in *Baillie v Wilson*[2] because on the particular point in question in the later case argument had not been put to the court in the earlier case. In the exchequer cause *Kerr's Trustees v Lord Advocate*[3] the court cast doubts on the correctness of concessions made by the Crown in two earlier cases[4], and Lord Fraser was of the opinion that because of the concessions those cases were not binding[5]. In *Carmichael v Boyle*[6] the High Court of Justiciary refused to give any weight as a precedent to *Stirling v Annan*[7], where the Crown had conceded the merits of the accused's appeal and the court had not delivered an opinion. However, if a concession relates to a matter of statutory interpretation, or possibly to a proposition of law, which the court must consider and construe in order to determine the issue before it, the decision may constitute a binding precedent, especially in the Outer House if the

Division which decided the earlier case expressly approved the concessio in law. Such cases may be distinguished from those in which a point of law has deliberately not been argued and therefore not considered judicially[8]. However, a concession that the laws of Scotland and of England are the same cannot be regarded as the basis for a binding precedent[9].

1 *Aldridge v Simpson-Bell* 1971 SC 87 at 95, 96, 1971 SLT 188 at 191–193.
2 *Baillie v Wilson* 1917 SC 55, 1916 2 SLT 252.
3 *Kerr's Trustees v Lord Advocate* 1974 SC 115, 1974 SLT 193.
4 Ie *Allan's Trustees v Lord Advocate* 1971 SC (HL) 45, 1971 SLT 62, and *Clark's Trustees v Lord Advocate* 1972 SC 177, 1972 SLT 190.
5 *Kerr's Trustees v Lord Advocate* 1974 SC 115 at 130, 1974 SLT 193 at 200, 201.
6 *Carmichael v Boyle* 1985 SCCR 58, 1985 SLT 399.
7 *Stirling v Annan* 1983 SCCR 396, 1984 SLT 88.
8 See *Elder v Elder* 1985 SLT 471, OH.
9 See para 272 above.

352. Defects in the report of the prior case. A court may obviate the necessity of having to seek a *ratio decidendi* of a prior case by pointing to defects in the report of the case. Clearly if a later court is not given an accurate account of a prior decision, it cannot begin its task of defining the issue before the earlier court and the proposition of law which the decision embodies. However, courts in later cases may carry out their own researches to amplify the background and detail of inadequately reported cases. In the *Wills' Trustees* case[1] considerable research, including examination of the various interlocutors, the Session papers and transcript notes of judges, was conducted to give more detail to *Grant v Duke of Gordon*[2].

Where it does not prove possible to improve on the details of a badly-reported decision, the decision may be later disregarded precisely because the court in the later case lacks sufficient detail to assess the prior case as a precedent. The reports contain many illustrations of this point. In *Wilson v Pagan*[3] the court pointed to the inaccuracies of the report of *Wilson v Wight* in Hume's *Decisions*[4]. In *Laing and Irvine v Anderson*[5] imperfections in the reports of two early cases[6] were given as reasons for ignoring them. In *Johnson v Tillie, Whyte & Co*[7] Lord Johnston noted that the 'case of *Leslie v Mollison*[8] has something rather apocryphal about it', and concluded that the report was incorrect. In *Fortington v Lord Kinnaird*[9] Lord Justice-Clerk Cooper refused to give too extensive an interpretation to a dictum of Lord Westbury in *Harvey v Farquhar*[10] which was contained in the report in *MacPherson* but which his Lordship had deleted from the opinion reported in the law reports.

In *Sinclair's Trustees v Sinclair*[11] the court consulted the Session papers to expand the 'somewhat meagre records' of *McKenzie v Holte's Legatees*[12], but refused to accept the argument that that case was authority for the *conditio si institus sine liberis decesserit* applying to a bequest by a testator to his stepson. In *Glasgow Corpn v Lord Advocate*[13] the court disregarded *Stirling v Earl of Lauderdale*[14], the entire report of which consists of ten words[15]. In *McLaughlin*[16] the court held that *Bell's Executor*[17] was not to be regarded as a precedent for other cases, and noted:

> 'We were also referred to a decision in *Bell's Executor*, reported only in 1960 SLT (Notes) 3, where a special sitting of a licensing court was ordered outside the statutory period. No opinions were delivered in that case and it is not possible to ascertain whether any question of principle was considered or upon what grounds precisely the court proceeded'.

1 *Will's Trustees v Cairngorm Canoeing and Sailing School Ltd* 1976 SC (HL) 30, 1976 SLT 162.
2 *Grant v Duke of Gordon* (1781) Mor 12820, 2 Pat 582, HL.

3 *Wilson v Pagan* (1856) 18 D 1096 at 1103.
4 *Wilson v Wight* (1816) Hume 537.
5 *Laing and Irvine v Anderson* (1871) 10 M 74, 44 SJ 53.
6 *Ord v Duffs* (1630) Mor 11083, Durie 492; and *Bruce v Jack* (1670) 1 Brown's Supp 609.
7 *Johnson v Tillie, White & Co* 1917 SC 211 at 219, 220, 1917 1 SLT 57 at 61.
8 *Leslie v Mollison* 15 Nov 1808 FC.
9 *Fortington v Lord Kinnaird* 1942 SC 239, 1943 SLT 24.
10 *Harvey v Farquhar* (1872) 10 M (HL) 26, 44 SJ 203.
11 *Sinclair's Trustees v Sinclair* 1942 SC 362 at 367, 1942 SLT 168 at 170.
12 *M'Kenzie v Holte's Legatees* (1781) Mor 6602, 2 Feb 1781 FC.
13 *Glasgow Corpn v Lord Advocate* 1959 SC 203 at 231, 232, 1959 SLT 230 at 244, 245.
14 *Stirling v Earl of Lauderdale* (1733) Mor 2930.
15 Ie *'Condictio indebiti* sustained to one who had paid *errore juris'*.
16 *McLaughlin* 1965 SC 243 at 246, 1965 SLT (Notes) 57 at 57.
17 *Bell's Executor* 1960 SLT (Notes) 3.

353. Change of circumstances: *cessante ratione cessat ipsa lex.* The maxim *cessante ratione cessat ipsa lex* also embodies a justifying reason for not following a prior case. It is a matter of dispute to what extent the Scottish courts do and should use the reasons stated in the maxim[1]; and to appreciate the points at issue in this debate, G Maher concludes that it is necessary to clarify a variety of different ideas to which the maxim has been applied, and T B Smith shares that view, if not all his deductions.

(1) One sense of *cessante ratione* is that where a rule of law has lost its underlying rationale because of changes in social or political circumstances, then the rule is no longer a valid rule of law and does not require to be followed or applied.

(2) A second sense of *cessante ratione* is that where a rule has lost its rationale because of changes in background circumstances, the rule has less weight or force and may be distinguished either on that or on some other basis. However, the rule remains valid until repealed by a competent authority.

(3) A third idea, to which it is submitted it is misleading to apply the maxim, is where a rule has been impliedly repealed by statute or has been impliedly overruled by a decision of a court with power to overrule it.

1 See G Maher *'Cessante Ratione Cessat Ipsa Lex'* 1978 SLT (News) 161; I D Willock 'Judges at Work: Making Law and Keeping to the Law' 1982 JR 240–243; A A Paterson and T St J N Bates *The Legal System of Scotland* (2nd edn, 1986) pp 341–345. Cf T B Smith *The Doctrines of Judicial Precedent in Scots Law* (1952) pp 100–102.

2 See *Miliangos v George Frank (Textiles) Ltd* [1976] AC 443 at 476, [1975] 3 All ER 801 at 820, 821, HL, per Lord Simon of Glaisdale.

354. Application of the maxim. As far as the extent to which the maxim *cessante ratione cessat ipsa lex* is used in judicial precedent, Maher considers that in the first sense indicated in the preceeding paragraph it is not followed at all and that there are good reasons of principle why it should not be used by courts. Scottish courts do, however, in his view appeal to reasons similar to those in the second sense there stated when considering whether or not to apply a decision *which is not binding in terms of stare decisis*. The third idea there noted is used by the Scottish courts, but this involves no more than the standard principles of the effect to be given to statute and to decisions of courts with power to overrule prior cases. He submits that the various cases mentioned in the discussion of this topic are consistent with this analysis.

In the first place he contends that it is difficult to find examples where a court has not applied a decision *otherwise binding* solely because of changes in the social or economic background to the *ratio decidendi* of the case. Indeed a system of precedent would be totally unworkable if general effect were given to *cessante*

ratione in this strong sense, for at least superficially there have been changes in
the social background to most decisions in the law reports. The difficulty in
accepting the legitimacy of the judicial use of *cessante ratione* is that judges are not
suitably placed to assess the essentially political question whether the particular
changes in the background to a rule justify not following that rule. This is a
question which Maher views as better left to the political process. Given the
radical nature of *cessante ratione* in this sense, it is hardly surprising that courts
seldom explicitly use it. It has been suggested[1], however, that the opinion of
Lord Wheatley in the Inner House in *M'Kendrick v Sinclair*[2] in 1972 is an
illustration of the use of the maxim in a strong sense. In that case an attempt was
made to use the form of action of assythment which had disappeared from
practice by the beginning of the nineteenth century. Lord Wheatley concurred
in the view stated by all members of the Second Division that the facts of the
present case did not fall four square into the scope of the action of assythment.
He added:

> 'For my own part, I would be prepared to dismiss the action on a more radical
> ground, namely that this form of action, which at best has been obsolescent for nigh
> on two hundred years, is now dead. When one looks at the nature of the action of
> assythment, and the true cases of it which are recorded, it was manifestly a creature
> of its times. Into it was woven the right of private prosecution, generally practised,
> and the basic principle was that it was the price which the culprit had to pay to the
> appropriate next of kin if, for one or other of the reasons stated by your Lordship,
> the law did not take its full toll. Remission might be granted as a result of the next of
> kin subscribing letters of slains, and in return they acquired the right of compen-
> sation in the form of assythment.
>   It is not surprising, therefore, to find such compensation was described as "blood-
> money". The political and social conditions of the times and the system of criminal
> administration then in common use may explain this concept, but I find it difficult,
> nay impossible, to believe that it can be carried forward, even in modified form, into
> our way of life today'[3].

Later in his judgment Lord Wheatley also noted:

> 'The only justification for keeping this form of action alive would seem to be that it
> gives to collaterals a right to sue for the death of a near relative, when they are
> excluded by the law of *Eisten*[4] from doing so. There are undoubtedly cases, and this
> may well be one, where the death of, say, a brother may cause just as much loss of
> support, and possibly just as much grief, as the death of, say, a father. It might seem
> unfair that the sufferers in such circumstances should be without a legal remedy. If it
> is thought, as I think, that this can result in injustice, the remedy seems to me to lie in
> legislation, whereby the limits imposed by *Eisten* can be broadened in the field of
> reparation. This would seem to me to be in conformity with the modern trend of
> legislation. I do not consider, however, that the answer is to be found by resurrect-
> ing a form of process which has been at least asleep for almost two hundred years,
> which is based on concepts and procedures which are outmoded, and which pro-
> ceeds on a principle which is obnoxious to our way of life in the 1970s. It may well be
> that, when it fell asleep, it quietly died without anyone paying particular notice,
> because there was no further justification for its survival. A new concept of repar-
> ation had been instituted and developed, and had replaced it'[5].

Lord Wheatley seems to hold that assythment is no longer a competent form of
action not only because of changes in the nature of society but also because *legal*
developments in the form of the rise of the concept of reparation, including the
then rule in the *Eisten* case, had replaced it and had impliedly overruled authorities, including decisions of the Full Bench of the Court of Session, which had
permitted assythment. The sorts of reasons to which Lord Wheatley was
appealing in the *M'Kendrick* case were not necessarily only social ones as such

but also changes in *legal* authority (which changes no doubt reflected changes in social circumstances). This, Maher concludes, is more like the third of the three senses of *cessante ratione* noted in the preceding paragraph than the first, and he notes that when the *M'Kendrick* case reached the House of Lords it was held by both Lord Reid and Lord Kilbrandon that in Scots law common law remedies could not be lost be desuetude or change of social circumstances.

T B Smith, on the other hand, notes the express stand of the Lord Justice-Clerk in the *M'Kendrick* case on 'a more radical ground' and his reference to 'political and social conditions of the times', and ventures with the greatest respect to question the views expressed by Lord Reid and Lord Kilbrandon in the House of Lords as to the possibility of common law remedies falling into desuetude — especially if these had been based on case law dating from a period before the doctrine of *stare decisis* had been recognised. This was an argument which they were not required to consider. Lord Wheatley expressed an individual view not adopted by his colleagues on the Bench at the time, but Smith regards it as more explicit than his co-author considers justified.

The second sense of *cessante ratione* which was noted in the preceding paragraph was that changes in the background to a rule may lessen its weight or force but does not affect its validity as a rule. Judicial acceptance of this sense of *cessante ratione* is possibly open to the same objection that courts are not well placed to assess the relevancy of changes in social or political circumstances which render a rule less useful. Nevertheless the courts in Scotland do adopt something very much like this approach. However, in Maher's view the exact approach of courts towards the maxim in this sense depends on the respective places in the judicial hierarchy held by the court in the instant case and that held by the court whose judgment is said to have lost its underlying rationale. If a court is not bound to apply a decision, it may give *cessante ratione* as the sole justifying reason for not following that decision in the instant case. If a court is bound by a previous decision, the maxim does not by itself on this view justify a court not following the precedent (which is *cessante ratione* in its strongest sense) but it does suggest that the court should look for accepted reasons for not following the case. T B Smith is not convinced that the observation of Lord President Cooper in the *Beith* case[6] to the effect that there was no need to convene a larger court to reconsider *Menzies v Murray*[7] did not in fact imply that the doctrine of *cessante ratione* — albeit not expressly referred to — did not justify overruling an outmoded precedent.

In the English *Miliangos* appeal[8] the House of Lords pointed to changes in commercial practice and fluctuations in the value of currency as justifying resort to its 1966 power[9] and overruled the *United Railways of Havana* decision[10]. In the *Miliangos* case Lord Fraser of Tullybelton, the sole Scottish judge in that case, noted that similar considerations applied also in respect of a decision of the House in the Scottish appeal *Hyslops v Gordon*[11]. In *Sugden v HM Advocate*[12] a Full Bench of the High Court of Justiciary was convened to consider, inter alia, the extent to which the court was bound by the Full Bench decision of *HM Advocate v Macgregor*[13]. Some of their Lordships thought that the *Macgregor* case could be distinguished, others that it had to be followed and could not be overruled, and others that it could and should be overruled. For example, Lord Justice-Clerk Aitchison noted:

'As I have already pointed out, the rule laid down in *Macgregor's* case was laid down in times that are far distant from our own, and under social and political conditions, affecting the purity of prosecutions, that have long since passed away. I cannot regard a rule so laid down one hundred and sixty years ago as fixed and unalterable, and so sacrosanct that it is beyond the power of this Court to declare that the rule no longer exists'[14].

This may well be a use of *cessante ratione* in its second, weaker sense, for Lord Aitchison also considered that the present court had power to review its previous decisions. There is the further factor which was not argued in the *Sugden* case that since the High Court of Justiciary in 1773 would not have regarded a single decision as a binding precedent, it would be anachronistic for a court sitting nearly two centuries later to regard the *Macgregor* case as sacrosanct. A distinction may possibly be made based not so much on the age of the precedent as on the doctrine of precedent accepted when the case was decided.

Another illustration of a court with power to review its decisions appealing to background circumstances of a prior case to justify not following it is the *McLaughlin* case[15], where Lord President Clyde observed:

> 'It was pointed out to us that in Purves on the Scottish Licensing Laws (8th edn) p 15, there is a reference to two unreported cases where the court in 1917 had ordered special sittings of a licensing court to deal with applications not timeously presented. But these were cases arising in war-time and the highly special circumstances directly attributable to the war enabled the court to reach the conclusion to which it came in these two cases. But this has no bearing on post-war conditions and these decisions cannot be invoked as precedents in ordinary peace-time conditions. Were we to do so, we should be enormously extending the powers and jurisdiction of this court to amend or repeal Acts of Parliament'.

Where a court is bound by rules of *stare decisis*, even if *cessante ratione* will not by itself permit the court to disregard a binding decision it may supply the court with reasons to find a way for not applying it. This is illustrated by *Coyle v Coyle*[16], where Lord Wylie in the Outer House referred to decisions, including the Inner House case of *Dickinson v Dickinson*[17], as having 'totally outlived their social usefulness'. However, his Lordship did not hold that this view was a sufficient reason for not following those cases but rather distinguished them as not stating a principle necessary for his decision in the instant case.

Commentators have also suggested that *cessante ratione* should also be applied as a description of the situation where a decision has been affected by subsequent legislation and by decisions of higher courts. Some consider it is misleading to use the expression *cessante ratione* in this context for danger of confusing it with *cessante ratione* in its strong sense. In the *Beith*[18] and *Commerzbank*[19] cases the maxim was not expressly invoked by the courts involved in the decisions but only by commentators (which in Maher's submission leads to confusion). In the *Beith's* case the First Division refused to follow *Menzies v Murray*[20], a decision of a court of seven judges, and Lord President Cooper noted:

> 'if it manifest that the *ratio decidendi* upon which a previous decision has rested has been superseded and invalidated by subsequent legislation or from other like cause, that *ratio* cease to be binding'[21].

He then argued that a number of statutes had deprived *Menzies v Murray* of its rationale, and as a result the case was no longer binding:

> 'We owe respect to previous decisions of superior or equal authority, but we also owe respect to Acts of Parliament; and if subsequent statutes have deprived a decision of its whole content, we have no duty to echo outmoded and superseded conceptions'[22].

If statute had expressly repealed the law laid down in the earlier case this had nothing to do with the doctrine of *cessante ratione*. Lord Keith, however, was unable to construe the statute referred to as depriving the earlier authority of effect. T B Smith accepts that the effect of statute law was the principal *ratio* expressed in the Lord President's opinion. However, although he did not expressly refer to the doctrine of *cessante ratione*, it seems at least possible that he had it in mind when, after referring to Lord Dunedin's dictum[23], he observed:

'I propose to apply this authoritative guidance . . . and to add this corollary that, if it is manifest that the *ratio decidendi* upon which a previous decision has rested has been superseded and invalidated by legislation or from other like cause that *ratio* ceases to be binding'[24].

Although the possibility of a second *ratio* in the *Beith's* case based on *cessante ratione* or obsolescence rather than abolition need not be overstressed, it seems to T B Smith to merit consideration. However G Maher's view is that the court in the *Beith* case did not explicitly use *cessante ratione* and that this doctrine was not necessary to the reasoning in that case.

In the *Commerzbank* case[25], a Full Bench of the Court of Session noted the comment of Lord Fraser of Tullybelton in the *Miliangos* case[26] concerning the House of Lords decision in *Hyslops v Gordon*[27] that: 'the case should, I think, be treated as one decided in accordance with a practice that existed in circumstances which were very different from those existing today and therefore as one not necessarily to be followed now'. In the *Commerzbank* case the court added: 'We agree with these observations and in our opinion the case of *Hyslops*, decided as it was in the context of conditions which no longer apply, does not bind this Court'[28]. The First Division did not regard *Hyslops v Gordon* as having been overruled by the House of Lords, and indeed it would be contrary to principle that the House should alter Scots law incidentally in an English appeal without argument on the issues involved[29]. Nevertheless, the fact that Lord Fraser, who alone of the Law Lords commented on *Hyslops v Gordon*, considered that its *ratio* was no longer binding because of changed circumstances, no doubt fortified the Division in adopting that view.

1 I D Willock 'Judges at Work: Making Law and Keeping to the Law' 1982 JR 242.
2 *M'Kendrick v Sinclair* 1972 SC (HL) 25, 1971 SLT 234, 1972 SLT 110.
3 1972 SC (HL) 25 at 39, 1971 SLT 234 at 239, 240.
4 *Eisten v North British Rly Co* (1870) 8 M 980, 42 SJ 575.
5 *M'Kendrick v Sinclair* 1972 SC (HL) 25 at 40, 41, 1971 SLT 234 at 240, 241.
6 *Beith's Trustees v Beith* 1950 SC 66 at 73, 1950 SLT 70 at 74.
7 *Menzies v Murray* (1875) 2 R 507.
8 *Miliangos v George Frank (Textiles) Ltd* [1976] AC 443, [1975] 3 All ER 801, HL.
9 *Practice Statement* [1966] 3 All ER 77, [1966] 1 WLR 1234, HL: see paras 283 ff above.
10 *Re United Railways of Havana and Regla Warehouses Ltd* [1961] AC 1007, [1960] 2 All ER 332, HL.
11 *Hyslops v Gordon* (1824) 2 Sh App 451, HL.
12 *Sugden v HM Advocate* 1934 JC 103, 1934 SLT 465.
13 *HM Advocate v Macgregor* (1773) Mor 11146.
14 *Sugden v HM Advocate* 1934 JC 103 at 112, 1934 SLT 465 at 470.
15 *McLaughlin* 1965 SC 243 at 245, 246, 1965 SLT (Notes) 57 at 57.
16 *Coyle v Coyle* 1981 SLT (Notes) 129, OH.
17 *Dickinson v Dickinson* 1952 SC 27, 1952 SLT 102.
18 *Beith's Trustees v Beith* 1950 SC 66, 1950 SLT 70.
19 *Commerzbank AG v Large* 1977 SC 375, 1977 SLT 219.
20 *Menzies v Murray* (1875) 2 R 507.
21 *Beith's Trustees v Beith* 1950 SC 66 at 70, 1950 SLT 70 at 72.
22 1950 SC 66 at 72, 1950 SLT 70 at 73.
23 *The Mostyn* [1928] AC 57 at 73, HL.
24 *Beith's Trustees v Beith* 1950 SC 66 at 70, 1950 SLT 70 at 72.
25 *Commerzbank AG v Large* 1977 SC 375, 1977 SLT 219.
26 *Miliangos v George Frank (Textiles) Ltd* [1976] AC 443, [1975] 3 All ER 801, HL.
27 *Hyslops v Gordon* (1824) 2 Sh App 451, HL.
28 *Commerzbank AG v Large* 1977 SC 375 at 382, 1977 SLT 219 at 223, 224.
29 For the effect of House of Lords decisions in English appeals on Scottish precedents, see paras 279 ff above. Lord Fraser's observations in the *Miliangos* case were not commented on by other members of the Appellate Committee.

3. CUSTOM AS A SOURCE OF LAW

(1) INTRODUCTION

355. Custom as a source of Scots law. To understand the place given to custom as a formal source of Scots law a historical perspective is essential. In a sense the story of custom as a source is the story of the common law of Scotland itself. It is also necessary to consider the various classifications of formal sources of law made in medieval Europe and, later, by the Scottish institutional writers. As little has been written in recent years on custom as a source in Scotland apart from an invaluable but controversial article by J T Cameron[1], the writer's own opinions on doubtful points are bound to intrude.

1 J T Cameron 'Custom as a Source of Law in Scotland' (1964) 27 MLR 306.

(2) HISTORICAL AND EUROPEAN BACKGROUND

(a) *Lex et Consuetudo*

356. *Lex et consuetudo*: written and unwritten law. 'Custom is older and stronger than statute', said Lord Justice-Clerk Moncrieff in 1878[1]. The remark was perhaps an odd one to make in the context of a nineteenth-century Scottish case, but it expresses an important historical truth. Throughout Western Europe in the Middle Ages statute law and custom (*lex et consuetudo*) were recognised as the twin sources of law, and of the two custom must often have appeared to be the stronger. In his study of custom as a source of law in medieval Europe, Professor Gilissen has given many examples of the juxtaposition of *lex* and *consuetudo* as sources of law from the time of Gregory of Tours in sixth-century Merovingian Gaul[2]. In England, the great treatise on the emergent common law known as 'Glanvill' (c 1200) is entitled '*De legibus et consuetudinibus regni Anglie*'[3]; two generations later Bracton's treatise (c 1270) too bears the title '*De legibus et consuetudinibus Angliae*'[4]. When Edward I gave judgment for John Balliol as king of Scots in 1292 at the end of the 'Great Cause' he founded on the '*leges et consuetudines utriusque regni*', that is, on the laws and customs of both England and Scotland[5]. The celebrated Declaration of Arbroath of 1320 refers to the succession of Robert Bruce to the throne '*iuxta leges et consuetudines nostras*'[6].

Lex was declared or promulgated by a ruler. Much early 'statute law' of this kind marked no new departure: it merely declared or clarified already existing custom. A comparison frequently made between *lex* and *consuetudo* was that *lex* was written down while customary law was not. According to Isidore of Seville (570–636), *Lex est constitutio scripta. Mos est vetustate probata consuetudo, sive lex non scripta. Consuetudo autem est ius quoddam moribus institutum, quod pro lege suscipitur cum deficit lex*[7]. Five centuries later Gratian wrote in his *Decretum* (c 1140): *Quae in scriptis redacta est, constitutio sive ius vocatur; quae vero in scriptis redacta non est, generali nomine consuetudo videlicet appellatur*[8]. The prime example of *lex* as *ius scriptum* was Civil or Roman law as set out in Justinian's *Corpus Iuris Civilis*. Thus the south of France, which relied heavily on Roman law, was known as *le pays de droit écrit* — the country of the written law — while the north of France, which relied to a far greater extent on customary law, was known as *le pays de coutumes* — the country of custom. However, the contrast between *lex* as *ius scriptum* and custom as unwritten law must not be pressed too far. In the course

of the Middle Ages much custom was committed to writing[9], while still
retaining its character as a customary source of law[10].

1 *Learmonth v Sinclair's Trustees* (1878) 5 R 548 at 560.
2 J Gilissen *La Coutume* (Turnhout, Belgium, 1982), being Fasc 41 (A–III, 1*) of *Typologie des Sources du Moyen Âge Occidental* (directeur L Genicot).
3 R de Glanvill *De legibus et consuetudinibus regni Anglie*, ed G D G Hall (Nelson's Medieval Text, 1965).
4 H de Bracton *De legibus et consuetudinibus Angliae*, ed G E Woodbine, trans S E Thorne (Cambridge, Mass, 1968–).
5 E L G Stones and G G Simpson *Edward I and the Throne of Scotland* 1290–1296 (1978) vol II, pp 246, 247.
6 J Fergusson *The Declaration of Arbroath* (1970) p 8.
7 Isidore *Etymologiarum*, ed Lindsay (1911) I, V, 3, 2 (see also *Gilissen* p 16) ('*Lex* is written regulation. *Mos* is custom proved by long existence, or unwritten law. *Consuetudo* is a type of legal right established by usage, which is received as law when *lex* is lacking').
8 Gratian *Distinctio* I, 5 (see also *Gilissen* p 16) ('What is reduced to writing is called *constitutio* or *ius*; what, indeed, is not reduced to writing, goes, it is clear, by the general description of *consuetudo*').
9 Two notable examples are the *Sachsenspiegel* of Eike von Repkow (c 1230) and the *Coutumes du Beauvaisis* of Philippe de Beaumanoir (c 1280).
10 *Gilissen* is invaluable on custom as a source of law in medieval Europe. Other useful works include the *Continental Legal History* series (1912, reprinted New York, 1968); C K Allen *Law in the Making* (7th edn, 1964); J H Baker *Introduction to English Legal History* (2nd edn, 1979); and R David and J E C Brierley *Major Legal Systems in the World Today* (3rd edn, 1985).

(b) The Diminishing Role of Custom

357. Custom and statute. As the Middle Ages progressed the role of custom
diminished and its ambit narrowed. At first it was possible to argue that custom
was stronger than statute in that statute merely declared already existing custom
or provided for emergencies or new situations as they arose. Thus statute could
be regarded as supplementary to custom. However, the capacity of statute for
innovation and alteration was gradually recognised and steadily exploited until,
by the end of the Middle Ages, custom could be better explained as ancillary to
statute. Even so, there was general recognition that contrary custom over a term
of years could derogate from statute. The introduction of codes of law in
modern times has altered this position in most European jurisdictions, but in
South Africa, where the law remains uncodified, the principle of derogation
from statute is still recognised as regards Acts passed before the Union of 1909[1].
In English law it has long been accepted that an Act of Parliament, once passed,
remains on the statute book until repealed by Parliament. This is no mere
academic doctrine: there have been several examples in recent years of the
interpretation and enforcement of elderly statutes such as the Justices of the
Peace Act 1361 (c 1) in circumstances beyond the imagination of their authors.
But even in England it was not always so. In the seventeenth century the great
Sir Edward Coke was prepared to concede the possibility that custom could
derogate from statute[2].

1 H R Hahlo and E Kahn *The South African Legal System and its Background* (Cape Town, 1968) p 174.
2 Co Litt 81b. See also C K Allen *Law in the Making* (7th edn, 1964) p 478, note 2.

358. The ambit of custom. In a different sense too the ambit of custom
narrowed. As the decisions of established courts came to be written, collected
and cited, and treatises written and relied on, it could be argued that case law (*la
jurisprudence*) and authoritative writing (*la doctrine*) constituted important

sources of law distinguishable from custom. In England, the concept of 'the common law of England', based essentially on the practice of the king's court, was well established by the end of the thirteenth century. Sir Edward Coke could describe common law as 'one of the main triangles of the laws of England', along with custom and statute[1]; although custom could equally be regarded as merely a part of the common law[2].

1 Co Litt 110b.
2 For useful works, see para 356, note 10 above.

(c) Custom in Early Scots Law

359. Emergence of the common law. There can be no doubt that a medieval Scots lawyer would have recognised and accepted the division of the sources of law into *lex* and *consuetudo*. However, in Scotland, as elsewhere in medieval Europe, the role of custom as a source of law gradually diminished. In Scotland, as in England, a significant feature was the emergence of the concept of the 'common law' of the realm. The English kings were pre-eminent in Europe in their early establishment of a strong central court staffed by professional lawyers, but the kings of Scots too were remarkably successful in moulding one nation from the diverse peoples over whom they ruled, and in integrating the separate customs of those peoples into one system of law. Professor Barrow has written, of the period from the death of King William the Lion in 1214, 'thenceforward, although feudal tenure and custom were irreversibly entrenched within the law of Scotland they would be interwoven with traditional rules and practice to form a distinctively Scottish common law'[1].

1 G W S Barrow *Kingship and Unity: Scotland 1000–1306* (1981) p 59.

360. Compilations of customary law. Early compilations of customary law include the thirteenth century *Leges Quatuor Burgorum*, closely related to the customs of Newcastle-on-Tyne, and the fourteenth century *Regiam Majestatem* and *Quoniam Attachiamenta*. Of these the most important was the *Regiam*. Although occasionally disowned by later authorities, including Sir Thomas Craig and Stair, it was generally accepted as a valuable statement of Scots law. The *Regiam* relies heavily on Glanvill[1], and in so doing no doubt reflects the practice of the Scottish king's court, which, as in England, must be seen as crucial to the development of the common law. But it also incorporates material from the Romano-Canonical tradition, as well as — at least in some manuscripts — various ancient pre-feudal rules, generally known as the *Leges inter Brettos et Scotos*, which fix a tariff and regulate compensation for slaughter and mutilation. The date and the purpose of *Regiam Majestatem* remain obscure, but it seems likely that it was a private work, or at best semi-official, compiled shortly after 1318. However, later generations, when they accepted its authority, tended to treat it as part of the *ius scriptum* and sometimes ascribed it unhistorically to King David I (1124–1153)[2].

1 As to Glanvill, see para 356 above.
2 See *Sources and Literature of Scots Law* (Stair Soc vol 1, 1936 ed H McKechnie); *Regiam Majestatem* (Stair Soc vol 11, 1947 ed Lord Cooper); *Introduction to Scottish Legal History* (Stair Soc vol 20, 1958). Lord Cooper's views on the *Regiam* must now be revised in the light of A A M Duncan 'Regiam Maiestatem: A Reconsideration' 1961 JR 199; P Stein 'The Source of the Romano-Canonical part of Regiam Maiestatem' 1969 Scottish Historical Review 107; and A Harding

'*Regiam Maiestatem* amongst Medieval Law Books' 1984 JR 97. *Regiam Majestatem* is specifically mentioned in a number of fifteenth and sixteenth century statutes and commissions in the context of digesting or amending the law: see eg APS II, 10 (1426); APS II, 97 (1469); and APS I, 29 (1566).

361. Early and local law and custom. Traces of pre-feudal law and of local or regional custom survived into the medieval period. The particular laws of Galloway were confirmed as late as 1384 in the Scots Parliament[1]. That same Parliament recognised the continuing validity of the 'Law of Clan Macduff', a set of archaic rules conferring special privileges on the kindred of the Celtic Earls of Fife, privileges claimed successfully as late as 1548[2]. In the Highlands and Islands, and particularly in the Macdonald Lordship of the Isles, customs based on Celtic law, such as fosterage and Celtic secular marriage, continued to flourish until the sixteenth century and later[3].

1 APS I, 551.
2 Balfour *Practicks* II, 511.
3 D Sellar 'Marriage, Divorce and Concubinage in Gaelic Scotland' Transactions of the Gaelic Society of Inverness, vol LI (1978–80) p 464; J Cameron *Celtic Law* (1937).

362. The common law of Scotland. However, there can be no doubt of the determination of both king and Parliament that the common law of the realm should be kept, and that it should prevail over other laws and customs, both local and extra-territorial. In 1399 Parliament complained of 'the mysgouvern-ance of the Reaulme and the defaut of the kepying of the common law'[1], and in 1426 it was ordained that the lieges should be:

> 'governyt under the kingis lawis and statutis of this realme alanerly [alone] and under na particular lawis na speciale privilegis na be na lawis of uther cuntreis nor realmis'[2].

In 1504 it was ordained that:

> 'all our soverane lordis liegis beand under his obesance and in speciale all the Iles[3] be Reulit be our soverane lordis aune lawis and the commoune lawis of the Realme And be nain other lawis'[4].

By the sixteenth century, therefore, the scope for custom as a source of law distinct from the common law of the realm was severely limited.

1 APS i, 572.
2 APS ii, 9.
3 By 'all the Iles' was probably intended the Hebrides.
4 APS ii, 244.

(d) The Source of Customary Rules

363. The origins of custom. There is always likely to be juridical debate about the precise sense in which custom as yet undeclared or unapproved by the courts or the legislature can be regarded as law at all. There will also be debate about the meaning of the proposition, accepted in some sense by all, that custom is based on the consent of the people: *Mores sunt tacitus consensus populi, longa consuetudine inveteratus*[1], in Ulpian's famous formulation[2]. Should custom be conceived of as deriving from the Sovereign by the tacit consent of the people, or as deriving directly from the people themselves? Is custom *Juristenrecht*, that is, recognised and declared by those skilled in the law, or is it *Volksrecht*, recognised and declared by the common people?

Perhaps it is best to cut the Gordian knot by taking a historical approach. In his telling discussion of custom as a source of law, Sir Carleton Allen has pointed out that it is impossible to think of feudal custom, 'perhaps the most important body of custom which has ever existed in Europe... as merely "broadbased upon a people's will"'[3], and that it is 'well known to legal historians nowadays that the "custom of the realm" [*scil* England] was in a very large measure the custom of the Courts not of the people'[4]. The medieval division of the sources of law into *lex* and *consuetudo* is comparable to the modern division into statute law and common law: all that is not known or perceived to be statute law is common law. Similarly all that was not known or perceived to be *lex* was *consuetudo*. The sources of customary law were various. Some customs derived from local usage, later more widely adopted, and some customs can be traced to earlier or indeed to rival systems of law. Some derived from mercantile usage and some from juristic writing. Many derived from the practice of the feudal courts and especially of the king's court. Some may have originated in forgotten royal ordinances and some may even have emerged by the tacit consent of the people[5].

1 Ie 'Customs arise by the tacit consent of the people, inveterate through long usage'.
2 Ulpian *Reg* pr 4. Recent research suggests that Ulpian may not, in fact, be the author of these *regulae*.
3 C K Allen *Law in the Making* (7th edn, 1964) p 92.
4 *Allen* p 124.
5 This section of the title owes much to *Allen*. For a recent and complex jurisprudential consideration of custom as a source of law, see J Finnis *Natural Law and Natural Rights* (1980) IX, 3.

(3) CUSTOM IN THE INSTITUTIONAL WRITERS

364. Craig. The basic classification made by Sir Thomas Craig in his *Jus Feudale* of the sources of the civil or municipal law of Scotland (*jus civile*) is between the written law (*jus scriptum*) and custom (*consuetudo*). He regards the statutes passed by the Scots Parliament as the prime and perhaps the only authentic example of *jus scriptum*, although he admits that a case might be made for the authority of Privy Council ordinances, and statutes passed by a Convention of Estates. He regards custom as a source of law distinctly secondary to statute, although he appreciates that this was not always so: 'when men first contracted into society, laws were not yet written, and custom and the tacit consent of the citizens settled all disputes'[1]. Now, however, he continues, even the oldest custom should not be followed in preference to the written statute law of the land. Craig's view of the relationship between custom and statute is a complex one, for although he states that custom (*consuetudo*) cannot overturn law (*lex*), but can only interpret it, he accepts that Scots statutes can go into desuetude, and that judicial practice repeatedly followed over a period of at least ten years can controvert the written law. For Craig, the prime example of custom is a settled course of judicial decisions, and the prime historical source of custom is the Feudal Law[2].

In his *De Unione Regnorum Britanniae* Craig discusses the sources of English law and says that on the whole they are very similar to those accepted in Scotland. He lists them in order of importance as statute, the common law of England (*Ius commune quod jus patrium dicitur*[3]), general legal maxims, local custom, judicial decisions (especially those of the King's Bench) and Equity. In discussing the place given to local custom in England he draws Scottish parallels, citing the hereditary leases of Glasgow and Paisley[4].

1 Ie '*cum primum inter homines contracta fuit societas, nec adhuc Leges scriberentur, consuetudo et tacitus civium consensus omnes dirimebat controversias*'.

2 Craig *Jus Feudale* I, 8 (I, 8, 6–I, 8, 15, and especially I, 8, 13 in Lord Clyde's translation). The present writer has preferred to consult the original latin in the London edition of 1655; the translation is his own.

3 Ie common law which is called the law of the land.

4 Craig *De Unione Regnum Britanniae Tractatus* (Scottish Historical Society, 1909 ed C Sandford Terry) pp 84 ff, 320 ff. Craig's reference to equity in England is to the Court of Equity (*Curia Conscientiae*).

365. Mackenzie. Sir George Mackenzie states that 'Our *Municipal Law* of *Scotland*, is made up partly of our *written*, and partly of our *unwritten Law*'[1]. The written law consists of Acts of Parliament, Acts of Sederunt and the *Regiam Majestatem*. The unwritten law comprehends '*the constant tract of decisions*, past by the Lords of Session', and ancient custom. 'Our *Ancient customs*', he writes, 'make up part of our *Unwritten Law*, which have been universally received among us. The *Tacite consent* of *King* and *People*, operating as much in these, as their *express concourse* does in making Laws'[1].

1 Mackenzie *Institutions* (1688 edn) I, 1.

366. Stair. In his discussion of sources of law Stair[1] gives first place to the law of nature and the law of nations and especially equity, as indeed did Craig before him, before discussing civil and municipal law. 'Yet surely they are most happy, whose laws are nearest to equity, and most declaratory of it, and least altering of the effects thereof'. But the laws of man are necessary, and of these, the best is custom, which Stair, the natural lawyer, contrasts favourably with statute law:

> 'Yea, and the nations are more happy, whose laws have entered by long custom, wrung out from their debates upon particular cases, until it come to the consistence of a fixed and known custom. For thereby the conveniences and inconveniences thereof through a tract of time are experimentally seen; so that which is found in some cases convenient, if in other cases afterwards it be found inconvenient, it proves abortive in the womb of time, before it attain the maturity of a law. But in statutes the lawgiver must at once balance the conveniences and inconveniences; wherein he may and often doth fall short: and there do arise *casus incogitati*, wherein the statute is out, and then recourse must be had to equity. But these are the best laws, which are approbatory or correctory of experienced customs. And in a customary law, though the people run some hazard at first of their judges' arbitrement; yet when that law is come to a full consistence, they have by much the advantage in this, that what custom hath changed, that is thrown away and obliterate without memory or mention of it: but in statutory written law, the vestiges of all the alterations remain, and ordinarily increase to such a mass, that they cease to be evidences and securities to the people, and become labyrinths, wherein they are fair to lose their rights, if not themselves; at least they must have an implicit faith in these, who cannot comprehend them, without making it the work of their whole life'[2].

Stair's discussion of the sources of civil law in Scotland owes much to the time-honoured distinction between *lex* and *consuetudo*.

> 'Next unto equity, nations were ruled by consuetude, which declareth equity and constituteth expediency, and in the third place, positive laws of sovereigns became accustomed, customs always continuing and proceeding, so that every nation, under the name of law, understand their ancient and uncontroverted customs time out of mind, as their first fundamental law'[3].

The English call these ancient and unquestionable customs their 'common law'. In Scotland too the term 'common law' may be used in this sense: 'In like manner we are ruled in the first place by our ancient and immemorial customs, which may be called our common law'[3]. Stair then gives several examples:

> 'By this law is our primogeniture, and all degrees of succession, our legitim portion of children, communion of goods between man and wife, and the division thereof at their death, the succession of the nearest agnates, the terces of relicts, the liferent of husbands by the courtesy, which are anterior to any statute, and not comprehended in any, as being more solemn and sure than those are'[3].

Stair's examples of ancient custom, *pace* Cameron, are not drawn 'direct from the civil or canon law' (although these would have been permissible quarries for Scots custom), but from the common feudal practice of both Scotland and England, described by Glanvill, repeated in *Regiam Majestatem*, and developed in the king's courts[4].

After ancient custom comes statute or Acts of Parliament, 'which in this are inferior to our ancient law, that they are liable to desuetude, which never encroaches on the other'. Stair also recognises recent custom as a source of law, and by this he means, above all, the settled practice of the Court of Session: 'but there is much difference to be made betwixt a custom by frequent decisions, and a simple decision, which hath not the like force'[5]. As has been seen[6], Craig and Mackenzie held similar views.

There are many references to custom, both ancient and recent, throughout the *Institutions*. Sometimes Stair emphasises custom as common law. Thus courtesy 'is introduced by our common law, which is our most ancient custom, whereof no beginning is known'[7]. Sometimes the emphasis is on recent custom: it was Craig's opinion[8] '. . . that in such cases the warrander should be liable in *quantum lucratus est*. But custom hath since cleared the contrary'[9]; 'but the decisions of the Lords [of Session] have been constantly observed since that King's [Charles II] return . . . and these things which Craig could but conjecture from the nature of the feudal rights, the customs of neighbouring nations, and the opinion of feudists, are now commonly known, and come to a fixed custom'[10]; 'and though that Act[11] was not restored, yet the Lords continued the custom as very convenient'[12]. Frequently Stair is at pains to relate the custom of Scotland to Roman law and to Canon law — sometimes in favour, sometimes adverse — and to the feudal law and the law of neighbouring nations[13].

Stair's account of custom as a source of law, therefore, is founded on the ancient distinction between *lex* and *consuetudo*, although, unlike Craig and Mackenzie, he makes little of the terminology which contrasts *jus scriptum* with the unwritten law. Stair's division of the sources of Scottish municipal law into ancient custom, recent custom and statute leaves little scope for custom as a source of law independent of the common law and judicial precedent. He did, however, recognise the existence and validity of local custom, and contrasts udal rights with the law and custom of Scotland: 'The udal rights of Orkney, by the peculiar customs of the isles of Orkney and Zetland, give the same rights as infeftments'[14].

---

1 For Stair as a jurist, see *Stair Tercentenary Studies* (Stair Soc vol 33, 1981), and also A H Campbell *The Structure of Stair's Institutions* (David Murray Lecture, Glasgow 1954), and three papers by N MacCormick: 'Law, Obligation and Consent: Reflections on Stair and Locke' Archiv für Rechts und Sozialphilosophie (1979) vol LXV, p 387 (reprinted in N MacCormick *Legal Right and Social Democracy* (1982)); 'The Rational Discipline of Law' 1981 JR 146; and 'Law and Enlightenment' in *The Origins and Nature of the Scottish Enlightenment* (1982, ed R H Campbell and A S Skinner) p 150. For Stair's account of the sources of law, see also H David *Introduction à l'Étude du Droit Écossais* (Paris, 1972) pp 191–195. The present writer, although generally in agreement with MacCormick, adopts a rather different standpoint from both MacCormick and David.

2 Stair *Institutions* I, 1, 15.
3 *Stair* I, 1, 16.
4 J T Cameron 'Custom as a Source of Law in Scotland' (1964) 27 MRL 306 at 311; and D Sellar 'English Law as a Source' in *Stair Tercentenary Studies* (Stair Soc vol 33, 1981) p 145.
5 *Stair* I, 1, 16.
6 See paras 364, 365 above.
7 *Stair* II, 6, 19.
8 Craig *Jus Feudale* II, 4, 10.
9 *Stair* II, 3, 46.
10 *Stair* II, 3, 3.
11 Act discharging letters of four forms (APS vi(1), 823) (1647).
12 *Stair* IV, 41, 6.
13 See eg *Stair* I, 9, 8, I, 12, 19, I, 13, 14, I, 14, 7 (Roman law); I, 10, 4 (Roman and Canon law); II, 1, 25, II, 8, 5–6 (Canon law); II, 11, 13 (Feudal law); II, 3, 19 (France); II, 4, 27 (France and England); and II, 6, 17 (England).
14 *Stair* IV, 22, 2. See also II, 3, 11. Cameron ('Custom as a Source of Law in Scotland' (1964) 27 MLR 306 at 319) is mistaken in stating that Stair does not treat local custom as a separate source and that that the first reference to local custom appears in Bankton.

367. Erskine. Erskine's account of custom relies much on Stair and Mackenzie but makes some separate points. The law of Scotland divides into written and unwritten, statutory and consuetudinary. Some customs are so well established that they need no proof, but others need to be proved in the courts.

> 'The most essential articles of our customary law are so interwoven with our constitution that they are notorious, and so require no evidence to prove them; as the laws of husband's primogeniture and deathbed, the order of legal succession, the legitim of children, the husband's courtesy and the widow's terce; but where any later usage which has been gradually gathering strength is pleaded upon as law, the antiquity and universality of that usage must be proved to the judge as any other matter of fact; for all customary law is founded on long usage, which is fact. No precise time or number of facts is requisite for constituting custom; because some things require in their nature longer time, and a greater frequency of acts to establish them than others'[1].

Custom may be either universal, applying throughout the jurisdiction, or, exceptionally, it may be local.

> 'There is hardly an instance of a local custom in any county, but in the udal right proper to the stewartry of Orkney and Zetland ... Certain usages are practised in particular boroughs, ... but have no authority elsewhere'[2].

Erskine notes that a uniform series of decisions of the Court of Session is considered by Mackenzie to be part of the customary law; his own view is that decisions of the Court of Session and of the House of Lords 'are frequently the occasion of establishing usages, which, after they have gathered force by a sufficient length of time, must, from the tacit consent of the state, make part of our unwritten law'[3].

Erskine, in fact, is very much a legal positivist. Custom, he says, 'is equally founded in the will of the lawgiver with written law'[4]. And again,

> 'Unwritten law is that which, without any express enactment by the supreme power, derives force from its tacit consent; which consent is presumed from the inveterate or immemorial usage of the community ... The authority, therefore, of customary law is not grounded on any presumption that what has been long observed must be just, as some lawyers choose to speak; for that presumption is alike applicable to written and unwritten law; but both one and the other derive their coercive force from this, that they are the ordinances, either express or implied, of the supreme power'[5].

Consonant with this view, Erskine says it is not necessary,

'as some writers have affirmed, that the custom be declared by the previous sentence [judgment] of a judge; for no court of justice can constitute law; and therefore any sentence declaring the customary law is of itself a clear proof that the law was constituted before'[6].

1 Erskine *Institute* I, 1, 44.
2 *Erskine* I, 1, 46. Erskine also discusses Udal law at II, 3, 18.
3 *Erskine* I, 1, 47.
4 *Erskine* I, 1, 45.
5 *Erskine* I, 1, 43.
6 *Erskine* I, 1, 44. MacCormick also considers Erskine's approach to sources of law and emphasises his positivist approach: 'Law and Enlightenment' in *The Origins and Nature of the Scottish Enlightenment* (1982, ed R H Campbell and A S Skinner).

368. Bankton. Bankton, like Stair, gives ancient and immemorial custom first place when discussing Scots civil or municipal law, and observes in his *Institute* that 'The ancient customs that have obtained with us, time out of mind, may well be termed our common law, in the same sense as the English lawiers do theirs'[1]. Next he considers statute. He then discusses customs which are not universal, and makes a distinction between the usages, customs and byelaws of royal burghs 'or other corporations' and 'the authorised customs of some parts of the country'[2]. The former are only binding so far as there is power to enact, and so far as not contrary to 'the publick laws of the nation'. (There seems to be a confusion between custom and delegated legislation here.) The latter, however, are received as part of the common law, even though they may be contrary to the general customs or maxims of the law. Thus, although it is a well-accepted principle of Scots law that infeftment is necessary to constitute a real right to heritage — *nulla sasina, nulla terra* — the custom of Udal law in Orkney and Shetland contrary to this has been recognised and sustained. Finally, Bankton accepts that a tract of decisions in the Court of Session can be regarded as establishing the law.

Elsewhere in his *Institute* Bankton discusses Udal law in greater detail[3]. He notes that much udal land has been feudalised since Stair's time and compares this to the disgavelling of land in Kent[4]. He has heard of two other features of udal custom which differ from Scots common law, namely that a man cannot sell udal land without first allowing his heir to offer for it, and that succession to land opens to *all* sons or brothers, with a *praecipuum* to the eldest[5]. He doubts, however, whether these customs are still in use. He notices Coke's division of English law into common law, statute and custom[6], and observes that 'such particular customs are in a more general sense, understood as part of the common law. And in the same manner with us, there are divers customs of burows [burghs] part of our common law'[7].

1 Bankton *Institute* I, 1, 59.
2 *Bankton* I, 1, 71, 72.
3 *Bankton* II, 3, 17–33.
4 *Bankton* II, 3, 33.
5 *Bankton* II, 3, 30.
6 See para 358 above.
7 *Bankton* II, 3, Observations on the laws of England 53.

369. Change in terminology. By the end of the eighteenth century the old terminology which contrasted *lex* and *consuetudo*, law and custom, or *jus scriptum* and 'unwritten law' as sources of law was falling into disuse. Instead a contrast between 'statute law' and 'common law' — both terms of considerable antiquity, as has been seen — seemed more apt, and this remains true today. 'The

Law of Scotland consists partly of enacted law . . .' runs the first sentence of *Gloag and Henderson* 'and partly of common law, which is recognised by the Courts as binding on some ground other than express enactment'[1]. The shift in terminology is explained by the growing perception of judicial decisions and learned writing — *la jurisprudence* and *la doctrine* of Continental legal theory — as separate sources of law, subsumed under the general heading of 'common law'. As already noted[2], the institutional writers from Craig to Erskine considered a settled course of judicial decisions to be a prime example of custom as a source of law. Now, however, judicial decisions would be considered under the head of 'precedent'[3]. The term 'custom' is no longer apt to describe the whole common law, but only a small part of it[4]. Finally, under this head, it is worth noting that the institutional writers do not appear to make a distinction between custom and usage[5].

1 W M Gloag and R C Henderson *Introduction to the Law of Scotland* (8th edn, 1980 by A B Wilkinson and W A Wilson) p 1.
2 See paras 364 ff above.
3 As to judicial precedent, see paras 247 ff above.
4 As to the growth of precedent as a source of law, see T B Smith *The Doctrines of Judicial Precedent in Scots Law* (1952).
5 See para 390 below.

(4) CUSTOM AS A SOURCE OF LAW IN ENGLAND

370. Introduction. Before examining the place of custom in modern Scots law[1] it is worth considering briefly custom as a source of law in England in order to underline the differences between the two systems[2].

1 See paras 375 ff below.
2 The main sources for this section of the title are Halsbury's Laws of England (4th edn), especially title CUSTOM AND USAGE (vol 12, paras 1 ff) by J W Wellwood; and C K Allen *Law in the Making* (7th edn, 1964).

371. Custom a local variation of the general law. In English law custom is always local: if a custom extends to the whole realm it is common law and not custom. 'Customs', writes Sir Carleton Allen, 'are local variations of the general law'. As they are variations, they differ from the general law, but they must not conflict with 'any fundamental principle of the Common Law', and cannot negate 'the very spirit of the law'[1]. As Allen observes, this can be a difficult balance to strike.

1 C K Allen *Law in the Making* (7th edn, 1964) p 131.

372. Tests of custom. Blackstone laid down a number of tests which custom must satisfy in order to be judicially recognised[1]. These are antiquity; peaceableness; continuance; reasonableness; certainty; compulsion; and consistency. These are still the hallmarks of custom in modern English law, although they are sometimes expressed differently. Of these tests the two which cause the most difficulty are antiquity and reasonableness. The difficulty as regards antiquity is peculiar to English law. In order to be judicially recognised, a custom must have existed since time immemorial, and the limit of legal memory has been fixed since the thirteenth century at the date of the accession of King Richard I in 1189! As is to be expected, this bizarre rule gives rise to difficulties. Although it is not necessary to provide proof positive that a custom has been observed since 1189, and although it is certain that many customs which have been recognised judicially must have arisen after that date, clear proof that the alleged custom cannot have existed in 1189 or, having existed then, has not been continuously observed, will result in its being unacceptable as law. The definition of 'time immemorial' also creates theoretical problems which are most obvious in the distinction which English law makes between custom and usage[2].

1 Blackstone *Commentaries on the Laws of England* (14th edn, 1803) vol 1, p 76.
2 See paras 374, 389, below.

373. The test of reasonableness. The difficulty as regards reasonableness, referred to by Allen as 'the last and most difficult test', is not peculiar to English law, but arises in all systems, including Scots law. Allen suggests that

'The true rule seems to be not that a custom will be admitted if reasonable, but that it will be admitted unless it is unreasonable. This is not a mere distinction without a difference, for it seriously affects the onus of proof. The party who has proved the existence of a custom is not under the further necessity of proving its reasonableness; it is for the party disputing the custom to satisfy the court of its unreasonableness'[1].

Although the standard of reasonableness to be applied has sometimes been expressed as 'fair and proper, and such as reasonable, honest and fair-minded men would adopt'[2], Coke's comment as to what is against reason that 'This is not to be understood of every unlearned man's reason, but of artificial and legal reason warranted by the authority of law'[3] has met with judicial approval[4]. It is accepted that the time to decide the reasonableness of a custom is the time of its origin. Allen has reviewed many cases on the reasonableness of custom from the fourteenth century onwards and concludes that it is rare indeed for a court to strike down a custom as unreasonable if the tests of antiquity and continuity are satisfied, although it is less rare to refuse a custom on the closely related ground of conflict with a fundamental principle of the common law[5].

The leading case on reasonableness, as on other aspects of custom in English law is the celebrated *Tanistry* case[6], in which the court struck down the Irish 'custom' of succession known as 'tanistry', by which the eldest and the worthiest (*senior et dignissimus*) of the kin succeeded, rather than the eldest son, as in feudal law. As has often been pointed out, this was not a simple case involving a local custom at odds with the common law. It was a case in which two cultures, and indeed two legal orders, were in conflict. Sir Henry Maine commented 'the Judges thoroughly knew that they were making a revolution, and they probably thought that they were substituting a civilized institution for a set of mischievous usages proper only for barbarians'[7]. A more recent English authority is *Johnson v Clark*[8].

1 C K Allen *Law in the Making* (7th edn, 1964) p 140.
2 *Produce Brokers Co Ltd v Olympia Oil and Coke Co Ltd* [1916] 2 KB 296 at 298, DC, per Horridge J.
3 Co Litt 62a.
4 *Johnson v Clark* [1908] 1 Ch 303 at 311, per Parker J.
5 See particularly *Allen* Appendix 'Reasonableness of Custom'.
6 *Tanistry Case* (1608) Dav Ir 28.
7 Sir H Maine *Early History of Institutions* (7th edn, 1905) Lecture VII, p 185.
8 *Johnson v Clark* [1908] 1 Ch 303.

374. Custom and usage. English law makes a firm distinction between custom and usage. Questions of usage in business or trade may arise in connection with the interpretation of contract. Thus it may be alleged that parties had a particular trade usage in mind in reaching agreement: for example, that it was a custom of the rabbit trade that 'one thousand' be taken to mean 1200[1]. Usage differs from custom in that it does not need to have existed from time immemorial and does not need to be confined to a locality. How far usage contrary to a particular rule or maxim of the common law can be accepted does not seem to be clear. The characteristics of usage, it is said, are notoriety; certainty; reasonableness; and 'legality' in that the usage in question must be in harmony with fundamental legal principle. It is difficult to resist the impression that were it not for the test of antiquity peculiar to English law applied to custom, the distinction between custom and usage would be superfluous. The test of antiquity also creates theoretical difficulties as regards the acceptance of general mercantile usage — usually a good deal more recent in origin than 1189 — as part of the common law[2]. In effect, the test of antiquity colours the entire English law on custom as a source, with the consequence that English cases on custom should be cited or followed in Scotland only with the utmost caution.

1 *Smith v Wilson* (1832) 3 B & Ad 728.
2 See *Brandao v Barnett* (1846) 12 Cl & Fin 787; *Crouch v Credit Foncier of England* (1873) 8 QB 374, and *Goodwin v Robarts* (1875) LR 10 Exch 337, Ex Ch, discussed by J T Cameron 'Custom as a Source of Law in Scotland' (1964) 27 MLR 396 at 309–311.

(5) CUSTOM IN MODERN SCOTS LAW

(a) Custom as Common Law

375. Custom and common law. In modern Scots law, custom as a source of law is usually conceived of as custom distinct from the general common law, custom which is local rather than universal. Those few of Stair's 'ancient and immemorial customs'[1] or Erskine's 'articles of our customary law . . . so interwoven with our constitution that they are notorious'[2] which still survive in the modern law, such as legitim, are not now normally referred to, or considered, as custom. General custom is simply the common law. This, it is thought, is as true of recent custom, once admitted, as of ancient custom. In Scotland, unlike England[3], there seems to be no reason, in theory or in practice, to prevent recent mercantile custom or usage simply being incorporated into, and considered as part of, the common law. Where judicial proof of the existence of such recent custom is required, it is submitted that the tests are the same as those which apply to local custom.

1 See para 366 above.
2 See para 367 above.
3 See para 374 above.

376. Desuetude. The doctrine that pre-Union statutes of the Scots Parliament can go into desuetude is still part of the law. Thus it is accepted that contrary custom over a term of years can derogate from statute and alter the general law[1]. The position as regards ancient legal remedies or modes of proof is more doubtful. In the celebrated English case of *Ashford v Thornton*[2] it was held that the right to trial by battle still existed, although it had not been exercised for centuries, and the Appeal of Murder Act 1819 (c 46) was passed in consequence. In the recent Scottish case of *M'Kendrick v Sinclair*[3] the majority of the judges were unwilling to declare that the remedy of assythment was no longer competent, and assythment was accordingly abolished by statute in 1976[4]. Lord Reid was of the view that:

'Loss of a common law remedy by desuetude would, I think, be a novelty in our law and I see no advantage in introducing such a principle. No one knows what may happen in the future'[5].

On the other hand it has been suggested that a doctrine or remedy which might have been discarded in the seventeenth or eighteenth century through the operation of judicial custom should not be regarded as sacrosanct in modern law[6].

1 *M'Ara v Edinburgh Magistrates* 1913 SC 1059, 1913 2 SLT 110: see para 381 below.
2 *Ashford v Thornton* (1818) 1 B & Ald 405.
3 *M'Kendrick v Sinclair* 1972 SC (HL) 25, 1972 SLT 110.
4 Damages (Scotland) Act 1976 (c 13), s 8.
5 *M'Kendrick v Sinclair* 1972 SC (HL) 25 at 54, 1972 SLT 110 at 113.
6 See para 256 above.

(b) Custom as a Distinct Source of Law

(A) CUSTOM AND FUNDAMENTAL LEGAL PRINCIPLE

377. Local custom may differ from the general common law. As already noted[1], the institutional writers are quite explicit in recognising that local custom, although differing from the general common law of the land, can be a valid source of law. The example which they commonly give is the Udal law or custom of Orkney and Shetland: it is a rule of the general common law that a real right to heritage cannot be acquired without infeftment; yet it is accepted that in Orkney and Shetland infeftment is not necessary to acquire title to udal land. The proposition that local custom can be a valid source of law has been recognised judicially in leading cases[2].

1 See paras 364 ff above.
2 See *Bell v Lamont* 14 June 1814 FC; *Learmonth v Sinclair's Trustees* (1878) 5 R 548; and *Bruce v Smith* (1890) 17 R 1000. The present writer has not been persuaded by Cameron's argument ('Custom as a Source of Law in Scotland' (1964) 27 MLR 306 at 314, 315) that the court in *Learmonth's* case was mistaken in taking *Bell v Lamont* to hold that local custom could create binding rules of law.

378. The test of legality. As already noted when considering custom in English law[1], it is difficult to strike a balance between the fact that local custom represents, by definition, a variation from the general law, and the proposition that custom should not contradict a fundamental principle of law. This difficulty exists in all systems. To suggest, as Cameron does, that 'a fundamental requirement of every custom or usage in Scots law is that it should be in accordance with the law'[2], is to beg the question. No matter what formulation is adopted to describe those parts or principles of the general law deemed so essential that they cannot be controverted by custom or usage, in effect much will depend on judicial discretion and the circumstances of each case. The present writer doubts Cameron's further statement, based on *Anderson v M'Call*[3], that 'The assertion that the common law cannot be altered by misunderstanding goes further than the English rule that custom must accord with the fundamental principles of the law'[4]. On the contrary, it is thought that the test of the 'legality' of the custom is similar in Scotland and in England.

Anderson v M'Call concerned an alleged custom of the grain trade in Glasgow which sought to effect the constructive delivery of goods by a delivery note in favour of the purchaser addressed by the seller to the storekeeper and custodier of the goods when that storekeeper was a servant of the seller. In these circumstances, the law then being that delivery was necessary to transfer ownership, the question was raised in a sequestration whether delivery had been properly effected and a valid title to the goods transferred to the purchaser. The Second Division had little difficulty in holding that it had not. Lord Justice-Clerk Inglis said that it was a clear rule of law that the property in goods could not pass while they were still in the seller's possession — *traditionibus non nudis pactis dominia rerum transferentur*. The so-called custom was based on a misunderstanding of the law, confined to one locality and one branch of trade. 'But that can never be a custom of trade. If it were so, I think that very few cases would be decided according to law'[5]. This seems fair comment. Lord Justice-Clerk Inglis continued, 'It is by just such misapprehensions of the law that litigations occur; and the only difference between this case and the ordinary case is that here the misunderstanding prevailed generally. But the general prevalance of a misunderstanding can never alter the common law'. As Cameron remarks[6] this appears to be a rejection of the maxim *communis error facit jus*, although that maxim was not referred to. In his opinion Lord Neaves remarked that 'The fundamental principle is, that the right of property in moveables does not pass by a consensual contract'[7]. The decision was followed in the *Dobell* case[8].

To be accepted, therefore, as a valid source of law, custom must not be in conflict with fundamental legal principle. Custom will also usually be local or restricted to a particular trade, although exceptionally it may involve a general mercantile usage[9]. There are four further tests which custom must satisfy: it should be certain[10], generally accepted[11], reasonable[12] and have existed for a tract of time[13]. All the tests of custom are to a considerable extent interconnected, the tests of legality and reasonableness very closely so, as Allen has shown in the English context.

1 See para 371 above.
2 J T Cameron 'Custom as a Source of Law in Scotland' (1964) 27 MLR 306 at 316.
3 *Anderson v M'Call* (1866) 4 M 765.
4 *Cameron* at 316.
5 *Anderson v M'Call* (1866) 4 M 765 at 769, 770.
6 *Cameron* at 316.
7 *Anderson v M'Call* (1866) 4 M 765 at 771.
8 *Dobell, Beckett & Co v Neilson* (1904) 7 F 281, 12 SLT 543.
9 See para 375 above and para 390 below.
10 See para 383 below.
11 See para 384 below.
12 See paras 385 ff below.
13 See paras 379 ff below.

(B) TRACT OF TIME

379. No equivalent to the English rule on the limit of legal memory. There is no doctrine of immemorial antiquity in Scots law corresponding to the rule in England which fixes the limit of legal memory in 1189. Scots law has never laid down a minimum period of time during which a custom must be observed before it can be accepted as law. Nor does it seem desirable to do so. The tract of time involved is only one factor to be considered along with others in testing the existence of custom. Some customs may become established and generally accepted very rapidly; others may take a long time.

380. Meaning of 'time immemorial'. Plucknett has commented that in so far as the phrase 'immemorial custom' 'implies that custom is or ought to be immemorially old it is historically inaccurate. In an age when custom was an active living factor in the development of society, there was much less insistence upon actual or fictitious antiquity. If we want the view of a lawyer who knew from experience what custom was, we can turn to Azo (d 1230), whose works were held in high respect by our own Bracton. "A custom can be called *long*", he says, "if it was introduced within ten or twenty years, *very long* if it dates from thirty years, and *ancient* if it dates from forty years" '[1]. Plucknett was writing about English law, but his remarks are generally valid. It was accepted by Scots common law that a period of forty years uninterrupted use was enough to satisfy the test of 'time immemorial' required for the prescription of a public right of way, and the same period of time was approved in the *Wills' Trustees* case[2] in connection with the use from time immemorial of a navigable river as a channel of communication or transportation[3].

1 T F T Plucknett *Concise History of the Common Law* (5th edn, 1956) pp 307, 308.
2 *Wills' Trustees v Cairngorm Canoeing and Sailing School Ltd* 1976 SC (HL) 30, 1976 SLT 162.
3 J Rankine *Law of Land-Ownership in Scotland* (4th edn, 1909) p 54. See also *Wills' Trustees v Cairngorm Canoeing and Sailing School Ltd* 1976 SC (HL) 30 at 126, 1976 SLT 162 at 191, per Lord Wilberforce, and at 165 and at 214 per Lord Fraser of Tullybelton. See further para 393 below.

381. Tract of time in leading cases. The tract of time involved has rarely been a contentious issue in the few reported cases on custom, and time has usually been referred to merely *en passant*. In the various cases concerning the 'kindly tenants' of Lochmaben there was no doubt that the custom was very old indeed, perhaps dating from the time of Robert Bruce[1]. In *M'Ara v Edinburgh Magistrates*[2], a case concerning the desuetude of a statute of 1606 through the operation of contrary custom, Lord President Dunedin noted that the statute had been in desuetude since time immemorial, and certainly since 1832. In the leading case of *Bruce v Smith*[3], although the sheriff-substitute found that the alleged custom was 'not sufficiently inveterate, uniform, or uninterrupted', the Second Division seems to have been convinced of the custom's antiquity and decided the case on other grounds[4]. In *Learmonth v Sinclair's Trustees*[5], where local Caithness custom was upheld that the price of woodwork added by an agricultural tenant to his 'houses and dwellings', including farm buildings, should be repaid by the landlord at the end of the lease, it was noted by Lord Gifford that the custom was claimed 'from time immemorial, and at least as far back as 1787', while Lord Justice-Clerk Moncrieff talked of 'immemorial custom or usage followed in the county of Caithness'.

1 See eg *Marquis of Queensberry v Wright* (1838) 16 S 439, and *Royal Four Towns Fishing Association v Dumfriesshire Assessor* 1956 SC 379, 1956 SLT 217.
2 *M'Ara v Edinburgh Magistrates* 1913 SC 1059 at 1075, 1076, 1913 2 SLT 110 at 117.
3 *Bruce v Smith* (1890) 17 R 1000.
4 See further paras 385 ff below.
5 *Learmonth v Sinclair's Trustees* (1878) 5 R 548 at 554, per Lord Gifford, and at 560 per Lord Justice-Clerk Moncrieff.

382. Tract of time relative. In Scots law then, antiquity of custom is purely relative, and Erskine's opinion still holds good, that 'No precise time or number of facts is requisite for constituting custom; because some things require in their nature longer time, and a greater frequency of acts to establish them than others'[1].

1 Erskine *Institute* I, 1, 44.

(C) CERTAINTY

383. The test of certainty. Erskine's opinion, just quoted[1], bears also on the next two tests which custom must satisfy in order to be accepted as a valid source of law: certainty and general acceptance. Before a custom can be established there must be certainty as to what the custom is. The custom must be definite and certain. This is no more than common sense, as is Erskine's observation that no precise number of facts is requisite: all depends on the circumstances of each case. In England, given the definition of the limit of legal memory, continuity is an essential test of custom, and a break in continuity will be fatal. In Scotland, by contrast, it is thought that evidence of interruption is only relevant in so far as it affects certainty and general acceptance.

1 See para 382 above.

(D) GENERAL ACCEPTANCE

384. The test of general acceptance. To be accepted as law, a custom must be generally accepted, or at least generally acquiesced in as having binding force. To demand that a custom be 'universally acquiesced in'[1] is perhaps to pitch the standard too high, but it will not fall far short of this. The test of general acquiescence is, it is submitted, essentially one of fact, although the court may not recognise an oppressive custom, unwillingly acquiesced in. What constitutes oppression touches on the question of reasonableness, as is clear from the case of *Bruce v Smith*[2].

1 Ie as is suggested by J Stevenson 'Custom and Usage' in 5 *Encyclopaedia of the Laws of Scotland* (1927–1935 ed Lord Dunedin and J Wark) 357.
2 *Bruce v Smith* (1890) 17 R 1000.

(E) REASONABLENESS

385. The test of reasonableness: *Bruce v Smith*. *Bruce v Smith*[1] is the leading case in Scots law on that 'last and most difficult test', the reasonableness of custom. It is not, unfortunately, a very satisfactory case, although it merits close attention, as the judicial opinions expressed raise many points crucial to a proper understanding of custom as a source of law. The action, in 1890, arose from a 'whale-drive' in Shetland — a not infrequent event in northern waters until the present century — by which a school of small pilot or 'caaing' whales were gradually driven into shallow water and killed by the shore by men wading waist deep. The pursuer was the owner of the land *ex adverso* the shallow water in question. He claimed that, 'conformably to the laws, usages, and rights of the islands' he was entitled as proprietor to one-third of the spoils. This, he alleged, had been the custom from time immemorial; the other two-thirds should be divided equally between the captors and the Crown. He relied, inter alia, on the earlier case of *Scott v Reid*[2], in which Lord Cockburn had upheld such a custom. In the event, and on appeal from the sheriff-substitute, the Second Divison (Lord Lee dissenting) found against the pursuer, the main ground on which the decision was based being that the custom failed the test of reasonableness.

According to Lord Justice-Clerk Macdonald there was

'no doubt that the customs of particular districts, though merely local, may have the force of law. But must not the custom, to have such force, commend itself as reasonable? Must it not be according to sound legal principle? Must the custom not be conform to good reason and justice? It may no doubt arise from the consent of the community in the locality, and in that case there is every presumption in favour of its reasonableness, and therefore in favour of its being in accordance with sound principle and justice. . . . On the other hand, the custom may be the result of compulsion; it may be forced on an unwilling community. I question whether the mere existence of a custom is sufficient to establish its legality without regard for the circumstances in which it is found existing. The nature of the custom, the relations of those who benefit by the custom and suffer from it respectively, the position of power of the one party to enforce and the position of feebleness of the other party effectively to resist, may all have a most important bearing on the question whether the custom is truly the outcome of a social *consensus*, or is, on the other hand, truly of the nature of an impost — the result of a law made by one part of the community as against the other, — which the other could not effectively resist'[3].

The Lord Justice-Clerk held that the existence of the custom was established, but he could find 'nothing in the evidence to shew that there is any basis of principle or of justice for the custom. It seems to be a thoroughly one-sided arrangement . . .'[4]. Although the custom was distinctly proved, he held 'that it was not the outcome of a consenting community but a practical tax, frequently protested against, and submitted to not willingly but as a choice of evils'.

Lord Young regarded the case as unique and described it as 'an action for money without alleging any contract, express or implied, with those against whom it is directed, against whom the claim is made, or any damage done which would entitle the claimant to reparation'[5]. The law of Scotland did allow for special customs to govern particular cases, but this rule of law was limited in its application, and generally involved contractual considerations. He noted that 'There is customary tenure of land certainly, but that is contract again'[6], and instanced the kindly tenants of Lochmaben. He was not prepared to go outwith existing principle — this seems to be a reference to contractual theory again — or 'outwith those considerations of utility and expediency and also of good sense upon which all the local customs or admissions of them hitherto by our Court have rested'[6]. He would not like to rest his judgment 'bluntly on the ground that a custom must in our opinion be reasonable in order to be admitted' — some mercantile customs might be admitted even though the court was not convinced of their reasonableness — he would rather put it that 'we are not within the region of custom here'[7].

Lord Rutherford Clark's opinion was more circumspect and learned. He quoted Voet that custom must be reasonable and not inconsistent with legal principle, as also Blackstone's *Commentaries*, Lord Chief Baron Pollock[8], and Broom's *Legal Maxims* to much the same effect. Lord Cockburn in the earlier Shetland case of *Scott v Reid* had wholly disregarded such considerations. A court of law should never approve of a custom which was unjust or unreasonable, however ancient and well-established that custom was. Lord Rutherford Clark held the custom in the instant case to be unreasonable and contrary to legal principle, long submitted to admittedly, but unwillingly, by fear or threat[9].

Lord Lee, dissenting, considered that the custom was not so unreasonable that it could not be recognised and enforced by law. He approved the doctrine of English law 'that a custom may be good though the particular reason of it cannot be assigned. It is enough if no good legal reason can be assigned against it'[10]. He believed that once the existence of a custom was proved, as in this case, then the onus of proving unreasonableness fell on the defenders. He also pointed out that 'the whole system of law in Shetland' was different from the common law of Scotland, except in so far as there had been assimilation by statute or gradual adoption[11]. He approved of Lord Cockburn's opinion in *Scott v Reid*.

1 *Bruce v Smith* (1890) 17 R 1000.
2 *Scott v Reid* 1838 (unreported).
3 *Bruce v Smith* (1890) 17 R 1000 at 1005, 1006.
4 (1890) 17 R 1000 at 1006.
5 (1890) 17 R 1000 at 1007.
6 (1890) 17 R 1000 at 1008.
7 (1890) 17 R 1000 at 1010.
8 *Cox v London Corpn* (1862) 1 H & C 338.
9 *Bruce v Smith* (1890) 17 R 1000 at 1010–1013.
10 (1890) 17 R 1000 at 1013.
11 (1890) 17 R 1000 at 1014.

386. Criticism of *Bruce v Smith*. There is much to be said for Lord Lee's dissenting opinion in *Bruce v Smith*[1]. Certainly the judgments of the majority of the judges are open to criticism, and it is difficult to extract from them a consistent *ratio decidendi*. Lord Young's opinion is at once idiosyncratic, and typical of the Victorian obsession with contract theory. The Lord Justice-Clerk's search for social consensus begs many questions about the nature and source of customary rules of law[2]. Social consensus, as contrasted with the test of general acceptance already outlined, could prove an unruly horse indeed. Two further criticisms of the majority opinions which require more detailed consideration are that they show little analysis of what is meant by 'reasonableness' in the context of custom, and little recognition that the so-called custom might have originated as part of a system of law distinct from Scots law.

It is notoriously difficult to define what is meant by 'reasonableness' in the context of custom. All are agreed that a large measure of discretion effectively remains with the judge. Even the great Hostiensis wrote *Utrum autem sit rationabilis vel non relinquo iudici nec certa regula possit tradi*[3]. However, there seems to be a considerable force in some of the rules which have been suggested by English lawyers: Coke's comment that the test of reasonableness 'is not to be understood of every unlearned man's reason, but of artificial and legal reason warranted by the authority of law'; Allen's suggestion that the true rule is not that a custom will only be admitted if it is reasonable, but that it will be admitted unless it can be shown to be unreasonable, thus affecting the onus of proof; and the general view that the time to decide the reasonableness of a custom is the time of its origin[4]. The criticism of the judges in *Bruce v Smith* is that, with the exception of Lord Lee, they do not appear even to have reflected on such matters. In truth, the custom in *Bruce v Smith*, although certainly inequitable to modern eyes, was no more unreasonable or oppressive than many other ancient customs once accepted as law.

1 *Bruce v Smith* (1890) 17 R 1000 at 1013.
2 See para 363 above.
3 Hostiensis *Summa Aurea* I, '*De Consuetudine*', 2, 3: 'Whether [a custom] is reasonable or not I leave to the judge, and it is not possible to lay down fixed rules'.
4 See paras 372, 373 above.

387. *Bruce v Smith* and Udal law. Only Lord Lee, of the judges in *Bruce v Smith*[1], noted that the whole system of law in Shetland had once been different from the common law of Scotland and considered that this might have a bearing on the matter. The majority does not appear to have considered that it made any difference whether the custom obtained in Shetland or in some part of mainland Scotland. It is true that the institutional writers instance custom in Orkney and Shetland as the leading example of local custom in Scotland[2]. But it is equally the case that most of the particular customs of Orkney and Shetland are based ultimately on Udal law, the system of law, Norwegian in origin, which obtained in the islands before they were pledged to the Scottish Crown in 1468 and 1469; and that, by and large, Scots law has recognised the continuing validity of Udal law, at least as regards the rights associated with the ownership of udal land[3]. Thus custom based on Udal law has been upheld this century in *Smith v Lerwick Harbour Trustees*[4] and *Lord Advocate v Balfour*[5].

There was, in fact, enough evidence available at the time of *Bruce v Smith*, although not all of it was cited, to indicate that the pursuer's claim to one-third of the proceeds of the whale-drive was in accord with a long-established tripartite division of whales and wrecks recognised by Udal law. More recently, arising out of the St Ninian's Isle Treasure case[6], it has been demonstrated by Professor Knut Robberstad and Sir Thomas Smith that the origin of the tripartite division, which included treasure as well as whales and wrecks, is to be sought in the *General Lawbook* of the Norwegian king Magnus 'the Law-Mender', first accepted by the Gulathing district of Norway in 1274, and adopted shortly after that date in the Faroe Islands and in Shetland and Orkney[7].

1　*Bruce v Smith* (1890) 17 R 1000.
2　See paras 366 ff above.
3　See further UDAL LAW.
4　*Smith v Lerwick Harbour Trustees* (1903) 5 F 680, 10 SLT 742.
5　*Lord Advocate v Balfour* 1907 SC 1360, 15 SLT 7, OH.
6　*Lord Advocate v Aberdeen University* 1963 SC 533, 1963 SLT 361.
7　T B Smith 'The Law relating to the Treasure' in *St Ninian's Isle and its Treasure* (1973, ed A Small, C Thomas and D M Wilson) p 149; K Robberstad 'Udal Law' in *Shetland and the Outside World* (1983, ed D J Withrington) p 49.

388. *Bruce v Smith* and the *Tanistry Case* compared. There is a clear parallel to be drawn between the leading case of *Bruce v Smith*[1] in Scotland and the leading *Tanistry Case*[2] in England. In both instances the 'custom' in dispute derived from a legal order distinct from the common law: Udal law as distinct from Scots common law in the one, and Irish 'Brehon law' as distinct from English common law in the other. This is not in itself surprising — much custom derives, as a matter of historical fact, from the law and practice of earlier or rival legal systems which have been loosely assimilated[3]. In both cases, moreover, it might be said that the so-called custom was based on law in the sense of *lex* rather than *consuetudo* in the alternative system; the legal basis for the custom of tanistry[4] being the ancient Irish law tracts, such as *Crith Gabhlach* and the *Senchus Mór*, and the basis for the three-fold right to treasure, whales and wrecks being the *Lawbook* of Magnus 'the Law-Mender' as adopted in Shetland. However, in finding against the custom in the *Tanistry Case* 'the judges', as already noted[5], 'thoroughly knew that they were making a revolution', whereas in *Bruce v Smith* it is doubtful if the majority of the judges had any notion that they were engaged in an exercise in legal imperialism as well as the elucidation of custom as a source of law.

1　*Bruce v Smith* (1890) 17 R 1000.
2　*Tanistry Case* (1608) Dav Ir 28: see para 373 above.
3　See para 363 above.
4　As to the custom of tanistry, see para 373 above.
5　See para 373 above.

(c) Custom and Usage

389. Custom and usage in English law. As has already been noted[1], English law draws a clear distinction in theory between immemorial custom and particular trade or local usages. This distinction appears to be very much the result of the rule peculiar to English law as to the measure of the antiquity of custom by which the limit of legal memory is fixed at the year 1189. In theory therefore, in English law particular trade or local usages of more recent origin cannot be regarded as sources of law: they do not meet the necessary test of antiquity. Instead, where recognised by law, they are regarded as terms to be implied in a contract. Such usages, it is said, must be certain, uniform, reasonable and notorious. The artificiality of this theory becomes increasingly obvious when a usage becomes so well known and accepted that it no longer needs to be proved judicially. Again, as already noted[1], the test of antiquity causes problems in English law as regards the recognition of general mercantile usage of comparatively recent origin.

1 See para 374 above.

390. Custom and usage in Scots law. It seems questionable whether it is necessary or desirable to distinguish between custom and usage in Scots law. Certainly the terms 'custom' and 'usage' do not appear to have become established as terms of art in Scotland, and the institutional writers do not make any distinction corresponding to that made in English law. In Scots law, as has been seen[1], the test of time presents no problem, and thus the main theoretical basis for the English distinction between custom and usage does not exist. Equally, there is no difficulty in Scots law in incorporating general mercantile usage into the main body of the common law. As already suggested[2], general mercantile usage, once accepted, simply becomes part of the common law, the tests for acceptance being identical to those of custom. The present writer agrees with Cameron[3] that the problems associated in English law with *Goodwin v Robarts*[4] do not arise in the same way in Scotland.

No doubt it may be necessary, in interpreting a contract, to distinguish between a 'custom' or 'usage' which has the force of law and must therefore be assumed to be within the contemplation of the parties, and trade usages which lack that force and which can only be incorporated into the contract by express or implied consent. This must be true of all systems; but it does not necessarily involve the English distinction between 'custom' and 'usage'. Nevertheless, over the past hundred years, Scots law does appear to have been affected by the English distinction. Thus in the House of Lords *Strathlorne Steamship* case[5], which was cited with approval by the First Division in *Cazalet v Morris & Co*[6], it seems to have been assumed that Scots law made the same distinction as English law between custom and usage. The Lord Chancellor, Lord Buckmaster, said[7]:

'In order that a custom or, to use a more exact phrase, a commercial usage, may be binding upon parties to a contract, it is essential that it should be certain, that it should be uniform, that it should be reasonable, and that it should be notorious. To use the words of Sir George Jessel in the case of *Nelson v Dahl*[8], "It must be so notorious that everybody in the trade enters into a contract with that usage as an implied term. It must be uniform as well as reasonable, and it must have quite as much certainty as the written contract itself".

I do not think it is necessary to consider in this case a matter which has been the subject of some slight discussion, as to whether or no this was a reasonable custom. I cannot help thinking that, when you are dealing with a custom of this description, which is nothing but a mercantile usage as between people engaged in a particular and important trade, if once it were established that the practice possessed the other attributes necessary for it to be recognised as a custom, the question of its reasonableness would be almost necessarily involved in the facts which were necessary to show that it was a uniform and accepted practice. Nor again do I wish to dwell upon the question of its being notorious. Notoriety in this connexion does not mean that it must be known to all the world, it does not even mean that it should be known to the persons against whom it is asserted; but it certainly does mean that it must be well known at the place to which it applies, and be capable of ready ascertainment by any person who proposes to enter into a contract of which that usage would form part. It is in fact to be regarded as though it were a term so well known in connexion with the particular transaction that it was nothing but waste of time and writing to introduce it into the contract'.

A number of other cases should be noticed in this context. In the *Peruvian Nitrate* case[9] it was held that the custom of the port of Iquique in Peru as regards 'working days' had not been incorporated into a charterparty. Lord President Inglis said: 'Now, the result of the authorities, both Scotch and English, is that where a custom is purely local it cannot be taken to control or explain the words of a written instrument unless it was known to both parties'. In the *Leith Cotton Seed Oil* case[10], which concerned the delivery of a mixed cargo of cotton seed, bone meal and Kurdee cake, an alleged custom of the port of Leith was rejected as indefinite and uncertain, not uniform, universal and notorious, and inconsistent with the terms of a written contract of affreightment. In *Cazalet v Morris & Co*[11] a practice of discharging esparto grass into railway wagons at Bristol was said to be not so certain, uniform, notorious and reasonable as to constitute the custom of the port. In *Clydesdale Bank v Snodgrass*[12] the well-known practice of The Stock Exchange as regards the contract of sale being between the ultimate seller and the ultimate purchaser was held to be recognised by the law. In *Wilkie v Scottish Aviation Ltd*[13] it was held that it was necessary to prove that an alleged custom regarding the scale of fees payable to a chartered surveyor in an arbitration was reasonable, certain and notorious; otherwise it was for the court to fix a reasonable remuneration.

Judicial dicta in Scottish cases have then — without close scrutiny of the juristic implications — gone a long way towards tacit acceptance of the distinction made in English law between custom and usage, although the distinction appears to be grounded on rules of English law which have no place in Scotland. It may be significant in this regard that South African law makes no such distinction[14]. Perhaps the position may yet be retrieved judicially, or at least be more clearly explained. In practice, the English tests which apply to usage are very similar to the Scottish tests for custom as a source of law, but difficulties might still arise in determining how far a usage contrary to existing law could be accepted, or in defining the circumstances in which a usage quite unknown to one of the parties could be implied into a contract.

1 See paras 379 ff above.
2 See para 375 above.
3 J T Cameron 'Custom as a Source of Law in Scotland' (1964) 27 MLR 306 at 311.
4 *Goodwin v Robarts* (1875) LR 10 Exch 337, Ex Ch.
5 *Strathlorne Steamship Co Ltd v Hugh Baird & Sons Ltd* 1916 SC (HL) 134, 1916 1 SLT 221.
6 *Cazalet v Morris & Co* 1916 SC 952, 1916 2 SLT 128.
7 *Strathlorne Steamship Co Ltd v Hugh Baird & Sons Ltd* 1916 SC (HL) 134 at 135, 136, 1916 1 SLT 221 at 221, 222.
8 *Nelson v Dahl* (1879) 12 Ch D 568 at 575, CA.
9 *Holman v Peruvian Nitrate Co* (1878) 5 R 657 at 671.
10 *Hugh Hogarth & Sons v Leith Cotton Seed Oil Co* 1909 SC 955, 1909 1 SLT 332.
11 *Cazalet v Morris & Co* 1916 SC 952, 1916 2 SLT 128.
12 *Clydesdale Bank (Moore Nominees) Ltd v Snodgrass* 1939 SC 805, 1940 SLT 46.
13 *Wilkie v Scottish Aviation Ltd* 1956 SC 198, 1956 SLT (Notes) 25.

14 'It will be seen that a trade usage is but a species of custom. It is a tacit term customarily implied in
   a contract, unless the parties have otherwise provided. Its requirements are the same as those of
   any other custom': H R Hahlo and E Kahn *The South African Legal System and its Background*
   (Cape Town 1968) p 303.

(d) Custom and Prescription

391. The doctrine of prescription. The doctrine of prescription applies to
constitute or to extinguish by the passage of time a right recognised by law.
Prescription is merely a necessary temporal test. It is not a source of law.
Custom, by contrast, even local custom, is concerned with general propositions
which, if accepted, give rise to many rights and obligations. Prescription,
characteristically, constitutes or extinguishes a particular right, real or personal,
of a natural or juristic person. Exceptionally, prescription may apply to rights
claimed by the public generally, as in the case of public rights of way[1], or to
rights expressed in terms of two parcels of heritage, as in the case of servitudes[2].
The law of prescription in Scotland is now mainly statutory[3].

   1 See para 393 below.
   2 See para 392 below.
   3 See generally PRESCRIPTION AND LIMITATION.

(e) Custom and Servitude

392. Servitudes. The law of servitudes[1] is a branch of the law of landowner-
ship and concerns rights over heritable property. A particular servitude right
must be expressed in terms of a dominant and a servient tenement. A servitude
right may be constituted by express grant, implied grant, or, in the case of
positive servitudes only, by the passage of time — that is, by prescription. The
prescriptive period is now laid down at twenty years by statute[2]. Custom,
except as synonymous with use over a period of time, plays no part in the
recognition of particular servitude rights. It is conceivable, however, that
custom as a source of law might lead to the recognition in Scots law of a new
class or type of servitude.

   1 See generally 'Servitudes and Rights of Way' in PROPERTY.
   2 Prescription and Limitation (Scotland) Act 1973 (c 52), s 3.

(f) Custom and Public Rights of Way

393. Public rights of way. A public right of way leads from one public place
to another and may be freely used by any member of the public[1]. It may be
constituted by grant or, more usually, by continuous use over a period of time
— that is, by prescription. The prescriptive period is now laid down at twenty
years by statute[2]. Similar to a public right of way is the public right to use
navigable rivers for communication or transportation, a right recognised by law
if the river in question has been so used from 'time immemorial' — a prescriptive period recognised in practice by the common law as forty years uninterrupted use[3].

1 See generally Servitudes and Rights of Way in the PROPERTY title.
2 Prescription and Limitation (Scotland) Act 1973 (c 52), s 3.
3 *Wills' Trustees v Cairngorm Canoeing and Sailing School Ltd* 1976 SC (HL) 30, 1976 SLT 162: see para 380 above.

4. EQUITY

(1) INTRODUCTION

394. The theory of equity. In juridical discourse 'equity' has a variety of connotations, some mutually compatible, some not. The theory of equity which was, in Milsom's words, 'a commonplace by the late sixteenth century' was

> 'that any general rule must work injustice in particular cases, and therefore that the application of positive law must be subject to some dispensing power in the interest of a higher justice. This idea, established on the continent but dramatised in England by the jurisdictional separation of law and equity, became part of the world's legal currency; and equity in this sense may appear, not necessarily administered by separate courts, in any legal system'[1].

This characterisation points to three recurrent themes: the individualisation of adjudication, the appeal to a higher justice, and the dispensing power[2].

1 S F C Milsom *Historical Foundations of the Common Law* (2nd edn, 1981) p 88.
2 See paras 395–397 below.

395. The individualisation of adjudication. Equity, where the ultimate value is said to be justice, is contrasted with *strictum ius*, where it is certainty[1]. Equity is typically identified with discretion and flexibility in the administration of justice, rather than the application of hard-and-fast rules. An extreme example is Blackstone, for whom equity depended 'upon the particular circumstances of each individual case' so that there could be 'no established rules and fixed precepts of equity laid down, without destroying its very essence, and reducing it to a positive law'[2]. A less extreme stance might be that a court of equity can be sensitive to circumstances which are irrelevant by the standard of strict law.

1 R A Newman (ed) *The Unity of Strict Law: A Comparative Study* (Brussels 1978) p 11.
2 Blackstone *Commentaries on the Laws of England* (14th edn, 1803), vol 1, p 61.

396. The appeal to a higher justice. Classically, the view was taken that equity transcended mere human or positive law. Equity was usually explicitly or tacitly identified with natural law or natural justice, particularly as manifested in the dictates of conscience.

397. The dispensing power. A third recurrent theme in accounts of equity is its capacity to override positive law in cases where the two come into conflict. Sometimes this was asserted baldly: positive laws contrary to natural law were said to be invalid. But the theory of the English common law proceeded by indirection: equity in effect overrode the common law, 'while affecting to treat it with the utmost deference' and purporting not to repeal it[1].

1   T E Holland *The Elements of Jurisprudence* (10th edn, 1906) pp 68, 69; S F C Milsom *Historical Foundations of the Common Law* (2nd edn, 1981) pp 91–93.

398. Equity as a source of law. However, equity is capable of losing any or all of these attributes in the course of the historical development of a legal system, as the English example shows. There the process of 'formalisation' or 'regularisation' of equity eventuated in a set of more or less determinate 'equitable' rules and principles, while the 'natural' conscience of the chancellors gave way to their 'civil' conscience. In short, equity becomes just another branch of positive law. At the same time general judicial notions of equity, in the sense of fairness or justice, retain significance in the legal system in several ways. First, generally because they are the product of an equitable jurisdiction, many rules of law incorporate 'equitableness' as a standard for decision-making. Secondly, an equitable spirit on the whole informs the interpretation of statutes and private legal instruments ('liberal' as opposed to 'literal' interpretation). And thirdly, in so far as judges commonly fall back upon their notions of justice and fairness to guide their decision-making in cases where authority is equivocal or absent, equity (or, more precisely, judicial conceptions thereof) remains a source of law, albeit a subordinate one.

399. Equity in Scots law. As will appear, the historical place of equity in the development of Scots law is no mere replication of the English position. No separate equity court appeared in Scotland. The Scottish commentators were given to searching for parallels to contemporary Scottish arrangements in the texts of Roman law. 'Equity' does not obviously exist as a distinct branch of law at the present day. Nevertheless, the status of equity *as a source of law* is nowadays much the same in Scotland and England.

(2) CIVIL LAW

(a) Stair

400. Introduction. In Stair's jurisprudence[1] there is a clear distinction between positive law, of which the law of Scotland is an instance, and the natural law, with which Stair identifies equity. Upon this distinction Stair's view of equity as a source of Scots law is founded.

1   See generally Stair *Institutions* (2nd edn, 1693, ed D M Walker 1981).

401. Natural law. The natural law, for Stair, is the 'dictate of reason, determining every rational being to that which is congruous and convenient for the nature and condition thereof'[1]. Divine law is that part of the natural law known intuitively to all men, being 'written by the finger of God upon man's heart'[2]; the law of reason is that part of the natural law deduced by reason from divine law[3]. The natural law is thus knowable, and Stair feels able to state its three first principles. The first of these is obedience: God is to be obeyed by man. The second is freedom: man may dispose of himself and all things, except in so far as he is restrained by his duty of obedience to God. The third is engagement: man's freedom may be restrained by his voluntary engagements, which he is bound to fulfil[4]. Stair recognises that equity is sometimes equated with 'the moderation of the extremity of human laws', but he himself holds that it 'doth truly comprehend the whole law of the rational nature'[5]. Hence the principles of the natural law are at the same time the principles of equity.

1 Stair *Institutions* I, 1, 1.
2 *Stair* I, 1, 3.
3 *Stair* I, 1, 4.
4 *Stair* I, 1, 18.
5 *Stair* I, 1, 6.

402. Positive law. Positive law, on the other hand, is the law of men, dependent on the will of men, and introduced 'either by tacit consent, by consuetude or custom, or by express will and command of those in authority, having the legislative power'[1]. Whereas the natural law is 'perfect and perpetual'[2], positive law is alterable, 'being dependent upon the will and pleasure of lawgivers'[3]. Whereas the natural law is *in aequo*, positive law is *in bono* or *utili*[4], that is, introduced 'for utility's sake'[5]. Whereas the natural law 'is not framed or fitted for the interest of any', many laws of men's choice are[6].

1 Stair *Institutions* I, 1, 10.
2 *Stair* I, 1, 15.
3 *Stair* I, 1, 17.
4 *Stair* I, 1, 18.
5 *Stair* I, 1, 10.
6 *Stair* I, 1, 6.

403. Scots law as positive law. The law of Scotland is, of course, a system of positive law. Its norms derive their legal authority primarily from human sources rather than equity. Like the English, 'we are ruled in the first place by our ancient and immemorial customs, which may be called our common law'[1]. This ancient law is more solemn and sure than any statute. 'In the next place are our statutes, or our acts of Parliament', which, unlike our ancient law, are liable to desuetude[1]. Then there are recent customs, constituted by frequent agreeing decisions of the Court of Session[1].

1 Stair *Institutions* I, 1, 16.

404. Equity as a source of Scots law. Equity, on the other hand, is a relatively minor source of Scots law. The dichotomy of the natural law and positive law enables equity to play a twofold part in Stair's thought. As long as it is *extraneous* to a system of positive law, equity is superior thereto. But *within* a system of positive law, equity plays a subordinate part. For if equity were to be allowed to override positive law within the latter's own sphere, the very *raison d'être* of positive law would be defeated. The point is that positive law exists not only to declare equity, but also to *depart from it*[1], and clearly this entails that within the system of positive law higher authority be assigned to custom and statute than to equity.

1 Cf D M Walker 'Equity in Scots Law' 1954 JR 103 at 115: 'Indeed the laws of man's constitution were only introduced to declare equity . . .'.

405. Theological foundation for positive law. Stair's account of the *raison d'être* of positive law has a theological foundation. Man in his lapsed state is incapable of living wholly by the natural law. 'If man had not fallen, there had been no distinction betwixt *bonum* and *aequum*: nor had there been any thing more profitable, than the natural law'[1]. But man 'being now depraved', there are five reasons why the introduction of positive law is necessary. First, positive laws are necessary to declare equity and to clarify its implications. Secondly, it would be impractical for positive law to enforce many rights competent to men in equity; hence, for example, positive law does not sanction 'the remuneratory obligations of gratitude'. Thirdly, 'that evident probation may be had', positive law imposes requirements of form that are no part of the natural law. Fourthly, most nations, 'for the flourishing of their families', practise primogeniture, even though 'by the law of nature, the right of succession doth belong to all'. And fifthly, positive law may permit things that are contrary to the natural, according to 'humours and inclinations' of a people[2]. In short the function of positive law is not only 'to declare equity, or make it effectual' but also 'in some cases to lay aside the effects of it'[3].

1 Stair *Institutions* I, 1, 18.
2 *Stair* I, 1, 15.
3 *Stair* I, 1, 17.

406. The authority of equity. Plainly it is possible to lay aside the effects of equity only if its authority within Scots law is inferior to that of custom and statute. This indeed is Stair's position. The authority of equity is confined to two situations. One is where judges modify 'exorbitant penalties' prescribed by men's laws. But judges will not presume to do this where 'law or custom hath excluded their modification'[1]. The other is where there occur *casus incogitati*: 'Where our ancient law, statutes and our recent customs are defective, recourse is had to equity ... and to expediency, whereby the laws are drawn, in consequence, *ad similes casus*. But if it appear that such cases have been of purpose omitted by the Parliament, the Lords will not sustain the same'[2]. From this it emerges that a law may be stretched to cover analogous cases (*ad similes casus*) where this would be equitable; but it emerges also that equity is of no avail when it can be inferred that the omission was intended by the legislator. Moreover it is noteworthy that Stair puts equity and expediency on a par with each other. This same coupling of equity and expediency occurs when Stair considers the authority of the civil, canon and feudal laws: 'none of these have with us the authority of law, and therefore are only received according to their equity and expediency, *secundum bonum et aequum*'[2]. So equity and expediency are of equal authority in Scots law, whereas in the natural law's own sphere equity alone is paramount.

1 Stair *Institutions* I, 1, 5.
2 Stair I, 1, 16.

407. Scots law equitable in content. According to Stair, therefore, equity is of limited authority in the law of Scotland. Nevertheless that law, in Stair's view, declares equity far more often than it derogates from it. Indeed the propinquity of the substance of Scots law to equity is such that the former may be expounded as a rational discipline by means of a structure that follows the latter[1]. This is the significance of Stair's famous remark that 'equity is the body of the law, and the statutes of men are but as the ornaments and vestiture thereof'[2]. At heart this is just an assertion that by and large Scots law is equitable in content.

1 D N MacCormick 'The Rational Discipline of Law' 1981 JR 146.
2 Stair *Institutions* I, 1, 17.

408. Conclusion. Stair's fundamental legal philosophy has been characterised in different ways. Carty is in no doubt that 'he was a legal positivist'[1]. Mac-Cormick, on the other hand, desires us 'to realise . . . how strongly Stair comes out against any positivistic or, rather, voluntaristic thesis which treats law as essentially dependant upon the arbitrary will of a lawgiver'[2]. In fact, Stair's account synthesises elements of both legal positivism and natural laws theory. Nevertheless, in the particular context of Stair's treatment of equity as a formal source of Scots law, positivistic elements necessarily have primacy. Most of the norms of Scots law draw their legal authority from human sources (ancient custom, statute and recent custom). They are legally authoritative because they are embodied in these human products, and not because (on the whole) they are equitable; indeed, in the final analysis, customary and statutory norms are authoritative whether or not they are equitable. At the same time, Stair's treatment of the formal sources of law does not rule out natural law altogether. There is (for Stair) such a thing as 'the' natural law, and it does perform a residual and supplementary function within the system of positive law.

1 A J Carty 'The Law of Nature and Nations as a Source' in *Stair Tercentenary Studies* (1981, ed D M Walker) pp 127–136 at p 127.
2 D N MacCormick 'The Rational Discipline of Law' 1981 JR 146 at 147. See also D N MacCormick 'Law and Enlightenment' in *The Origins and Nature of the Scottish Enlightenment* (1982, ed R H Campbell and A S Skinner) pp 150–166 at p 152.

(b) Bankton and Erskine

409. Bankton. Like Stair, Bankton regards 'equity' as a synonym for the law of nature[1]. However, Bankton's theoretical stance is more thoroughgoingly committed to doctrines of natural law than is Stair's, in that in the final analysis he feels constrained to acknowledge the supremacy of the law of nature. On the one hand, 'in arbitrary and indifferent cases the will of the lawgiver is sufficient to impose an obligation'[2]. On the other hand:

> '. . . where the positive law is plainly repugnant, in our apprehension, to the law of GOD, whether natural or revealed, it is not binding to an active obedience, because that were inconsistent with the indispensible obligation to the divine law, and in such case the rule is, We must obey GOD rather than man'[3].

That Bankton felt some unease at this resolution of the problem we may infer from his next remarks:

> 'At the same time, we are not absolved from our allegiance to the sovereign power in respect of an unjust law, or which we imagine perhaps only to be such; for that would unhinge all government, to the ruin of the publick tranquility: we ought therefore in such case, as dutiful subjects, to submit to the law by a passive obedience, with which we have not freedom to comply by an active. But one ought rather, if possible, by all means to leave the territory'[3].

Bankton does not elaborate this crucial but fragile distinction between active and passive obedience.

1 Bankton *Institute* I, 1, 24.
2 *Bankton* I, 1, 65.
3 *Bankton* I, 1, 66.

410. Erskine. Erskine's account of the relationship between positive and natural law is founded on the distinction between the *concessive* and the *preceptive* law of nature. Concessive natural law gives rights, without requiring their exercise. These rights may be given up by agreement. Hence, by entering into civil society, a person is understood to vest the legislature with the power to take away his concessive natural rights, if the common interest requires it.

Preceptive natural law imposes duties, and positive law cannot forbid or dispense with what the law of nature commands. No earthly lawgiver has the right to abrogate it. 'Obedience, therefore, to any enactment which is plainly adverse to the preceptive law of nature, is rebellion against God.' 'Hence it may be concluded, that things which natural law has left mankind at liberty either to do or to forbear, and these alone, are the matter of positive law'[1].

Again, this attributes higher status to natural law than Stair would have allowed. But Erskine's apparently unequivocal position must be read in the light of his subsequent remarks on statutory interpretation:

> '... statutes can in no case be explained into a sense which infers injustice or absurdity, or which, if admitted, would render them of no effect; for laws enacted by the wisdom of a nation, must be presumed to be agreeable to the immutable laws of nature, consistent in themselves, and made for some salutary purpose'[2].

This canon of interpretation no doubt enjoins an 'equitable' approach to the interpretation of statutes. It may also be observed, however, that the requirement that statutes must be 'presumed to be agreeable to the immutable laws of nature' effectively neutralises the implications of Erskine's theoretical account of the relationship between positive and natural law: for in practice, it seems, conflict between positive and natural law will not be acknowledged.

1 Erskine *Institute* I, 1, 20.
2 *Erskine* I, 1, 50.

(c) Kames

411. Introduction. Kames's jurisprudence by no means makes a clean break with the natural law tradition in its entirety. But he differs in two major respects from his Scottish juristic predecessors. First, the laws of nature are to be discovered, as Ross puts it, 'not by reason but by experience'[1]. Secondly, Kames's work displays greater awareness of the relationship between social change and legal development[2]. This is not to say that Stair's perspective is altogether ahistorical[3] — only that Kames's historical sense is deeper and more pervasive.

1 I S Ross *Lord Kames and the Scotland of His Day* (1972) p 102.
2 P Stein 'Legal Thought in Eighteenth-Century Scotland' 1957 JR 1; W C Lehmann *Henry Home, Lord Kames and the Scottish Enlightenment* (The Hague 1971) pp 206 ff.
3 D N MacCormick 'The Rational Discipline of Law' 1981 JR 146 at 156, 157.

412. Development of the common law. In his *Principles of Equity*, first published in 1760, Kames explicitly sets his account of equity's role in the legal system in the context of his vision of social and legal progress. He advances a four-stage scheme. The first stage is the establishment of civil society:

> 'After states were formed, and government established, courts of law were invented ... to enforce duties essential to the existence of society; such as that of forbearing to do harm or mischief. Power was also given to enforce duties derived from covenants and promises, such of them at least as tend more peculiarly to the well-being of society'[1].

This was the original scope of the common law. Gradually, however, the jurisdiction of courts of law was extended 'till it embraced every obvious duty arising in ordinary dealings between man and man'. But in this second stage 'it was extended no farther'[2].

These first two stages of legal development reflect a relatively simple division of labour and a rough-and-ready moral code:

> 'Among a plain people, strangers to refinement and subtilties, law-suits may be frequent, but never are intricate. Regulations to restrain individuals from doing mischief, and to enforce performance of covenants, composed originally the bulk of the common law; and these two branches, among our rude ancestors, seemed to comprehend every subject of law. The more refined duties of morality were, in that early period, little felt, and less regarded'[3].

1 Kames *Principles of Equity* (5th edn, 1825) p 2.
2 *Kames* p 3.
3 *Kames* p 5.

413. Resort to equity. The third stage is one of 'enlightenment' and 'humanisation'. The connections among individuals become more varied and complex, and the duties to which they give rise are more clearly perceived. Now 'law ripens gradually with the human faculties; and by ripeness of discernment, and delicacy of sentiment, many duties formerly neglected, are found to be binding in conscience'[1]. This is where equity comes in. For 'a court of equity commences at the limits of the common law, and enforces benevolence where the law of nature makes it our duty'[2]. Indeed, equity 'comprehends every matter of law that, by the common law, is left without remedy'[3]. By resort to equity, therefore, the law is brought into conformity to the needs of a more refined age.

1 Kames *Principles of Equity* (5th edn, 1825) p 5.
2 *Kames* p 8.
3 *Kames* p 4.

414. Equitable rules becoming customary rules. The fourth stage, like the third, is a continuing one. Rules whose authority was originally founded on equity gradually become customary rules, and thus part of the common law:

> 'In England, where the courts of equity and common law are different, the boundary between equity and common law ... will remain always the same. But, in Scotland ... where equity and common law are united in one court [the Court of Session], the boundary varies imperceptibly; for what originally is a rule in equity, loses its character when it is fully established in practice; and then it is considered as common law'[1].

Hence actions once regarded as equitable in character, and therefore reserved to the Court of Session, come to be sustained in inferior courts[2]. But as equity loses old rules it creates new ones: 'by cultivation of society, and practice of law, nicer and nicer cases in equity being daily unfolded, our notions of equity are preserved alive; and the additions made to that fund, supply what is withdrawn from it by common law'[3].

1 Kames *Principles of Equity* (5th edn, 1825) p 17.
2 *Kames* p 21.
3 *Kames* p 18.

415. Limits of equity. Equity, therefore, is the source upon which judges draw in order to make new law. This equitable jurisdiction is not, however, unbounded. Kames's assertion that 'a court of equity, accompanying the law of nature in its gradual refinements, enforces every natural duty that is not provided for at common law'[1] goes much too far, as Walker has observed[2]. Indeed, it cannot be taken at face value, because Kames himself was well aware that many equitable obligations (such as those of gratitude, compassion and friendship) were no part of the business of any court. In fact, elsewhere in his writings he acknowledges that 'the municipal law of all countries is so little regardful of the laws of nature, as to adopt but a very few of them'[3].

Kames proffers an explanation for this state of affairs. In the first place, municipal laws 'cannot reach the heart, nor its intentions, further than as exprest by outward acts'[3]. So equity is legally irrelevant save in so far as it addresses outward acts. Secondly, equity is not to be enforced for its own sake, but for the good of society. Hence equity is inadmissible when it is at odds with social utility:

> 'It is, indeed, the declared purpose of a court of equity, to promote the good of society by an accurate distribution of justice: but the means ought to be subordinate to the end; and, therefore, if, in any case, justice cannot be done by using means that tend to the hurt of society, a court of equity ought not to interpose'[4].

Thirdly, equity cannot be taken into account when it is incapable of yielding a general rule. This is the trouble with 'the more conscientious duties' as opposed to duties connected with goods or riches:

> 'The duties arising from the connection last mentioned, are commonly ascertained and circumscribed, so as to be susceptible of a general rule to govern all cases of the kind. This is seldom the case of the other natural duties; which, for that reason, must be left upon conscience, without receiving any aid from a court of equity. [For example, charity]... the extent of this duty depends on such a variety of circumstances, that the wisest heads would in vain labour to bring it under general rules'[5].

That being so, judicial enforcement of such natural duties 'would open a wide door to legal tyranny and oppression'[5].

It emerges, then, that the equitable jurisdiction of the Court of Session is not uncircumscribed. Kames does not see the judges as free agents with *carte blanche* to incorporate the principles of equity within positive law. Only subject to the qualifications just adumbrated will equity 'supply the defects of the common law' (as Kames defines it) and 'correct its rigour or injustice'[6].

1 Kames *Principles of Equity* (5th edn, 1825) p 8.
2 D M Walker 'Equity in Scots Law' 1954 JR 103 at 119, 120.
3 Kames *Essays on the Principles of Morality and Natural Religion* (1751) p 132.
4 Kames *Principles of Equity* p 365.
5 Kames *Principles of Equity* p 15.
6 Kames *Principles of Equity* p 27.

416. Conclusion. In retrospect, it is apparent that Kames's theory of equity is an attempt to make sense of the legal system's response to the commercialisation of Scottish society. His *Principles of Equity* is a rationalisation of the phenomenon which a later, more positivistic age, would characterise as 'judicial legislation'. Kames, however, did not regard judicial decisions as authoritative *per se*. He adhered to the traditional conception of the common law as custom, and respected its rules as authoritative because they were customary. How then to account for the authority of those recent decisions which manifestly lacked any foundation in custom? Kames's answer was to attribute their authority, not to the will of the judges, but to the objective principles of equity. To Kames it was self-evident that the judges did not invent these principles, but merely 'enforced' them selectively under appropriate circumstances. Courts of equity did not make law; their genius lay in 'seconding the laws of nature'[1].

1 Kames *Principles of Equity* (5th edn, 1825) p 21.

(d) The Downgrading of Equity

417. Neglect of equity in the nineteenth century. It appears, as Walker puts it, 'that any general conception of equity and equitable influence in Scots law had been lost sight of by the nineteenth century, although it was still admitted that various doctrines were equitable in nature'[1]. Nineteenth-century Scottish jurisprudence neglected equity as a source of law.

This neglect was a logical consequence of the ideological triumph of Benthamite and Austinian legal positivism. The old theory was that the common law was custom. Precedents were not inherently authoritative, but authority might be imputed to a uniform series of decisions as constituting 'an Evidence of the Greatest Weight in ascertaining our Customes'[2]. The difficulty of attributing authority to recent, innovative precedents on this basis is obvious. Therefore it was useful to recognise equity or natural law as authoritative, and to rationalise certain judicial decisions on this alternative basis.

1 D M Walker 'Equity in Scots Law' 1954 JR 103 at 116.
2 *The Decisions of the Court of Session from its Institution till the Year 1764* (1774) p v. See generally J C Gardner *Judicial Precedent in Scots Law* (1936) pp 23–38; T B Smith *The Doctrines of Judicial Precedent in Scots Law* (1952) pp 6–10; and paras 247 ff above.

418. Equity and judicial authority. The new theory depicted precedents as authoritative in themselves; in unprecedented cases judges possessed and exercised legislative powers, although these were to be used as infrequently and restrainedly as possible. But if judicial authority is a source of law in its own right, custom and equity are largely redundant. The outcome is described by MacCormick:

'Custom slides off the stage altogether save as an aid to the construction of private contracts. "Equity" ceases to be seriously recognisable as a source of law, and becomes either the name of a particular set of judicially legislated rules, or the name of a particular power of law-making vested in judges'[1].

1 N MacCormick *Legal Reasoning and Legal Theory* (1978) pp 60, 61.

419. Subjective character of equitable notions. The relegation of equity was also encouraged by scepticism about the very notion of equity as a body of objective principles, ascertainable and with determinate implications. Legal positivists often alluded to the subjective, and hence variable or even capricious, character of notions of equity. In the Scottish context this is well exemplified by the remarks of Dove Wilson:

'At no very distant time it was the custom to suppose that under municipal law there lay a so-called law of nature, which was believed to be common to all men, and ingrained as it were in the human conscience. ... When that so-called law of nature was analysed it was found to consist in little else than a few general maxims, undoubtedly sound and true, but common to every kind of human conduct. ... The law of nature as so understood, though harmless enough, went no way to explain the existence of municipal law'[1].

How far equity is to be reckoned with in present-day Scots law we shall consider after an examination of the *nobile officium*[2].

1 J Dove Wilson 'The Sources of the Law of Scotland' 1892 JR 1.
2 See paras 426 ff below.

(3) CRIMINAL LAW

420. Moral and juridical criminal behaviour. *Mutato nomine*, equity has played an important part in the development of Scottish criminal law. The distinction between *mala in se* and *mala prohibita* presupposes a natural law approach, and Scottish judges asserted the power to 'declare' *mala in se* to be crimes according to the law of Scotland. The concept of a 'crime' in Scots law was not defined exclusively by reference to the infraction of positive law; instead the old idea was that conduct might be 'criminal' independently of positive law, and prior to the explicit recognition of its criminality within the sphere of positive law. Indeed it seems that in Scottish criminal jurisprudence crime as a juridical notion has still not been wholly emancipated from crime as a moral notion.

421. Mackenzie. In Mackenzie's account in 1678[1], 'That is a Crime whereby the publick peace is immediatly disquieted. Or whereby the Law of Nature is violated'. Indeed, 'the Law of God is the first fountain of our Criminal Law'. From this it followed that iniquitous conduct might be punished as criminal, even in the absence of positive legal authority for this. So it was that 'Incests, and Rapts, were accounted Crymes with us, before they were declared to be such by an express Law'[2]. If the crime was against natural rather than positive law this would appear in the indictment. The usual indictment began: 'Albeit by the laws of this and every other well-governed realm . . .', but the indictment for sodomy or bestiality began: 'Albeit by the Law of the Omnipotent God . . .'[3]. Likewise 'the lybel in single Adultery is only founded upon the Law of God'. In the case of usury, on the other hand, 'we lybel upon the Municipal Law, and the Law of God joyntly'[4].

1 Sir George Mackenzie *The Laws and Customes of Scotland in Matters Criminal* (1698).
2 *Mackenzie* I, I, III.
3 *Mackenzie* I, XV, IV.
4 *Mackenzie* I, I, III.

422. Kames. A century after Mackenzie it was still possible for natural law in its own right to be regarded as a criterion of criminality by Kames: 'Every crime against the law of nature may be punished at the discretion of the judge, where the legislature has not appointed a particular punishment'[1].

1 Kames *Principles of Equity* (5th edn, 1825) Appendix, 'Principles founded on in this work'.

423. Hume. David Hume's position was less clear-cut. He asserted the existence of the declaratory power, but failed to identify its basis:

'. . . the Supreme Criminal Court have an inherent power as such, competently to punish, (with the exception of life and limb), every act, which is obviously of a criminal nature; though it be such which in time past has never been the subject of prosecution'[1].

How, in the absence of any positive legal authority, the criminal nature of an act can be 'obvious' was not explained by Hume. On his formulation the basis of the declaratory power might be natural law; but it might equally just be judicial intuition or common sense.

1 Hume *Commentaries on the Law of Scotland, Respecting the Description and Punishment of Crimes.* (1797) I, iii.

424. The court's power to declare an action criminal. Nevertheless Hume's remark was quoted with warm approval by several of the judges in 1838 in the leading case, *Greenhuff*[1], where the decision was strongly influenced by natural law ideas. Here a court of six judges, with only one dissentient, asserted the existence of the declaratory power and exercised it to designate as criminal the keeping of a public gaming house. The decision proceeded on the footing that this activity was not only *malum in se*[2], but also a 'public evil'[3], 'noxious to society'[4], 'injurious to society in the highest degree'[5]. Lord Cockburn's dissenting judgment was a clear statement of the philosophy of legal positivism:

> 'There was perhaps a time in the history of this country . . . in which Courts were apt, or rather were obliged, to proceed in the declaration of crimes, upon nothing better than their own views of expediency. When the proper departments of the legislative and judicial powers are unsettled, and urgent evils require speedy remedies, and Courts have little else to direct them than instinctive feelings of morality, — this last ground for the interference of the judicial authority is made reasonable by being necessary. Courts are compelled to do whatever appears just and useful; and this is justified by being ascribed to the law of nature — the only light that they then have'[6].

But such judicial legislation was, in Cockburn's view, no longer legitimate. It was a trespass on the domain of Parliament, and hence 'inconsistent with the proper constitutional limits' on the courts, upon whom it was incumbent to 'proceed upon the principles which the long, regular, practice of the law has introduced'[7].

1 *Greenhuff* (1838) 2 Swin 236.
2 2 Swin 236 at 262 per Lord Meadowbank, at 266 per Lord Moncrieff and at 269 per Lord Mackenzie.
3 2 Swin 236 at 266, per Lord Moncrieff.
4 2 Swin 236 at 268, per Lord Mackenzie.
5 2 Swin 236 at 270, per Lord Medwyn.
6 2 Swin 236 at 271, 272.
7 2 Swin 236 at 272, 274, 275.

425. The declaratory power today. The *Greenhuff* case[1] is plainly incompatible with the principle of *nulla poena sine lege*, and for this reason modern academic commentators have evinced little enthusiasm for that decision. Smith argues that Lord Cockburn's dissenting opinion has 'probably prevailed' in the sense that the declaratory power 'would and should not' be invoked nowadays[2]. Certainly in this century there have been occasions on which the court declined to exercise the power[3]; but the High Court of Justiciary has not impeached the authority of *Greenhuff*, and in 1934 in *Sugden v HM Advocate*[4] a modern decision[5] was explained as an exercise of the declaratory power, Lord Justice-Clerk Aitchison remarking that it is 'not a usurpation of the powers of the Legislature, it is a prerogative of the Justiciary derived from its history'[6]. That the declaratory power has not been avowedly exploited in modern times is attributable not only to positivistic and constitutional scruples, but also to the ease with which the Court of Justiciary has been able to enlarge the scope of the criminal law by claiming to apply established principles (expansively defined) to novel circumstances[7].

1 *Greenhuff* (1838) 2 Swin 236: see para 424 above.
2 T B Smith *A Short Commentary on the Law of Scotland* (1962) pp 127, 131. See further G H Gordon *The Criminal Law of Scotland* (2nd edn, 1978) p 26.
3 *HM Advocate v Semple* 1937 JC 41, 1937 SLT 48.
4 *Sugden v HM Advocate* 1934 JC 103, 1934 SLT 465.
5 *Strathern v Seaforth* 1926 JC 100, 1926 SLT 445.
6 *Sugden v HM Advocate* 1934 JC 103 at 109, 1934 SLT 465 at 468.
7 See *Gordon* pp 32–43; and *Khaliq v HM Advocate* 1983 SCCR 483, 1984 SLT 137.

(4) THE *NOBILE OFFICIUM*

426. Ordinary and extraordinary equitable jurisdiction. Modern commentators contrast the *ordinary* or *general* equitable jurisdiction of the Court of Session with its *extraordinary* or *special* jurisdiction — its *nobile officium*[1]. The distinction is somewhat elusive. According to Walker, ordinary equitable jurisdiction is administered 'in and through and along with common law; it is widespread but concealed'[2]. In the case of the extraordinary equitable jurisdiction, on the other hand, 'equity is openly and avowedly acknowledged'[3]. In support of his view Walker refers to Stair, Bankton and Kames[4].

1 D M Walker 'Equity in Scots Law' 1954 JR 103 at 125; T B Smith *Scotland: The Development of its Laws and Constitution* (1962) p 45; D Maxwell *The Practice of the Court of Session* (1980) p 126. The High Court of Justiciary has a parallel jurisdiction in matters criminal: C N Stoddart 'The Nobile Officium of the High Court of Justiciary' 1974 SLT (News) 37.
2 D M Walker 'Equity in Scots Law' 1954 JR 103 at 125.
3 D M Walker *Equity in Scots Law* Ph D Thesis (University of Edinburgh 1952) p 229.
4 See paras 427–429 below.

427. Stair. In fact the historical foundations of Walker's distinction are not wholly secure. Stair, to be sure, distinguished between the *officium ordinarium* of the Court of Session and its *officium nobile*. But it is evident that by the former term he understood the court's common law jurisdiction, and by the latter its entire equitable jurisdiction. Thus Stair identifies the *officium ordinarium* with custom, whereas exercise of the *officium nobile* entails 'recourse from strict law to equity', which is appropriate 'in new cases, [where] there is necessity of new cures'[1]. The *nobile officium* is 'competent to no inferior court', but every sovereign court must have it, unless there is a separate equity court as in England: 'Other nations do not divide the jurisdiction of their courts, but supply the cases of equity and conscience, by the noble office of their supreme ordinary courts, as we do'[1]. It is clear, then, that the modern distinction would have been alien to Stair, for whom equity was a source of law upon which the Court of Session alone might draw[2].

1 Stair *Institutions* IV, 3, 1.
2 Erskine *Institute* I, 3, 22 is to the like effect.

428. Bankton. Bankton, on the other hand, does distinguish between the *nobile officium* and that equitable jurisdiction of the Court of Session which is part of its *officium ordinarium*. Speaking of the court's power to ordain witnesses to be examined *ad rimandam veritatem*, he says:

'This is a supereminent power, founded in their high jurisdiction, in order to the discovery of truth, and cannot be said only to proceed upon their equitable powers. Equity is a favourable construction of the law, and may be prayed by either party;

but no party is intitled to demand, as his right, an examination *ex officio*; he may suggest it, but he cannot ask it as a point of right'[1].

Plainly this distinction — between what may be demanded as of right and what may not — is not the same as that propounded by Walker.

1 Bankton *Institute* IV, 7, 23.

429. Kames. For Kames also, equitable jurisdiction was in principle a monopoly of the Court of Session[1], but he acknowledged that departures had been made from this principle. Inferior courts were in general confined to common law, but equitable defences might be pleaded in them, and certain firmly established actions of equitable origin (such as the *actio negotiorum gestorum*) were now commonly sustained in them. This state of affairs Kames attributed to imitation of the supreme court, the inconvenience of moving a process to another court, and the tendency of well established equitable rules to become part of the common law[2]. Since Kames's day the sheriff courts have encroached much further on to terrain once exclusively occupied by the Court of Session, and this development is perhaps the only real justification of the modern distinction whereby ordinary equitable jurisdiction denotes that equitable jurisdiction common to the sheriff courts and Court of Session, while the extraordinary equitable jurisdiction denotes those equitable powers that remain exclusive to the Court of Session — its *nobile officium*.

1 Kames *Principles of Equity* (5th edn, 1825) p 20; Kames *Historical Law-Tracts* (4th edn, 1792) pp 228 ff.
2 Kames *Principles of Equity* p 21: see para 414 above.

430. Early exercise of the *nobile officium*. Ordinary equitable jurisdiction is equitable only in the attenuated sense that its exercise consists of the application of rules which incorporate equitableness as a standard of adjudication or which are equitable in terms of historical origin. Before the nineteenth century, however, the *nobile officium* of the Court of Session was an authentic equitable jurisdiction. In Erskine's words:

'The session is a court of equity, as well as of law; and as such may and ought to proceed by the rules of conscience, in abating the rigour of the law, and in giving aid . . . to those who can have no remedy in a court of law'[1].

Many instances of the exercise of the *nobile officium* are enumerated by Stair[2], Bankton[3] and Kames[4]. There was uncertainty over the theoretical basis of the *nobile officium*[5], but this did not prevent its vigorous exercise in practice when the occasion demanded[6]. Nevertheless, even in its heyday the *nobile officium* did not entitle the judges to 'contraveen the direct ordinance of the law'[7].

1 Erskine *Institute* I, 3, 22. See also Stair (para 406 above) and Kames (para 415 above).
2 Stair *Institutions* IV, 3, 1.
3 Bankton *Institute* IV, 7, 24.
4 Kames *Principles of Equity* (5th edn, 1825) *passim*.
5 See Stair IV, 3, 1; *Erskine* I, 3, 22; *Bankton* IV, 7, 26–27; Kames *Principles of Equity* p 20; Kames *Historical Law-Tracts* pp 228 ff.
6 For example when 'the spirit of mutiny' showed itself among the brewers of Edinburgh, and 'the inhabitants might apparently have been reduced to the greatest straits for want of drink': Kames *Principles of Equity* pp 336, 339; *Bankton* IV, 7, 25.
7 *Bankton* IV, 7 [Observations] 4; IV, 7, 28.

431. Modern exercise of the *nobile officium*. In the nineteenth century, under the influence of positivism, the *nobile officium* became stereotyped[1], and judicial restraint in its exercise has been the practice ever since. Lord Wark summarised his view of the modern *nobile officium* as follows:

'It is theoretically unlimited, and although the tendency in recent times has been to restrict it to cases where there is a direct or analogous precedent, it is not to be assumed that it will be so restricted where there is a manifest necessity for the intervention of the Court'[2].

While we may agree that the *nobile officium* is not necessarily incapable of novelty, it goes too far to characterise it as 'theoretically unlimited'. It is no less true today than formerly that it is incompetent for the court to exercise the *nobile officium* 'in order to override the express provision of a statute'[3]. The *nobile officium* may be invoked to meet a *casus improvisus* in a statute, but not 'to alter the statutory provisions of an Act of Parliament or enable anything to be done which is expressly rendered ineffective by the Act'[4]. And in those cases where the exercise of the *nobile officium* most closely approaches the exercise of legislative powers — as when a *casus improvisus* in a statute is supplied or when the provisions of a trust deed are varied to deal with unanticipated circumstances — the court must exercise its power in conformity to the presumed intention of Parliament[5] or to realise the main purpose of the trust[6]. The most that the *nobile officium* permits is the sympathetic adaptation to unforeseen circumstances of legal norms made by others.

1 W Bell *Dictionary and Digest of the Law of Scotland* (4th edn, 1838) sv 'Equity'.
2 Lord Wark 'Law of Nature' in *Sources and Literature of Scots Law* (Stair Soc vol 1, 1936) p 249 at p 254.
3 *Adair v David Colville & Sons Ltd* 1922 SC 672 at 677, 1922 SLT 532 at 536, per Lord Justice-Clerk Dickson. See also *MacGown v Cramb* (1897) 24 R 481, 4 SLT 289; *Crichton-Stuart's Tutrix* 1921 SC 840, 1921 SLT 132; *B's Executor v Keeper of the Registers and Records of Scotland* 1935 SC 745, 1935 SLT 476; *Smart v Registrar General* 1954 SC 81, 1954 SLT 213. Likewise the *nobile officium* of the High Court of Justiciary 'may never be invoked when to do so would conflict with statutory intention, express or clearly implied': *Anderson v HM Advocate* 1974 SLT 239 at 240, per Lord Justice-General Emslie.
4 *McLaughlin* 1965 SC 243 at 245, 1965 SLT (Notes) 57.
5 See eg *Lloyds and Scottish Finance Ltd v HM Advocate* 1974 JC 24, 1974 SLT 3.
6 See eg *Gibson's Trustees* 1933 SC 190, 1933 SLT 166.

(5) CONCLUSION

432. The modern role of equity in Scots law. Walker advances two theses regarding the role of equity in Scots law. One is that equity, administered through common law forms, has always been a 'material formative influence' in Scots law[1]. His evidence for this is:

'In numerous branches of Scots law the basis or justification of the rule in observance has been ascribed to "equity", "natural justice", "substantial justice", "reason and justice" and similar phrases, and . . . there are repeated acknowledgments of this fact in judgments and the most authoritative text-writers'[2].

One hesitates to concede that the mere description of a rule as 'equitable' necessarily makes it so. More importantly, however, as Walker himself recognises, rules of an equitable character in today's legal system may be no more than the vestiges of the recognition of equity as a source of law in the more or less distant past.

This brings us to his second thesis which is that 'the creative function of equity in Scots law is ended. No substantial new doctrine or change in common law seems now possible, save by statute'[3]. Here Walker seems to exaggerate the fixity of the common law. Judges will inevitably respond to changing economic and social patterns by engaging in interstitial, incremental law-making, and in doing so they will be guided by their conceptions of equity and justice *inter alia*.

Smith, in contrast to Walker, contended that 'equity is still a valid, valuable and unexhausted source of Scots law'[4]. The concept of equity itself he is content to identify with 'reason' or 'natural justice'[5]. This will hardly do. One cannot turn back the clock, and reconstruct a belief in the *objective* existence of principles of equity. The fact is that equity is qualitatively different from the sources of law usually regarded as 'formal'[6]. It is not one of the authoritative materials of the law; rather it is on a par with such things as common sense, expediency, public policy and the public interest. Judicial conceptions of such matters are, when all is said and done, subjective and dependent on judicial values, although it may well be that to an appreciable extent there is among judges a common set of values.

Modern attempts to rehabilitate equity as a formal source of law proceed by postulating some sort of societal value-consensus upon which judges may draw. They seek to salvage equity by substituting a sociological conception for a metaphysical one. Allen, for example, redefined equity as 'some kind of common denominator of just instinct in the community'[7]. It need scarcely be remarked that such a conception of equity is highly problematic in sociological terms. Such attempts are bound to continue, however, in view of the unavoidability of judicial law-making and the felt need to find a legitimation for it. Whether we like it or not, judges will go on developing the law to meet the needs of the times as they see them[8]; and when they have exhausted the authoritative materials of the law some of what they do will be done under colour of equity, even if that concept nowadays lacks a coherent basis.

1 D M Walker *Equity in Scots Law* Ph D Thesis (University of Edinburgh 1952) pp 6, 186.
2 D M Walker 'Equity in Scots Law' 1954 JR 103 at 145.
3 D M Walker 'Equity in Scots Law' 1954 JR 103 at 147. Cf GENERAL LEGAL CONCEPTS.
4 T B Smith *A Short Commentary on the Law of Scotland* (1962) p 46.
5 *Smith* p 43.
6 D Sellar, Book Review 1977 SLT (News) 94 at 95.
7 C K Allen *Law in the Making* (7th edn, 1964) p 387. For another example, see Lord Devlin 'Judges and Lawmakers' (1976) 39 MLR 1.
8 Lord Reid 'The Judge as Law Maker' (1972) 12 JSPTL (NS) 22.

5. LEGAL LITERATURE

The present writer acknowledges valuable advice and criticism from Professor D M Walker, whose treatise The Scottish Jurists *(1985) contains the only comprehensive account of Scottish legal literature to be published to date.*

(1) INTRODUCTION

433. Legal literature in general. In general legal literature in the form of books and articles seeking to expound or clarify the law on a topic is not an authoritative source of law in the sense that a court is obliged to accept the author's statement of the law as binding upon it. Statements in treatises on the law may have considerable persuasive force, according to the eminence of the author and the cogency of his reasoning, in assisting a court to reach a decision. The judges may expressly accept an author's formulation of what the law is or should be, but it is the pronouncement of the court which gives the statement of the law authority. However, by way of exception, the treatises of a few favoured writers have come to be regarded as primary sources of law to be accepted by judges — except those in the highest courts — as actually prescribing the law to be applied. This is probably a phenomenon not encountered in the jurisprudence of any other jurisdiction, and peculiar to Scots law as it has developed since about 1840. The favoured category of authoritative authors is usually referred to in modern times as the 'institutional writers' — a designation which is terminologically confusing. It seems to have no exact counterpart in other legal systems[1] and to be incapable of precise formulation[2]. The form and scope of a treatise may satisfy the dictionary meaning of an *Institute*, but it may never attain the rank of an authority. On the other hand, a treatise may be of the highest authority, whilst falling short of that comprehensiveness which the definition requires.

1 H David *Introduction à l'Etude du Droit Ecossais* (Paris 1972) p 293.
2 A C Black 'The Institutional Writers' in *Sources and Literature of Scots Law* (Stair Soc vol 1, 1936 ed H McKechnie).

(2) HISTORICAL AND COMPARATIVE

434. Institutional writing: the European context. To appreciate the modern doctrine of 'institutional writers' or 'institutional works' as a source of law, a brief account of the historical and comparative context and also of terminological difficulties seems essential. Between the sixteenth and eighteenth centuries throughout Western Europe the phenomenon is recognisable of publications describing the national laws of particular states, based on native rather than Roman sources, although largely based on the pattern of Justinian's *Institutes*. These works sought to expound the basic principles of law in a clear and systematic manner. They were comprehensive in their treatment of private law and were frequently intended as introductory material for legal education[1]. Scottish authors participated in this European movement[2], although because Scots law was in a formative stage and had to resist pressures for assimilation with the doctrinally distinct system of English law, invocation of the Civil or Roman law as a subsidiary source and reference to the *ius commune* of Europe was more apparent in Scottish legal writings than in some West European counterparts. Distinct from the elementary and introductory 'institutes', such as the *Institutions* of Mackenzie[3] and the works designated *Principles* published by Erskine and by Bell, were the more substantial systematic expositions of Scots law contained in the *Institutions* of Stair and the *Institute* of Bankton and of Erskine. These works may be regarded as more analogous to those by authors on the Pandects rather than to those whose model was the *Institutes* of Justinian. The distinction between the introductory and fuller expositions of national systems which have been regarded as 'institutional' is not a characteristic of Scots law alone. Writing of 'institutes' in general, Lawson observed 'One must beware of attaching much importance to terminology. The terms "Institutes" and "Institutions" cover a large number of miscellaneous writings on law, some of which . . . are too encyclopaedic to be considered institutional; and many works that would normally be considered institutional are not so named, but include "commentaries", "introductions", "principles" or "elements"'[4].

1 K Luig 'The Institutes of National Law in the Seventeenth and Eighteenth Centuries' 1972 JR 193; K Luig 'Stair from a Foreign Standpoint' in *Stair Tercentenary Studies* (Stair Soc vol 33, 1981) p 239.
2 J W Cairns 'Institutional Writings in Scotland Reconsidered' (1983) 4 J Legal Hist 76, which deals comprehensively and in detail with Scottish institutional writings.
3 H L MacQueen 'Mackenzie's *Institutions* in Scottish Legal History' (1984) 29 JLSS 498.
4 F H Lawson 'Institutes' in *Festschrift für Imre Zajtay* (Tübingen 1982) p 333.

435. Legal writing as a source of law. These comprehensive works as well as specialist treatises on particular branches of the law were regarded as sources of law in Western Europe in the era before codification[1]. 'Works of legal scholarship *(la doctrine)* were for a long time the fundamental sources of law in the Romano-Germanic family. As a matter of fact it was essentially in the Universities that the principles of law emerged between the thirteenth and seventeenth centuries. Only comparatively recently has the primacy of doctrinal writing given way to that of enacted law'[1]. However, legal literature *(la doctrine)* did not in general have binding power. An exception was the *Opus Tripartitum Juris Consuetudinarii Inclyti Regni Hungariae*, prepared by the sixteenth-century Hungarian judge and jurist Werböczy on royal mandate. Both in his lifetime and after his death it was accepted in effect as a code[2].

1 R David and J E C Brierley *Major Legal Systems in the World Today* (2nd edn, 1978) p 134.
2 I Zajtay *Introduction à l'Etude du Droit Hongrois* (Paris 1953) pp 89 ff.

436. Affinities between Scots law and Roman Dutch law. At least in the field of private law Scots law has close affinity with the legal systems of Southern Africa. In these systems a distinction is drawn between the works of certain authors known as the Old Authorities and legal literature in general. 'In South Africa the treatises of a large number of Dutch jurists, written in the seventeenth and eighteenth centuries, are so authoritative that our common law, the Roman-Dutch law, consists in fact of the rules of law stated in their books. The foremost of these writers was Grotius, Voet, Van Leeuwen, Huber, Bynkershoek, Van der Keesel and Van der Linden. It was by custom that the people in the Netherlands recognised and accepted these writings, and custom continued the process in the Cape. Legislation has also assisted in the recognition'[1]. The writings of Grotius and Voet in particular had a considerable influence on Scots law in its formative period[2].

1 G Wille *Principles of South African Law* (7th edn, Cape Town 1977 by J T R Gibson) pp 11, 12. See also H R Hahlo and E Kahn *The South African Legal System and its Background* (Cape Town 1968) pp 324, 325.
2 The influence of these and other Roman Dutch authors is discussed by Lord Macmillan in *Stewart's Executrix v London, Midland and Scottish Rly Co* 1943 SC (HL) 19 at 38, 39, 1944 SLT 13 at 20. Unfortunately the court misunderstood the authors' exposition of *actio injuriarum*.

437. Historical development in Scotland. Certain works of a few Scottish authors have in modern times been recognised as having special authority, approximating to the decision of a bench of judges. Lord Normand commented:

> 'Stair, Erskine and Bell are cited daily in the courts and the court will pay as much respect to them as to judgments of the House of Lords, though it is bound to follow a judgment of the House of Lords whatever the institutional writers may have said'[1].

The emergence of that special status has been traced particularly in relation to Viscount Stair, who published the first edition of *The Institutions of the Law of Scotland* in 1681. Evaluation of the authority of other writers — Craig and Mackenzie in the seventeenth century, Bankton, Erskine, Hume and Kames in the eighteenth century and Bell in the early nineteenth century — has been related to the recognition of Stair as pre-eminent. All these authors were experienced practitioners. Stair and Bankton were judges. Although Erskine, Hume and Bell had been Professors of Scots Law at Edinburgh University, Hume subsequently was appointed to the Bench, and Bell would have been appointed likewise but for his involvement with proposals for the reform of the Court of Session[2]. There was thus no separate tradition of *Professorenrecht* distinct from court practice as in some European systems[3]. One may generalise in respect of other writers from what has been written of Stair:

> 'The reputation of a legal writer cannot be separated from the use made by lawyers at any particular time of legal writings in general. The development of a reputation is bound up with the degree to which writings are used, the uses to which they are put, the reasons why some writings are preferred to others and the way in which writings are combined with or preferred to other materials such as the decisions of the courts or unexpressed tradition among those concerned with the law. Stair's reputation as a jurist in Scotland is influenced by, and is itself part of, the way in which these factors have varied since the late seventeenth century'[4].

Although Stair was cited even in his lifetime, after his death his views were often cited in conjunction with those of other authors to indicate consensus of opinion, or cited to indicate what the law was at the time when he wrote — indicating a phase in legal development. Subsequent writers might express dissent from his views, which might also in the eighteenth century be rejected without much concern by a court. This was consistent with judicial attitudes to precedent. In the eighteenth century single decisions of a court were not regarded as binding, although a tract of decisions might establish 'modern' or 'learned' custom which, although not sacrosanct for all time, would normally be respected[5]. In a sense the most respected authors were accepted by the judiciary as partners in developing 'learned custom'. Kames, who at one time contemplated publishing a new edition of Stair's *Institutions*, envisaged a continuing relationship between development of the law by judicial decision and periodical publication of up-to-date institutional works:

> 'What greater service to his country can a lawyer in high estimation perform, than to bring their substance into a new institute, leaving nothing to the student but to consult the original when not satisfied with his author'[6].

The according of special authority to a restricted number of Scottish authors was a nineteenth-century development[7]. Before that development Stair, Erskine, Bell and the other now privileged Scottish writers were cited on much the same footing as other Scottish, English and Continental treatises relevant to the matter to be decided by a court[8].

---

1 Lord Normand 'The Scottish Judicature and Legal Procedure' (address to the Holdsworth Club, Birmingham 1941).

2 See references in N T Phillipson *The Reform of the Court of Session* (PhD dissertation, Cambridge 1967) p 314.

3 Indeed, past professorial status enhanced judicial regard for the views of those later appointed to the Bench, eg Hume and Irvine (Lord Newton) (*Kerr v Martin* (1840) 2 D 752), and Professor Bell was referred to with high regard by the Bench even in his lifetime (*Kerr v Martin* above; see also *Thomson v James* (1855) 18 D 1 at 23).

4 J W G Blackie 'Evaluation of the Institutions' in *Stair Tercentenary Studies* (Stair Soc vol 33, 1981) p 207. This contribution analyses the evolution of a category of 'authoritative writers'.

5 See references in T B Smith *The Doctrines of Judicial Precedent in Scots Law* (1952) pp 4 ff. See also paras 247 ff above.
6 Kames *Select Decisions of the Court of Session 1752–68*, Preface.
7 However, it was accepted in the eighteenth century that certain authors had authority or were authorities just as much as were decisions of the courts: D M Walker *The Scottish Jurists* (1985) p 428.
8 T B Smith 'Authors and Authority' (1972) 12 JSPTL (NS) 3 at 9 ff.

(3) TERMINOLOGY

438. Terms describing writers and their works. During the seventeenth and eighteenth centuries the authors who are now accorded a special status would be referred to — as were others — as 'lawyers' or 'writers' or a variant such as 'text writers' or 'law writers of authority'. If the expression 'institutional writer' was used it indicated the author of a type of literary work rather than indicating his special authority because of the standing of his treatise[1]. The expression 'institutional' has, moreover, been used in the later nineteenth century to indicate works which are neither institutional in format nor composed by authors recognised as specially authoritative[2]. Moreover, in fields such as consistorial law, even the value of Stair has been discounted[3]. 'Authority' and 'authorities' are terms which have sometimes been used indiscriminately or analogously when referring to legal treatises[4], while in other cases 'authority' has been given precise meaning to restrict the value of a particular work or author[5].

1 Blackie observes 'While there may be earlier examples it is striking that the words "institutional writer" begin to appear in a number of different types of material only from the first years of the nineteenth century': J W G Blackie 'Evaluation of the Institutions' in *Stair Tercentenary Studies* (Stair Soc vol 33, 1981) p 207 at 210, 211.
2 See eg *Murdoch & Co v Greig* (1889) 16 R 396 at 401, where Lord President Inglis seemingly refers to Lord Elchies and Mungo Brown as 'institutional writers'.
3 Lord Fraser *Husband and Wife* (2nd edn, 1876) p 3 seemingly includes Balfour and Dirleton among 'institutional writers' and discounts the value of other 'institutional writers', including Stair, on consistorial matters because they do not appear to have regarded the law administered in the Commissary Court with much interest.
4 See eg *Wills' Trustees v Cairngorm Canoeing and Sailing School Ltd* 1976 SC (HL) 30 at 45, per Lord Maxwell, 1976 SC (HL) 30 at 79, 80, 1976 SLT 162 at 172 per Lord President Emslie, at 92, 93, 98 and at 178, 180 per Lord Cameron, at 117 and at 187 per Lord Wilberforce, and at 163 and at 212 per Lord Fraser. See also D M Walker 'Principle and Authority as Sources of Norms' 1982 JR 198. On the earlier use of the term 'authorities', see eg *Fisher v Dixon* (1840) 2 D 121 at 135; *Kerr v Martin* (1840) 2 D 752 at 788, 792; *Thomson v James* (1855) 18 D 1.
5 *Royal College of Surgeons of Edinburgh v Royal College of Physicians of Edinburgh* 1911 SC 1054 at 1060, 1911 2 SLT 134 at 137, per Lord President Dunedin ('There is no authority for it in any text writers — because the note that was quoted of a very learned editor of "Erskine" is not an authority . . .'); *Sugden v HM Advocate* 1934 JC 103, 1934 SLT 465, per Lord Mackay, Lord Wark and Lord Carmont ('We are quite unable to accept Mr MacLaurin as an institutional writer'); *Kerr v Martin* (1840) 2 D 752 at 792, of Commissary Wallace's *System of the Principles of the Law of Scotland* (1760) ('Wallace, it is true, differs. But it is the first time I ever heard of that worthy man as an authority of any weight. He is more, I think, of a speculative philosopher than a lawyer'). Contrast *Fortington v Lord Kinnaird* 1942 SC 239 at 276, 1943 SLT 24 at 40, per Lord Mackay: 'As regards history and authority . . . I personally assign a good deal of weight . . . to the place . . . of Mr John S More . . . whose *Notes on Stair* were published . . . in 1832 . . . the work carries almost the authority of a separate Institution'. As to the status of Hume's *Lectures*, see the opinion of the consulted judges concurred in by Lord President Normand at 1942 SC 254 and at 1943 SLT 30: 'The publication of these lectures . . . cannot be held to have made available to us and our successors a new and authoritative source of Scots law' (see also para 440, note 5 below).

(4) AUTHORITATIVE WRITINGS IN SCOTS LAW

439. Meaning of 'authoritative' and 'institutional'. The emergence of a specially recognised class of legal literature as authoritative was seemingly a nineteenth-century development[1]. Although reference will, no doubt continue to be made by others to 'the institutional writings', the present author prefers the formula 'authoritative writings', partly because not all the works of a particular writer may be regarded as authoritative and partly because not all 'authoritative writings' are institutional in format. On the other hand, there seems to be no fundamental reason why the term 'institutional' should be restricted to comprehensive works on private law and not extended to comprehensive treatment of a specialised aspect of private law such as sale or insolvency. Moreover, the designation 'institutional writer' implies that the courts have recognised an individual as a partner in law-making and that by implication all his writings are entitled to special respect unless judicial pronouncement qualifies recognition.

1 J W G Blackie 'Evaluation of the Institutions' in *Stair Tercentenary Studies* (Stair Soc vol 33, 1981) p 207; T B Smith 'Authors and Authority' (1972) 12 JSPTL (NS) 3 at 10 ff; T B Smith 'Authors as Authority' in *Huldigunsbundel Paul van Warmelo* (Pretoria 1984) p 180 at 189 ff.

440. Judicial recognition. Special recognition of a category of authoritative writings is essentially a sub-category of judge-made law[1]. In the last resort even statute law is enforceable within the parameters of judicial construction, but recognition of the authority of certain authors or treatises has no other foundation than judicial recognition. As the judiciary is free to reformulate the doctrines of judicial precedent by which it will be bound, subject to subordination only to decisions of the judiciary higher in the hierarchy of courts[2], so presumably the courts may regulate and vary the recognition to be accorded to legal writing. They have not as yet promulgated an equivalent of the Valentinian law of citations whereby the authority of privileged writers, in the case of conflict, is to be evaluated by reference to a majority view or special respect for the eminence of a particular author within the class of recognised jurists. Nor has the judiciary extended the procedures for overruling dubious precedents to rejecting statements of the law by privileged writers. These can be disregarded on grounds of obsolescence or rejected by a bench of judges.

It would seem that until the 1840s judges and writers were partners in developing 'learned custom', but as the Scottish courts developed stricter doctrines of judicial precedent and accorded a modified acceptance of *stare decisis* to the decisions of Divisions of the Court of Session the judiciary considered the weight to be given to the opinions of certain authors entitled to special respect. At this period the influence of Hume and Bell, who died in 1843, was apparent in the respectful attitude of the judges to their erstwhile professors, while the pre-eminence of Stair had emerged[3], a recognition in part fostered by Bell. Whereas Bankton had paid tribute to Stair, he had felt free to prefer his own opinions. While Erskine and Kames assessed Stair's work in a historical perspective and by rational analysis, Bell associated his major ideas with those of Stair as 'fountainhead of the law'. Recognition of 'authoritative writings' or authors entitled to declare the law largely depends on uncontradicted dicta of individual judges[4], although paradoxically the actual decision of a single judge has in Scots law no binding authority. Only in such cases as *Fortington v Lord Kinnaird*[5] and *Sugden*[6] have Seven Judges or the Whole Court considered authoritative writing comprehensively. There is no real discussion of what confers authoritative or 'institutional' status, but only of what excludes it. It is thought that the category of privileged writers was closed by the mid-nineteenth century, not because there was no possibility of a subsequent work of outstanding legal scholarship, but because the circumstances of recognition could not be repeated. The re-organisation of the courts and improved reporting had made it expedient to formulate new rules on judicial precedent, and the basic principles of the laws of Scotland had been definitively formulated by certain approved authors in partnership with the judiciary. Accelerating development of the law in the future would largely be the province of statute and precedent. English case law would increase in influence as the reform of the English courts and procedure seemed to make their decisions more comprehensible to Scottish lawyers. 'Authoritative writings' formulated the basic principles which justified recognition of Scots law as a system. In the absence of conflicting authority they were to be applied. Other means would develop it. This conclusion is, however, more justifiable in the context of civil than in criminal law. Scots criminal law has resisted the influences — statutory and otherwise — which might tend to assimilate it to English law, and as far as serious crime is concerned remains based on common law. Recognition of further 'authoritative writing' on the lines of Hume and Alison cannot be excluded as a possibility.

1 This may be contrasted with the situation in South Africa, where acceptance of certain 'Old Writers' is not only judicial but in part statutory. For the attitude of contemporary judges to 'institutional' writings, see R Black 'Practice and Precept in Scots Law' 1982 JR 31 at 43 ff.

2 As to judicial precedent, see paras 247 ff above.

3 J W G Blackie 'Evaluation of the Institutions' in *Stair Tercentenary Studies* (Stair Soc vol 33, 1981) p 207 at 225.

4 The process was gradual. Lord Justice-Clerk Boyle, referring to Stair, Erskine and Bell, had observed 'I am not bold enough, for one, to set opinion against the greatest luminaries of our law even if I differed from them, which I do not' (*Ross v Heriots Hospital Governors* 6 June 1815 FC 393 at 412); and Lord President Blair said 'these questions Lord Stair, that oracle of the Law of Scotland, has long ago answered' (*Routledge v Carruthers* 19 May 1812 FC 572 at 588). A Lord Ordinary who is reluctant to accept Stair's opinion feels that he should report the case (*Barbour v Halliday* (1840) 2 D 1279). Later observations by single judges include Lord Benholme in *Drew v Drew* (1870) 9 M 163 at 167 ('When on any point of law I find Stair's opinion uncontradicted, I look upon that opinion as ascertaining the Law of Scotland'), and Lord President Inglis in *Kennedy v Stewart* (1889) 16 R 421 at 430 ('The principles of equity as systematised by Lord Kames I look upon as the equity law of Scotland').

5 *Fortington v Lord Kinnaird* 1942 SC 239 at 254, 1943 SLT 24 at 30, where the opinion of the consulted judges was delivered by Lord President Normand who, having referred to the authority of Stair, Bankton, Erskine and Bell as 'institutional writers' and accorded the same status to Hume in respect of his *Commentaries on the Law of Scotland, Respecting the Description and Punishment of Crimes* (1797), declined to accord the same authority to his *Lectures on the Law of Scotland* published by the Stair Society a century after his death. The grounds were that he had had ample opportunity to publish them in his lifetime had he so wished but he withheld final authority and approval. Posthumous publication would not by itself deprive a work of institutional status, and indeed Erskine's *Institute* was published posthumously. Lord Justice-Clerk Cooper at 265 and at 35 agreed with the consulted judges that Hume's *Lectures* were not entitled to 'the veneration attaching to our recognised institutional works'. He thought that the *Lectures* were entitled to be regarded as 'authority of very great weight' and as 'decisive evidence of the general and understood state of the law' at the time Hume lectured and put them in the same class as Mackenzie's *Observation on Acts*, More's *Notes on Stair* and Ivory's *Notes on Erskine*. Hume's *Lectures* have been cited frequently since 1942: see eg *Pettigrew v Harton* 1956 SC 67, 1956 SLT 25; *Mill's Trustees v Mill's Trustees* 1965 SC 384, 1965 SLT 375; and *Balshaw v Balshaw* 1967 SC 63, 1967 SLT 54.

6 *Sugden v HM Advocate* 1934 JC 103, 1934 SLT 465, where the institutional status of Mackenzie, Stair, Erskine, Bell, Hume and Alison are clearly recognised, and approval seems to extend to Erskine's *Principles*. Forbes, Fountainhall and Maclaurin are referred to as 'institutional writers' by Lord Anderson but not by the other judges, and Maclaurin is expressly rejected by Lord Mackay, Lord Wark and Lord Carmont.

441. The canon. The canon of 'authoritative writing' is not beyond controversy, but the following seem beyond challenge. Sir Thomas Craig _Jus Feudale_ (1655); Viscount Stair _The Institutions of the Law of Scotland_ (1st edn 1681, 2nd edn 1693); Andrew McDouall, Lord Bankton _An Institute of the Laws of Scotland_ (1751–1753); Professor John Erskine _An Institute of the Law of Scotland_ (1772); Professor George Joseph Bell _Commentaries on the Law of Scotland and on the Principles of Mercantile Jurisprudence_ (1804), and _Principles of the Law of Scotland_ (1829). Especially if authority is attributed to a writer in respect of his status (as is the case with regard to judicial decisions) the canon should also include Sir George Mackenzie _The Institutions of the Law of Scotland_ (1684)[1] and Erskine _Principles of the Law of Scotland_ (1759)[2]. Although he also wrote extensively on other matters, at least Henry Home, Lord Kames _Principles of Equity_ (1760) also merits inclusion in the canon. Baron Hume's _Lectures on the Law of Scotland_ have been refused 'institutional' status for reasons unrelated to the author's own authority[3].

In the field of criminal law may be included Sir George Mackenzie _The Laws and Customs of Scotland in Matters Criminal_ (1678); Baron David Hume _Commentaries on the Law of Scotland Respecting the Description and Punishment of Crimes_ (1st edn 1797, 3rd edn 1829); and Archibald Alison _Principles of the Criminal Law of Scotland_ (1832) and _Practice of the Criminal Law of Scotland_ (1833).

Authority attaches only to the text prepared by the author, and not to editorial additions or notes — which may, however, have persuasive value and even be commended judicially[4]. Editorial errors had impaired the value of the text of Stair's _Institutions_, and the only reliable edition is the second edition (1693) prepared by Stair and made available in 1981 in a text carefully edited for accuracy by Professor D M Walker. The Guthrie (10th) edition of Bell's _Principles_ contains unwarranted additions[5], and the only altogether reliable edition is the 4th, the last to be edited by Bell himself, although the 5th edition edited by his son-in-law using Bell's last recorded reflections has special value.

1 Mackenzie's _Institutions_ is seemingly regarded as a work of 'institutional authority' by Lord Hunter (Lord Ordinary) and without contradiction in the Second Division by Lord Mackintosh in _Lord Advocate v Aberdeen University_ 1963 SC 533 at 559, 1963 SLT 361 at 366; and was cited by counsel in _Inland Revenue Comrs v Graham's Trustees_ 1970 SLT 149 at 152, LVAC. On the importance of the work as a basic medium of instruction, see H L MacQueen 'Mackenzie's _Institutions_ in Scottish Legal History' (1984) 29 JLSS 498.
2 Erskine's _Principles_ was cited in _Sugden v HM Advocate_ 1934 JC 103, 1934 SLT 465.
3 See para 440, note 5 above.
4 In _Fortington v Lord Kinnaird_ 1942 SC 239, 1943 SLT 24, Ivory's _Notes on Erskine_ and More's _Notes on Stair_ were regarded, especially by Lord President Cooper and Lord Mackay, as entitled to special respect, but not to 'institutional' status. On judicial regard for More's _Notes on Stair_, see further _Forrest v Forrest_ (1863) 1 M 806.
5 Thus the law of error as stated in the Guthrie edition differs so substantially from the author's text as to have misled Lord Carmont in _Ritchie v Glass_ 1936 SLT 591 at 593, OH.

(5) LEGAL LITERATURE IN GENERAL

442. Legal literature as a secondary source of law. Apart from the authoritative or 'institutional' works, legal literature is not a primary source of law. The views of particular authors may, however, be adopted in argument as correct expressions of the law, and the court may accept or reject views expressed by authors. They are thus a persuasive source of law, and the weight to be attached to any statement in a treatise or other text depends on the reputation of the author and also on whether the work has been recognised as a reliable guide to the chapter of the law which it seeks to expound. Works such as R Candlish Henderson's *Principles of Vesting in the Law of Succession* (2nd edn, 1938) and W M Gloag's *Law of Contract* (2nd edn, 1929), for example, have been held in high esteem for over fifty years[1].

1 See Lord Cooper *Selected Papers 1922–1954* (1957) pp 129, 190. See also *Errol v Walker* 1966 SC 93, 1966 SLT 159. Later writers are perhaps less enthusiastic — especially regarding Gloag's treatment of error and fraud.

443. Suggested anomalous restrictions. Although legal treatises have long been referred to in the Scottish courts during an author's lifetime, some contemporary authors have expressed the opinion that Scottish practice recognised a rule that because his writings were not strictly 'authority' an author could not be cited to the court unless he was dead or had been elevated to the Bench[1]. Such a rule has been well described[2] as 'of the same order of rationality as trial by ordeal'. It reflects an outdated English rather than a Scottish attitude to the citation of treatises on the law — an attitude which gained some acceptance among a few Scottish judges prone to accept English doctrines uncritically. Especially in the first half of the nineteenth century before reported judicial precedents proliferated it was normal practice in Scotland to cite a wide range of text writers, Scots and foreign, without differentiating except by reference to the cogency of their reasoning and reliability in stating what the law was when the author wrote. During their lifetime the works of Hume and Bell were freely cited by Bench and Bar, as were the works of other authors who commanded respect. The English view was expressed by Lord Wright as recently as 1936 when he referred to Pollock's *Law of Torts* as 'fortunately not yet an authority'[3], implying that the author was still in life. Even an English peer in an appeal to the House of Lords referred to Bell as 'that most enlightened author who (though no authority for their Lordships) is still to be looked on with greatest deference'[4]. These statements tend to blur the distinction between binding and persuasive authority. At all events the most eminent judges in England now welcome the assistance of legal literature, and there is no justification for extending an anachronistic rule of English law — where judicial precedents were and are much more prolific than in Scots law — to Scottish practice.

1 See eg A C Black 'The Institutional Writers' in *Sources and Literature of Scots Law* (Stair Soc vol 1, 1936 ed H McKechnie) p 59, especially footnote; W A Wilson 'Knowing the Law and Other Things' 1982 JR 259 at 267. Cf W M Gloag and R C Henderson *Introduction to the Law of Scotland* (8th edn, 1980 by A B Wilkinson and W A Wilson) p 12; D M Walker *The Scottish Legal System* (5th edn, 1981) pp 402–404.
2 W A Wilson 'Knowing the Law and Other Things' 1982 JR 259 at 267.
3 *Nicholls v Ely Beet Sugar Factory Ltd* [1936] Ch 343 at 349, CA.
4 *Gardner v Cutherbertson* (1824) 2 Sh App 291 at 298, HL.

444. Works of scholarship. After the era when professors were closely integrated with the practising profession the Scottish judiciary was for a period — under English influence — somewhat circumspect in its attitude to writings by contemporary academic writers[1]. However, in 1944 Lord Mackay, who was a judge of somewhat conservative judicial views, expressed his opinion on academic writing as follows:

'A question of the weight of a living academic writer is a somewhat curious one, although it seems to me well settled. For myself, I would agree quite readily that the academician has often the facility of expressing some new distinction or some new principle which, if it appeals to the Judge, may well be adopted as his own, but the authority does not run farther'[2].

This harmonises with Professor Walker's conclusion, which the present writer shares:

'If a court accepts the view of a text-writer that view becomes authoritative, not because the text-writer wrote it but because the court has adopted and approved it, and it thereby acquires the authority of case-law'[3].

It is not, however, inappropriate to refer to the text writer's view as 'persuasive authority', comparable to views expressed in English or other foreign precedents cited for their persuasive value.

Further encouragement to the citation of academic works and comparative materials was given in Edinburgh in 1972 by Lord Reid, who commented:

'In the House of Lords at least we turn a blind eye to the rule that an academic writer is not an authority until he is dead because then he can no longer change his mind. May I suggest to text book writers and editors that they could usefully promote appreciation of academic work by practising members of the profession by increasing their citations from academic works as well as from authorities in other comparable jurisdictions because it is not always easy for busy counsel to lay their hands on these'[4].

1 W A Wilson 'Knowing the Law and Other Things' 1982 JR 259 at 267; T B Smith 'Authors as Authority' in *Huldigunsbundel Paul van Warmelo* (Pretoria 1984) 180 at 185 ff.
2 *Steel v Glasgow Iron and Steel Co Ltd* 1944 SC 237 at 263, 1945 SLT 70 at 81.
3 D M Walker *The Scottish Legal System* (5th edn, 1981) p 344.
4 Lord Reid 'The Judge as Lawmaker' (1972) 12 JSPTL (NS) 22.

445. Criteria for evaluation. Legal literature is of uneven quality, and a work written at the end of an author's life distilling his reflections and experience may have greater influence than a work composed in his youth when warmed by enthusiasm for a particular point of view[1]. The fact that an author has been elevated to the Bench may also influence respect for his work — including contributions to encyclopaedias — although his judicial duties may be in a different field from his writings[2]. Articles in learned journals may also be considered in appropriate cases, although it is for the court to decide what weight to give to particular views expressed[3]. Comment on particular decisions in treatises accorded respect may influence subsequent developments in the law[4], while judicial disapproval of passages in legal literature may diminish a work's or part of a work's persuasive authority[5]. As legislation increases in complexity, a case has been argued[6] for published 'restatements' — official or unofficial — to expound statute law which is not readily comprehensible because of drafting techniques and parliamentary procedure. An unofficial restatement of consumer credit law has been published to this end[7]. To exclude citation of such works would not further the administration of justice, but they could not be regarded as a substitute for judicial interpretation.

1 T B Smith 'Authors and Authority' (1972) 12 JSPTL (NS) 3 at 20, 21.
2 *Coat's Trustees v Lord Advocate* 1965 SC (HL) 45 at 69, 1965 SLT 145 at 153, per Lord Guest, referring to Lord Wark; *Wills' Trustees v Cairngorm Canoeing and Sailing School Ltd* 1976 SC (HL) 30 at 53, per Lord Maxwell (not reported on this point in 1976 SLT 162), referring to Lord Keith of Avonholm, one of the authors of the title WATER AND WATER RIGHTS in the Dunedin *Encyclopaedia of the Laws of Scotland* (1935).

3 See W A Wilson 'Knowing the Law and Other Things' 1982 JR 259 at 266, 267. He uses by way of illustration an article in 1956 SLT (News) 89 by the present writer which was brought to the attention of the House of Lords by Viscount Simonds in *Attorney-General v Prince Ernest Augustus of Hanover* [1957] AC 436 at 464, 472, [1957] 1 All ER 49 at 55, 56, 61, HL.

4 *Dempster's Trustees v Dempster* 1949 SC 92 at 95, 1949 SLT 110 at 112, per Lord Jamieson; *M'Elroy v M'Alister* 1949 SC 110 at 135, 1949 SLT 139 at 149, 150, per Lord President Cooper.

5 *Bentley v Macfarlane* 1964 SC 76, 1964 SLT 58; *Kerr v Martin* (1840) 2 D 752 at 792.

6 F A R Bennion 'Legislation: Principles and Methods' in *Proceedings and Papers, 5th Commonwealth Law Conference* (1977) p 53.

7 It is somewhat paradoxical that a draftsman should make legislation intelligible in book form rather than in the statute drafted.

SOURCES OF LAW
(GENERAL AND HISTORICAL),
LEGAL METHOD AND REFORM

1. INTRODUCTION

501. Sources of law. The term 'sources of law' is a compendious one, and care must be taken to distinguish between the different contexts in which it can be used[1]. Here, our concern is with the distinction between the historical sources and the legal or formal sources of law. The latter may be defined as the agencies which give a rule the force of binding law or whose sanction allows the inquirer to conclude that the rule he has found will be applied as law by the courts. In short, the legal or formal sources tell us both what the law is and by what means it may be changed in the future. In Scots law, these sources are legislation[2], precedent[3], authoritative or institutional writings[4] and custom[5]; equity[6] is also normally included in their number.

  1 See further D M Walker *The Scottish Legal System* (5th edn, 1981) pp 342–345.
  2 See paras 523 ff below, and paras 101 ff above.
  3 See paras 539 ff below, and paras 247 ff above.
  4 See paras 534 ff below, and paras 439–441 above.
  5 See paras 529 ff below, and paras 355 ff above.
  6 See paras 546, 547, below, and paras 394 ff above.

502. Historical sources. The historical sources of law are of a somewhat different nature. They have no necessary connection with the formal validity of legal rules, but they do explain their origins. They are the factors which contribute to the development of a legal system during its formative years and which account for its ultimate form and character. Yet none of these historical sources is ever authoritative in itself. Scots law, for example, has borrowed much from Roman law; the historical source of these rules is therefore the Roman system but their validity as rules of Scots law rests on their absorption by one or other of the formal sources.

    This part of the title will be concerned with the historical sources of Scots law and with the history and development of its formal sources. The Scottish legal system is the product of many centuries of development during which it has been subject to a variety of influences, internal and external, legal and non-legal. Political and economic conditions peculiar to Scotland have left their mark as, for example, the Wars of Independence at the end of the thirteenth century and the Union with England of 1707. But Scots law did not develop in isolation. It also participated in the legal history of Europe, borrowing as appropriate from other legal systems and reacting to events such as the Reformation and the Industrial Revolution which had a wider European dimension and which produced similar reactions in the other states of Europe. The result is a legal system which, like any other, has its own characteristics but which must also be set in a broader, European context if its history and evolution are to be understood properly[1].

  1 See generally O F Robinson, T D Fergus and W M Gordon *An Introduction to European Legal History* (1985).

2. THE HISTORY OF SCOTS LAW: AN OUTLINE

(1) PRE-FEUDAL SCOTLAND

503. Celtic law. Little is known of the early laws of Scotland, although it seems clear that they consisted largely of tribal customs, varied and unwritten. Early Scottish society was predominantly Celtic in its orientation, and it is likely that laws of the Celtic type featured prominently and that they were related to the laws of Celtic Ireland, about which much more is known. Celtic law represents law at an early stage of its development. Wrongs such as assault and theft were still a matter for the individual concerned and his kin, although the private vengeance of primitive times had gradually been replaced — perhaps due to the influence of Christianity — by an elaborate system of pecuniary penalties, the amount payable depending on the nature of the wrong and the rank of the party wronged. Evidence of this system is to be found in an early collection known as the *Laws of the Brets and Scots*[1]. Again, although detailed knowledge is lacking, it is clear that land-holders owed military service as well as burdens in kind to their overlords. Obscure, too, are the courts and their procedures. We have evidence of the existence of the *brehon* (or judge) but not of his functions, although, like his Irish counterpart, he probably acted as a law-speaker, declaring the law of the tribe. Proof by compurgation was a feature of Celtic procedure generally and is likely to have been widely used in Scotland; there is evidence that it survived well into the feudal period in Galloway[2].

1 These are printed in APS I, 663–665.
2 W E Levie 'Celtic Tribal Law and Custom in Scotland' (1927) 39 JR 191 at 197.

504. Survival of Celtic law. It is difficult to say how long Celtic law and customs survived and to assess their contribution to the development of modern Scots law. The coming of feudalism did not destroy Celtic society and it is therefore likely that Celtic customs prevailed for quite some time. Indeed, there is evidence from the early seventeenth century that Celtic marriage customs, at odds with the rules of the Roman Church, were still being widely followed in the Highlands and Islands[1].

1 See W D H Sellar 'Marriage, Divorce and Concubinage in Gaelic Scotland' (1978–80) 51 Transactions of the Gaelic Society of Inverness 464.

(2) FEUDAL SCOTLAND

505. The coming of feudalism. Feudalism came to Scotland during the eleventh century, taking as its model the feudalism established in England after the Norman Conquest. Tenure of land was transformed into feudal tenure and government developed along the lines of that of the Anglo-Norman state. Unlike England, however, the coming of feudalism to Scotland was a peaceful process and for that reason gradual. At first it was confined to the more accessible regions of the south and east, and it was only slowly that it spread northwards and westwards. Nor was the older, Celtic order swamped by the new regime. The native aristocracy survived alongside the incoming Anglo-Norman lords and acquired feudal status. Many of the feudal incidents found in the charters are simply the Celtic burdens and duties in feudal guise[1].

1 W C Dickinson *Scotland from the Earliest Times to 1603* (3rd edn, 1977 revised by A A M Duncan) p 82.

506. Feudal national administration. Feudal tenure of land[1] and the influence of Anglo-Norman law in Scotland[2] will be considered below. Here, we shall concentrate on the administration of justice. In feudal theory the king was the fount of all secular justice; justice could only be administered by others to the extent that they had been granted the right to do so. In practice, such delegation was common. The king could not be everywhere at once while other matters of state also demanded his attention. The king, of course, had his own court, the *curia regis*, a body composed of his chosen advisers which dealt with both administrative and judicial business. This court — or council — could be augmented on occasions by others called by the king, and by the end of the thirteenth century such enlarged sittings were being described as *in parliamento*. As well as other matters, Parliament dealt with judicial business both at first instance and on appeal by the process of 'falsing the doom' (judgment) of a lower court. Indeed, in some respects Parliament was superior to the council as a court of law. It was a properly constituted feudal court (whereas the council was not), and so could deal with matters of fee and heritage.

1 See paras 587 ff below.
2 See paras 597 ff below.

507. Feudal local administration. In the localities, royal justice was administered by the justiciar and the sheriff[1]. The justiciar, the superior official, was an itinerant judge going on periodic circuits or ayres and exercising both a civil and a criminal jurisdiction. It was in his court alone that the pleas of Crown could be heard. Normally there were two justiciars, one for the region north and one for that south of the Forth and, in theory, each held his ayre twice annually. In the later middle ages, however, there is evidence that the system was not working well; frequent Acts enjoining the regular holding of the ayres would seem to suggest continued non-observance of the regular pattern.

1 As to the sheriff, see para 508 below.

508. The sheriff. A sheriffdom was an administrative division of the kingdom, having as its centre (or *caput*) a royal castle or, later, a burgh which had grown up round such a castle. The establishment of sheriffdoms throughout Scotland was a slow process, and it was only in the thirteenth century that they began to be created in the remoter northern and western parts of the country. In charge of the sheriffdom was the sheriff, the king's officer in the locality. Appointment lay initially with the Crown, although in some sheriffdoms the office became hereditary. Sheriffs were permitted to appoint deputies to act for them, and this soon became common practice; in the course of time, some sheriffs became merely figureheads. The sheriff was charged with a variety of functions, administrative and judicial, and among these was the regular holding of the sheriff court. This court dealt with a wide variety of civil and criminal business, although certain matters such as the pleas of Crown were reserved for the court of the justiciar[1], to which appeals from the sheriff court also went in the first instance. In addition, the sheriff was charged with the oversight of the inferior courts within his sheriffdom, from which appeal to his court lay.

1 As to the justiciar, see para 507 above.

509. The lord. Feudal tenure of land also entailed the administration of justice for, in feudal theory, a lord who had tenants was entitled to hold a court for them; in Scotland, however, it may be that this right had to be specifically conferred[1]. At his court, disputes between the lord's free tenants concerning their holdings and matters incidental thereto were dealt with, as well as minor criminal matters, while less formal meetings were devoted to his unfree tenantry — those who held and worked his land on a tenure that was not strictly feudal. In addition, a feudal lord might exercise franchisal justice; that is, he might be granted cognisance of matters normally reserved for the Crown. The extent of such grants depended on the terms of each lord's charter, but characteristically they included the right to deal with criminal matters involving the death penalty. By the early fourteenth century a lord who so held was often described as holding *in liberam baroniam* (in free barony); his holding was a barony and he a baron. Grants more extensive still were also made, being described as *in liberam regalitatem* (in free regality). In its most extreme form, the regality was almost a 'petty kingdom'. The baron dealt with all criminal matters, save only treason, and might have his own chancery for the issue of brieves in connection with civil disputes. As a result, the king's writ did not run in the regality and it was outwith the jurisdiction of justiciar and sheriff.

1 W C Dickinson *The Court Book of the Barony of Carnwath 1523–1542* (Scottish Historical Society 1937) p xi.

510. The burghs. The Scottish burghs also had their own courts. A burgh was a town which had been granted the special status of burgh. The first burghs were royal creations. They were trading centres, and to encourage their mercantile activities they and their inhabitants were accorded various rights and privileges. As well as the general law of the land, the burgh court administered the law and customs of the burgh — the special law which contained the privileges of the community and which dealt with matters concerning trade and commerce. One example of burgh law is the code known as the *Laws of the Four Burghs*[1], the oldest part of which derives from the customs of Newcastle-on-Tyne and was probably introduced into Scotland by David I (1124–1153). The burgh courts themselves were subject to the supervision of the chamberlain while above them was the Court of the Four Burghs which gradually expanded to include most of the Scottish burghs and which dealt with disputes between burghs and pronounced on doubtful points of burgh law[2].

1 The *Laws of the Four Burghs* are printed in APS I, 333–356.
2 In time the court became more of a debating chamber and less of a court of law. During the sixteenth century it was transformed into the Convention of Royal Burghs.

511. Church courts. The courts dealt with so far have all been secular courts, but the courts of the Church were also important in medieval Scotland. They had exclusive cognisance of matters such as questions of marriage and status which are today the province of the lay courts, but their activities, and those of the men who staffed them, were not limited to the strictly ecclesiastical sphere. In contrast to the royal and feudal courts, the courts of the Church were largely manned by trained lawyers, clerics who had been educated in one or both of Roman and canon law. The Church could therefore offer justice that was both learned and sophisticated by comparison with that of other courts, and it seems likely that, due to the preference of litigants, many cases which in England would have gone to the lay courts were in Scotland disposed of either in the Church courts or through the offices of an ecclesiastical arbiter.

512. Legal literature. The feudal period also saw the beginnings of a native legal literature. This development was not peculiar to Scotland, as throughout western Europe the thirteenth century witnessed the appearance of treatises devoted to the local feudal and customary law. But the Scottish texts have received less scholarly attention than their European counterparts and the two principal works, *Regiam Majestatem* and *Quoniam Attachiamenta* are at present available only in unsatisfactory modern editions[1].

Regiam Majestatem, a treatise probably compiled in the early fourteenth century[2], is essentially a commentary on the procedures of the royal courts. It is, however, neither wholly original nor wholly Scottish, being based on the later twelfth-century English treatise, the *Tractatus de legibus et consuetudinibus regni Anglie* attributed to Ranulf de Glanvill[3]. Yet it is more than a re-issue of the English work between Scottish covers. Some of the Glanvillian material has been edited to take account of Scottish conditions and there is a section which has no counterpart in Glanvill and which appears to have been drawn from a Roman or Romano-canonical source[4]. Associated with *Regiam Majestatem* is the treatise known as *Quoniam Attachiamenta*. Unlike *Regiam* it appears to be a wholly Scottish work. Its subject matter is again procedural, and its inclusion of the procedures of the baron courts probably accounts for its alternative title, the *Leges Baronum*.

1 APS I, 597–659; and *Regiam Majestatem and Quoniam Attachiamenta* (Stair Soc vol 11, 1947 ed Lord Cooper).
2 See A A M Duncan '*Regiam Majestatem* — a Reconsideration' 1961 JR 199.
3 Nelson's Medieval Texts 1965, ed G D G Hall.
4 See P Stein 'The Source of the Romano-canonical part of *Regiam Majestatem*' (1969) 48 Scot Hist Rev 107; and Stair Soc vol 11, Introduction.

(3) THE DARK AGES?

513. Legal development. With the Wars of Independence — the Scottish reaction to the attempt by Edward I to impose himself on Scotland — it has often been assumed that Scots law entered a 'dark age' from which it did not emerge until the later sixteenth century[1]. This view is, however, questionable. Certainly Scotland's legal development was affected by the political and other problems she experienced during the later middle ages, but if progress was slow there are signs that, at least from the fifteenth century onwards, there was progress of a sort and not the stagnation of the traditional view[2].

The evidence comes from a variety of sources. From the early fifteenth century the parliamentary records reveal a concern for the provision of accurate and authentic texts of the law in force, both contemporary statute law and the 'Auld Lawes' — that is, the various pre-fifteenth-century treatises and collections of native assizes circulating in manuscript form — and on a number of occasions commissions were appointed to deal with the matter[3]. It is true that nothing substantial was produced until the later sixteenth century when various collections of statutes were published, and it was not until 1609 that the 'Auld Lawes' appeared in print in the editions prepared by Sir John Skene[4]. But the fifteenth-century attempts at codification and revision do at least evidence a concern and so point to development of a limited kind.

1 See Lord Cooper *The Dark Age of Scottish Legal History 1350–1650* (David Murray Lecture, Glasgow 1952); and G C H Paton 'The Dark Age, 1329–1532' in *An Introduction to Scottish Legal History* (Stair Soc vol 20, 1958) pp 18 ff; but contrast G W S Barrow 'The Scottish Justiciar in the Twelfth and Thirteenth Centuries' 1971 JR 97.

2 See J J Robertson 'The Development of the Law' in *Scottish Society in the Fifteenth Century* (1977) p 136.
3 *Robertson* p 143.
4 J Skene *Regiam Majestatem Scotiae, Veteres Leges et Constitutiones* (1609); J Skene *Regiam Majestatem, The Auld Lawes and Constitutions of Scotland* (1609).

514. Statutes. The statutory records of the period also contain a number of reforming Acts dealing with such matters as prescription and security of tenure under lease[1]. Taken together their number is not large, but they do show that Parliament, or a section of it, was aware of deficiencies in the law and was prepared to try to remedy these. Attempts were also made to make adequate provision for legal education. It is likely that the foundation of Scotland's three oldest universities in the fifteenth century was motivated by a desire to make university education in law more readily available by establishing native law schools[2], while an Act of 1496, imposing on landowners of substance the duty of securing an education in law for their sons and heirs, seems to have been intended to ensure that those who would later exercise an inherited jurisdiction would do so with at least some training behind them[3].

1 Husbandmen Act 1429 (c 2) (APS II, 17); Leases Act 1449–50 (c 6) (APS II, 35); Prescription Act 1469 (c 4) (APS II, 95); Diligence Act 1469 (c 12) (APS II, 96); Prescription Act 1474 (c 9) (APS II, 107).
2 See para 552 below.
3 Education Act 1496 (c 3) (APS II, 238).

515. The Council and the Lords of Council. It is also in the fifteenth century that the origins of the Court of Session are to be found. As we have seen, the king administered justice in person either through the Council or, more formally, in Parliament. Parliament, however, had other matters to attend to, and by the mid-fifteenth century it was normal for it to appoint two committees to deal with judicial business; one *ad iudicia contradicta* (for the falsing of dooms) and one *ad causas et querelas* (for cases at first instance). The competence of these committees lasted only while Parliament was in session; at other times, the judicial work of the Crown fell to the Council. The pressure of business on the Council seems to have been considerable, and steps were taken to alleviate it. At first the device of appointing sessions was tried; that is, a group of men were appointed to sit — or hold sessions — to dispose of judicial business on behalf of the Council[1]. Unfortunately, we have little information about the activities or effectiveness of the sessions, although it does seem that they ceased altogether during the 1470s. Further developments came from within the Council itself, and by the early sixteenth century a specialised group of councillors was beginning to emerge whose sole duty was to deal with judicial business; in 1528 it was laid down that Lords of Council not appointed to this group were to be excluded from its sessions[2]. It was this body which was transformed into the College of Justice in 1532 and whose members, as Lords of Council and Session, formed the nucleus of what was not a new, but rather a reconstituted, Court of Session[3].

At the same time the judicial arm of the Council began to absorb the functions of the parliamentary committees. The committee for the falsing of dooms gradually became redundant as a simpler method of appeal directly to the Council developed, while by the end of the fifteenth century it is clear that the committee for cases at first instance had been taken over by the Council to the extent that it was simply the judicial Lords of Council sitting under another name. After 1544, this latter committee ceased altogether to be appointed.

1 See eg the Lords of Session Act 1425–26 (c 19) (APS II, 11).
2 A A M Duncan 'The Central Courts before 1532' in *An Introduction to Scottish Legal History* (Stair Soc vol 20, 1958) p 336.
3 As to the establishment of the College of Justice, see the College of Justice Act 1532 (c 2) (APS II, 336).

(4) THE MODERN ERA

516. Introduction. With the sixteenth century we enter the modern era in the history of Scots law for, although the description of the preceding centuries as a 'dark age' is not apposite, it is from this time that Scots law slowly began to develop into a self-contained national system. Many factors contributed to this process and the more important of these will be dealt with below[1]. Here we shall consider the changes affecting the structure and powers of the courts.

1 See paras 523 ff below.

517. The early Court of Session. In 1532 the Court of Session consisted of the Chancellor of Scotland, the Lord President of the Court, fourteen Lords Ordinary and a number of Extraordinary Lords[1]. In theory the Chancellor presided but in practice this duty fell to the Lord President, whose position as senior judge was confirmed in 1707 when the Chancellorship went into abeyance. At first, the Lords Ordinary consisted of clerics and laymen. The clergy, with their superior legal training, had made an important contribution to the judicial work of the Council, and it is therefore not surprising that they continued to act after 1532. The first four Lords President of the Court were churchmen and its last clerical member was Archbishop Burnet of Glasgow, appointed an Extraordinary Lord in 1664, who died in 1668. The Extraordinary Lords were Crown nominees, appointed more for political reasons than on the grounds of suitability for judicial office. As early as 1533 the court expressed dissatisfaction with this arrangement and their number was reduced to four. But it was not until 1723 that such appointments were abolished altogether.

1 For what follows on the Court of Session, see Lord Cooper 'The Central Courts after 1532' in *An Introduction to Scottish Legal History* (Stair Soc vol 20, 1958) pp 341 ff.

518. The modern Court of Session. Until the early nineteenth century the structure of the Court of Session remained much as it had been in the sixteenth; that is, it was a unitary court whose members acted as one, even though individual Lords might be absent on ancillary business. But a heavy case-load together with an excessive reliance on written pleadings created delays and the need for reform. Accordingly, during the earlier part of the nineteenth century the court was restructured and took on its modern form of a largely appellate Inner House consisting of two Divisions and an Outer House comprising a number of Lords Ordinary sitting singly to deal with cases at first instance[1]. Its collegiate character[2], however, was preserved by the provision for sittings of the Whole Court to deal with particularly difficult matters. Procedural reform, too, was forthcoming; for example, the closed record was introduced and the practice of taking all oral evidence on commission abandoned.

1 Court of Session Act 1808 (c 151), ss 1, 5.
2 As to the collegiate nature of the court, see para 286 above.

519. Absorption of other courts. The Court of Session is Scotland's supreme civil court, but for much of its history its competence was restrained by the existence of a number of other courts whose jurisdiction was both specialised and exclusive. The nineteenth century saw the disappearance of most of these courts and the absorption of their jurisdiction, in whole or in part, by the Session.

In the aftermath of the Reformation, commissary courts had been created as successors to the consistorial jurisdiction of the pre-Reformation Church. That at Edinburgh was the principal court, having exclusive jurisdiction in causes involving marriage and status and an appellate jurisdiction over the local commissary courts which dealt with remaining matters such as the confirmation of testaments. By 1836 these courts had gone, the duties of the Edinburgh court being taken over by the Session[1] and those of the local commissaries by the sheriff court[2]. Likewise, the jurisdiction of the Scottish Court of Admiralty was distributed among the Courts of Session and Justiciary as well as to the English Court of Admiralty[3].

Also of interest in this context is the Scottish Jury Court. Scotland has always known the criminal jury but by the end of the sixteenth century trial by jury in civil cases had all but disappeared. In 1810, however, it was recommended that Scotland consider the adoption of the civil jury as a desirable improvement, the main impetus coming from the House of Lords, accustomed to English practice. Effect was given by statute to these recommendations[4]. At first, a separate Jury Court was established, but in 1830 it ceased to function as an independent tribunal, being incorporated into the Court of Session[5].

1 Commissary Court of Edinburgh Act 1836 (c 41), s 1.
2 Commissary Courts Act 1823 (c 97), ss 6–9.
3 Court of Session Act 1830 (c 69), s 21.
4 Jury Trials (Scotland) Act 1815 (c 42); Jury Trials (Scotland) Act 1819 (c 35). See N T Phillipson 'Scottish Public Opinion and the Union in The Age of Association' in *Scotland in the Age of Improvement* (ed N T Phillipson and R Mitchison, 1970) pp 125 ff; 'Nationalism and Ideology' in *Government and Nationalism in Scotland* (ed J N Wolfe, 1969) pp 167 ff.
5 Court of Session Act 1830, s 1.

520. The High Court of Justiciary. In the seventeenth century Scotland acquired her supreme criminal court, the High Court of Justiciary. In 1524 the Lord Justice-General (the Justiciar) had been instructed to remain continually at Edinburgh or with the king to deal with criminal business[1]. In practice most of the work was done by his deputies, and by the 1660s it was accepted that the Lord Justice-Clerk, an officer who rose to the Bench from humble beginnings as clerk of court, presided in the absence of his superior. The administration of criminal justice in the localities, however, was at best sporadic and *ad hoc*, and by the 1660s the situation called for reform. In 1672 the establishment of the High Court of Justice, consisting of the Lord Justice-General, the Lord Justice-Clerk and five Lords of Session, was formally ratified[2]. The new court was based at Edinburgh, but provision was also made for the holding of circuits throughout the country. In 1830 the office of Lord-Justice General was combined with the presidency of the Court of Session, and from 1877 all Lords of Session were also made Lords Commissioners of Justiciary[3].

1 Administration of Justice Act 1524 (c 8) (APS II, 286).
2 Courts Act 1672 (c 40) (APS VIII, 80).
3 Court of Session Act 1830 (c 69), s 18; Criminal Procedure (Scotland) Act 1887 (c 35), s 44.

521. The sheriff. From the sixteenth century the sheriff and his court attracted a good deal of criticism; lack of training on the part of both sheriffs and their deputies together with the heritable nature of the shrieval office was not conducive to an efficient or impartial discharge of duties. Reform came in the eighteenth century when heritable jurisdictions were abolished by statute in the aftermath of the Jacobite Risings[1]. The heritable sheriffs were replaced by advocates of at least three years' standing, and under them were the sheriff-substitutes to whom in practice fell much of the day-to-day work of the sheriffdom. In 1825 and in the light of complaints received it was laid down that the substitutes, too, must be legally qualified[2]. The nineteenth century also saw the expansion of the jurisdiction of the sheriff court towards its present level.

1 Heritable Jurisdictions (Scotland) Act 1746 (c 43).
2 Sheriff Courts (Scotland) Act 1825 (c 23), s 9.

522. The baron court. From the later middle ages the baron court (with the exception of the more important regalities) began to decline as the Court of Session and, later, the High Court of Justiciary became established. By the early seventeenth century the baron court had ceased to deal with anything more than minor disputes and the maintenance of the laws of good neighbourhood; that is, the supervision of the well-being of the community of the barony, including such matters as common pasturage, the repair of boundary walls and a host of similar domestic issues. The heritable feudal and franchisal jurisdictions were abolished in 1746[1]. Only the baron court survived, but with a much attenuated jurisdiction which has long since fallen into desuetude.

1 Heritable Jurisdictions (Scotland) Act 1746 (c 43).

3. THE FORMAL SOURCES OF SCOTS LAW

(1) LEGISLATION

523. Introduction. Legislation[1], according to Stair, is that part of the law introduced 'by express will or command of these in authority, having the legislative power'[2]. Today, legislation comprises the statutes of Parliament, delegated legislation and the prerogative legislation of the Crown. In addition, the accession of the United Kingdom to the European Communities has added a further tier to the enacted law of Scotland, member states being bound to observe the legislation of the Communities[3]. Of these legislative sources, the statutes of Parliament are the most important; they are the primary source of law in the sense of the source to which (with the exception of Community legislation) all others must yield, and the principal means of change and inno-vation. But this has not always been the case. The law of Scotland, like that of any other early legal system, originally consisted of unwritten custom and, when it came, enacted law was at first the exception. It was also largely derivative in that, often, it did little more than restate or clarify existing custom. Nor was any overt distinction drawn between legislation proper and judicial decision; both were aspects of the Crown's role as declarer of the law and, for example, the early Scottish assizes attributed to David I, William the Lion and Alexander II contain, without distinction, enactments of both types[4].

1 As to legislation, see further paras 101 ff above.
2 Stair *Institutions* I, 1, 10.
3 European Communities Act 1972 (c 68), s 2.
4 These are printed in APS I, 313–325, 367–384, 395–404. See also T M Cooper 'Early Scottish Statutes Revisited' (1952) 64 JR 197.

524. Parliamentary legislation. Legislation originated as a formal enactment of the king made in the presence of his advisers. In time, however, Parliament came to be considered as the normal forum for such activity. Parliament, after all, was a full and formal meeting of those summoned by the king to advise him and sat, among other things, to 'show' the law applicable to cases brought before it; and, as we have seen, there was originally no qualitative difference between declaring the law applicable to the matter in hand and, as circumstances demanded, declaring what was to be law for the future. Many of the enactments of the medieval Scottish Parliament have to do with administrative matters and with the public peace but, certainly by the fifteenth century, Parliament is also to be found legislating on points of substantive law[1]. By the early seventeenth century the authority of Parliament in this sphere had become established to such an extent that Craig could write:

'The decrees and statutes passed by the three estates of the realm with the royal assent form the proper material of the written law of Scotland . . . in Scotland we have no other body of positive written law of comparable authority'[2].

Parliament, however, was not the only source of enacted law and, until its demise in 1707, the Scottish Privy Council regulated many matters[3]; for Craig, though, its ordinances were inferior to the Acts of Parliament and he held that 'they have no legal validity in any point concerning life, liberty, or estate, and that personal and private affairs are unaffected by them'[4].

1 See para 514 above.
2 Craig *Jus Feudale* I, 8, 9.
3 See eg F J Shaw 'Sumptuary Legislation in Scotland' 1979 JR 81.
4 *Craig* I, 8, 9.

525. Statutory sources of Scots law. The statutory sources of Scots law consist of the Acts of the Scottish Parliament prior to the Union Agreement of 1707, the Acts of the Parliament of Great Britain from 1707 to 1800 and those of the Parliament of the United Kingdom, commencing in 1801. The study of the early Scottish Acts, however, is surrounded by difficulties. The extant original records of Parliament only commence in 1466 and are incomplete until 1578. From the sixteenth century, various collections of the Acts began to appear in print, but these are not always reliable[1], and it was only in the nineteenth century that a comprehensive and scholarly edition appeared with the publication of the *Acts of the Parliaments of Scotland, 1124–1707*[2].

1 See *Sources and Literature of Scots Law* (Stair Soc vol 1, 1936 ed H McKechnie) pp 5–9.
2 *Acts of the Parliaments of Scotland 1124–1707* (Record edn 1814–75, ed C Innes and T Thomson), 12 volumes (APS).

526. Pre-Union legislation. The Acts of the pre-Union Parliament have two notable characteristics. First, their style is usually terse and laconic and, compared with modern statutes, their terms are general. As such, they must of necessity be interpreted liberally and are not subject to the same rules of construction as later statutes[1]. Their provisions are normally considered as

exemplary and not restrictive and, as Lord Dunedin commented, their interpretation must be 'of the spirit and not of the letter'[2]. Secondly, early Scots
statutes are subject to tacit repeal by desuetude[3]. Desuetude involves more than
mere non-observance of a provision; as Lord Mackay put it, it requires 'a very
considerable period, not merely of neglect, but of contrary usage of such a
character as practically to infer such completely established habit of the community as to set up a counter-law or establish a quasi-repeal'[4]. Examples of
statutory provisions which have gone into desuetude include provisions dealing
with Sunday observance and an Act of 1581 requiring landed gentlemen to
reside at their country seats[5]. The doctrine of desuetude of statute is recognised
in the *ius commune* but is not accepted in English law, and it is doubtful if it
applies to legislation passed since the Union of 1707[6].

1 See *Thomas v Thomson* (1865) 3 M 1160 at 1165, per Lord Inglis.
2 *George Heriot's Trust Governors v Paton's Trustees* 1912 SC 1123 at 1135, 2 SLT 116 at 122.
3 Erskine *Institute* I, 1, 45.
4 *Brown v Edinburgh Magistrates* 1931 SLT 456 at 458, OH. See also J R Philip 'Some Reflections on
   Desuetude' (1931) 43 JR 260.
5 Residence of Land Owners Act 1581 (c 21) (APS III, 222).
6 H F Jolowicz *Roman Foundations of Modern Law* (1957) pp 28–32; T B Smith *A Short Commentary
   on the Law of Scotland* (1962) p 30.

527. The Union. In 1707 the Parliaments of Scotland and England were
replaced by the new Parliament of Great Britain. With the exception of regulations governing trade, customs and excises, the Treaty of Union stipulated
that the law of Scotland was to 'remain in the same force as before' although
subject to legislation by the new Parliament; in matters of private right,
however, statutory change was only to be permissible if 'for the evident utility
of the Subjects within Scotland'[1]. Despite this provision, legislation has been
one of the ways in which English law has influenced Scots law, not always to the
'evident utility' of the latter system. At the same time, statute has grown
increasingly important as a source of law; the nineteenth century in particular
saw much legislation on matters of both public and private law and by the
opening of the twentieth century legislation had acquired its primacy as a source
of law.

1 Treaty of Union 1707, art 18.

528. Acts of Sederunt. Among the legislative sources of Scots law are Acts of
Sederunt. When the College of Justice was founded in 1532, the Court of
Session was authorised to regulate its own procedure. This power was ratified in
1540, when the court was permitted to make 'sic actis statutis and ordinancis as
thai sall think expedient for ordouring of process and haisty expeditioun of
Justice'[1]. The power thus granted resulted, over the following centuries, in a
prodigious number of such enactments, or Acts of Sederunt. On occasions the
court exceeded the terms of its authority and issued Acts which dealt with what
were, in effect, matters of substantive and administrative law. Examples include
an Act against alienations by bankrupts and regulations concerning imprisonment for debt[2]. But, certainly by the later eighteenth century, Acts of Sederunt
were being restricted to their proper scope. In 1913 an Act of Sederunt revised
and consolidated all such previous enactments and provided what virtually
amounted to a 'code of civil procedure'[3]. This, in its turn, was superseded by the
Rules of Court of 1936[4] (revised in 1948[5] and 1965[6]). The High Court of
Justiciary exercises a similar rule-making power in the form of its Acts of
Adjournal[7].

1 College of Justice Act 1540 (c 10) (APS II, 371).
2 These and other examples are cited in J I Smith 'The Transition to the Modern Law, 1532–1660' in *An Introduction to Scottish Legal History* (Stair Soc vol 20, 1958) p 28.
3 Act of Sederunt to Consolidate and Amend the Acts of Sederunt 1913, SR & O 1913/638: see D Maxwell 'Civil Procedure' in *An Introduction to Scottish Legal History*, p 424.
4 Rules of Court enacted by Act of Sederunt dated 18 March 1936, SR & O 1936/88.
5 Act of Sederunt (Rules of Court, consolidation and amendment) 1948, SI 1948/1691.
6 Act of Sederunt (Rules of Court, consolidation and amendment) 1965, SI 1965/321, made under the Administration of Justice (Scotland) Act 1933 (c 41), s 16.
7 See the Criminal Procedure (Scotland) Act 1975 (c 21), s 282.

(2) CUSTOM

529. Introduction. 'The municipal law of Scotland', wrote Erskine, 'may be divided, after the example of the Romans, into written and unwritten'[1], and from what follows it is plain that by written he means statute and by unwritten, custom. Earlier, Stair drew a similar distinction. 'We are ruled in the first place', he tells us, 'by our ancient and immemorial customs ... [and] in the next ... [by] our statutes'[2]. It is also clear that he valued custom above statute. For Stair, correspondence with equity was the desirable end of all law and, in his view, custom 'declareth equity and constituteth expediency'[2]. Thus, both Stair and Erskine include custom as one of the constituent elements of Scots law and in addition give it a greater prominence than would be usual today. Custom is therefore one of the sources of law the history of which falls to be considered here. First, however, we must try to define our terms for, as has been noted, 'there is no more certain, but at the same time elusive, source of Law than Custom'[3].

1 Erskine *Institute* I, 1, 30.
2 Stair *Institutions* I, 1, 16.
3 Lord St Vigeans 'Custom' in *Sources and Literature of Scots Law* (Stair Soc, vol 1, 1936 ed H McKechnie) p 163. As to custom, see further paras 355 ff above.

530. Meaning of 'custom'. Custom is grounded in generally accepted usage and practice but, beyond that, 'custom' may be used in a variety of senses. Sometimes reference is made to custom to explain the historical origins of a legal institution or rule in circumstances where its formal validity depends on statute or some other authoritative source. Thus, for Erskine, history explained the contents of the codified customs of France but their authority rested on 'the explicit enactment of the supreme power' which had the additional effect of converting them from unwritten to written law[1]. Then there is what is usually termed legal custom, custom which is binding in and of itself without reference to any other formal authority. According to Erskine it is 'that which, without any express enactment by the supreme power, derives force from its tacit consent; which consent is presumed from the inveterate or immemorial usage of the community'[2]. Thus, in Erskine's view, tacit consent as evidenced by long use was the authority behind customary law and, by implication, there was nothing to prevent new rules being created in this way. Erskine also notes that legal custom may be universal (or general) or local; universal when it applies throughout Scotland, local when only in a particular district, as with the udal law of Orkney and Shetland[3].

1 Erskine *Institute* I, 1, 30.

2 *Erskine* I, 1, 43.

3 *Erskine* I, 1, 46. See, however, paras 355 ff above, and UDAL LAW.

531. Erosion of custom as a source of law. It seems to be generally accepted that in primitive legal systems all law was customary law, communal life being regulated by standards and practices which were widely accepted and treated as binding. These customs might, if the need arose, be declared judicially, but such confirmation was not required to establish them as law. As we have also seen, early enacted law was often little more than the redaction of existing custom. This was largely true of the Twelve Tables of Roman law and is likely to have been the case with the earliest Scottish legislation. However, as soon as custom is reduced to formal writing, such as royal enactment, a change occurs. The authoritative source of the rule becomes the writing, and custom, now crystallised, is relegated to the status of historical custom, the factor which explains the appearance and form of the rule. The result is that the importance of custom as a formal source of law is gradually reduced as more and more of it is reduced to writing. We may recall here Erskine's remarks on the French customs[1].

1 See para 530 above.

532. Custom and the institutional writers. Juristic treatment of custom as a source of Scots law begins with the 'institutional' writers. Stair draws a primary distinction between 'our ancient and immemorial custom' and 'our recent customs and practiques'. As examples of the former, he quotes, among other things, 'primogeniture, and all degrees of succession, our legitim portion of children, [and the] communion of goods between man and wife'[1]. Similarly, Erskine compares 'the most essential articles of our customary law . . . [which] are notorious, and so require no evidence to prove them' and 'later usage . . . which must be proved to the judges as any other matter of fact'[2]. In respect of Stair's 'ancient and immemorial' and Erskine's 'essential' custom, and the examples thereof, it has been suggested that 'it can scarcely be affirmed that the technical rules [cited] . . . were ever the product of custom in the sense of the practice of the community. These rules were developed by courts and writers, and a considerable number of them are drawn direct from the civil or canon law'[3]. This, however, is to miss the important point that Stair's and Erskine's conception of custom was not necessarily that of the modern lawyer.

While it is true to say that some of the ancient customary law of Scotland was 'drawn from the civil and canon law' (one might also add feudal law), this does not necessarily imply that Stair and Erskine had a clouded perception of custom. The importance of these systems in the development of Scots law cannot be denied, but it must also be remembered that in the institutional scheme none of them is admitted to be authoritative *per se*; indeed canon law, having been largely abrogated at the Reformation, could not be. Stair considered the backbone of Scots law to be equity, and its formal sources statute and custom, a construct which, once adopted, dictated that the received Roman, canon and feudal law could only be accommodated on the grounds that it was equitable custom. As he tells us, 'our customs . . . are also from the civil, canon, and feudal laws. . . . But none of these have with us the authority of law; and therefore are only received according to their equity and expediency'[4]. In other words, for Stair and those who followed his scheme, the written texts of the learned laws were undoubtedly the historical source of much of Scots law but their formal, juristic source could be none other than custom.

Again, it cannot be denied that the customary law of Scotland 'was developed by courts and writers'. It is to be found in legal treatises from *Regiam Majestatem* onward, while the Court of Session undoubtedly played a part in clarifying it and drawing out its consequences. In this task, the court frequently sought guidance from juristic literature, both Scottish and continental. Thus, arguably, some of the customary law existed in writing while the more technical contributions made to its development by jurists and the court cannot, in any real sense, be said to be grounded in the practice of the community. However, legal treatises were not written law, strictly speaking; in Stair and Erskine (unlike Justinian[5]) written law signifies statute only and so any other source must logically be explained as evidencing custom. We must also remember that Stair and Erskine would have construed the term 'custom' to include its wider, European sense of learned legal custom, or the law as developed by jurists and the practice of courts[6]. This latter is not custom in modern Scottish parlance, but for the 'institutional' writers it was the only way to justify the contribution of these agencies to a system whose only other formal source was statute.

1 Stair *Institutions* I, 1, 16.
2 Erskine *Institute* I, 1, 44.
3 J T Cameron 'Custom as a Source of Law in Scotland' (1964) 27 MLR 306 at 311.
4 *Stair* I, 1, 16.
5 Justinian *Institutes* I, 2, 3.
6 T B Smith 'Authors and Authority' (1973) 12 JSPTL 3 at 9.

533. Ancient and recent custom. As previously mentioned, the 'institutional' writers drew a distinction between ancient and recent custom. The distinction is primarily one of proof. Ancient custom is notorious custom. It has been accepted for so long that no further proof of its validity is required; as Stair comments, it 'may be called our common law'[1]. Recent custom, on the other hand, requires to be proved like any other matter of fact. Stair appears to equate recent custom with a series of like decisions of the Court of Session, the latter constituting the necessary proof of the former [1]. Erskine, in a fuller discussion, is more cautious. He acknowledges the probative value of such a series but, recognising that recent custom is more than the learned legal custom discussed above, adds that 'neither is it necessary . . . that the custom be declared by the previous sentence of a judge; for no court of justice can constitute law; and therefore any sentence declaring the customary law is of itself a clear proof that the law was constituted before'[2]. In other words, recent custom does not coincide completely with what today would be termed case law. Prior decision, although useful, is only one method of establishing that a usage, by tacit consent, has acquired the mantle of law.

Thus in the 'institutional' scheme, custom would appear to have a broader significance than it does in modern Scots law. The difference, it is suggested, may be explained historically. Until the nineteenth century the only recognised formal sources of Scots law were statute and custom[3]; anything which affected the development of the law other than legislation had therefore to be subsumed under the latter. It was only during the nineteenth century that this construct broke down as the decisions of the courts became formal sources in their own right with the development of the doctrine of precedent, and certain jurists began to acquire formal authority as 'institutional writers'. Thereafter the role of custom was much reduced. Statute, as we have seen, gained ground as a tool of legal development, so perhaps taking account of usage that was beginning to crystallise, while precedent and 'institutional' writings — in one sense the offspring of custom — acquired an independent formal status.

1 Stair *Institutions* I 1, 16.

2 Erskine *Institute* I, 1, 47.
3 T B Smith 'Authors and Authority' (1973) 12 JSPTL 3 at 9.

(3) THE 'INSTITUTIONAL' WRITERS

534. Introduction. A distinction must first be drawn between 'institutional writers' and writers who wrote what may be described as institutional works. In Scotland 'institutional writers' is a term of art and signifies a small group of writers whose works — or at least some of whose works — are regarded as formal sources of Scots law. Most of these writings also qualify as institutional works, but this is not a prerequisite of their formal status. Institutional works, on the other hand, have a broader European significance and this must be understood in order to place developments in Scotland and the Scottish institutional writers in their proper context[1].

During the early modern period the various states of western Europe began to break with the traditions of the *ius commune* and to fashion for themselves self-contained national systems of law[2]. Naturally, the process varied from country to country, as did the precise blend of indigenous law and elements preserved from Roman, canon and feudal law ultimately contained in these systems. But of importance for it everywhere was the production of institutional works; that is, literature usually in the vernacular rather than Latin which set out the municipal law in a systematic and comprehensive way on the analogy of Justinian's *Institutes*. Often, like their Roman model, these works had a didactic purpose, being intended for use as textbooks in the universities of Europe.

1 See generally J W Cairns 'Institutional Writings in Scotland Reconsidered' (1983) 4 J Leg Hist 76.
2 See K Luig 'The Institutes of National Law in the Seventeenth and Eighteenth Centuries' 1972 JR 193.

535. Craig. The first of the Scottish institutional writers, Sir Thomas Craig of Riccarton (1538–1608)[1], owes his place in the canon to a work which was not institutional in the sense described in the preceding paragraph. Craig's reputation rests on his *Jus Feudale*, first published in 1655 although completed some fifty years earlier. The work was written in Latin, not English, and dealt with feudal law only. Nor did Craig confine himself to Scots law; rather he wrote a general work on the feudal law of Europe with specific reference to Scotland. Nevertheless, the *Jus Feudale* is a landmark in Scottish legal writing. It acquired a considerable reputation on the continent, and its systematic approach presages the future, placing it in an altogether different world from that of the digest *Practicks*.

1 As to Craig and the other 'institutional writers', see A C Black 'The Institutional Writers, 1600–1829' in *Sources and Literature of Scots Law* (Stair Soc vol 1, 1936) pp 59 ff.

536. Stair. Of greater importance for the development of Scots law was Sir James Dalrymple, Viscount of Stair (1619–95). Stair's contribution to Scots law lies chiefly in his *Institutions of the Law of Scotland*, first published in 1681. This was the first work of its kind to be devoted to the municipal law; as Stair tells us, his design was to 'give a description of the law and customs of Scotland, such as might not only be profitable for judges and lawyers, but might be pleasant and useful to all persons of honour and discretion'[1]. Native sources, particularly in the form of the decisions of the Court of Session, have a prominent place in the exposition. Roman, canon and feudal law are not — and indeed could not be — ignored, while the continental jurists, particularly the Dutch civilians, were also among the sources used. But the importance of Roman or other non-native sources must not be overrated. The *Institutions* was not a work based on the *ius commune* with Scottish annotations, but 'an exposition of Scots law based predominantly on native sources'[2]. In addition, Stair's approach was that of the early natural lawyers. He considered law to be none other than 'the dictate of reason'[3] and, taking equity as his guiding criterion, he set out to construct a system that accorded with the principles of natural law. He also held that law 'should be handled as a rational discipline, having principles from whence its conclusions may be deduced'[4]. His presentation was therefore reasoned and systematic.

1 Stair *Institutions* I, 1, preamble.
2 D M Walker, Introduction to Stair's *Institutions* (1981) p 21. It must be remembered, however, that these native sources (particularly case law) had already absorbed much from the *ius commune*.
3 *Stair* I, 1, 1.
4 *Stair* I, 1, 16.

537. Other writers. Stair's text was an institutional work in the continental sense of the term, and its appearance both marked the emergence and aided the further development of Scots law as a national system. It also stands at the beginning of a long tradition of Scottish legal literature which continued this work of development. Much, but not all, of this literature consisted of similar institutional works. It is from the jurists of this tradition that the writers who achieved formal 'institutional' or authoritative status are drawn. However, it appears that the canon of Scottish institutional writers and writings is not settled beyond a doubt[1]. Craig's *Jus Feudale*, Stair's *Institutions*, Bankton's *Institute*[2], Erskine's *Institute*[3] and Bell's *Commentaries*[4] would appear to have an assured place. But some commentators also include Mackenzie's *Institutions*[5], while there is also uncertainty about the status of Erskine's *Principles*[6] and Kames's *Principles*[7]. Other notable writers, such as Forbes[8], seem never to have been considered for inclusion. Similar uncertainty surrounds writers of authority on the criminal law[9].

1 J W Cairns 'Institutional Writings in Scotland Reconsidered' (1983) 4 J Leg Hist 76 at 99. As to legal literature, see also paras 433 ff above.
2 Andrew McDouall, Lord Bankton *An Institute of the Laws of Scotland* (3 vols, 1751–53).
3 John Erskine *An Institute of the Law of Scotland* (2 vols, 1773).
4 George Joseph Bell *Commentaries on the Law of Scotland and on the Principles of Mercantile Jurisprudence* (1804) and *Principles of the Law of Scotland* (1829).
5 Sir George Mackenzie of Rosehaugh *The Institutions of the Law of Scotland* (1684).
6 John Erskine *Principles of the Law of Scotland* (1754).
7 Henry Home, Lord Kames *Principles of Equity* (1760).
8 William Forbes, who was appointed Professor of Civil Law in the University of Glasgow in 1713, produced *The Institutions of the Law of Scotland* (1722) and *The Great Body of the Law of Scotland* (unpublished).
9 Mackenzie's *Laws and Customs* (Sir George Mackenzie of Rosehaugh *The Laws and Customs of Scotland in Matters Criminal* (1678)) and Hume's *Commentaries* (David Hume *Commentaries on the Law of Scotland, Respecting the Description and Punishment of Crimes* (2 vols, 1797)) are usually considered institutional. More doubtful is the position of Alison's *Principles* and *Practice* (Archibald Alison *Principles of the Criminal Law of Scotland* (1832) and *Practice of the Criminal Law of Scotland* (1833)).

538. Conclusion. What, then, has determined whether a particular writer or a particular text should be regarded as formally authoritative, given that an institutional writer is not merely nor exclusively one who wrote an institutional work?

It would appear that the category of institutional writer was a creation of the Scottish Bench during the nineteenth century[1]. Initially, Stair and the other jurists mentioned above had no particular authority or standing beyond the quality of their work. They were certainly referred to and cited in court, but so were other writers, both Scottish and foreign. In the continental tradition, the contribution of jurists to legal science was highly valued; their work represented one strand of legal custom and offered ready guidance on many points[2]. During the nineteenth century, however, a change took place as certain works began to cross the line from much-used sources of reference to sources possessing a degree of authority in their own right, as the judiciary found itself more and more reluctant to depart from the views found therein. The change may have been due partly to the rise of *stare decisis*; that is, as decision gained formal authority a need was felt to bestow like authority on frequently-used and often-followed works of reference[3]. Thus in 1815 Lord Boyle, referring to Stair, Bankton and Erskine stated that 'I am not bold enough, for one, to set my opinion against those of the great luminaries of our law, even if I had differed from them'[4]; by 1870 Lord Benholme could pronounce that 'when on any point of law I find Stair's opinion uncontradicted, I look upon that opinion as ascertaining the law of Scotland'[5]. In short, as a matter of custom and practice, the judiciary began to regard certain jurists and works in a special light and to elevate them to the status of authoritative sources. The corollary was that increasingly less attention came to be paid to those not thus singled out. The process was, however, gradual — almost a matter of unconscious growth — with the result that no clear criteria were ever ascertained by which an 'institutional' — in the sense of authoritative — writer might be identified. The doubts referred to above therefore remain, as does the possibility of the inclusion of a new writer in the class.

1 See J W G Blackie 'Stair's Later Reputation as a Jurist' in *Stair Tercentenary Studies* (Stair Soc vol 33, 1981) p 207; and T B Smith 'Authors and Authority' (1973) 12 JSPTL 3 ff. Generally as to legal literature see paras 433 ff above.
2 See para 532 above.
3 Thus, in Smith's view, 'the authority of an institutional writer is approximately equal to that of a decision by a Division of the Inner House of the Court of Session': T B Smith *A Short Commentary on the Law of Scotland* (1962) p 32.
4 *Ross v Heriot's Hospital Governors* 6 June 1815 FC 393 at 412.
5 *Drew v Drew* (1870) 9 M 163 at 167.

(4) PRECEDENT

539. Practicks. The decisions of the Court of Session began to attract attention from an early date. In 1574, for example, a commission appointed to compile a written statement of Scots law was instructed to base its work on the 'decisions befoir the sessioun' as well as the 'bukis of the law [and] actis of parliament'[1]. Apart from the official records, the earliest collections of the decisions of the court took the form of *Practicks*[2]; that is, records of its work compiled by one of its members. *Practicks* normally go under the name of their compiler. The earliest surviving collection, covering the period 1540 to 1549, is Sinclair's *Practicks*. Other examples include Maitland's *Practicks* (1550–80) and Hope's *Practicks* (1610–19). *Practicks* are the ancestor of the modern Scottish law reports, although they were originally compiled for private use and not intended for publication. Nor should their appearance be construed as a commitment to precedent, in the strict sense of the term, on the part of the Bench; the aim was rather the promotion of a degree of consistency in judicial decision-making.

1 Act 1574 APS III, 89. It has been suggested that Balfour's *Practicks* were the outcome of this commission.
2 As to *Practicks*, see H McKechnie 'Practicks, 1469–1700' in *Sources and Literature of Scots Law* (Stair Soc vol 1, 1936) pp 25 ff.

540. Digests. Towards the end of the sixteenth century, *Practicks* of a different kind began to appear. In contrast to the earlier type, these *Practicks* attempted to digest the law, subject by subject, and as well as the decisions of the Session their compilers drew on the Acts of Parliament and the Auld Lawes. The first of their kind were the *Practicks* of Sir James Balfour, compiled in the later 1570s[1]. Others include the *Major Practicks* of Sir Thomas Hope[2] and the *Practicks* of Sir Robert Spottiswoode[3].

1 Sir James Balfour of Pittendreich *Practicks or System of the More Ancient Law of Scotland* (1754; Stair Soc vols 21, 22, 1962, 1963, ed P G B McNeill).
2 Sir Thomas Hope of Craighall *Major Practicks* (Stair Soc vols 3, 4, 1937, 1938, ed J A Clyde).
3 Sir Robert Spottiswoode *Practicks of the Law of Scotland* (1706).

541. The development of precedent. The instructions to the commission of 1574[1] and at least the digest *Practicks*[2] would suggest that, if only in a loose sense, the decisions of the Court of Session were coming to be considered as one of the sources of Scots law during the sixteenth century. It is, however, important to grasp the nature of their status at this early stage and, above all, to avoid the conclusion that regard for prior decision necessarily indicates a commitment to precedent in the form of the rules of *stare decisis*, or something akin to it. Prior decision was important for two reasons, but neither of these involve precedent in its modern sense.

1 See para 539 above.
2 See para 540 above.

542. Judicial consistency. First, as already noted, reference to decided case was an aid to judicial consistency, a goal desirable in any legal system. Thus in the case of *Carmichael v Lermonth* in 1622, although the Court of Session decided contrary to an earlier case in point, it also took care to state that 'the Lords . . . in time coming . . . would decide, where the like question occurred, conform to the last Decision'[1]. It has been argued that this 'looks like an acceptance of the doctrine of *stare decisis*'[2], but that is to interpret the evidence in the light of modern and not seventeenth-century conceptions; it is more likely to have been an indication that, without necessarily feeling bound to do so, the Bench would normally have regard to prior decision in the interests of consistency and certainty. To this end, the practice of the courts, particularly in the early modern period, provided a useful guide. Kames noted that in the absence of an extensive body of written law 'our judges depend, in a great measure, upon practice and precedent as their guides'[3] while, earlier, Craig commented that prior decision could be a useful aid to the interpretation of statute. 'Practice', he wrote, 'affords the best rule of interpretation of obscurities and ambiguities in native written law. . . . Once a decision putting a particular interpretation upon a statute has been arrived at, it is not lightly gone back on'[4]. In short, at this stage commitment to prior decision was a commitment to consistency and not authority.

1 *Carmichael v Lermonth* (1622) Durie 28.
2 J C Gardner *Judicial Precedent in Scots Law* (1936) p 25.

3 Kames *Dictionary of Decisions* (1741) vol 1, Preface.
4 Craig *Jus Feudale* I, 8, 14.

543. Precedent and custom. Secondly, prior decision was useful as a means of establishing custom. Erskine, as we have seen, drew a distinction between ancient custom which did not require proof, and later usage which did[1]. For the institutional writers the principal mode of proof was prior decision of the Court of Session. But a single decision was not of itself sufficient; rather a series of like decisions was demanded. Mackenzie noted that 'our unwritten Law, comprehends the constant Tract of Decisions, past by the Lords of Session'[2] while Stair drew a distinction between 'a custom by frequent decision, and a simple decision, which hath not the like force'[3]. The same point is made by Erskine[4] but he also takes care to point out that past decisions 'have no proper authority in similar cases' and that they 'create no obligation on the judges to follow in the same tract, if it shall appear to them contrary to law'. Thus by the mid-eighteenth century it seems that a series of like decisions had considerable probative value in respect of custom, but that such a series (let alone a single decision) had not, as yet, acquired binding authority even if, in practice, the court would normally 'follow in the same tract'.

1 See para 533 above.
2 Mackenzie *Institutions* I, 1, 10.
3 Stair *Institutions* I, 1, 16.
4 Erskine *Institute* I, 1, 47.

544. Modern doctrines of precedent and *stare decisis*. The modern doctrine of precedent and the adoption of the rules of *stare decisis* would appear to be a development of the nineteenth century. The process, however, was a gradual one and one which is not always easy to follow. At first, judicial opinion appears to have been divided about the force of precedent, some judges clinging to the institutional approach that regard need only be had to uniform series of decisions[1]. But by 1828 there is evidence that at least a decision of the Whole Court was considered as binding for the future[2]. English law, in which the rules of precedent had been established at an earlier date, probably influenced developments in Scotland, as did the appellate jurisdiction of the House of Lords and the creation of an appellate structure within the Court of Session itself. A hierarchical court structure meant that a lower court would feel prompted to take special note of the work of a higher court to which it was subject; conflict would normally result in the overturning of the decision of the former by the latter. At first it is unlikely that lower courts felt strictly bound by the decisions of those above them, but equally they would feel that even a single decision was highly persuasive and not to be departed from lightly. From this, it was but a short step to admitting the binding force of such precedent and converting invariable practice into legal theory. By the mid-nineteenth century, for example, it appears that the sheriff court regarded decisions of the House of Lords and of the Inner House, if not as absolutely binding, at least as extremely weighty authority[3].

1 See *Bulloch v Smith* 31 Jan 1809 FC at 116 per Lord Craig.
2 See J C Gardner *Judicial Precedent in Scots Law* (1936) p 36, and the authorities there cited. As to judicial precedent, see also paras 247 ff above.
3 *Gardner* p 40.

545. Law reporting. A system which relies on precedent requires sound law reports[1]. It is, however, difficult to say which is the cause and which the effect; it is more likely that each contributes to the development of the other. Systematic law reporting did not begin until the early eighteenth century, although previously individuals such as Stair and Dirleton had compiled collections of decisions of the Session[2]. In 1705 William Forbes was appointed by the Faculty of Advocates to report the decisions of the Court of Session; and he was succeeded by other Faculty reporters whose work is represented by the series of reports known as the *Faculty Collection*[3] and *Faculty Decisions*[4]. Latterly these Faculty reports were tardy in appearing and in the nineteenth century they were overtaken by the *Session Cases*[5]. The form of the reports naturally changed over the years, and of particular importance for the development of precedent was the inclusion of the full opinions of the judges. The Bench had long been reluctant to allow this and, despite the efforts of the Advocates, it was only in 1825 that the reports took on their modern form.

1 As to law reporting, see J S Leadbetter 'The Printed Law Reports, 1540–1935' in *Sources and Literature of Scots Law* (Stair Soc vol I, 1936) pp 42 ff.
2 Stair's *Reports* (2 vols) cover the period 1661–81, and Dirleton's *Decisions* the period 1665–77.
3 *Faculty Collection* covers the period 1752–1825 in twenty-one volumes.
4 *Faculty Decisions* covers the period 1825–1841 in sixteen volumes.
5 *Session Cases* comprises reports by Shaw (16 vols, 1821–38), Dunlop (24 vols, 1838–62), Macpherson (11 vols, 1862–73), Rettie (28 vols, 1873–98) and Fraser (8 vols, 1898–1906), and the modern *Session Cases* (from 1907).

(5) EQUITY

546. Law and equity. Unlike English law, Scots law has never clearly differentiated between law and equity[1]. The two have always been administered together, equity being called in where necessary to temper the rigidities of law. Thus, for example, the courts have intervened on equitable grounds 'to modify exorbitant conventional penalties, to permit irritancies to be purged at the Bar, and to grant redress by decree of interdict or specific implement'[2]. Equity, in the form of the dictates of reason or natural justice, is therefore among the sources of Scots law, but the way in which it is applied has had the substantive result that its standing as a separate and distinct source of law has been obscured. As Lord Kames, one of the few Scottish writers to deal with equity in its own right, noted, 'In Scotland and other countries where equity and common law are united in one court, the boundary varies imperceptibly; for what originally is a rule in equity, loses its character when it is fully established in practice; and then it is considered as common law'[3].

1 As to equity, see further paras 394 ff above.
2 T B Smith *A Short Commentary on the Law of Scotland* (1962) p 44.
3 Kames *Principles of Equity* (3rd edn) p 26.

547. The *nobile officium*. In addition to the application of equitable considerations in the course of its normal business, the Court of Session also exercises a special equitable jurisdiction known as the *nobile officium*[1] (noble office); and a similar jurisdiction in criminal matters is exercised by the High Court of Justiciary. The origins of this jurisdiction are historical. In medieval times the Crown, as the fount of justice, was bound to provide a remedy where the lower courts could not or would not; as well as intervening when a subordinate tribunal failed to do justice, the king could thus step outwith the bounds of strict law where justice demanded. Latterly, the Crown's residual equitable jurisdiction was exercised through the Scottish Privy Council, but in 1708 this body ceased to exist when a new Privy Council for Great Britain was created. The powers of the new Council were to be those previously exercised by the English Privy Council, which had lost all jurisdiction in England and Wales in the mid-seventeenth century. The jurisdiction of the Scottish Privy Council therefore disappeared, no arrangements being made to confer it on other courts. As a result, 'many matters were, by the abolition of the council, left without remedy'[2]. Certainly, as urged by Kames[3], the Court of Session stepped in and by default assumed the equitable jurisdiction of the abolished Council, but its exercise of the *nobile officium* has always been cautious and, in practice, gradually became virtually restricted to established precedent.

1 As to the *nobile officium*, see paras 426 ff above. See also ADMINISTRATIVE LAW, vol I, para 332.
2 P G B McNeill 'The Passing of the Scottish Privy Council' 1965 JR 263 at 264.
3 Kames *Historical Law-Tracts* (4th edn, 1792) pp 231, 232.

4. THE HISTORICAL SOURCES OF SCOTS LAW

(1) ROMAN LAW

548. Introduction. Scotland, like much of western Europe, experienced a reception of Roman law that contributed materially to the development of her law. However, the nature of this process of reception has not always been appreciated. Roman law was never authoritative in Scotland; rather it was received *imperio rationis* — by reason of its inherent rationality and as a source of equitable principle. Again, the reception involved a good deal more than an intellectual awareness of Roman law and a knowledge of its sources and literature. Roman law, after all, was part of the cultural heritage of the West and, with canon law, it was for long the only system of law taught in the universities of Europe. Acquaintance with Roman law was thus widespread, but this did not inevitably produce reception. The step from knowledge to reception is marked by two processes, one practical and one theoretical. The practical step occurs when courts and litigants begin to look with increasing frequency to Roman rules and procedures to settle disputes, the theoretical when a municipal system is given a Roman-based systematic structure; when, for example, its material is ordered according to the scheme of Justinian's *Institutes*, or Roman definitions are coined for institutions of the native law, thus casting them in a distinctly Roman mould.

549. The Roman law of medieval Europe. The Roman law that came to Scotland was not the Roman law of antiquity but Roman law as developed in medieval Europe. At its heart lay the texts of the *Corpus Iuris Civilis*[1], the great revision and codification of Roman law carried out by the Emperor Justinian (527–565). The *Corpus Iuris*, however, was the product of the Eastern Empire (Justinian himself ruled from Constantinople), and in the West it remained largely neglected until the rediscovery of its most important component, the *Digest*, at the close of the eleventh century. Thereafter Roman law was studied, first at Bologna and the other Italian universities, whence it spread throughout Europe. The aim was to use the texts as sources of legal principle for contemporary practice, but in some ways they were unsuited for their new work. They represented, for example, a legal system which knew nothing of medieval feudalism nor the law of the Roman Church; in short, they took no account of many factors which were an integral part of medieval civilisation. Some adaption and some discarding was therefore necessary, and what emerged from the Italian law schools was in effect a hybrid Romano-Italian law which was to prove useful precisely because of its flexibility. Together with canon law and the learned elements of feudal law, this medieval brand of Roman law constituted the *ius commune* — the common law of Europe which stood above its local laws.

1 The *Corpus Iuris Civilis* consists of the *Digest* or *Pandects*, the *Institutes*, the *Code* (*Codex Repetitae Praelectionis*) and the *Novels* (*Novellae Constitutiones*): see further W W Buckland *Textbook of Roman Law* (3rd edn, 1966 by P Stein) ch I.

550. Reception of Roman law in Europe. Throughout Europe the reasons for and the process of reception of Roman law were broadly similar. Essentially, Roman law was received because it stood available to fill a need. At a time when the indigenous laws of Europe were localised, comparatively undeveloped and often consisted of unwritten custom, but when something more was coming to be demanded, Roman law offered a written and mature system of law that could be quarried with profit. The agents of reception were university-trained men. At first these graduates tended to pursue careers in the service of Church or state, but gradually they were drawn into the administration of justice. Litigants preferred them and the law and procedures they had to offer, and slowly the higher courts of Europe were taken over by learned men and the learned law. Roman law, of course, could not normally be applied in the face of local law, but the latter could be — and was — interpreted strictly and against a background of Roman ideas. In addition, when the native law was obscure or silent — or was deemed to be so — Roman law was available to fill the gap. The extent of the reception in the various states of Europe was determined by the capacity of the indigenous law of each to resist, or assimilate, these Romanising influences.

551. Roman law in Scotland. During the middle ages Scotland was not untouched by the continental revival of Roman law, but it was some time before its doctrines began to exert any direct or substantial influence. The contents of *Regiam Majestatem*[1] and the other medieval law books are primarily feudal and customary, and there is little in them to suggest that Roman law was, in any systematic way, beginning to affect the substantive law or the procedures of the lay courts. They do contain Roman terminology and the occasional extract from Roman or Romano-canonical sources[2], but these only illustrate that the Roman law of the *ius commune* was not considered as alien but part of an intellectual tradition with which Scotland was in touch.

When Roman law first began to influence legal development, it was not directly but through canon law. Canon law was itself partly derived from Roman law and so argument based on Roman law had a place in the Church courts. For example, instances of claims based on prescription and cases of sale being set aside on the ground of enorm lesion have been noted[3]. The proceedings of the Church courts, of course, had no necessary effect on the secular law, but the use of Roman law there did at least accustom litigants to it and the advantages it had to offer. More importantly, the Church was responsible for the reception in Scotland of Romano-canonical procedure, a procedure which was based on that of the courts of the later Roman Empire. Churchmen, as we have seen, made an important contribution to the judicial work of the royal Council, and it seems likely that their presence there led to the use of a canonically-based procedure. The clergy continued to act in a judicial capacity after the foundation of the College of Justice with the result that the refurbished Court of Session continued to employ a procedure akin to that of canon law.

By the later fifteenth century there are signs that Roman law was beginning to have a direct, even if generalised, influence on the law of Scotland. For example, statutes of 1469 and 1474 introduced respectively rules on prescription and tutory which have Roman pedigrees[4]. But it was not until the sixteenth century that the reception proper began, and, as elsewhere, it was largely the work of those trained in the learned laws.

1 As to *Regiam Majestatem*, see para 512 above.
2 See P Stein 'The Influence of Roman Law on the Law of Scotland' 1963 JR 205 at 207–209.
3 *Stein* at 210. 'Enorm lesion' means substantial injury to an estate.
4 Prescription Act 1469 (c 4) (APS II, 95); Tutors Act 1474 (c 6) (APS II, 106). The Roman source of the rules is not acknowledged in the Acts.

552. The universities. Until the fifteenth century Scotland had no universities of her own; accordingly Scots received their legal education abroad. At first many of these students concentrated on canon law with a view to ecclesiastical preferment on their return but, during the fifteenth century, something of a change took place as university-trained men began to look to the lay rather than the Church courts for employment. Their numbers were initially small, but it was with them that the future lay. It is from this time that we can begin to trace the emergence of what was to become the Faculty of Advocates, as a small but discrete body of men began to practise as professional pleaders in the higher courts. The fifteenth century also saw the foundation of Scotland's three senior universities, St Andrews (1413), Glasgow (1451) and Aberdeen (1496). It was intended that each should offer instruction in Roman and canon law, but these hopes remained largely unfulfilled, whether because of inadequate financial provision or because of a continuing preference for foreign travel. Scots students continued to go abroad in substantial numbers, and it was only during the eighteenth century that the teaching of law in the Scottish universities began to revive and the practice of seeking legal education on the continent to decline.

553. Roman law and the Scottish courts. The Scottish reception of Roman law was accomplished largely through the practice of the courts, particularly the Court of Session. As the court became more firmly established during the sixteenth century so the attractions of a career at the Bar increased; the Reformation effectively closed the door on the alternative of ecclesiastical preferment. By the end of the century there were some fifty advocates practising at the Bar and their numbers were growing. At first it seems that Roman law was used more by advocates in the presentation of their arguments than by the judges in reaching their decisions. But the Bench was also well-disposed towards Roman law; increasingly its members were graduates who had started their careers at the Bar. The judiciary, of course, did not have a free hand, being bound to apply the law of Scotland as found in the Scots statutes and treatises devoted to the feudal and customary law. However, statute law was still the exception, and much of the indigenous law remained uncertain; it did not exist, for example, in a form comparable to the codified customs of France. Nor, some statute law apart, was it a particularly mature or sophisticated law. Thus in default of other guidance the judiciary turned to the *ratio scripta* (written reason) of Roman law. As one sixteenth-century Lord of Session remarked, 'this far to the lawis of the Realme we are restricted, gif ony cummirsum or trubilsum cause fal out, as oft chances, quhilke can nocht be agriet be our cuntrey lawis, incontinent quhatevir is thoct necessar to purify this controversie, is cited out of the Roman lawis'[1].

1 John Lesley (appointed to the Bench in 1564), cited by P Stein 'The Influence of Roman Law on the Law of Scotland' 1963 JR 205 at 216.

554. Roman law and legal literature. The importance of Roman law is also reflected in legal literature. In 1590 William Wellwod, professor of civil law at St Andrews, produced *The Sea Laws of Scotland*. His sources included the law merchant as well as appropriate Scottish material, but his greatest debt was to Roman law. Somewhat later, the institutional and other Scottish legal writers also provide evidence of its contribution. Roman law was not acknowledged as a formal source, but a good deal of what they have to say is shot through with civilian doctrine while the presentation of their material has clearly been influenced by the structure of Justinian's *Institutes*.

555. Decline in influence of Roman law. From the beginning of the eighteenth century the direct impact of Roman law began to decline. By then Scots law was emerging as a coherent national system; much of what Roman law had to offer had already been absorbed, while native writers and the practice of the courts offered a more immediate *corpus* of source material, making direct reference to the civilian sources increasingly unnecessary. In addition it was from this time that Scots law began to be influenced by English law and to look to its southern neighbour for solutions to new legal problems, particularly in the commercial sphere. Yet resort to Roman law did not cease altogether and it still occasionally happens that argument on court is founded directly on its rules[1].

1 See eg *Sloans Dairies Ltd v Glasgow Corpn* 1977 SC 223, 1979 SLT 17.

556. Conclusion. Important though Roman law has been, care must be taken not to exaggerate its influence. The use of Roman terminology alone does not necessarily indicate the adoption of a Roman institution. Scots law, for example, employs the Roman term 'interdict', but the remedy to which it refers is a very different one in each system. Again, Scots law has adopted the provisions of the *Lex Rhodia* which are also found in the Roman sources, but this does not necessarily indicate direct borrowing; the provisions of the *Lex* were part of the general mercantile custom of Europe and would probably have come to Scotland even if Roman law had not[1]. These cautions noted, it is still possible to trace the influence of Roman law on many branches of Scots law. Examples include the law of moveable property and some aspects of heritable property such as servitudes, the law of guardian and ward and that of contract and quasi-contract.

1 See D B Smith 'Roman Law' in *Sources and Literature of Scots Law* (Stair Soc vol 1, 1936 ed H McKechnie) pp 171, 172.

(2) CANON LAW

(a) Introduction

557. Scope of section. Before there can be an appreciation of the influence of the canon law of the Roman Catholic Church on the law of Scotland, there must be an appreciation of the origins and development of the canon law of the Church. There will, therefore, be given a general conspectus of canon law. This will be divided into four parts: (1) the nature of canon law[1]; (2) canon law from apostolic times to the *Decretum* of Gratian[2]; (3) canon law from Gratian to the Council of Trent[3]; and (4) post-Tridentine canon law[4]. Thereafter there will be a discussion of the relevance of canon law on the development of law in Scotland[5].

1 See paras 558, 559, below.
2 See paras 560 ff below.
3 See paras 564 ff below.
4 See paras 577 ff below.
5 See paras 580 ff below. For the historical sources, see T L Bouscaren, A C Ellis and F N North
   Canon Law, A Text and Commentary (4th edn, Milwaukee 1963) pp 1–14; P Andrieu-Guitrancourt *Introduction Sommaire à l'Etude du Droit en général et du Droit Canonique Contemporain en
   particulier* (Paris, 1963) pp 569–896; V del Giudice *Nozioni di Diritto Canonico* (12th edn, Milan
   1970) pp 33–61.

(b) The Nature of Canon Law

558. Meaning of 'canon' and 'canon law'. Where there is society, there is
law; therefore, where there is a Christian society there must be laws for the good
ordering of that society. From the earliest days of the Christian Church, that is,
the society of the believers in Christ dispersed throughout the world, rules were
developed for determining matters of faith and conduct. These rules were called
canons. The Greek word 'canon' originally meant a rod for measuring or
putting right what was crooked. It came to mean a norm or rule of belief or
conduct, especially when promoted by the Church.

A modern definition of canon law is 'the complex of laws given either by God
or by the competent ecclesiastical authority, by which the Church is constituted
and ruled or the activities of the baptised are regulated towards the proper ends
of the Church, the ultimate end being eternal life'[1].

1 E F Regatillo *Institutiones Iuris Canonici* (7th edn, Santander 1963) I, 9.

559. The authority of the Church. In the apostolic times of the first century,
Rome was the centre of an expanding empire. Rome, not Jerusalem, became the
centre of the Christian mission. To Rome went Peter and Paul. Christ, it was
said, in the institution of the Church, had endowed Peter and his successors with
the authority for making laws for the faithful — 'Whatsoever you shall bind
upon earth shall be bound also in heaven: and whatsoever you shall loose upon
earth shall be loosed also in heaven'[1]. The implications of this injunction, if
accepted, are awesome. It gave to the bishops of Rome, from apostolic times to
the present day, the authority to legislate for Christ's 'faithful people dispersed
throughout the world'[2], in other words, the Roman Catholic Church.

To the Pope, as Bishop of Rome, is entrusted the complex of laws, either
divine or human, the object of which is the faith, morals and discipline of the
Christian people. All who are baptised are Christians; therefore, it is claimed
that all Christians, whether obedient or not to the Church, are the subjects of
canon law.

1 Matt 18:18.
2 St Augustine: see V Del Giudice *Nozioni di Diretto Canonico* (12th edn, Milan 1970) p 15, note 2.

(c) Canon Law from Apostolic Times to the
Decretum of Gratian (1140)

560. Establishment of canon law. In the period from apostolic times to the
time of Gratian the sources of the canon law were established. The lack of a
systematic co-ordination of the sources is characteristic of the period.

Prior to the Edict of Milan in 312 there had been, from the late first century, an increasing recourse from local bishops to the Bishop of Rome to settle disputes on disciplinary matters. Papal letters concerning such disputes survive from the papacy of Clement I (c 90–99). Aprocryphal material attributed to the apostles also appeared. There was the *Didache* or Doctrine of the Twelve Apostles (c 70–160) composed either in Syria or Palestine. In Rome about the year 218 appeared the *Traditio Apostolica* written by St Hippolytus. Perhaps the best known of these early collections are the *Constitutiones Apostolorum* which include the *Canones Apostolorum*, compiled in Syria or Palestine around the year 400.

561. Ecumenical councils. The Edict of Milan in 312 established religious toleration throughout the Roman empire. The Church, centred in Rome, was now free from persecution. This promoted a rapid development in legal organisation. Between the Council of Nicea in 325 and the Second Lateran Council of 1139 there were ten ecumenical councils. These councils, under the leadership of the Popes, not only defined articles of faith but also promulgated many disciplinary laws for the whole Church.

562. Local collections of canons. In addition to the rules of the general councils, many collections of local canons appeared between the fourth and the twelfth centuries. Collections survive from many parts of Europe such as France, Italy and Spain. There are also collections from England and Ireland. In England there is the *Liber de remediis peccatorum* attributed to Egbert of York, who died in 767. In Ireland in the eighth century appeared an influential collection of legal canons and moral precepts known as the Synod of St Patrick. Nothing survives in Scotland from this period, but it is not unreasonable to suggest there may have been collections derived from, or similar to, the Irish material.

The main feature of this early period of development of western canon law, especially between the fourth and the eighth centuries, is lack of co-ordination. This is not surprising given the unsettled state of Europe after the decline of the Western Roman empire. It must nevertheless be stressed that despite the extensive emergence of local canon laws, the overall jurisdiction of the Bishop of Rome was paramount. Local churches adapted general canons to suit local conditions. The local canons were within the framework of the general law.

563. The need for uniformity. From the eighth to the eleventh centuries the policy of the Popes was to establish their authority over Western Christendom. There was a need to produce a systematic and uniform body of canon law. Order had to be brought into the diverse local customs. There are many facets to this movement. An example is the compilation of the *Decretales Pseudo-Isidorianae*, probably in Le Mans about the year 850, which created a corpus of canon law, the authority of which was deliberately but falsely attributed to the decrees of early councils and Popes.

Systematic collections of canons were being prepared. Canon law was being recognised as a discipline in its own right distinct from theology. Perhaps the most important compilation prior to Gratian was the *Decretum* of Burchard of Worms produced between 1008 and 1012. This work, consisting of twenty books devoted to legal matters, heralded the revolution in canon law which was to take place in the twelfth century.

(d) Canon Law from Gratian to the Council of Trent 1545–63

564. Gratian. The eleventh and twelfth centuries in Europe experienced what can now be called the Papal Revolution[1]. The Papacy asserted its independence from secular control and established its spiritual supremacy over Western Christendom. This fundamental change necessitated a fundamental change in the development of the law of the Church. The *ius antiquum* of the first millenium of the Church was superseded by the *ius novum*. The creator of the *ius novum* or reformed canon law was Ioannes Gratianus — the 'divine' Gratian. He was a Camaldolese monk who taught in the new law school at Bologna. About 1140 he produced the monumental *Concordantia discordantium canonum*, more simply entitled the *Decretum*[2]. As Berman has stated:

> 'The work, which in a modern edition fills over 1400 printed pages, was the first comprehensive and systematic legal treatise in the history of the West, and perhaps in the history of mankind — if by "comprehensive" is meant the attempt to embrace virtually the entire law of a given polity, and if by "systematic" is meant the express effort to present that law as a single body, in which all the parts are viewed as interacting to form a whole'[3].

The *Decretum* was a new beginning of ecclesiastical jurisprudence. Thenceforth canon law was a discipline separated from theology.

1 H J Berman *Law and Revolution, The Formation of the Western Legal Tradition* (Harvard 1983) pp 85–119.
2 The *Decretum* is to be found in the *Corpus Iuris Canonici* (ed A Friedberg and A L Richter) (2 vols, Leipzig 1879, reprinted Graz 1959).
3 *Berman* p 143.

565. The *Decretum*. Gratian's *Decretum* is divided into three parts. The mode of reference identifies the part. It should be noted that the name of Gratian and, in the subsequent additions to the *Decretum*, the names of the Popes, for the most part, are not given in the references. The first part has 101 *distinctiones* or divisions in which the nature of law and jurisdictions are considered[1]. The second part deals with thirty-six problems or *causae*. These are questioned and analysed with a view to achieving harmonisation[2]. The third part has five *distinctiones*, all concerned with the title 'consecration'[3].

1 The mode of reference is by canon and distinction. Thus 'c 3 D 1' refers to Part 1, canon 3 of Distinction 1, which is *Quid sit lex?*
2 The mode of reference is by canon, cause and question. Thus 'c 27, C 2, q 6' refers to Part 2, canon 27 of cause 2, question 6, which is *Iniuste appellans omnino puniendum est.*
3 The mode of reference, incorporating the sign 'de cons' (which stands for 'consecration') is by canon and distinction, followed by title. Thus 'c 5, D 1, *de cons*' refers to Part 3, canon 5 of Distinction 1, which is *Sine auctoritate summi Pontificis nova non dedicetur ecclesia.*

566. Decretals. Although the *Decretum* was an unofficial compilation it soon became the primary source for the subsequent development of canon law. With the growing importance of the Roman Curia as the supreme court of Christendom, the *decretals* or decisions of later Popes were added to the *Decretum*. Many of these Popes such as Innocent III and Gregory IX were canon lawyers.

Five books of *Decretals* compiled by St Raymond of Pennafort OP (the patron saint of lawyers) were promulgated by Gregory IX in 1234, the contents being summarised in the verse '*Iudex, iudicium, clerus, connubia, crimen*'. This collection was originally called the *Liber Extra* since it was 'outside' the *Decretum*[1]. In 1300 Boniface VIII added a sixth book, the *Liber Sextus*, which contains five books[2].

1 The mode of reference therefore includes the sign 'X' (for *Extra*). Thus 'c 6, X, I, 43' refers to the *Decretals* of Gregory IX, chapter 6, book I, title 43, which is *Arbiter non habet potestatem iudicandi ultra comprehensa in compromisso* — a decretal given to the Bishop of St Andrews and the Abbot of Arbroath.

2 The mode of reference includes the sign 'in VI°'. Thus 'c 5, i, 19, in VI°' refers to the *Decretals* of Boniface VIII, chapter 5, book I, title 19, which is *Mandatum generale ad negotia, etiam ad judicia se extendit*.

567. *Clementinae* and *Extravagantes*. In 1317 John XXII promulgated in five books the constitutions made by Clement V in the Council of Vienne (1311 to 1312). These are known as the *Clementinae*[1]. In 1500 the canonist John Chapuis added two more collections, the *Extravagantes* of John XXII[2] and the five books of the *Extravagantes communes* of decretals from Boniface VIII to Sixtus IV (who died in 1484)[3].

1 The mode of reference includes the sign 'in Clem'. Thus 'c 6, II, 12, in Clem' refers to the Constitutions of Clement V, chapter 6, book II, title 12, which is *Prosecutio appellationis desertae non impedit*.

2 The mode of reference is by chapter and title. Thus 'c 2, I, in Extravag Ioan XXII' refers to chapter 2 of title I, which is *Beneficio Vacante*.

3 The mode of reference is to chapter, book and title. Thus 'c 1, V, 6 in Extravag com' refers to chapter 1, book V, title 6, which is *Alchemia hic prohibentur et puniuntur facientes*.

568. The *Corpus Iuris Canonici*. All the material from the *Decretum* to the *Extravagentes* was formally promulgated as the *Corpus Iuris Canonici* on 1 July 1580 by the bull *Cum pro munere pastorali* of Gregory XIII. The *Corpus Iuris Canonici* reflects the development within the Church of a judicial system for the resolution of disputes. Prior to the twelfth century contentious matters were referred to the Pope or to the local bishop for adjudication, but there was little or no uniform procedure or system. After the 'Papal Revolution' a highly efficient papal Curia in Rome co-ordinated and harmonised the administration of the Church throughout Western Christendom. In Rome, between the twelfth and fifteenth centuries, there had developed three separate supreme tribunals for hearing cases either at first instance or on appeal from diocesan courts.

569. Dioceses in Scotland. The diocesan courts reflect the systematic creation of dioceses throughout Europe in the twelfth century. Scotland exemplifies this. Prior to the twelfth century there was an ill-defined diocesan structure. During the twelfth and thirteenth centuries the Scottish diocesan structure was clearly established. It must be noted that in 1218 a Bull of Honorius III confirmed the church in Scotland as the 'special daughter' of the apostolic see 'with no intermediary'[1]. This Bull was the culmination of a series of papal bulls (particularly the Bull *Super anxietatibus* of Alexander III of 1176) which liberated the Scottish Church from the jurisdiction of any archbishop — especially York. Henceforth, any appeals from cases heard before Scottish diocesan courts could be taken only to Rome. The decisions and procedures of the Roman supreme courts were therefore a potential source of major influence on the development of law in Scotland. The practice of making appeals to Rome became so well established that the erection of St Andrews and Glasgow into archbishoprics in 1472 and 1492 seems, from the evidence of appeals taken to the *Sacra Romana Rota*, to have had no effect in diminishing the great volume of such appeals.

1 G Donaldson *Scottish Historical Documents* (1970) p 31; A A M Duncan *Scotland: The Making of the Kingdom* (1975) p 264.

570. Diocesan courts in Scotland. With the creation of the Scottish dioceses came also the creation of the diocesan courts. The judge in these courts was known as the 'official'. He was appointed by the bishop. Of the twelve Scottish dioceses, officials had been appointed to ten of the dioceses between 1172 and 1266[1]. The competence of these courts was extensive. Apart from matters of a purely ecclesiastical nature, matters concerning, among other things, status, testaments and arbitrations were heard by these courts. Appeals could be taken to Rome or Rome could appoint judges–delegate to hear cases in Scotland[2]. It is of interest to note that five of the *Decretals* of Gregory IX relate to Scottish cases. They are (1) to the Bishop of St Andrews and the Abbot of Arbroath concerning an arbitration[3]; (2) to the Bishop of St Andrews concerning donations[4]; (3) to the King of Scotland concerning the immunity of churches[5]; (4) to the Archdeacon of St Andrews concerning gifts between husband and wife[6]; and (5) to the Abbot of St Andrews concerning the sentence of excommunication[7].

1 D E R Watt *Fasti Ecclesiae Scoticanae* (2nd draft 1969) p 23 *et passim*.
2 Lord Cooper *Select Scottish Cases of the Thirteenth Century* (1944) pp xxx–xxxix.
3 *Decretals* c 6, X, I, 43. As to the mode of reference, see para 566, note 1 above.
4 *Decretals* c 9, X, III, 24.
5 *Decretals* c 6, X, III, 49.
6 *Decretals* c 6, X, IV, 20.
7 *Decretals* c 28, X, V, 39.

571. The superior tribunals of the Church. Owing to the fragmented state of the surviving archival material, the record of the supreme tribunals of the Church is incomplete[1]. Due to the growing volume of referrals to Rome, it is evident that from the thirteenth century the Popes were delegating the adjudication of cases to specialised tribunals. Three supreme tribunals had clearly emerged by the fifteenth century[2]. They were the *Segnatura Iustitiae*[3], the *Sacra Penitentiaria Apostolica*[4] and the *Sacra Romana Rota*[5].

1 As part of a project directed by Professor Ian B Cowan of the University of Glasgow to recover from the Vatican Archive all material relating to Scotland, J J Robertson of the University of Dundee has been responsible for the identification of Scottish material in the archives of the *Rota* and the *Penitentiaria*. This material is now being analysed in Dundee and Glasgow.
2 For a history of these tribunals, see N Del Re *La Curia Romana Lineamenti Storico-Giuridici* (3rd edn, Rome 1970) pp 227–274.
3 See para 572 below.
4 See para 573 below.
5 See para 574 below.

572. The *Segnatura Iustitiae*. The medieval archive of the *Segnatura Iustitiae* has not survived. The work of the *Segnatura*, in its judicial capacity, was of primary importance. It seems to have been a 'clearing house' for cases which were to be raised in the *Sacra Romana Rota*. Before a litigant could proceed in the *Rota* he had to lodge with an auditor of the *Rota* a commission from the *Segnatura* authorising him to proceed. It is yet to be ascertained whether this initial reference was purely formal or whether a *probabilis causa* had to be established before the case was transmitted to the *Rota*.

573. The *Sacra Penitentiaria Apostolica*. The *Sacra Penitentiaria Apostolica* was also a supreme tribunal. The archive of the *Penitentiaria*, which is now part of the Vatican Archive, survives from the beginning of the fifteenth century. Owing to the fact that the *Penitentiaria* was intimately involved with matters arising out of the confessional, the archive remained closed to scholars until 1983. After a prolonged debate which commenced in 1929, the medieval archive, which does not deal with the forum of conscience, is now accessible for examination. An examination of this archive has revealed that Scottish matrimonial cases involving divorce, cases concerning dispensations for marriage within the forbidden degrees and matters involving dispensations from the effects of illegitimacy were dealt with by the *Penitentiaria*. A full analysis of these cases has yet to be made. It should be noted that this discovery must now qualify the traditional view that Scottish matrimonial cases were heard by the *Sacra Romana Rota*. Only one Scottish matrimonial case has been discovered in the archive of the *Rota*. This is in sharp contrast to the great number of Scottish matrimonial cases and cases related thereto which have now been identified in the archive of the *Penitentiaria*. The paucity of matrimonial cases before the *Rota* has also been observed by J T Noonan, who has estimated that 'marriage cases were less than 5 per cent of its load'[1]. The discovery of the extensive jurisdiction of the *Penitentiaria* in matrimonial cases probably explains the small number of such cases heard by the *Rota*.

1 J T Noonan *Power to Dissolve* (Harvard 1972) p 48.

574. The *Sacra Romana Rota*. The *Sacra Romana Rota* appears to have been the busiest of all the tribunals. By the fifteenth century it had omnicompetence in matters referred to it for decision. Cases, either of first instance or of appeals from the diocesan courts, came from all of Christendom. By the fifteenth century the *Rota* was made up of a college of twelve judges or auditors. Cases were initially heard by individual auditors. Each auditor had his own notary who acted as clerk of court. The notaries kept the records in *Manualia*. The *Manualia* survive from 1464. From an examination of the *Manualia* between 1464 and 1560, which is the effective date of the Protestant Reformation in Scotland, it is clear that Scottish litigants were making frequent recourse to the *Rota*. The estimated number of cases originating from Scottish dioceses in that period is as follows:

DIOCESE	NUMBER OF CASES
Aberdeen	25
Brechin	14
Candida Casa	26
Caithness	5
Dunblane	16
Dunkeld	28
Glasgow	89
Moray	9
Ross	17
St Andrews	141
Conjoined dioceses[1]	4
	374

No cases have been identified as coming from Argyll and the Isles. Nearly all of these cases are concerned with disputes to benefices. There are only two cases which deal with marriage and succession. It should be noted that between 1464 and 1540, which is the effective date of the English Reformation, the estimated number of English cases recorded in the *Manualia* is approximately twenty. From the disparity between the great number of Scottish cases and the small number of English cases, it can be suggested that there were many more Scottish procurators both in Scotland and in Rome who were more familiar with canonist procedures than their English counterparts. This familiarity with canonist procedures explains the extensive influence of canonist procedure in the development of civil procedure as outlined by Stair in his *Institutions*.

1 Ie where the rubric of the case shows that litigants came from more than one diocese, eg Glasgow and Aberdeen.

575. The teaching of canon law. The pre-eminence of canon law after the Papal Revolution is further reflected in the widespread diffusion of literature on, and teaching of, canon law in the universities which were being founded throughout Europe from the twelfth century. By the late fifteenth century the universities of St Andrews, Aberdeen and Glasgow were teaching canon law[1].

1 R G Cant *The College of St Salvator* (1950); *William Hay's Lectures on Marriage* ed J C Barry (Stair Soc vol 24, 1967), p xi; J Durkan and J Kirk *The University of Glasgow 1451–1577* (1977) pp 127–130.

576. The Protestant Revolution. The Papal Revolution was followed by the Protestant Revolution of the sixteenth century. The papal response to this was given in the decrees of the Council of Trent which sat from 1545 to 1563.

(e) Post-Tridentine Canon Law

577. The *Ius Novissimum*. The Council of Trent introduced the *ius novissimum*. Many new disciplinary measures were introduced to the corpus of the law. Due to the advent of printing it was possible to preserve and disseminate papal enactments and legal decisions. The decisions of the *Sacra Romana Rota* have been published from the beginning of the seventeenth century, creating a vast collection of case law.

578. The *Codex Iuris Canonici*. By the beginning of the twentieth century the vast bulk of canon law which had accumulated since Gratian's time was in a state of confusion. The confusion is summarised in Benedict XV's constitution, *Providentissima Mater Ecclesia* of 27 May 1917 which promulgated a new Code of Canon Law, the *Codex Iuris Canonici*. The constitution states that 'canonical enactments had so increased in number and were so disconnected and scattered that many of them were unknown not only to the people but to many among the most learned experts themselves'. Pius X was responsible for creating, in 1904, the commission of cardinals to which was entrusted the task of producing the code. There were 2,411 canons in the code, which was divided into five books, entitled General Rules, Persons, Things, Procedure and Crimes.

579. The constitution *Sacrae Disciplinae Leges*. The Code of 1917 has itself been replaced with a new code. On 25 January 1959 John XXIII announced his decision to reform the 1917 Code to reflect the renewal of Christian life. A commission of cardinals was created to implement this decision. On 25 January 1983 the new code was promulgated by John Paul II. In the constitution *Sacrae Disciplinae Leges*, John Paul II states that the code is

'the Church's fundamental legislative document, and because it is based on the juridical and legislative heritage of revelation and tradition, the Code must be regarded as the essential instrument for the preservation of right order, both in individual and social life . . . . The Code fully accords with the nature of the Church, particularly as presented in the authentic teaching of the Second Vatican Council . . . and especially in its ecclesiological doctrine'[1].

There are 1,752 canons in the new code, which is divided into seven books entitled General Norms, the People of God, the Teaching Office of the Church, the Sanctifying Office of the Church, the Temporal Goods of the Church, Sanctions in the Church and Processes.

  1 *The Code of Canon Law* prepared by The Canon Law Society of Great Britain and Ireland (1983) p xiii.

(f) The Relevance of Canon Law to the Development of Scots Law

580. Canon law and Scots law before 1560. Prior to 1560 and from the twelfth century Scotland was an integral part of a united Christendom. The foundations of a national legal system were being laid at this time. All medieval kingdoms were, however, within the supra-national jurisdiction of the Roman Church. The remark made by Lord Hailes in the eighteenth century that 'the Canon Law is not the law of Scotland' would be meaningless in medieval Scotland[1]. Canon law was being applied, practised and taught in Scotland until papal jurisdiction was abolished in 1560. Canon law was therefore a direct source of law in Scotland prior to 1560. The canon law on marriage and on testamentary succession to moveable property was the law which regulated these matters in pre-Reformation Scotland[2]. The post-Reformation development of the law in these areas continued to be indirectly influenced by canon law and canonist procedures.

  1 S Ollivant *The Court of the Official in Pre-Reformation Scotland* (Stair Soc vol 34, 1982) p 130.
  2 *William Hay's Lectures on Marriage* ed J C Barry (Stair Soc vol 24, 1967) pp xxxi–xlvi. For a historian's account of a canon lawyer and Auditor of Causes at work in Scotland and the materials available to him in the fifteenth century, see L J Macfarlane *William Elphinstone and the Kingdom of Scotland 1431–1514* (1985) ch 2, 3.

581. Canon law after the Reformation. William Hay's lectures on the sacrament of marriage[1], given in the University of Aberdeen in the early sixteenth century, give evidence that the post-Reformation law of marriage contained, and still contains, elements derived from canon law. This is especially so on the fundamental aspect of the exchange of consents as the basis of the modern Scots law of marriage. Canonist attitudes to impediments to marriage, especially through impotence, to separation and to legitimation are all reflected — sometimes rather dimly — in modern Scots law. In the law of succession, the administration of moveable estate was regulated by the canon law. The detailed regulation of confirmation of executors and the duties of executors are to be found in the surviving statutes of the Provincial Synods and General Councils of the Scottish Church[2]. After the Reformation the procedures were, in general, retained by the Commissary Courts. The powers and jurisdiction of these courts in matters of moveable succession were eventually transferred to the sheriffs who then acted as commissaries. Final abolition was deferred until the Sheriff Courts (Scotland) Act 1876 (c 70) after which the only survivor was the Commissary Clerk of Edinburgh who continued to confirm testaments of persons dying furth of Scotland[3].

  1 *William Hay's Lectures on Marriage* ed J C Barry (Stair Soc vol 24, 1967).

2 *Statutes of the Scottish Church* ed D Patrick (Scottish History Soc, 1907). The older opinion that these statutes contained the whole body of Scottish canon law to the exclusion of the general canon law can no longer be maintained. As F P Walton has stated, the statutes 'form merely an addendum to the *jus commune* of the canon law': see 'The Courts of the Officials and the Commissary Courts, 1512–1830' in *Sources and Literature of Scots Law* (Stair Soc vol 1, 1936 ed H McKechnie) pp 135, 138.

3 As to the transfer of functions, see G Donaldson 'The Church Courts' in *An Introduction to Scottish Legal History* (Stair Soc vol 20, 1958) p 371.

582. Canon law and procedural law. It is more difficult to assess the extent of the influence of canon law on the general development of Scots law. Further research is here required. Nevertheless in the light of recent research it can be suggested that much of Scottish legal procedure is directly derived from canon law[1]. The procedure followed in the officials' courts and in the cases taken by Scots to the *Sacra Romana Rota* is essentially the procedure which is outlined by Stair in the fourth book of his *Institutions*. The cases which were taken to Rome were generally prepared by Scottish procurators in Rome. The practice and procedures of the *Rota* were well known to Scots. The legal experience of these men must have influenced legal practice and procedure in Scotland. The names *advocatus, procurator* and *solicitor* are derived from rotal terminology.

1 S Ollivant *The Court of the Official in Pre-Reformation Scotland* (Stair Soc vol 34, 1982) pp 129–133; J J Robertson 'Canon Law as a Source' in *Stair Tercentenary Studies* ed D M Walker (Stair Soc vol 33, 1981) pp 119, 120.

583. Canon law and the Court of Session. It is also suggested that the constitution of the *Sacra Romana Rota* may have influenced the constitution of the Court of Session in 1532. The *Rota* was at that time a collegiate body of twelve auditors. The Court of Session was a collegiate body of fifteen judges. Seven of the fifteen judges had to be churchmen. The Church played an important part in the institution of the Court of Session as the supreme civil court in Scotland. It is almost inconceivable that the churchmen who were involved in the creation of the Court of Session were not to some extent using the *Rota* as a model. Mackay made this point in 1877 when he stated that the Court of Session 'resembled the Rota Romana'[1]. Recent research in the archive of the *Rota* tends to confirm this. The pioneering work of R K Hannay[2] on the origins of the Court of Session must now be amplified to take into account an assessment of the extent to which the *Rota* was a model for the Court of Session.

There has never been in Scotland a separate court of equity as in England. The Court of Session dispenses equity through its *nobile officium*. The origins of the *nobile officium* have not as yet been examined. It is suggested that this rests on a canonical foundation. That a judge must dispense equity is a feature of canonist procedure[3]. It is incumbent upon judges of superior courts, especially the *Rota*, to judge *ex aequo et bono*[4].

1 A J G Mackay *The Practice of the Court of Session* (1877) I, 22.
2 R K Hannay *The College of Justice* (1933).
3 P Andrieu-Guitrancourt *Introduction Sommaire à l'Etude du Droit en général et du Droit Canonique Contemporain en particulier* (Paris 1963) pp 1181–1194.
4 *Dictionnaire de Droit Canonique* ed R Naz (Paris 1935–65) V, 399.

584. Decline in influence of canon law. The conclusion of R D Ireland respecting the lessening of canonical authority on post-Reformation marriage law can be adapted to apply to the general influence of canon law on Scottish legal development. He states that the 'reason for the neglect of the canon law was the growth, during the 17th and 18th centuries, of a native Scottish law . . . created partly by Parliament and partly by the decisions of Courts. With this body of authority . . . it became less necessary and more difficult to penetrate to the canonical principles which, in many cases, lay at the root of the law . . .'[1].

The areas where this influence survived, as reflected in Stair's *Institutions*, were in commissary practice, marriage law, procedure and the law of teinds.

1 R D Ireland 'Husband and Wife' in *An Introduction to Scottish Legal History* (Stair Soc vol 20, 1958) p 83; J J Robertson 'Canon Law as a Source' in *Stair Tercentenary Studies* ed D M Walker (Stair Soc vol 33, 1981) p 120.

585. The Officials' Courts. The Reformation abolished the Officials' Courts in Scotland[1]. After 1560 the Commissary Courts were established to deal with the matrimonial jurisdiction of the Officials' Courts. With the restoration of the Scottish Roman Catholic hierarchy in 1878 the Officials' Courts were restored by the Roman Catholic Church to deal with litigation within the Scottish Roman Catholic community. On 11 June 1970 a single *Tribunal Nationale Scoticanum* was constituted. It sits permanently in Glasgow to deal at first instance with 'not only cases of nullity of marriage . . . but also cases of separation of husband and wife, contentious cases and criminal cases'[2]. Cases on appeal, or at second instance, are heard either by the Metropolitan Tribunal of Birmingham or by the *Sacra Romana Rota*.

1 Papal Jurisdiction Act 1560 (c 2) (APS II, 534).
2 Constitution prepared by the Scottish Episcopal Conference, art 2, *erigendum decernit*. The constitution was approved by Paul VI in an audience given to the Cardinal Prefect of the *Segnatura Apostolica* on 3 July 1970.

586. Conclusion. With the growth of interest in Scottish legal history over the past fifty years — an interest which has accelerated with the growth of the law faculties within the Scottish universities — it is now being appreciated that canon law has exerted an important formative influence on the development of Scots law. Much is now known of the areas of general influence such as marriage and procedure, but much more historical study is required of the abundant source material which is now available, especially the material from the Vatican repositories. In the field of Scottish legal history, canonist studies have a continuing and growing importance. It is further submitted that the modern canon law, particularly after the promulgation of the new code in 1983[1], may yet have a place in Scottish legal studies. Modern canonists are concerning themselves with important matters of general and particular legal interest. For instance, there is much concern about fundamental aspects of justice within human society; there is comment on general principles of equity and the practical application of such principles; there is debate on error in the contracting of marriage and exploration into physical incapacity in marriage; there is also a developing doctrine on compensation arising out of illicit acts. In the past, Scots law has shown an enlightened approach to examining and assimilating external legal influences. It may be that canonist studies should again be introduced into the Scottish universities for the benefit they could give to jurisprudential studies.

1 See para 579 above.

(3) FEUDAL LAW

587. The meaning of 'feudalism'. The term 'feudalism' has been used in many contexts. Here we shall be concerned with military feudalism as it developed in Western Europe from the eighth century onward. Medieval feudalism permeated many aspects of life; it was as much a social as a tenurial structure. For the legal historian, however, its importance lies in its system of land tenure and the law stemming therefrom. It is this which constitutes feudalism in the strict legal sense.

588. Feudal land law. Land lay at the heart of the feudal system. Its basis was the grant of land by one party to another for a specified *reddendo*, or return. The classic, although not the only, form of feudal tenure was military tenure; that is, land was granted in return for military service, the estate given being deemed sufficient to support the required number of fighting men. The feudal relationship was thus tenurial, but not purely so; there was a second, more personal strand. The grantee also became the man, or vassal, of the grantor by performing homage and swearing fealty to him. In other words, he recognised the grantor as his lord and undertook to perform faithfully the services required of him and, generally, to do nothing to his prejudice. In return, the lord undertook to maintain and sustain his man, an obligation normally (but not invariably) discharged by the grant of land — the vassal's benefice or, more usually, his fief.

589. Lord and vassal. The relationship between lord and man was thus bilateral and highly personal; originally it did not survive the lifetime of either. But in time the interests of property prevailed. The loyalty of a vassal whose estate could not be passed to his heirs and whose own tenure was not assured after the death of his lord might prove lukewarm and so, by feudal custom, the fief gradually became heritable. There were, however, qualifications which reflect the original importance of the personal bond and the purpose for which the fief was granted. On the lord's death, the vassal required to seek confirmation of his holding from his successor and to renew his homage and fealty. If the vassal died, his heir similarly required to become the man of the lord and to be invested with the deceased's fief, a procedure accompanied by the payment to the lord of a sum of money — the relief — by way of indication that the succession was not his by unquestionable right. In addition, feudal succession was governed by its own rules. An estate given for military service required that it be held by one who could perform it and, further, that it be not divided up to such an extent as to destroy its character as the alimentary portion of one or more warriors. Accordingly, whatever the rules of non-feudal customary law may have been, the primary rule of feudal succession was that of male primogeniture.

590. Spread of feudal law. Feudalism originated in the Merovingian and Carolingian kingdoms of the eighth and ninth centuries and from there it spread throughout Western Europe. With it spread feudal law — the law of fiefs and matters incidental thereto. It was thus essentially a system of land law, having little to say about obligations or even moveable property. Nor was feudal law everywhere identical; the underlying structure was the same but the details varied according to the practice of the courts and the extent to which local and non-feudal custom impinged on it. As Erskine noted, 'every kingdom hath formed to itself such a scheme of feudal rules as best agreed with the genius of its own constitution'[1]. Nevertheless, feudal law did attain a wider European dimension. At Bologna, the home of the medieval revival of Roman law, the feudal law of northern Italy attracted the interest of the jurists, and in the mid-twelfth century one Obertus de Orto compiled the *Libri Feudorum* (Books of the Feus). His text was thereafter dealt with in a way similar to the Roman texts, and when it was included as an appendix to the *Corpus Iuris* it came to be considered and used as part of the learned laws of Europe.

1 Erskine *Institute* II, 3, 6.

591. Feudalism in Scotland. As we have seen, feudalism came to Scotland during the twelfth century and, particularly from the time of David I (1124–1153), the Crown is to be found granting lands — often to Anglo-Norman incomers — in feudal tenure. By the thirteenth century it had become the normal, if not the invariable, practice for such grants (or their subsequent confirmations) to be recorded formally in a charter, detailing the land given and the returns owed. Not surprisingly, many of these charters were carefully preserved and survive to provide us with much of our knowledge of Scottish feudal practice.

592. Subinfeudation. It was not only the Crown which gave land in feudal tenure. A tenant-in-chief (that is, one who held directly of the Crown) could himself acquire vassals by granting out, or subinfeudating, part of his holding. This process could then be repeated and a chain of feudal relationships, stretching from the Crown downwards, formed. In England, the creation of sub-tenancies in this way was effectively curtailed by the Statute of *Quia Emptores* of 1290; thereafter substitution replaced subinfeudation. Scotland, however, was never subject to a similar provision, but there were restrictions[1]. By feudal law a tenant who alienated so much of his fief as to make impossible the performance of the services due from it risked forfeiture; it thus became prudent practice to obtain the consent of one's lord to subinfeudation, a consent which normally had to be purchased. And until 1874[2] it was competent for subinfeudation to be prohibited by the terms of a tenant's charter.

1 See I A Milne 'Heritable Rights: the Early Feudal Tenures' and H H Monteath 'Heritable Rights: from Early Times to the Twentieth Century' in *An Introduction to Scottish Legal History* (Stair Soc vol 20, 1958) pp 151, 160.
2 Conveyancing (Scotland) Act 1874 (c 94), s 22.

593. Military tenure. As in England, the classic form of feudal tenure in Scotland was military tenure[1] or, as it later became known, wardholding. By Stair's time this tenure was presumed in cases of doubt[2]. However, the continuing importance of wardholding did not lie in the services due but in the feudal incidents attaching to it; that is, in the prestations, subsidiary to the principal *reddendo*, which a feudal superior could exact. These included relief, the right to the wardship of a minor vassal and the right to arrange his, or a female heir's, marriage. All of these rights were sources of profit. In other words, wardholding continued because of the fiscal advantages to be derived from its incidents rather than its military nature.

1 See para 588 above.
2 Stair *Institutions* II, 3, 31.

594. Other forms of tenure. There were other tenures, but the terms used here to denote them were not used consistently in the early charters, and there would appear to have been no clear rule about the incidents attaching to each. Systematisation only came later. These tenures included:

(1) *Mortification*, the tenure by which the pre-Reformation Church held its land. Its principal feature was that no *reddendo* was expected other than the saying of prayers and masses for the granter and his family. Mortification disappeared after the Reformation.

(2) *Blench-ferme*, the tenure of land for a nominal return such as 'a rose in the season of roses'.

(3) *Burgage*, the tenure of burgh land. Originally carrying certain privileges, this tenure was assimilated with feu-ferme in 1874[1].

1 Conveyancing (Scotland) Act 1874 (c 94), s 25. As to feu-ferme tenure, see para 595 below.

595. Feu-ferme tenure. The principal Scottish tenurial development was the rise of feu-ferme. This tenure, in the sense of land held in return for a rent, can be traced back to the twelfth century and may originally have been used to give feudal form to the older Celtic burdens on land. But it was only during the later middle ages that feu-ferme can be said to have emerged as a distinct tenure. The reasons are complex, but it was the tenure that was best suited to an economy that was becoming increasingly money-based. Land was coming to represent an investment and was required to produce a return in cash; this feu-ferme provided, offering not only a guaranteed annual rent but, normally, a sizeable lump-sum, the *grassum*, when the tenure was first created. From the middle of the fifteenth century the Crown set much of its land in feu, while in the century or so before the Reformation the Church dealt with its land in a similar way. In the process, many who had previously held by lease converted their holdings into feudal tenure, becoming landed proprietors for the first time. For the tenant feu-ferme also offered the opportunity to speculate in land; having invested his *grassum* he could hope to make his land yield a profit, either by working it himself or by further subinfeudation.

596. Abolition of tenures. By the seventeenth century feu-ferme tenure had become widespread although wardholding still remained, particularly in northern Scotland. Then, in the aftermath of the Jacobite Risings, came the Tenures Abolition Act 1746. Tenure by wardholding with its accompanying feudal incidents was abolished[1]; land so held of the Crown was converted to blench-ferme[2] and that held of a subject-superior to feu-ferme[3].

1 Tenures Abolition Act 1746 (c 50), s 1.
2 Ibid, s 2.
3 Ibid, s 4.

(4) ENGLISH INFLUENCE

597. Introduction. Scotland has been influenced by English law twice during her history, once during the Anglo-Norman period and once as a result of the Union with England, consolidated by the Union Agreement of 1707. The Union has been the more important influence, but historically the contribution made by Anglo-Norman law was also significant. Indeed, had it not been for the Wars of Independence, it is not impossible that Scots law might have continued to develop along English lines and so taken a very different course.

598. English influence in the Anglo-Norman era. The Anglo-Norman era saw important innovations in legal procedure, the most notable of which were the introduction of the brieve and the inquest. In one respect Scotland was following the lead set by England where procedure by inquest upon writ (as the brieve was known there) was establishing itself as the normal method of initiating action in the royal courts. It would, however, be a mistake to assume that Scotland slavishly copied England's example; the evidence rather points to a process of parallel development. Scotland certainly borrowed from England, but that borrowing was selective and subject to adaption.

599. The brieve system. The brieve was in origin an executive device, a royal order commanding or prohibiting a course of action. Our concern, however, is with the judicial brieve — the brieve purchased out of Chancery by a subject-litigant in order to initiate judicial process by the submission of a written issue to a sworn inquest (or assize) presided over by a royal official. The procedure thus replaced the older, irrational methods of proof with the verdict of the assize on the questions put to it. The brieve system was a formulary system; that is, process upon brieve was only possible if the pursuer's claim corresponded with the form of an existing remedy. Naturally, new forms were introduced as the system became established, and often it seems these were suggested by English writs. But the copying was not always exact. In contrast to England, Scotland appears to have been content with fewer basic forms of action, but to have made these do more work than their English counterparts. It may also be that Scotland was unable to keep abreast with developments in England. There the writ system was to become a highly complex and technical apparatus, moulded and administered in the central courts by a trained judiciary and professional Bar. Scotland lacked these judicial resources. The royal judges were largely untrained laymen, and there was nothing approaching an established central court until the fifteenth century. In short, as both systems developed, it seems they grew further and further apart as England strove for a level of sophistication that Scotland could not match.

Procedure by brieve was well established by the fourteenth century and 'the fifteenth century seems to have been the heyday of the brieve system'[1], with existing brieves regularly being called into service and new forms being introduced. However, by 1500 it was beginning to decline. The brieve was never a method of initiating procedure in Parliament or Council, while an Act of 1491 restricted the use of brieves to those already in existence and forbad the introduction of new forms[2]. At the same time, the brieve was beginning to give way to the summons *via* the brieve of citation[3]. That is, a brieve initially designed to secure the attendance of witnesses gradually acquired the more substantive function of summoning the defender to court. The advantage was that the pursuer did not need to fit his case into the formula of an existing brieve; he had only to state that he had been wronged, leaving the details of his claim until a later stage. Accordingly, the mediaeval forms of action gradually disappeared and are now virtually redundant.

1 H McKechnie *Judicial Process upon Brieve 1219–1532* (David Murray Lecture, Glasgow 1956) p 18.
2 Brieves Act 1491 (c 5) (APS II, 224).
3 See D Maxwell 'Civil Procedure' in *An Introduction to Scottish Legal History* (Stair Soc vol 20, 1958) pp 415, 416.

600. The effect of the Union. On the death of Elizabeth Tudor in 1603, James VI of Scotland succeeded to the throne of England. In 1707 the personal union of the two kingdoms under the one monarch was taken a step further by the creation of a new state with a united Parliament of Great Britain. The Union with England was of fundamental importance for the future of Scotland. For Scots law it resulted in the gradual replacement of Roman law by English law as the principal external factor in its development. Some view this with regret, arguing that the purity of Scots law has been sullied by contact with England. Certainly the civilian and institutional basis of Scots law is very different from the common law of England, and on occasions the introduction of English doctrine has jarred. But at other times Scotland has profited from the connection, and from the availability of English law as a source of comparative principle as an aid to development. During the eighteenth century, for example, Scottish trade began to expand, and the country found itself in need of a more mature mercantile law than it hitherto possessed. England, where mercantile law had been so brilliantly developed in the judgments of Lord Mansfield, proved a useful model, as is illustrated by Bell's use of and reliance on English authorities in his *Commentaries*.

601. Legislation from Westminster. Voluntary borrowing apart, the principal means by which English law has come to Scotland are statute and decisions of the House of Lords. In some instances Scots law has suffered as a result of the legislation of the predominantly English Westminster Parliament. In 1708, for example, the Scots law of treason was abrogated and replaced by the unsatisfactory English provisions[1], based on a statute of 1351[2]. Again, many would argue that the original Scots law of sale was superior to that which resulted from the Sale of Goods Act 1893 (c 71). But on other occasions Scots law has benefited even from statutes which, although common to both countries, contain predominantly English rules. Examples include the mercantile statutes of the later nineteenth century[3].

1 Treason Act 1708 (c 21).
2 Treason Act 1351 (c 2).
3 Eg the Bills of Exchange Act 1882 (c 61). See however J J Gow *Mercantile and Industrial Law of Scotland* (1964), especially ch 2; T B Smith *Property Problems in Sale* (1978); Lord Kilbrandon *Scots Law seen from England* (Child Oxford Lecture 1980–81).

602. Appeals to the House of Lords. Prior to 1707, appeal for 'remeid of law' lay from the Court of Session to the Scottish Parliament. The Treaty of Union 1707 provided that the Court of Session and the other Scottish courts were to remain for all time as they then were, subject only to future statutory regulation for the better administration of justice[1]. It also provided that 'no causes in Scotland be cognisable by ... any ... court in Westminster Hall; and that the said courts ... shall have no power to cognosce, review, or alter the Acts or Sentences of the Judicature of Scotland'[1]. This, however, left unclear the question of appeals from the Court of Session. Before 1707 the judicial powers of the English Parliament were exercised by the House of Lords and, in the absence of express provision in the Treaty, it was open to question whether the new Parliament, acting through the Lords, was entitled to consider itself heir to the judicial powers of the former Scottish Parliament and so entertain Scottish appeals. Nor did the prohibition against the hearing of Scottish cases by English courts which sat in Westminster Hall strike against this possibility; unlike, for example, the Courts of Chancery and King's Bench, the House of Lords did not sit there and so was not included within the proscription. The matter was soon tested and by 1710, when the Lords overturned the prior decision of the Session in the case of *Greenshields*, the right to take Scottish appeals in civil matters to the House of Lords had been established[2].

The decisions of the Lords had the potential to influence Scots law, particularly with the rise in the nineteenth century of the doctrine of precedent. But this influence has not always been beneficial. The Lords was a predominantly English body and did not necessarily contain anyone acquainted with Scots law[3]. Consequently, even when dealing with Scottish cases, it tended to think and reason in terms of English law and sometimes to assume that the English solution was, by definition, the natural solution. The result has been decisions based on English rules unknown to Scots law and out of line with its principles, as in *Bartonshill Coal Co v Reid*, by which Scotland was forced to accept the English doctrine of common employment[4]. On the other hand, the contribution of the Lords does not lie completely on the debit side. Some judges evidently tried to apply Scots law[5], while some of the work of the House of Lords concerned statutory matters common to both countries and so provided useful guidance.

In 1856 a committee appointed to review the appellate jurisdiction of the Lords took the opportunity to investigate the possible inclusion of a Scottish judge in the House. Somewhat surprisingly, opinion obtained from Scotland was divided and no firm decision was taken, despite the committee's sympathy for the change. The first Scottish judge to sit in the Lords, Lord Colonsay, only took his seat in 1867, and it was not until the Appellate Jurisdiction Act of 1876 that statutory provision for the appointment of a Scottish Law Lord was introduced[6].

1 Treaty of Union 1707, art 19.
2 *Greenshields v Edinburgh Magistrates* (1710–11) Robin 12. On the appellate jurisdiction of the House of Lords, see generally A J MacLean 'The 1707 Union: Scots Law and the House of Lords' (1983) 4 J Leg Hist 50; and as to the history of appeals to the House of Lords, see COURTS AND COMPETENCY.
3 Until the 1840s, lay peers were entitled to take part in the judicial business of the House of Lords. Thereafter the convention grew up that lay peers would not participate in this class of business.
4 *Bartonshill Coal Co v Reid* (1858) 3 Macq 266. The doctrine was abolished by the Law Reform (Personal Injuries) Act 1948 (c 41), s 1.
5 E J MacGillivray 'The Influence of English Law' in *Sources and Literature of Scots Law* (Stair Soc vol 1, 1936 ed H McKechnie) p 219.
6 Appellate Jurisdiction Act 1876 (c 59), ss 6, 25.

(5) FRENCH AND DUTCH INFLUENCES

603. Introduction. Historically, Scotland has had close links with both France and the Netherlands. Those with France stemmed from the 'Auld Alliance', the diplomatic and military alliance first formed in 1295, while those with the Netherlands were founded on trade. These links influenced many aspects of Scottish life; our concern is with the nature and extent of that influence on the development of Scots law. Here, the contribution of Scotland's continental neighbours was of two kinds, direct and indirect, and it was the latter that was to prove the more important by far. It may be described as an influence of method and approach rather than one involving the direct borrowing of substantive rules of law.

604. Education of Scottish law students. As we have seen, Scottish law students were largely educated abroad until well into the eighteenth century. Many found their way to the universities of France and the Netherlands. In France, the important law school at Orléans was particularly popular and at one time the Scots formed a separate nation within the university. Later, Scots also attended the University of Bourges, the home of the French humanist lawyers. After the Reformation the preference was for the universities of Protestant Europe, and most favoured were those of the Netherlands, especially Utrecht and, above all, Leyden. It has been estimated that between 1600 and 1800 some 1,600 Scots students attended the latter[1].

The way in which the Scots obtained their legal education had important consequences for the future of Scots law. They attended some of Europe's most notable law schools, and those who returned home to practise did so armed with an up-to-date knowledge of the best in European civilian scholarship. In short, the continental connection was one of the avenues by which Roman law came to Scotland. At the same time, these students also gained some insight into the legal systems of their hosts and the way in which the *ius commune* and indigenous law were each contributing to the emergence of an identifiably French or Dutch law. This experience was also to prove valuable.

1 See J C Gardner 'French and Dutch Influences' in *Sources and Literature of Scots Law* (Stair Soc vol 1, 1936 ed H McKechnie) p 233.

605. France. In France, Scots became acquainted with the customary law as found in the medieval customals and, later, in the codified texts produced during the sixteenth century[1]. They were also able to observe the mixture of Roman and customary law being applied in the higher French courts. Thus, in addition to their academic education in Roman law, Scots witnessed its practical application against a background of native and non-Roman custom — a process that was to be repeated in Scotland. It is therefore not surprising that Scots lawyers made use of French material[2]; Fountainhall's *Reports* and Spottiswoode's *Practicks*, for example, contain references to French jurists and the decisions of the French courts. Likewise, from its foundation, the Library of the Faculty of Advocates held a comprehensive collection of French material which would thus appear to have been among the sources regularly consulted by both Bench and Bar. Individual Scottish jurists also evidence the influence of French legal scholarship; Craig, for example, followed the French humanist scholar, François Hotman (1525–90), on a number of points, most notably in his insistence on the equal reality of *dominium directum* and *dominium utile*. It may also be that Sir John Skene's edition of the *Auld Lawes* was inspired by the codified French customs, being an attempt to provide a written and therefore certain statement of Scottish customary law at a time when the courts were turning increasingly to Roman law[3].

1 Following a royal ordinance, the customs of the North of France (the *pays de coutumes*) were formally reduced to writing during this period.
2 For what follows, see D B Smith 'Roman Law' and J C Gardner 'French and Dutch Influences' in *Sources and Literature of Scots Law* (Stair Soc vol 1, 1936 ed H McKechnie) pp 174–177, 230–231.
3 See the epistles dedicatory which preface J Skene *Regiam Majestatem, The Auld Lawes and Constitutions of Scotland* (1609) and *Regiam Majestatem Scotiae, Veteres Leges et Constitutiones* (1609).

606. The Netherlands. In the Netherlands the Roman law studied by Scots was the Roman law of the *usus modernus hodiernum*; that is, Roman law as developed for contemporary practice in the light of existing custom. Thus, as well as a grounding in the law of the *Digest*, Scottish students gained first-hand experience of that blending of law that was to emerge as the Roman-Dutch law of the Netherlands. This was particularly apposite as the period of the popularity of the Dutch universities coincided with Scotland's reception and the increasing application of Roman law by the Scottish courts to a system based on indigenous statute and custom. Accordingly, the works of the great Dutch civilians were brought back to Scotland and featured prominently in the Advocates' collection, which contained the treatises of such notable Dutch jurists as Voet, Grotius, Huber, Noodt, Vinnius and Van Leeuwen[1]. Again, and indeed to a greater extent than their French counterparts, Dutch jurists were frequently founded on in forensic argument. In sum, as with France, Scotland's connection with the Netherlands was an important factor in determining the course of her reception.

1 See D B Smith 'Roman Law' in *Sources and Literature of Scots Law* (Stair Soc vol 1, 1936 ed H McKechnie) p 177.

607. Borrowed law. Did Scotland in addition borrow directly from the native laws of France and the Netherlands? There is no evidence of borrowing from the Netherlands, but there is some to suggest that French practices found their way to Scotland. However, caution is necessary when assessing the nature and extent of this influence. Often similarities between French and Scots law are not due to direct borrowing but can be explained by the common origins of each system in Germanic and feudal custom as well as the *ius commune*. If the evidence is examined closely there is, in fact, little to suggest that French law exerted a sustained and extensive influence on Scotland; and what instances of borrowing there are have more to do with procedure and terminology than with rules of substantive law. Examples include the provision of counsel for the poor, introduced into Scotland in 1424[1], a few years after a similar French regulation, and the use of such phrases as *liege poustie*[2] and *chaude melle*[3] as useful terms of art.

1 Poor's Counsel Act 1424 (c 24) (APS II, 8).
2 *Liege poustie* is a state of health sufficient to justify the making of a will or conveyance, derived perhaps from the French *en vive pouste*.
3 *Chaude melle* is a phrase which indicates that a crime was committed *in rixa* and not wilfully.

(6) THE LAW MERCHANT

608. Origins of the law merchant. The origins of the law merchant lie in the mercantile usages developed by communities of traders and applied in their courts. It thus started life as local, and therefore diverse, custom. Gradually, however, the more important features of European mercantile custom became generalised. During the eleventh and twelfth centuries European trade began to expand, becoming an activity which increasingly crossed regional and national boundaries. The commercial links thus fostered highlighted the inconveniences of diversity of mercantile usage and created a corresponding need for a measure of uniformity. Accordingly, a more general European law merchant slowly developed to exist alongside local custom; that is, the uniformity achieved was a uniformity of institutions rather than rules, the latter still remaining subject to national and local regulation.

The law merchant consisted of two strands, maritime custom[1] and the usages of inland trade[2].

1 See para 609 below.
2 See para 610 below.

609. Maritime custom. Maritime custom is associated principally with the Mediterranean ports of Spain and Italy where, from an early date, written codes of maritime custom were produced. The importance of the more significant of these collections lies in their gradual acceptance throughout Europe; they thus provided the basis for an international law of maritime commerce which consisted partly of medieval custom and partly of provisions either drawn from Roman law or developed out of its institutions. The principal text was undoubtedly the *Consolato del Mare* of Barcelona, which dates from the thirteenth century. It was translated into Latin, French and Italian and achieved a European-wide circulation, becoming 'a basis and norms for all marine contracts by all the people of Europe engaged in commerce'[1]. Other leading collections included the *Charte d'Oléron* and the *Waterrecht* of Wisby, which itself drew extensively on the *Consolato* and was widely used in the ports of northern Europe.

The influence of the maritime customs of Europe is apparent in Scotland from the middle ages. It was administered in courts presided over by the magistrates of seaward burghs and, latterly, in the court of the Admiral of Scotland. Its provisions are reflected in statute from the fifteenth century[2], and it is clear that the leading continental codes, particularly those of Oléron and Wisby, were well known and widely used by theorists and practitioners alike. A number of the early manuscript sources contain, among other material, collections of sea laws which are based on them, as is a similar section in Balfour's *Practicks*[3]. In 1613 there appeared William Wellwod's *An Abridgement of All Sea Laws*, a revised and enlarged version of his *Sea Laws of Scotland*, first published in 1590; among his sources were the laws of Oléron, appropriate Roman material and the relevant Acts of the Scottish Parliament.

Wellwod wrote in a European tradition — his treatise evidently circulated in England and part of it was translated into Latin under the title *De dominio maris* — but in modern times maritime law has largely lost its international character, its institutions and principles having been absorbed into the national legal systems of Europe. In Scotland, the special jurisdiction of the Court of Admiralty in matters maritime declined from the eighteenth century, to be taken over by the Courts of Session and Justiciary in the nineteenth[4]. Maritime law thus came to be administered as part of the municipal law of Scotland and its further regulation the concern of the national legislature. But if the formal authority of maritime law is now that of domestic law, it is also the case that the historical source of much of it lies in the marine customs of Europe. Examples include marine insurance, the law of general average and such maritime documents as bills of lading and bonds of bottomry.

1 *Consulate of the Sea and Related Documents* (Alabama 1975, ed S S Jados) p xv, quoting earlier opinion.
2 Eg Charterparty Act 1466 (c 4) (APS II, 87); and Shipping Act 1487 (c 15) (APS II, 178). See also Lord Murray 'The Law Merchant' in *Sources and Literature of Scots Law* (Stair Soc vol 1, 1936 ed H McKechnie) p 243.
3 Balfour *Practicks* (Stair Soc vol 22, 1963 ed P G B McNeill) pp 614–644.
4 See ADMIRALTY, vol 1, paras 404, 405.

610. Inland trade. Inland trade also contributed to the law merchant. From the twelfth century, prompted by the revival of trade in Europe, towns grew to importance as existing centres expanded and new ones were founded. The largest were in southern Europe, but the north also saw urban expansion, albeit on a smaller scale. Towns developed as centres of trade and manufacture and their commercial life was regulated by its own customs and courts. In addition, trade was conducted at the fairs of Europe, for example those of medieval Champagne. Fairs were more characteristic of the north than the south; usually they were annual events, taking place at urban centres and, unlike the more regular domestic markets of the towns, attracting foreign merchants. The granting of a fair was a regalian right and the grant characteristically included jurisdiction, the right to hold a court to deal with matters arising from the fair.

It was from the customs and usages of merchants and their courts that the second strand of the law merchant developed; its elaboration was the work of the medieval jurists, many of whom lived and worked in the cities of Europe. Although inland trade did not produce the same community of rules as maritime commerce, institutions did develop which, in outline at least, acquired general acceptance. Often these had to do with money and were associated with fairs as they became centres for the raising of credit and transfer of capital. In them lie the origins of the mercantile law of Scotland, as of Europe. For example, the needs of commerce produced negotiable instruments such as the bill of exchange; these were accepted in principle into Scots law although their detailed regulation has always been a domestic matter. Again mercantile custom, in the interests of expediency, allowed contracts *in re mercatoria* to be concluded with the minimum of formality, and this is reflected in the modern Scottish rules governing proof of such obligations. On the other hand, there are aspects of the law merchant which Scotland has declined to follow. One example is the rule that a buyer in good faith, purchasing in the open market, acquired good title regardless of any defect in that of the seller; this rule, perhaps due to civilian influences, has never been part of Scots law although it was accepted in England.

(7) THE LAW OF THE BIBLE

611. Introduction. Religion and the Bible have influenced law since the advent of Christianity. In mediaeval times, however, this influence was largely indirect, its principal medium being canon law[1]. Change came with the Reformation. In Scotland the Reformation Parliament of 1560 abolished the authority of the Pope in the country and thus by implication the efficacy of all future legislation of the Roman Church[2]. In 1567 Parliament also abrogated 'all and quatsumever lawis actis and constitutionis canone civile or municipale' which were not in accord with the reformed faith[3]. The controlling factor was Scripture, which the reformers deemed to be the sole and sufficient guide necessary 'to instruct and mak the man of god perfyte'[4]. Canon law, on the other hand, in addition to the Bible, was founded on the traditions and legislation of the Church and the writings of the Church fathers. These latter sources were not, strictly speaking, scriptural, and if canonical provisions based on them were out of step with the Bible — as interpreted by the reformers — they need no longer be regarded as binding. In short, it was directly to the Scriptures that the reformers looked for inspiration.

1 As to canon law, see paras 557 ff above.
2 Papal Jurisdiction Act 1560 (c 2) (APS II, 534).
3 Religion Act 1567 (c 2) (APS II, 548).
4 APS II, 531 (Confession of Faith presented to Parliament in 1690).

612. Marriage. The effect of this on Scots law was chiefly felt in the area of marriage. Prior to the Reformation, marriage was within the exclusive jurisdiction of the Church and the rules governing it part of canon law. The Reformation did not abolish the entire canonical system and, indeed, Scots law preserved the fundamental canonical principle that consent of parties was the very essence of marriage, 'the one thing sufficient and indispensable to its completion'[1]. But reform came on other points. The canonical rules governing prohibition on marriage by reason of an existing relationship between intending spouses were very wide and, although grounded in Scripture, had been extended far beyond its express precepts. On the eve of the Reformation marriage was forbidden to parties related, either by consanguinity or affinity, in the fourth degree or nearer, as it was to those whose relationship was spiritual; that is, the relationship created between spiritual parents and the child they presented for baptism or confirmation. Change came in 1567 when Parliament permitted marriage to parties related in the second degree or beyond, provided the contemplated union did not conflict with the word of God — in effect, the scriptural rules contained principally in the eighteenth chapter of Leviticus[2]. This rider was necessary as an earlier Act of the same year had rendered incestuous and punishable by death unions proscribed by that chapter[3], and included within its prohibitions was the union of aunt and nephew, otherwise lawful as being between parties related in the second degree.

The remaining rules in this area were the result of judicial interpretation, a course made necessary by the fact that Leviticus did not lay down its prohibitions in a general way but framed them in terms of particular relationships. Taken literally, it created some anomalies and appeared to permit some unions that were clearly *contra bonos mores*. It was therefore treated judicially as laying down general principles — the particular instances being read as examples only of these — and applied accordingly. Thus, as construed, the chapter was held to preclude marriage between ascendants and descendants, between uncle and niece, and with the siblings of ascendants remoter than parents. At the same time, and despite some doubt, it was finally settled that the rules governing consanguinity were to apply equally to relationships by affinity[4]. Relaxation of these rules in the latter case was only introduced in the twentieth century.

1 Hume's *Lectures* (Stair Soc vol 5, 1939) p 22.
2 Marriage Act 1567 (c 16) (APS III, 26). See Lev 18:6 ff.
3 Incest Act 1567 (c 15) (APS III, 26).
4 Hume's *Lectures* (Stair Soc vol 5, 1939) p 74; APS IX, 128 c 24, s 4.

613. Divorce. The pre-Reformation Church never recognised divorce *a vinculis*. Marriage was in principle indissoluble and could only be set aside by reason of nullity. Scripture, however, does contain some references to divorce and, although the texts are not always easy to interpret, it is at least possible to construe them as permitting it on the grounds of adultery and desertion[1]. This was the interpretation placed on them by the reformers. Divorce for adultery appears to have been permitted from an early date[2], and while divorce for desertion was sanctioned by a statute of 1573, its terms also suggest that it was merely confirming what had been the practice of the courts for some years[3]. Conform to Scripture, however, these remained the only lawful grounds of divorce until the statutory innovations of the twentieth century.

1 See Mt 5:32, 19:9; Mk 10:2–12; Lk 16:18; 1 Cor 7:15.
2 R D Ireland 'Husband and Wife: Divorce, Nullity of Marriage and Separation' in *An Introduction to Scottish Legal History* (Stair Soc vol 20, 1958) p 95.
3 Divorce for Desertion Act 1573 (c 1) (APS III, 81).

614. Conclusion. The Reformation thus gave Scripture a primary and direct authority both in matters of doctrine and in questions touching conduct and morals. Scots law reacted accordingly and, as well as the important area of marriage, the influence of the Bible can be detected in such aspects of the law as blasphemy, Sunday observance and witchcraft[1].

1 Much of the law relating to these latter topics is, of course, no longer extant.

5. LEGAL METHOD

615. Meaning of 'legal method'. The idea of legal method has two distinct meanings. The first, with which this title is not concerned, relates to the ways in which the methods of empirical research used by social scientists are applied to the investigation of the law in practice. Although traditionally lawyers have not been trained in legal method in this sense, it has been argued that an increasingly important function of the academic lawyer is to conduct empirical research[1]. Equally significant has been the recognition given by law reform bodies such as the Scottish Law Commission to the need to carry out socio-legal research to allow for a coherent and comprehensive set of proposals for changes in legal rules and principles[2].

A second meaning of 'legal method' which will be examined in the remainder of this section of the title is concerned with the application of legal technique often referred to as 'legal reasoning' or 'judicial reasoning'. Professor D M Walker defines 'legal method' in this sense in the following way:

'The problem of legal method consists in ascertaining what methods can best or indeed should be adopted to find the principles of law relevant to the solution of some legal difficulty'[3].

It must be emphasised that legal method is of concern not only to the judge or to the practising lawyer (although typically those engaged in professional legal practice will employ this method more frequently than others). Rather, legal method is deployed by anyone who wishes to use the law as a means of solving some problem. This point about the range of persons who use legal method leads on to another point of some significance, namely, that legal method is a specialised form of reasoning which stands in marked contrast to many of the types of reasoning used in everyday life.

This is so for two related reasons. The first is that legal systems usually restrict the aspects of criteria to which appeal can be made when using legal method to certain specified legal sources and will not allow appeal to other sources (for example political principles or religious tenets). The second is that the law itself defines the categories in which legal problems are to be conceptualised. Thus legal method is concerned both with the specialised ways in which legal problems are constructed and the ways in which these problems are to be solved.

1 W A Wilson 'Knowing the Law and Other Things' 1982 JR 259 at 271, 272.
2 See eg the extensive empirical research commissioned by the Scottish Law Commission as part of its review of the law of diligence: Scot Law Com Memorandum no 47 (1980) App A.
3 D M Walker *The Scottish Legal System* (5th edn, 1981) p 443.

616. Legal method and facts. Traditionally the study of legal method has concentrated on the ways in which a correct legal solution to a problem can be found. More recently it has been accepted that the realm of fact is also a significant component of legal method. One important feature of the ways in which legal method deals with fact is that many rules of law disallow methods of inference and fact-finding which are employed in other, everyday contexts. For example, in attempting to discover the identity of a person who has committed a crime, ordinary methods of reasoning (which will be used by the police at the investigative stage of the criminal process) would make inferences from the past criminal records of likely suspects. In terms of legal proof, this form of reasoning would not, in general terms, be permitted. Many of the rules of the law of evidence do not accord with accepted methods of fact-finding, and some forbid the use of these methods. Although much work requires to be done on the rationale of these rules, it is clear that one aim of the law in imposing such limitations on fact-finding is to promote the ideas of justice and fairness.

Another significant feature about legal method and fact-finding is that many legal systems, including the Scottish and the English, embody a particular conception of reasoning (which might be called 'common sense' reasoning) which is to be distinguished from forms of reasoning advanced in theories of psychology and mathematical probability[1].

1 For a discussion of the reasons why law does not permit the direct use of theories of psychology, see M Stone *Proof of Fact in Criminal Trials* (1984). There is at present a lively debate about the concept of probability which the British legal systems use: see eg the papers in W Twining (ed) *Facts in Law* (Wiesbaden 1983).

617. Legal method and law. The methods used to determine the, or a, legally correct answer to a problem is at the focus of much attention in current legal theory, and it is beyond the confines of this title to describe the full details of this debate. What will be presented is an outline of some of the more central positions adopted in the discussions[1].

1 See paras 618 ff below.

618. The deductive reasoning view. There are two contrasting extreme views about legal method and the law, namely, the deductive reasoning and the indeterminate law view. The first such view is that the ordinary methods of deductive reasoning from a major premise (namely the appropriate legal rule or principle) and a minor premise (the facts) to a conclusion apply in all instances of legal reasoning. On such a view the law is complete and presents no special difficulties in its application. This view has few, if any, adherents in current thinking and has been rejected by even the legal profession itself, including members of the judiciary. Lord Reid once stated in an extra-curial address:

'There was a time when it was thought almost indecent to suggest that judges make law — they only declare it. Those with a taste for fairy tales seem to have thought that in some Aladdin's cave there is hidden the Common Law in all its splendour and that on a judge's appointment there transcends on him knowledge of the magic words Open Sesame. Bad decisions are given when the judge has muddled the pass word and the wrong door opens. But we do not believe in fairy tales any more.

So we must accept the fact that for better or worse judges do make law and tackle the question how do they approach their task and how should they approach it'[1].

1 Lord Reid 'The Judge as Lawmaker' (1972) 12 JSPTL 22. See also the views on discretion expressed by members of the House of Lords in A A Paterson *The Law Lords* (1982) pp 190–195.

619. The indeterminate law view. A directly conflicting view to that which asserts that deductive reasoning can be applied to all legal problems asserts that law is so inherently indeterminate that it can never lead solely to one solution. On this view, purported justifications of answers to legal problems by reference to legal rules and principles are merely *ex post facto* rationalisations of decisions which could have gone in more than one way. But again this approach seems too exaggerated to stand up to scrutiny, and it fails to meet two crucial objections. First, it ignores the many instances of legal reasoning where the law clearly gives a single solution to a problem. A client who seeks guidance from a solicitor on how to make a valid will leaving his estate to his wife or on how to sell his house will be given advice which will reflect the (relatively) clear rules of law on these (and on many similar) matters. Secondly, the view that the law is completely indeterminate cannot account for the fact that on occasions lawyers employing legal reasoning reach conclusions with which they disagree, a feature which would scarcely arise if legal rules always permitted decisions either way. Consider, for example, the remarks of Lord Justice-Clerk Wheatley in *Dick v Falkirk Burgh*[1] that he shared the doubts and criticisms made about the case of *Darling v Gray & Sons*[2] but that it was not for the Inner House of the Court of Session to create artificial grounds for refusing to follow the admittedly unsatisfactory decision of the House of Lords.

1 *Dick v Falkirk Burgh* 1976 SC (HL) 1 at 4, 1975 SLT 110 at 112, 113.
2 *Darling v Gray & Sons* (1892) 19 R (HL) 31.

620. The appeal to principle view.

Most commentators accept that in many instances the rules and principles of law are clear and that ordinary methods of deductive reasoning can be used in respect of them. Disagreement occurs over the ways in which legal method does and should deal with the unclear or difficult cases where a problem cannot be easily resolved by reference to an uncontroversially applicable legal rule. One view, which has been advanced by Professor Ronald Dworkin, is that in such 'hard' cases lawyers discover the answer by appealing to the principles of law which the accepted rules embody and that resort to this method will lead to a single, correct answer to every such disputed question of law[1]. Although Dworkin's position appears very much to accord with the traditional Scottish emphasis on legal principle, it must be noted that for Dworkin the idea of a legal principle is used in the highly specialised sense of a standard which sets out rights of individuals (in contrast to other sorts of justification, such as arguments of social policy) and that his arguments about there always being a single correct answer to a question of law depend on controversial philosophical assumptions. Furthermore, Dworkin has himself admitted that his theory is not completely successful as a description of how judges in Britain do decide hard cases[2].

1 R Dworkin *Taking Rights Seriously* (revised edn 1978) ch 4.
2 R Dworkin 'Political Judges and the Rule of Law' (1978) 64 Proc Brit Acad 259. It should be noted, however, that Dworkin's main concern is with the normative rather than descriptive adequacy of his theory of adjudication.

621. The public interest view.

Another influential theory of legal reasoning, which is based on decisions of the English courts, has been advanced by Professor John Griffith[1]. Griffith argues that in unclear cases judges will decide on the basis of their conception of what the public interest requires. Griffith believes that this view of the public interest is not determined by legal rules but is rather permeated by particular political values which tend to favour the interests of the state, to protect property rights, and to promote the political values associated with the Conservative Party.

1 J A G Griffith *The Politics of the Judiciary* (3rd edn, 1985).

622. Reasoning and the requirements of consistency, coherence and consequences.

Another recent contribution to this debate which deserves particular attention is that of Professor Neil MacCormick, for MacCormick uses many Scottish illustrations for his theory of legal method in difficult cases[1]. MacCormick brings out that much of legal method consists of traditional deductive reasoning. He argues that, for a variety of reasons, there are also cases where no obvious answer is provided to a legal problem, but he disagrees both with the idea that the decision on such a problem is entirely discretionary and also with Griffith's view that it is purely a matter of a political conception of the public interest. MacCormick believes that a decision in a hard case must accord with the demands of formal justice, that is, it must appeal to a legal standard which is capable of being universally applied.

Two further requisites are those of what MacCormick calls consistency and coherence. He explains these ideas in the following way. The requirement of consistency is that the standard to which appeal is made to resolve a hard case must not conflict with an accepted rule of the legal system, and he illustrates this feature by examining both the dissenting and the majority judgments in the Second Division case of *Temple v Mitchell*[2]. Furthermore, a decision in a hard case must conform to the requirement of coherence, that is, the standard appealed to must have a general 'fit' with the other rules of the system. One illustration of this feature is the case of *Steel v Glasgow Iron and Steel Co Ltd*[3], where the Court of Session reasoned that it should accept the argument that a person attempting to rescue others endangered by an unlawful act of a third person did not voluntarily undertake the risk of injuries suffered in so doing. The court accepted that the position was coherent with the view, already accepted as part of the Scots law of delict, that attempting to save property in similar circumstances did not amount to a voluntary assumption of risk.

MacCormick's view is that by following these requirements legal method structures but does not completely determine answers to difficult questions of law, for there might still be competing standards which all satisfy these conditions. His further argument is that the choice between these competing standards is made on a consequentialist basis: the standards are assessed in terms of the consequences which would follow from adopting each as a general rule and the various consequences are compared with each other. MacCormick shows that many cases illustrate this feature and suggests that the speeches in *Donoghue v Stevenson*[4] can profitably be read in this light.

1 N MacCormick *Legal Reasoning and Legal Theory* (1978).
2 *Temple v Mitchell* 1956 SC 267, 1957 SLT 169. See *MacCormick* pp 200–203.
3 *Steel v Glasgow Iron and Steel Co Ltd* 1944 SC 237, 1945 SLT 70. See *MacCormick* pp 161–163.
4 *Donoghue v Stevenson* 1932 SC (HL) 31, 1932 SLT 317. See *MacCormick* pp 108–128.

6. LAW REFORM

(1) GENERAL

623. Aims and methods. The making of new law is necessary because society is not static and must respond to philosophical and moral developments, to new social habits and patterns, to scientific and technological changes, to more complex commercial relationships and to European Community and international obligations. Changes in the law may result from judicial reformulation of principle, and sometimes in response to the contribution of legal literature which has identified problems and propounded solutions for the rationalisation and improvement of the law. In the course of administering justice between litigants the judiciary has always taken an active part in reforming, albeit mainly cautiously and within self-imposed limits, the legal system under review. During the eighteenth and early nineteenth centuries in particular there was a partnership in developing the system between the Scottish judiciary and certain authors of comprehensive works on Scots law. Some such works are accepted as formal sources of law[1]. The main instrument of law reform has, however, been legislation[2]. Those who have advocated law reform through their writings have more often depended on the legislator than on the judiciary to implement their policies. Often their style has been polemical rather than detached, and, although they have created a climate for reform, the reforms which they had advocated have eventually been implemented only in part and only after scrutiny by objective commissions or committees guided by lawyers who have assessed the reforms proposed in the context of the legal system as a whole.

1 As to legal literature as a source of law, see paras 433 ff above.
2 Lord Hunter 'Law Reform: The Meaning and the Methods' in *Proceedings and Papers of the 5th Commonwealth Law Conference* (1977) p 1.

624. Responses to Benthamism. Perhaps the most influential of writers on law reform in Britain was Jeremy Bentham (1748–1832)[1], a jurist and utilitarian philosopher who had abandoned legal practice in disgust. Although the main targets for his criticism on grounds of conservatism and antipathy to reform were Blackstone and the English judiciary, the reform movement which he initiated had effects throughout the United Kingdom. His suggestions for reform were, however, not implemented in their entirety or in the form which he wished. He advocated the wholesale demolition of the structure of English law and its replacement by comprehensive codes based on principles of utility. In fact such reforms as were given effect had been scrutinised by commissions, using the talents of lawyers who were masters of the existing legal system, and these reforms were enacted piecemeal in such a way as to harmonise with that system. The underlying policy of those who actually enacted the reforms of the first half of the nineteenth century was based on the belief that workable reforms in the law can best be recommended by legal experts who can evaluate the theoretical merits of proposed reforms but have also sufficient knowledge of the existing system to work deductions from theory into the technical context of the law as a whole. This policy has, on the whole, also been given effect subsequently in evaluating reforms advocated by individuals or pressure groups whose concerns are with particular interests and apparent injustices irrespective of wider perspectives. It is relatively easy to analyse the existing law and identify defects. It is more difficult to establish new laws which do not create new problems and adverse consequences. Since the law reform movement was initiated, largely by Bentham at the beginning of the nineteenth century, projects for reform have been submitted to the scrutiny of various bodies. These in the past have been mainly constituted *ad hoc* — as in the case of royal commissions or departmental committees[2]. Some committees have had greater continuity of membership than others but have been empowered only to examine projects remitted to them from time to time. Reference to a commission or committee may be resorted to by government to avoid or postpone taking action on a sensitive issue, while in the last resort recommendations for reform depend for implementation on the goodwill of ministers and civil servants whose legislative priorities may be determined by considerations other than the merits of the proposals recommended.

1 W S Holdsworth *History of English Law* vol XIII, references in App 1; W H Hurlburt *Law Reform Commissions in the United Kingdom, Australia and Canada* (Edmonton 1986) pp 18 ff. This valuable work considers law reform in a historical and comparative dimension and should be consulted generally on all aspects of law reform.

2 Lord Hunter 'Law Reform: The Meaning and the Methods' in *Proceedings and Papers of the 5th Parliamentary Law Conference* (1977) p 2.

625. The Law Commissions. The creation of the Law Commissions by the Law Commissions Act 1965[1] did not altogether reflect the policies envisaged by those who had proposed the establishment of the Law Commission for England and Wales. They had contemplated its inclusion within the structure of government itself[2] — a solution which was rejected. Had it been accepted the wider organisational structure of administrative departments would have reinforced the commission's overview of the law as a whole and possibly fostered closer co-operation with ministers and administrators. This policy had not been proposed for the Scottish Law Commission. Systematic law reform resulting from proposals by experienced lawyers after meticulous research and careful consultation with all interests concerned is the underlying philosophy of the established statutory Law Commissions. Commissioners and legal staff are experienced lawyers, and account is taken of economic, sociological and other non-legal factors by commissioning research projects undertaken by experts in the appropriate field. Although examination of particular problems in isolation was not excluded from commissioners' responsibilities, it was envisaged that they should be primarily concerned with 'programme subjects' comprehensive in scope. Especially since commissioners are independent of government, the problem of implementation of comprehensive commission reports has not been resolved. Neither politicians nor administrators are greatly interested in proposals for law reform unless they have obvious popular appeal, and, unless they are urgent, may not be regarded as politically important. Divergent developments of law in Scotland and England are viewed with impatience. Administrators, moreover, prefer short pragmatic solutions rather than comprehensive and systematic proposals. The factors of parliamentary time and parliamentary scrutiny cannot be disregarded. Each government is primarily concerned with its legislative programme as a whole, which is likely to contain political measures to which it attaches priority. The legislative function of Parliament is inevitably subordinated to its role as the arena for a power struggle. This situation is unfavourable for the implementation of comprehensive proposals by the Law Commissions. The Scottish Law Commission has to overcome additional obstacles in that influential Whitehall departments such as the Department of Trade and Industry[3] seek to assert a measure of control over aspects of Scots law such as the sale of goods or security over moveables. They are disposed to support proposals for reform only if the outcome will be a substantial assimilation of Scots and English law, despite basic conceptual divergencies in the areas of law involved. Moreover, where an international or European Community dimension is involved, law reform policy of Scotland may be subordinated to what is acceptable to Whitehall departments from the standpoint of English lawyers. Harmonisation of law may often be desirable, especially in a commercial context, but it should preferably be based upon compatibility or preferability of principle[4] rather than on political advantage. Arguments which might have been relevant to support policies of assimilating mercantile law within Great Britain are much less cogent in a European Communities context. In that context — unlike a United Kingdom context — English law is a minority system rather than that of the majority.

1 Law Commissions Act 1965 (c 22), ss 1, 2. As to the Scottish Law Commission, see paras 665 ff below, and Lord Kilbrandon 'The Scottish Law Commission' (1968) 2 Ga LR 194.
2 G Gardiner and A Martin *Law Reform Now* (1963) pp 7–10; W H Hurlburt *Law Reform Commissions in the United Kingdom, Australia and Canada* (Edmonton 1986) pp 50 ff.

3 T B Smith 'Law Reform in a Mixed "Civil Law and Common Law" Jurisdiction' (1975) 35 La
  LR 927, 958; *Report of the Royal Commission on the Constitution* (the Kilbrandon Report) (1973)
  (Cmnd 5460) p 723; *Hurlburt* pp 86 ff.
4 See the Kilbrandon Report referred to in note 3 above. Lord Kilbrandon has discerned that
  imposing English mercantile law solutions on Scots law for the sake of uniformity may be
  prejudicial: *Scots Law seen from England* (Child Lecture 1980–81) pp 5, 6. What is 'desirable' or
  'necessary' to the Department of Trade and Industry may be the converse of reform from the
  viewpoint of Scots law.

626. 'Codification'. Codification was the preferred solution of Bentham to
law reform, and the Law Commissions are required by statute to 'take and keep
under review all the law with which they are respectively concerned with a view
to its systematic development and reform, including in particular the codification of such law, the elimination of anomalies, the repeal of obsolete and
unnecessary enactments and generally the simplification and modernisation of
the law'[1].

The negative function — the repeal of what is obsolete and unnecessary — is
an important aspect of law reform[2]. Statute law reform is of particular importance. Thus the doctrine of desuetude in relation to legislation of the pre-Union
Scottish Parliament and the recognition of special policies for statute law
revision and statute law repeal have made important contributions to reform.

What was implied by the positive policy of codification was not defined. It
may be that no more was contemplated than 'codifying statutes' such as the Sale
of Goods Act 1893 (c 71) (now 1979 (c 54)). This aimed to present comprehensively, but in the context of the general law, solutions worked out by the
English courts[3]. However, statutory restatement rather than reform does not
seem to be what the Law Commission Act 1965 required. The Law Commissions' early and abortive joint venture to formulate a Contract Code illustrates the difficulties of attempting to reform, unify and codify substantial
chapters of the law in two legal systems — especially when there is no agreement on what 'codification' implies nor on the style in which it should be
drafted. The commissions did not even reach the stage of seeking parliamentary
enactment of a code and thus did not face the formidable problems both of
parliamentary time and jealous parliamentary scrutiny of the measure clause by
clause. One Scottish Law Commissioner involved has noted: 'The history of
codification suggests that the successful enactment of codes depends on strong
political motivation. It is doubtful, however, whether at the present time,
codifying statutes would strike the imagination either of Parliament or the
general public'[4]. Moreover, 'To put the matter at its lowest, therefore, the
successful enactment of codes may require the development of new Parliamentary procedures'. Lord Hunter, a former Chairman of the Scottish Law Commission, has also observed that there 'seems no escape from the conclusion that,
in any of the legal systems served by Westminster, codification (in any proper
sense of the term) must remain a pipe dream until new methods of drafting, new
legislative approaches and machinery and new principles of interpretation are
introduced and accepted'[5]. In short, the Law Commissions are likely to prove
important sources of law reform, but the power to reorganise the effective
machinery of law reform — the legislative process — is beyond their control.
Their full potential can only be realised in the context of constitutional reform
such as that which in a historical context has provided the necessary climate for
codification and comprehensive law reform generally. In particular this is the
case where by 'codification' is implied a self-contained statement of the main
chapters of the law to be construed without reference to law developed in a more
general context. Such a development cannot be readily envisaged in relation to
Scots law within the framework of the present constitution.

1 Law Commissions Act 1965 (c 22), s 3(1).
2 See paras 698 ff below.
3 The uncritical inclusion of Scotland in this legislation at the Bill stage was an unhappy after-thought and has created confusion, especially in relation to its property provisions. See T B Smith *Property Problems in Sale* (1978) passim.
4 A E Anton 'Obstacles to Codification' 1982 JR 15, 27.
5 Lord Hunter 'Law Reform: The Meaning and the Methods' in *Proceedings and Papers of the 5th Commonwealth Law Conference* (1977) p 1 at p 7.

(2) REFORM FROM MEDIEVAL TIMES
TO THE UNION OF 1707

627. Reform commissions. Statute law revision and the creation of com-missions for 'codification of the law' have been characteristic of Scottish law reform from medieval times. As far back as 1425 Scotland's first law reform statute set up a commission[1] 'to se and examyn the bukis of law of this realme, that is to say, *Regiam Majestatem* and *Quoniam Attachiamenta*, and mend the lawis that nedis mendment'. The commission established in 1425 was fruitless and in 1469[2] (or 1487) the project for revision of the laws by a commission was renewed, the material to be examined comprehending 'the Kingis Lawis, *Regiam Majestatem*, Actis, Statutis and uthir Bukis'. This commission also laboured in vain. However, in 1556 a further commission was set up to 'visit sycht and correct the lawis of this Realme', and this commission at least produced a printed edition of statutes from the time of James I to 1564. Further commissions[3] constituted in 1574 and 1578 were required to consider 'the bukis of the Law, Actis of Parliament, and Decisionis before the Session' and to compile a body of laws 'meet and convenient to be statute', while in 1592 Skene was appointed to a commission concerned with the publication of an authentic edition of the Acts of Parliament as they had been interpreted. The compilation of Acts was completed in 1597 and Parliament ensured the dissemination of this work. However, the by-products of the labours of these commissions had their effect, albeit not in legislation. Balfour's *Practicks*, although not published until 1754, circulated in manuscript from about 1580[4]. This work almost certainly resulted from Balfour's researches as commissioner. Skene's version of the '*Auld Lawes and Constitutions of Scotland*', although not published until 1609 (after sharp representations made to the Scottish Privy Council by James VI), had been included in the remit to the 1574 commission and was published with parliamentary authority. Balfour's *Practicks* was in effect an archaic legal en-cyclopaedia comprising statutes and decisions, and an exposition of 'auld laws', and was a valued professional repository for development of the law — in effect, though very different in style, a forerunner of 'institutional' writing. Skene's *Regiam Majestatem* was also of professional value as an authorised work. In unauthorised versions it had often been cited in the sixteenth century, but was waning in relevancy by 1609. Indeed in 1628 the Privy Council set up a new commission[5] to revise the laws, narrating that 'the customs and consuetude of the said kingdom ar in manie things so obscure and uncertaine that the same has need to be explained and cleared'. The commission was directed to consider 'the Acts, Decreets of the Lords of Session and Justice-General' and 'the book entitled *Regiam Majestatem* which conteaneth a record of the ancient lawes and customs observed within the said kingdome'. In 1649 a somewhat similar remit was made to another commission which included Stair. The commission was 'to revise and consider all the laws and statutes and Acts of Parliament' as well as customary law, and was to 'collect draw up and compile a formal mode and frame of a book of just and equitable laws'. It is possible that work for that commission may have motivated Stair to start work on his *Institutions*[6]. On balance it seems more probable that he embarked on this enterprise about 1657 when he was first appointed a judge — albeit the remit to the commission may have influenced his decision[7]. The influence of Stair's *Institutions* on the survival and development of the law of Scotland is inestimable, and, if it was the by-product of a project for law reform, it is in a class by itself.

1 Statute Law Revision Act 1425 (c 10).
2 Remit to Committee Act 1469 (c 20). See T M Cooper 'Regiam Majestatem and the Auld Lawes' in *Sources and Literature of Scots Law* (Stair Soc vol 1, 1936) pp 70, 71.
3 See generally Cooper's paper referred to in note 2 above, and *Regiam Majestatem* (Stair Soc vol 11, 1947, ed Lord Cooper). See also T B Smith 'British Justice: A Jacobean Phantasma' 1982 SLT (News) 157.
4 Balfour's *Practicks* (Stair Soc vol 21, 1962, ed P G B McNeill) p xxxiii.
5 *Regiam Majestatem* (Stair Soc vol 11, 1947, ed Lord Cooper) p 4.
6 G M Hutton 'Purposes and Pattern of the Institutions; 1. Stair's Aim in writing the Institutions' in *Stair Tercentenary Studies* (Stair Soc vol 33, 1981) p 79 at p 82.
7 *Hutton* at p 81.

628. Projects for unification. After acceding to the throne of England in 1603, James VI and I expressed to the English House of Commons in the following year his aspiration to unify the laws of the two kingdoms as one aspect of his great design 'at my death to leave one worship to God; one kingdom entirely governed; one uniformity of laws — *unus rex unus grex una lex*'[1]. There was a certain amount of theoretical support for the project of legal unification both in Scotland and England, the English supporters being largely of civil law background in the Bartolist tradition whose followers envisaged modernising and civilianising the laws of England. The most substantial support among Scottish writers came from the publication of Sir Thomas Craig's *De Unione Regnorum Britanniae Tractatus* in 1604. He discerned similarities between the two systems of jurisprudence, and while not specifically recommending assimilation, considered that the project was feasible and should not be discouraged. However, the commissioners appointed by the legislatures of the two countries to treat on closer union were more cautious and more suspicious, while the English common lawyers jealously asserted the supposed superiority of their system against civilian influences. Each Parliament gave effect in 1607 to the commissioners' proposals for elimination of laws of one country hostile to the other state, but this agreement did not extend to reconciliation of laws which were not hostile. Work on preliminary compilation of digests comparing the laws of Scotland and England progressed in 1607, but even the King's advisers such as Bacon expressed reservations. Two different approaches to legal union had emerged in England during that year — the first favouring a gradual process of unification while respecting essential differences and the second advocating subjection of Scots law to English law[2]. Neither plan prevailed. The decision of the English judges in *Calvin's Case*[3] recognising the naturalisation in England of Scotsmen born after the Union of 1603 was based on allegiance of the subject to the king and not to a legal system, and by 1608 the project of unification of law had lapsed as a practical objective. However, even after the project was dead, James in 1615 assured his English subjects that his desire was 'to conform the laws of Scotland to the law of England ... my intention was always to effect union by uniting Scotland to England and not England to Scotland'[4].

The policy of unification which had been defeated in the early seventeenth century was revived by Cromwell in mid-century, and he probably envisaged unification of laws as an aspect of his project for full parliamentary union.

However, most leading Scots lawyers refused to subscribe to the Tender of Union, and Cromwell's commissioners administered Scots law as they understood it. They left no imprint on the substance of the law[5]. However, from this period one may probably date the commencement of the compilation of the *Institutions* of Stair, who was himself one of the Usurpation judges and who was in effect to restate the law of Scotland as a coherent system as more than a match for English law on its merits.

In 1670 Charles II authorised the appointment of Scottish and English commissioners to negotiate a parliamentary union[6]. The Scottish commissioners, reflecting the views of the leading lawyers, resisted a solution which would impair the independence of Scots law. Indeed Mackenzie maintained that nations seeking to unite with others should strive 'to retain their supremacy which they have enjoyed and to have distinct laws and Parliaments'[7]. The Scottish assertion of severalty of administration of justice was unacceptable to the English commissioners. Consequently the union project was abandoned in 1671, and its one apparent practical consequence was the provision of safeguards for Scottish legal institutions in the Union Agreement of 1707. By this time, due largely to the labours of Stair and Mackenzie, the merits of the Scottish system were more apparent than they had been a century before.

Although projects for the unification of the laws of Scotland and England were in the seventeenth century at times associated with the reform and simplification of each system, the latent motif was 'conforming the laws of Scotland to the Law of England', and this, though a potential source of new law, was not necessarily a source of law reform. This motif has, since the Union, been too often apparent in 'law reform' projects.

1 Journals of the House of Commons i, 171.
2 B P Levack 'The Proposed Union of English Law and Scots Law in the Seventeenth Century' 1975 JR 97; T B Smith 'British Justice: A Jacobean Phantasma' 1982 SLT (News) 157.
3 *Calvin's Case* (1608) 7 Co Rep 1a.
4 James I *Works* p 329, cited in E J Cowan 'The Union of the Crowns and the Crisis of the Constitution in 17th Century Scotland' in *The Satellite State* (1979) p 125.
5 Lord Cooper 'Cromwell's Judges and their Influence on Scots Law' in *Selected Papers 1922–1954* (1957) p 115.
6 *Levack* 1975 JR 97 at 113.
7 G Mackenzie 'Discourse concerning the Three Unions between England and Scotland' in *Works*, vol 2 (1722) pp 637, 662.

629. Legislative landmarks. Ephemeral legislation on ecclesiastical, constitutional and fiscal matters promoting sectional interests has little relevance to law reform. Of more significance are the Acts passed to regulate bankruptcy, entails, trusts and the registration of land rights. The Bankruptcy Act 1621 (c 18) was modelled on the *actio pauliana* of Roman law and was aimed at annulling deeds granted in fraud of creditors, while the Bankruptcy Act 1696 (c 5) was designed to restrict the possibility that a debtor in embarrassed circumstances might grant a deed in favour of one particular creditor to the prejudice of others before insolvency could be proved. The solution was to establish the concept of 'notour' or notorious bankruptcy which could be inferred from certain facts and to invalidate voluntary deeds granted by a debtor in favour of a creditor within a prescribed period of notour bankruptcy. The Diligence Act 1661 (c 344) and the Judicial Sale Act 1681 (c 83) were concerned with heritable property and designed to put on an equal footing diligences carried out in competition. The Blank Bonds and Trusts Act 1696 (c 25) prohibited actions of declarator of trust unless the trust could be established by the oath or signed declaration of the trustee.

Related to the problems of bankruptcy is the concept of tailzie or entail. The Entail Act 1685 (c 26) was designed, according to Mackenzie, to establish a register of entails to protect creditors against dishonest heirs of entail who had raised loans on secretly entailed estates. However it was widely welcomed as a device to protect the estates of an impoverished landed class from forfeiture, debt or profligate heirs. The Act was complemented by another in 1690[1] designed to protect the heir of entail against forfeiture for political reasons. About half a century later the device became extremely controversial. Its critics regarded it as an intolerable burden on commerce, preventing heirs of entail from granting satisfactory leases, raising money for improvements or making adequate provision for their families.

Among the most notable law reform measures of the seventeenth century must be recognised the Acts of 1617[2] and 1681[3], and in particular the Register of Sasines Act 1693[4], relating to registration for publication of conveyances of land. The 1693 Act making the date of registration the criterion of preference as to title was rightly regarded as 'the keystone of the Scottish system of land rights'.

1 Persons Forfeited Act 1690 (c 104).
2 Registration Act 1617 (c 16).
3 Registration in Burgh Act 1681 (c 13).
4 The Register of Sasines Act 1693 was designated the Registration Act 1693 (c 24) in the Chronological Table of the Acts of the Parliaments of Scotland 1424–1707, pursuant to the Statute Law Revision (Scotland) Act 1964 (c 80), which assigned short titles to Scots Acts then in force. See generally H H Monteath 'Heritable Rights from Early Times to the Twentieth Century' in *An Introduction to Scottish Legal History* (Stair Soc vol 20, 1958) p 156 especially at p 159.

(3) REFORM FROM THE UNION OF 1707
TO THE 'REFORM ACTS' OF 1832

630. Qualified respite from legislation in the eighteenth century. The development of Scots law during the eighteenth century, especially in the field of private law, owed little to projects of statutory law reform. Nevertheless, or because of this, it was the Golden Age of Scots law. The law was restated and developed in a series of 'institutional treatises' reflecting the formulation of learned custom in a series of judicial decisions. In this period of freedom from legislative interference Scotland was one of the least 'governed' countries of Europe. Between 1709 and 1746 (although with substantial gaps) a Scotsman had been appointed third Secretary of State, but the last occupant of the office was dismissed in 1746. Those who had held this office had exercised disproportionate power over Scottish affairs, which were otherwise of little concern to government in London.

Legislative intervention immediately after the Union of 1707 reflected the imposition of the policies of government in London regardless of Scottish interests. The application to Scotland of the barbarous English treason laws by the Treason Act 1708 (c 21) and the introduction of lay patronage in Scotland by the Church Patronage (Scotland) Act 1711 (c 21), were bitterly resented, while a proposal in actual breach of the Union Agreement to levy a malt tax in 1711 caused such adverse reaction that it was for a time suspended, but not before a motion to dissolve the Union was very narrowly defeated in the House of Lords in 1713. Perhaps influenced by such reactions subsequent governments until the end of the century rarely intervened by legislation in Scottish affairs unless on

Scottish initiative and after consulting Scottish interests. Among the rare exceptions were the abolition of the Extraordinary Lords of the Court of Session by the Court of Session Act 1723 (c 19), and the abolition of ward holding by the Tenures Abolition Act 1746 (c 50) and of the heritable jurisdictions by the Heritable Jurisdictions (Scotland) Act 1746 (c 43). Among the consequences of the abolition of the heritable jurisdictions were reorganisation of the sheriff court, the requirement of legal qualification for its judges and the transference of the duties of the inferior commissary courts to the sheriffs. These Acts, which could be recognised as reforms, were passed predominantly by English legislators with little concern for specifically Scottish interests, and the same may be true of the extension by implication of the Thellusson Act 1800[1] to accumulations of moveable property in Scotland. By contrast, other legislation applicable to Scotland was discussed but not enacted until approved by the various branches of the Scottish legal profession and the freeholders — the small landowning electorate which discussed legislative policies in their Michaelmas head courts and regarded themselves as custodians of the constitution.

1 Ie the Accumulations Act 1800 (c 98). See generally R Burgess *Perpetuities in Scots Law* (Stair Soc vol 31, 1979).

631. Law reform measures prior to 1832. Statutory law reform prior to 1832 affecting Scotland in particular concerned employment, bankruptcy, entails and the Court of Session[1].

1 See paras 632–635 below.

632. Employment. The bond status of salters and colliers was finally abolished by Acts passed in 1775 and 1799[1], the former measure having been introduced at the instigation of coal owners. The status of slavery had, however, always been rejected in Scots law by judicial pronouncements[2] much wider than those of Lord Mansfield in *Sommersett's Case*[3].

1 Colliers (Scotland) Acts 1775 (c 28) and 1790 (c 56).
2 See T B Smith 'Master and Servant' in *An Introduction to Scottish Legal History* (Stair Soc vol 20, 1958) p 130 at pp 137, 138.
3 *Sommersett's Case* (1772) 20 St Tr 1. See generally N Wilson 'Legal Attitudes to Slavery in Eighteenth Century Britain; English Myth; Scottish Social Realism and their Wider Comparative Context' (1970) 11 Race 463.

633. Bankruptcy. On the whole mercantile law was not extensively developed in Scotland during the greater part of the eighteenth century. When George Joseph Bell wrote his *Commentaries on the Law of Scotland and on the Principles of Mercantile Jurisprudence* (1804) he made extensive use of English materials. Lord Mansfield had developed substantially the mercantile law of England during the eighteenth century, drawing on earlier Scottish and Continental sources[1] and on the experience of London merchants. However, Bell took as the basis of his writings on mercantile law the situations created by bankruptcy, and the Scots law of bankruptcy had been regulated by a series of statutes enacted between 1772 to 1814. The Bankruptcy (Scotland) Act 1772 (c 72) was one of the landmarks in this branch of the law. It was enacted 'for rendering the payment of creditors of insolvent debtors more equal and expeditious and for regulating the diligence of the law by arrestment and poinding'. However, it continued the policy of segregating heritable property in bankruptcy situations. The Payment of Creditors (Scotland) Act 1783 (c 18), although it restricted the process of sequestration to traders, rendered it applicable to their heritable property. Experience indicated that the law of bankruptcy had to be adapted constantly to commercial developments, and a further Payment of Creditors (Scotland) Act was enacted in 1814 (c 137). This Act began the involvement of the sheriff court in the progress of sequestration and *inter alia* provided for commissioners to assist the trustee and also for the discharge of a bankrupt. Bankruptcy has, however, continued to demand further attention by those concerned with law reform in Scotland up to modern times[2].

1 C H S Fifoot *Lord Mansfield* (1936) p 30 and *passim*.
2 See eg the Bankruptcy (Scotland) Act 1985 (c 66), giving effect with modifications to the Report of the Scottish Law Commission *Bankruptcy and Related Aspects of Insolvency and Liquidation* (Scot Law Com no. 6, 1982).

634. Entails. Reform of the law of entail is of particular social interest in the context of the civic leadership of post-Union Scotland. The role of the Faculty of Advocates and that of the landowners whose interest in parliamentary elections was predominant were of particular significance[1]. The Entail Act 1685 (c 26) had served a useful purpose, but by 1740 the restraints which it imposed on commerce and land development were strongly criticised by an influential section of the community, and the Faculty of Advocates was particularly concerned. In 1764 the Dean of Faculty convened a special meeting to approve his proposal that a Bill be drafted to bring an end to perpetuities created by entail. If the draft of the Bill were approved it was to be sent to the Courts of Session and Exchequer, to the Writers to the Signet, to provosts of royal burghs, to the sheriffs and to the county freeholders for approval, and thereafter when in final draft form to peers, members of Parliament and the Law Officers. By a substantial majority the Faculty agreed that such a Bill be drafted. In proposing to abolish perpetuities on the death of the possessor and heirs of entail living at the time of its creation the Faculty was consciously seeking to change the social and economic development of the country. In Phillipson's words:

> 'the paradox was that the very system which had been devised to protect ancient families from economic extinction before the Union would become an instrument to destroy them. Liberty and the interests of Scotland's most ancient families, it was argued, could only be preserved if the interests of landed society, like those of the commercial world were regulated by market forces. These alone would encourage men to improve their estates and maximise their wealth, their power and that of the commonwealth'[2].

However, the ideological opposition to the Bill proved more powerful at Westminster, where the Bill foundered without even securing a first reading[3]. Subsequently the Entail Improvement Act 1770 (c 51) merely extended the powers of management of the heir of entail, without affecting the perpetuity element, while the Entail Provisions Act 1824 (c 87) allowed him to burden the rental of the estate with provisions for his wife and children. Real change affecting the perpetuation of entail came only after 1832 with the Entail Amendment Act 1848 (c 36) and the Entail (Scotland) Act 1914 (c 43), which prohibited new entails altogether.

1 N Phillipson 'Lawyers, Landowners and Civic Leadership of Post-Union Scotland' 1976 JR 97.
2 *Phillipson* at p 116.
3 Thus, as Ross observes, Kames and those who thought like him were more than a century and a half ahead of their successful Scottish adversaries: I S Ross *Lord Kames and the Scotland of His Day* (1972) pp 210–212, 255, 343, 364.

635. Reform of the Court of Session. Reform of the Court of Session was seen to be expedient in the last decades of the eighteenth century[1]. There was inefficient use of judicial resources as well as procedural anomalies, including unrestrained powers of the court to review its own decisions, and insufficient machinery to ascertain fact. The Court of Session sat as a collegiate court of not less than nine judges and often of all fifteen — a situation 'better calculated for debate than discussion', in Islay Campbell's words. Consequent delays in the administration of justice resulted in multiplication of appeals to the House of Lords, a procedure which already seemed attractive to those who saw a sporting chance in resorting to an ultimate appellate tribunal unfamiliar with Scots law. An abortive first step was taken by the introduction of a Judges' Bill in 1785 which proposed to reduce the size of the bench from fifteen judges to ten, and to use the money thus saved to augment the salaries of the remaining judges. This measure, which had been introduced without consultation with Scottish legal and landed interests, provoked deep resentment among those interests which had previously been consulted regarding proposed legislative reforms. They regarded it as an attempt to subvert the constitution. The Bill was withdrawn, but fresh proposals for reform of the Court of Session were pressed. The controversy was further complicated by the activities of Scottish Whigs (including a substantial number of lawyers) who desired reform of the Court of Session by imitating English models and in particular to make provision for civil jury trial. Their reforming programme had been directed towards 'including Scotland within the constitution', by which they meant bestowing upon their fellow countrymen the same sort of liberties as they believed were enjoyed by Englishmen. An ill-prepared Bill instigated by Whigs and presented by Grenville was presented in Parliament without consideration of the reactions of the Scottish judges. However, in 1807 the Lord President and two senior Senators were summoned to be questioned at the Bar of the House of Lords — a procedure regarded as particularly offensive because English judges when consulted were seated on the woolsacks[2]. Grenville's Bill fell with his ministry in 1807, and when Lord Eldon assumed responsibility the procedures appropriate to rational law reform were observed. By the Court of Session (Scotland) Act 1808 (c 151), enacted after full consultation, the Inner House was divided into two Divisions, and the Act also authorised the appointment of commissioners 'to make full Enquiries into the Forms of Process in the Court of Session and to report in what cases and in what manner and form it appears that Jury Trial could be most usefully established in that Court'. Jury trial was introduced by the Jury Trials (Scotland) Act 1815 (c 42). As the result of the work of several commissions[3] the Court of Session (Scotland) Act 1825 prescribed an Inner House of two Divisions with seven permanent Lords Ordinary in the Outer House[4], reduced to five in 1830[5]. Moreover in 1830 the civil jurisdiction of the Admiralty Court was transferred to the Court of Session and to the sheriff court[6] and the Admiral's criminal jurisdiction to the High Court of Justiciary and sheriff court[7]. Prize jurisdiction had already been appropriated by the English Admiralty Court in 1825[8], partly as an indirect consequence of the jealousy shown by the Court of Session to the Scottish Admiralty Court but mainly due to the imperial pretensions of the English jurisdiction.

1 J G Mackay *The Practice of the Court of Session* (1877) I, pp 30 ff. See generally N T Phillipson *The Reform of the Court of Session 1785–1830* (unpublished PhD thesis, Cambridge University 1967). Contributions based on this thesis are published in J N Wolfe (ed) *Government and Nationalism in Scotland* (1969) pp 167 ff, and J N Phillipson and R Mitchison *Scotland in the Age of Improvement* (1970) pp 125 ff.

2 *Phillipson Thesis* pp 202, 203.

3 *Report of the Committee appointed to search the Lords Journals for Proceedings respecting the Judicature of the Court of Session in Scotland* (1808) III, 129–154; *Report of the Commissioners appointed for inquiring*

into the Administration of Justice in Scotland (1810) ix; *First, Second and Third Reports of the Lord President of the Court of Session, the Lord Justice-Clerk and the Lord Chief Commissioner respecting the Jury Court* (1816) viii; *Report of the Commissions for inquiring into the Forms of Process in the Courts of Law in Scotland* (1824) x.
4 Court of Session Act 1825 (c 120), s 1.
5 Court of Session Act 1830 (c 69), s 20.
6 Ibid, s 21: see ADMIRALTY, vol 1, para 404.
7 Ibid, s 21; Circuit Courts (Scotland) Act 1828 (c 29), s 16 (which had already given concurrent jurisdiction). See ADMIRALTY, vol 1, para 405.
8 Court of Session Act 1825 (c 120), s 57. See ADMIRALTY, vol 1, para 406; 'Pretensions of English Law as Imperial Law' in CONSTITUTIONAL LAW vol 5, para 714; PRIZE.

636. Subsequent developments. Whig policies identifying law reform for Scotland with conforming the system to English solutions became more apparent beyond the fields of electoral and judicial reform, after extension of the franchise extinguished the close relationship between constituency and member of Parliament which had been of constitutional significance in Scotland since the Union of 1707. Representation by 'carpet bagger' was a consequence of the Representation of the People (Scotland) Act 1832 (c 65)[1]. Moreover, industrial, economic and social developments in the nineteenth century presented new problems which seemed to require common solutions on either side of the Border.

1 As to the pre-1832 electoral system, see 'The Post-Union Electoral System' in CONSTITUTIONAL LAW, vol 5, paras 467–470; ELECTIONS.

(4) REFORM FROM 1832 TO THE MID-TWENTIETH CENTURY

(a) General

637. Introduction. 1832 was a year particularly noted for the electoral reform provided by the Representation of the People (Scotland) Act 1832 (c 65)[1]. The nineteenth century from that period is famous for its major social measures[2], but it was also an era remarkable for statutory reform of Scots substantive law, as well as for reforms developed by the courts and expounded by writers[3]. The sources of reform were various. A Bill presented to Parliament might have its origins in the work of a private individual, professional organisations or other pressure groups[4], or of royal commissions, departmental committees, government departments or any combination of these.

The use by government of royal commissions and departmental committees became increasingly significant. These bodies have been defined in the following terms:

'Royal commissions and departmental committees are *ad hoc* advisory committees appointed by virtue of non-statutory powers of the Crown and its ministers respectively. As such, they represent one of the oldest and most numerous of all the institutions of government in Britain'[5].

In the early nineteenth century about one royal commission was being appointed each year, but by the mid century the annual rate of appointment had increased on average by seven-fold, and a peak was reached in 1859 when thirteen royal commissions were created[6]. These commissions were given particular terms of reference and came to an end on submission of their final reports. Their membership ranged from three to thirty persons, but averaged between ten and twenty members. The appointment of a commission was an opportunity for lay experts and representatives to be involved gratuitously in the formulation of public policy. This did not necessarily mean, however, that well-balanced representation was always achieved in the government's appointment of a commission[7]. Nor were the reports of royal commissions always successfully implemented[8], although many did lead to some legislation.

Royal commissions may be distinguished from departmental committees in their method of appointment. The former are appointed by the Crown, the latter by a government minister. The practical distinction between the two is that a departmental committee is likely to fall with a government, whereas this need not be so with a royal commission, which has in theory been appointed by the Crown. Royal commission reports are also certain to be presented to Parliament as Command Papers, but departmental committee reports are more likely to be non–parliamentary papers[9]. Royal commissions also tend to be more prestigious and larger than departmental committees. In any event, both institutional devices have been used by government in the preparation of reform of Scots substantive law. A notable example of such a royal commission was that first appointed in 1833[10] under the chairmanship of Professor George Joseph Bell with terms of reference which ranged from court and professional practices to diligence and conveyancing. This body, as has been the case with other royal commissions, has been referred to as 'the Law Commission'[11]. It produced three reports in 1834, 1835 and 1838 respectively. Equally substantial reform over a period of twelve years was attained through the work of the Lord Advocate's Conveyancing (Departmental) Committee, chaired throughout by Sir George Paul, with half a dozen statutes to its credit, from the Entail (Scotland) Act 1914 (c 43) to the Conveyancing (Scotland) Act 1924 (c 27)[12].

1 As to the history of the Scottish electoral system, see 'The Post-Union Electoral System' in CONSTITUTIONAL LAW, vol 5, paras 467–470; ELECTIONS.

2 See *The Edinburgh History of Scotland* (1978), vol 4, ch 9–11.

3 See Will C Smith 'Scots Law in the Victorian Era' (1901) 13 JR 152, and Lord Blackburn 'The Development of the Law' (1933) 49 SL Rev 339, 377.

4 For instance the Scottish Law Amendment Society was formed in 1868, combining all branches of the legal profession, along with commercial and agricultural interests, with the aim of identifying and suggesting reform of the law and criticising measures proposed. See 1868 J Juris 655.

5 T J Cartwright *Royal Commissions and Departmental Committees in Britain* (1975) p 1.

6 *Cartwright* p 37. At p 35 the author also notes 'Reliable detailed information from 1800 to the present can be obtained only in the case of royal commissions; in the case of departmental committees, detailed information is available only from 1900 onwards'.

7 Eg initial reaction to the appointment of the Royal Commission on the Courts of Justice in Scotland was scathing, as seen in editorial comment in the 1868 J Juris at 651: 'The objection is not that a majority of the Commissioners are Tories, but that it consists of men whose minds are already made up on the chief subjects of the inquiry, who are all, with two or three exceptions, sure to stand upon the old ways, and — we say it with respect but with boldness — some of whom are the very men under whose guidance and control the judicial institutions of our country have fallen into disgrace'. In the light of that and other criticisms the Lord Advocate advised the government to recall the commission and issue a new one, changing the terms of reference and increasing its membership: see at 710–712.

8 Eg the commission appointed in 1896, chaired by Lord Law, which recommended in 1897 the introduction, in relation to land registration, of a process of photo-zincography for the reproduction of deeds lodged for registration. This met with strong opposition from the legal profession and led to the eventual withdrawal of a Bill which had been designed to implement the recommendation. See 'Land Registration in Scotland' (1902) 18 SL Rev 101; J Erskine 'A Bill to improve the System of Registration of Writs relating to Heritable Property in Scotland' (1903) 19 SL Rev 96; A R Prentice 'A Project for a Printed Register of Sasines' (1904) 20 SL Rev 115.

9 *Cartwright* p 27.

10 There were further appointments in 1834 and 1837.

11 See L Ockrent *Land Rights: An Enquiry into the History of Registration for Publication in Scotland* (1942) p 115. See also 'The New Law Commission' (1897) 13 SLR 247, referring to the Commission on Procedure in the Law Courts of Scotland.

12 The other enactments were the Feudal Casualties (Scotland) Act 1914 (c 48), the Intestate Husband's Estate (Scotland) Act 1919 (c 9), the Married Women's Property (Scotland) Act 1920 (c 64), and the Trusts (Scotland) Act 1921 (c 58). See C Mackintosh 'The Conveyancing (Scotland) Act 1924' 1924 SLT (News) 153.

638. Blue Books and White Papers. 'Blue Book' is a term normally reserved for a large publication prepared for or by government, such as the report of a royal commission or departmental committee. The colloquial reference to 'Blue Book' stems from the protective cover used on such publications, although Her Majesty's Stationery Office has also employed colours other than blue. Of the term 'White Paper' it has been stated:

'In its broad sense, a White Paper is merely a Parliamentary Paper not thick enough to require a protective cover. Nowadays, however, it is used, more often than not, to refer to a statement of Government policy'[1].

The extent to which government is committed to the statement of policy in a White Paper, or is seeking further reaction from the public or organisations, tends to vary with the policy under consideration and whether it has been preceded by any earlier consultation. An example of this kind of publication is the White Paper on *Intellectual Property and Innovation*[2].

 1 J G Olle *Introduction to British Government Publications* (2nd edn, 1973) p 58.
 2 (1986) Cmnd 9712.

639. Green Papers. The term 'Green Paper' is attributed to Michael Stewart[1], who in 1967 defined it as:

'A statement by the Government not of policy already determined but of propositions put before the whole nation for discussion'[2].

The first example of such a document was a joint publication in 1967 of the Department of Economic Affairs and the Treasury called '*The Development Areas: a proposal for a regional employment premium*'. A Green Paper may precede the publication of a White Paper. This was the case with the White Paper cited above on intellectual property[3], which took account of the comments of a wide range of consultees who responded to the 1983 Green Paper *Intellectual Property Rights and Innovation*[4]. Governments may use Green Papers to consult the public on the most controversial issues of the day[5].

 1 J G Olle *Introduction to British Government Publications* (2nd edn, 1973) p 58.
 2 Debate in the House of Commons on regional employment premiums on 5 June 1967.
 3 See para 638 above.
 4 (1983) Cmnd 9117. See *Intellectual Property and Innovation* (1986) (Cmnd 9712) p 3.
 5 Eg *Paying for Local Government* (1986) (Cmnd 9714).

(b) Mercantile Law

640. The Mercantile Law Amendment Acts of 1856. During George Joseph Bell's professorship in Scots law at the University of Edinburgh from 1822 to 1843, his *Principles* and *Commentaries* were published. These leading works are particularly important for their accounts of Scots common law as it affected commerce. Since that period significant inroads have been made into Scots mercantile law by statute. In the mid and late nineteenth century some opinion within the profession in England and Scotland favoured assimilation and 'codification' of Scots and English mercantile law. Indeed in 1853 a royal commission[1] was appointed with the remit to 'report whether it will be expedient that any, and what, alterations shall be made in the Mercantile Laws of the United Kingdom, in those respects in which the laws of Scotland differ from those of England and Ireland'. In 1855 a report was submitted by the commission making a number of practical recommendations, about half of which were adopted in the Mercantile Law Amendment Act, Scotland of 1856[2] and its English equivalent[3]. The Act affected a variety of areas, making changes in the law of sale, guarantees and cautionary obligations, bills of exchange, the liability of carriers, and aspects of shipping law. Although some attempt was made by the royal commission to assimilate Scots with English law (and this was purportedly done more to remove glaring anomalies than to assimilate for its own sake[4]), the courts, nonetheless, interpreted certain changes in the common law restrictively.

Section 5 of the 1856 Act was a notable example of an attempt to bring Scots law into line with that of England. In the Scots common law of sale there was an implied term of 'priceworthiness' whereby the buyer was entitled to expect that the quality of goods purchased would be commensurate with their price. The seller was under an obligation 'to supply a good article without defect, unless there are circumstances to show that an inferior article was agreed on'[5]. Under section 5 of the 1856 Act, however, if at the time of sale the seller did not have knowledge that the goods were defective or of bad quality, the goods with all faults were bought at the risk of the purchaser, unless they had expressly been sold for a specified and particular purpose, in which case the seller was to be taken to have warranted them as fit for that purpose. But the courts, when faced with this provision, restricted its application to the sale of specific goods, having a definite quantity or *corpus*, and also excluded its application where the goods failed to comply with their description under the contract[6]. Thus the impact of section 5 was minimised.

Similarly section 1 of the 1856 Act sought to assimilate Scots law to some extent with that of England. Under English law a purchaser could become the owner of goods on the completion of a consensual contract of sale. Under Scots law, ownership was achieved on delivery of the goods to the buyer. In Scotland, unlike England, this meant that if the buyer had paid the price for the goods but the seller became bankrupt he could not enforce delivery of the goods against the seller's creditors, but merely had to rank as a creditor himself. Section 1 of the 1856 Act did not seek to change the basic Scots common law rule on the passing of property, but rather provided a special rule to the effect that once goods had been sold, but remained in the custody of the seller, it would not be competent for a creditor of the seller to attach those goods by diligence or other process. Until the House of Lords case of *M'Bain v Wallace & Co* in 1881[7] the Court of Session gave this provision very limited application[8]. It is perhaps not surprising that piecemeal reform which was in conflict with the general principles of the common law did not meet with immediate success[9].

1 This is sometimes known as the 'Mercantile Law Commission'.
2 The commission leading to the Mercantile Law Amendment Act, Scotland, 1856 (c60) is assessed by one writer: 'they submitted about fifty-two practical recommendations, but of these about twenty-two only were adopted': J K 'On the Codification of Mercantile Law' 1880 J Juris 638 at 640.
3 Ie the Mercantile Law Amendment Act 1856 (c97).
4 See H Aitken 'The Present Position of Mercantile Law in Scotland' 1909 SLT (News) 5 at 8.
5 *Whealler v Methuen* (1843) 5 D 402 at 406, per Lord Justice-Clerk Hope. See also Lord Kilbrandon 'The Honest Merchant' (1967) 20 *Current Legal Problems* p 1.
6 *Jaffé v Ritchie* (1860) 23 D 242, and at 249 per Lord Justice-Clerk Inglis; *Hutchison & Co v Henry and Corrie* (1867) 6 M 57, 40 SJ 36. See also J J Gow *The Mercantile and Industrial Law of Scotland* (1964) pp 161–162, noting also that when the Mercantile Law Amendment Act Scotland 1856, s 5, was relevant it was applied rigorously.

7 *M'Bain v Wallace & Co* (1881) 8 R (HL) 106, 6 App Cas 588.

8 For a discussion of the case law, see 'The House of Lords on the Mercantile Law Amendment Act (section 1)' 1882 J Juris 25.

9 Lord Kilbrandon has even suggested that the Mercantile Law Amendment Act, Scotland, 1856 could have been struck down by the Court of Session as unconstitutional, in view of the Treaty of Union between Scotland and England, art 18: see Lord Kilbrandon *Scots Law seen from England* (Child Lecture 1980–81) p 6.

641. Bills of exchange. Reform of mercantile law did not stem merely from the reports of public bodies such as royal commissions. Several important statutes derive their existence from the work of private individuals and organisations. The historical accident of the English origins of this work and the initial English drafting of legislation ultimately destined to apply in Scotland as well as England have not been without significance for the way in which Scots commercial law has evolved.

This development can be seen initially in the work of Judge Chalmers, of the Birmingham County Court, who in the 1870s produced a digest of the English law on bills of exchange. The Institute of Bankers and the Associated Chambers of Commerce were impressed by this work and wished to see it have legislative authority. Chalmers drafted a 'codifying' Bill which was introduced into Parliament by a private member[1]. The Bill then was also applied to Scotland. At the time of the Bill's introduction the Faculty of Advocates, in making suggestions for its improvement in its application to Scotland, regretted that it had been originally drafted solely from the standpoint of the law of England and Ireland[2]. The result, however, was the Bills of Exchange Act 1882 (c 61) which in its principal provisions applies to both Scotland and England.

1 H Aitken 'The Present Position of Mercantile Law in Scotland' 1909 SLT (News) 5 at 12.

2 *Report by the Committee of the Faculty of Advocates on the Bills of Exchange Act 1882* in 1882 J Juris 381: 'It might with advantage have been framed from the first, as a British code upon its subjects, intended, after due comparison and selection, to write and combine the different local systems into one national whole. The expediency of having the same laws for the three Kingdoms with regard to instruments of such commmon occurrence as bills of exchange is plain; and though Scottish lawyers are placed at some disadvantage in being asked, after the measure has been prepared in terms of English law and upon English authorities exclusively, to consider whether it can be accepted for Scotland, there is fortunately less difficulty in this than in almost any other branch of law in arriving at substantial uniformity'.

642. Partnerships. A similar history can be seen with the Partnership Act 1890 (c 39), with the writings of Sir Frederick Pollock being the basis for a private member's Bill, which also applied to Scotland[1]. Although the 1890 Act has done much to assimilate English and Scots law, certain Scottish concepts, such as the personality of the firm as distinct from individual partners, were preserved as were areas of the common law affecting partnerships[2].

1 H Aitken 'The Present Position of Mercantile Law in Scotland' 1909 SLT (News) 5 at 12.

2 See J B Miller *The Law of Partnership in Scotland* (1973) pp 1, 2.

643. Sale of goods. Of greatest significance was the further work of Judge Chalmers in drafting in 1888 a Sale of Goods Bill which was intended to restate the English common law on sale. It was first introduced in Parliament in 1889[1] and at that time did not extend to Scotland. Significantly, however, from that first introduction, some members of the legal profession in Scotland took an interest in the Bill on the basis that its extension to Scotland could be expected[2]. In the House of Lords, Lord Watson, a Scots lawyer keen to see a gradual process of assimilation of Scots and English law[3], pressed for the extension of the Sale of Goods Bill to Scotland. An academic writer of the time analysed what this would mean for Scots law[4], given, in particular, that the Bill had the effect that property in goods could pass to the buyer at the time the contract was made, as opposed to the principle of Scots law that property passed only with delivery of the goods. Lord Watson proposed assimilation by yielding the Scottish principle[5]. He also favoured the introduction of the *actio quanti minoris*, which was recognised under English but not Scots law[6]. In 1892 the Bill was extended to Scotland. Lord Watson was not alone among prominent Scottish lawyers in favouring such changes, and his views were echoed by Lord McLaren[7]. Indeed, Richard Brown commented at the time:

> 'In regard to tradition it is surprising that the suggested adoption of the English principle has met with so little opposition in Scotland'[8].

In 1894 the Sale of Goods Act 1893 (c 71) came into force, providing for Scots, as well as for English law, that property passed under the contract, and that the *actio quanti minoris* should be a remedy of the buyer. The statute also throughout uses the English terminology of 'conditions' and 'warranties', although for Scots law any legal distinction between these terms was removed by interpretation provisions. This approach in the legislation did not aid certainty in the subsequent application of Scots law[9]. Criticism of this method of law reform is made by Aitken:

> 'To codify the law of one country is, as I have shewn, a work of the greatest difficulty. How immensely is that difficulty increased when we propose in one enactment to codify two separate and in many respects irreconcilable systems of law! And this had to be done, not by building up an Act from start to finish embracing both systems; but by taking an Act framed in view entirely of the law of England and endeavouring, by inserting a clause here and a clause there, to mould it so as to embrace Scots law. And the parties in Scotland who were consulted had no power to alter the Bill. All that they were asked to do, and did do, was to make suggestions, and these suggestions were then considered by the English lawyers who had drafted the Bill. Some suggestions were adopted and many were not'[10].

1 (1894) 10 SL Rev 59. J Mackintosh warned against the dangers of extending the Bill to Scotland in *Roman Law of Sale* (1st edn, 1892) Preface p vi.
2 See J G S 'Sale of Goods Bill' (1889) 1 JR 310, where it is observed at 311: '. . . the Committee of the Faculty of Advocates, which was appointed a few weeks ago to report upon the Bill, have wisely resolved, with the consent of the Faculty, to undertake the revision of the Bill, in the expectation that it may be ultimately extended to Scotland. More recently the Writers to the Signet and the Society of Solicitors before the Supreme Court have offered to co-operate with them in the work of revision, and the offer has been cheerfully accepted'. Contrast *Mackintosh*.
3 See the address of Lord Watson in 1883 to the Glasgow Juridical Society, published as 'Recent Legal Reform' in (1901) 13 JR 1 at 11, 12. His views have been criticised by T B Smith in *Property Problems in Sale* (1978) generally, and in 'Retention of Title: Lord Watson's Legacy' 1985 SLT (News) 105.
4 R Brown 'Assimilation of the Law of Sale' (1891) 3 JR 297.
5 *Brown* at 298. Yet 'property' is nowhere defined in the Act in relation to Scots Law.
6 *Brown* at 303.
7 John McLaren 'Lord President Inglis' (1892) 4 JR 14 at 18: '. . . we ought to give up the theoretical distinction that the risk only, and not the general property, is transferred by the contract of sale'.
8 R Brown 'The Sale of Goods Bill' (1892) 8 SL Rev 149 at 150. In this article he also discusses 'the elaborate report' of the Bills Committee of the Glasgow Faculty of Procurators, 'specially devoted to the adaptation of the bill to Scotland'.
9 See *Sale and Supply of Goods* (Scot Law Com Consultative Memorandum no. 58) at paras 2.33–2.36.
10 H Aitken 'The Present Position of Mercantile Law in Scotland' 1909 SLT (News) 5 at 13. He also notes that even when it was intended from the start to apply the Marine Insurance Act 1906 (c 41) to both countries the Bill was drafted by English lawyers with exclusive reference to English law. See also T B Smith *Property Problems in Sale* (1978) pp 12–17.

644. Assimilation of Scots and English mercantile law. These attempts at assimilation of the mercantile laws of Scotland and England were, therefore, somewhat one-sided in approach. Moreover, even as regards English law they were not measures of codification in the continental sense of a comprehensive set of legal rules relating to an entire area of the law, but rather were collections of the principal rules on a given topic supplemented by the common law, which of course differed in both jurisdictions. Although there may have been some support in Scotland for assimilation of commercial law with that of England, and for 'codification', the history of legal development in that area from the mid-nineteenth to the early twentieth century was not that of systematic law reform.

645. Bankruptcy and debt recovery. Just as commercial development in Scotland required greater sophistication in mercantile laws to regulate the wealth-creating aspects of that progress, so also there was a need to develop the statutory rules governing the consequences of economic failure. Thus the law of bankruptcy was subject to a considerable number of reforms throughout these times. An example of this was the Bankruptcy (Scotland) Act of 1839[1], the drafting of which had been under the supervision of George Joseph Bell. Its aims were to make sequestration more generally available, to reduce expense and delay in the operation of the sequestration process and to extend sequestration to the estates of deceased debtors[2]. Also of great importance was the reforming and consolidating Bankruptcy (Scotland) Act 1856 (c 79). Reforms under this Act were to render sequestration not only competent in relation to the moveable estates of trading debtors, as under the previous law, but to widen the process to include the moveable and heritable estates of all debtors, whether they were traders or not, and whether they were alive or dead. The sheriff courts, moreover, were given jurisdiction to hear applications for sequestration regarding debtors within their respective jurisdictions. Subject to court approval, it was also made competent for a sequestration to be held annulled and the estate wound up under a deed of arrangement agreed on by a majority of the creditors[3]. The 1856 Act remained the key piece of bankruptcy legislation throughout the nineteenth century, but it was subject to considerable amendment and addition[4].

An important change in the character of debt recovery came with the Debtors (Scotland) Act 1880 (c 34) which abolished imprisonment for civil debt, with the notable exceptions of sums decerned for aliment and debts in the form of taxes, fines and penalties owed to the Crown, or for rates or assessments[5]. This also had significance for the process of personal diligence for a civil debt known as *cessio*. This was governed by the Cessio (Scotland) Act 1836 (c 56), and had been a means of avoiding imprisonment for debt by the debtor surrendering all his property to his creditors, including that subsequently acquired, and obtaining discharge only when his creditors had been paid in full[6]. *Cessio* differed from sequestration in that it was conducted exclusively in the sheriff courts and the creditors played a passive role, having no direct control over the estate, this being managed by the trustee as an officer of the court rather than as a representative of the creditors[7]. Following the 1880 reform came the Bankruptcy and Cessio (Scotland) Act 1881 (c 22), under which, as Fyfe explains:

'... Cessio had become — nominally a summary process for the distribution of a debtor's estate amongst all his creditors — but really in practice a form of diligence for exacting payment of an individual creditor's debt'[8].

The law on imprisonment for alimentary debts was changed by the Civil Imprisonment (Scotland) Act 1882 (c 42). Imprisonment by personal diligence for this kind of debt was abolished as such, although it was still possible by means of a direct warrant of the sheriff in cases of failure to pay aliment for which decree had been granted when the debtor had the means of paying.

Appeals for further reform of the law of bankruptcy were made in the late nineteenth century[9] and in 1907 a private member's Bill was introduced, but it did not reach the Statute Book. In 1908, however, the Secretary of State for Scotland appointed a Departmental Committee on the Bankruptcy Laws, chaired by Sheriff (later Lord) Cullen[10]. The committee reported in 1910 and its recommendations led to the Bankruptcy (Scotland) Act 1913 (c 20). For some this Act was a disappointment[11], as its reforms were not radical and its importance was more as a consolidating measure. Significantly, however, it abolished the process of *cessio* and introduced a new summary sequestration in the sheriff courts for estates whose assets, it was estimated, did not exceed £300[12]. At that time Goudy hoped that the 1913 Act paved the way for a bankruptcy code for the United Kingdom, the laws of both jurisdictions by then having been assimilated in many respects[13].

1 The Bankruptcy (Scotland) Act 1839 (c 41) was amended by the Bankruptcy (Scotland) Act 1853 (c 53).
2 See H Goudy *The Law of Bankruptcy in Scotland* (4th edn, 1914 by T A Fyfe) p 4.
3 *Goudy* p 5; J J Gow *The Mercantile and Industrial Law of Scotland* (1964) p 617.
4 See the Bankruptcy (Scotland) Amendment Act 1860 (c 33); Conveyancing (Scotland) Act 1874 (c 94); Bankruptcy (Scotland) Act 1875 (c 26); Conveyancing (Scotland) Act 1874 Amendment Act 1879 (c 40); and the Conveyancing (Scotland) Acts (1874 and 1879) Amendment Act 1887 (c 69). See T A Fyfe *The Bankruptcy Code* (1913) p 2.
5 *Goudy* at p 7: 'The Act was also declared not to apply to persons bound by an obligation *ad factum praestandum*, nor to affect proceedings under *meditatione fugae* warrants. In respect of none of the excepted cases was a debtor to be imprisoned for a larger period than one year'.
6 A Mackenzie *Manual of the Law of Cessio* (1887) p 1.
7 *Goudy* p 8.
8 *Fyfe* p 3.
9 'Bankruptcy Reform' (1887) 3 SL Rev 113.
10 1910 SLT (News) 100.
11 See 'Bankruptcy Reform' (1913) 29 SL Rev 125, and W Wallace 'The New Bankruptcy Bill' (1913) 25 JR 136.
12 See *Fyfe* at pp 4, 5.
13 *Goudy* p 11.

(c) Land Law

646. Entails. An important area of the law governing land tenure, which saw progressive reform throughout the nineteenth century and into the early twentieth century, was that of the law of entails or tailzies. Entails were a means whereby a proprietor of heritable property could regulate the order of succession to that property. Menzies explains this system:

'Entails were a necessary consequence of the feudal system, and of the law of primogeniture, which was indispensable to the maintenance of that system. The object being to perpetuate estates in the same families, the purpose of the entail is to determine, throughout the future succession, what particular person shall be the proprietor to the exclusion of all others, and so to limit his powers of disposal and administration as to prevent alienation or mortgage of the estate during the successive generations. Thus, by the limitation of the succession to one heir, the estate was preserved from disruption by being divided and it was secured against dilapidation and alienation by the fetters imposed upon every succeeding proprietor'[1].

The Entail Act 1685 (c 26) was the statutory base from which the system of entails grew[2]. Gradually more and more land became the subject of entails[3]. The restrictions of this system of land holding soon were seen, however, to lead to serious economic problems for both proprietors and society at large. The proprietor's inability to raise finance on the security of his land to make improvements and the status of entailed land as *extra commercium*, at a time when land was probably the most important of commodities, were sources of economic stagnation which required to be alleviated[4]. The first statutory qualifications to strict entail came with the Montgomery Act of 1770[5] and the Aberdeen Act of 1824[6]. The general objectives of these enactments were to give the entailed proprietor greater power to grant leases, expend money on improving the estate and grant excambions, exchanging limited portions of the estate for other land. Power was also given to the proprietor to grant an annuity from the estate for the benefit of his wife, and to make financial provision for those children who would not succeed to the estate. These were the first in a series of reforms.

Following the failure of a House of Commons select committee of 1828, whose Bill of 1829 for the reform of entails was rejected on the grounds of its defects, a further select committee was appointed which reported in 1833[7]. Its Bill, drafted with the aim of the assimilation of the Scots law of entails with that of England, and in English terminology, was not only criticised on that account, but also because its provisions would not have cured the ills it sought to amend[8]. Although the power of the heir of entail of leasing and of excambion were developed further in the Rosebery Act of 1836[9], it was not until an Act of 1848[10], sponsored by Lord Rutherfurd, that substantial reform was achieved. By this Act irrevocable entail was overtaken by the possibility of disentail. The statute also introduced rules whereby if an entail were defective in one respect it was to be deemed invalid and ineffectual in all respects. Thus there were created opportunities of striking down an entail through some technical defect in its constitution or of extinguishing it by the heir of entail exercising his option of disentail. Of the practical effects of this reform, however, McLaren later was to comment:

> 'I do not believe it will accomplish the object which its author is understood to have had in view — the gradual extinction of entail; and for this reason, that its provisions are merely permissive, and they can only be put in force by the heirs of entail themselves — that is, by the parties who are most strongly interested in maintaining the system. According to Lord Rutherfurd's Act an heir born after 1st August, 1848, on coming into possession of the estate, and being of full age, may disentail the estate. But, as the law stands, he may immediately re-entail it, either upon the same or upon a different series of heirs; and the new entail, on being recorded, will be binding until the estate shall come into the possession of an heir born after its date — that is, at least, for two generations. It will be binding not only against the maker and his successors, but against creditors whose rights are subsequent to it in date. No doubt the power of disentailing will be largely used for the purpose of paying off or securing family provisions; but there is just as little doubt that, as soon as those objects are accomplished, the estate will be re-entailed, and very little entailed land will find its way into the market. The effect of Lord Rutherfurd's Act, when it comes into full operation, is to place the law of entail in Scotland on the same footing as that of England; and the practice in England has been, to settle a property after getting as much money as is required secured upon it. The effect of such a system upon the cultivation of the soil is even worse than that of a system of strict entail'[11].

McLaren saw the real difficulty, therefore, as being the power to re-entail the estate, and he argued that the only way by which the land of the country really could become a marketable commodity was the removal of the landowner's power to entail. Reforms relating to entails throughout the remainder of the nineteenth century, however, were merely refinements of procedure or further removals of the restrictions of entails[12]. Problems stemming from entails meanwhile kept the legal profession in Scotland busy[13]. It was not until the Entail (Scotland) Act 1914 (c 43), which was the fruit of the labours of the Lord Advocate's Conveyancing Committee, that the power to entail was finally abolished[14].

1 A Menzies *Conveyancing according to the Law of Scotland* (4th edn, 1900 by J S Sturrock) p 719. 'The word Entail, or Tailzie, is derived from the French *tailler*, to cut, and it expresses an act or deed by which the legal line of succession to a property is cut off, and an arbitrary series of heirs fixed to take the inheritance in their order to the exclusion of the heirs-at-law': p 720.

2 Although there is debate as to the source of entails in Scots law, T B Smith identified origins through Roman law in 'Trusts and Fiduciary Relationships in the Law of Scotland' in his *Studies Critical and Comparative* (1962) pp 204, 205, whereas others have seen them as a creation of statute (*Menzies*, p 719), or as a development under the feudal law which was secured by statute (R Burgess *Perpetuities in Scots Law* (Stair Soc vol 31, 1979) pp 62–64, 69–80; J H R 'Entails in Scotland' (1896) 3 SLT (News) 284; A M Bell *Lectures on Conveyancing* (3rd edn, 1882) p 104).

3 J H R 'Entails in Scotland' (1896) 3 SLT (News) 284 refers to the work of Patrick Irvine WS *Considerations on the Inexpediency of the Law of Entails in Scotland* (1826), where he stated 'about one-half of the territorial property of the kingdom is now, or will very soon be, under the fetters of entail, and the proprietors subjected to all the inconveniences attending their restricted rights of property'.

4 Of the theory of entails John (later Lord) McLaren was to state in a paper of the Scottish Law Amendment Society 'On the Law of Entail' 1869 J Juris 436 at 439, 440: 'When a legislator has desired to tie the hands of his successors, the pretension has appeared inconsistent and futile. Yet this privilege has been successfully claimed by private individuals who, in pure caprice, have adjected conditions to the enjoyment of estates which are of no possible benefit to society, and are, for the most part, either vexatious or frivolous. It is, of course, impossible that any one should pretend to know what conditions of possession are fit to be observed by his successors generations after he has ceased to exist; and it is equally impossible that he should know what are the proper uses to which his property can be applied under unforeseen conditions and states of society'.

5 Ie the Entail Improvement Act 1770 (c 51).

6 Ie the Entail Provisions Act 1824 (c 87).

7 See *Burgess* at p 105.

8 That was the conclusion of the Lords of Session in their reply when consulted on the Entails (Scotland) Bill 163 Parl Papers (1835) xlvi; *Burgess* p 105.

9 Ie the Entail Powers Act 1836 (c 42), amended by the Entailed Lands etc (Scotland) Act 1841 (c 24).

10 Ie the Entail Amendment Act 1848 (c 36).

11 John McLaren 'On the Law of Entail' 1869 J Juris 436 at 440, 441.

12 See the Entail Amendment Act 1853 (c 94); the Entail Amendment (Scotland) Acts 1868 (c 84), 1875 (c 61) and 1878 (c 28); and the Entail (Scotland) Act 1882 (c 53).

13 Eg between the years 1876 and 1878, as regards proceedings before the Court of Session relating to entails, the average annual number of petitions was ninety-three, and there were also from twenty to thirty actions annually depending on the court. See 'The Entail Amendment (Scotland) Bill 1879' 1879 J Juris 350 at 360.

14 For a discussion of the persistence of old entails into the twentieth century, see H H Monteath 'Heritable Rights from Early Times to the Twentieth Century' in *An Introduction to Scottish Legal History* (Stair Soc vol 20, 1958) p 156 at p 177; and *Burgess* pp 109, 110.

647. Conveyancing. Conveyancing reform had as its aim the simplification and rationalisation of the law relating to the transfer of interests in land, yet the overall approach adopted to further that objective was a long history of piece-meal legislative attempts. Loewensohn comments:

'According to the "Table of Conveyancing Statutes" no less than 52 conveyancing Statutes were passed during the period of less than 80 years (1845–1924). The reason for this deplorable state of legislation is that these Statutes contain mostly amend-ments of amendments arising from a spirit of opportunism rather than looking to the future. Thus the conveyancing reforms are more like a patch-work which cannot last for a considerable time'[1].

The origins of the initial reforms of this period, however, were in the recommendations of the royal commission, appointed in 1837 and reporting in 1838, under the chairmanship of George Joseph Bell. These recommendations were implemented in stages[2]. One of the first significant enactments in this series was the Infeftment Act 1845 (c 35), which dispensed with the ceremony of symbolical delivery in the transfer of land. In its place sasine and infeftment could be acquired by a new form of precept of sasine, authorising a notary public to grant sasine, which he could do by recording an instrument of sasine at any time during the life of the party in whose favour it was made out. In turn the instrument of sasine was to become superfluous under the Titles to Land (Scotland) Act 1858, whereby it was competent and sufficient for a person in whose favour a conveyance had been granted to record the conveyance itself in the Register of Sasines. This was to have the same force and effect as if the recording of the conveyance had been followed by the recording of an instrument of sasine[3]. These provisions were later to be re-enacted in the Titles to Land Consolidation (Scotland) Act 1868 (c 101)[4], and are examples of the simplification of conveyancing procedures which gradually were facilitated.

In respect of the administration of conveyancing, there was considerable debate over a period of years within the legal profession regarding the centralisation of the Register of Sasines. From the late 1850s individuals and professional bodies sought abolition of the local land registers. It was argued that the local registers were often inaccurately kept and that in any event their very existence caused extra expense and inconvenience necessitated by the double searching of both the particular and the general registers. A select committee of the House of Commons heard conflicting arguments on the desirability of one central register, but in 1866 reported in favour of this solution. Under the Land Registers (Scotland) Act 1868 (c 64) the local registers were phased out[5] and a comprehensive General Register of Sasines was established[6].

Another important statute of this period was the Conveyancing (Scotland) Act 1874 (c 94). Significantly under this Act the period for positive prescription was reduced from forty to twenty years, but subject to a reservation, in favour of persons under the age of majority or subject to legal disability, suspending the running of time during such periods of disability, and extending the prescriptive period up to a maximum of thirty years. This thirty-year period for positive prescription in practice became the rule, however, rather than the exception. The removal of this relaxation for periods of legal disability came with the Conveyancing (Scotland) Act 1924 (c 27), which resulted from the work of the Lord Advocate's Conveyancing Committee[7]. Of note among the reforms contained in the 1924 Act was a reduction in the period of the long negative prescription from forty to twenty years. This did not apply to all claims, but only to those relating to heritable right and title, with the exception of servitudes, public rights of way and other public rights. Following the objective of the simplification and modernisation of conveyancing, the statute rendered notarial instruments unnecessary, extended the function of warrants of registration, provided that all entries in the personal registers were to prescribe in five years[8] and, generally, sought to shorten deeds.

One important area of conveyancing where reform was not achieved in this period, however, related to the question of the introduction of a system of registration of title. In 1906 a royal commission under the chairmanship of Lord Dunedin was appointed to consider this question. The commission reported in 1910, but was divided in its opinion on the desirability of registration of title, and the matter was taken no further at that stage[9].

1 L Loewensohn 'Recast of the Conveyancing Statutes' (1942) 58 SL Rev 129 at 130.

2 'Once a beginning was made, one Act followed another, in rapid succession, with the final result that many unnecessary proceedings have been abolished or superseded, and short forms of writ substituted for the burdensome and verbose deeds which were formerly the products of our system of conveyancing. From an intellectual point of view, conveyancing has, as a result of the statutory conveyancing under the guidance of this Commission, become more a science than an art': L Ockrent *Land Rights, An Enquiry into the History of Registration for Publication in Scotland* (1942) pp 115, 116.

3 Titles to Land (Scotland) Act 1858 (c 76), s 1 (repealed). The conveyance was to be presented for registration with a warrant for registration.

4 See also the Titles to Land Consolidation (Scotland) Amendment Act 1869 (c 116).

5 The last local register was phased out by December 1871.

6 See *Ockrent* pp 139–142.

7 See C Mackintosh 'The Conveyancing (Scotland) Act 1924' 1924 SLT (News) 153; and 'The Conveyancing (Scotland) Act 1924' (1924) 40 SL Rev 261, 293.

8 The Conveyancing (Scotland) Act 1874 had introduced a five-year restriction only for inhibitions, thus in all other respects still requiring a forty-year search of the personal registers against the seller and all previous proprietors, covering their respective periods of ownership within the prescriptive period.

9 'The ideal of registration of title was not advanced by this report. The lack of unanimity amongst the Commissioners themselves for one thing, and the overwhelming opposition of the legal profession for another . . . put an end, temporarily at least, to any hopes that Scotland would fall into line with other countries in accepting a system of registration which is steadily encircling the globe': *Ockrent* p 155. See also R Whyte 'Conveyancing Bill' 1912 28 SL Rev 121. For further details of the reforms of this period, see *Ockrent* pp 109–160, and H H Monteath 'Heritable Rights from Early Times to the Twentieth Century' in *An Introduction to Scottish Legal History* (Stair Soc vol 20, 1958) p 156.

(d) Family Law

648. The married woman. Social reform in the nineteenth century witnessed the beginning of the legal emancipation of the married woman. There was plenty of scope for reform, as is explained by Clive:

'In 1830 the husband's legal supremacy was undoubted. The wife's moveable property became his property: the children of the marriage were, for purposes of guardianship, custody and access, his children: the wife's domicile followed that of her husband automatically: she had hardly any contractual capacity: she was "in a manner, in a state of wardship or minority under the husband" — a "peculiar and inferior condition"'[1].

Although some of these inequalities were not to be removed until the mid-twentieth century, law reform first concerned itself with the property consequences of marriage.

In the absence of an antenuptial or postnuptial contract to contrary effect, on marriage an implied assignation operated in the husband's favour giving him complete control of his wife's moveable estate for most practical purposes[2]. This was known as the *ius mariti*[3], from which was excepted only the wife's 'paraphernalia', or personal effects and their repositories. Even as regards moveable property which was effectively retained by the wife, her paraphernalia and heritable estate, the husband still retained a curatorial right of administration, or *ius administrationis*. Under this regime all the wife's acts in relation to her property required the consent of her husband, although he was under a duty to exercise his power in her interests and could not withhold his consent arbitrarily.

The first reform restricted the husband's *ius mariti* and his *ius administrationis*, and came with the Conjugal Rights (Scotland) Amendment Act 1861 (c 86). This limited the *ius mariti* in situations where the wife acquired right to property other than by her own efforts, such as by succession or donation, to the effect that the husband had no claim to it unless he made reasonable provision from the property for his wife's maintenance, this having been requested by her[4]. The *ius administrationis* was also excluded where the wife had been deserted and had obtained a protection order against her husband, as regards property acquired after desertion, or as regards property acquired after a decree of separation[5]. In respect of the signing of deeds relating to the wife's estate, the court could also dispense with the husband's consent where the wife had been deserted or the spouses had separated by consent.

Then came the Married Women's Property (Scotland) Act 1877 (c 29), under which the wife was freed of the *ius mariti* and *ius administrationis* as regards earnings from her own employment, business or other exercise of skills[6]. Further, the Married Women's Policies of Assurance (Scotland) Act 1880 (c 26) permitted a married woman to take out insurance on her own life or that of her husband, the policy vesting in her without being subject to the *ius mariti*. Finally, the Married Women's Property (Scotland) Act 1881 (c 21) abolished the *ius mariti*, and the Married Women's Property (Scotland) Act 1920 (c 64)[7] abolished the *ius administrationis*[8].

1 E M Clive *The Law of Husband and Wife in Scotland* (2nd edn, 1982) p 11.
2 The restriction was that 'he could not do any deed which injured his wife's interest without any benefit to himself or which took effect against her only as at his death': G C H Paton 'Husband and Wife: Property Rights and Relationships' in *An Introduction to Scottish Legal History* (Stair Soc vol 20, 1958) p 99 at p 100.
3 See Lord Fraser *Husband and Wife* (2nd edn, 1876) pp 676, 679.
4 See *Fraser* pp 830–836.
5 See *Paton* pp 104, 105.
6 Ie provided these earnings were independent from any business association with her husband: *M'Ginty v M'Alpine* (1892) 19 R 935; *Dryden v M'Gibbon* 1907 SC 1131, 15 SLT 125.
7 This Act also abolished the common law rule that donations between spouses were revocable during the donor's lifetime, with the exception of donations made less than a year and a day before the donor's sequestration, which were to remain revocable at the instance of the donor's creditors.
8 For further details on these reforms, see *Paton* pp 100–108; *Clive* pp 295–299; and *Matrimonial Property* (Sc Law Com Consultative Memorandum no. 57) (1983) pp 2–9.

649. Marriage and divorce. Reform of the law relating to marriage proceeded in piecemeal fashion[1], but a gradual widening and secularisation of the procedure leading to marriage was introduced. The Marriage (Scotland) Act 1834 (c 28) permitted priests or ministers who were not of the established Church to celebrate marriage. The Marriage Notice (Scotland) Act 1878 (c 43) introduced a form of notice to a registrar regarding intention to marry, as an alternative to the use of wedding banns[2], and the Marriage (Scotland) Act 1939 (c 34) provided for civil marriage before an authorised registrar[3]. The 1939 Act also abolished irregular marriages[4], with the exception of marriage by cohabitation with habit and repute.

In 1850 a Royal Commission on Divorce was appointed, which reported in 1853. In Scotland the reforms which followed were primarily of a procedural nature. For instance, the Conjugal Rights (Scotland) Amendment Act 1861 (c 86) enabled a Lord Ordinary to hear in one action not only proceedings for divorce, but also a husband's claim for damages and expenses from his wife's paramour, in cases of adultery, and further to settle the custody of pupil children of the marriage. By the Sheriff Courts (Scotland) Acts of 1907 (c 51) and 1913 (2 & 3 Geo 5 c 28) the sheriff courts also gained jurisdiction to hear actions for separation and aliment, adherence and aliment, interim aliment and custody[5].

On the substantive law of divorce, since the Act of the Scots Parliament of 1573[6] the grounds of divorce had been adultery and desertion, but this was altered by the Divorce (Scotland) Act 1938 (c 50). Added to the matrimonial offences justifying divorce were cruelty, sodomy and bestiality; the period for desertion was shortened from four to three years; and divorce could also be granted on the ground of the incurable insanity of a spouse. The 1938 Act further permitted the dissolution of a marriage on the ground of the presumed death of a spouse[7].

1 E M Clive *The Law of Husband and Wife in Scotland* (2nd edn, 1982) pp 8–10.
2 This followed the recommendations of the Royal Commission on the Laws of Marriage, which was appointed in 1865 and reported in 1868.
3 This followed recommendations made as far back as 1868 by the Royal Commission on the Laws of Marriage, but also followed those of the Departmental Committee on the Marriage Laws of Scotland (the Morison Committee), which was appointed in 1935 and reported in 1937.
4 Ie as recommended by the 1868 royal commission and the Morison Committee.
5 See *Clive* pp 12–14.
6 Divorce for Desertion Act 1573 (c 1).
7 See *Clive* pp 11, 12.

(5) THE LAW REFORM COMMITTEE FOR SCOTLAND

650. Constitution. The Law Reform Committee for Scotland was set up by the Lord Advocate on 2 December 1954. It had both an initiating and a responsive function: to bring to the attention of the Lord Advocate aspects of the law which seemed to require consideration; and to consider these or other aspects of the law which might be remitted to the Committee by the Lord Advocate[1]. The committee was a part-time body, comprising about a dozen members of varied legal experience. It was presided over by a Court of Session judge[2], and included representatives of the senior and junior Bar, the sheriff court bench, the Law Society of Scotland and the universities. The secretariat was provided by the Lord Advocate's Department. Because of its part-time membership the committee's work tended to concern relatively small areas of the law, rather than the wide-ranging, comprehensive reviews undertaken later by the Scottish Law Commission.

1 See the *First Report of the Law Reform Committee for Scotland* (1957) (Cmnd 88) p 5.
2 The first Chairman was Lord Walker, who in fact presided over the committee during the preparation of all its fourteen reports. He was succeeded in 1964 by Lord Kissen. Upon the setting up of the Scottish Law Commisson in June 1965 the committee was not formally abolished, but was given no further work to do. In the early 1970s it was wound up at Lord Kissen's suggestion.

651. The 1st report: occupiers' liability. The first report of the Law Reform Committee for Scotland concerned the law relating to:
(1) the liability of an occupier of land or other property to persons suffering injury while on the property, and
(2) the obligations of a lessor towards third persons invited, or allowed, by the lessee to be on the subjects let[1].
At common law the liability of an occupier of premises for loss, injury or damage was merely an aspect of *culpa*. In 1929, however, the English categories of invitee, licensee and trespasser were superimposed upon the common law by the House of Lords decision in the *Addie* case[2]. The main feature of the post-1929 law was that, as a general rule, an occupier owed no duty to a trespasser.

Subsequently the new law was widely criticised as having introduced narrow, rigid and ambiguous distinctions[3]. In particular, it was scarcely apt to deal with cases of injury to small children. Strong criticism was advanced in both Divisions of the Inner House[4]. The Law Reform Committee for Scotland recommended that these categories should be abolished, and that the standard of care should be determined by the whole circumstances of the particular case — in effect, that liability should depend on the broad general principle of *culpa*[5]. The committee's recommendations were implemented by the Occupiers' Liability (Scotland) Act 1960 (c 30).

1 *First Report of the Law Reform Committee for Scotland* (1957) (Cmnd 88).
2 *Dumbreck v Robert Addie & Sons (Collieries) Ltd* 1929 SC (HL) 51, 1929 SLT 242. Both Viscount Dunedin and Lord Shaw of Dunfermline expressly stated that these three categories formed part of the law of Scotland.
3 See eg *First Report* para 22.
4 *M'Phail v Lanarkshire County Council* 1951 SC 301 at 314, 1951 SLT 32 at 36, per Lord President Cooper, and at 319 and at 38 per Lord Keith; *Mooney v Lanarkshire County Council* 1954 SC 245 at 250, 1954 SLT 137 at 139, per Lord Justice-Clerk Thomson; *Plank v Stirling Magistrates* 1956 SC 92 at 104, 1956 SLT 83 at 85, 86, per Lord Justice-Clerk Thomson.
5 *First Report* para 24.

652. The 2nd report: actions of removing and ejection. The second report of the Law Reform Committee for Scotland concerned procedural law relating to actions of removing and actions of ejection[1]. The committee interpreted this remit as excluding matters of substantive law affecting the rights and obligations of landlord and tenant, but as embracing all forms of process whereby owners of heritable property sought to recover possession from occupiers. The most important recommendation was that one form of action should be provided. This proposal was subsequently endorsed by the Grant Committee[2] and was implemented by the Sheriff Courts (Scotland) Act 1971, which applied the new summary cause procedure to such actions[3]. Other recommendations, dealing with the period, form and content of notices terminating tenancies, the right or title of parties to give notice and take recovery proceedings, the effect of decrees, and the requirement of caution for violent profits, have not been implemented[4].

1 *Second Report of the Law Reform Committee for Scotland* (1957) (Cmnd 114).
2 *The Sheriff Court* (1967) (Cmnd 3248).
3 Sheriff Courts (Scotland) Act 1971 (c 58), s 35.
4 The Scottish Law Commission has recently returned to this theme: see its Consultative Memorandum no. 59 (1984), and the Research Paper on Actions of Ejection and Removing prepared by A G M Duncan WS and published for the commission in January 1984.

653. The 3rd report: interest on damages. In a brief third report on the rules governing the date from which interest on an award of damages is, or may be, ordered by the court to run[1], the Law Reform Committee for Scotland recommended that the courts be given a discretion to award interest on damages from the date of citation. The previous practice had been for interest to be awarded from the date of decree. The recommendation was implemented by the Interest on Damages (Scotland) Act 1958 (c 61)[2].

1 *Third Report of the Law Reform Committee for Scotland* (1957) (Cmnd 141).
2 The courts' powers were extended by the Interest on Damages (Scotland) Act 1971 (c 31) so that interest may now be awarded from the date when the right of action arose.

654. The 4th report: insurance law. The fourth report of the Law Reform Committee for Scotland concerns the effect on the liability of insurance companies of special conditions and exceptions in insurance policies and of non-disclosure of facts by persons effecting such policies[1]. The committee was principally concerned with the contractual right of the parties to make any term material, whether or not it was in fact material to the risk; and with the effect of the insured's failure to disclose material facts. On the second point the common law test is that the insured must disclose any fact 'which any reasonable man might suppose could in any way influence the insurers in considering and deciding whether they will enter into the contract'[2]. The committee did not recommend any change to the law, and accordingly no legislation ensued. More recently the Law Commission (for England and Wales) has made recommendations *inter alia* on these aspects of insurance law[3], but its report has not yet been implemented.

1 *Fourth Report of the Law Reform Committee for Scotland* (1957) (Cmnd 330).
2 *Life Association of Scotland v Foster* (1873) 11 M 351 at 359, per Lord President Inglis.
3 *Insurance Law: Non-disclosure and Breach of Warranty* (Law Com no. 104; Cmnd 8064 (1980)).

655. The 5th report: reciprocal enforcement of maintenance orders. The fifth report of the Law Reform Committee for Scotland concerned the need for provision allowing the enforcement in Scotland of orders for maintenance made by the courts of other Commonwealth countries (except England and Wales) and, reciprocally, the enforcement in those other countries of orders for aliment made by Scottish courts[1]. The object of the committee's recommendations was to facilitate the reciprocal enforcement in Commonwealth countries of orders for aliment made by the Scottish courts, and *vice versa* — a course which had previously been recommended by the Royal Commission on Marriage and Divorce[2]. Arrangements of this nature had existed between other parts of the United Kingdom and Commonwealth countries since 1920[3], but were not at that time extended to Scotland. The committee's recommendations were implemented by the Maintenance Orders (Reciprocal Enforcement) Act 1972 (c 18).

1 *Fifth Report of the Law Reform Committee for Scotland* (1956) (Cmnd 449).
2 *Marriage and Divorce* (1955) (Cmnd 9678).
3 See the Maintenance Orders (Facilities for Enforcement) Act 1920 (c 33).

656. The 6th report: taxation of damages. The sixth report of the Law Reform Committee for Scotland concerned the relevance, in a question of the assessment of damages, of any liability to tax of the person entitled to the damages, with particular reference to the decision in *British Transport Commission v Gourley*[1]. The committee's remit followed on the decision of the House of Lords in that case[2] that, under English law, in assessing damages for loss of earnings through personal injuries, there should be taken into account the liability to tax which the injured person would have incurred if he had received the lost earnings. Subsequently that case was distinguished in the Inner House[3]. Subject to reservations expressed in the appendix to its report, the committee endorsed the principle laid down in the *Gourley* case, without recommending legislation.

1 *Sixth Report of the Law Reform Committee for Scotland* (1959) (Cmnd 635).
2 *British Transport Commission v Gourley* [1956] AC 185, [1955] 3 All ER 796, HL.
3 *Spencer v Macmillan's Trustees* 1958 SC 300, 1959 SLT 41. See T B Smith *A Short Commentary on the Law of Scotland* (1962) pp 864, 865.

657. The 7th report: actions of aliment in the sheriff courts. In its seventh report the Law Reform Committee for Scotland turned its attention to the procedure in actions in the sheriff court between spouses for payment of aliment[1]. The Royal Commission on Marriage and Divorce had recommended[2] that a simplified procedure should be introduced in the sheriff courts where a wife claims aliment on behalf of herself or her children; and the committee was asked to consider how this recommendation might be implemented. The committee's proposals envisaged that the old small debt procedure should apply, and this was achieved by the Sheriff Courts (Civil Jurisdiction and Procedure) (Scotland) Act 1963[3]. The financial limits in the 1963 Act have been regularly updated, and the summary cause procedure now applies[4].

1 *Seventh Report of the Law Reform Committee for Scotland* (1959) (Cmnd 907).
2 *Marriage and Divorce* (1955) (Cmnd 9678) Recommendation 68.
3 Sheriff Courts (Civil Jurisdiction and Procedure) (Scotland) Act 1963 (c 22), s 3.
4 Ibid, s 3, was amended by the Divorce (Scotland) Act 1976 (c 39), s 8, and the Sheriff Courts (Civil Jurisdiction and Procedure) (Scotland) Act 1963 (Interim Aliment) Order 1983, SI 1983/1445, and substituted by the Family Law (Scotland) Act 1985 (c 37), s 23, so that the limits are now £70 per week (claim by wife or child over the age of eighteen) and £35 per week (claim on behalf of child under the age of eighteen).

658. The 8th report: floating charges. The eighth report of the Law Reform Committee for Scotland concerned the constitution of security over moveable property, and also floating charges[1]. At common law it was not possible for a debtor to create in favour of his creditor a real security over corporeal moveables without delivery or its equivalent. This meant that a real security could not be created if the debtor was to retain the use and benefit of the property. The committee therefore recommended the introduction of the floating charge, which could be created over all or any of the borrowing company's property (whether heritable or moveable). At that time no recommendation was made for the introduction of receivers[2]. The committee's recommendations were implemented by the Companies (Floating Charges) (Scotland) Act 1961 (c 46)[3].

1 *Eighth Report of the Law Reform Committee for Scotland* (1960) (Cmnd 1017).
2 This was later recommended by the Scottish Law Commission: *Report on the Companies (Floating Charges) (Scotland) Act 1961* (Scot Law Com no. 14; Cmnd 4336 (1970)): see para 680 below.
3 See now the Companies Act 1985 (c 6), Pt XVIII (ss 462–487).

659. The 9th report: powers of trustees and variation of trust purposes. The ninth report of the Law Reform Committee for Scotland concerned the powers of trustees to sell, purchase or otherwise deal with heritable property, and the variation of trust purposes[1]. Under the Trusts (Scotland) Act 1921[2], as interpreted, the extent of a trustee's power to sell heritable property was uncertain, in the absence of a specific power in the trust deed. That Act conferred no power on a trustee to purchase heritable property: in the absence of a specific power in the trustee, a trustee might have recourse to the *nobile officium* of the Court of Session. The committee therefore recommended that there should be a general power to purchase heritable property, and that purchasers should have no concern with the power of trustees to sell heritable property. The committee further recommended that the Scottish courts be given wide powers to approve the variation and revocation of trust purposes. These recommendations were implemented by the Trusts (Scotland) Act 1961 (c 57).

1 *Ninth Report of the Law Reform Committee for Scotland* (1960) (Cmnd 1102).
2 Trusts (Scotland) Act 1921 (c 58), s 4.

660. The 10th report: damages for injuries causing death. The tenth report of the Law Reform Committee for Scotland concerned the title of a person's relatives to sue in respect of the death of that person, with particular reference to *Laidlaw v National Coal Board*[1], and the right to solatium for the death of a relative or spouse[2]. The committee made recommendations to extend further the rights of relatives to sue for solatium and damages for loss of support. A mother was to have a right to sue in respect of the death of her child during the father's lifetime, and *vice versa*; and the parents of an illegitimate child were to have the same rights to sue in respect of his death as if he were legitimate. These recommendations were implemented by the Law Reform (Damages and Solatium) (Scotland) Act 1962 (c 42)[3].

1 *Laidlaw v National Coal Board* 1957 SC 49, 1957 SLT 125.
2 *Tenth Report of the Law Reform Committee for Scotland* (1960) (Cmnd 1103).
3 A more fundamental review of this branch of the law was later undertaken by the Scottish Law Commission: see para 676 below. This resulted in the Damages (Scotland) Act 1976 (c 3), which replaced the 1962 Act.

661. The 11th report: employer's right to recover damages for injury to employee. In its eleventh report the Law Reform Committee for Scotland dealt with the desirability of enabling an employer to recover damages for loss suffered by him in consequence of a wrong done to his employee by a third person[1]. It considered the rule that an employer cannot recover damages in these circumstances, and concluded that the rule should not be changed. No legislation was accordingly recommended.

1 *Eleventh Report of the Law Reform Committee for Scotland* (1963) (Cmnd 1997).

662. The 12th report: animals. In its twelfth report the Law Reform Committee for Scotland considered the law relating to civil liability for loss, injury and damage caused by animals[1]. It recommended that the legal distinction between wild and tame animals should be abolished, and that civil liability for loss, injury or damage caused by animals should instead depend on failure to exercise reasonable care; that the Winter Herding Act 1686 (c 21) should be re-enacted in modern form; that liability under the Dogs Act 1906 (c 32) and the Dogs (Amendment) Act 1928 (c 21) should attach to the animal's keeper as well as to its owner; and that there should be a defence for anyone who shot a dog in defence of cattle or poultry. Legislation has been passed only on the last of these points[2].

1 *Twelfth Report of the Law Reform Committee for Scotland* (1963) (Cmnd 2185).
2 See the Civic Government (Scotland) Act 1982 (c 45), s 129. A more fundamental review of the law as it affects animals has been conducted by the Scottish Law Commission: see *Obligations: Civil Liability in relation to Animals* (Scot Law Com no. 97). The report is implemented in the Animals (Scotland) Bill (1987).

663. The 13th report: dangerous agencies escaping from land. The thirteenth report of the Law Reform Committee for Scotland concerns the law relating to civil liability for loss, injury and damage caused by dangerous agencies escaping from land[1]. The committee considered the development of the common law on this subject, but concluded, with one dissenting opinion, that no change was desirable. Accordingly no legislation ensued[2].

1 *Thirteenth Report of the Law Reform Committee for Scotland* (1964) (Cmnd 2348).

2 The law has now been clarified by the House of Lords in *RHM Bakeries (Scotland) Ltd v Strathclyde Regional Council* 1985 SLT 214, HL. In particular it was stated by Lord Fraser of Tullybelton at 217 that the decision of the House in *Rylands v Fletcher* (1868) LR 3 HL 330 'has no place in Scots law, and the suggestion that it has, is a heresy which ought to be extirpated'.

664. The 14th report: diligence of goods not belonging to a debtor. In its fourteenth report the Law Reform Committee for Scotland considered the position in relation to diligence of creditors of goods in the possession of, but not belonging to a debtor[1]. The committee recommended that no change be made in the general rule that a creditor cannot poind goods not belonging to the debtor, but recommended that the landlord's hypothec should be restricted to goods owned by the tenant. This last recommendation has not been implemented.

1 *Fourteenth Report of the Law Reform Committee for Scotland* (1964) (Cmnd 2343).

(6) THE SCOTTISH LAW COMMISSION

(a) Introduction

665. Constitution. The Scottish Law Commission was set up on 16 June 1965 by the Law Commissions Act 1965 for 'the purpose of promoting the reform of the law of Scotland'[1]. There is 'a Chairman and not more than four other Commissioners'[2] appointed by the Lord Advocate[3]. The commissioners are to be persons appearing to the Lord Advocate to be suitably qualified by the holding of judicial office or by experience as an advocate or solicitor or as a teacher of law in a university[4]. The appointment is for up to five years and is renewable[5]. Commissioners are disqualified for membership of the House of Commons[6].

1 Law Commissions Act 1965 (c 22), s 2(1). See generally W H Hurlburt *Law Reform Commissions in the United Kingdom, Australia and Canada* (Edmonton, 1986) pp 50 ff, 86 ff, 360 ff, 401 ff. The role of the Scottish Law Commission falls to be contrasted with the role of '*the* Law Commission' (sc for England and Wales), which is to promote 'the reform of *the* law': s 1(1) (emphasis added). It is not clear whether, or to what extent, the functions of the Law Commission extend to reforming the law of Northern Ireland.
2 When originally constituted in 1965 the commission comprised four commissioners.
3 Law Commissions Act 1965, s 2(1) (amended by the Transfer of Functions (Secretary of State and Lord Advocate) Order 1972, SI 1972/2002). Until this amendment Scottish Law Commissioners were appointed by both the Secretary of State for Scotland and the Lord Advocate. The Lord Advocate alone now has this responsibility.
4 Law Commissions Act 1965, s 2(2). In practice the Chairman is always a Court of Session judge.
5 Ibid, s 2(3). As to remuneration and pensions, see s 4. As to staff and expenses, see s 5.
6 House of Commons Disqualification Act 1957 (c 20), s 1(1)(f), Sch 1, Pt II; Law Commissions Act 1965, s 6(1).

666. Duties of the commission. It is the statutory duty of the Scottish Law Commission 'to take and keep under review all the law with which [it is] concerned with a view to its systematic development and reform, including in particular the codification of such law, the elimination of anomalies, the repeal of obsolete and unnecessary enactments, the reduction of the number of separate enactments and generally the simplification and modernisation of the law'[1]. In practice the commission has been seen as a suitable body for examining areas of private law and, to a much lesser extent, criminal law. It is relatively rarely involved in consideration of areas of public law[2], and it has seldom considered aspects of court procedure except where such matters arise incidentally in the course of a review of a branch of substantive law[3].

There are five prescribed methods whereby the commission may become involved in a review of a particular branch of the law. For this purpose the commission is under a duty:

(1) to receive and consider any proposals for the reform of the law which may be made or referred to it[4];

(2) to prepare and submit to the Lord Advocate from time to time programmes for the examination of different branches of the law with a view to reform, including recommendations as to the agency (whether the commission or another body) by which any such examination should be carried out[5];

(3) to undertake, pursuant to any such recommendations approved by the Lord Advocate, the examination of particular branches of the law and the formulation, by means of draft Bills or otherwise, of proposals for reform therein[6];

(4) to prepare from time to time at the request of the Lord Advocate comprehensive programmes of consolidation and statute law revision, and to undertake the preparation of draft Bills pursuant to any such programme approved by him[7];

(5) to provide advice and information to government departments and other authorities or bodies concerned at the instance of the government with proposals for the reform or amendment of any branch of the law[8];

(6) to obtain such information as to the legal systems of other countries as appears to the commissioners likely to facilitate the performance of any of their functions[9].

Of these the most important paragraph is (2), under which three programmes of law reform have been approved. These programmes cover the greater part of the private law of Scotland. The First Programme[10], for example, includes evidence and obligations — the latter comprehending the entire law of contract and delict. The Second Programme[11] includes bankruptcy, succession, diligence and family law. The Third Programme[12] consists of private international law, and is the source (*quoad* Scotland) of a substantial number of projects in this field carried out jointly by the two Law Commissions. The approval of these programmes constitutes a standing continuing authority to the commission to review any topic which falls within a programme subject, whenever this is thought necessary either by the commission or by a government department[13].

The other important paragraph is (5), under which a number of specific requests have been made by ministers. Examples of reports on such requests include *Divorce: the Grounds Considered*[14]; *Liability for Antenatal Injury*[15]; *Liability for Defective Products*[16]; *The Law of Incest in Scotland*[17]; and *Irritancies in Leases*[18]. On occasions a law reform proposal has been received from a professional body such as the Faculty of Advocates or the Law Society of Scotland, and in these circumstances paragraph (1) constitutes sufficient authority to enable the commission to embark upon a law reform project. The commission's series of consultative memoranda on corporeal moveables sprang partly from such a proposal[19]. It would, no doubt, be possible for ministers or government departments to make a proposal to the commission under paragraph (1), but in practice paragraph (5) is always used for this purpose.

The Lord Advocate must lay before Parliament any programme prepared by the commission and approved by him, and any proposals for reform formulated by the commission pursuant to such programmes[20]. The commission must make an annual report to the Lord Advocate, which he must lay before Parliament with such comments, if any, as he thinks fit[21]. In the exercise of their functions each of the Law Commissions must act in consultation with the other[22].

 1 Law Commissions Act 1965 (c 22), s 3(1).
 2 An exception was *Remedies in Administrative Law* (Scot Law Com Consultative Memorandum no. 14). This was, however, of limited scope, falling far short of a major review of administrative law. Its genesis was a desire in England and Wales to re-examine their prerogative writs. Consultative Memorandum no. 32 set forth the commission's comments on the White Paper *Our Changing Democracy: Devolution to Scotland and Wales* (1975) (Cmnd 6348), and also included earlier comments on devolution, Scots law and the role of the commission.
 3 *The Second Programme of Law Reform* (Scot Law Com no. 8) (1968) included criminal procedure, but in the event this work was entrusted on the commission's recommendation under the Law Commissions Act 1965, s 3(1)(b), to a departmental committee under the chairmanship of Lord Thomson.
 4 Ibid, s 3(1)(a).
 5 Ibid, s 3(1)(b).
 6 Ibid, s 3(1)(c).
 7 Ibid, s 3(1)(d).
 8 Ibid, s 3(1)(e).
 9 Ibid, s 3(1)(f).
10 *The First Programme of the Scottish Law Commission* (Scot Law Com no. 1) (1965).
11 *The Second Programme of Law Reform* (Scot Law Com no. 8) (1968).
12 *The Third Programme of Law Reform* (Scot Law Com no. 29) (1973).
13 A number of joint projects from the two Law Commissions sprang from Scottish Law Commission programme subjects and from references under the Law Commissions Act 1965, s 3(1)(e), to the Law Commission (for England and Wales). Examples are *Exemption Clauses in Contracts: 1st Report: Amendments to the Sale of Goods Act 1893* (Law Com no. 24; Scot Law Com no. 12 (1969)), and *Exemption Clauses: 2nd Report* (Law Com no. 69; Scot Law Com no. 39 (1975)).
14 Scot Law Com no. 6; Cmnd 3256 (1967): see para 683 below.
15 Scot Law Com no. 30; Cmnd 5371 (1973): see para 675 below.
16 Law Com no. 82; Scot Law Com no. 45; Cmnd 6831 (1977): see para 677 below.
17 Scot Law Com no. 69; Cmnd 8422 (1981): see para 695 below.
18 Scot Law Com no. 75; Cmnd 8760 (1983): see para 681 below.
19 The series also sprang partly from the programme subject Obligations (Scot Law Com Consultative Memoranda nos. 24–31 (1976)). In the course of the commission's examination of the law of prescription the Law Society of Scotland suggested that the law of prescription should be clarified as it affects corporeal moveables. The *Report on Powers of Judicial Factors* (Scot Law Com no. 59; Cmnd 7904 (1980)) also arose out of a suggestion made by the Law Society of Scotland: see para 694 below. The consultative memorandum on rights of relief arose from a proposal made by the Faculty of Advocates. See also *Civil Liability: Contribution* (Scot Law Com Consultative Memorandum no. 73) (1986).
20 Law Commissions Act 1965, s 3(2).
21 Ibid, s 3(3).
22 Ibid, s 3(4).

(b) Reforms recommended by the Scottish Law Commission

667. Introduction. In this section it is proposed to examine the principal reforms recommended by the Scottish Law Commission. No description is given of current law reform projects — that is, those projects on which the commission has not yet reported — but a full list of published memoranda is to be found at the end of the section[1].

 1 See para 696 below.

668. Evidence of sexual offences. In 1983 the Scottish Law Commission made recommendations to restrict the range of evidence which may be led in cases of rape and other sexual offences[1]. As a general rule, the court should not admit questioning or evidence which shows or tends to show that a complainer has at any time been of bad character, has associated with prostitutes or engaged in prostitution, or has engaged in sexual behaviour not forming part of the subject matter of the charge. These prohibitions should not, however, apply to questioning, or evidence being adduced, by the Crown. Nor should they apply where the questioning or evidence is relevant to the charge, or where it may be contrary to the interests of justice to exclude it. These recommendations were implemented by the Law Reform (Miscellaneous Provisions) (Scotland) Act 1985[2].

1 *Report on Evidence in Cases of Rape and other Sexual Offences* (Scot Law Com no. 78 (1983)).
2 See the Criminal Procedure (Scotland) Act 1975 (c 21), ss 141A, 141B, 346A, 346B (added by the Law Reform (Miscellaneous Provisions) (Scotland) Act 1985 (c 73), s 36).

669. Presumption of death. Under the old common law a person was presumed to have lived, in the absence of proof to the contrary, to an advanced age[1]. By statute a person might be presumed dead after seven years for certain limited purposes, including the obtaining of title to land[2] and divorce[3]. In a report the Scottish Law Commission recommended the adoption of the seven-year rule for all legal purposes except in relation to criminal responsibility[4]. The report dealt comprehensively with the various ancillary matters arising out of a decree of declarator of death of a missing person. The commission's recommendations were implemented by the Presumption of Death (Scotland) Act 1977 (c 27).

1 This has not been authoritatively decided, but was said by the institutional writers to be either eighty or a hundred years: see eg Stair *Institutions* IV, 45, 19.
2 Presumption of Life (Limitation) (Scotland) Act 1891 (c 29), s 3 (repealed).
3 Divorce (Scotland) Act 1938 (c 50), s 5 (repealed).
4 *Report on Presumption of Death* (Scot Law Com no. 34 (1974)).

670. Exemption clauses in contracts. In conjunction with the Law Commission (for England and Wales) the Scottish Law Commission re-examined the content of the implied terms in contracts of sale and considered the extent to which, if any, it should be competent to contract out of those terms[1]. Most of the problems identified in the implied terms concerned the implied term of quality[2]. Under the Sale of Goods Act 1893 an implied term of quality arose only in respect of goods which it was in the course of the seller's business to supply. The commissions took the view that, if a retailer sells an article in the course of a business, he should be answerable for its quality, whether or not he has previously traded in that line of goods[3]. Under the 1893 Act the term 'merchantable quality' was undefined; the commissions proposed a statutory definition[4]. Under that Act it was possible to contract out of these implied terms, although their incorporation in the Act was intended to impose certain rules of fair dealing[5]. The habit of ousting the implied terms by express contractual provision had become a widely practised technique at all levels of commerce, and had received a 'steadily growing impetus from the ubiquitous appearance of standard contracts on the economic scene'[6]. The commissions recommended that in a consumer sale a seller should not be permitted to contract out of the terms implied by statute[7]. The commissions disagreed, however, on whether the right to contract out of these terms in non-consumer sales should be restricted. Five of their number[8] favoured complete freedom of contract; five[9] favoured control by a reasonable test[10]. The latter view prevailed in Parliament[11]. Attempts to contract out of the implied term as to title[12] were to be void in all contracts of sale. The commissions' recommendations, with the modifications noted above, were implemented by the Supply of Goods (Implied

Terms) Act 1973, which also reformulated the statutory implied terms in hire purchase agreements and contained similar provisions for controlling attempts to contract out of these implied terms.

In the Second Report on Exemption Clauses[13] the commissions considered the extent to which contracting out should be permitted in respect of the corresponding terms implied in certain other contracts for the supply of goods (although not the actual content of these terms, which are implied at common law)[14]. They recommended the same types of control as were introduced by the 1973 Act. 'Negligence' clauses — in context, the breach of a duty or obligation imposed by the common law or by contract to take reasonable care or to exercise reasonable skill — were to be subject to a reasonableness test[15]. Provisions excluding or restricting liability, incurred in the course of a business, for death or personal injury due to negligence were to be void in certain circumstances, for example in a question with employees or passengers. This recommendation was extended in Parliament to all cases of death or personal injury where the breach of duty arose in the course of any business or from the occupation of any premises used for business purposes[16]. One major mischief identified by the commissions was the widespread use of standard form contracts, which often removed, by the use of clauses in small print, the apparent benefit conferred on the customer by the presentation of the contract as a whole. Accordingly the commissions recommended, in a similar range of contracts, that the reasonableness test was to apply to terms which (1) excluded or restricted liability for breach of contract, or (2) enabled a party to render no performance, or to render a performance substantially different from that which the consumer or customer reasonably expected from the contract[17]. These recommendations were implemented with minor modifications by the Unfair Contract Terms Act 1977. In particular the controls were not extended to insurance contracts[18].

1 *Exemption Clauses in Contracts: 1st Report: Amendments to the Sale of Goods Act 1893* (Law Com no. 24; Scot Law Com no. 12; Cmnd 4949 (1969)).
2 See the Sale of Goods Act 1893 (c 71), s 14, and, now, the Sale of Goods Act 1979 (c 54), s 14.
3 *Report*, para 31.
4 This definition now appears in the Sale of Goods Act 1979, s 14(6).
5 *Report*, para 64.
6 *Report*, para 65.
7 Ie by the Sale of Goods Act 1893, ss 13–15, and, now, the Sale of Goods Act 1979, ss 13–15.
8 Four of these were Scots Commissioners.
9 Four of these were English Commissioners.
10 Thus a term excluding or restricting the seller's liability for breach of any of these implied terms would not be enforceable to the extent that it is shown that it would not be fair or reasonable in the circumstances of the case to allow reliance on the term.
11 See the Sale of Goods Act 1893, s 55 (substituted by the Supply of Goods (Implied Terms) Act 1973 (c 13), s 4). The proposal contained in the report was modified by the introduction of five 'guidelines' to assist the court. The substance of this reform is now contained in the Unfair Contract Terms Act 1977 (c 50), s 20, Sch 2. In addition, s 24 further modifies the reasonableness test.
12 See the Sale of Goods Act 1893, s 12, and, now, the Sale of Goods Act 1979, s 12.
13 *Exemption Clauses: 2nd Report* (Law Com no. 69; Scot Law Com no. 39; Cmnd 8422 (1975)).
14 The relevant contracts in Scots Law are hire and barter. The implied terms in hire purchase contracts are codified in statutory form in the Supply of Goods (Implied Terms) Act 1973, which extended the same controls to consumer and non-consumer hire purchase agreements as it did to contracts of sale.
15 The Scottish Law Commission recommended that this control should apply only to contracts for the supply of goods, contracts of service and apprenticeship, contracts for services of all types, contracts of insurance and licences to enter upon or use land: Unfair Contract Terms Act 1977, s 15.
16 Unfair Contract Terms Act 1977, s 16 (which applies only to Scotland, and which is subject to the range of contracts specified in s 15).

17 Ibid, s 17(1) (which applies only to Scotland).
18 More detailed amendments to the law of insurance, which would have the effect of protecting the customer in consumer insurance contracts, have been proposed by the Law Commission (for England and Wales), but have not yet been implemented. See *Non-disclosure and Breach of Warranty* (Law Com no. 104; Cmnd 8064 (1980)).

671. Rectification of documents. In 1983 the Scottish Law Commission recommended that the courts should have wider powers to order the rectification of a document which has been defectively expressed[1]. In particular, the court should have power to order the rectification of a document intended to give effect to a prior agreement, when it is satisfied that the document does not accurately express the common intention of the parties. The proposals did not extend to testamentary writings. The report also sought to provide adequate protection for third parties. The recommendations were implemented by the Law Reform (Miscellaneous Provisions) (Scotland) Act 1985[2].

1 *Report on Rectification of Contractual and Other Documents* (Scot Law Com no. 79 (1983)).
2 See the Law Reform (Miscellaneous Provisions) (Scotland) Act 1985 (c 73), ss 8, 9.

672. Prescription and limitation. In 1970 the Scottish Law Commission recommended the modernisation of the law on prescription and limitation and its statement in a single comprehensive statute[1]. The commission's recommendations were implemented by the Prescription and Limitation (Scotland) Act 1973. In Part I of the Act the various short prescriptions[2] were replaced by a uniform five-year short negative prescription running from the date when loss, injury or damage occurred[3], which was to extinguish the relevant rights and obligations[4]. The long negative prescription, running from the date when loss, injury or damage occurred, remains at twenty years[5]. Part II of the Act merely consolidated the rules of limitation affecting personal injuries actions[6].

Further examination in England of the rules in personal injuries actions[7] led to the introduction, in England and Wales, of a judicial discretion to disregard the three-year time limit[8]. This in turn led to a further review of the position in Scotland by the Scottish Law Commission, and while consultation was taking place a similar discretion was introduced into Scots law[9]. The commission's subsequent report[10] recommended a simplification of the existing principles of the law, notably the three-year limitation period and the circumstances in which it might be extended. The report did, however, recommend a number of minor changes, including the disapplication of the long negative prescription to personal injuries claims. The Prescription and Limitation (Scotland) Act 1984 (c 45) implemented the commission's recommendations. The judicial discretion introduced in 1980 is retained.

1 *Report on Reform of the Law relating to Prescription and Limitation of Actions* (Scot Law Com no. 15 (1970)).
2 Eg the three-, five- and six-year prescriptions, which were in fact limitations, in that they did not extinguish the relevant rights but imposed limitations on the mode of proof.
3 Alternatively the period was one running, if later, from the date when the creditor first became, or could with reasonable diligence have become, aware of the loss etc.
4 Prescription and Limitation (Scotland) Act 1973 (c 52), ss 6, 11. Part I embraces ss 1–16.
5 Ibid, ss 7, 8, 11.
6 Ibid, ss 17–23.
7 *Interim Report on Limitation of Actions in Personal Injury Claims* (20th Report of the Lord Chancellor's Law Reform Committee) (1974) (Cmnd 5630).
8 See the Limitation Act 1975 (c 54), the main provisions of which are now consolidated in the Limitation Act 1980 (c 58), ss 11–44, 28, 33.
9 See the Law Reform (Miscellaneous Provisions) (Scotland) Act 1980 (c 55), s 23.
10 *Prescription and the Limitation of Actions: Report on Personal Injuries Actions and Private International Law Questions* (Scot Law Com no. 74 (1983)).

673. Negligent misrepresentation. It was held by the First Division in *Manners v Whitehead*[1] that a contracting party cannot recover damages from another contracting party on the grounds of misrepresentation unless the misrepresentation was fraudulent. However, under the modern law of delict negligent misrepresentation is actionable. Developments from *Donoghue v Stevenson*[2] onwards have shown the decision in *Manners* to be anomalous and out of date, but those judges who have had to consider the question have — with the exception of Lord Dunpark[3] — regarded *Manners* as still binding on the Outer House and on the sheriff courts. The Scottish Law Commission has accordingly recommended legislation to reverse the rule in the *Manners* case[4]. The recommendation was implemented by the Law Reform (Miscellaneous Provisions) (Scotland) Act 1985[5].

1 *Manners v Whitehead* (1898) 1 F 171, 6 SLT 199.
2 *Donoghue v Stevenson* 1932 SC (HL) 31, 1932 SLT 317.
3 Ie in *John Kenway Ltd v Orcantic Ltd* 1980 SLT 46, OH.
4 *Report on Negligent Misrepresentation* (Scot Law Com no. 92 (1985)).
5 See the Law Reform (Miscellaneous Provisions) (Scotland) Act 1985 (c 73), s 10.

674. Breach of confidence. In 1973 the Scottish Law Commission was asked by the government to consider the law on breach of confidence, and the related question of information unlawfully obtained. After many years' study the commission[1] reached no concluded view on whether it should be left to the courts to develop the principles of the common law, or whether the common law should be supplemented by legislation. In case legislation appeared to the government to be desirable, the commission included in its report a draft Bill, setting out a number of general principles for creating obligations of confidence, the most notable feature of which was that any person to whom or to whose interests the information related would be entitled to enforce the obligation. No legislation has yet ensued, the government having concluded that legislation is not necessary at present.

1 *Breach of Confidence* (Scot Law Com no. 90; Cmnd 9385 (1984)).

675. Liability for antenatal injury. In December 1972, at the height of the controversy over the drug Thalidomide, which was alleged to have caused deformities in unborn children, the Scottish Law Commission was requested to review the law on antenatal injury. Unusually, the commission did not issue a consultative memorandum but proceeded directly to the preparation of a report[1]. This was the consequence of the commission's terms of reference. The commission was asked (1) what was the present law regarding liability for injury caused to a child before birth?; (2) if the present law gave rights of reparation for such injury, was redress competent when the acts causing the injury occurred before the child's conception?; (3) should there be liability if there was none under the present law? The commission's conclusions on questions (1) and (2) in effect superseded discussion of question (3). As regards both question (1) and question (2) the commission concluded that there is liability under the present law and that legislation should only be considered if it was thought desirable to put the matter beyond argument. In the event, no legislation ensued.

1 *Liability for Antenatal Injury* (Scot Law Com no. 30; Cmnd 5371 (1973)).

676. Damages for personal injuries. In 1973 the Scottish Law Commission published a report[1] designed to overhaul the law on damages arising out of fatal accidents. At that time the category of dependent relatives entitled to claim damages was artifically narrow: there had to be a prestable legal obligation of support (as opposed to a history of actual support), and a number of close relatives, notably brothers and sisters, could not claim. There were also procedural barriers to a dependant's claim where the deceased had raised an action in his lifetime which was carried on by his executors. Under the commission's scheme the executors' claim was to be confined to patrimonial loss up to the date of death; the link with the law of aliment in determining the category of dependants was to be broken; and the category of those entitled to sue for loss of support widened to include (in addition to spouses, parents and children) other descendants and ascendants, collaterals and divorced spouses. A narrower category was to be entitled to sue for the new non-patrimonial loss of society award (replacing solatium): only spouses, parents and children[2]. The commission's recommendations were implemented by the Damages (Scotland) Act 1976.

In 1978 the commission published a further report[3] dealing principally with the admissibility of claims for services. The principal defect in the law was that the unpaid services of a housewife were not quantified in terms of money, so in practice an injured married woman who did not work would only be able to claim *solatium*. The commission accordingly recommended that, where a person has been deprived by reason of his injuries of the ability to render personal services to members of his family, he should be able to recover damages. In the event of a fatal accident the person's dependants can claim for the loss of personal services. Similarly, where a member of the family renders services to an injured person, the injured person can recover a reasonable sum by way of remuneration for those services. The commission's recommendations were implemented by the Administration of Justice Act 1982[4].

The final intromission of the commission in this area of the law was to seek to resolve a major procedural difficulty arising out of the Damages (Scotland) Act 1976[5]. Section 5 of the Act laid down provisions for the avoidance of more than one action arising out of the same death. A pursuer was placed under a duty to serve notice of the action on 'every connected person of whose existence and connection with the action the pursuer is aware or could with reasonable diligence have become aware'[6]. The words 'and connection with the action' were thought by the commission, which drafted the Bill on which the 1976 Act was modelled, to limit the duty to 'genuine' claimants[7]. These words were, however, omitted from the Act of Sederunt which regulated the procedure in the Court of Session[8], thus rendering the duty extensive and onerous. After six years section 5 of the 1976 Act was prospectively repealed[9], and after a further two years new rules of court were introduced both for the Court of Session[10] and for the sheriff court[11].

1 *Report on the Law relating to Damages for Injuries causing Death* (Scot Law Com no. 31 (1973)).
2 Cohabitants as well as spouses may claim damages for both loss of support and loss of society, and for the new heads of damage introduced by the Administration of Justice Act 1982 (c 53), Pt II (ss 7–14) (see below): see ss 7–9, 13(1). The Scottish Law Commission had recommended in its report in 1973 that, *inter alia* because of the risk of fraudulent claims, cohabitants should not have a dependant's claim.
3 *Damages for Personal Injuries: Report on (1) Admissibility of Claims for Services; (2) Admissible Deductions* (Scot Law Com no. 51 (1979)).
4 Administration of Justice Act 1982, Pt II (ss 7–14).
5 *Report on Section 5 of the Damages (Scotland) Act 1976* (Scot Law Com no. 64 (1981)).
6 Damages (Scotland) Act 1976 (c 13), s 5(6).
7 Ie as distinct from remote relatives of every description, by affinity as well as consanguinity, and of the half blood as well as the whole blood.

8 RC 75B (added by AS (Rules of Court Amendment No 12) (Intimation under Damages (Scotland) Act 1976) 1976, SI 1976/2020).
9 Administration of Justice Act 1982, s 75(1), Sch 9, Pt I.
10 RC 75B (substituted by AS (Amendment of Rules of Court No 5) (Intimation in fatal accident cases) 1984, SI 1984/920).
11 OCR 145 (added by AS (Damages) 1984, SI 1984/921).

677. Liability for defective products. The two Law Commissions were asked by the government to consider whether the existing law governing compensation for personal injury, damage to property or any other loss caused by defective products is adequate, and to recommend what improvements were needed. Under the present law an injured person must generally establish that the manufacturer was at fault. It is said that most modern products are so complex that evidence of fault is very difficult to obtain. Where several members of a family are injured, only one — the purchaser — may be able to recover damages, because he or she can sue the seller for breach of contract; whereas the other members of the family must establish fault, generally against the manufacturer.

The commissions' examination of this subject took place against the background of two separate attempts in Europe to achieve some measure of uniformity in the laws of European states. The first of these, the fruits of whose work the commissions largely endorsed, took place under the aegis of the Council of Europe in Strasbourg. The Council of Europe was responsible for a draft convention[1] which sought to impose strict liability[2] on producers of goods for death or personal injuries caused by a defect in a product[3]. The term 'product' included all moveables, natural or industrial, whether raw or manufactured, even though incorporated into another moveable or into an immoveable[4]. Liability was to apply even where the manufacturer could not have taken steps, in the light of current human knowledge and experience, to eradicate the defect in his product (that is, there was to be no 'state of the art' defence). This stems from the view that the risk of injury from defective products should be borne by those who can most conveniently ensure against it. The Council of Europe made no proposals for strict liability for other forms of loss, injury or damage, such as damage to property or economic loss.

The second European initiative was a proposal for a European Community directive on liability for defective products[5], which differed in important respects from the convention. For example, it sought to provide a 'state of the art' defence.

In their report[6] the Law Commissions were in substantial agreement in criticising the draft directive, but differed in their attitude to the convention, which the Scottish Law Commission found unsatisfactory in several respects. The directive has now been adopted[7], albeit in a form very different from the draft which the commissions considered. It is being implemented by Part I of the Consumer Protection Bill which is before Parliament in 1987.

1 European Convention on Products Liability in regard to Personal Injury and Death (Strasbourg, 27 January 1977; ETS 91). The convention is set out in Appendix A to the Law Commissions' report cited in note 6 below.
2 Ie irrespective of fault.
3 Convention, art 3(1).
4 Convention, art 2(b).
5 The draft directive is set out in Appendix B to the Law Commissions' report cited in note 6 below.
6 *Liability for Defective Products* (Law Com no. 82; Scot Law Com no. 45; Cmnd 6831 (1977)).
7 EC Council Directive 85/374 (OJ L210, 7.8.85, p 29).

678. Bankruptcy. Until the publication of the Scottish Law Commission's report on bankruptcy[1], there had been no systematic review of this area of Scots law since before the 1914–18 war[2]. The commission's report is one of the largest it has produced, extending to almost six hundred pages. It does not recommend major changes in the structure of the law, which dates from 1839. The principal innovations proposed are, first, that there should be an interim trustee in every case (superseding the largely ineffective procedure for interim preservation of the bankrupt's estate[3]); secondly, that the state should meet some of the cost of personal bankruptcy (previously met out of the estate); thirdly, that Crown preferences should be abolished; and fourthly, that the bankrupt should automatically be discharged five years after his sequestration. The commission's recommendations were implemented, with certain modifications, by the Bankruptcy (Scotland) Act 1985 (c 66). Certain Crown preferences are retained, and a bankrupt is to receive an automatic discharge after three years.

1 *Report on Bankruptcy and Related Aspects of Insolvency and Liquidation* (Scot Law Com no. 68 (1982)).
2 *Report of the Departmental Committee appointed to inquire into the Bankruptcy Law of Scotland and its Administration* (the Cullen Committee) (1910) (Cd 5201). The Bankruptcy (Scotland) Act 1913 (c 20) was based largely on that committee's representations.
3 See ibid, ss 14, 15.

679. Diligence. In 1980 the Scottish Law Commission published a comprehensive series of five consultative memoranda on diligence[1]. In the commission's report[2] a number of reforms were recommended. These were, first, the 'diligence stopper', which would enable the debtor to apply to the court for the substitution of an instalment decree for an existing open decree. Secondly, the commission proposed the introduction of debt arrangement schemes to cover cases of multiple debt. A scheme would only come into force on the application of the debtor himself, approved by the court. The consent of the creditors would not be necessary. Thirdly, the commission recommended restrictions on poindings. There should be no sales in the debtor's home; the exemptions on domestic plenishings which can be poinded would be widened; and the sheriff would have discretion to refuse warrant of sale on the grounds, for example, of hardship to the debtor or the limited value of the article. Fourthly, the commission recommended the introduction of arrestment of wages by continuous diligence, which would extend to the recovery of regular maintenance payments. Fifthly, imprisonment for rates and taxes would be abolished. Finally, the general organisation of officers of court would be retained. The commission's recommendations are being implemented by the Debtors (Scotland) Bill before Parliament in 1987, subject to modifications of which the most significant is the omission of provisions giving effect to the proposals for debt arrangement schemes.

1 Scot Law Com Consultative Memoranda nos. 47–51.
2 *Report on Diligence and Debtor Protection* (Scot Law Com no. 95 (1985)).

680. Floating charges. In 1967 the Scottish Law Commission was asked by the government to consider and advise on the provisions of the Companies (Floating Charges) (Scotland) Act 1961 (c 46). In its report in 1970[1] the commission recommended a number of changes to the Act, and in particular the introduction of receivers in Scotland[2]. The commission's recommendations were implemented by the Companies (Floating Charges and Receivers) (Scotland) Act 1972[3].

1 *Report on the Companies (Floating Charges) (Scotland) Act 1961* (Scot Law Com no. 14; Cmnd 4336 (1970)).
2 See the *Eighth Report of the Law Reform Committee for Scotland*, and para 658 above.
3 The Companies (Floating Charges and Receivers) (Scotland) Act 1972 (c 67) was revoked by the Companies Consolidation (Consequential Provisions) Act 1985 (c 9), s 29, Sch 1, and replaced by the Companies Act 1985 (c 6), Pt XVIII (ss 462–487).

681. Irritancies in leases. In 1976 the Scottish Law Commission was asked by the government to advise on the operation of irritancies clauses in commercial leases of heritable property. In a subsequent report[1] the commission recommended that for the purpose of terminating a lease a landlord should not be entitled to rely on a tenant's default in making any monetary payment unless he served written notice on the tenant specifying a period of not less than fourteen days for payment. In the case of any other kind of default, a landlord should not be entitled to rely on the tenant's default unless no fair and reasonable landlord would seek so to rely. The recommendations were implemented by the Law Reform (Miscellaneous Provisions) (Scotland) Act 1985[2].

1 *Irritancies in Leases* (Scot Law Com no. 75; Cmnd 8760 (1983)).
2 See the Law Reform (Miscellaneous Provisions) (Scotland) Act 1985 (c 73), ss 4–7.

682. Jurisdiction in family law actions. A married woman used to take the domicile of her husband, a rule much criticised as discriminatory and contrary to the modern principle of the equality of the sexes. The two Law Commissions therefore recommended in 1972[1] that the rule be changed for the purposes of jurisdiction in most consistorial actions. In the event Parliament abandoned the rule generally: a married woman now has an independent domicile for all purposes[2]. The commissions also recommended that the rules for jurisdiction in these actions should be rationalised. As a result the Scottish courts now have jurisdiction if (and only if) either party to the marriage is domiciled in Scotland on the date when the action is begun, or was habitually resident in Scotland throughout the period of one year ending with that date[3]. The reports also made recommendations to ease conflicts of jurisdiction within the United Kingdom.

1 *Family Law: Report on Jurisdiction in Consistorial Causes affecting Matrimonial Status* (Scot Law Com no. 25 (1972)). The English recommendations were contained in a separate report, *Family Law: Report on Jurisdiction in Matrimonial Causes* (Law Com no. 48 (1972)).
2 Domicile and Matrimonial Proceedings Act 1973 (c 45), s 1(1).
3 Ibid, s 7. See also s 8, which allocates jurisdiction between sheriff courts.

683. Grounds of divorce. The Scottish Law Commission began its work on examining the grounds of divorce at the end of 1966. At that time divorce could only be awarded on the ground of a matrimonial fault, such as adultery, cruelty or desertion. The commission's original views[1] underwent modification, both within and without the commission, mainly because of developments in England[2]. During the 1970s a number of private members' Bills were unsuccessfully introduced until, eventually, the Divorce (Scotland) Act was passed in 1976. This Act introduced, at any rate in theory, a single ground of divorce (irretrievable breakdown of marriage)[3], which is taken to be established[4] by one of five facts: adultery; unreasonable behaviour; desertion for two years; separation for two years where the defender consents to decree of divorce; and separation for five years (irrespective of consent).

1 *Divorce, The Grounds Considered* (Scot Law Com no. 6; Cmnd 3256 (1967)).
2 See the Divorce Reform Act 1969 (c 55) (repealed).

3 Divorce (Scotland) Act 1976 (c 39), s 1(1).
4 Ibid, s 1(2).

684. Aliment and financial provision. In 1981 the Scottish Law Commission published a report[1] dealing with aliment and financial provision on divorce. The first part sought to simplify the common law rules governing aliment. It recommended that the scope of alimentary obligations should be much reduced: in future, a person should be liable to aliment only his spouse and his child (including an illegitimate or adopted child and a child accepted by him as a child of his family). The obligation would cease when the child reached the age of eighteen (or twenty-five if receiving further education). Title to sue on behalf of a child would be conferred on the child himself, his parent, tutor, or any person entitled to, seeking or having custody or care of the child.

As to financial provision on divorce, the existing law conferred an unfettered discretion on the courts, and was widely criticised as not providing sufficient guidance for the assessment of financial provision. The commission accordingly recommended the following principles for assessing financial provision: (1) normally, equal sharing of matrimonial property; (2) due recognition of contributions made for the economic benefit of the other party and of economic disadvantages sustained in the interests of the other party or of the family; (3) fair sharing of the economic burden of caring for children under the age of sixteen; (4) a 'rehabilitation' provision to enable a spouse who has been financially dependent to adjust to independence over a period of not more than three years from the date of divorce; and (5) if a party seems likely at the time of divorce to suffer serious financial hardship as a result of the divorce, a suitable award. The award is to take the form, where possible, of a lump sum (payable, if necessary, by instalments) or a transfer of property. An award in the form of a periodical allowance is only to be made under principles (3), (4) and (5), and can be made for a fixed period.

These recommendations were implemented by the Family Law (Scotland) Act 1985 (c 37).

1 *Family Law: Report on Aliment and Financial Provision* (Scot Law Com no. 67 (1981)).

685. Financial provision after foreign divorce. Until 1984 the Scottish courts had no power to make an order for financial provision after a foreign divorce[1]. If a husband went to a foreign country and obtained a divorce there, his wife might not be awarded financial provision in the foreign proceedings. If the divorce fell to be recognised in Scotland, his wife could not claim financial provision in a Scottish court. The Scottish Law Commission therefore recommended[2] that the Scottish courts should have jurisdiction, in strictly limited circumstances, to entertain an action for financial provision after a valid foreign divorce[3]. The commission's recommendations were implemented by the Matrimonial and Family Proceedings Act 1984[4].

1 The resulting legislation refers to divorce in an 'overseas country', defined as a country or territory outside the British Islands (Matrimonial and Family Proceedings Act 1984 (c 42), s 30(1)). 'British Islands' means the United Kingdom, the Channel Islands and the Isle of Man: Interpretation Act 1978 (c 30), s 5, Sch 1.
2 *Family Law: Report on Financial Provision after Foreign Divorce* (Scot Law Com no. 72 (1982)).
3 Ie notably where the applicant is domiciled or habitually resident in Scotland on the date when the application is made; and where the other party is or was domiciled or habitually resident in Scotland on the date of the application or on the date when the parties last lived together as husband and wife. An alternative ground of jurisdiction is where the other party owned, was a tenant of or had a beneficial interest in property in Scotland which had at some time been the matrimonial home. The application would be competent only if *inter alia* the marriage had a

substantial connection with Scotland. See the Matrimonial and Family Proceedings Act 1984,
s 28.
4 Ibid, Pt IV (ss 28–31).

686. Liability for adultery and enticement of a spouse. In connection with
the reforms to the grounds of divorce, which were the subject of two Bills
before Parliament in 1976, the Scottish Law Commission recommended[1] the
abolition of a husband's rights (1) to claim damages from his wife's paramour
for patrimonial loss arising from the adultery; and (2) to cite him as a co-
defender in an action of divorce. These recommendations were implemented by
the Divorce (Scotland) Act 1976[2]. A proposal to abolish actions of enticement
(the competence of which was, in any event, hypothetical) was implemented by
the Law Reform (Husband and Wife) (Scotland) Act 1984[3].

1 *Family Law: Report on Liability for Adultery and Enticement of a Spouse* (Scot Law Com no. 42
   (1976)).
2 Divorce (Scotland) Act 1976 (c 39), s 10.
3 Law Reform (Husband and Wife) (Scotland) Act 1984 (c 15), s 2.

687. Occupancy rights in the matrimonial home and domestic violence.
Until 1981 Scots law did not recognise rights of occupancy in a matrimonial
home arising by virtue of the status of spouse. A spouse had such a right only if
he or she was the sole or joint owner or tenant of the home. The lack of a legal
right compelled many wives to endure intolerable conduct at the hands of their
husbands as the price of remaining, with their children, in the home. The
Scottish Law Commission therefore made radical proposals to deal with this
kind of problem[1]. The commission's report was implemented, with certain
modifications, by the Matrimonial Homes (Family Protection) (Scotland) Act
1981, under which a 'non-entitled spouse'[2] is given a statutory right of occupancy in a matrimonial home by virtue of the status of spouse during the
marriage, irrespective of the legal title to the home[3], together with certain
ancillary rights, such as paying rent and rates and carrying out essential repairs[4].
The court is given wide powers to regulate the occupation of the home and the
use and possession of the furniture and plenishings[5]. The report contained a
number of specific proposals designed to deal with practical conveyancing
problems, notably that the non-titled spouse should be entitled to give notice of
occupancy rights by registering a matrimonial home notice in the Land Register
or the Sasines Register. This recommendation was, however, rejected, partly
on the ground of alleged expense, and partly because it was doubted whether the
system would be widely used. The solution chosen by Parliament, however,
has led to certain practical difficulties which are slowly being resolved. Under
the Act the statutory occupancy rights of the non-entitled spouse remain
unaffected by any dealing of the entitled spouse in the property, unless he or she
has consented or consent has been dispensed with[6]. The Act goes beyond the
recommendations contained in the report, by creating limited occupancy rights
in favour of cohabiting couples[7].

1 *Report on Occupancy Rights in the Matrimonial Home and Domestic Violence* (Scot Law Com no. 60
   (1980)).
2 In the Bill appended to the commission's report the expression used was 'non-titled spouse'. The
   expressions 'titled' and 'non-titled' were objected to by certain members of the Upper House,
   notably Lord Scarman, a former chairman of the Law Commission (for England and Wales), on
   the strange ground that 'titled' should be reserved for members of that House, as being an
   indication of noble rank. Reference was made to the Oxford English Dictionary, which has not
   hitherto been regarded as sound authority for Scottish legal terminology. A cursory glance at
   Chambers Twentieth Century Dictionary (1977 edn) would have revealed that 'title' means, *inter
   alia*, a right to possession, and that 'titled' means simply having a title.

3 Matrimonial Homes (Family Protection) (Scotland) Act 1981 (c 59), s 1(1).
4 Ibid, s 2.
5 Ibid, s 3.
6 Ibid, s 6.
7 Ibid, s 18.

688. Matrimonial property. In 1983 the Scottish Law Commission published a substantial consultative memorandum[1] which reviewed the law on matrimonial property in Scotland and in many overseas countries. In a subsequent report[2] most of the radical possibilities, such as the introduction of a community property system, or of statutory co-ownership of the matrimonial home and/or of household goods, were rejected on the overwhelming advice of those consulted. The commission recommended a short Act to reaffirm the principle that, in modern times, marriage does not affect property rights or legal capacity[3]; and to lay down a presumption of equal shares in household goods[4] and in money and property derived from a housekeeping allowance[5]. These recommendations were implemented by the Family Law (Scotland) Act 1985.

1 Scot Law Com Consultative Memorandum no. 57.
2 *Family Law: Report on Matrimonial Property* (Scot Law Com no. 86 (1984)).
3 See the Family Law (Scotland) Act 1985 (c 37), s 24.
4 See ibid, s 25, which will be brought into force at the same time as the provisions of the Debtors (Scotland) Bill.
5 See the Family Law (Scotland) Act 1985, s 26.

689. Married women's policies of assurance. The Law Society of Scotland, among others, proposed to the Scottish Law Commission that the Married Women's Policies of Assurance (Scotland) Act 1880 (c 26) should be amended. Accordingly in 1978 the commission recommended certain extensions to the Act, notably to enable a woman to effect policies under the Act on her own life for the benefit of her husband or children[1]. The Commission's recommendations were implemented by the Married Women's Policies of Assurance (Scotland) (Amendment) Act 1980 (c 56).

1 *Report on the Married Women's Policies of Assurance (Scotland) Act 1880* (Scot Law Com no. 52; Cmnd 7245 (1978)).

690. Illegitimacy. Until recently there were still several ways in which the law discriminated against an illegitimate child. For example, his succession rights were restricted: he could not inherit from his grandparents, brothers or sisters if they died intestate. He had no legal guardian unless one was appointed by the court. The Scottish Law Commission recommended[1] that nearly all remaining areas of discrimination should be removed[2]. The Guardianship Acts should be repealed, and in their place should be substituted a short Act, applying to all children, setting out the principle of legal equality of children; making provision for parental rights and their exercise; and for court orders as to parental rights (preserving the principle that the welfare of the child is the paramount consideration). These recommendations were implemented by the Law Reform (Parent and Child) (Scotland) Act 1986[3].

1 *Family Law: Report on Illegitimacy* (Scot Law Com no. 82 (1984)).
2 The exceptions include British nationality, titles of honour and domicile: see the Law Reform (Parent and Child) (Scotland) Act 1986 (c 9), ss 1(4)(a), 9(1). See also the British Nationality Act 1981 (c 61), s 50(9).
3 Among the Acts repealed in their entirety by ibid, s 10(2), Sch 2, are the Bastards (Scotland) Act 1836 (c 22), the Guardianship of Infants Acts 1886 (c 27) and 1925 (c 45), the Illegitimate Children (Scotland) Act 1930 (c 33), the Children and Young Persons (Scotland) Act 1932 (c 47) and the Custody of Children (Scotland) Act 1939 (c 4).

691. Legitimation. Until 1968 Scots law, while accepting in principle that a child who was born before the marriage of his parents is legitimated upon the marriage taking place, refused to legitimate him when, at the date of his conception or birth, his parents were not free to marry. The Scottish Law Commission recommended that this bar to legitimation should be removed[1]. This recommendation was implemented by the Legitimation (Scotland) Act 1968[2].

1 *Reform of the Law relating to Legitimation per Subsequens Matrimonium* (Scot Law Com no. 5 (1967) (Cmnd 3223)).
2 See the Legitimation (Scotland) Act 1968 (c 22), ss 1, 4. See also the Law Reform (Miscellaneous Provisions) (Scotland) Act 1968 (c 70), s 5.

692. Custody of children. In 1985 the two Law Commissions made recommendations for uniform rules of jurisdiction in civil proceedings relating to the custody of children, and for recognition and enforcement throughout the United Kingdom of custody orders made in England and Wales, Scotland and Northern Ireland[1]. At present there is a wide variety of rules under which courts in different parts of the United Kingdom may assume jurisdiction to make custody orders, with the result that courts in more than one country may have jurisdiction at the same time. The proposed rules confer jurisdiction on the courts of the country with which the child has the closest long-term connection. Otherwise, the main recommendations are that the courts should continue to have jurisdiction to make custody orders in the course of proceedings for divorce, nullity and separation; if there are no such proceedings, jurisdiction should be conferred on the courts of the country where the child is habitually resident. An emergency jurisdiction would be conferred on the courts of the country in which the child is present, if an order is considered necessary for the child's immediate protection. The scheme recommended by the Law Commissions is implemented by the Family Law Act 1986 (c 55).

1 *Family Law: Custody of Children: Jurisdiction and Enforcement within the United Kingdom* (Law Com no. 138; Scot Law Com no. 91; Cmnd 9419 (1985)).

693. Private international law. Over the years the Scottish Law Commission has made a substantial number of recommendations in the field of private international law, almost all of them in reports prepared jointly with the Law Commission (for England and Wales)[1]. The first of these reports[2] concerned the ratification of the Hague Convention on the Recognition of Divorces and Legal Separations[3]. Under the previous law recognition by a Scottish court generally depended on the divorce having been granted by a court of the husband's domicile. The rule in the convention was that a foreign divorce or legal separation should be recognised if either spouse was habitually resident in, or a national of, the country in which it was obtained[4]. In a report published in 1981[5] the commissions examined two Council of Europe conventions, on foreign money liabilities[6] and on the place of payment of money liabilities[7], but recommended that the United Kingdom should not become a party to either of them. By the time of the report it was competent in both jurisdictions for a court to give judgment in a foreign currency where the claim was properly formulated in that currency. In a report published in 1984[8] the commissions recommended that the grounds for recognition of foreign nullity decrees should be the same as those for recognition of foreign divorces and legal separations. The next year the commissions published a report on conflicts of jurisdiction affecting the custody of children[9], and in another report[10] recommended that a potentially polygamous marriage entered into by a person domiciled in part of the

United Kingdom should be valid. Examination of various other branches of private international law is still in progress. Current projects include the choice of law rules in delict[11]; domicile[12]; and choice of law rules relating to marriage[13].

1 *The Third Programme of Law Reform* (Scot Law Com no. 29 (1973)) constitutes continuing authority for work in this field.
2 *Report on the Hague Convention on the Recognition of Divorces and Legal Separations* (Law Com no. 34; Scot Law Com no. 16; Cmnd 4542 (1970)).
3 Convention on the Recognition of Divorces and Legal Separations (The Hague, 1 June 1970; TS 123 (1975); Cmnd 6248).
4 The convention was implemented for the United Kingdom by the Recognition of Divorces and Legal Separations Act 1971 (c 53).
5 *Council of Europe Conventions on Foreign Money Liabilities 1967 and on the Place of Payment of Money Liabilities* (Law Com no. 109; Scot Law Com no. 66; Cmnd 8318 (1981)).
6 European Convention on Foreign Money Liabilities (Paris, 11 December 1967; ETS 60).
7 European Convention on the Place of Payment of Money Liabilities (Basle, 16 May 1972; ETS 75).
8 *Recognition of Foreign Nullity Decrees and Related Matters* (Law Com no. 137; Scot Law Com no. 88; Cmnd 9341 (1984)).
9 *Family Law: Custody of Children; Jurisdiction and Enforcement within the United Kingdom* (Law Com no. 138; Scot Law Com no. 91; Cmnd 9419 (1985): see para 692 above.
10 *Polygamous Marriages: Capacity to contract a Polygamous Marriage and Related Issues* (Law Com no. 146; Scot Law Com no. 96; Cmnd 9595 (1985)).
11 *Choice of Law in Tort and Delict* (Law Com Working Paper no. 67; Scot Law Com Consultative Memorandum no. 62 (1984)).
12 *The Law of Domicile* (Law Com Working Paper no. 88; Scot Law Com Consultative Memorandum no. 63 (1985)).
13 *Choice of Law Rules in Marriage* (Law Com Working Paper no. 89; Scot Law Com Consultative Memorandum no. 64 (1985)).

694. Powers of judicial factors. The Law Society of Scotland drew the attention of the Scottish Law Commission to the difficulty which faced a judicial factor when he had to consider whether the exercise of a statutory power[1] would conflict with the terms or purposes of his appointment. The commission recommended in 1980[2] that in these circumstances the factor might apply for the consent of the Accountant of Court. This recommendation was implemented by the Law Reform (Miscellaneous Provisions) (Scotland) Act 1980[3].

1 Ie specified in the Trusts (Scotland) Act 1921 (c 58) s 4.
2 *Report on Powers of Judicial Factors* (Scot Law Com no. 59; Cmnd 7904 (1980)).
3 See the Law Reform (Miscellaneous Provisions) (Scotland) Act 1980 (c 55), s 8.

695. Incest. In 1977 the Scottish Law Commission was asked by the government to review the law on incest, which derives from an Act of 1567[1]. The commission recommended[2] the retention of incest as a separate crime, and that the prohibition should be confined to a narrow range[3] of blood relationships[4], but not relationships by affinity. The prohibition should extend to illegitimate and adopted children. It should be a separate offence for a step-parent or former step-parent, or for a person over the age of sixteen in a position of trust or authority who is a member of the same household, to have sexual intercourse with a child under the age of sixteen. The commission's recommendations were implemented by the Incest and Related Offences (Scotland) Act 1986[5].

1 See the Incest Act 1567 (c 15), which was repealed by the Incest and Related Offences (Scotland) Act 1986 (c 36), s 2(2), Sch 2. The Act of 1567 was based on Leviticus ch 18 in the text of the Geneva Bible of 1562.
2 *The Law of Incest in Scotland* (Scot Law Com no. 69; Cmnd 8422 (1981)).

3 Ie between ascendants and descendants, brothers and sisters, uncles and nieces, and aunts and nephews.
4 Ie both of the full blood and of the half blood.
5 See the Sexual Offences (Scotland) Act 1976 (c 67), ss 2A–2D (added by the Incest and Related Offences (Scotland) Act 1986, s 1).

(c) Law Commission Reports and Memoranda

696. Statutory provisions relating to commission proposals. Many of the proposals and recommendations of the Scottish Law Commission have resulted in legislation, as is shown in the list below. Reports produced jointly with the Law Commission (for England and Wales) are marked with an asterisk.

MEMORANDA AND REPORTS, WITH DATE OF PUBLICATION	STATUTORY PROVISION
Proposals for Reform of the Law of Evidence relating to Corroboration (Scot Law Com no. 4 (20.4.67))	Law Reform (Miscellaneous Provisions) (Scotland) Act 1968 (c 70), s 9
Reform of the Law relating to Legitimation *per Subsequens Matrimonium* (Scot Law Com no. 5; Cmnd 3223 (20.4.67)) (see para 691 above)	Legitimation (Scotland) Act 1968 (c 22); Law Reform (Miscellaneous Provisions) (Scotland) Act 1968, s 5
Restrictions on the Creation of Liferents (Scot Law Com Consultative Memorandum no. 3 (5.5.67))	Law Reform (Miscellaneous Provisions) (Scotland) Act 1968, s 18
Applications for Planning Permission (Scot Law Com Consultative Memorandum no. 4 (11.5.67))	Town and Country Planning (Scotland) Act 1969 (c 30), s 79
Divorce: The Grounds Considered (Scot Law Com no. 6; Cmnd 3256 (12.5.67)) (see para 683 above)	Divorce (Scotland) Act 1976 (c 39)
*Sea Fisheries (Shellfish) Bill: Report on the Consolidation of certain Enactments relating to Shellfish Fisheries and Shellfish (Scot Law Com no. 6A; Cmnd 3267 (11.5.67))	Sea Fisheries (Shellfish) Act 1967 (c 83)
*Trustee Savings Banks Bill: Report on the Consolidation of the Trustee Savings Banks Acts 1954 to 1968 (Scot Law Com no. 10; Cmnd 4004 (17.4.69))	Trustee Savings Banks Act 1969 (c 50)
*Interpretation of Statutes (Law Com no. 21; Scot Law Com no. 11 (11.6.69))	none
*Exemption Clauses in Contracts: First Report: Amendments to the Sale of Goods Act 1893 (Law Com no. 24; Scot Law Com no. 12 (18.9.69)) (see para 670 above)	Supply of Goods (Implied Terms) Act 1973 (c 13)
Companies (Floating Charges) (Scotland) Act 1961 (Scot Law Com no. 14; Cmnd 4336 (22.4.70)) (see para 680 above)	Companies (Floating Charges and Receivers) (Scotland) Act 1972 (c 67)
Reform of the Law relating to Prescription and Limitation of Actions (Scot Law Com no. 15 (27.11.70)) (see para 672 above)	Prescription and Limitation (Scotland) Act 1973 (c 52)
*Hague Convention on Recognition of Divorces and Legal Separations (Law Com no. 34; Scot Law Com no. 16; Cmnd 4542 (1.12.70)) (see para 693 above)	Recognition of Divorces and Legal Separations Act 1971 (c 53)
*Coinage Bill: Report on the Consolidation of certain Enactments relating to Coinage (Law Com no. 38; Scot Law Com no. 18; Cmnd 4544 (26.11.70))	Coinage Act 1971 (c 24)

MEMORANDA AND REPORTS, WITH DATE OF PUBLICATION	STATUTORY PROVISION
★Vehicles (Excise) Bill: Report on the Consolidation of certain Enactments relating to Excise Duty on Mechanically Propelled Vehicles and the Licensing and Registration of such Vehicles (Law Com no. 39; Scot Law Com no. 19; Cmnd 4547 (2.12.70))	Vehicles (Excise) Act 1971 (c 10)
★National Savings Bank Bill: Report on the Consolidation of Enactments relating to the National Savings Bank (Law Com no. 41; Scot Law Com no. 20; Cmnd 4574 (13.1.71))	National Savings Bank Act 1971 (c 29)
★Taxation of Income and Gains derived from Land (Law Com no. 43; Scot Law Com no. 21; Cmnd 4654 (23.4.71))	(in part) Finance Act 1972 (c 41), s 82
★Road Traffic Bill: Report on the Consolidation of certain Enactments relating to Road Traffic (Law Com no. 46; Scot Law Com no. 22; Cmnd 4731 (26.7.71))	Road Traffic Act 1972 (c 20)
Town and Country Planning (Scotland) Bill: Report on the Consolidation of certain Enactments relating to Town and Country Planning in Scotland (Scot Law Com no. 24; Cmnd 4949 (20.4.72))	Town and Country Planning (Scotland) Act 1972 (c 52)
Family Law: Report on Jurisdiction in Consistorial Causes affecting Matrimonial Status (Scot Law Com no. 25 (29.9.72)) (see para 682 above))	Domicile and Matrimonial Proceedings Act 1973 (c 45)
★Statute Law Revision: Fourth Report: Draft Statute Law (Repeals) Bill (Law Com no. 49; Scot Law Com no. 26; Cmnd 5108 (28.9.72))	Statute Law (Repeals) Act 1973 (c 39)
Liability for Antenatal Injury (Scot Law Com no. 30; Cmnd 5371 (30.8.73)) (see para 675 above))	none required
Report on the Law relating to Damages for Injuries causing Death (Scot Law Com no. 31 (24.10.73)) (see para 676 above)	Damages (Scotland) Act 1976 (c 13)
★Statute Law Revision: Fifth Report: Draft Statute Law (Repeals) Bill (Law Com no. 57; Scot Law Com no. 32; Cmnd 5493 (6.12.73))	Statute Law (Repeals) Act 1974 (c 22)
Report on Presumption of Death (Scot Law Com no. 34 (3.9.74)) (see para 669 above)	Presumption of Death (Scotland) Act 1977 (c 27)
★Friendly Societies Bill: Report on the Consolidation of the Friendly Societies Acts 1896 to 1971 and certain other Enactments relating to Societies to which those Acts apply (Law Com no. 59; Scot Law Com no. 35; Cmnd 5634 (27.6.74))	Friendly Societies Act 1974 (c 46)
★Statute Law Revision: Sixth Report: Draft Statute Law (Repeals) Bill (Law Com no. 63; Scot Law Com no. 36; Cmnd 5792 (5.12.74))	Statute Law (Repeals) Act 1975 (c 10)
★Supply Powers Bill: Report on the Consolidation of certain Enactments relating to Supply Powers (Law Com no. 66; Scot Law Com no. 38; Cmnd 5850 (6.1.75))	Supply Powers Act 1975 (c 9)
★Exemption Clauses: Second Report (Law Com no. 69; Scot Law Com no. 39 (2.10.75)) (see para 670 above)	Unfair Contract Terms Act 1977 (c 50)
★Statute Law Revision: Seventh Report: Draft Statute Law (Repeals) Bill (Law Com no. 70; Scot Law Com no. 40; Cmnd 6303 (8.12.75))	Statute Law (Repeals) Act 1976 (c 16)

MEMORANDA AND REPORTS, WITH DATE OF PUBLICATION	STATUTORY PROVISION
Family Law: Report on Liability for Adultery and Enticement of a Spouse (Scot Law Com no. 42 (23.6.76)) (see para 686 above)	(in part) Divorce (Scotland) Act 1976, s 10
*Statute Law Revision: Eighth Report: Draft Statute Law (Repeals) Bill (Law Com no. 80; Scot Law Com no. 44; Cmnd 6719 (6.1.77))	Statute Law (Repeals) Act 1977 (c 18)
*Liability for Defective Products (Law Com no. 82; Scot Law Com no. 45; Cmnd 6831 (15.6.77)) (see para 677 above)	none
*Statute Law Revision: Ninth Report: Draft Statute Law (Repeals) Bill (Law Com no. 87; Scot Law Com no. 58; Cmnd 7189 (11.5.78))	Statute Law (Repeals) Act 1978 (c 45)
Electricity (Scotland) Bill: Report on the Consolidation of certain Enactments relating to Electricity in Scotland (Scot Law Com no. 49; Cmnd 7178 (23.5.78))	Electricity (Scotland) Act 1979 (c 11)
Adoption (Scotland) Bill: Report on the Consolidation of certain Enactments relating to Adoption in Scotland (Scot Law Com no. 50; Cmnd 7187 (3.5.78))	Adoption (Scotland) Act 1978 (c 28)
Damages for Personal Injuries: Report on (1) Admissibility of Claims for Services; (2) Admissible Deductions (Scot Law Com no. 51 (18.7.78)) (see para 676 above)	Administration of Justice Act 1982 (c 53), Pt II (ss 7–14)
Report on the Married Women's Policies of Assurance (Scotland) Act 1880 (Scot Law Com no. 52; Cmnd 7245 (27.7.78)) (see para 689 above)	Married Women's Policies of Assurance (Scotland) (Amendment) Act 1980 (c 56)
*Interpretation Bill: Report on the Interpretation Act 1889 and certain other Enactments relating to the Construction and Operation of Acts of Parliament and Other Instruments (Law Com no. 90; Scot Law Com no. 53; Cmnd 7235 (8.6.78))	Interpretation Act 1978 (c 30)
*Customs and Excise Management Bill: Report on the Consolidation of the Enactments relating to the Collection and Management of the Revenues of Customs and Excise (Law Com no. 93; Scot Law Com no. 54; Cmnd 7418 (7.12.78))	Customs and Excise Management Act 1979 (c 2)
Report on Lost and Abandoned Property (Scot Law Com no. 57 (16.1.80))	(in part) Civic Government (Scotland) Act 1982 (c 45), Pt VI (ss 67–79)
Education (Scotland) Bill: Report on the Consolidation of certain Enactments relating to Education in Scotland (Scot Law Com no. 58; Cmnd 7688 (2.4.80))	Education (Scotland) Act 1980 (c 44)
Report on Powers of Judicial Factors (Scot Law Com no. 59; Cmnd 7904 (3.7.80)) (see para 694 above)	Law Reform (Miscellaneous Provisions) (Scotland) Act 1980 (c 55), s 8
Report on Occupancy Rights in the Matrimonial Home and Domestic Violence (Scot Law Com no. 60 (17.7.80)) (see para 687 above)	Matrimonial Homes (Family Protection) (Scotland) Act 1981 (c 59)
*Judicial Pensions Bill: Report on the Consolidation of certain Enactments relating to the Pensions and other Benefits payable in respect of Service in Judicial Office (Law Com no. 105; Scot Law Com no. 62; Cmnd 8097 (27.11.80))	Judicial Pensions Act 1981 (c 20)
*Statute Law Revision: Tenth Report: Draft Statute Law (Repeals) Bill (Law Com no. 106; Scot Law Com no. 63; Cmnd 8089 (10.12.80))	Statute Law (Repeals) Act 1981 (c 19)

MEMORANDA AND REPORTS, WITH DATE OF PUBLICATION	STATUTORY PROVISION
Report on Section 5 of the Damages (Scotland) Act 1976 (Scot Law Com no. 64 (29.4.81)) (see para 676 above)	Administration of Justice Act 1982, Pt II (ss 7–14)
★Trustee Savings Banks Bill: Report on the Consolidation of the Trustee Savings Banks Acts 1969 to 1978 (Law Com no. 108; Scot Law Com no. 65; Cmnd 8257 (11.6.81))	Trustee Savings Banks Act 1981 (c 65)
★Council of Europe Conventions on Foreign Money Liabilities 1967 and on the Place of Payment of Money Liabilities 1972 (Law Com no. 109; Scot Law Com no. 66; Cmnd 8318 (28.7.81)) (see para 693 above)	none required
Family Law: Report on Aliment and Financial Provision (Scot Law Com no. 67 (5.11.81)) (see para 684 above)	Family Law (Scotland) Act 1985 (c 37)
Report on Bankruptcy and Related Aspects of Insolvency and Liquidation (Scot Law Com no. 68 (26.2.82)) (see para 678 above)	Bankruptcy (Scotland) Act 1985 (c 66)
Law of Incest in Scotland (Scot Law Com no. 69; Cmnd 8422 (23.12.81)) (see para 695 above)	Incest and Related Offences (Scotland) Act 1986 (c 36)
Family Law: Report on Financial Provision after Foreign Divorce (Scot Law Com no. 72 (28.10.82)) (see para 685 above)	Matrimonial and Family Proceedings Act 1984 (c 42), Pt IV (ss 28–31)
Prescription and Limitation of Actions: Report on Personal Injuries Actions and Private International Law Questions (Scot Law Com no. 74 (10.2.83)) (see para 672 above)	Prescription and Limitation (Scotland) Act 1984 (c 45)
Irritancies in Leases (Scot Law Com no. 75; Cmnd 8760 (17.2.83)) (see para 681 above)	Law Reform (Miscellaneous Provisions) (Scotland) Act 1985 (c 73), ss 4–7
Family Law: Report on Outdated Rules in the Law of Husband and Wife (Scot Law Com no. 76 (12.5.83))	Law Reform (Husband and Wife) (Scotland) Act 1984 (c 15)
★Medical Bill: Report on the Consolidation of the Medical Acts 1956–78 and certain Related Provisions (Law Com no. 120; Scot Law Com no. 77; Cmnd 8839 (24.3.83))	Medical Act 1983 (c 54)
Report on Evidence in Cases of Rape and Other Sexual Offences (Scot Law Com no. 78 (21.7.83)) (see para 668 above)	Law Reform (Miscellaneous Provisions) (Scotland) Act 1985, s 36
Report on Rectification of Contractual and Other Documents (Scot Law Com no. 79 (28.7.83)) (see para 671 above)	Law Reform (Miscellaneous Provisions) (Scotland) Act 1985, ss 8, 9
The Mental Element in Crime (Scot Law Com no. 80; Cmnd 9047 (23.11.83))	none required
Family Law: Report on Illegitimacy (Scot Law Com no. 82 (26.1.84)) (see para 690 above)	Law Reform (Parent and Child) (Scotland) Act 1986 (c 9)
★Amendment of the Companies Acts 1948–83 (Law Com no. 126; Scot Law Com no. 83; Cmnd 9114 (21.12.83))	Companies Acts (Pre-Consolidation Amendments) Order 1983, SI 1983/134; Companies Act 1985 (c 6)
★Dentists Bill: Report on the Consolidation of the Dentists Acts 1957 to 1983 (Law Com no. 129; Scot Law Com no. 84; Cmnd 9119 (18.1.84))	Dentists Act 1984 (c 24)

MEMORANDA AND REPORTS, WITH DATE OF PUBLICATION	STATUTORY PROVISION
*Road Traffic Regulation Bill: Report on the Consolidation of the Road Traffic Regulation Act 1967 and certain Related Enactments (Law Com no. 133; Scot Law Com no. 85; Cmnd 9162 (21.2.84))	Road Traffic Regulation Act 1984 (c 27)
Family Law: Report on Matrimonial Property (Scot Law Com no. 86 (21.6.84)) (see para 688 above)	Family Law (Scotland) Act 1985 (c 37)
*Further Amendments of the Companies Acts 1948 to 1983 (Law Com no. 136; Scot Law Com no. 87; Cmnd 9272 (25.6.84))	Companies Acts (Pre-Consolidation Amendments) (No 2) Order 1984, SI 1984/1169; Companies Act 1985 (c 6)
*Private International Law: Recognition of Foreign Nullity Decrees and Related Matters (Law Com no. 137; Scot Law Com no. 88; Cmnd 9341 (19.9.84)) (see para 693 above)	Family Law Act 1986 (c 55), Pt II (ss 44–54)
Breach of Confidence (Scot Law Com no. 90; Cmnd 9385 (20.12.84)) (see para 674 above)	none
*Family Law: Custody of Children: Jurisdiction and Enforcement within the United Kingdom (Law Com no. 138; Scot Law Com no. 91; Cmnd 9419 (15.1.85)) (see para 692 above)	Family Law Act 1986, Pt I (ss 1–43)
Obligations: Report on Negligent Misrepresentation (Scot Law Com no. 92 (24.1.85)) (see para 673 above)	Law Reform (Miscellaneous Provisions) (Scotland) Act 1985, s 10
Criminal Law: Art and Part Guilt of Statutory Offences (Scot Law Com no. 93; Cmnd 9551 (18.7.85))	none
*Report on the Consolidation of the Housing Acts: Housing Bill; Housing Associations Bill; Landlord and Tenant Bill (Law Com no. 144; Scot Law Com no. 94; Cmnd 9515 (10.5.85))	Housing Associations Act 1985 (c 69)
Report on Diligence and Debtor Protection (Scot Law Com no. 95 (14.11.85)) (see para 679 above)	Debtors (Scotland) Bill (1986)
*Private International Law: Polygamous Marriages: Capacity to Contract a Polygamous Marriage and Related Issues (Law Com no. 146; Scot Law Com no. 96; Cmnd 9595 (8.8.85)) (see para 693 above)	none
Obligations: Report on Civil Liability in relation to Animals (Scot Law Com no. 97 (8.11.85))	Animals (Scotland) Bill (1987)
*Statute Law Revision: Twelfth Report: Draft Statute Law (Repeals) Bill (Law Com no. 150; Scot Law Com no. 99; Cmnd 9648 (14.11.85))	Statute Law (Repeals) Act 1986 (c 12)
Evidence: Report on Corroboration, Hearsay and Related Matters in Civil Proceedings (Scot Law Com no. 100 (22.5.86))	none

697. Consultative memoranda. The following consultative memoranda have been prepared by the Scottish Law Commission and circulated for comment and criticism. Those marked with an asterisk were prepared by the commission jointly with the Law Commission (for England and Wales).

1966	1	Probates or Letters of Administration as Links in Title to Heritable Property under the Succession (Scotland) Act 1964
	2	Expenses in Criminal Cases
1967	3	Restrictions on the Creation of Liferents
	4	Applications for Planning Permission
	5	Damages for Injuries causing Death
	6*	Interpretation of Statutes

1981	52	Irritancies in Leases
1982	53	Family Law: Illegitimacy
	54	Some Obsolete and Discriminatory Rules in the Law of Husband and Wife
	55	Civil Liability in relation to Animals
	56*	Polygamous Marriages (Capacity to contract a Polygamous Marriage and the Concept of the Potentially Polygamous Marriage)
1983	57	Matrimonial Property
	58*	Sale and Supply of Goods
1984	59	Recovery of Possession of Heritable Property
	60	Mobbing and Rioting
	61	Attempted Homicide
	62*	Private International Law: Choice of Law in Tort/Delict
1985	63*	Private International Law: The Law of Domicile
	64*	Private International Law: Choice of Law Rules in Marriage
	65	Legal Capacity and Responsibility of Minors and Pupils
	66	Constitution and Proof of Voluntary Obligations and the Authentication of Writings
	67	Child Abduction
1986	68	Computer Crime
	69	Intestate Succession and Legal Rights
	70	The Making and Revocation of Wills
	71	Some Miscellaneous Topics in the Law of Succession
	72	Floating Charges and Receivers
	73	Civil Liability: Contribution

(7) CONSOLIDATION AND STATUTE LAW REFORM

698. Consolidating statutes. A consolidation Act is an enactment which, without making any changes in the law, brings together in one Act the statutory provisions relating to a particular topic and repeals the former enactments. The object of the Act is to tidy up the statute book and make the statutory provisions concerned more accessible to the user. Being an Act which does not alter the existing law, it has the benefit of accelerated procedure in Parliament, thus saving valuable parliamentary time. The procedure consists of introduction and formal second reading in the House of Lords, followed by consideration by a joint committee of both Houses[1] which has the function of satisfying itself that no changes have been made in the law. After the Bill has been approved by the joint committee, it is not open to detailed debate at any subsequent stage in either House, and the only amendments that can be made to the Bill are:

(1) an amendment to change the date on which the Bill is to come into operation;

(2) an amendment which would make the words of the Bill express the existing law more clearly; and

(3) an amendment seeking to bring the law into conformity with the existing law if the Chairman of the Joint Committee was satisfied that the Bill, as it had left that committee, would nevertheless have effected an alteration in the law[2].

Consolidation has been carried out, more or less on a regular basis, since the setting up in 1868 of the Statute Law Committee which was made responsible for the quality of the statute book. Until 1949 the only Bills entitled to the benefit of the accelerated procedure were 'pure consolidations', that is Bills which contained no changes in the law at all, it being necessary to consolidate even doubts and anomalies in the law[3].

1 Ie the Joint Committee on Consolidation etc Bills: see CONSTITUTIONAL LAW, vol 5, para 438.

2 See Erskine May *Parliamentary Practice* (20th edn 1983, by C Gordon) pp 558, 559. The rule that no change to the existing law is allowed in a consolidation Bill is subject to the modifications mentioned in paras 699–701 below.

3 The 'Scotland only' pure consolidations at present in force are the Nurses (Scotland) Act 1951 (c 55); the Housing (Scotland) Act 1966 (c 49); the Police (Scotland) Act 1967 (c 77); the Housing (Financial Provisions) (Scotland) Act 1968 (c 31); the Criminal Procedure (Scotland) Act 1975 (c 21); the Sexual Offences (Scotland) Act 1976 (c 67); the National Health Service (Scotland) Act 1978 (c 29); the Slaughter of Animals (Scotland) Act 1980 (c 13); the Water (Scotland) Act 1980 (c 45); the Solicitors (Scotland) Act 1980 (c 46); the Mental Health (Scotland) Act 1984 (c 36); the Foster Children (Scotland) Act 1984 (c 56); and the Rent (Scotland) Act 1984 (c 58).

699. 1949 procedure for consolidation Bills. Because of the unsatisfactory result often produced by a pure consolidation, machinery was introduced by the Consolidation of Enactments (Procedure) Act 1949 whereby a consolidation Bill was permitted to contain, in order to facilitate the consolidation of the enactments concerned, 'corrections and minor improvements'[1], that is amendments whose effect was 'confined to resolving ambiguities, removing doubts, bringing obsolete provisions into conformity with modern practice, or removing unnecessary provisions or anomalies which are not of substantial importance, and amendments designed to facilitate improvement in the form or manner in which the law is stated, and ... any transitional provisions which may be necessary in consequence of such amendments'[2]. Under this procedure the Lord Chancellor lays before Parliament a memorandum setting out the proposed amendments, on which parties affected have a right to make representations[3]. The memorandum and the Bill reflecting the proposals, together with any representations which have been received, are then referred to the Joint Committee on Consolidation etc Bills[4]. The joint committee, at the end of proceedings before it, informs the Lord Chancellor and the Speaker which amendments it is prepared to approve and, provided the Lord Chancellor and the Speaker concur, the Bill is reported to Parliament[5]. At this stage the amendments are deemed to have become law as if they had been made by an Act[6]. The amendments therefore cannot be debated and the Bill is open only to the very limited degree of amendment allowed in the case of pure consolidation[7]. The Act, however, provides that the joint committee is not to approve any amendments unless it is satisfied that the amendments do not effect any changes in the existing law of such importance that they ought, in its opinion, to be separately enacted by Parliament[8]. Generally speaking, the 1949 Act has been construed narrowly, the view being taken that, since the justification for having the amendments is 'in order to facilitate the consolidation', the consolidation must be virtually impossible without them[9].

1 Consolidation of Enactments (Procedure) Act 1949 (c 33), s 1(1).

2 Ibid, s 2. The 'Scotland only' consolidations enacted under the 1949 Act and at present in force are the Land Compensation (Scotland) Act 1963 (c 51) and the New Towns (Scotland) Act 1968 (c 16).

3 Consolidation of Enactments (Procedure) Act 1949, s 1(1)–(3).

4 Ibid, s 1(3).

5 Ibid, s 1(4).

6 Ibid, s 1(6).

7 See para 698 above.

8 Consolidation of Enactments (Procedure) Act 1949, s 1(5).

9 A much more robust approach, however, was taken in the case of the Industrial and Provident Societies Act 1965 (c 12), where there were about fifty proposals for amendment approved by the joint committee, of which about twenty were Scottish.

700. Consolidation on proposals of the Law Commissions. The restricted scope of what can be done under the Consolidation of Enactments (Procedure) Act 1949 led to its being largely replaced[1] in 1966 by a new process of consolidation with amendments proposed by either of the Law Commissions or by the two Law Commissions acting jointly, as appropriate[2]. Under this procedure the Law Commissions' recommendations for the changes in the law which are thought necessary to facilitate a satisfactory consolidation are laid before Parliament in a command paper at the same time as the consolidation Bill which reflects the recommendations. However, unlike amendments proposed under the 1949 Act, the amendments proposed by the recommendations are not deemed to be part of the existing law so that, even after they have been approved by the Joint Committee on Consolidation etc Bills they can be amended or rejected by either House, or, if rejected by the joint committee, can be restored by either House. In practice Parliament has almost never interfered with recommendations which the joint committee has approved.

In theory there is no limit to the kind of change which can be recommended by the Law Commissions, but in practice there are limits to what the joint committee is likely to approve. It has been said that Law Commission recommendations 'should be for the following purposes: to tidy up errors of the past, to remove ambiguities and generally to introduce common sense on points where the form of drafting in the past appeared to lead to a result which departed from common sense; though not to introduce any substantial change in the law or one that might be controversial — indeed nothing that Parliament as a whole would wish to reserve for its consideration'[3]. In one doubtful case the risk that the joint committee would decide not to approve a Law Commission recommendation on the ground that the matter was a proper one for Parliament itself to decide was avoided by the introduction of the Bill without anything implementing the recommendation; an amendment to implement the recommendation was moved at a stage after the Bill and the unimplemented recommendation had been considered by the joint committee[4]. The same procedure was followed in another Bill, but in that case the joint committee did not consider the unimplemented recommendation[5].

1 The procedure under the Consolidation of Enactments (Procedure) Act 1949 (c 33) was used in the New Towns (Scotland) Act 1968 (c 16) and the British Airways Board Act 1977 (c 13).
2 As to the Law Commissions, see paras 665 ff above. The 'Scotland only' consolidations enacted under this procedure and currently in force are the Town and Country Planning (Scotland) Act 1972 (c 52); the Adoption (Scotland) Act 1978 (c 28); the Electricity (Scotland) Act 1979 (c 11); and the Education (Scotland) Act 1980 (c 44).
3 Report 5 by the Joint Committee on Consolidation etc Bills on the Rent Bill (HL Paper (1976–77) no. 169; HC Paper (1976–77) no. 387).
4 Recommendation 7 of the Joint Law Commission Report on the Sea Fisheries (Shellfish) Bill (Cmnd 3267) (1967).
5 Recommendation 2 of the Report on the Judicial Pensions Bill (Law Com no. 105; Scot Law Com no. 62; Cmnd 8097 (1980)).

701. Consolidation of the Companies Acts. Yet another consolidation procedure was introduced by the Companies Act 1981 to facilitate the consolidation of the Companies Acts. That Act enabled an Order in Council to make such amendments of the Companies Acts and of any other enactments relating to companies as the two Law Commissions might jointly recommend as desirable to enable a satisfactory consolidation of the Companies Acts to be produced[1]. In fact the amendments recommended by the two Law Commissions[2] under this procedure were no more adventurous than the sort of amendments that they have recommended under the 'consolidation with Law Commission recommendations' procedure[3]; and the Law Commission in its Annual Report for

1982–83 stated that many of the suggestions for amendments of the Companies Acts which it had received seemed to it to fall outside the confines of what it could properly recommend as 'desirable to enable a satisfactory consolidation ... to be produced'[4].

1 Companies Act 1981 (c 62), s 116 (repealed). This provision is not reproduced in the Companies Act 1985 (c 6).
2 Report on Amendment of the Companies Acts 1948–83 (Law Com no. 126; Scot Law Com no. 83; Cmnd 9114 (1983)).
3 See para 700 above.
4 Law Commission 18th Annual Report 1982–83 (Law Com no. 131).

702. Consolidation and repeal. On some occasions consolidation has been combined in a single Bill with the repeal of enactments which are spent or obsolete[1]. It should also be noted that the consolidation procedure has been used to re-enact an Act applying throughout Great Britain, shortly after it has received the royal assent, as an Act applying only to Scotland[2].

1 Eg the Police (Scotland) Act 1967 (c 77); the Reserve Forces Act 1980 (c 9) and the Representation of the People Act 1983 (c 2).
2 Ie the Town and Country Planning (Scotland) Act 1959 (c 70), re-enacting the Town and Country Planning Act 1959 (c 53); and the Land Compensation (Scotland) Act 1973 (c 56), re-enacting the Land Compensation Act 1973 (c 26).

703. Statute Law Revision Acts and Statute Law (Repeals) Acts. The purpose of Statute Law Revision Acts and Statute Law (Repeals) Acts is basically to remove the dead wood from the statute book. The Bills for these Acts pass through Parliament in the same way as the Bills for pure consolidations[1]. Statute law revision in effect started during the nineteenth century, but in those days the enactments which qualified for express repeal were restricted to those which had ceased to be in force or had 'by lapse of time and change of circumstances become unnecessary'[2]. Despite such restriction, no less than 13,000 whole Acts were expressly repealed by this means between 1861 and 1908. Thereafter the interest in statute law revision declined, and only one Statute Law Revision Act was enacted between 1908 and 1948[3]. In 1948 the categories of enactments which could be repealed by Statute Law Revision Bills was widened from enactments which were unnecessary to include:
(1) expired enactments;
(2) spent enactments;
(3) enactments repealed by the operation of an enactment expressed only in general terms;
(4) an enactment which is inconsistent with, or is rendered nugatory by, a later one;
(5) superseded enactments; and
(6) obsolete enactments[4].
The new categorisation enabled enactments to be repealed by a Statute Law Revision Bill which would not have been possible before 1948. Despite this, however, difficult arguments arose over the categories of enactments qualifying for repeal in relation to the Statute Law Revision (Scotland) Bill 1963, which was a Bill to repeal enactments of the Parliament of Scotland[5].

1 See para 698 above.
2 Eg the Statute Law Revision Act 1874 (c 35) and the Statute Law Revision (No 2) Act 1874 (c 96).
3 Statute Law Revision Act 1927 (c 42).
4 Memorandum to the Statute Law Revision Bill (1948).

5 See the minutes of evidence taken before the Joint Committee on Consolidation etc Bills (HL Paper (1963–64) no. 57-IV; HC Paper (1963–64) no. 270-1). As a result of proceedings before the joint committee the Bill had to be withdrawn and was introduced the following session without the references to enactments relating to Church doctrine. The Bill then became the Statute Law Revision (Scotland) Act 1964 (c 80).

704. Statute law revision and the Law Commissions. By virtue of the Law Commissions Act 1965 statute law revision became the responsibility of the two Law Commissions[1]. In its First Programme of Consolidation and Statute Law Revision[2] the Law Commission (for England and Wales) stated 'The scope of statute law revision has of recent years been somewhat extended, but we think there is room for a still more forceful approach: we propose to work systematically through the existing statutes with a view to recommending the repeal not only of matter which can be treated as inoperative, but also of matter that no longer serves any useful purpose'. The Scottish Law Commission in its first such report[3] associated itself with this approach, which in effect replaced the old categories[4] by the single test of whether an enactment continued to serve any useful purpose[5]. The decision as to whether an enactment continued to be of practical utility fell to be taken in the first place by the Law Commissions, and a new type of Bill was therefore devised — to repeal, in accordance with recommendations of the Law Commissions (or one of them as appropriate), enactments which are no longer of practical utility[6]. These Bills, to distinguish them from Statute Law Revision Bills, are described as Statute Law (Repeals) Bills[7]. Since their inception in 1969, nine Statute Law (Repeals) Bills have been enacted.

1 Law Commissions Act 1965 (c 22), s 3(1)(d): see para 666 above.
2 Law Com no. 2.
3 Scot Law Com no. 2.
4 See para 703 above.
5 This concept of 'usefulness' very soon became formally known as the concept of 'practical utility'.
6 This in effect corresponds to the procedure of consolidation with Law Commission recommendations: see para 700 above.
7 Statute Law (Repeals) Bills have since 1969 really replaced Statute Law Revision Bills, although the latter are still possible: two Northern Ireland Statute Law Revision Bills have passed into law since 1969.

TIME

1. THE CALENDAR

801. Introduction. A calendar has been defined as a 'system according to which the beginning and length of successive civil years, and the subdivision of the year into its parts, is fixed', or, more particularly, 'a table showing the divisions of a given year into its months and days, and referring the days of each month to the days of the week; often also including important astronomical data, and indicating ecclesiastical or other festivals, and other events belonging to individual days'[1]. A knowledge of how the modern calendar has evolved is essential to an appreciation of the legal significance of time.

The passage of time is to be perceived at its most fundamental in the transition of the light of day into the dark of night, with the moon and stars taking the place of the sun in the sky. However, observation has demonstrated that the motion of the sun and the phases of the moon are independent. It is this independence which has produced the problems which have attended the devising of a systematic calendar, and in particular have necessitated one year in four being longer than the others.

The day is the basic unit of time. Its duration is determined by the rotation of the earth about its axis, as measured by the passage of the sun across the meridian. Most early civilisations regarded the day as commencing at sunrise, although some deemed it to commence at noon, and others at sunset or midnight. The division of the day into twenty-four periods or hours probably originated in Egypt, but the duration of those periods was flexible until mechanical clocks became widespread and necessitated regularity. Only from the thirteenth century AD onwards have hours, whether of light or dark, been periods of equal length. The duration of the solar day has been accurately measured as 24 hours, 3 minutes and 56.55 seconds, the excess over twenty-four hours being consequent upon the earth's motion around its own axis.

The foundation of the month is the lunation, the period from one new moon to the next. This period, which is dependent upon the orbital motion of the moon about the earth, has been calculated to be 29.53059 solar days. The lunar month was a more generally accepted grouping of days than the period now termed the week. The duration of the week varied among early communities, probably in consequence of its origin being the interval between the holding of markets, and it settled into a seven-day form in Rome only in the first century BC. The lunar month, being capable of easy recognition, was used to determine recurring religious festivals, and is still used to fix the date of Easter. The earliest calendars were groups of months, with various schemes being used to eliminate the inconvenient fraction of a day.

The seasons are determined by the orbital motion of the earth about the sun. Their duration depends upon the location of the observer and they do not provide an accurate means of measuring the passage of time, although any such means must have regard to their recurring nature. A cycle of seasons will amount to a tropical year, the duration of which is measured as the period between successive passages of the sun across the celestial equator in spring (the vernal equinox), and amounts to 365.242199 solar days.

It will be evident that it is impossible to construct a calendar in which each year is of equal duration and is divided into months of equal duration, while also keeping in step with the seasons, as measured by the recurrence of the vernal equinox. Achieving the best possible compromise is the task which has faced those entrusted with devising calendars.

1 See the Oxford English Dictionary.

802. The Roman Republican calendar. A consequence of the incompatibility of the solar day, the lunar month and the tropical year is that, in any calendar which is to be based on them and which is also to keep in step with the recurrence of the seasons, extra days will have to be intercalated at appropriate points. One method of doing this, which featured in an early Babylonian calendar, was to have months of twenty-nine and thirty days alternately. The calendar employed in Republican Rome was based on the lunar month and consisted of four months of thirty-one days, seven months of twenty-nine days, and one month of twenty-eight days, a total of 355 days. As a year of such duration rapidly became out of step with the seasons, twenty-two or twenty-three extra days were intercalated alternately each second year. In a four-year cycle there would thus be 1,465 days, an average of 366.25 days per year. Unfortunately the pattern of intercalation was not strictly adhered to, largely due to mismanagement by the pontiffs to whom the task was entrusted[1]. A regular system of intercalation was essential to the construction of a coherent calendar.

1 H F Jolowicz *Historical Introduction to the Study of Roman Law* (3rd edn, 1972 ed B Nicholas), p 89.

803. The Julian Calendar. Around 50 BC Julius Caesar invited the Alexandrian astronomer Sosigenes to reform the Republican calendar. He first required to eliminate the accumulated errors which had arisen due to the mistakes made by the pontiffs. This was done by intercalating ninety days in 46 BC. His solution to prevent the problem recurring was to base the calendar on the solar year with an assumed length of 365.25 days. The normal year was to have 365 days, the quarter days being gathered together and intercalated as one extra day each fourth year. As February had been the principal month for intercalation in the Republican calendar, it continued to be so after the reforms, with the extra day being inserted not at the end of the month, but, as formerly, between the twenty-third and twenty-fourth days. The pontiffs again failed to follow the simple rules of intercalation, with the result that, although the edict introducing what became termed 'the Julian Calendar' was pronounced in 45 BC, the calendar as originally intended did not come into operation until Augustus had identified and corrected the error in AD 4.

It is not entirely clear how the lengths of the individual months were fixed. The basic scheme was that which applied in the Republican calendar, but this is believed to have been modified on a number of occasions, partly in order to provide an element of regularity (thirty-day and thirty-one-day months alternately) and also to ensure that months named after emperors (July after Julius Caesar and August after Augustus) were equal in length. February normally had twenty-nine days, but one day was removed in order that August could have an extra day and thereby be the same length as July, which already had thirty-one days. With the exception of those months, the pattern became, as it still is, alternate thirty-day and thirty-one-day months.

804. The Gregorian Calendar. As a more correct estimate of the length of the solar or tropical year is 365.242199 solar days, there was an error inherent in Sosigenes's 365.25-day year. That error accumulated over the centuries, resulting in the calendar again falling out of step with the seasons. This produced problems, particularly in regard to the fixing of religious feasts such as Easter which has traditionally been related to the spring equinox. The Council of Trent in 1545 authorised Pope Paul III to seek a solution, but so difficult did this prove that it was not until 1582 that his successor, Pope Gregory XIII, was able to promulgate a Bull introducing what is now termed 'the Gregorian Calendar', and which is still in use.

By 1582 the accumulated error (at eleven minutes and fourteen seconds per year) amounted to ten days. To eliminate these days, the Bull provided that 5 October was to be renumbered 15 October. The length of the year was then accepted as being 365.2422 days. This was still not correct, but was more accurate. The difference between the Julian and Gregorian year was 0.0078 of a day per year, a figure in itself insignificant but which, when multiplied, would produce a deferred error of 3.12 days in four centuries. Normally centennial years are leap years, but to prevent this potential error the Bull decreed that only every fourth centennial year should be a leap year. The year 1600 was designated a leap year as will be 2000 and 2400, but the intervening centennial years are all common years.

805. The calendar in Great Britain. The Gregorian calendar was rapidly adopted throughout Catholic western Europe. However, its reception into Protestant and Orthodox countries was much slower, and it was not adopted in Great Britain and the British Dominions until 1 January 1752.

By 1750 the difference between the Julian and Gregorian calendars had reached eleven days. To correct this, and to introduce certain consequential reforms, Parliament passed the Calendar (New Style) Act 1750 which bears to have been passed because

'a Method of correcting the Calendar in such manner, as that the Equinoxes and Solstices may for the future fall nearly on the same nominal Days, on which the same happened at the Time of the said General Council [of Nicaea in AD 325] hath been received and established, and is now generally practised by almost all other Nations of Europe[1]'.

It also recognised that conformity with such other nations would be 'of general Convenience to Merchants, and other Persons corresponding with other Nations and Countries'. The eleven accumulated days were eliminated by providing that the day following 2 September 1752 should be reckoned as 14 September[2], a procedure which was, apparently, so unpopular that crowds took to the streets demanding 'Give us back our eleven days'. It also led to the legend of the flowering of the Glastonbury thorn on the 'real' Christmas

Day, 5 January. The error was prevented from recurring by the introduction of the rule that centennial years, with the exception of the year 2000 and every fourth centennial year thereafter, should be common years instead of leap years[3]. The Calendar (New Style) Act 1750 also contained provisions to prevent prejudice arising from the renumbering process[4]. The Calendar Act 1751 introduced further such provisions to deal with situations which had been overlooked when the principal Act was passed[5].

It should be noted that the Calendar (New Style) Act 1750 introduced the Gregorian Calendar to Scotland as well as to England and the Dominion territories, contrary to the assertion of subsequent commentators[6].

1 The Calendar (New Style) Act 1750 (c 23). In *Statutes at Large* this Act is ascribed to 1751.
2 Calendar (New Style) Act 1750, s 1.
3 Ibid, s 2.
4 Ibid, s 4 (amended by the Statute Law (Repeals) Act 1986 (c 12), s 1(1), Sch 1, Pt I) (holding of markets, fairs and marts), Calendar (New Style) Act 1750, s 5 (opening and enclosing of common land), s 6 (payments of rents, annuities, sums of money, interest etc).
5 Eg the presentation and swearing in of the Lord Mayor of London: Calendar Act 1751 (25 Geo 2 c 30), s 4. In *Statutes at Large* this Act is ascribed to 1752.
6 D M Walker *Oxford Companion to Law* (1980), p 1219; 45 Halsbury's Laws of England (4th edn) para 1102, n 2.

806. The commencement of the year. The Gregorian Calendar provided that the calendar year was to commence on 1 January, but this merely gave effect to what had become the practice in Rome. In the earliest Roman calendars the year had begun in March, and this was carried into the Republican calendar, possibly because that was originally when the new consul took office. In 153 BC this was transferred to 1 January and that date also became the commencement of the year.

The tradition of the year commencing in March had been widespread. It may have been associated with the spring equinox and the beginning of the growth of crops. Prior to the exodus of the Children of Israel from Egypt, the Jewish year had commenced in Tishri, approximately our September/October. However, immediately prior to the Passover Moses and Aaron were commanded to make the month of Passover the 'beginning of months'[1]. That month was Abib[2], which means 'green ears' (of corn), more commonly known by its Babylonian name Nisan or Nisanu.

Although, under Roman influence, both Scotland and England had adopted the Julian Calendar, the year was deemed to commence on 25 December until the fourteenth century, when it moved to 25 March. Scotland and England were thus out of step with their continental neighbours. Possibly in consequence of the close ties between Scotland and France and the custom of Scots lawyers being educated on the continent, the correction was made in Scotland many years before it was made in England. On 17 December 1599 the Privy Council of Scotland, assembled by James VI, issued an Ordinance changing the first day of the year to 1 January with effect from 1600[3]. This was expressly stated as being in order to bring Scotland into line with the practice on the continent. However, no such change was effected in England until 1752[4]. For a period of over 150 years there was, therefore, a discrepancy in the legal commencement of the year in Scotland and England, a fact of importance in considering the dates of documents executed in those countries during that period.

1 Exodus 12:2.
2 Exodus 13:4.
3 Register of the Privy Council, 1st series, vol 6 (1599–1604), p 63.
4 Calendar (New Style) Act 1750 (c 23), s 1.

807. Numbering of years. The concept of the consecutive numbering of years, commencing with and by reference to the birth of Christ, was probably devised by the sixth-century scholar Dionysius Exiguus. At that time it was generally held that the year now numbered 1 BC was the year of the birth of Christ. The concept was introduced into the West by the Venerable Bede and became an integral part of the Gregorian Calendar.

808. Easter. The Crucifixion having taken place on the day prior to the Passover, the date of Easter, which celebrates the Resurrection and occurs three days thereafter, must also be dependent on the date of the Passover. The Jews celebrated this on the fourteenth day of their month Nisan (or Abib), that is the lunar month the fourteenth day of which falls on or next after the spring equinox. The Christians' desire to ensure that Easter was always celebrated on a Sunday necessitated a departure from the strict rule and the introduction of more elaborate methods, which differed in the Churches of the East and the West, for fixing the feast. An attempt to resolve the conflicts in determining this most important of Christian festivals was made at the Council of Nicaea in 325, which provided that Easter should be celebrated on the Sunday immediately following the full moon which fell on or after the vernal equinox, which was presumed to take place on 21 March. If that day coincided with either the actual day upon which the Jews were celebrating the Passover, or the day which the Eastern Churches had traditionally treated as Easter day, the celebration was to be postponed by one week. The Eastern Churches, holding that Easter must neither coincide with nor precede the Jewish Passover, refused to accept this ruling, and continued, as they still do, to celebrate the festival independently.

In order to satisfy the need of the Church to be able to determine for many years in advance the date upon which Easter would fall, a highly complex scheme was developed. It involved calculating upon which day of the week any date in the year would fall, and also ascertaining the date of the full moons in each year. This was done by assigning to each year a dominical letter which depended upon the date upon which the first Sunday in January fell, and aligning that dominical letter in astronomical tables of what were termed 'golden numbers', which themselves were derived from cycles of the moon. The procedure was fallacious and was eventually abandoned when the Gregorian Calendar was introduced in 1582. However it remained in the Book of Common Prayer of the Church of England until 1752[1].

The Gregorian Calendar confirmed a system which had been in use unofficially for some years before 1582. It still depended on tables, but these were based on the number of days from the last new moon of the old year to the first new moon of the following January, known as the epact of that new year, from the Greek 'epagein', to intercalate. This system was introduced into England by the Calendar (New Style) Act 1750[1], but there does not appear ever to have been any statutory method of fixing Easter in Scotland. The provision is expressly applied to 'that part of Great Britain called England' and the dominions of Britain only, to the exclusion of Scotland, thereby implying that the provisions of the Gregorian Calendar had already been adopted in Scotland. The Act prescribed a new Table of Moveable Feasts for the Book of Common Prayer[2], and this is still valid. This table has not been reproduced in the Alternative Service Book 1980, which is content with a simple Table of Dates of Easter for years from 1981 to 2025, stipulated to be valid 'unless other provision is made'. The Prayer Book of the Scottish Episcopal Church (1929) also contains a simple Table of the Moveable Feasts for Fifty Years to the year 2000.

This method of determining Easter, which is now accepted throughout the West, means that the date can vary from 22 March to 25 April. The name

'Easter' is said to have been adapted from the Old English 'eastre', which was a heathen festival held at the vernal equinox in honour of the Teutonic goddess of dawn, named 'Eostre' by the Venerable Bede.

The flexibility of Easter has been widely criticised and suggestions have been made that it should be a defined date, as is Christmas Day (which would inevitably mean that it would frequently fall on a day other than Sunday) or, more popularly, that it should be calculated by a more logically defensible method. The Easter Act 1928 provided that Easter Day is to be the first Sunday after the second Saturday in April[3]. However, the provisions of this statute are not to come into force until an Order in Council so enacts[4], and this is unthinkable until unanimity among all the Churches has been reached. The Second Vatican Council declared in 1963 that the Church of Rome was in favour of a fixed date, but agreement with the Eastern Churches, which still use the Julian Calendar for fixing Easter, seems as distant as ever.

1 Calendar (New Style) Act 1750 (c 23), s 3.
2 Ibid, Schedule.
3 Easter Act 1928 (c 35), s 1.
4 Ibid, s 2(2).

2. LEGAL TIME

809. Greenwich mean time. Greenwich mean time is a species of standard or zone time, a method of time calculation based on twenty-four meridians, starting at Greenwich and each fifteen degrees apart. Between any two adjacent zones there is a difference of one hour. Greenwich mean time is based on noon occurring when the mean sun passes over the meridian at Greenwich Observatory.

Whenever an expression of time occurs in a statute, statutory instrument, deed or other legal instrument or document, the time referred to is, unless otherwise specifically stated or the provisions of the Summer Time Act 1972 (c 6) apply, held to be Greenwich mean time[1].

1 Interpretation Act 1978 (c 30), ss 9, 23(3).

810. Summer time. Summer time is a statutory variant of Greenwich mean time, designed to enable greater use to be made of the hours of daylight. Such a measure was advocated in the United States in the eighteenth century by Benjamin Franklin, but its introduction into Great Britain is generally attributed to the efforts of William Willett (1856–1915), aided by the exigencies of war. As a result of Willett's lobbying, a Daylight Saving Bill was introduced into Parliament in March 1908 to provide for time to be advanced by eighty minutes during spring and summer. The Bill was never passed despite being re-introduced in 1909 and 1911, but the matter was raised again in 1916 when Germany, to assist its war effort, enacted a similar provision. Britain swiftly followed suit, the clock being advanced by one hour from 2 am on 21 May 1916[1]. Although the Summer Time Act 1916 applied initially for only one year, its provisions could, by an Order in Council, be extended annually[2]. This was done by a combination of Orders in Council and statute each year until 1925, when the measure was made permanent[3]. Summer time was deemed to begin at 2 am Greenwich mean time on the day after the third Saturday in April (or, if that was Easter Day, the day after the second Saturday in April) and end at 2 am Greenwich mean time on the day after the first Saturday in October[4].

This system continued until the outbreak of war in 1939. As a measure to save fuel and increase the hours available for production, summer time commenced in 1940 on 25 February, was increased to double summer time (that is, two hours in advance of Greenwich mean time) in 1941, and continued thus until 1945. Double summer time was reintroduced for a period in 1947[5]. In 1961 the period of summer time was extended by six weeks[6].

For a continuous period from 27 October 1968 to 31 October 1971, summer time was made permanent[7]. Renamed British Standard Time, it was intended to replace Greenwich mean time[8]. The British Standard Time Act 1968 provided that standard time should expire on 31 October 1971 unless an Order in Council directed otherwise[9]. Public opinion was opposed to standard time, and the Act was allowed to expire.

The Summer Time Act 1972 (c 6) repealed the British Standard Time Act 1968 and consolidated previous enactments. It provides that summer time, defined as being one hour in advance of Greenwich mean time, is to commence at 2 am, Greenwich mean time, the day after the third Saturday in March or, if that day is Easter Day, the day after the second Saturday in March, and end at 2 am, Greenwich mean time, the day after the fourth Saturday in October[10]. This period may be varied by Order in Council, but no such Order may be made unless, after copies of a draft of it have been laid before Parliament, each House presents an address to the Crown praying that the Order be made[11]. To facilitate the harmonisation of the commencement of summer time in all the countries of the European Economic Community in the years 1981 to 1988, the provisions of the Summer Time Act 1972 have been varied by Orders in Council which provide that in those years summer time is to commence at 1 am, Greenwich mean time, on the fourth Sunday of March[12]. Agreement has not yet been reached among the members of the Community on a common date of cessation, although the Orders effected a minor variation by providing that summer time should, in the years to which they apply, end at 1 am, Greenwich mean time, on the fourth Sunday of October. Double summer time may also be reintroduced by the Order in Council procedure[13].

During summer time, any reference to a point of time in any enactment, Order in Council, order, regulation, rule, byelaw, deed, notice or other document is to be reckoned in accordance with summer time[14]. However, Greenwich mean time is preserved for the purposes of astronomy, meteorology and navigation, and for the construction of documents relating thereto[15].

1 Summer Time Act 1916 (c 14), s 1(1) (repealed).
2 Ibid, s 1(2) (repealed).
3 Summer Time Act 1925 (c 64), s 1(1) (repealed).
4 Ibid, s 3(1) (repealed).
5 Summer Time Act 1947 (c 16), s 1(2) (repealed).
6 Ibid, s 1(2) (repealed); Summer Time Order 1961, SI 1961/71.
7 British Standard Time Act 1968 (c 45), s 4(2) (repealed).
8 Ibid, s 1(1) (repealed).
9 Ibid, s 4(2) (repealed).
10 Summer Time Act 1972 (c 6), s 1(1), (2).
11 Ibid, s 2.
12 Summer Time Order 1980, SI 1980/1089; Summer Time Order 1982, SI 1982/1673; Summer Time Order 1986, SI 1986/223; EC Council Directive 82/399 (OJ L173, 19.6.82, p 16); EC Council Directive 84/634 (OJ L331, 19.12.84, p 33).
13 Summer Time Act 1972, s 2(1)(b).
14 Ibid, s 3(1).
15 Ibid, s 3(2).

3. DIVISIONS OF TIME

811. Year. A year is the period of time taken by the earth to complete one revolution of the sun. The precise duration of a year depends on the mode of measurement adopted. If measurement is by reference to the time taken by the sun to return to the same equinox, termed variously the tropical equinoctial, solar, natural, or astronomical year, the duration is 365 days, 5 hours, 48 minutes and 46 seconds (otherwise 365.242199 solar days). If measurement is by reference to the time taken by the sun to travel from a given position in relation to another star to the same position again, termed the astral or sidereal year, the duration is 365 days, 6 hours, 9 minutes and 9.6 seconds. The excess over 365 days occurs due to the rotation of the earth around its own axis.

However, for all practical and legal purposes, the duration of a common year is taken as 365 days and of a leap or bisextile year as 366 days. A leap year, which is designed to correct the error inherent in the Gregorian Calendar, occurs every fourth year and is any year whose date is divisible exactly by four, except those which are divisible exactly by 100 but not by 400.

Since 1600 in Scotland[1] and since 1752 in the remainder of Great Britain and its dependent territories the calendar year has begun on 1 January[2]. Whether the expression 'year' refers to a calendar year or to a period of 365 days commencing on an arbitrary date will depend on the facts of each individual case[3]. When the latter interpretation applies, a year is calculated not by the number of days but by the return of the day of the same denomination in the next year, leap years making no difference in this respect[4]. There is no authority on when the anniversary of an event (such as a birth) which occurred on 29 February should be celebrated in a common year, but on general principles the appropriate date is 28 February, being the 365th day after the event[5].

'Financial year' means, in relation to the Consolidated Fund, the National Loans Fund, or moneys provided by Parliament, or to the Exchequer, or to central taxes or finance, the twelve months ending with 31 March[6]. The financial year of a Scottish regional, islands or district council is also the period of twelve months ending with 31 March, or such other period as the Secretary of State may specify[7].

'Financial year' means, in relation to corporation tax, the period beginning on 1 April in one year and ending on 31 March in the following calendar year[8]. 'Year of assessment' means, in relation to income tax and capital gains tax, the period beginning on 6 April in one year and ending on 5 April in the following year[9]. Various other statutes contain arbitrary definitions of the term 'year'[10].

1 Register of the Privy Council, 1st series, vol 6 (1599–1604), p 63.
2 Calendar (New Style) Act 1750 (c 23), s 1.
3 *Shankland v Airdrieonians Football and Athletic Society* 1956 SLT (Sh Ct) 69.
4 *Lady Bangour v Hamilton* 1681 Mor 248; Stair *Institutions* (5th edn, 1832, ed by John S More), II, notes, p 305; Erskine *Institute* (1871, ed by J B Nicolson) II, 12, 30.
5 The Calendar (New Style) Act 1750, s 6, refers to this, but seems to apply only to anomalies created by the removal of eleven days from 1752.
6 Interpretation Act 1978 (c 30), s 5, Sch 1.
7 Local Government (Scotland) Act 1973 (c 65), s 96(5) (amended by the Local Government (Scotland) Act 1975 (c 30), s 18).
8 Income and Corporation Taxes Act 1970 (c 10), s 527(1).
9 Ibid, s 526(5); Capital Gains Tax Act 1979 (c 14), s 155(1).
10 See eg the definition of 'benefit year' in the Social Security Act 1975 (c 14), s 13(7).

812. Quarter. A quarter is the period of approximately three months which elapses between two quarter days. In Scotland, the quarter days are Candlemas (2 February), Whitsunday (15 May), Lammas (1 August) and Martinmas (11

November). In spite of the variations in the duration of the four quarters, they still appear in leases as the dates for commencement and cessation of tenancies and the payment of rent[1]. The Scottish quarter days must be distinguished from those of England, which are Lady Day (25 March), Midsummer Day (24 June), Michaelmas Day (29 September) and Christmas Day (25 December).

In relation to value added tax, quarters are the periods of three months ending at the end of March, June, September and December[2].

1 Proposals for reform are contained in *The Scottish Term and Quarter Days: A Statutory Definition* (Scot Law Com Consultative Paper, 1986).
2 Value Added Tax Act 1983 (c 55), s 48(1).

813. Month. The term 'month' may be variously interpreted depending upon the context in which it is employed. As has been seen, one of the bases for the construction of early calendars was the lunation, the cycle of the phases of the moon. The most primitive of calendars were, in effect, collections of lunations with various devices being adopted to even out the irregularities produced by the duration of a lunation being approximately twenty-nine and a half days. A 'month' may, therefore, be one of the twelve named divisions of the calendar year, with a duration of from twenty-eight to thirty-one days.

Notwithstanding the duration of the lunation, a 'lunar month' is a period of exactly twenty-eight days. A 'solar month' is the period which the sun takes to pass through one of the twelve signs of the zodiac, and is approximately thirty days. A 'calendar month', where circumstances make clear that the reference is not to one of the named divisions of the year, is a period of from twenty-eight to thirty-one days commencing on any day other than the first day of a named calendar month and terminating on the corresponding day in the succeeding named calendar month. When the period starts towards the end of a named calendar month which contains more days than the following named calendar month, the period expires on the last day of that following month. So a period of one month from 29, 30 or 31 January will terminate, in a common year, on 28 February and, in a leap year, on 29 February.

There has been debate on the meaning of the bare word 'month' at common law in Scotland. It has been held that it means a calendar and not a lunar month[1]. However in *Campbell's Trustees v Cazenove*, Lord Young stated that 'primarily, it means a period of twenty-eight days'[2]. No authority was vouched for this proposition and the point was specifically not decided by the other judges of the Second Division. Lord Young advanced the same view, although rather more tentatively, in *Farquharson v Whyte*[3] but the majority of the court opined to the contrary.

The Interpretation Act 1978 provides that in any Act, unless the contrary intention appears, 'month' means calendar month[4]. In England this definition is applied to deeds, contracts, wills, orders and other instruments[5]. The definition has not been so extended to Scotland, a fact which lends support to the view that at common law the term has always meant calendar month.

1 *Smith v Robertson and Jeffrey* (1826) 4 S 442.
2 *Campbell's Trustees v Cazenove* (1880) 8 R 21 at 23.
3 *Farquharson v Whyte* (1886) 13 R (J) 29 at 32.
4 Interpretation Act 1978 (c 30), s 5.
5 Law of Property Act 1925 (c 20), s 61.

814. Week. The origin of the period now known as a week is most obscure. It has been described as an intruder into other measures of time, for it consists of a fixed number of complete days but pays no regard to months or years. It may have astrological origins, although a much more popular theory is that it derives from the intervals between market days, these being events which occurred with regularity in most early civilisations. However, the concept of a week as a period of seven days is probably related to the four seven-day phases of the lunation. Such a week was certainly the custom in Babylon and was adopted by the Jews and thereafter, in the first century BC, by the Romans[1].

At common law, a week is a period of seven days, commencing at midnight on Saturday and terminating at midnight on the next following Saturday. This calendar week will apply unless statute, context, or trade custom dictate otherwise[2]. The term may also apply simply to any period of seven consecutive days.

1 For a discussion of the origin of the week, see F H Colson *The Week* (1926).
2 *Shanks Fleming v Lochgelly Iron and Coal Co Ltd* (1902) 4 F 890, 10 SLT 114; *John McCue v Barclay, Curle & Co Ltd* (1902) 4 F 909, 10 SLT 116.

815. Day. A day is a period of twenty-four hours. In Scotland, at common law a day begins at midnight, and the period is termed a 'natural day'. However, for most primitive civilisations the day began at dawn with the rising of a new sun; for the early Christians, as for the Jews, it began at sunset; and until 1925 astronomers reckoned the day as beginning at noon. Where context so dictates, a day may be any arbitrary period of twenty-four hours.

Statutes may provide that when calculating a period numbered in days, certain intervening days (such as Sundays and holidays) are to be excluded[1]. When an Act or a provision of an Act is stated to come into force on a particular day, it does so at the beginning of that day[2].

1 Local Government (Scotland) Act 1973 (c 65), s 208(1); Criminal Procedure (Scotland) Act 1975 (c 21), s 451 (substituted by the Criminal Justice (Scotland) Act 1980 (c 62), s 34, Sch 3, para 10).
2 Interpretation Act 1978 (c 30), s 4(a).

816. Periods less than a day. The law will interpret the terms 'hour', 'minute' and 'second' as they are normally understood. Whether intervals of such duration are to be taken into account when calculating the lapse of a period of time will depend on the principle of computation adopted.

4. SUNDAY AND HOLIDAYS

817. Sunday. The common law maxim *dies dominicus non est juridicus* is not of consistent application in Scotland. The statement that 'bargains made on a Sunday are not illegal though judicial acts are', although an accurate reflection of the opinions of earlier writers[1], is now incorrect. It is clear that private acts are valid although taking place on a Sunday. Whether steps in a judicial process are so valid will depend on the terms, if any, of the governing statute. Stair was of the opinion that arrestment[2], horning[3] and poinding[4] were all invalid if carried out on a Sunday, and this remains the position[5]. A debtor may be apprehended on a warrant *in meditatione fugae* on a Sunday[6], but a debtor may not be arrested on that day on an ordinary warrant for civil imprisonment[7]. When an act requires to be carried out at the expiry of a given period, there is a general rule that if that period expires on a Sunday then the act need not be performed until the following day[8].

When calculating a period of time, Sundays are not normally excluded[9], but there are exceptions to this general rule[10].

The principle underlying the common law maxim is, of course, observance of the Fourth Commandment[11]. This is clearly enunciated by Hume who regarded 'the open profanation of the Lord's day' as a species of the offence of profanity, and constituted 'by the doing of such acts thereon, whether for lucre or amusement, as are inconsistent with the command of God on that head, and with the salutary ends which that institution is excellently fitted to promote'[12]. This principle was embodied in a succession of statutes, commencing in pre-Reformation days and extending to the middle of the seventeenth century, which prohibited certain specific activities on Sunday[13].

In contrast to the plethora of enactments which once regulated Sunday observance, there are now few statutory provisions. The Factories Act 1961 prohibits the employment on a Sunday of a young person (defined as a person who has not attained eighteen) in a factory or in connection with any other business carried on by a factory occupier[14]. This is subject to a variety of exceptions, in particular in regard to factories where food is processed[15]. There are also exceptional provisions applicable where both the factory occupier and the employee are Jews[16]. The Shops Act 1950 contains restrictions regarding the carrying on of business as a hairdresser, there again being special exemptions for Jews[17].

Premises in respect of which a public house licence or a refreshment licence is in force can open on Sundays between 12.30 pm and 2.30 pm and between 6.30 pm and 11.00 pm provided that the local licensing board has granted an application to this effect[18]. Premises in respect of which a hotel licence, a restricted hotel licence, a restaurant licence or an entertainment licence is in force, seamen's canteens and registered clubs, may open between those hours without special permission being sought[19]. However, where a licensing board is satisfied that the use of licensed premises is the cause of disturbance or public nuisance, having regard to the way of life in the community in the locality on a Sunday, it may make a Sunday restriction order reducing or completely eliminating all permitted hours for all of such premises[20]. Such provisions enable the local community to retain at least some control over one aspect of Sunday observance which still causes controversy in certain areas of Scotland.

1   Erskine *Institute* III, 1, 10n (d).
2   Stair *Institutions* III, 1, 37.
3   *Stair* III, 3, 11.
4   *Stair* IV, 47, 27.
5   J Graham Stewart *Law of Diligence* (1898), pp 317, 338.
6   Stewart, p 697.
7   Stewart, p 713.
8   See also para 823 below.
9   *Hutton v Garland* (1883) 10 R(J) 60.
10 See the Criminal Procedure (Scotland) Act 1975 (c 21), s 451 (substituted by the Criminal Justice (Scotland) Act 1980 (c 62), s 34, Sch 3, para 10), which provides that, for the purpose of calculating periods of days in appeals and other applications under the Act, Sundays and public holidays are to be excluded.
11 Exodus 20:8.
12 Hume *Commentaries* I, 572.
13 The list of statutes cited by Hume, and repeated by subsequent commentators, was incomplete. The complete list is the Fairs Act 1503 (c 28; 12mo c 83); Sunday Acts 1579 (c 8; 12mo c 20), 1594 (c 8; 12mo c 201) and 1661 (c 281; 12mo c 18); Market-days Act 1592 (c 17; 12mo c 124); Markets on Sundays Act 1592 (c 6; 12mo c 163); Justices of the Peace Act 1661 (c 338; 12mo c 38); Markets Act 1663 (c 42; 12mo c 19); Profaneness Acts 1672 (c 58; 12mo c 22), 1690 (c 55; 12mo c 25), 1693 (c 64; 12mo c 40), 1695 (c 16; 12mo c 13), 1696 (c 31; 12mo c 31) and 1700 (c 12; 12mo c 11); Confession of Faith Ratification Act 1690 (c 7; 12mo c 5); and the Scottish Episcopalians Act 1711 (c 10). The majority of these Acts were repealed by the Statute Law Revision (Scotland) Act 1906 (c 38), s 1, Schedule, and the Statute Law Revision (Scotland) Act 1964 (c 80), s 1, Sch 1. However, the Confession of Faith Ratification Act 1690 remains in force. See the statement by

the Solicitor General to the House of Commons made on 24 November 1983 (1984 SLT (News) 11).
14 Factories Act 1961 (c 34), s 93 (amended by the Sex Discrimination Act 1986 (c 59), s 9(2), Schedule, Pt III).
15 See the Factories Act 1961, ss 96, 112, 113 (as so amended), and the Baking and Sausage Making (Christmas and New Year) Regulations 1986, SI 1986/1709.
16 Ibid, s 60.
17 Shops Act 1950 (c 28), s 67 (amended by the Shops (Early Closing Days) Act 1965 (c 35), s 4(1)(c)).
18 Licensing (Scotland) Act 1976 (c 66), s 53(2), Sch 4.
19 Ibid, s 53(3).
20 Ibid, s 53(2), Sch 4, para 19.

818. Holidays. Holidays, formerly 'holy days of obligation' upon which Roman Catholics were obliged to attend Mass and refrain from work, may arise as a result of statutory enactment, or contractual agreement.

The days designated Bank Holidays in Scotland are New Year's Day if it is not a Sunday or, if it is a Sunday, 3 January; 2 January if it is not a Sunday or, if it is a Sunday, 3 January; Good Friday; the first Monday in May; the first Monday in August; Christmas Day if it is not a Sunday or, if it is a Sunday, 26 December[1]. Upon these days no person can be compelled to make any payment or do any act which he could not be compelled to do on Christmas Day or Good Friday. Any obligation to make such a payment or do such an act is complied with if done on the next following day[2]. The Factories Act 1961 provides that women and persons under eighteen who work in factories are to be permitted six weekday holidays in the year[3]. Two of these holidays must be taken upon days, not less than three months apart, fixed by the district council[3].

Contracts of employment should stipulate the holidays to which employees are entitled, including public holidays and holiday pay[4]. In regard to those industries for which there are wages councils, holidays and holiday remuneration will be regulated by orders made by the councils[5]. Shop assistants are entitled to at least one half day holiday each week[6]. For other offices and employments, holidays may be as negotiated nationally by trade unions and modified to suit local custom, or as agreed between employee and employer.

1 Banking and Financial Dealings Act 1971 (c 80), s 1(1), Sch 1, para 2.
2 Ibid, s 1(4).
3 Factories Act 1961 (c 34), s 94(3) (amended by the Local Government (Scotland) Act 1973 (c 65), ss 155(4), 237(1), Sch 29).
4 Employment Protection (Consolidation) Act 1978 (c 44), s 1(3)(d)(i).
5 Wages Councils Act 1979 (c 12), s 14.
6 Shops Act 1950 (c 28), s 17(1).

5. COMPUTATION OF TIME

819. General. When calculating the precise extent of a period of time it is necessary to determine, first, the method of computation which is to be employed (which may be *naturalis computatio* or *civilis computatio*); second, when the period commences; and, third, when it terminates. The second and third points are closely linked and may conveniently be dealt with together.

The law relating to the computation of time has developed in a piecemeal fashion and there are still a number of significant ambiguities. In so far as a general rule can be enunciated, it is that a period of time which is to be counted in units of a day or longer is to be calculated by *civilis computatio*, the whole of the first day is to be excluded, and the last day is to be included. Whether the whole of the last day is to be included, or the maxim *dies inceptus pro completo habetur* is to be applied, will depend on the circumstances, but inclusion of the whole day is to be preferred although the general tenor of the decisions may be to the contrary.

Except where statute has placed the matter beyond doubt, it is essential to look at each time limit independently, and ascertain the computation principles applicable thereto from an examination of the decided cases or by analogy from similar situations. A general statutory provision would be of great assistance. In the context of time limits in criminal procedure, the Court of Appeal has expressed the hope that

'in any reconsolidation of the Scottish legislation on criminal procedure, this matter (the clear definition of time limits) will be attended to, since express provision on the matter should remove all possibility of doubt or misunderstanding on the part of those who, often under considerable pressure, have to operate in practice our system of criminal procedure'[1].

Similar sentiments may be expressed in regard to private law and procedure.

1 *McMillan v H M Advocate* 1982 SCCR 309 at 312, 1983 SLT 24 at 26.

820. *Naturalis computatio* and *civilis computatio* distinguished. According to *naturalis computatio*, time is calculated *de momento in momentum*. The effect of this is that

'in reckoning time *de momento in momentum*, the prescribed period, say sixty days, will run from a particular hour on the first day to the same hour on the sixty-first day. Where the solar day is taken as a unit of time, and hours are neglected, the mode of reckoning the period of sixty days will be the same, except that the time will run from any hour on the first to any hour on the sixty-first day. Under this mode of computation the error in hours can never amount to a whole day, and is therefore a minimum'[1].

When the point of commencement of the period is not known exactly, the period is calculated from the last moment of the day, month or even year:

'Where the bond or obligation expresses the year in which it was granted, or that in which it was to be performed by the debtor, without mention of the month or term, the last day of that year is presumed to be understood in favour of the creditor'[2].

Naturalis computatio is employed only in exceptional circumstances. It is the appropriate mode of computation only when either the period is to be calculated in units of an hour or less (for example the commencement of the *induciae* of an action which, in terms of the Citation Amendment (Scotland) Act 1882, is to be reckoned from twenty-four hours after the time of posting[3]), or the intention of the parties clearly so implies. Although some institutional writers state that prescription runs *de momento in momentum*, it is questionable whether prescription is a true example of *naturalis computatio*. However the attainment of the age of majority is determined by *naturalis computatio*.

According to *civilis computatio*, time is calculated *de die in diem*. This is the normal method of calculating a period of time. Bell asserted that there is

'a general rule that time is calculated not *de momento in momentum* (*naturalis computatio*) but *de die in diem* (*civilis computatio*), ie that fractions of days are not to be reckoned, but computation is to the midnight following or preceding the last day of the specified term'[4].

Generally accepted though this proposition now is, in Bell's day there was a paucity of authority to support it[5].

 1 *Greig v Anderson* (1883) 20 SLR 421 at 423 per Lord McLaren.
 2 Erskine *Institute* III, 7, 30, founding upon *Ogilvie v Ogilvie* 1630 Mor 6541.
 3 Citation Amendment (Scotland) Act 1882 (c 77), s 4(2).
 4 Bell *Principles* (10th edn, 1899, by W Guthrie) s 46 (note).
 5 See *Pugh v Duke of Leeds* (1777) 2 Cowp 714 at 720, per Lord Mansefield; *Lester v Garland* (1808) 15 Ves 248; *Re Railway Sleepers Supply Co* [1885] 29 Ch D 204 at 205, per Chitty J.

821. Inclusion and exclusion of *dies a quo* and *dies ad quem* generally. In computing any period of time it is essential to establish precisely at what point the period commences, the *terminus a quo*, and when it terminates, the *terminus ad quem*. The essence of *naturalis computatio* being reckoning *de momento in momentum*, ascertainment of the point of commencement, and hence also of the point of cessation, will not usually present any problem. Where the precise *terminus a quo* is not known, the period must be computed from the end of the first hour or such longer period as is, consequent upon the duration of the total period, taken to be the unit of computation.

822. Excluded days. In *civilis computatio* fractions of a day are ignored and the general rule is that the day from which the period runs is excluded, the period being deemed to commence at midnight on that day. This principle was enunciated in cases relating to reductions *ex capite lecti* under the Death Bed Act 1696 (c 4) (repealed), which provided that a testamentary deed could not be reduced under the law of deathbed if the granter had lived for sixty days after the date of the deed. Lord Ivory wrote:

> 'The ground of decision in the House of Lords is important, as fixing the rule of computation, "that the *terminus a quo*, mentioned in the act, is descriptive of a period of time, viz the date or day of death, which is indivisible; and *sixty days after* is descriptive of another and subsequent period, which begins when the first period is completed. The day of making the deed must therefore be excluded" '[1].

The same principle was applied in the context of the law of bankruptcy where preferences granted within the sixty days prior to notour bankruptcy could be reduced under the Bankruptcy Act 1696 (c 5) (repealed). It should be noted that, due to a misinterpretation of the facts in *Blaikie v Clegg*[2], Bell stated the rule incorrectly[3]. A correct statement was given by Lord Ivory:

> 'The day of the bankruptcy is excluded; and, counting from it, the sixty days are held as complete, provided there intervene (1) fifty-nine entire days, reckoning backwards from midnight to midnight; and (2) any portion, however small, of the sixtieth free day'[4].

The general rule has been reinforced by both specific statutory provisions and judicial interpretation of potentially ambiguous statutes. The Bankruptcy (Scotland) Act 1913 stated: 'Periods of time in this Act shall be reckoned exclusive of the day from which such period is directed to run'[5]. So where an arrestment was executed on 20 April and sequestration followed on 19 June, the arrestment was subsequently reduced[6]. On a number of instances within the Bankruptcy (Scotland) Act 1913, immediately one time limit expired another commenced. For example, s 121 provided that immediately upon the expiry of four months from the date of sequestration, the trustee was to make up a statement of the bankrupt's estate which was to be examined by the commissioners within fourteen days of the expiry of the four-month period. Section 124 provided that within eight days of the expiry of the fourteen-day period, the trustee must give notice in the Edinburgh Gazette of the time and place of payment of the first dividend. In *Lipman & Co's Trustee*[7] the four-month period expired on 25 May but the Gazette notice required by the Bankruptcy (Scotland) Act 1856 (c 79), s 127 (which differed from the Bankruptcy (Scotland) Act 1913, s 124, in that the notice had to be published in the Gazette published *next* after the expiry of the fourteen-day period), was not published until 13 June, although the Gazette had been printed on 9 June, the fifteenth day after the expiry of the four-month period. It was held that the notice had not been published timeously. Lord McLaren stated:

> 'I understand the meaning of the statute to be that consecutive periods of time are to be computed according to the ordinary rules of arithmetic, that is to say, you are to add or subtract just as in any ordinary calculation. Now here the period of four months expired on 25th May, and adding 14 to 25 gives 39, and if from that you substract the 31 days of May, you reach the 8th of June. I cannot suppose that the statute means that between two consecutive periods of time there should intervene a day, which belongs neither to the one period nor to the other'[8].

Where a penal statute provides that 'not less than' so many days must elapse before some act is done, it has been held that both the first day and the last day are to be excluded in computing the period[9]. There is no distinction between this phrase and the more commonly encountered 'not less than (so many) clear days'.

In a prosecution under the Sale of Food and Drugs Act 1875 (c 63), s 6 (repealed), for the sale of adulterated milk, the court had to consider the phrase 'not exceeding twenty-eight days from the time of the purchase' of a test sample where it occurred in the Sale of Food and Drugs Act Amendment 1879 (c 30), s 10 (repealed), this being the period within which the summons had to be served[10]. It was argued that the use in the statute of the word 'time' instead of the more usual 'date' implied that computation should be *de momento in momentum*, but the court held that:

> 'In the ordinary sense of our criminal law the word "time" means the day on which the fact or offence occurred, and the rule of law applies, that in computing a period from the time or day of the occurrence of any event, the day of that occurrence is not to be counted. The running of the time is to be counted as from midnight of that day, and therefore any proceedings raised before midnight of the day when the statutory period expires are timeously instituted'[11].

When a period is stated to run 'from' a given date, that date itself is excluded and the period runs from midnight on that date[12]. When an event is to take place 'not earlier than' a specified number of days from a prescribed date, that date is excluded and the phrase is the equivalent of 'clear days'[13].

However, when interpreting such words regard must always be had to the context in which they are employed, which may have the effect of negating the general rule. In one case the court had to consider the meaning of 'from' as occurring in the phrase 'commencing from the 8th September, at which date' a chartered vessel was to be available[14]. The court found that the phrase 'from the 8th September' was ambiguous, but that the ambiguity was cleared up by the qualifying words 'at which date'. 'At a date' or 'at a time' was held to mean 'from the period when the date or time begins to run' and was contrasted with the bare word 'on' which was held to mean 'at any time within the day or date'. Accordingly the phrase in question meant 'from the commencement of 8 September', that is from midnight on 7 September. The opinion was also expressed that when a period of time is set forth in a contract as beginning at a specified hour, it begins at the commencement of that hour and not its close[15]. The decision in *S Appellants*[16] accords with this interpretation. The Social Work (Scotland) Act 1968 (c 49), s 49(1), provides that a child or his parents who are dissatisfied with the decision of a children's hearing may appeal to the sheriff 'within a period of three weeks beginning with the date of' the decision. It was held that in consequence of the use of the words 'beginning with', the whole of the day upon which the hearing at which the decision was made must be included, and that accordingly when the hearing had taken place on 18 February the period of three weeks expired on 9 March[17].

An exception to the general rule is also found in the Interpretation Act 1978 (c 30), s 4, which provides that an Act or provision of an Act comes into force at the beginning of the day upon which it is stated to come into force or, if no specific provision is made for its coming into force, at the beginning of the day upon which the Act receives the royal assent.

1 Note to Erskine *Institute* III, 8, 96, commenting on *Ogilvie v Ogilvie* 1630 Mor 6541, where a deed was reduced where the grantor had survived its execution for fifty-nine days and three hours.
2 *Blaikie v Clegg* 21 January 1809, FC.
3 Bell *Commentaries* II, 168.
4 Note to *Erskine* IV, 1, 41. This approach was followed in *Scott v Rutherfurd* (1839) 2 D 206.
5 Bankruptcy (Scotland) Act 1913 (c 20), s 3 (repealed).
6 *Stiven v Reynolds & Co* (1891) 18 R 422, interpreting the Bankruptcy (Scotland) Act 1856 (c 79), s 108 (repealed).
7 *Lipman & Co's Trustee* 1893 20 R 818.
8 *Lipman & Co's Trustee* (1893) 20 R 818 at 820.
9 See *McMillan v H M Advocate* 1982 SCCR 309, 1983 SLT 24, in which, in the context of the Road Traffic Act 1972 (c 20), s 10(3), the statement at para 1041 of 'Time' by J R Philip in Dunedin *Encyclopaedia of the Laws of Scotland* (1933), vol 14, pp 441–449 was approved.
10 *Frew v Morris* (1897) 24 R(J) 50, 4 SLT 342.
11 *Frew v Morris* (1897) 24 R(J) 50 at 51, 4 SLT 342, per Lord Justice-Clerk Macdonald.
12 *Sickness and Accident Assurance Association v General Accident Assurance Corpn* (1892) 19 R 977.
13 *Wilson* (1891) 19 R 219.
14 *Mackenzie v Liddell* (1883) 10 R 705. See also *Cook's Trustee* 1985 SLT 33.
15 *Mackenzie v Liddell* (1883) 10 R 705 at 714, per Lord Craighill. See also *Hough v Athya & Son* (1879) 6 R 961.
16 *S Appellants* 1979 SLT (Sh Ct) 37.
17 See also *Hare v Gocher* [1962] 2 QB 641, [1962] 2 All ER 763; *Trow v Ind Coope (West Midlands) Ltd* [1967] 2 QB 899, [1967] 1 All ER 19.

823. The termination of the period. When computation is made *de momento in momentum*, little difficulty should attend determining when a period of time concludes, for it will end at the precise *terminus ad quem*[1]. When computation is by *civilis computatio* and the day upon which the period commenced has been excluded, it is to be expected that the final day will be included, and this is the general rule. However, problems attend deciding at what point on that day, notwithstanding that computation is not to be made *de momento in momentum*, the period is to be deemed to have terminated. There are three possibilities; at the beginning of the day, at the conclusion of the day, or at some intermediate point.

The first possibility, that a period of time will expire at the earliest moment of the final day, on the principle that *dies inceptus pro completo habetur*, is the one which is applied most commonly. But the maxim will apply only when a right is being acquired, not when a right is being lost. Lord Justice-Clerk Moncrieff gave the classic exposition of the principle:

'The general rule is, *in favoribilibus dies inceptus pro completo habetur,*—*in favoribilibus*, ie where a party has a presumption in his favour. But where a presumption or a limitation operates so as to cut off a right which a party would otherwise have had, the brocard does not apply'[2].

The difficulty is that the expiry of a period of time may cut off the rights of one party while completing those of another. To whose benefit is the rule then to operate? Bell, drawing on Savigny, appreciated that the application of the maxim must be limited:

'Commentators on the Roman law have gathered from the instances which occur in the law sources the further rule, that when, as in usucaption, a right is acquired by the lapse of a period of time, the preceding midnight is to be taken as its termination (*dies inceptus pro completo habetur*), because the person acquiring is entitled at any moment of the calendar day to regard the acquisition as completed; but that if, as in the prescription of actions, a right is lost by the lapse of the period, the following midnight is the end of the term, because the person who has the right of action may assert, by reason of the uncertainty inherent in the limitation put upon his right, that he can still bring his action at any moment of the last day. This holds, it is said, in ordinary cases where the lapse of a period of time is made the condition of a change in the rights of a party; but if the condition expressly requires the period of time to be completed and overpassed, then even in regard to the acquisition of a right the following midnight is the limit, because, as the calendar day is indivisible, it can only be said on the next day that the period has been exceeded'[3].

It was no doubt uncertainty as to the precise duration of a year that led to the adoption in certain contexts of a period of a year and a day, the expiry of which would ensure that at least a year had elapsed. This did not, however, guarantee that disputes would not arise, because the extra day could, on occasion, be crucial[4].

Under the law of deathbed, the sixty-day period prescribed by the Death Bed Act 1696 (c 4) (repealed) expired at the first moment of the sixtieth day[5]. Similarly, it has been held that a deed granted in preference of creditors on or before the sixtieth day prior to the constitution of notour bankruptcy could not be challenged under the Bankruptcy Act 1696 (c 5) (repealed)[6]. The *dies inceptus* principle applies generally throughout the many time limits involved in bankruptcy law.

The second possibility is that a period of time will not terminate until the final moment of the last day. As already noted, where a right is to be lost by the lapse of a prescriptive period, that period will not expire until the last moment:

'The years of prescription must be fully completed, before any right can be either acquired or lost by it; so that interruption made on the last day of the fortieth year will break its course: for no person ought to be stripped of his property by building one fiction upon another; first by holding a man to have abandoned his right, from his not having exercised it for forty years; and then, by considering him to have neglected his property for full forty years, when in truth that term is not completely run'[7].

It should be noted that in the same passage, Erskine stated that 'prescription runs *de momento in momentum*'. This statement does not accord with authority and must be held to be incorrect. In *Simpson v Marshall* Lord Moncrieff commented:

'The expression *de momento in momentum*, as used by Erskine, means no more than this, that every moment of the years of prescription is to be counted; it does not (as I understand it) mean that the years of prescription necessarily begin to run from the moment or minute or hour that infeftment is completed'[8].

In the same case, Lord Justice-Clerk Macdonald stated:

'The running of prescription is to be counted not from a moment of time on the day of recording, but by the days following on the date. That, as it appears to me, is the sound view, and the day itself is a *dies non* in the computation'[9].

The matter has been placed beyond doubt by the Prescription and Limitation (Scotland) Act 1973 which provides that if the commencement of a prescriptive period would fall at a time in any day other than the beginning of the day, the period is to be deemed to have commenced at the beginning of the next following day[10]. The Act also provides that the principles of computation which are to be applied to the periods of prescription regulated by the Act are those which applied for the purposes of the Prescription Act 1617 (c 12)[11]. Erskine notwithstanding, Walker is correct to state that: 'Negative prescription runs *de die in diem*, and therefore commences to run from the earliest moment of the next day to the last moment of the day of the same number in the same month five years later'[12]. This principle applies to the computation of all prescriptive periods.

The third possibility is that a period of time may terminate at neither the beginning nor the end of the final day but at some intermediate point. There are two situations in which this is most likely to occur. The first is where there is a contractual agreement between parties as to the precise end of a period within which some act must be done. This is frequently encountered in missives for the purchase and sale of heritable property. Where an offer (or a counter-offer which is frequently termed a qualified acceptance) is stated to be open for acceptance until a stated time, acceptance by that time is essential to the conclusion of the bargain. Such acceptance may be constructive, as by posting the letter prior to the stipulated time, but this will not be adequate if the offeror uses words such as 'open for acceptance to reach me not later than' a stated time.

The second situation is where, because of the nature of the act, it can be done only during a restricted period, such as business hours or the hours for which a public office is open, of the final day. So a notice of appearance, defences, or a notice of appeal are timeously lodged only if delivered to the clerk of court's office during the hours when that office is open for business. If merely pushed through a letter box they are held to be received the following business day[13].

There are many occasions on which the last day of a period falls to be excluded wholly. This is most likely to occur where, in a statute, words such as 'clear days', 'not less than (so many) days', 'not less than (so many) clear days', 'at least (so many) days' are employed. J R Philip wrote: 'Where so many "clear days" or "not less than" so many days must elapse before some act is done, not merely the first but the last day is excluded'[14], a passage which has been expressly approved by the High Court in the context of the Road Traffic Act 1972 (c 20), s 10(3)[15]. The High Court also described as 'similar in meaning and effect to the Scottish principle already referred to', a passage from Halsbury's Laws of England[16] which had been quoted with approval by Lord Parker CJ: 'When a period is fixed before the expiration of which an act may not be done, the person for whose benefit the delay is prescribed has the benefit of the entire period, and accordingly, in computing it the day from which it runs as well as the day on which it expires must be excluded.'[17]

1 *Blair v Edinburgh Magistrates* 1704 Mor 3468.
2 *Thomson v Kirkcudbright Magistrates* (1878) 5 R 561 at 563.
3 Bell *Principles* s 46.
4 *Waddell v Salmond* 1680 Mor 3465; *Lady Bangour v Hamilton* 1681 Mor 3467.
5 *Ogilvie v Mercer* 1798 Mor 3336.
6 *Scott v Rutherfurd* (1839) 2 D 206.
7 Erskine *Institute* III, 7, 30.
8 *Simpson v Marshall* (1900) 2 F 447 at 459.
9 *Simpson v Marshall* (1900) 2 F 447 at 457.
10 Prescription and Limitation (Scotland) Act 1973 (c 52), s 4(1)(c).
11 Prescription and Limitation (Scotland) Act 1973, s 4(1)(e).
12 D M Walker *The Prescription and Limitation (Scotland) Act 1973* (2nd edn, 1976), p 56.
13 *Neilson v Robertson* (1891) 19 R 301; *Mackenzie v Munro* (1894) 22 R 45; *S Appellants* 1979 SLT (Sh Ct) 37; *Charleson v Duffes* (1881) 8 R (J) 34.
14 *Encyclopaedia of the Laws of Scotland* (1913) vol 37, para 1041.
15 *McMillan v H M Advocate* 1982 SCCR 309 at 312, 1983 SLT 24 at 25. The Road Traffic Act 1972 (c 20), s 10(3) was substituted by the Transport Act 1981 (c 56), s 25(3), Sch 8.

16 45 Halsbury's Laws of England (4th edn) para 1132.
17 *R v Long* [1959] 3 All ER 559 at 560, [1960] 1 QB 681 at 683, CCA.

824. Attainment of majority. It has been held that the attainment of majority is to be calculated *de momento in momentum*:

> 'The years of minority are computed in *de momento in momentum*, both because one
> cannot in proper speech be called major till the twenty-one years of minority be
> completely run, and because that manner of computation is most profitable to the
> minor'[1].

Accordingly a bond executed on 23 November 1622 by a person born on
24 November 1601 fell to be reduced due to the minority of the granter[2]. The
same principle presumably applies in Scotland to the calculation of any age,
not only to majority, and the age is not attained until the anniversary of the
precise moment of birth.

1 Erskine *Institute* I, 7, 36. By the Age of Majority (Scotland) Act 1969 (c 39), s 1 the age of majority
  was reduced to eighteen.
2 *Drummond v Cunningham-Head* 1624 Mor 3465, approved in Stair *Institutions* I, 6, 33.

825. Effect of Sundays and holidays. In general, no speciality attaches to
Sundays or holidays which occur within a period of time; the period is not to be
extended to compensate for them[1]. However there are important statutory
exceptions to this rule[2].

Difficulties may arise if a period of time which is to be measured in days
terminates on a Sunday or holiday and the act which should be performed
before the expiry of the period cannot be performed on such a day, for instance
due to a public office being closed. In such an event the period is extended to the
first day upon which the act could be performed, on the principle that 'when a
limited time is allowed by the legislature for the exercise of (a right) . . . that
must always be subject to the implied condition that it is possible to perform the
act in question within the specified time'. This principle has been reaffirmed by
Lord President Clyde:

> 'where a certain number of days are prescribed as the period within which a
> particular step must be taken, the Court has repeatedly construed the limitation to
> mean that, if the last day of the period so prescribed is one on which the step cannot
> be taken or completed, then an additional day may be allowed in order to admit of
> the final step being effectively taken or completed'[3].

However the principle is subject to an important qualification; it applies only
where the period is specified in days. It has been held that where a statute
provided that an action must be commenced within six months of an accident
taking place, that six-month period expired on the day of the sixth month
bearing the same number in that month as the day of the accident, and no
allowance was to be made for that day being a Sunday:

> 'I can find nothing in a limitation which is measured by months to warrant my
> holding that such limitation implies, not merely that in each of the unit months there
> shall be opportunity of performing and completing the act, but that there shall be on
> each of the days composing such unit, or, to bring the matter to the crucial point, on
> the last of the days composing the last unit, opportunity of performing and complet-
> ing the act. I see no more reason to suppose that that is the result with regard to a
> prescribed period of six months than to suppose that, in the case of a prescribed
> period of six days, every hour, and in particular the last hour of the sixth day, must
> be available for the purpose of performing and completing the act'[4].

The principle, in its unqualified form, has been accorded statutory authority by the Local Government (Scotland) Act 1973 which provides that where the day or the last day on which anything to which that Act relates is required or permitted by that Act to be done is a Sunday, Christmas Day, New Year's Day, Good Friday, bank holiday, public holiday or day appointed for public thanksgiving or mourning, the requirement or permission is to relate to the first day thereafter which is not one of such days[5]. However the same section specifically retains the general rule that, unless otherwise expressly provided in the Act, such days are not to be excluded when computing a period of time for the purposes of the Act.

1 *Hutton v Garland* (1883) 10 R (J) 60.
2 Criminal Procedure (Scotland) Act 1975 (c 21), s 111A (added by the Criminal Justice (Scotland) Act 1980 (c 62), s 83(2), Sch 7, para 31) provides that where the last day of any of the periods specified in the Criminal Procedure (Scotland) Act 1975, s 75 (substituted by the Criminal Justice (Scotland) Act 1980, s 12, Sch 4) (notice of trial diet), the Criminal Procedure (Scotland) Act 1975, s 76 (as so substituted) (notice of a matter necessitating a preliminary diet), s 76A (as so added) (appeal against a decision taken at a preliminary diet) or s 80 (as so substituted) (notice of objection to a witness) of the Act falls on a Saturday, Sunday or court holiday, the period is extended to and includes the next day which is not a Saturday, Sunday or court holiday. See *H M Advocate v McDonald* 1984 SCCR 229. The Criminal Procedure (Scotland) Act 1975, s 451 (substituted by the Criminal Justice (Scotland) Act 1980, s 34, Sch 3, para 10) provides that in calculating the periods of days in appeals and other applications under the Act, Sundays and public holidays are to be excluded.
3 *M'Niven v Glasgow Corpn* 1920 SC 584 at 588, 1920 2 SLT 57 at 59. See also *Russell v Russell* (1872) 2 R 82; *Hutton v Garland* (1883) 10 R (J) 60; *McVean v Jameson* (1896) 23 R (J) 25; *Blackburn v Lang's Trustees* (1905) 8 F290.
4 *M'Niven v Glasgow Corpn* 1920 SC 584 at 588, 1920 2 SLT 57 at 59, per Lord President Clyde.
5 Local Government (Scotland) Act 1973 (c 65), s 208(1).

826. Construction of expressions. Upon an analysis of the decided cases, it is possible to catalogue various expressions relating to the computation of periods of time which have been judicially construed. There is, however, no guarantee that the same meaning will always be ascribed to a word or phrase, for regard must always be had to the context, statutory or otherwise, within which it occurs.

(1) *'After'* a specified day. The day is not counted and the period of time commences at the first moment of the following day[1].

(2) *'At'* a specified time. 'At a date or at a time means from the period when the date or time begins to run . . . When the occurrence is to happen at a date or at a time, this means, as I think, the opening of the specified period'[2].

(3) *'At least'* a specified period must elapse. Both the first and the last days of the period are to be excluded. It has been held that, when a notice of appeal in the context of the Valuation of Lands (Scotland) Act 1854 (c 91), s 9 (repealed) required to be given 'six days at least before such appeal is heard', there must be six clear days' notice[3]. Lord Dundas stated: 'The appellants were thus duly certiorated that, if they meant to appeal, they must give six days' notice before the 10th of September — that is, not later than 3 September 1909'[4].

(4) *'By'* a specified day. The whole of the day is to be included, not merely that portion during which business can be transacted. Where an offer was open for acceptance 'by Monday 6th inst.' it was held to have been accepted by the posting of an acceptance on that day, although it was not received until noon the following day.

'When the offeror names a time such as a certain day of the month, there is given to the person to whom the offer is made the whole of that day to make his decision, and that if within that day he accepts in a manner to bind himself, the bargain is closed. Up to the end of the time named, the consent of the offerer must be held to subsist, so that it may be taken advantage of by the other party'[5].

(5) *'Clear days'.* 'Where so many "clear days" . . . must elapse before some act is done, not merely the first but the last day is excluded'[6].

(6) *'From' or 'commencing from' a specified date.* 'From' has been described as 'an ambiguous expression undoubtedly; for consistently with ordinary use of the word, it may mean from the beginning so as to include the whole, or from the termination so as to include no part of that day'[7]. The ambiguity can be removed only by examining the context in which the expression is used. It has been stated that the primary meaning of 'from' a date is 'from the expiry of' the date[8], but this was in the context of a contract of insurance where the risk which had been insured against had come to pass on the disputed date, to the knowledge of both insurer and insured, and had therefore ceased truly to be a risk but had become a certainty. Where the phrase 'within twenty-eight days from the time' occurred in a penal statute it was held that the whole of the twenty-eight days fell to be included[9]. Where the words 'commencing from' were qualified by 'at which date' the ambiguity was held to be resolved in favour of including the whole of the first day[10].

(7) *'Not earlier than' or 'not less than' a specified number of days.* Both phrases are synonymous with 'clear days' and the first and last days must be included[11].

(8) *'On' a specified day.* 'A thing that is to happen on a day or date, may occur at any time within the day or date'[12].

(9) *'Within' a specified time.* Where an act must be performed within a specified number of days, it can be timeously performed at any time up to midnight on the final day of the period, the period being calculated exclusive of the *terminus a quo*. This has been held to apply to the serving of a complaint[13]. However this principle does not apply to an application for a stated case under the Criminal Procedure (Scotland) Act 1975, s 442 which, in terms of s 444(1) of that Act must be made within one week of the final determination of the proceedings[14]. Such an application is not deemed made until it is in the hands of the clerk of the court; if posted within the week but received outwith that period, the application has not been made timeously[15].

1 *Stiven v Reynolds & Co* (1891) 18 R 422; Bills of Exchange Act 1882 (c 61), s 14(2).
2 *Mackenzie v Liddell* (1883) 10 R 705 at 714.
3 *Watson, Gow & Co Ltd v Glasgow Assessor* 1910 SC 807, 1910 2 SLT 189, LVAC.
4 *Watson, Gow & Co Ltd v Glasgow Assessor* 1910 SC 807 at 809, 1910 2 SLT 189 at 190, LVAC.
5 *Jacobsen Sons & Co v Underwood & Son Ltd* (1894) 21 R 654 at 657, per Lord Justice-Clerk Macdonald.
6 Dunedin *Encyclopaedia of the Laws of Scotland* (1933), vol 14, p 449; quoted and approved in *McMillan v H M Advocate* 1982 SCCR 309 at 311, 1983 SLT 24 at 25.
7 *Mackenzie v Liddell* (1883) 10 R 705 at 714, per Lord Craighill.
8 *Sickness and Accident Assurance Association Ltd v General Accident Assurance Corpn Ltd* (1892) 19 R 977 at 985, per Lord President Robertson.
9 *Frew v Morris* (1897) 24 R (J) 50, 4 SLT 342.
10 *Mackenzie v Liddell* (1883) 10 R 705.
11 *McMillan v H M Advocate* 1982 SCCR 309, 1983 SLT 24. See also *Cook's Trustee* 1985 SLT 33.
12 *Mackenzie v Liddell* (1883) 10 R 705 at 714, per Lord Craighill.
13 *Frew v Morris* (1897) 24 R (J) 50, 4 SLT 342; *Lockhart v Bradley* 1977 SLT 5.
14 The Criminal Procedure (Scotland) Act 1975 (c 21), ss 442, 444(1) are replaced, respectively, by the Criminal Justice (Scotland) Act 1980 (c 62), s 34, Sch 3, paras 1, 3.

15 *John Elliot* 1984 SCCR 125, 1984 SLT 294, but cf *Charleson v Duffes* (1881) 8 R (J) 34; and see M Christie 'Applying for a Stated Case' 1984 JLSS 457.

6. THE EUROPEAN CONVENTION ON THE CALCULATION OF TIME-LIMITS

827. Introduction. In an attempt to harmonise the methods of calculating time limits in the member states of the Council of Europe, a committee of experts set up by the European Committee on Legal Co-operation prepared a draft Convention on the Calculation of Time-Limits which was adopted by the Committee of Ministers of the Council of Europe in January 1972 and opened for signature in Basle, Switzerland on 16 May 1972 on the occasion of the Seventh Conference of European Ministers of Justice. Although the Convention has not yet been signed by the United Kingdom, it provides an insight into the manner in which the problem of calculating time limits has been tackled on an international plane and its provisions may eventually be of relevance in Scotland.

There are severe limitations to the scope of the Convention. It applies to a 'time-limit' which is conceded in the Explanatory Report published along with the Convention to be an unsatisfactory translation of the French term 'delai'[1]. No satisfactory definition of 'time-limit' could be devised although various possibilities were canvassed. Among the situations which might be regarded as time limits but which are not to be covered by the Convention are the calculation of the moment of the attainment of majority (so the discrepancy between the rules applicable in Scotland and England noted in para 824 above would not be removed), the calculation of limited periods of time for which a person is to be liable for payment of maintenance, and the calculation of a period for which a contract, such as hire, lease or employment, was concluded. The calculation of the qualifying periods necessary for social security benefits and for entitlement to hold certain employments and public offices are excluded. The Convention would not apply to time limits calculated retroactively. The substantial restrictions on the application of the Convention must raise serious doubts as to its potential utility.

The preamble narrates that the Convention has been entered into because its signatories are 'convinced that the unification of rules relating to the calculation of time limits, both for domestic and international purposes, will contribute to the attainment' of greater unity among Members of the Council of Europe. The scope of the Convention is defined in article 1 and it is stated to apply to the calculation of time-limits in civil, commercial and administrative matters where limits have been laid down by statute, judicial or administrative authority, arbitral body, or by parties who have not agreed some alternative method of calculation or between whom there is no alternative established practice. The apparently wide ambit of the Convention must, of course, be read subject to the restrictive interpretation of 'time limit' noted above. However the Explanatory Report concludes that the Convention would apply to prescriptive periods, a time limit for acceptance of an offer, and time limits in court proceedings[2].

1 *Explanatory Report on the European Convention on the Calculation of Time Limits* (Council of Europe, Strasbourg) 1973, para 5.
2 Ibid, para 15.

828. *Dies a quo* and *dies ad quem*. Article 2 of the European Convention on the Calculation of Time-Limits defines the terms *dies a quo* and *dies ad quem*, neither of which will present any problems in Scotland. Article 3(1) states: 'Time-limits expressed in days, weeks, months or years shall run from the *dies a quo* at midnight to the *dies ad quem* at midnight'. Accordingly, in Scottish terminology, *civilis computatio* is to be adopted, and all ambiguity which can attend defining the termination of the period is removed. The maxim *dies inceptus pro completo habetur* is not applied. The Convention contains no provisions relative to periods calculated in hours. The time limit applicable to an act which can be performed only during normal business or office hours (such as lodging a notice of appearance or appeal) will expire at the conclusion of those normal hours[1] even though this is earlier than midnight on the *dies ad quem*[1]. Whether a document such as an acceptance of an offer must actually reach the person to whom it is addressed by midnight on the *dies ad quem* or whether it is sufficient if posted before that time is a matter for the national law and is not covered by the Convention.

1 European Convention on the Calculation of Time-Limits, art 3(2).

829. Rules for the calculation of periods of time. Article 4 of the European Convention on the Calculation of Time-Limits contains detailed rules for the calculation of periods expressed in weeks, months, years or fractions thereof. Where the period is expressed in weeks, the *dies ad quem* is the day of the last week whose name corresponds to that of the *dies a quo*. Where a period is expressed in months or years, the *dies ad quem* is the day of the last month or year whose date corresponds to that of the *dies a quo* or, when there is no corresponding date, the last day of the last month. Where fractions are specified, whole months are counted first, and then days or fractions of a month, a month being deemed to consist of thirty days.

830. Saturdays, Sundays and holidays. Article 5 of the European Convention on the Calculation of Time-Limits applies to Saturdays, Sundays and official holidays the principle applicable in Scotland to such days when the total period is calculated in days. When calculating a period of time they are to be counted as normal, but if the *dies ad quem* of a period before the expiry of which some act is to be performed falls on such a day, and performance on the day is impossible, the period is extended to the first working day thereafter. Articles 6 to 14 are of a formal nature.

831. Effect of the Convention in Scotland. Ratification of the European Convention on the Calculation of Time-Limits by the United Kingdom should cause few problems in Scotland. It would introduce certainty into the termination of a period calculated by *civilis computatio*. Presumably *naturalis computatio* would continue to be applied to periods calculated in hours. There is no good reason for the Convention not being applied to all time-limits, in addition to those encompassed by the term 'delai'. If this was not done, then alternative modes of computation would be preserved, causing unnecessary confusion. There is also no reason why the Convention should not be applied to periods computed retroactively.

INDEX

SOCIAL WORK

Accommodation. *See also* HOMELESS PERSON; RESIDENTIAL CARE
hostel, for probationers, 34. *See also* HOSTELS
mentally handicapped person—
community sheltered, 31
remand centre—
young person, committal, 33
secure—
child, for—
registration by Secretary of State, 33
young person, for—
local authority duty to provide, 16
temporary—
person in need, Social Work (Scotland) Act 1968 . . . 13
young person on remand—
local authority provision, 32

Adoption
agency—
report of placement, 19
freeing procedure, 18
local authority, role, 19
panel, decisions, 19
placement for, 19
reports for court, 19
services, generally, 19
timescales, procedures, absence, 18
social worker, role, 18
voluntary organisations, role, 19
welfare of child, 18, 19

After-care
child detained at direction of Secretary of State, 36
family placement—
child released at direction of Secretary of State, 36
licence, duration, 36
mandatory, groups to which applicable, 36
mental disorder, person with—
local authority, duty to provide, 30
voluntary organisations, co-operation with local authority, 30
planning before offender's release, 36
residential unit—
child released at direction of Secretary of State, 36
Secretary of State—
child detained at direction of, 36

After-care—*contd*
Secretary of State—*contd*
notification to—
social worker, by—
after-care licence, supervision, 36
social worker—
statutory duty—
young offenders to which applicable, 36
supervisory role, 36
young offender—
social worker, statutory duty, 36
young offender's institution, person released from, 36

Appeal
residential home, refusal of registration, 16

Assistance in kind
child under 18—
local authority duty, exercise, discretion, 13
preventing child coming into care, 13
conditionally given—
local authority, 13
emergency, 13
entitlement, statutory, 13
home meals service as, 27. *See also* HOME MEALS SERVICE
local authority, discretion to provide—
matters required to be considered in exercise, 13
repayment—
local authority, 13

Bail
social worker, access to person on—
condition of bail, as, 32
refusal—
application by social worker to court, 32

Burial
expenses, recovery—
local authority, by—
deceased estate, 15
person liable to maintain, 15
local authority—
payments, discretionary to assist/attend, 15
power to arrange, of person in care, 15

References are to paragraphs

Capital expenditure
central government loan, 16
day facilities, 16
residential facilities, 16
**CCETSW (Central Council for Edu-
cation and Training of Social
Workers)**
establishment, 11
functions, 11
Secretary of State, appointment of members, 11
Younghusband Report, 11
Charitable organisations. See also VOL-
UNTARY ORGANISATIONS
historical background—
provision of services, 1
Child
abuse, see CHILD ABUSE
adoption, see ADOPTION
after-care supervision—
release after detention at direction of
Secretary of State, 36
assistance in kind—
local authority, duty to exercise discretion, 13
preventing child coming into care, 13
care—
generally, 17–22
historical background, 1, 2
legal basis—
social worker, duty to assess appropriate, 18
local authority duties, 17–22
reception into, see CHILD IN CARE
compulsory removal—
procedure, 18
social worker, evidence, 18
conviction—
detention at direction of Secretary of
State—
placement, local authority function,
33
custody. See CUSTODY
day care, 21. See also DAY FACILITIES
detention—
direction of Secretary of State, 33
placement after conviction—
local authority function, 33
principles, 33
neglect—
McBoyle Committee recommendations, 4
person in need, as—
Social Work (Scotland) Act 1968 . . . 13
place of safety, committal by court to, 33

Child—contd
release, Secretary of State, recommendations, 33
residential care, 13, 17, 36. See also RESI-
DENTIAL CARE
risk, at—
McBoyle Committee recommendations, 4
secure accommodation—
Secretary of State, registration with,
33
social work department—
duties to child—
care, provision, 17. See also CHILD IN
CARE
generally, 17–22
supervision by social worker, 21
under 17—
local authority, duty to provide care,
17
welfare, 1, 18, 19, 20
Child abuse
assessment, level of risk—
social worker, 1
children's hearing, time limit for—
place of safety warrant, after, 22
co-ordination of services to protect children, 22
criticisms of social work intervention, 1
place of safety—
social worker, application for warrant,
22
risk—
duty, social worker, to investigate, 22
social worker—
discretion, problems in exercise, 1
duty to investigate report of, 22
intervention, generally, 1
Child in care
assistance in kind—
local authority, discretion, 13
preventing child coming into care, 13
boarding out facilities—
local authority duty to provide, 17
visiting of child, regulation, 17
criteria for reception into, 17
decisions relating to—
criteria, 18
social work department, duty, 18
foster parents—
local authority duty to assess, 17
Kilbrandon Committee report, 5
local authority—
exercise of duty to receive into care, 17
parental contact—
Secretary of State, Code of Practice, 15

References are to paragraphs

References are to paragraphs

References are to paragraphs

References are to paragraphs

References are to paragraphs

References are to paragraphs

References are to paragraphs

References are to paragraphs

References are to paragraphs

References are to paragraphs

References are to paragraphs

SOURCES OF LAW (FORMAL)

Acts of Parliament
citation, 169
commencement—
　enactment distinguished, 155
continuing Acts—
　expiring Acts, for, 166
duration, 156
enactment—
　commencement distinguished, 155
　formula, 153
　legal validity, effect, 153
European Communities legislation—
　implementation by, 221
　precedence, 214
expiry—
　continuing Acts, 166
　effect, 165
judicial notice—
　as public Act, 168
operation, generally, 153–170
parent legislation, as, *see* LEGISLATION;
　STATUTORY INSTRUMENTS
preamble, 154
presumption of application to Scotland,
　170
promulgation, 167
proof, 168
re-enactment after repeal, 164
repeal—
　effect—
　　accrued rights etc, on, 161
　　common law, on, 163
　　Interpretation Act 1978 ... 159
　　subordinate legislation, on, 160, 183
　　substitute provisions for enactment
　　　repealed—
　　　duration, repealed enactment, 164
　express, 156, 157
　implied, 156, 158
　re-enactment, 164
repeal of repealing enactment—
　effect, 162
Scotland—
　application to, 170
　presumption of application to, 170
territorial extent, 170
Adjournal, Acts of
subordinate legislation—
　High Court of Justiciary, 187
statutory instruments, when, 187
Alison, Archibald
'authoritative writings', inclusion in
　canon of—
　Practice of Criminal Law of Scotland, 441
　Principles of Criminal Law of Scotland,
　　441

Appellate jurisdiction. *See also* HOUSE
　OF LORDS; JUDICIAL COMMITTEE OF
　THE PRIVY COUNCIL; JUDICIAL
　PRECEDENT
House of Lords, generally, 270–285
precedent in appeals, 265–333
Thomson Committee on Criminal
　Appeals in Scotland—
　recommendations, 319
Assythment, action of
precedent—
　reasons for not following prior
　　decisions—
　　cessante ratione cessat ipsa lex, 354
Attorney-General
England and Wales—
　reference to Court of Appeal, point of
　　law, 319, 320
Lord Advocate—
　analogous powers of reference—
　　High Court, on point of law, 319,
　　　320
Authoritative writings. *See* INSTI-
　TUTIONAL WRITERS; LEGAL
　LITERATURE

Bankton, Andrew McDouall, Lord
An Institute of the Laws of Scotland—
　'authoritative writings', inclusion in
　　canon of, 441
　common law—
　　custom distinct or part of, 368
　custom as formal source of law, 131,
　　368
　desuetude, doctrine of, 131
　equity as synonym for law of nature,
　　409
　formal source of law, as, 434
　nobile officium, 428, 430
　precedent—
　　as gloss upon statute, 136
　　as practice or custom, 251
　special authority of, 437, 440
　Union legislation as fundamental
　　law—
　　objection to thesis, 147
Bell, Professor George Joseph
*Commentaries on the Law of Scotland and on
　the Principles of Mercantile
　Jurisprudence*—
　'authoritative writings', inclusion in
　　canon of, 441
Principles of the Law of Scotland, 441
special authority of writings, 437, 440,
　441
Stair, assessment, 440

References are to paragraphs

Benthamism
legal positivism—
   neglect of equity as result, 417
Brehon law
English common law and, 338
Tanistry Case, 388
Udal law—
   validity in Scots common law, com-
      parison, 388
Byelaws
authenticity, 190
commencement, 190
confirmation, 191
confirming authority—
   powers, 189
enactment, 189
local authority, 189–193
public authority, 189–193
publicity, 190
review—
   requirement, local authority, ten-
      yearly intervals, 193
revocation—
   procedure, 192
ultra vires—
   challenge not vitiated by con-
      firmation, 191
validity, generally, 191

Case law. *See* JUDICIAL PRECEDENT
Civil law
criminal proceedings, arising in—
   precedent, 303
equity, part in development, 400–419.
   See also EQUITY
Codes of Practice, Statutory
formula, 197, 199
functions, 196
health and safety at work, 200
Highway Code, 197, 198
industrial relations, 199
promulgation, 197
self-regulation by, 196
status, generally, 197
statutory guidance for, 201
subordinate legislation, whether, 195
College of Justice
Sederunt, Acts of—
   purported powers conferred on judges
      of Court of Session, 187
Senator—
   Court of Session decisions—
      record, sixteenth and seventeenth
         centuries, 251

Commercial law
custom and precedent, influence, 260
precedent—
   reasons for not following prior
      decisions—
      cessante ratione cessat ipsa lex, 354
      Commerzbank case, 354
      Miliangos case, 354
Common law
Bankton—
   custom as common law, 368
Coke, Sir Edward—
   description of common law, 358
Craig, Sir Thomas—
   sources of English law, 364
custom as formal source in Scotland—
   displacement by sixteenth century,
      362
   generally, 355–359
desuetude, doctrine of, 376. *See also* DE-
   SUETUDE, DOCTRINE OF
displacement of custom as source of law
   by, 362
eighteenth   century   change   in
      terminology—
   custom, relationship to, 369
emergence distinctively in Scotland, 359,
   362
enforcement—
   King and Parliament, 362
English—
   Coke's description, 358
   custom and usage as source—
      distinguished, 372, 374, 389, 390
   Tanistry Case, 388
   test of antiquity—
      'from time immemorial', 372, 373
King and Parliament—
   determination to enforce, 362
legal custom differing from—
   local custom still a valid source of law,
      377
lex et consuetudo, 356
mercantile usage, incorporation into,
   375, 390
modern Scots law—
   desuetude, doctrine of, 376, 381
   England, contrasting reception of
      custom as, 375
   general custom as, 375, 376
prevalence over other laws and
      customs—
   King and Parliament, determination,
      362
repeal of statute, effect, 162

References are to paragraphs

References are to paragraphs

References are to paragraphs

References are to paragraphs

References are to paragraphs

References are to paragraphs

References are to paragraphs

References are to paragraphs

References are to paragraphs

References are to paragraphs

References are to paragraphs

References are to paragraphs

Legislation—*contd*
subordinate—
codes of practice, statutory, 195–201.
    See also CODES OF PRACTICE,
    STATUTORY
delegated powers, 175
European Communities legislation,
    implementation by, 221
generally, 175–201
meaning, 175
repeal of enabling Act, effect, 160
statutory instruments, 176–187. *See
    also* STATUTORY INSTRUMENTS
subordinate instruments not statutory
    instruments—
    autonomic/autonomous legislation,
    194
    byelaws, 189–193. *See also* BYELAWS
    status, 188
Union—
fundamental law, as—
    academic logic, 152
    assertion and proof, 151
    difficulties, Universities (Scotland)
        Act 1853 . . . 149
    generally, 144–146
    judicial review, competence, 150
    objections to thesis of—
        Dicey, 148
        institutional writers, 147
        political realism, 152
    Union Agreement as constituent
        document, 145
    intention, 146
validity, 111
Lord Advocate
Attorney General in England—
analogous power of reference—
    Court of Appeal, 319
reference to High Court—
    point of law, 319
    Thomson Committee on Criminal
        Appeals in Scotland—
        recommendation, 319
Lyon Court
appeal from—
    Court of Session, to, 325
    House of Lords, to—
        Court of Session, from, 325
Court of Session—
    jurisdiction to review proceedings,
    325
High Court of Chivalry, comparison,
    325
jurisdiction, 325

Lyon Court—*contd*
Lord Lyon—
authority, comparison—
    Earl Marshal of England, 325
    jurisdiction to reduce own decrees, 325
precedent—
    binding decisions—
        Court of Session, 325
        High Court of Justiciary, 325
        House of Lords in Scottish
            appeals, 325
    power to distinguish decisions incon-
        sistent with authority, 325
review of proceedings—
    Court of Session, jurisdiction, 325
Mackenzie, Sir George. *See also* INSTI-
    TUTIONAL WRITERS
criminal law—
    crime against natural or positive law,
        distinction, 421
    equity, part in development, 421
    *The Laws and Customs of Scotland in
        Matters Criminal*—
        canon of 'authoritative writings',
            inclusion, 441
custom and statute—
    sources of law, tension as, 130
desuetude, doctrine of, 130
Institutions of the Law of Scotland—
    canon of 'authoritative writings',
        inclusion, 441
precedent, view of, 251
special authority of writings, 437, 441

Nationality
Scottish—
pre-Union legislation—
    Union Agreement of 1707, effect—
        House of Lords as court, binding
            decisions, 275
Natural law
authority of equity in, 406
Bankton—
    equity as synonym for law of
        nature, 409
criminal law—
    Kames, 422
    Mackenzie, 421
    mala in se and *mala prohibita*, distinc-
        tion, 420
divine law and, 401
Erskine—
    positive and natural law—
        relationship, foundation, 410
Kames's *Principles of Equity*, 411–416

References are to paragraphs

Natural law—*contd*
Stair's jurisprudence—
  equity as a source of law, 400, 401,
    406, 408
  meaning, 401
  principles identical with those of
    equity, 401

Order in Council
judicial review—
  exercise, ministerial powers conferred
    by, 173
prerogative legislation, 171
Privy Council—
  by and with advice of, 171
royal proclamations contrasted, 171
Orkney and Shetland
customary law—
  distinction from common law of Scot-
    land, 387
  reasonableness—
    Bruce v Smith, 385–388
  udal rights—
    Bankton, *Institutes,* 368
    Erskine, *Institutes,* 367
    modern cases, 385–388
    Stair's *Institutions,* 366
Udal law—
  Bruce v Smith—
    reasonableness test of custom, 385–
    388
  distinction from common law of Scot-
    land, 387
  local custom, as, 387
  origin, 387
  Scots law, recognition—
    continuing validity, Udal law, 387

Parliament. *See also* ACTS OF PARLIA-
  MENT; LEGISLATION
legislative supremacy—
  critical scrutiny—
    Accession of United Kingdom to
    European Communities, 120,
    214
    Act of Union of England and Scot-
    land, 120
  fundamental postulate, 120
Scots—
  customary law, confirmation, 361
Pension Appeal Tribunals
precedent—
  binding authority, 332
war pension cases—
  stare decisis doctrine, application, 332

Positive law
equity—
  principles of natural law distinguished,
    402
Erskine—
  positive and natural law—
    foundation of relationship, 410
Kames's *Principles of Equity,* 411–416
meaning—
  Stair's *Institutions,* 402
natural law, distinction, 402
Scots law as—
  Stair's *Institutions,* 403
Stair's *Institutions,* 402–408
theological foundations, 405
Prerogative. *See* LEGISLATION
Prescription
custom and, 391
doctrine, 391
public rights, application to, 391
servitudes—
  prescriptive period, 392
statutory basis in modern Scots law, 391
Presumption
Act of Parliament—
  application to Scotland, 170
statutory endorsement of precedent,
  137–140
Public interest
legislation—
  intention as to contracting out—
    competing concepts, public interest,
    125
Public policy
precedent, 'cross-border'—
  House of Lords, decisions—
    Scots and English law, 277
Public rights of way
custom and—
  'time immemorial', 380, 393
meaning, 393
prescription—
  application of doctrine, 391, 393

Registration of Voters Appeal Court
absent voter—
  interpretation of entitlement, 326
authority, binding, own decisions—
  sheriff court, on—
    appeal from electoral registration
    officer, 326
decisions binding on, 326
Restrictive Practices Court
decisions binding on, 327
institution, 327

References are to paragraphs

References are to paragraphs

References are to paragraphs

SOURCES OF LAW (GENERAL AND HISTORICAL), LEGAL METHOD AND REFORM

References are to paragraphs

References are to paragraphs

References are to paragraphs

Company law
floating charges, 658, 680
Law Reform Committee for Scotland—
  1960 report—
    floating charges, 658
    security over moveable property,
      658
Scottish Law Commission recommendations—
  floating charges, 680
Confidence
breach of—
  Scottish Law Commission consideration of law, 674
Confirmation of testaments
commissary courts, local, 519
Contract law
exemption clauses, 670
implied terms, 670
rectification of documents, 671
Sale of Goods Act 1893 . . . 640, 643, 670.
  See also MERCANTILE LAW
Scottish Law Commission recommendation for reform, 670, 671
Unfair Contract Terms Act 1977 . . . 670
Conveyances of land, *see* LAND LAW
Council of the king
churchmen, participation, 551
College of Justice—
  development from, 515
curia regis, 506, 515
judicial function, 506, 515
Lords of—
  inclusion in fifteenth century sessions,
    515
sessions, appointment to facilitate
  judicial business, 515
Court of Session
absorption of other courts—
  nineteenth century, 519, 635
Admiralty court—
  jurisdiction partly transferred to, 519,
    609, 635
appeal from—
  House of Lords, 602, 635
appellate jurisdiction—
  before 1707 . . . 602
  generally, 518
  within—
    development of precedent, 544
canon law, influence—
  constitution, on—
    Sacra Romana Rota, 583
  procedure, on, 551
Chancellor of Scotland—
  abeyance of chancellorship, 517
  theoretical president, 517

Court of Session—*contd*
College of Justice, nucleus of reconstituted, 515
collegiate character, 518
commissary court, principal—
  absorption, 519
curia regis—
  sessions of—
    fifteenth century origins, 515
damages for personal injuries, action—
  procedural reforms—
    Scottish Law Commission, 676
description—
  eighteenth century composition, 635
equitable jurisdiction, special—
  nobile officium, 547, 583
Extraordinary Lords—
  abolition, 517, 630
  Crown nominees, 517
first instance, as court of, 518
functions, 518
House of Lords—
  appellate jurisdiction from, 602
Inner House, 518, 544, 635
jury trial, introduction, 635
Law Reform Committee for Scotland—
  judge as president of, 650
Lord President—
  clerical background, sixteenth century, 517
  Lord-Justice General—
    office incorporated in presidency,
      520
  sixteenth century, 517
Lords Commissioners of Justiciary—
  Lords of Session, as, 520
Lords of Council—
  inclusion, fifteenth century sessions,
    515
Lords Ordinary—
  reforms, nineteenth century, 635
  sixteenth century, 517
nineteenth century restructuring, 518,
  635
nobile officium—
  canonical foundation, suggested, 583
  special equitable jurisdiction, 547, 583
  origins, 515
Outer House, 518, 635
Practicks, 539, 540. *See also* PRECEDENT
precedent, generally, 539–545. *See also*
  PRECEDENT
procedural reforms, 518, 635
reform, generally, 518, 635
Rules of Court of 1936 (revised), 528
Sederunt, Acts of, 528. *See also* STATUTORY SOURCES OF SCOTS LAW

References are to paragraphs

Court of Session—*contd*
sixteenth century composition, 517, 583
stare decisis doctrine—
  development, 541
  modern rules—
    Whole Court, decisions, 544
structure, 518, 519
Whig proposals—
  eighteenth century reform, 635
Whole Court, 518, 544
Craig of Riccarton, Sir Thomas, *see*
  INSTITUTIONAL WRITERS
Criminal justice. *See also* HIGH COURT
  OF JUSTICIARY
Adjournal, Acts of—
  High Court of Judiciary, procedure,
    528
administration—
  seventeenth century generally, 520
circuit sittings—
  High Court of Justice, 520
High Court of Justice—
  jurisdiction, 520
High Court of Justiciary—
  Acts of Adjournal, 528
  jurisdiction, 520
incest, review of law—
  Scottish Law Commission, 695. *See
    also* INCEST
Lord-Justice General—
  combination of office with presidency,
    Court of Session, 520
  functions, 520
Cromwellian period
law reform, attempted—
  unification proposals—
    Scots and English law, 628
Stair's *Institutions*, commencement, 628
Tender of Union—
  refusal of Scots lawyers to subscribe
    to, 628
Crown, the
bankruptcy, preferences—
  limited retention, 678
equitable jurisdiction—
  modern exercise, 547
Extraordinary Lords—
  nomination to Court of Session, 517
feudal law, position, 591, 592, 596
judicial role, original, 523
prerogative legislation, 523
nobile officium—
  Court of Session—
    exercise, Crown's equitable juris-
      diction, 547
royal commission, appointment, 637

Custom
ancient—
  proof as distinction from modern, 533
'ancient and immemorial'—
  Stair's view, 532
binding, 530
constituent element of Scots law, as, 529
Court of Session—
  role in clarification, 532
equitable, 532
erosion as source of law, 531
Erskine—
  analysis, 529–532
'essential'—
  Erskine's view, 532
formal source of law, as, 501, 529–533
French customary law—
  admixture with Roman law—
    influence, education, Scottish law
      students, 604
'institutional' writers—
  juristic treatment, 532, 533. *See also*
    'INSTITUTIONAL' WRITERS
legal treatises, development through,
    532
local legal, 530
marine, 608, 609. *See also* MERCANTILE
  LAW
meaning, 530
modern—
  proof as distinction from ancient, 533
notorious—
  ancient custom as, 533
precedent and, 543
proof of validity, 533
Reformation, effect, 532
sources of Scottish customary law—
  canon law, 532
  civil law, 532
  feudal law, 532
Stair's *Institutions*—
  evaluation of custom, 529, 532, 533
Udal law—
  Orkney and Shetland, 530
universal legal, 530

Damages
antenatal injury, liability—
  Scottish Law Commission report, 675
cohabitant as claimant—
  personal injuries action, 676
employer's right to recover—
  injury to employee, 661
  Law Reform Committee for Scotland
    1963 report, 660

References are to paragraphs

References are to paragraphs

References are to paragraphs

Feudal law—*contd*
military tenure—*contd*
  fiscal advantages, 593
  prestations attached to, 593
mortification tenure, 594
Parliament—
  curia regis, contrast, 506
  judicial role, 506
primogeniture, male—
  succession, rule, 589, 646
reddendo—
  military tenure, 588, 593
  mortification tenure, 594
Scotland—
  charters, survival, 591
  growth, 591
sheriff, role, 507, 508. *See also* SHERIFF
spread in Western Europe, 590
subinfeudation—
  consent of lord to, 592
  description, 592
  prohibition clause in tenant's charter,
   592
  Statute of *Quia Emptores*, curtailment
   by, 592
  substitution replacing, 592
tenant—
  lord's powers, administration of justice, 509. *See also* TENANT
tenure—
  abolition of tenures, 596
  blench-ferme, 594, 596
  burgage, 594
  feu-ferme, 595, 596
  land, generally, 506, 509, 588, 593. *See
   also* land tenure, above
  military, 588, 593, 596. *See also* military tenure, above
  mortification, 594
  wardholding, 593, 596
variations in Europe, 590
vassal—
  oath of fealty, 588
wardholding—
  abolition, 596, 630
  fiscal advantages, 593
Floating charges. *See* COMPANY LAW
Formal sources
custom, generally, 501. *See also* CUSTOM
definition, 501
enumeration, 501
equity, generally, 501. *See also* EQUITY
'institutional' writers, generally, 501. *See
  also* 'INSTITUTIONAL' WRITERS
legislation, generally, 501. *See also*
  LEGISLATION

Formal sources—*contd*
precedent, generally, 501. *See also*
  PRECEDENT
Freeholders
legislative policies—
  post-Union governments—
   opportunity to approve, 630
Michaelmas head courts—
  approval, legislative policies—
   post-Union governments, 630
French influences
'Auld Alliance' as basic link, 603
borrowing, direct from French law, 607
Bourges, University—
  humanist lawyers, 604
customary law—
  Roman law, admixture, 605
education of Scottish law students, 604
Faculty of Advocates—
  Library collections, 605
historical sources of Scots law, 603, 604,
  605, 607
legal literature in Scotland, 605
Orléans law school, 604
Roman law, entry into Scots law
  through, 604

Head courts
freeholders—
  approval, legislative policies—
   post-Union governments, 630
Michaelmas sittings—
  freeholders as landowning electorate
   approval, legislative policies—
    post-Union governments, 630
Heritable jurisdictions
abolition, 630
commissary courts, inferior—
  transfer to sheriff court on abolition,
   630
feudal law, origin, 589
effects of abolition, 630
judges, requirement of legal qualification—
  on abolition, 630
sheriff court—
  reorganisation on abolition, 630
High Court of Justiciary
Adjournal, Acts of, 528
Admiralty Court—
  transfer, partial, jurisdiction, 519, 609,
   635
criminal jurisdiction, origins, 520
equitable jurisdiction, special, 547
Lord Justice-Clerk, functions, 520

References are to paragraphs

References are to paragraphs

References are to paragraphs

References are to paragraphs

References are to paragraphs

References are to paragraphs

References are to paragraphs

Procedural law—*contd*
damages for personal injuries claims—
    contd
  Scottish Law Commission re-
    commendations, 676
  sheriff court, 676
reform—
  Law Reform Committee for
    Scotland—
    actions of removing and ejection,
      652
  Scottish Law Commission—
    damages for personal injuries
      claims, 676
removing and ejection, actions of—
  Law Reform Committee for Scotland
    1957 report, 652
royal courts—
  Regiam Majestatem, 512
terminology—
  derivation from rotal law, 582
Products liability
European Communities draft directive,
  677
European Convention on Products
  Liability in regard to Personal Injury
  and Death, 677
Scottish Law Commission recommen-
  dations, 677

Roman law
advocates, use of arguments based on—
  assisting reception into Scots law, 553
bankruptcy legislation, effect, 629
canon law—
  admixture, 549
  influence of Roman law in Scotland
    through, 551
contract law, influence traceable in, 556
Corpus Iuris Civilis, 549
decline of influence, 555
direct influence, development, 551
Dutch influence, entry into Scots law
  through, 604, 606
feudal law, admixture, 549
French influence, entry into Scots law
  through, 604
generally, as source, 502
guardian and ward, law of—
  influence traceable in, 556
historical source of Scots law, as, 502,
  548–556
ius commune of Europe, origins, 549
Justinian's *Institutes*, 534, 548, 554
legal literature—
  content/presentation, importance in,
    554

Roman law—*contd*
medieval Europe—
  arrival in Scotland through develop-
    ment in, 549
property law—
  influence traceable in areas of, 556
ratio scripta—
  influence on Scottish courts in default
    of other guidance, 553
reception in Europe—
  through professional lawyers, 550
reception in Scotland—
  canon law, influence through, 551
  imperio rationis, 548
  ius commune of Europe, as, 551
  practice of the courts, through, 553
  professional lawyers, through influ-
    ence, 551
terminology, use—
  different meanings in Scots law, 556
universities—
  continental—
    training of Scots lawyers until eight-
      eenth century, 552
  Scottish—
    failure to teach Roman law, 552. *See
      also* UNIVERSITIES
Royal Commission. *See* LAW REFORM
Royal courts
contrast in administration with church
  courts, 511
curia regis, description, 506
procedure—
  Regiam Majestatem, 512

Sale of goods, *see* CONTRACT LAW;
  MERCANTILE LAW
Scottish Law Commission
animals, civil liability in relation to, 662
assimilation of Scots and English law—
  central government—
    administration, attempts to secure,
      625
bankruptcy law reform, 633, 678
codification—
  statutory requirement to consider, 625
Commissioners—
  disqualification from membership,
    House of Commons, 665
  qualifications, 665
  term of appointment, 665
confidence, law on breach—
  consideration by, 674
consolidating statutes—
  generally, 698–704
  meaning, 698

References are to paragraphs

References are to paragraphs

TIME

References are to paragraphs

Contract—*contd*
duration—
European Convention on the Calculation of Time-Limits, 827
employment—
duration, 827
European Convention on the Calculation of Time-Limits—
dies ad quem, meaning, 828
duration, 827
hire/lease—
duration, 827
offer/acceptance—
termination, precise period, 823, 828
termination at specified hour, 823
Criminal procedure
appeal—
calculation, period of days for, 817
applications, time limits—
calculation of period of days, 817
stated case, application—
'within' a specified time, 826
time limits generally, 817, 819, 822

Date. *See also* DAY
'at a date', 822
'at which date', 822
'beginning with the date of', 822
clear days, meaning, 822, 823, 826
'commencing from' a specified date, 826
'from' a specified date, 826
meaning, 822
'time' distinguished, 822
Day
'after' a specified day, 826
'at least (so many) days', 823
'by' a specified day, 826
common law, at, 815
dies a quo, definition, 828, 829
dies ad quem, definition, 828, 829
dies inceptus pro completo habetur, 828
division—
origin, 801
duration—
determination, 801, 815
European Convention on the Calculation of Time-Limits—
dies a quo, 828, 829
dies ad quem, 828, 829
first—
exclusion/inclusion, computation of
period, 819, 820, 821, 822
incalation—
pattern to construct coherent calendar,
802, 803

Day—*contd*
intervening—
disregarded calculating periods numbered in days, 815
last—
exclusion/inclusion, computation of
period, 819, 820, 821, 822, 823,
825
part—
dies inceptus pro completo habetur, 819,
822, 823
legislation coming into force on particular day—
time of commencement, 815
less than a day, period, 816, 822
natural day, 815
'not earlier than' a specified number of
days, 826
'not exceeding 28 days from date of . . .',
822
'not less than' a specified number of days,
826
'not less than (so many) clear days', 822,
823
'on' a specified day, 826
Scotland—
common law, at, 815
solar—
accurate measurement, 801
incompatibility with solar day/
tropical year, 801, 802
statutory provisions, 815
Daylight saving
historical background, 810
legislation, 810
Definitions
'at a time', 822, 826
clear days, 822, 823, 826
dies a quo, 828
dies ad quem, 828
judicial construction of expressions, 826
list, 826
time, 822

Easter
Church of England—
Book of Common Prayer, 808
description, 808
Eastern churches, 808
etymology, 808
fixed date, views, 808
fixing date, 804, 808
Gregorian calendar, 808
Julian calendar, 808
legislation governing date, 808
Scotland, fixing date in, 808

Easter—*contd*
Scottish Episcopal Church—
    Prayer Book, 808
Second Vatican Council, 808
summer time, effect on calculation, 810
Western churches, 808
Employment
contract—
    duration, 827
    European Convention on the Calcu-
        lation of Time-Limits, 827
    terms, holidays/holiday pay, 818
holiday pay, 818
holidays—
    statutory requirements, 818
Sundays—
    restrictions, 817
wages councils—
    regulatory powers, 818
**European Convention on the Calcu-
lation of Time-Limits**
attainment of majority, 827
business hours, 828
bankruptcy law, 827
civilis computatio, 828, 831
contract—
    acceptance/offer, 828
    duration—
        hire/lease/employment, 827
definitions, problems, 827
dies a quo, definition, 828, 829
dies ad quem, definition, 828, 829
generally, 827–831
limitations on scope, 827, 831
maintenance payments, period of liab-
    ility, 827
month, calculation, 829
purpose, 827
ratification by United Kingdom, 827,
    839
retroactively calculated time limits, 827
Scotland, effect on ratification, 830
signatories, 827
social security benefits—
    qualifying periods, 827
Sundays, principle of counting, 830
week, calculation, 829
year, calculation, 829
European Economic Community
legal time, 810
summer time—
    harmonisation, 810

Festivals. *See also* HOLIDAYS
calendar, inclusion, 801
Christmas, 805. *See also* CHRISTMAS

Festivals—*contd*
Easter, 804, 808. *See also* EASTER
ecclesiastical, 801, 804
Passover, 808

Greenwich Mean Time
basis of calculation, 809
legal time, as, 809, 810
overriding summer time as legal time—
    documents, purposes etc to which
        applicable, 810
purposes for which overrides summer
    time as legal time, 810
summer time defined in terms of, 810

Holidays
bank—
    obligation to make payment falling
        on—
        compliance, 818
    Scotland, designation, 818
contractual agreement, by, 818
employment contracts—
    designated days, 818
    holiday pay, 818
European Convention on the Calcu-
    lation of Time-Limits, 830
exclusion, calculating period numbered
    in days, 815
holy days of obligation, origin, 818
payment, employee, 818
public—
    criminal law, application/appeal—
        exclusion, calculation, time limits,
        817
statutory enactment, by, 818
termination of period on holiday—
    measured in days, 825
    qualification to principle of exclusion,
        825
within a period—
    calculation, total period, 825
Hotel
Sunday opening—
    control, 817
    local licensing board, 817
Hour
de momento in momentum, 820, 823
meaning, 816
naturalis computatio, period calculated in,
    819, 820, 831
Hume, Baron
validity of acts performed on Sunday,
    817

References are to paragraphs

References are to paragraphs

Saturday
European Convention on the Calculation of Time-Limits, 830
Seasons
cycle, 801
duration, determination, 801
tropical year—
cycle of seasons as, 801
vernal equinox—
Easter, to fix date, 808
recurrence as measurement, 801, 804, 806
Second
meaning, 816
Social security
qualifying periods for benefit—
European Convention on the Calculation of Time-Limits, effect, 827
Stair, Lord
validity of acts performed on Sunday, 817
Standard time
British Standard Time, 810
Greenwich mean time as species, 809
Summer time
British Standard Time, as, 810
daylight saving—
historical background, 810
description, 810
European Economic Community—
harmonisation, 810
Greenwich mean time, variant, 810
legal time, as—
generally, 810
purposes for which not legal time, 810
statutory basis, 809, 810
Sunday
common law maxim, 817
criminal law—
exclusion, Sunday, calculation, time limits, appeal/application, 817
employment—
statutory prohibitions, 817
European Convention on the Calculation of Time-Limits, 830
exclusion, calculating period numbered in days—
exception, general rule, 815, 817
expiry day of given period for act—
performance, following day, 817
hotel licence/restricted licence, premises, opening, 817
invalid acts performed on, 817
Jews, exemptions from prohibitions, 817
judicial acts, validity, 817

Sunday—*contd*
licensed premises, generally, opening, 817
local licensing board—
powers, opening hours, 817
private acts, validity, 817
profanity, offence, 817
prohibition of specific activities on—
statute, by, 817
public house, licensed premises, opening, 817
refreshment licence, premises, opening, 817
statutes, extant, affecting prohibition, specific activities, 817
termination of period on—
measured in days, 825
qualification to principle of exclusion, 825
validity, steps in a judicial process, 817
within a period—
calculation, total period, 825
woman, employment, 817
young person, employment, 817

Taxation
capital gains tax, 811
corporation—
financial year, 811
financial year, 811
income tax, 811
value added tax, *see* VALUE ADDED TAX
'year of assessment', 811
Termination of period
bankruptcy law, 823
business hours etc, defined by, 823
civilis computatio, 823
contract, as term, 823
dies inceptus principle, 823
generally, 819, 820, 821, 822, 823
holiday, on, 825
last day, exclusion, 823, 825
naturalis computatio—
de momento in momentum, 823
prescriptive period—
where right to be acquired/lost by lapse, 823, 825
presumption, 823
right to be acquired/lost by lapse of prescriptive period, where, 823, 825
Sunday, on, 825
Testamentary deed
exclusion, day of making—
computation, period, survivorship of granter, 822
expiry, sixty-day period—
law of deathbed, 823

References are to paragraphs

References are to paragraphs